THE ZETETIC METHOD
PROVING THE EARTH FLAT
By LLOYD HUNT

The Zetetic Method

Copyright 2023 Lloyd Hunt

ISBN:

The material in this publication is fair use. Any part of this publication may be used in arguments for or against the subject or transmitted in any form or by any means, including photocopying, recording, or other electronic or mechanical methods.

Publisher: Kindle Direct Publishing

Printed in the United States

Author's website: Flatearthlogic.net

The Zetetic Method

To my loving mother, who did right by us as best she could. I love you mama. Dorothy Mae Hennigan 1951-2021

Table of Contents

INTRODUCTION..1
  What is the Zetetic Method..1
  It's what you can and can't prove..3
FORWARD...5
  The scientific method..7
  Where's the logic?...10
  What is the Black Swan?...11
CHAPTER 1: FLAT OR BALL..14
  Flat Water/Flat Earth..15
  The BLACK SWAN...24
Curvature..25
Curveless ball...25
THE QUOTED MEASUREMENT OF EARTH'S CURVATURE BY OUR
"ESTABLISHED SCIENTISTS"..26
  The Black Swan..35
  Compass on a ball...35
  Dear invisible curvature..38
  The Black Swan..42
  The Great Plains...43
  Plane Surveying..50
The Great Plains Black Swan...52
  Earthquakes..54
Lighthouses..55
Black Swan..57
  Railroads, bridges and canals..57
  Lake Pontchartrain bridge..60
  The Black Swan..63
Aeronautics..63
  The Black Swan..64
  The Laws of Perspective..67
  Bill Nye the Pseudo-science Guy...68
  The laws of perspective..68
  Fitting 14 feet into 8 inches..72
  Laws of perspective experiment...74
  Sunset between New York and LA..75
  Story Time..76
The Black Swan...76
Sailing over a ball earth using flat earth math..77
Sextant and plane trigonometry...77
  CHAPTER 2: MAP/FLIGHTS..81

The flat earth maps..83
All but one scale..86
Southern flights go North..87
Emergency landings on a globe map vs a flat map..........................92
Fly to China on a ball..94
Don't worry the plane's not going down..98
Flat earth author's conversation with a professor about a flight........99
Gyroscope..101
The Black Swan...101
CHAPTER 3: ANTARCTICA...102
Antarctica...103
Captain Cook done went too far...104
The 24-hour sun..106
How do we have all that ice..107
The one unbreakable treaty..110
The Black Swan...113
CHAPTER 4: THE ABOVE SITUATION...114
Assumptions in the sky keep on turning..115
Is it written in the Stars...118
The case of the missing star parallax..120
Flat earth in court..128
To spin or not to spin..131
Coriolis effect..132
Don't aim for the deer or you'll miss it...136
The Black Swan...137
The revolving pendulum or the revolving Earth..............................139
Meteorites..142
Back to the stars, lights or burning balls of gas.............................144
The Sun..144
The sun's not going down on me...145
The sun, far or near..152
The Black Swan...153
Moon happenings..154
The moon, cheese or light bulb..156
Craters..156
Moon being a reflector..160
Tides but nothing else..161
Lunar eclipses...166
The flipping moon...166
Sextant calculations..166
The Black Swan...167
Seasons...167

What causes seasons?..168
The Analemma...175
The Black Swan...178
CHAPTER 5: GRAVITY..179
To fall or to settle..180
How does one pull gas..183
The vacuum vs the gravitational pull..188
What can you prove..194
The Black Swan...200
CHAPTER 6: THE FIRMAMENT..202
The firmament or open space...203
Air pressure and gas gradient in our atmosphere......................................205
The Black Swan...210
CHAPTER 7: NASA..212
Trust...214
Things that make you go hmmm..214
That after moon landing glow... 218
Moon rocks or old kindling wood...223
Pictures vs images..225
When telling the truth can get you killed..237
Here's some more NASA fallacies...241
What about other space agencies..246
Honest and noble confessions..252
The Black Swan...253
CHAPTER 8: SATELLITES...254
Satellites..255
Google satellite cables..263
Satellite balloons...265
The Black Swan...268
CHAPTER 8.5: GOVERNMENT DOCUMENTS...269
CHAPTER 9: DISINFORMATION AGENTS...289
Disinformation agents or truth seekers..290
Why the lie...292
Truth fears no investigation...293
Disinformation agents...294
The Flat Earth Society...300
A lying government??? What?..301
Book burning...302
The Black Swan...305
To ball earthers that refuse to even listen..306
The Illuminati card game and Hollywood truths...306
Illuminati rituals...306
Truth in Hollywood..313

CHAPTER 10: RIDICULOUS CLAIMS ... 326
- Calculated assumptions over experiments ... 327
- Ridiculous claims ... 329

CHAPTER 11: THE SCRIPTURES ... 354
- The Bible, flat earth book or flying ball book ... 355
- Claims ... 356
- Sun, the greater light ... 359
- God's flying footstool ... 362
- The Firmament ... 365
- Heaven's doors ... 368
- Stars ... 370
- Where's the Up and DOWN ... 373
- The day the sun stood still ... 374
- Flat earth Qur'an ... 380
- Realize the greatness of your mind ... 381

CHAPTER 12: Comments and Arguments ... 383

CHAPTER 13: Dear Flat Earthers ... 395
- Arguments vs "debating" ... 397
- "Here's my link" ... 400
- Show me the math ... 401
- People can change their minds ... 402

CHAPTER 14: Evolution ... 404
- These are not the bones you are looking for ... 405
- It's a matter of matter being intelligent ... 409
- You can dress up and put on cologne all you want, but that doesn't make dating carbon a "sure thing" ... 416
- The lonely cell ... 420
- The claim that all scientists believe in evolution ... 428
- The case with fossils ... 434
- A Dino tale ... 436
- The Great Flood ... 438
- The Black Swan ... 441

CHAPTER 15: Gotta Have Faith ... 445
- REAL SCIENCE DOESN'T CARE IN YOUR BELIEF SYSTEM, PSEUDO-SCIENCE ON THE OTHER HAND REQUIRES IT ... 446
- Require faith and a belief system ... 447
- The Black Swan ... 449

CONCLUSION ... 450

Recommendation ... 454

The Zetetic Method

"Crossing the Rubicon" by Luca Fezzi

The Zetetic Method

"Beliefs is yours to have, what you think is yours to have, but here you will require evidence." Judge Judy Sheindlin

"It is the mark of an educated mind to be able to entertain a thought without accepting it." Aristotle

"Conspiracy Theorist- A person that researches a subject and then uses logic and critical thinking skills to form an educated opinion instead of just blindly believing whatever they saw on TV." Eric Dubay

INTRODUCTION
(My pre-book rant)

What is the Zetetic Method

The term "Zetetic" means to search, proceed by inquiry. to trace out, or to examine. For truth seeking this is better than the word "theoretic," which means imaginary, speculative, supposing but not proving.

My desire in this book is to establish the fundamental principles of Zetetic science. The foundation of any science or any system of knowledge should be based on established facts that are proven and not assumed. That way we won't need faith in things we have no way of knowing. "Trust the science" is the most anti-science statement ever. Questioning science is how you do science.

As one flat earther put it oh so nicely: "None can doubt that by making special experiments and collecting manifest and undeniable facts, arranging them in logical order, and observing what is naturally and fairly deducible, the result will be far more consistent and satisfactory than by framing a theory or system and assuming the existence of causes for which there is no direct evidence, and which can only be admitted "for the sake of argument."

As Zetetic truth seekers, we want to go off physical evidence and facts, not emotions or an appeal to authority. I love the way this author, M. Dabney, puts it in her book "The Forgotten Gift of Life":

"Though at times delusion may eclipse truth, truth remains obvious, because it is simply the recognition of what is. I need only to open myself to recognize truth without judgment or expectation built from my experience of the past." M. Dabney

First, I would just like to say, that if you still believe two planes took down three buildings and passports can survive explosions that plane engines can not, then you're to far taken, this book is not for you. For the rest of you who might be questioning authoritarian claims because of our recent scam, then take a look at this. This is a dark world but we can illuminate it with knowledge.

I want to switch people's brains to self-thinking mode and create a greater interest in Zetetic research with no government filters telling them what to believe; to cause individuals to think for themselves, and find out which is true and which is false using physical based evidence. And by doing so, I hope that honest thinkers will choose that 'belief', which will be shown to be supported by facts, that the earth that we live on is flat, stationary and enclosed.

Unproven ideas, that we have been taught since infancy, have to be gotten rid of before we can entertain the new. The evidence of science should be sound and established on facts not theories. How are we to have a system of knowledge when our science is theoretical? A foundation of truth is key.

Here's the globe model proving system they use, in a nutshell. (A) is the main theory, (B) and (C) are also theories used to 'prove' (A). If you ask them to prove (A), they will simply quote you (B) and (C); if you then ask them to prove (B), you'll get (A) and (C) quoted to you. If you want (C) proven, guess what will happen, they will repeat (A) and (B).

"It's like writing a fictional story and supporting the fiction world with 'facts' from the fiction universe."

Remember, indoctrination is not knowledge. Degrees mean nothing if all someone can do is repeat. And if you can't figure out that all you are doing is simply repeating, then there's nothing anyone can do for you.

If you call them on this trickery, they will call you a science denier. I have researched the globe and flat earth models for almost six years now and this is the method the globers and government established 'scientists' alike use. Flat earthers on the other hand give out observable provable content.

It's easier to be told, to suppose than to prove, to speculate rather than search for truth, but it's a good way to be misled. But truth can be obtained through research of facts. By adopting the Zetetic Method and taking nothing for granted, and trying to find facts to back them up, we keep on solid ground, a foundation built upon physical facts.

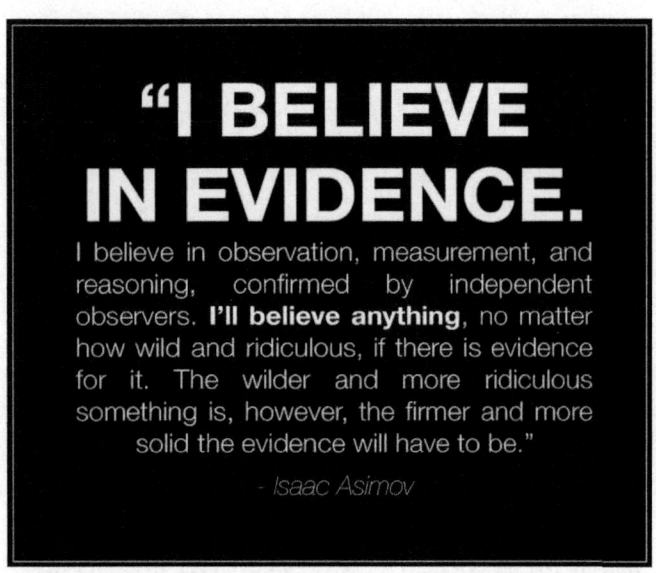

It's what you can and can't prove

It's all about what YOU can and can't prove without taking someone's word for it that matters.

1) What you CAN prove is that the horizon is flat.
   What you CAN'T prove is that the horizon is curved.
2) What you CAN prove is that sizable bodies of contained water are flat and level.
   What you CAN'T prove is that the ocean is wrapped around a ball.
3) What you CAN prove is the ship comes back into view with zooming.
   What you CAN'T prove is that the ship goes behind a curve of water.
4) What you CAN prove is that the atmosphere is moving in all different directions simultaneously at different speeds.
   What you CAN'T prove is that the atmosphere is spinning 1000 mph on a flying ball earth.
5) They tell you the space station is about the size of a 747 plane and is around 240 miles up. What you CAN prove is that you can barely see a 747 at 35,000feet up.
   What you CAN'T prove is that you can see it at 240 miles up.
6) What you CAN prove is that things fall.
   What you CAN'T prove is that gravity makes us orbit a ball of burning gas, and the Milky Way while leaving the Big Bang.
7) What you CAN prove is that sun spots exist.
   What you CAN'T prove is that the sun is 93,000,000 miles away.
8) What you CAN prove is that the north star doesn't move.
   What you CAN'T prove is that we're wobbling and flying in three directions.
9) What you CAN prove is that the plane is flying flat and level when cruising.
   What you CAN'T prove is that the plane is gradually dipping to account for invisible curvature.
10) What you CAN prove is that the star constellations are always the same and on the same course.
    What you CAN'T prove is that the universe is expanding.
11) What you CAN prove is that the pendulum is moving.
    What you CAN'T prove is that the earth is turning under the pendulum rather than the pendulum turning over the earth.
12) What you CAN prove is numbers 1 through 12.
    What you CAN'T prove is the Big Bang theory.

I have yet to read or see any real 'proof' from the globalist scientists, that does not require faith and an acceptance. I have to put aside my common-sense and reasoning powers and use pure imagination to even consider what's been presented to me as a theory AND the "proof" that comes with it. If I break it down with real questions, the whole fairytale would fall to pieces.

At this point, without proof of these ridiculous claims, we are going along to get along.

It is impossible for any serious truth-seeker to gain any truth by getting 'information' from someone else without the physical evidence to back it up. If physical evidence is not provided, then it should be rejected. If one trusts another to obtain their knowledge, then the one becomes their sheep. Simple as that. Ask yourself, are the theories we are taught confirmed by facts? Are they taught to make us more intelligent or keep us dumbed down?

Using the Zetetic Method, we will only stick to logical, reasonable and provable claims. No imaginary speculation, supposing but not proving. No mathematics built on assumptions making them worthless. No theoretical science posing as facts, theoretical science is not real science. The globe model doesn't even sound logical, reasonable or even provable. It can't be recreated and is definitely not observable. That in itself is a red flag.

Reality is a great teacher if people would just look at it and notice what it has to say. Let's do that right now shall we.

Here's an example. Continental drift is false. Reality shows it. Here's how. If you're drifting on an iceberg around the ocean you can't tell if the sea level is up or down. The iceberg doesn't help in the least because it's drifting on the very thing you want to measure. Therefore you have no way of measuring.

However, when you drift by some land, you see the seashore exposed. Now you are allowed to measure the sea level and see that it is low. You can measure the sealevel simply because the land is anchored to the Earth. That's how you know you have high tide and low tide. Every seashore in the world has these tides because they are fastened to the Earth. See, reality can prove or disprove theories. Let's look at some other examples and see where the evidence points to and how the globe holds up.

Examples

1) If you tell me that the ship is going behind curvature but I show you in long distance photography that it is not, then who's basing their knowledge on facts?

2) If you tell me there's a downward curvature to the world and I tell you the horizon line is at eye level on the beach then again on a plane, all observable. That we see more land straight ahead instead of downward as we would if the earth were actually curving downward, then who's basing their knowledge on facts?

3) If you tell me that we're flying in three different directions and wobbling and I say we're staying put and the lights are moving; then I show you perfect star trail circles all year long, with no star parallax or the north star not shifting whatsoever, then who's basing their knowledge off facts?

4) If you tell me the earth is flying around the sun and I say no it's the other way around then I show you a time-lapse video of the sun booking it across the sky and neither one of us feels any movement whatsoever then who's basing their knowledge off facts?

Let us skip the hearsay and go off observable provable facts for this book shall we.
This book does not endorse any religion, although, I do include a Bible chapter showing that the Bible does indeed support flat earth, for the religious truth seeker. The bible proves to be a flat earth book but does not prove the earth is flat, writing can't do that, it's objective reality and true independently verifiable science that supports a motionless level plane. One should not give up a more authenticated model for a more speculative one.

Also you hear people say "You should be more open minded." Children are open minded and will believe anything you tell them, especially after the natural questioning curiosity they have is taken out of them by the indoctrination system that we call a school. So let's try a different approach. Let's try a filter of source coupled with the open minded. A filter that consists of logic, reasoning and common sense.

In all observable ways there is so much truth in our favor that we do not have to believe in a flat stationary earth because we do nothing but observe it and even fly over it. However the globe is something of a different matter isn't it? You have to believe.
You can not observe any curvature whatsoever. You can not observe or feel any movement. So you're left with taking the government's word for it. They control the education system and the science industry. And control your thoughts if you let them. But I'm sure they have your best interest at heart.

"Your mind is programmable. If you're not programming your mind, someone else will program it for you." Jeremy Hammond

I want you to research what they claim that you think debunks what I say, and see if they can prove this claim AND/OR if they just make yet another unproven assumption to back up the previous claim. Keep asking why and how with ALL of their claims, and see if it matches physical reality. The higher the education is, the harder it is to break out of your indoctrination because they put so much faith and money into it. I don't care how much education you have or how high your IQ is or what your job title is, if you don't seek to prove the claims of your authoritarians, then you're just a sheep being led.
ZETETIC, to seek by inquiry.

FORWARD
"The Modern Skeptic: The Greek word 'skeptic' means investigation. By calling themselves skeptics, the ancient skeptics thus described themselves as investigators. They also called themselves 'those who suspend', thereby signaling that their investigations lead them to suspension of judgment. They do not put forward theories, and they do not deny that knowledge can be found. At its core, ancient skepticism is a

way of life devoted to inquiry. It is as much concerned with belief as with knowledge. As long as knowledge has not been attained, the skeptics aim not to affirm anything. This gives rise to their most controversial ambition: 'a life without belief'. Skeptic does not mean him who doubts, but he who investigates or researches as opposed to him who asserts and thinks that he has found." Miguel de Unamuno, "Essays and Soliloquies," 1924 from the book "Flat Earth: Investigation Into A Massive 500 Year Heliocentric Lie" by James W. Lee

    If you want to control a society, you have to control the education system, the media and the banks. It's simple, teach them as children so they will accept it, control their information as adults and keep them in debt to keep their minds and bodies busy.
    Man is firmly convinced that he is awake; in reality, he is caught up in a web of lies and false knowledge, woven by trust in his government, thus he's fast asleep and in a dream reality, where talking monkeys live on a spinning wobbling flying ball. Ahhh, but facts are stubborn things that don't listen to opinions or claims, they just are. If what you're saying is not taken from reality then it's a hypothesis taken on faith.
    Let every man possessing eyes and senses may make himself aware, only then he can not be fooled that easily. Your mind is your most precious asset and that's because it is free from all external influence. You HAVE to give your consent to be tricked.

Over the years science has proven its usefulness to mankind. Using it, we've created medicine, tools, better ways of living; I could go on and on. The nature of science is open and always evolving. This is fact-based science that has done this.

    Some branches of science are not fact based and not even real science anymore. It has morphed into Scientism. Scientism is the belief that scientists are correct and should be trusted and if spoken out against you should be shunned and looked at as a science denier.
    NOAA, the climate change research organization, got caught lying a few years back, about the temperature data in order to fit conclusions that would go alone politically. Most accepted it without demanding proof. That's Scientism.

THE SCIENTIFIC METHOD

sci·en·tif·ic meth·od

noun

• a method of procedure that has characterized natural science since the 17th century, consisting in systematic observation, measurement, and experiment, and the formulation, testing, and modification of hypotheses.

•

"criticism is the backbone of the scientific method"

Is science the great liberator from ignorance or is science like a dark cloud that has hidden the truth from our eyes?

"The scientific method is an empirical method of acquiring knowledge that has characterized the development of science since at least the 17th century. It involves careful observation, applying rigorous skepticism about what is observed, given that cognitive assumptions can distort how one interprets the observation." Wikipedia

True science is the scientific method or empirical data. Science is about observing, testing and re-creating, etc. Scientism on the other hand it's something completely different, often with an agenda attached. What passes as science today is nothing of the sort. Its claims and mathematics build on assumptions that we are pushed to believe in without showing us a dilly swat of real physical evidence. We cannot recognize the truth anymore and criticize the people who point it out. We have to realize that not all science is fact-based, and has done nothing but deceive mankind and take away knowledge that is rightly ours. You can't rely on anyone but yourself, we must relearn.

Empirical evidence is information acquired by observation or experimentation. Scientists record and analyze this data. The process is a central part of the scientific method, leading to the proving or disproving of a hypothesis and our better understanding of the world as a result.

Remove the empirical component from the scientific method and it becomes far easier to perpetuate fairy tales.

Too big, too small, too old. How does one adequately verify current models if observation is beyond our scope? There's always an excuse why WE, the common man, can't prove, so we leave the thinking to someone else. I call BS!

It's funny to think that a flat, stationary plane is currently the default model given that it's the only one with empirical evidence that we can all verify. We can't trust the governments or their puppet Pseudo-scientist, therefore we should not hand them over our thinking power to THEM.

"Those that wish to have us believe heliocentrism has simply made the numbers over time, so huge, so enormous, that humans have no relative experience to comprehend what such large numbers even mean. NASA can make up any number they want, and no one can question the validity of their outrageous statements of "facts." Author James Lee

Our inner thoughts/consciousness is what separates us from other animals. A consciousness that helps us understand the meaning of life. Faith in Pseudo-scientist, that present this non-fact-based science, has directed our inner thoughts into what they want them to be. We've become slaves to a belief system. The worst kind of slavery because we're not even aware of it. To make you feel like an object, a speck of dust, instead of the highest conscious being on this great earth realm, so you can be easily controlled and manipulated.

But in order for this to happen we have to give our consent. No one can change your mind or make you think whatever they please without your agreement. If you fly all over the world and see a flat ocean at every part and they tell you it's wrapped around a ball, they can't make you disregard your senses and believe such rubbish, it's your free will that does so. They change your perception of reality to get you to change your mind, it's just that simple.

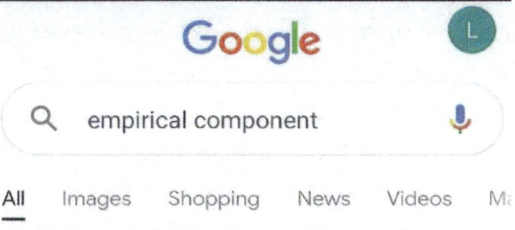

Here's some examples of hypotheses and assumptions being made in order to support these unsound unproven astronomical claims that scientism have made.

Example #1: In "Modern Science and Modern Thought," by S. Laing: "What is the material universe composed of? Ether, Matter, and Energy. Ether is not actually known to us by any test of which the senses can take cognizance, but it is a sort of mathematical substance WHICH WE ARE COMPELLED TO ASSUME IN ORDER TO ACCOUNT for the phenomena of light and heat."

This claim must be discarded because it's untrustworthy, because it's not based on facts but is assumed.

Example #2: Scientism Priest once said that the stars were motionless, but the science magazine, Science Siftings, back then tells us "as soon as it was CONJECTURED that the stars were subject to the law of gravitation, it was inferred that they were not motionless."

Example #3: Professor T. H. Huxley made an assumption to account for the disappearance of ships at sea. If he would have actually taken the time and thought about it just a little, he might have realized that the laws of perspective answers this perfectly well and can be proven and without the use of assuming that the earth is a ball that seems curve less.

Professor Huxley states: "We assume the convexity of the water, because we know of no other way to explain the appearance and disappearance of ships at sea."

Now how is that science? When it comes to science and truth, wouldn't it be better to admit ignorance than to assume anything? This same Professor, in his book "Science and Culture" says "the assertion which outstrips evidence is not only a blunder but a crime." HA!

Here's what a real scientist sounds like: "Knowledge is gained by practical investigation and experience, and has no need of the assistance of assumption to provide an excuse for ignorance." Thomas Winship

Let honest truth-seeking individuals, who want to learn the truth for themselves by practical investigation into the physical evidence set forth in this book, read it with a clear thinking mind. I ask anyone to successfully dispute it with real evidence. I'm a man looking for truth, therefore I court no favor and fear no foe, scientific or otherwise. All I ask for is careful attention to what is claimed and what is proven.

They want you to ignore the loopholes in their theories that aren't as solid as you might think they are. We'll be looking at some of these theories to see how they hold up with physical reality. The greatest danger for a scientism priest, is individuals who use their mind to judge and analyze, to wonder and seek the truth. To use the Zetetic Method.

As someone told me once, "We reached this point, mainly, because science is no longer science anymore. What started as science back then, has evolved into something that we cannot recognize anymore, we can't understand it, or break it into small bits, and all we are pushed to do is to believe in it!"

There's an information war that's going on right now about so many things, if we want the truth then we have to KEEP IT REAL! Use the Zetetic method of investigating, starting with known FACTS, accept no speculations, assumptions or premature deductions. Then we'll get a more accurate and trustworthy view of reality. Leave your opinions and emotions out of it

To Apply Occam's Razor:

1. Determine how many assumptions and conditions are necessary for each explanation to be correct.

2. If an explanation requires extra assumptions or conditions, demand evidence commensurate with the strength of each claim.

3. Extraordinary claims require extraordinary evidence.

In this book I will be taking on one of those issues. And that's our earth. Has government scientists baffled humanity? It's not that hard to do. Humanity trusts appointed leaders who are 'supposed' to be trusted. This nasty little habit is used against us.

We should look at the globe earth theory as if it's on trial in court. Look at the evidence very strongly, and decide if it's REALLY provable evidence. How do you know the Earth is a ball when the curve cannot be established even though there's a formula for measuring it?

WHERE'S THE LOGIC

Wouldn't it be more logical to think that the perfect star trail circles are there because the stars(lights) are rotating around Polaris and not this massive gigantic world of land and water with all its stock, spinning 1000mph?

Wouldn't it be more logical to think that we live on an observable curve less stationary plane instead of a spinning wobbling flying ball where the curvature can't be observed?

All the observable provable evidence points to a flat stationary earth so why believe otherwise

 Different science websites have different numbers so we'll just pick one. There is 57,308,738 square miles of land, above sea level, here on earth and 139.5 million square miles of ocean. How could we possibly believe that this massive gigantic world, with all its stock, is a spinning wobbling flying ball? What/where is the real life evidence, not government hearsay, are we basing this incredible claim on exactly? Where can I obtain this observable provable evidence? There should be stockpiles of evidence that doesn't need a belief system to exist. Again, one should not give up a more authenticated model for a more speculative one.

There should be more evidence for these claims:
1. Earth is spinning at 1000mph
2. Earth orbits the sun at 67,000mph
3. All of this is spiraling around the Milky Way around a black sucking hole at 500,000mph
4. And all while being shot out by a Big Bang at 670,000,000mph through an endless universe.

That's a grand total of 670,568,000mph in different directions. How is it that we need to take someone's word for such a huge claim? HOW? This is pure faith based.

I'm not telling you to forget what you've learned, but instead to DEEPLY QUESTION what you've learned and to seriously think about it. The Globe requires unproven theories and your blind faith. Flat Earth only requires an open filtered mind and common sense, the rest is observable and your faith is not required.

What is "The Black Swan"

I will be using the term "Black Swan" here and there in this book. Here's what I mean by "Black Swan." If you say no black swans exist, only white ones, then I bring you a black swan, your theory just got destroyed and should be rejected, correct? Here's where the phrase came from.

An experiment was done a while back, with a zoomed camera showing oil platforms in a distance of 9 miles, with the horizon line yet another mile further back. At 9 miles, we supposedly have a curvature of 54 feet. Yet the horizon line is a mile or so behind said oil platforms, thus debunking the given curvature that has been taught to us. This is your Black Swan.

This Black Swan, which is actually the disproving of the ball earth and all the assumptions that come with it, is all over this book. One only has to debunk curvature for the rest to crumble, but we'll still be looking at the other assumptions and theories.

Here's a good comment in the comment section explaining more on the Black Swan.

"The black Swan photo is a photo of a black Swan event i.e. if you were to assert that only white swans exist, I need only to show one black Swan to disprove the notion.

So, if only white swans exist- if the Earth is a ball with radius 3959 miles then every distance to horizon measurements can be no more than 1.2 times the observer's height in feet.

The black Swan is the photograph which is actually a screen from a video taken from 1 foot above the water level. In the photo it shows two oil platforms, the furthest one over 9 miles away with the horizon clearly visible beyond 10 miles. This is the black Swan. The horizon need only be shown once to NOT be the physical Earth curve of a ball for it not to be. It can't be a geometric physical position one day, and apparent ie moves with altitude and weather the next.

The black Swan argument destroys the Radius value. The distance to other supposed physical celestial bodies are all derived using that Radius. That radius is gone. The Black Swan destroys the ball. The sextant proves it's flat in the fact angles need straight lines. You cannot take a measurement if one of the lines is the curved Earth."

How can indoctrination come into existence with nothing for a foundation, not one observation to be found upon, no physical evidence to justify it whatsoever; but only the word of authoritarians? How can this baseless structure slip under so many minds?

There are however some retired military personnel and some not retired military who have said that they know it's flat. And some pilots have come out saying the same. One such pilot wanted to open up a non-government funded school teaching flat earth but was stopped by the government. Why? Truth fears no investigation or opposition.

One scientist said (wasn't talking about flat earth but was talking about evolution) that scientists have financial handcuffs on. Another said "the conversations we have backstage is a lot different then what we have at the podium." Remember some of the doctors who got online and spoke out against covid or the vaccine, lost their medical license. When the government has a noose around your wallet, or neck for that matter, you learn to play the script.

I've read science books that are 100 to 150 years old. Some scientists back then said that the government is infiltrating the science department and turning it into an industry, they're taking over financially and bringing in their own scientists who are ruining science.

When the government controls scientists through financing, then you have no peer review. Real peer review has been bought and paid for.

The Zetetic Method

The term 'conspiracy theorist' itself has gotten a lot of laughs and is designed to do just that. Our society has been programmed, indoctrinated and hypnotized so bad that they assume and perceive every critical thinker as a conspiracy theorist. To discredit someone who has looked into something and has found that things don't seem exactly right or doesn't add up. People are so busy laughing at conspiracy theorists that the concern has moved from those responsible for the conspiracy to those calling upon it. Isn't that convenient for those who are responsible and want to conceal the truth? To convince the masses to laugh instead of opening their eyes and listening? We can have all the proof and physical evidence in the world, but it would still be worthless, if their eyes and minds remain closed.

The greatest weapon ever devised is not a missile or virus, but mind control. It can convince the unthinking masses that they are at peace when they actually are being warred upon. Their minds and freedoms are being controlled and they're not even aware of it. This forms a political religion of sorts that the masses unquestioningly supports because they can't see how it all ties in together or believe that it ever would.

If flat earth is so easily debunked with globe earth proof, then why are more and more globers turning into flat earthers? Are people dumbing down suddenly or waking up? And 5 years ago, people were calling all of us flat earthers crazy, but too many people are waking up now, we can't all be crazy can we? I'll ask that again at the end of this book.

If you still believe in the official 9/11 story and have NO doubts that the moon landing is real, then this book is not for you, as for the rest of us diet woke puppies, let's dive into this flat earth subject and see what else they're lying about. Please read each photo as well. Each one makes a good point.

Real science is provable. My object is to discover and hold on to that only which is true beyond doubt. Scientists aren't showing you anything, they're telling you. I'm showing you. Let's start shall we.

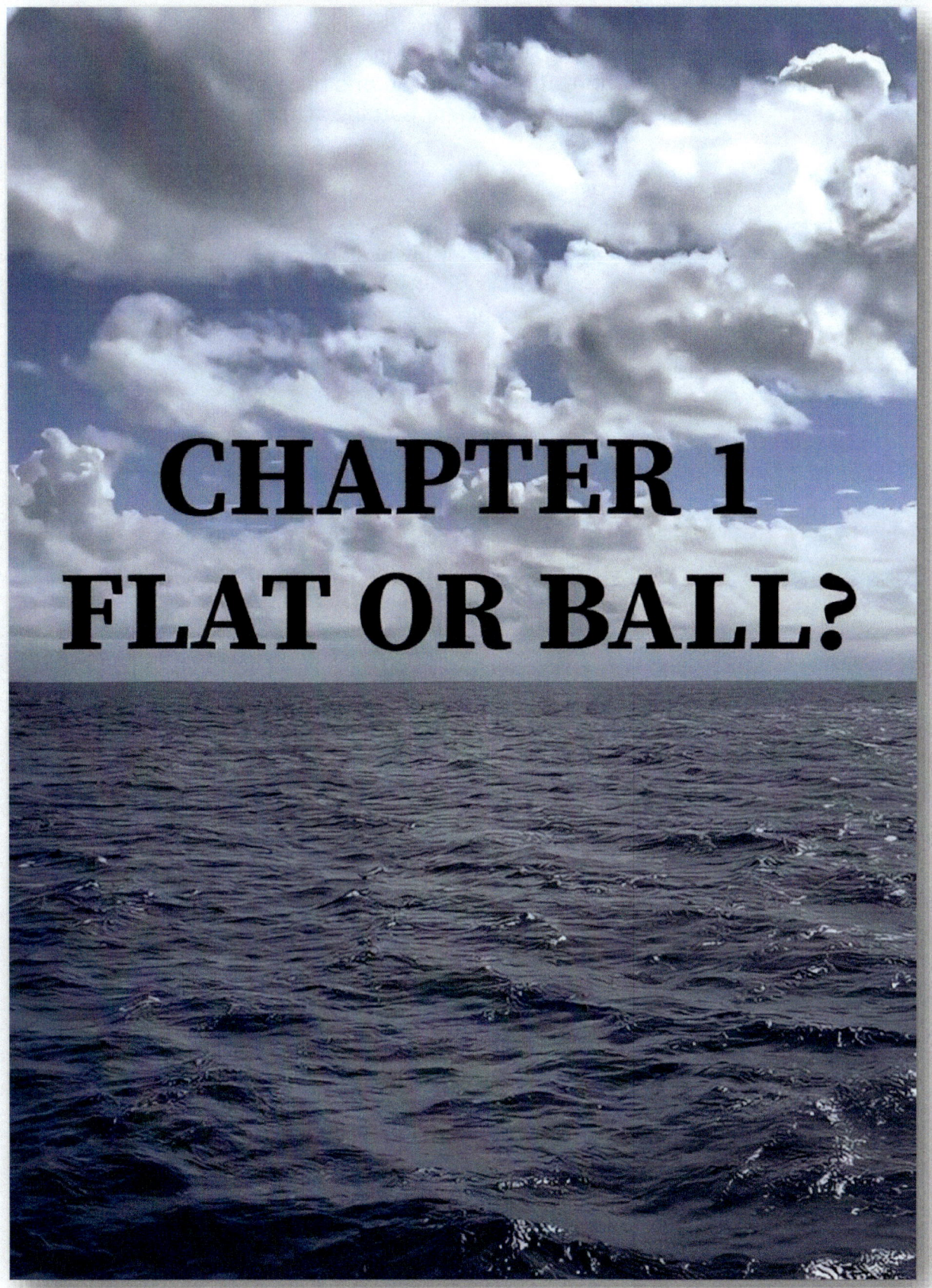

The Zetetic Method

FLAT WATER/FLAT EARTH

"The great and theory-destroying fact was quickly discovered that the surface of standing water was perfectly horizontal. Here was another death-blow to the unnatural ideas and speculations of pseudo-philosophers." Author Thomas Winship

Water always finds its level is NOT a conspiracy theory, it's a proven fact! This next statement couldn't be more true.

The ability of water to always finds its lowest level and flatten out is an observable, measurable, testable and repeatable scientific fact and objective reality backed with solid evidence.
A proofless magical, nature-defying spinning globe with curving, adhesive oceans impossibly wrapped around it rocketing aimlessly through a vacuum IS a conspiracy theory, it is ALL based on theory-tales and beliefs, a belief is a faith, a religion. The globe Earth is just an image in books and on a tel-a-vision, and does not actually exist in reality. Earth is demonstrably level and stationary and not a ball!

Water

I have nothing against true science. I love science. It's the assumptions of science; ie pseudo-science that I'm against. The very theoretical science which manufactured the hypothetical globe nonsense that helps control the world now. The indoctrination system that we call an education system.

The Zetetic Method

Water seems to be a thorn in the ball earth that's slowly flattening it. Let's look at this observable flat proof.

Ok now I want you to stop me when my observable provable claims run out:
1. Toilet water is flat.
2. Tub water is flat.
3. Lake and pond water is flat.
4. Ocean is wrapped around a ball.

The natural physics of water is to find its level and flatten out. All experiments that I've seen prove the surface of contained standing water to be flat and level. If you have one to show otherwise, please share.

If the earth were a ball then the oceans would be curved from North's tip to South's tip, but instead no matter where you're at on this earth you'll see a eye level flat horizon line on a ocean, whether it be on the beach, equator, on a plane or 121,000 feet up.

One of these is observable testable and one is not.

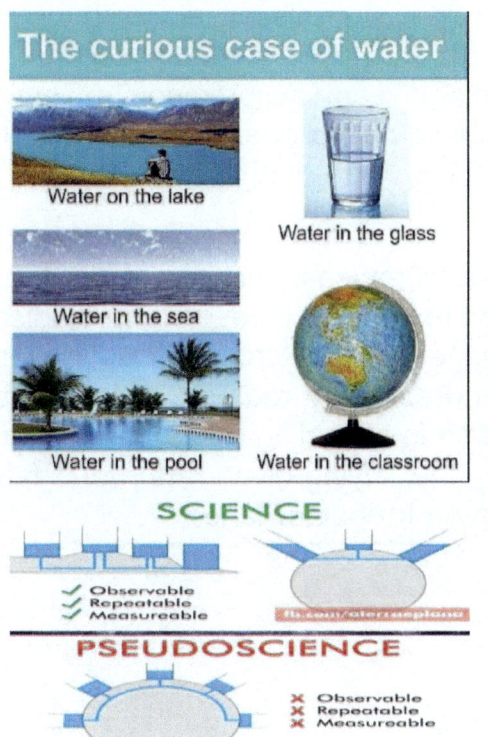

If water was actually curved around a big ball earth then it could be proven and not have to be assumed. The proof and evidence would be piled up instead of being debunked by flat earth realists. Those who deny observable measurable proof have to make assumptions to defend their whirling ball of water.

Water will travel 1000s of miles to find seaLEVEL. Every time experiments have been conducted standing water has proven to be perfectly flat and level. You have NEVER seen a curved ocean, only a horizon line. It's flat and at eye level on the beach and flat and still at eye level in a plane going over the ocean, flat and at eye level flying over the equator. No downward curvature whatsoever means no ball. It's as simple as that.

Rivers run down to sea-LEVEL because of the incline of their beds, sometimes 1000s of feet above sea-level.

16

If the world were a globe however, the Amazon in South America, that flows in an easterly direction, would sometimes be running uphill and sometimes down, according to the movement of the globe. All rivers form ponds and lakes. All from flowing down hill, not upwards. Then the Congo in West Africa, flows a westerly course to seaLEVEL, would also be running alternately up and down. There are plenty of other long rivers but I think you get my point.

They both would be running upward but when the globe takes a half turn, they would both be running downward. But no one ever sees any such changes. But experiments and physical reality SHOWS us that water will find its level and flatten out just like the horizon line on an ocean. I'll go with the observable evidence.

There are rivers that flow for hundreds or even a 1000 miles towards seaLEVEL without failing more than a few feet, notably, the Nile, which, in a thousand miles falls but a foot. That's 666,666 feet of missing curvature. This fact alone should tell you someone's lying.

These flat land rivers would have to be flowing up the ball earth at some points. There's no reason to assume that they are, because this problem does not exist on a flat earth. No curvature, no ball.

"The surface of all water, when not agitated by natural causes, such as winds, tides, earthquakes etc., is perfectly level. The sense of sight proves this to every unprejudiced and reasonable mind. Can any so-called scientist, who teaches that the earth is a whirling globe, take a heap of liquid water, whirl it round, and so make rotundity? He cannot. Therefore it is utterly impossible to prove that an ocean is a whirling rotund section of a globular earth, rushing through 'space' at the lying-given-rate of false philosophers." William Thomas Wiseman (The Earth An Irregular Plane)

Water never has convexity like it would have to on a ball earth. All oceans, seas, lakes and ponds have zero convexity to them. This is because water is level and flat, hence the term 'water level.'

Periscopes are another example that water level does not have a downward curvature to it. They typically don't rise high out of the water, they instead rely on magnification to see further. How are they ignoring the curvature of the earth?

Lake Baikal, Siberia

Pack work on the pack ice.
© NVANIER TAIGA

If water curves, why don't big frozen lakes have a curve on them? Lake Baikal in Siberia is about 400 miles long; it is also one of the flattest places on earth when frozen. That's 106,666 feet of missing curvature. It creates a mirror image where you can see for almost 100 miles, that's 6,666 feet of missing curvature. We use instruments that use water to make sure things are level across its length and breadth.

Lake Baikal in the south of Siberia is not only the oldest and deepest lake in the world, but during colder months it freezes and forms one of the flattest surfaces on Earth. During the Russian Civil War in 1920, the White Russian Army fled the pursuing Red Army by crossing the frozen lake southward to China.

Land has mountains, hills and valleys, so we must turn to the ocean to prove or disprove, by way of sight and measurements, the earth's curvature, because it is the same elevation all over, which is sea-level. Although you can debunk ball-Earth with land, we'll get to that in a little while.

Curvature is the very thing that requires to be seen to establish the globe theory; but it is the very thing that has never been seen. But it MUST exist for the ball Earth theory to be proven.

No matter whether on the beach, on a boat or on a plane, when we look out at the sea, the water extends in one straight line on a flat surface, as far as the eyesight can reach, from straight ahead and from left to right.

Ships are seen with scopes and binoculars, at distances much further than the allowance would be for the supposed curvature. When a ship or any other object recedes from the observer on a level surface the highest part is always seen last by reason of perspective. So that the masts and sails of a receding vessel on a flat surface should be in view long after the hull has become invisible to the naked eye, but they will never appear to lean like they would be doing on a ball. They're always vertical.

I love how curvature is never left and right, it's always in front of you, till you zoom in that is. If you can see the ship go over curvature from sea shore at 3 to 5 miles out, then wouldn't the ocean be dropping away quite noticeably when you're flying over it at 500 mph?

Nothing ever looks tilted like it would if it going over curvature. Everything is always vertical, even when almost completely gone it's still standing or sailing straight vertical.

If you can stand at sea level and see the ship go over the curve, what does that say about the size of the globe? How can it hold even North America much less the other land masses and massive oceans?

The ocean is a body of water that has reached a level, therefore it has a SURFACE. Oceans are connected and contained. It is one level of ocean, one huge body of water, sharing the same horizontal surface. When water is added to it, the ocean level rises. This big "puddle" is filling up and the shorelines of our continents adapt accordingly. Puddles don't curve when they get bigger. Prove me wrong.

Some islands have already vanished completely under the flat surface of the rising ocean level. This fact alone proves the existence of a container allowing a surface to exist within it. This is real. It's simple physics of contained water and land.

The oceans are physically connected as a huge body of water, surrounding our continents equally and leveling up to the shoreline. All seashores are level together.

Every contained body of water naturally establishes a horizontal surface when at rest. Sea level is the actual surface, the beach is the point where water has stopped because of the continental shelf, thus holding the water. The continents are islands, visible above a flat ocean. They are connected and contained. It is one level of ocean, one huge body of water, sharing the same horizontal surface between our continents.

The ocean is contained and enclosed by Antarctica. Antarctica is the shelf that holds the ocean. Antarctica is 7000-9000 feet above sea level. This fact makes it the most elevated landmass on earth. The perfect container for the ocean. We'll discuss Antarctica more a little later.

Observable physical reality shows that all bodies of standing water have a level surface with no one part higher than the other. Seeing as how all the oceans are connected together, they are all virtually of the same level. If the earth is 70% water then it's acknowledged that the world is a plane and not a sphere.

People continue to tell me that the ship going out of view bottom first is a sure proof the earth is a ball. But flat earthers have video recorded themselves running a leveled blank all the way down the beach. As our eyes tell us, there is no curvature. This experiment shows that the ship is not going behind any curvature. Once again, when such an unproven theory goes against all experiments, experience and common sense, it is high time to drop the theory.

If you can see a ship go behind the curvature straight ahead then you should see twice the curvature from left to right. If there's no curvature from left to right then how can there be any curvature at HALF the distance? The experiment showed however, that no such curvature existed, just as our eyes have shown us. No curvature, only deception.

There is no curvature from left to right as a leveled blank down the beach showed, therefore there is none half that distance straight ahead, as a good zoom camera can show.

SPHERICAL TRIGONOMETRY DICTATES THE SURFACE OF ALL STANDING WATER MUST CURVE DOWNWARD EQUALLY IN ALL DIRECTIONS.

IT'S CALLED "SEA LEVEL" FOR GOOD REASON.

BECAUSE THERE IS NO CURVATURE FROM LEFT TO RIGHT, THERE CANNOT BE CURVATURE FROM NEAR TO FAR OR ANY OTHER DIRECTIONS.

THE EARTH IS PAPER TOWEL ROLL SHAPED

Nick Havok

The Navy brags about shooting a target at 80 to 100 miles away with their rail guns, by locking on with a laser. How, when 100 miles has 6,666 feet of curvature? I wonder if any of the "sailors" ever think of that. I asked one and he simply deflected the question. Another Navy sailor said all their weapons are designed for a plane. He is a flat earther as well.

On clear days you can see the Chicago skyline from sea level even though it's almost 60 miles across Lake Michigan. That's 2,320 feet of missing curvature. Notice the buildings are upright and not tilted slightly as it would be if going over a curved earth.

After a photographer, Joshua Nowicki, posted a picture of the skyline, the News weatherman announced that you can't see Chicago because of the curvature, and that it is a superior mirage. However, fellow flat earther, Rob Sika proved them wrong. He and some other flat earthers jumped on his boat and video recorded themselves going across the lake with the skyline in view. It was not a mirage.

The Zetetic Method

This weather man told us this was a mirage. Rob Skiba hopped into a boat with a camera crew and proved him WRONG. This city should be 2320 feet below curvature.

Two real mirage.

The fact that water is flat, when undisturbed, and proven so, is one of the anchors and solid proofs of a flat earth. If people reject that provable fact, it's a personal choice based on authoritarian hearsay. The globe earth is simply a delusion of modern theoretical astronomy. I challenge any globe earth believer to prove large bodies of water to be convex, and I'll concede.

It is this annoying flat water that keeps defying all astronomical attempts to make this earth plane into a sphere. Water thus proves that the earth is indeed a plane and not a whirling ball.

Will any scientist, by a practical experiment upon standing water, give us one proof that this world is an "oblate spheroid?" A flat ocean can be verified with the scientific method, but the whirling ball claim cannot. Please prove me wrong with the scientific method.

Many have told me a drop of water proves the ocean's curved. Rain drops and drops of water on a surface is called water/surface tension. Using surface tension, from drops of water as proof of an ocean wrapped around a whirling ball is called desperation. It's proof of a successful indoctrination.

Why aren't people demanding demonstration and real physical based evidence for the globe model? Flat earthers did, and got nothing but censorship and discrediting campaigns for their questioning. No politician or Pseudo-scientist likes a denier/debunker.

Water is flat. It doesn't require a belief system. This is an irrefutable fact that can be tested and replicated by anyone. The ball theory is a lie. It's not even a mistake or miscalculation. It's a flat out lie. We need a practical demonstration with a body of water at rest displaying measurable convexity. Till then you are a flat earther, whether you believe it or not.

The BLACK SWAN

This is only ONE of the simplest flat earth proofs. For the flat levelness of water meets us on every hand at every location. We can do nothing but prove it and recreate it. If you can disprove this "Black Swan" then do so, until then the ball earth sinks under flat and level water by way of buoyancy, but that's another chapter further on.

Congrats to all the higher conscious mammals who woke up to flat water.

"When you're creating a bullshit story you don't have physical evidence." Eric Dubay

CURVATURE
"This is why it must be admitted that beliefs resting entirely on statements from NASA and other national space agencies, true or not, are in fact demonstrations of blind faith in the trustworthiness, goodness, and competence of government and the politicians that run government.

With our nearly blind faith in place, the major governments of the world are in a position to insert beliefs into our collective minds at their pleasure without restraint. Let's all hope the governments of the world and the politicians that run them are all benevolent, kind, competent, and beyond all capacity for wrongdoing." Author John Andrew Reed

CURVELESS BALL?
To paraphrase Gabrielle Henriete, if we want to ascertain the shape of the floor of any large room we get down to the floor itself, and do not go about measuring the light bulbs or spots on the ceiling.

In this book the reason some of the distances and speeds, to and from, are quoted differently each time is because different science books and science websites have different claims. So I'll share this absurdity with you. If they went off facts this wouldn't be the case, would it?

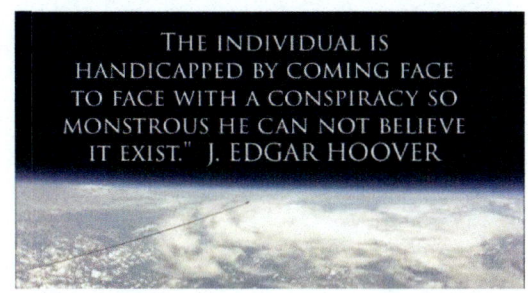

When I'm discussing flat earth with people, most will point to the sky. They know they can't prove curvature. But I'll point to the sky later on, but for now let's look downward to the observable provable flat earth.

If the earth were a ball at 25,000 miles in circumference at the equator, there would have to be downward curvature at 8" per square mile. This IS NOT flat earther's claim as some think, it is the government established scientist claim. People are debunking this claim in different ways. We'll look at some of these ways in this chapter.

THE QUOTED MEASUREMENT OF EARTH'S CURVATURE BY OUR "ESTABLISHED" SCIENTISTS

To find the curvature for any number of miles not given on this chart, simply square the number of miles, multiply that by 8 and then divide by 12. Example: 5 miles/ 5x5=25, 25x8=200, 200÷12=16.66 feet of curvature.

Look at the picture below this chart I made. At the top it says the chart they made is Pythagorean proof for curvature of a ball....... But this chart has been debunked in many ways. Measurements put on a chart are not proof of the measurements.

MILES	CURVATURE DROP IN INCHES THEN FEET
1	8"
2	32"
3	6'
4	10'
5	16'
6	24'
7	32'
8	42'
9	54'
10	66'
20	266'
30	600'
40	1,066'
50	1,666'
60	2,400'
70	3,266'
80	4,266'
90	5,400' (1.02 miles)
100	6,666' (1.26 miles)
120	9,600' (1.82 miles)

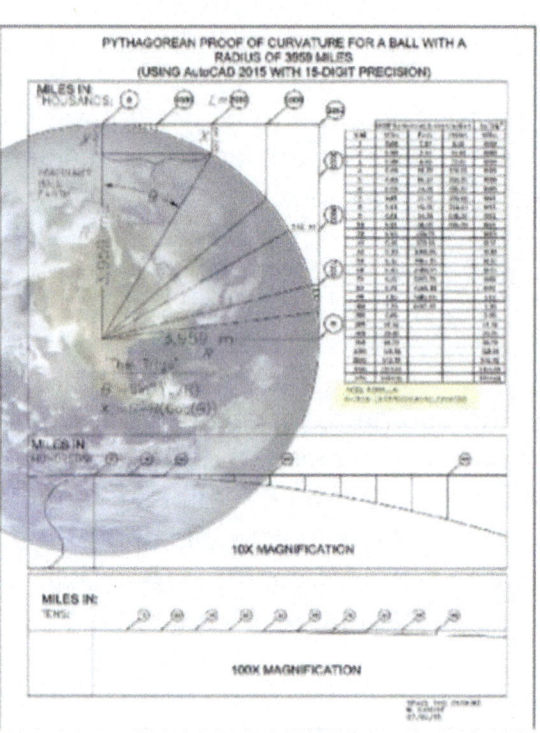

IF the earth is a globe, and is 25,000 English statute miles in circumference, the surface of all standing water must have a certain degree of convexity--every part must be an *arc of a circle*. From the summit of any such arc there will exist a curvature or declination of 8 inches in the first statute mile. In the second mile the fall will be 32 inches; in the third mile, 72 inches, or 6 feet, as shown in the following diagram:

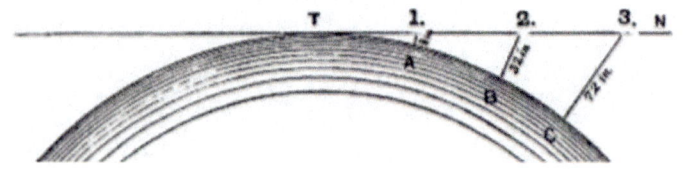

"In the world of science, a fact is a legal tender. Before you can assert a legal tender, you must demonstrate a fact. A fact must be established as such before it is legal tender." Ingersoll

Earth's curvature of 8" per squared mile is figured by the radius which is figured by the diameter. However long distance photography, a level blank down a beach, plane sailing, a plane ride, the Great Plains of Earth, water, etc have all debunked it. There is no established curvature though there's a formula for it. That's proves it's math build on assumptions of curvature. And it's been debunked.

Right now, if everyone, all over the world that's on a plane, simultaneously took pictures of the flat horizon line they were viewing and put them all together would we have a sphere? If not, how many flat horizons lines does it take to create a sphere?

The stretch of land view on a plane is between 300 to 500 miles, depending on atmosphere and height. Let's go in-between and say a 400 miles stretch is seen. That's 106,666 feet of missing curvature. These flat horizons are all across the world.

Look at all these flat horizon lines. Remember, they go on and on as the plane fly's. How can anyone think they can dig their way to blue skies?

If you were laying on the beach the flat horizon line would be at eye level. If you were to fly over the beach the horizon line would remain flat and at eye level. Sphere horizon lines drop downward and roll away from you, not rise with you.

On an unmanned amateur balloon, at 121,000 feet with a non-gopro cam, the horizon line is still flat and at eye level. The horizon line on a ball should be fixed, not continuously being extend as the observer rises. Where's the downward curvature at the beach? Or on the plane? How about the balloon?

No matter how big the ball is, the horizon has to drop downward and away from you, there's no physical way to do otherwise. The fact that it doesn't destroys the ball theory.

How can there be so many flat surfaces, that go for such great distances, on a ball? On an extended level plane, the horizon would always remain level with a ratio of 50% sky to 50 % land, just as we see it. If it was concave, the horizon would be concave, not horizontal, if it was a ball, the horizon would be convex, not a straight flat line, and the sky/land ratio would change the higher you ascended, not stay the same.

The priests of Scientism have people believing that Australians are 'down under' underneath us, their feet opposite of ours. But you can fly flat and level, with the horizon line at eye level the entire trip, all the way to Australia and see that it's NOT the land from "down under" on an imaginary ball, but simply across the way. There's no digging your way to blue skies folks. Wake up, they're lying.

If the earth is 25,000 miles around at the equator and you flew around the ball earth at the equator, then the amount of curvature you have to account for is 416,666,666 feet. Do you think your plane would do that, or do you think it would fly flat and level, like it always does?

You can fly to and over the equator and observe a flat horizon line just like you see on the beach. This world is covered in flat horizon lines that remain at eye level. If you can prove we're on a ball I'm listening.

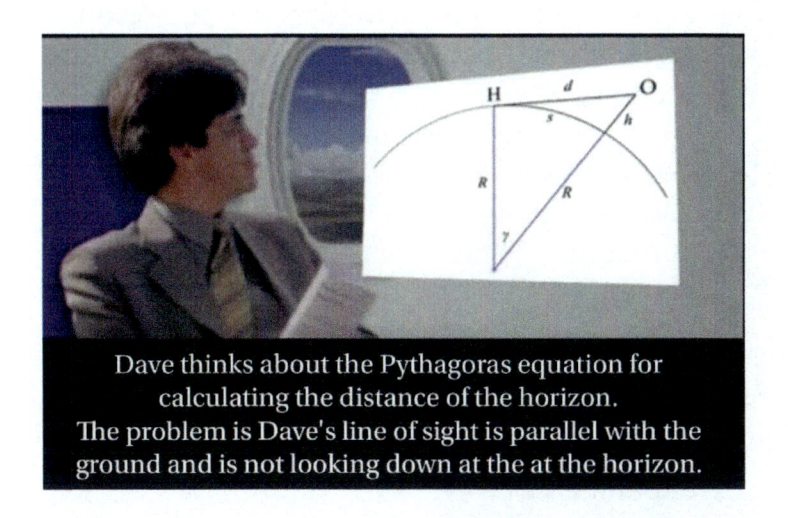

Dave thinks about the Pythagoras equation for calculating the distance of the horizon.
The problem is Dave's line of sight is parallel with the ground and is not looking down at the at the horizon.

So how is it that Dave can see the horizon in his window at 35,000 feet above sealevel if the ground beneath him is shaped like a ball?

Picture Credit Aerotime.aero

This jet has a speed of mach 3.2, which is 2455.26 mph. That's over 40 miles a minute, which means it has to account for a little over 1066 feet of curvature per minute or it'll start ascending into "space." Do you think it does this? I've seen videos of them flying over the ocean and it was not.

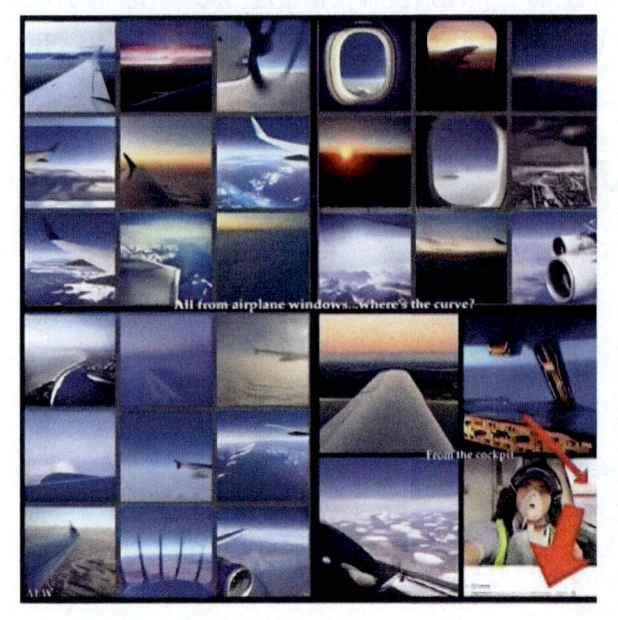

Flat earthers have taken to doing their own experiments and video recording it, since the government puppet Pseudo-scientist can't be trusted.

One such experiment was taking a flat blank and two sawhorses and going down the beach leveling the blank to see if there was any curvature. There was none, just like our senses tells us; the ocean is flat and we can prove it in several ways; no need to take anyone's word for it. AT ALL! Can you say the same for the ocean being wrapped around a ball? Where are the globe believers' experiments?

Scientist Carl Sagen did an experiment where he clued two sticks on a flexible board, and showed a light of the board with the board curved. The shadows were different lengths. Carl Sagen then said that this could ONLY happen if the earth was a sphere. A flat earther did the same experiment on a flat board and showed it was the positioning of the light source, not curvature, that made the difference.

Don't ever think that a Scientist is smarter than you just because he talks with big words, quoting useless math, with a white coat on and indoctrinated heavily with degrees. I can trash their theories with my GED education using reality.

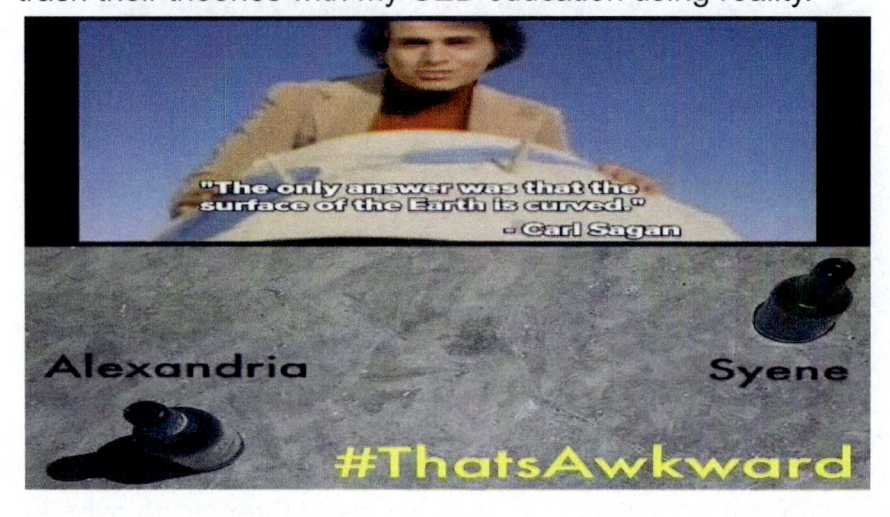

I have a video on my YouTube channel, "flatearthlogic dot net," that has quite a few experiments debunking curvature done by scientists. It's called "Experiments that prove flat earth." Go check it out. These experiments are mostly laser test.

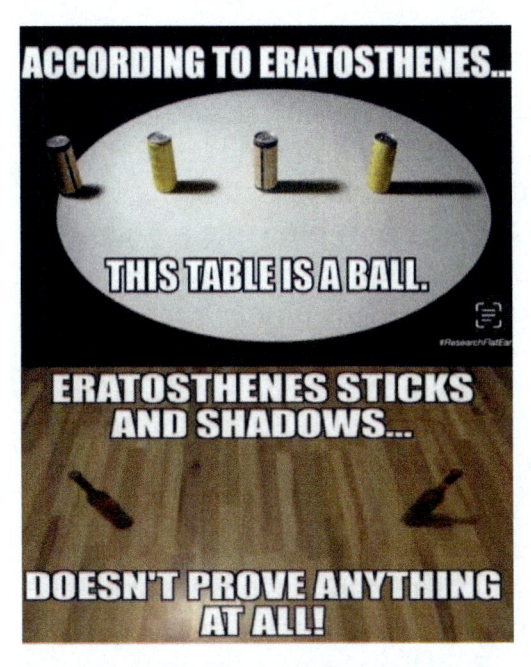

Some of these scientists on the video are from Brazil. The scientists in Brazil seem to be coming out and proving flat earth while in America they're staying silent. Our scientists are waking up but quietly, and for good reason, but that's another story.

Survey says that there are about 11,000,000 flat earthers in Brazil. Or should I say 11,000,000 who know they're flat earthers.

That's what happens when the government doesn't have a strong grip around the pocket books of the science industry. The truth seems to get out more.

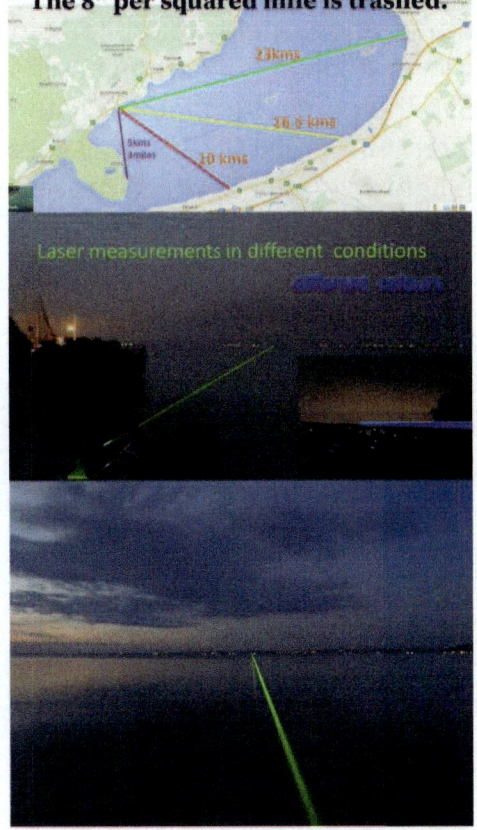

Then we have the old Bedford Level experiment that proved conclusively the canal's water to be completely flat over a 6-mile stretch. Dr. Samuel Rowbotham stood in the canal with his telescope held 8 inches above the surface of the water, then his friend in a boat with a 5 foot tall flag sailed the 6 miles away. If Earth were a ball 25,000 miles in circumference the 6 mile stretch of water should have comprised an arc exactly 6 feet high in the middle, so the entire boat and flag should have ultimately disappeared, when in fact the entire boat and flag remained visible at the same height for the entire journey.

Twice the altitude of a commercial aircraft and yet the horizon is still and always will be flat.
https://www.nbcnews.com/mach/science/experimental-glider-smashes-record-high-altitude-flight-ncna907586

How did sailors, for many centuries, use a flat earth map for navigation if it is incorrect and earth is actually a ball? If the Antarctic treaty prevents a Antarctica circumference trip then how can we prove the southern hemisphere trips are the same as the northern? Once again, we have to take someone's word for it. Captain Cook and other expeditions reported around 60,000 miles, give or take, around Antarctica before the treaty. What about their claims?

Sailors used, and can still use, star constellations that have been unchanging in recorded history. If the earth was flying about in three different directions, this would not be the case. Reality shows us the truth. We're being lied to. But more on the stars later.

Some people give me the argument that the bottom of the clouds lid up at sunset, proves globe earth because the sun is going around the curvature and can hit underneath the clouds. Let's have a look at this shall we.

Let's do an experiment. If you lay under the porch and someone held a mobile light above the porch, the top of the porch would be lid but not the bottom. If that person begins to walk away, still holding the light the same distance above the porch, the sides will start to light up and less on the top. Then as they walk away even further, the bottom will light up and it will be in your eye. The top is even less. Also the light will "appear" to be moving downward. It's not. It's moving away from you.

It's just that simple folks. The sun can now hit the bottom of the clouds as it moves away, whereas before the sun was located on the top of the clouds and couldn't get to the bottom. If you think the sun is going behind any curvature, fly west and debunk that illusion.

The Zetetic Method

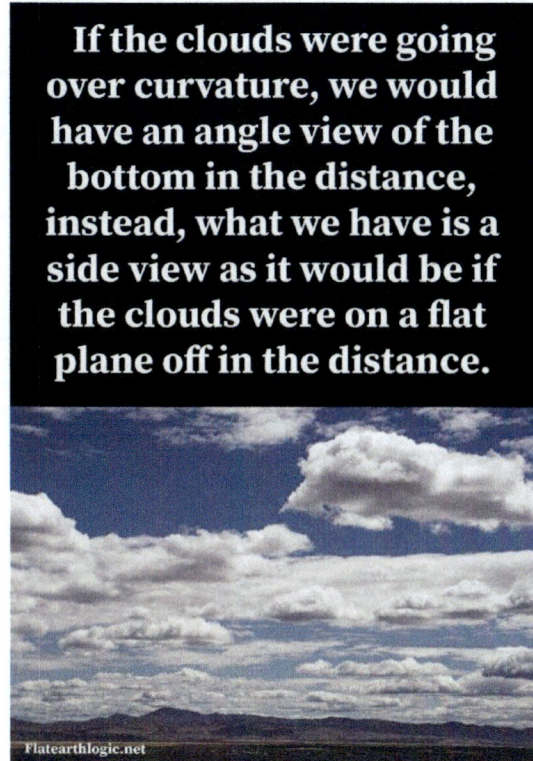

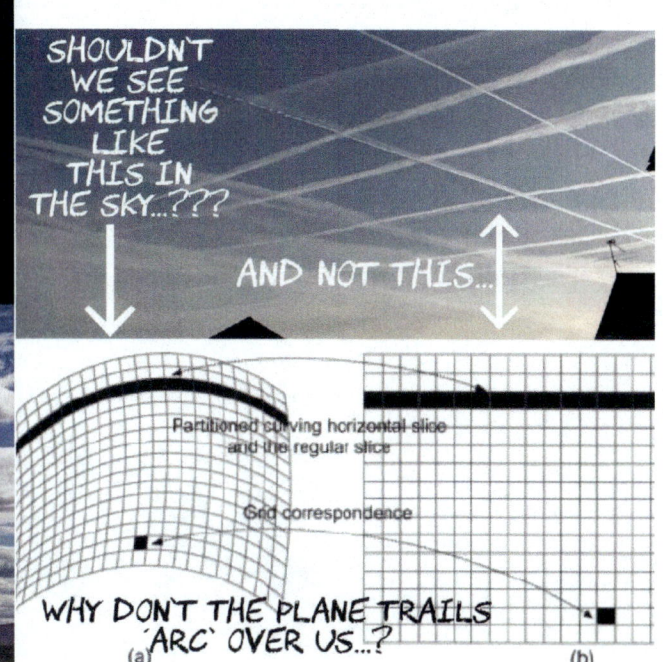

> If the clouds were going over curvature, we would have an angle view of the bottom in the distance, instead, what we have is a side view as it would be if the clouds were on a flat plane off in the distance.

Same with chemtrails as with clouds, if they were going over a curved earth we would see a different view, would we not? More like the underside of them; but instead, the view we get is that of a straight line going off in the distance. As you drive down the road following them, they'll be straight and flat.

Furthermore, if planes follow the supposed invisible curvature of earth, then as the plane flies away from us, it wouldn't just appear to go towards the horizon like we see it, it would have to lower its nose slightly, otherwise it would fly off into space. So, we would start seeing more of the bottom of the plane. But as physical evidence would have it, the plane's nose stays tilted 3º upward to prevent the wind from catching the nose and pushing it downward. The wings lower and raise the plane when needed, but the nose remains tilted upward. This makes sense on a flat earth, but on a ball earth the plane has to lower its nose to make for downward curvature.

Take a basketball and a small object and move the object around the ball while keeping the nose tilted upward. Do you see what I mean?

34

The BLACK SWAN

I'm not really sure if you can read the writing on these pictures after publishing. This is my first book and I have no idea how the final work it's going to turn out, so I'll repeat it here:

Earth's curvature of 8" per square mile is figured by the radius which is figured by the diameter. However, long distance photography, a level blank down a beach, plane sailing, a plane ride, water, the Great Plains of Earth, railroad and bridge design, etc. have all debunked it. There is no established curvature though there's a formula for it. That's proof that it's math built on assumptions of curvature, not the reality of it. And it's been debunked.

COMPASS ON A BALL?

If you're in the southern hemisphere how can your compass point to the north pole? It has to go through 1000s of miles of land and water and you have to point it towards your feet, not hold it flat like you're supposed to. There are no fixed East or West point's just as there's no fixed South. The North central pole is the only fixed point on our flat earth. Hold your compass flat in your hand like you're supposed to and tell me it's not pointing into space if we're on a ball. If the earth were globular, it would point into the sky at both ends. Compass only makes sense on a flat earth.

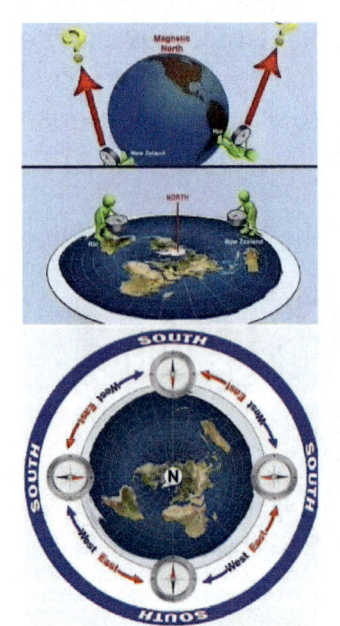

They claim the core of the ball Earth (another assumption, seeing as how we've only dug 8 miles in) creates a magnetic effect with a magnetic pole at the top and an opposite magnetic pole at the bottom. This magnetic sphere however, with opposite poles, cannot be found anywhere in nature, only bar magnetics do this. Ring magnetics exist and are shaped just like the flat earth model. Ring magnetics have the magnetic pole in the center and the opposite pole everywhere along the circumference, like a loudspeaker. You can prove one magnetic pole, you can prove no curvature; these two proven physical facts make the compass a useful tool, until slapping a compass on the bottom of a ball, then.....

Something to think about from author James Lee: "The Sun acts as the positive (+) electromagnetic energy causing 'low-tide' and the moon acts as the negative (-) electromagnetic energy. This alternating current also causes the high and low tides of the oceans. The reason that lakes, rivers and streams do not experience tidal action is due to salinity, or salt. The ocean conducts the needed sodium to connect the negative charge magnetic (anode) of the North Pole with the positive charge (cathode) of the Antarctic region, just like how a common ring magnet loudspeaker works."

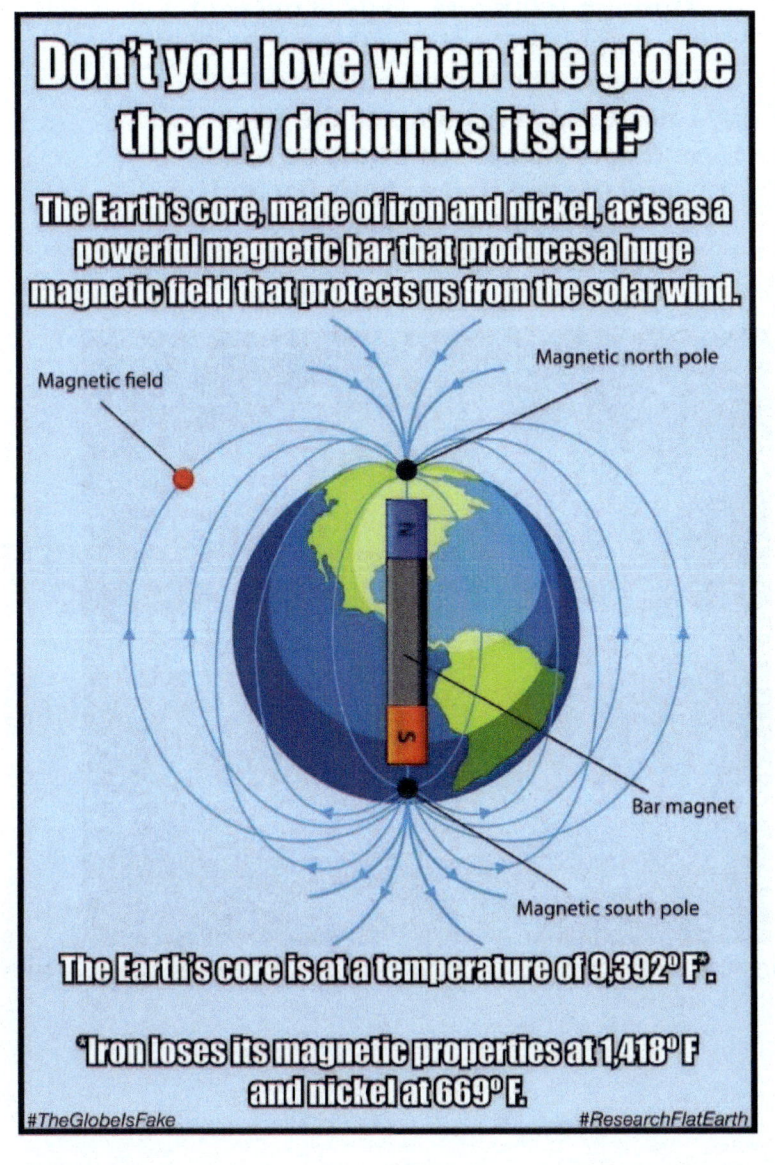

Don't you love when the globe theory debunks itself?

The Earth's core, made of iron and nickel, acts as a powerful magnetic bar that produces a huge magnetic field that protects us from the solar wind.

- Magnetic field
- Magnetic north pole
- Bar magnet
- Magnetic south pole

The Earth's core is at a temperature of 9,392° F.

Iron loses its magnetic properties at 1,418° F and nickel at 669° F.

#TheGlobeIsFake   #ResearchFlatEarth

The North pole is the only magnetic pole on our flat earth and in real life. The poles' other end is not the south pole as reality proves. People say it's the Earth's magnetic lines that makes the compass point north. Put a magnet next to a compass and it will point to the magnet instead of North, now take it away and it points back to North, and only north, once more.

As someone pointed out in a conversation I was following: "It is well known that magnetism acts in a straight line. This of itself is sufficient to prove that the earth cannot be a globe; because on a globe, wherever the magnetic influence came from, the needle would point in that direction; sometimes down through the ship's keel, and always at an angle that would render it useless to the navigator."

The fact that the Compass needle would always have to point North and not space like it would on a ball, and the fact that water is flat and always finds its own level, conclusively proves that the Earth is flat and not a revolving Planet.

If you use the scientific method on curvature, it fails every time. Long distance photography has trashed the quoted non-scientific assumed curvature time and time again. We only have to debunk curvature, for all other assumptions, that can only exist with the ball, to be disregarded.

People say it's the Earth's magnetic lines that makes the compass point north around the ball. Well that offers nothing to the conversation does it? Yes the compass gets pulled north and only north, no one's denying that? It doesn't contribute to the subject of the compass pointing through 1000s and 1000s of miles of water and land to point north though. The fact that the Compass needle always points to the North and not space like it would on a ball, and the fact that water is flat and always finds its own level, conclusively proves that the Earth is flat and not a revolving Planet.

Flat earthers are using the P900 camera to debunk the curvature math; other people as well but they don't even realize it.

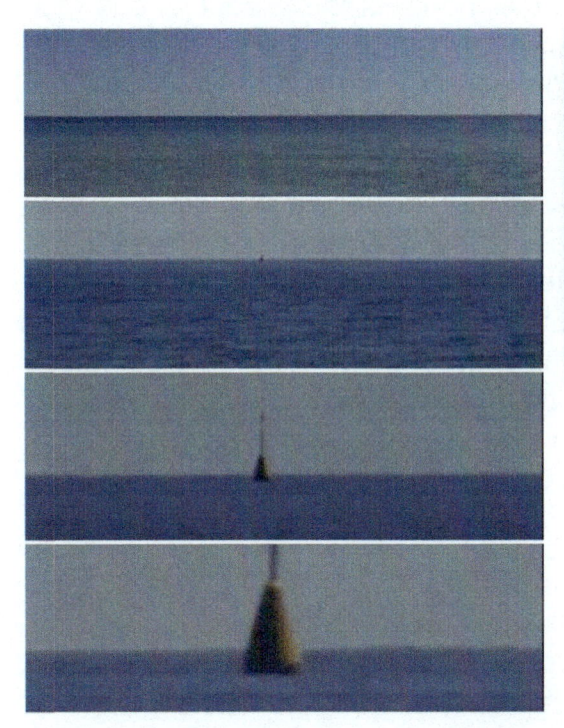

Dear Invisible Curvature

1. How come pilots, railroad and bridge engineers don't have to account for you?
2. How can I believe in you when I've never seen you and all your photos and videos are catfished by NASA and the people who promote you are proven liars?
3. Curvature, how come you're never left to right on the beach, just straight ahead? And why, when I zoom in, you disappear?
4. How come you don't curve downward but instead remain at eye level when the observer rises? Doesn't that make you NOT a curve?

The Zetetic Method

Curvature is the foundation of the heliocentric globe model. It is the root of it in fact. Demonstrations of a curved ocean should be an easy enough task, one would think, but when asked for it, all they tell us is "the ships going behind the curvature you deny," but then long-distance photography with a good scope or a plane rider can debunk it. Is this the best they have?

If they quote the ball earth at being 25,000 miles in circumference at the equator, then that means the curvature has been defined and measured; yet when citizens measure the said curvature, it's missing. Are we to ignore this and go with "authoritarian knows best?" If it's not based on physical facts and reasoning, then it's based on authority.

Luckily, we don't have to take anyone's word for the world we live in. All physical based facts lay in the favor of a flat earth. This is shown to be true when we challenge the earth's rotundity theory to be proven with facts and nothing else.

The theory of Earth's curvature and mobility go hand and hand. If one is proven untrue then the other one must be disregarded as well.

When such an unproven theory goes against all experiments, experience and common sense, it is high time to drop the theory.

If the Earth's circumference is 25,000, and there are 360° in a circle, then each 1° equal 69 miles. Thus, if we see an horizon that covers 500-600 miles, we should see an 8° curve to the horizon. But we don't. It's debunked easily without much effort.

"It is good to pass from fiction to fact—to have, instead of a rotten plank, a strong bridge on which to cross the stream—in lieu of panting in the foggy atmosphere of impossible Theory, to breathe the pure air of heavenly Truth."   I forgot where I got this gem from.

The Zetetic Method

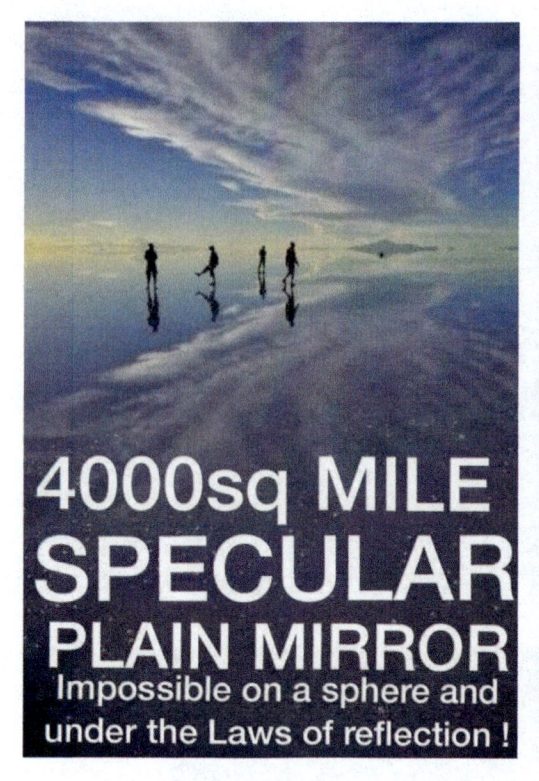

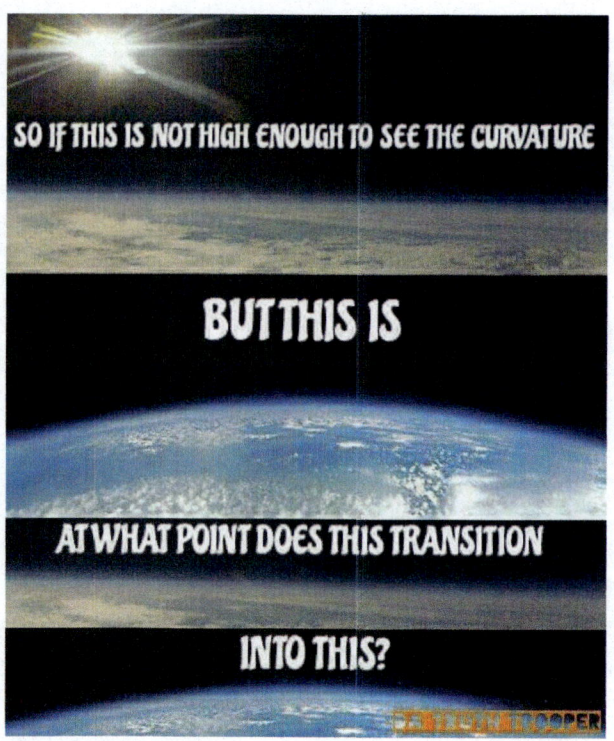

NASA shows a lot of curvature at 75,000 feet and said so in their article, but Neil Degrasse Tyson said you can't see curvature until you get to around 128,000 feet or so. So I'm assuming once again that NASA has released a gopro image of earth with a false claim with it, or are they both full of it? On the video the inside has one view but the outside another. Hmmm

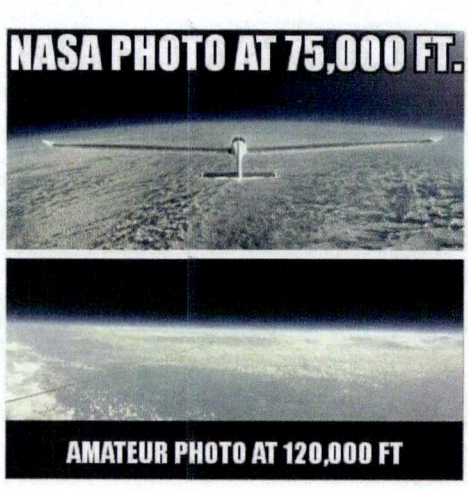

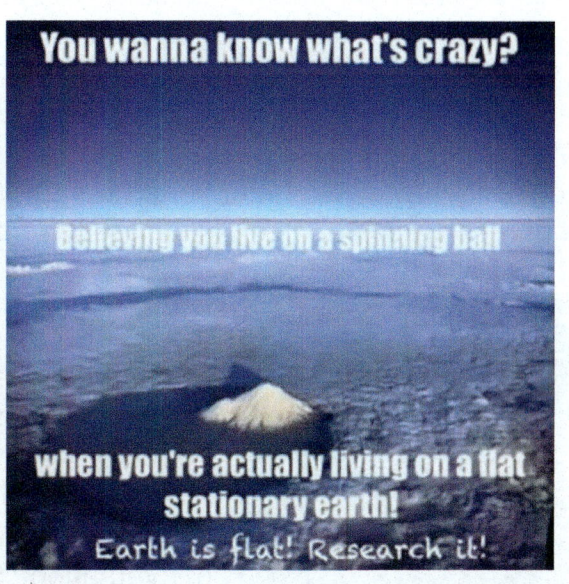

The BLACK SWAN
Curvature is debunked with experiments (such as long distance photography and lasers), and physical based reality, such as a horizon line that remains at eye level like it would on an extended plane, instead of dropping away from you like it would on a sphere earth. This is a solid proof in itself. Observable and provable.

THE GREAT PLAINS

"It will be seen that my reasons for thinking that the earth is round are rather precarious ones. Yet this is an exceptionally elementary piece of information. On most other questions I would have to fall back on the expert much earlier, and would be less able to test his pronouncements. And much of our knowledge is at this level. It does not rest on reasoning or on experiment, but on authority. And how can it be otherwise, when the range of knowledge is so vast that the expert himself is an ignoramus as soon as he strays away from his own specialty? Most people, if asked to prove that the earth is round, would not even bother to produce the rather weak arguments I have outlined above. They would start off by saying that 'everyone knows' the earth to be round, and if pressed further, would become angry. … This is a credulous age, and the burden of knowledge which we now have to carry is partly responsible." George Orwell

I was discussing flat earth vs globe earth with an ex Navy soldier, who was bragging, saying he used to shoot railguns. He could not answer any of my questions though and it wasn't going too well for him. So then he said "You flat earthers always want to talk about water, you never want to talk about land. It's because it doesn't fit your flat earth narrative."

He didn't realize he just admitted that water fits the flat earth "narrative." So I told him I was talking about water because he was in the Navy and I thought he had knowledge to share, but that I was wrong. So I mentioned the Great Plains of the world. The very next comment out of his mouth was him pointing to the sky.

So that conversation gave me the idea to add this subchapter on the Great Plains of the biggest beautiful plain of them all, Earth. Land may not be FLAT, but it doesn't go by any claim of Earth's curvature either. Let's dig in and see what conversation, about land, he was trying to avoid shall we.

There's a section of Europe extending from the German Sea, through Prussia, Poland, and Russia, towards the Ural Mountains, regarded by geographers as ONE VAST PLANE. So flat is the general profile of the region, that it has been remarked, "IT IS POSSIBLE TO DRAW A LINE FROM LONDON TO MOSCOW, WHICH WOULD NOT PERCEPTIBLY VARY FROM A DEAD LEVEL."

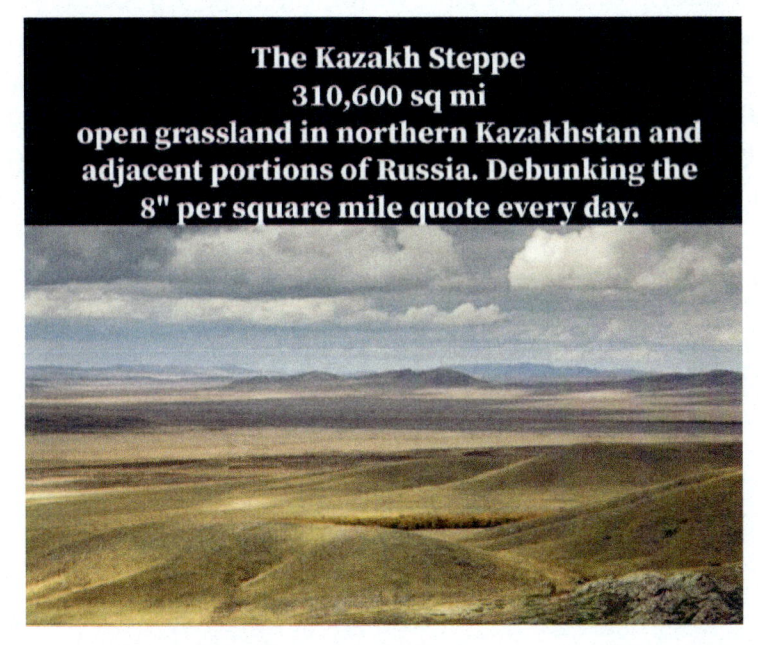

The Kazakh Steppe
310,600 sq mi
open grassland in northern Kazakhstan and adjacent portions of Russia. Debunking the 8" per square mile quote every day.

From the "Atlas of Physical Geography," by the Rev. T. Milner, M.A.: "The plains of Venezuela and New Granada, in South America, chiefly on the left of the Orinoco, are termed llanos, or level fields. Often in the space of 270 square miles THE SURFACE DOES NOT VARY A SINGLE FOOT." "The Amazon only falls 12 feet in the last 700 miles of its course; the La Plata has only a descent of one thirty-third of an inch a mile."

Cloncurry, Australia: The outback in Australia is famous for its vast, almost unending flat plains. Getting across them requires driving along strips of tarmac in a seemingly endless stretch of sameness that can make some drivers go bananas and question whether they are really getting any closer to their destination.

When talking about the railways of South America E. F. Knight says: "There are no curves on the way, the rails being carried in one perfectly straight line across the level plains." As the South America plains are known to be for thousands of square miles."

THE TRANS-AUSTRALIAN RAILWAY HAS THE LONGEST STRAIGHT STRETCH OF RAILTRACK IN THE WORLD

301 MILES WITHOUT A SINGLE CURVE

In a book titled "Nature and Man," by Professor W B. Carpenter, he writes: "Nothing seems to have struck the "Challenger" surveyors more than the extraordinary FLATNESS (except in the neighborhood of land) of that depressed portion of the earth's crust which forms the FLOOR OF THE

GREAT OCEANIC AREA.....If the bottom of mid-ocean were laid dry, an observer standing on any spot of it would find himself surrounded BY A PLAIN, only comparable to that of the North American prairies or the South American pampas.....The form of the depressed area which lodges the water of the deep ocean is rather, indeed, to be likened to that of a FLAT WAITER or TEA TRAY, surrounded by an elevated and deeply-sloping rim, than to that of the basin with which it is commonly compared."

Makgadikgadi salt pans, Botswana:
The 16,000sq km Makgadikgadi Salt Pans in north-eastern Botswana flood seasonally and are not a single pan, but consist of many saltpans divided by sandy desert. Idiot drivers are discouraged, as it's easy to become bogged or lost and with little hope of rescue.

WIKIPEDIA

Abyssal plain

Article Talk

An **abyssal plain** is an underwater plain on the deep ocean floor, usually found at depths between 3,000 metres (9,800 ft) and 6,000 metres (20,000 ft). Lying generally between the foot of a continental rise and a mid-ocean ridge, abyssal plains cover more than 50% of the Earth's surface.[1][2] They are among the flattest, smoothest, and least explored regions on Earth.[3] Abyssal plains are key geologic elements of oceanic basins (the other elements being an elevated mid-ocean ridge and flanking abyssal hills).

Scientists today have mentioned about the sea beds of the Atlantic, the Pacific, and the great Southern Ocean, the Abyssal Plain one is called, being a vast plane surface for tens of thousands of square miles.

The ocean is one great plain. The Abyssal plains can range as far as thousands of kilometers, forming huge plateaus beneath the sea. Look at this article. This sea bed is one of the flattest, smoothest places on earth. How so on a sphere? Exactly how is anyone buying the globe? Please read this article.

Guinness World Records website list the Abyssal Plain as one of the flattest places in the world:

"Abyssal plains are vast expanses of flat, featureless terrain found at the deepest parts of the ocean. They cover approximately 40% of the ocean floor at depths of 4,000–5,000 m (13,000–20,000 ft). The uniform flatness is caused by the accumulation of sediments, up to 5 km (3 miles) thick in places, which overlies the basaltic rocks of the oceanic crust. This means that there is less than 1.5 m (5 ft) of vertical variation for every mile, with an overall average gradient of 1:1,000."

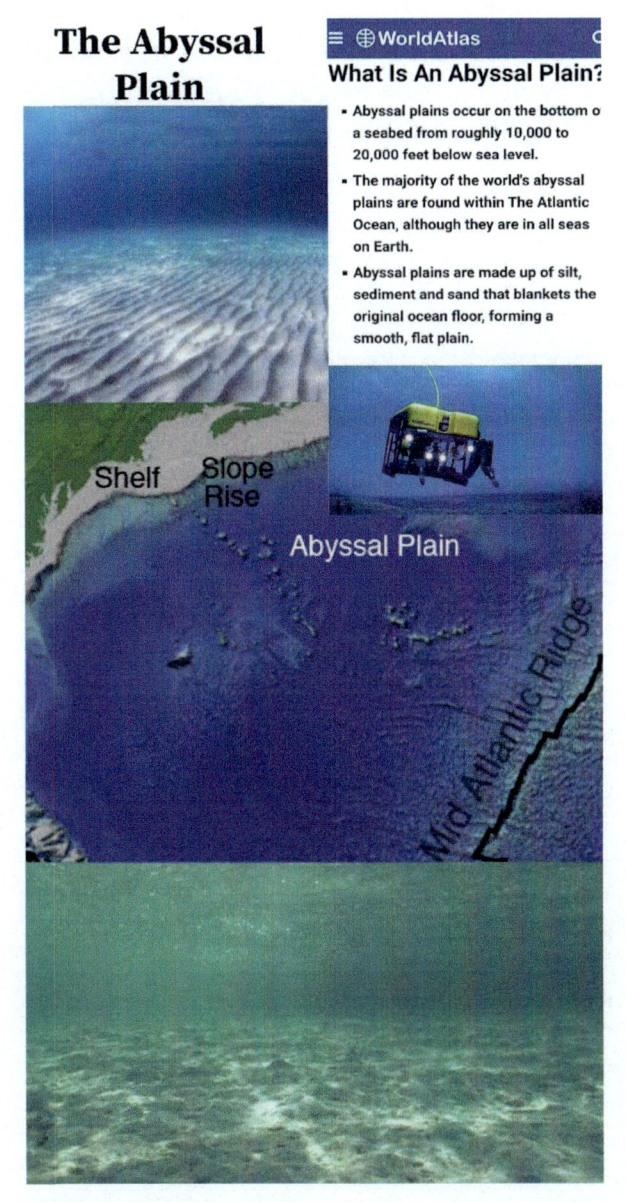

All this observable flat oceans, ocean beds, canals and bridges, lakes and eye level horizon lines from planes, at what point do we see proof of curvature? I guess we'll have to see them in NASA photos, right? I'll get to that a little later.

And once again, it is these level intervening surfaces that defies the astronomical attempts to change this great almighty plain, called earth, to a whirling ball.

Professor W. B. Carpenter's work, "The Deep Sea and its contents": "Nothing seems to have struck the Challenger's surveyors more than the extraordinary flatness (except in the neighborhood of land) of that depressed portion of the Earth's crust which forms the floor of the ocean area."

How does sonar work with directional variable change on a globe vs just depth and directions on a flat earth? Whale sonar can go 10,000 miles. How can that occur on a ball? Wouldn't the Earth's curvature make short work of that?

10,000 miles

A Traveling Music

One of the interesting things about the humpback whale song is how far the song can travel. Researchers estimate that some of the lowest frequency sounds can travel through the ocean as far as **10,000 miles** without losing their energy.
Jul 13, 2018

https://www.bodyglovehawaii.com › ...

All About Whale Song | Body Glove Hawaii

How can a Navy submarine use sonar for Military testing for 1000s of miles? Even covering 80% of earth's oceans.

https://www.exploratorium.edu/theworld/sonar/sonar.html

Flat long-distance surfaces such as that of the sea or the African desert is reason enough to question the ball earth theory.

The Danakil Desert is a desert in northeast Ethiopia, southern Eritrea, and northwestern Djibouti. Situated in the Afar Triangle, it stretches across 100,000 square kilometres (10,000,000 ha) of arid terrain. The area is known for its volcanoes and extreme heat, with daytime temperatures surpassing 50°C. The Danakil Desert is one of the lowest and hottest places on Earth.

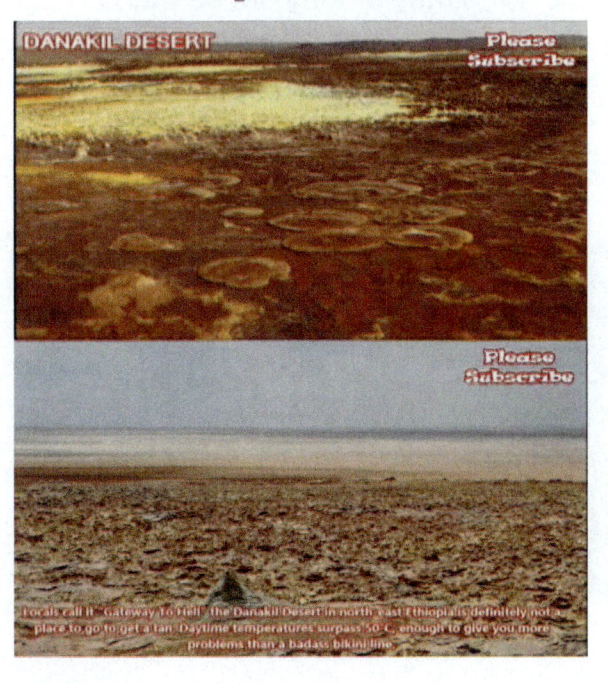

The Zetetic Method

Asia has flatlands all throughout the continent and especially central Asia which is mostly flat. Almost all of Tibet is flatlands. There are continents with 1000s of miles of flatlands. Where's the globe exactly? If you stand at point A note the attitude then get to point B at the end of the horizon and note the attitude, if point A and B matches then that means Earth is flat.

Bonneville salt flats, Utah:
If you want to drive really fast, and we mean really fast, say 900kph for example, then this is the place to do it. Located in north-western Utah, the 121sq km flats are famous for the Bonneville Speedway where various daredevils since 1912 have strapped themselves into speed machines – some jet-propelled – and blasted themselves across the vast flats and into the halls of speed fame. In 1965, professional racecar driver Craig Breedlove topped 966kph in his jet-propelled machine.

How could a tsunami make its way around a ball? Look at the strong currents and their courses that go in every direction, all throughout the world's oceans; how could they be so strong, or even exist at all, if the earth were a ball? Are we supposed to believe that a current will travel 1000s upon 1000s of miles while making for curvature? The curvature would have an end to it. Think about it.

The earth may or may not be round like a plate, but flat water, a rising horizon line and a heck of a lot of flat plains proves it's not a ball. A lot of the ocean beds are gigantic plains.

PLANE SURVEYING

When someone tells you geodetic surveying proves globe earth ask them how. How is the curvature figured into the equation and why don't railroad engineers use it? I have and he couldn't answer it, which means that he doesn't have to do it, he was just defending his belief poorly. Geodetic surveying proves flat earth.

What Is Plane Surveying?

C. Mitchell
Date: July 14, 2022

Plane surveying is a common method of calculating land composition and topography that involves considering a set expanse of land as a flat plane. This kind of land surveying works best for small areas of land, in large part because the Earth is not actually flat. A plane survey conducted over a vast expanse of land is likely to be inaccurate, because it is incapable of accounting for the natural curvature of the earth. In some circles, aerial

This article says plane surveying is done in short distances because of Earth's curvature; but, like plane trigonometry in sailing, you measure flat from A to B then B to C then C to D, etc., etc. etc., and what you end up with is a flat earth. You also have plane surveying on an actual plane to measure longer distances. Hmmm! It would seem logical to use sphere surveying if we lived on a sphere.

Nullabor Plains Australia 800 kms x 400 kms
Zero curvature to be found

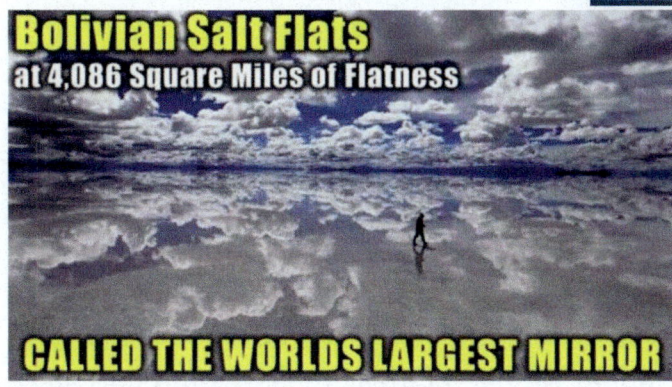

Bolivian Salt Flats at 4,086 Square Miles of Flatness
CALLED THE WORLDS LARGEST MIRROR

The Zetetic Method

The Maldives is another one of the flattest places on earth. Google flattest places on earth. Reality debunks lies. They can't change THAT, they can only change your perception of what you see.

**The Maldives is a nation of islands in the Indian Ocean, that spans across the equator. The country is comprised of 1192 islands that stretch along a length of 871 kilometers.
One of the flattest places in the world is on the equator, who would have thunk?**

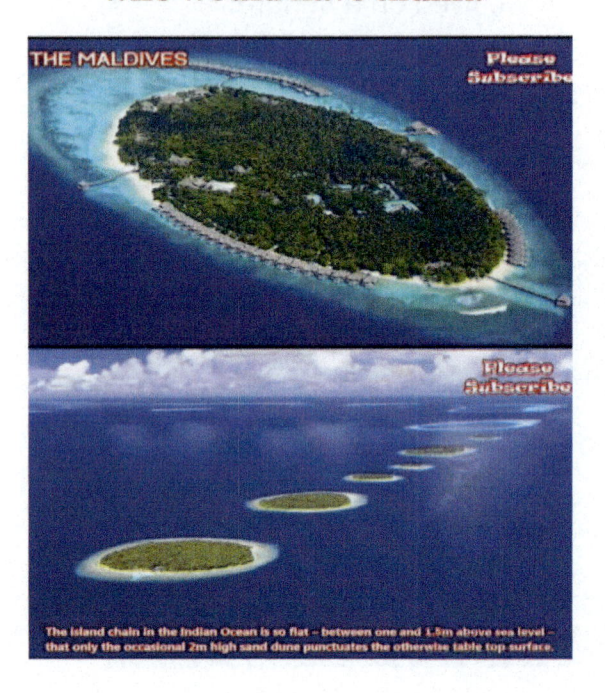

Here's a comment I found, from a flat earther talking to a globe believer, that I liked and 100% agree with, "Ok, it doesn't get any more simple than this and most people don't seem to get it but I'll try to reach you. If the earth is a sphere or even close to being a sphere then it must curve. If something doesn't curve then it is flat. your table doesn't curve, so it is flat. Your tires curve so they are round. Now IF the earth is not flat then it must curve somewhere. So you're at the beach and you see the boat disappear. You think it went beyond the curve. Great, if the earth curves over such a small distance, you should have no difficulty finding places on the earth that we can actually measure the curvature from. Measuring is scientific. A scientist would measure an amount of a chemical or a distance or any quality or quantity of something. So instead of us proving the earth is flat, maybe you can prove to us that it is curved."

The Great Plains BLACK SWANS

1. So we have all of the airplanes views, from all over the world, of horizontal flatness, we have a 121,000 feet elevation gain with nothing but horizontal flatness, at every turn we have a body of water view of horizontal flatness, we have an ocean bed of great flatness, and now the Earth's Great Plains of flatness.

At what point are we on a sphere again? How many of these does it take to make a sphere? It's time to wake up and look around! They're lying to us and our ancestors were correct.

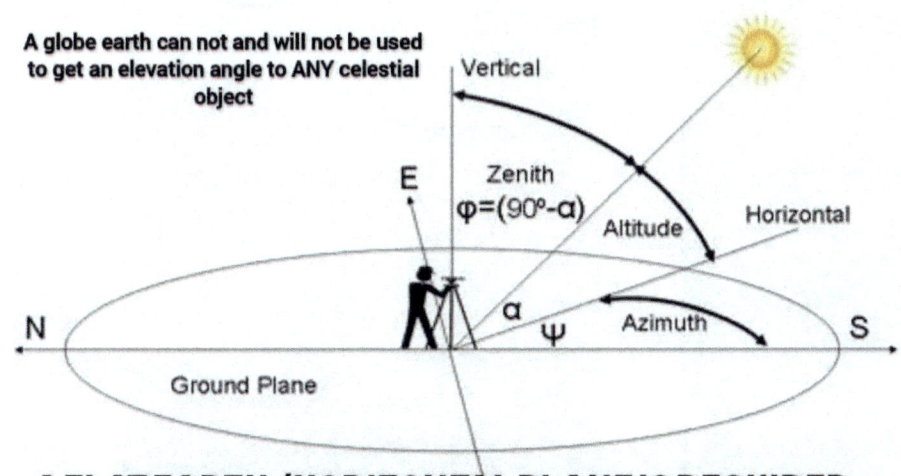

A globe earth can not and will not be used to get an elevation angle to ANY celestial object

$\varphi = (90° - \alpha)$

A FLAT EARTH/HORIZONTAL PLANE IS REQUIRED.

2. The sentence "Geodetic surveying is being done all over the ball earth with flat earth calculations," makes NO sense. And it's not happening because the Earth is flat.

3. Not only does the Great Plains of Earth mentioned here debunk the 8" per square mile, but think of all the other plains not mentioned here. Examples would be the Great Plains of Texas, Kansas, a lot of Montana, all others you can think of from all across the world. If you add all of these together you do not get a ball of earth but rather a flat plain with flat water. All these together make the biggest Great Plain of them all, the Earth Plain.

At 10,582sq km in size and about 100km across, Salar de Uyuni in Bolivia – the world's largest salt flat – is roughly the size of Jamaica. The salt crust ranges from three to 10m thick, amounting to about 10 billion tons of salt.

Wadi Rum, Jordan: Wadi Rum is a valley cut into the sandstone and granite rock in southern Jordan 60 km (37 mi) to the east of Aqaba; The 720sq km of desert valley is walled by sheer sided sandstone and granite mountains. Locals call it the Valley of the Moon.

The Everglades of Florida: Native Americans called it the "grassy waters", others the "River of Grass", which describes the Everglades located in southern Florida, one of the flattest parts of America. Over 60 miles wide and 100 miles long the waters flow south over a limestone shelf to the Florida bay.

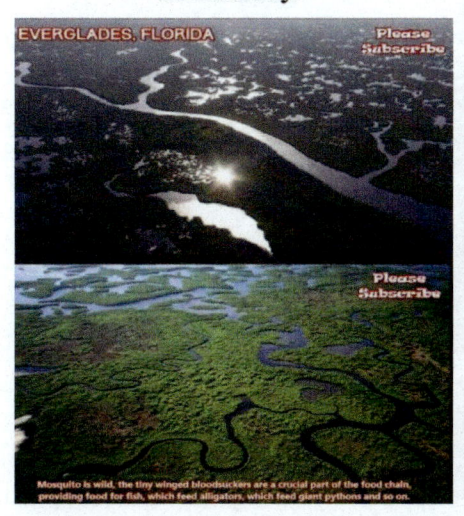

Schleswig-Holstein mudflats, Germany: The mudflats in northern Germany's Schleswig-Holstein Wadden Sea National Park are the largest continuous mudflats on the earth. With an area of 4410 km ^{2} it is by far the largest national park in Germany. The national park extends from the German-Danish maritime border in the north down to the Elbe estuary in the south. In the north there are mudflats are 40 km wide in places.

EARTHQUAKES

Ball earthers have said to me that earthquakes prove a globe earth. Does it really though? How? Is it because of the core of the earth that they assume is a hot molten ball? How would they "know" this when we've only dug 8 miles into the earth? The fact they think plates!!! are shifting and that proves a ball earth is hilarious.

I like the way one flat earther put it so I stole it. "The entomological meaning of the word planet is 'wandering star.' Our Plane-t is a plane, which is why to this day we still call the oceans, Sea-level, and flying crafts are called aero-planes and Earth's mantles are called plate-tectonics. Ancient Greek etymology uses the letter "T" for Terra, or land, so a Plane-T means a plane land or Flat Earth!"

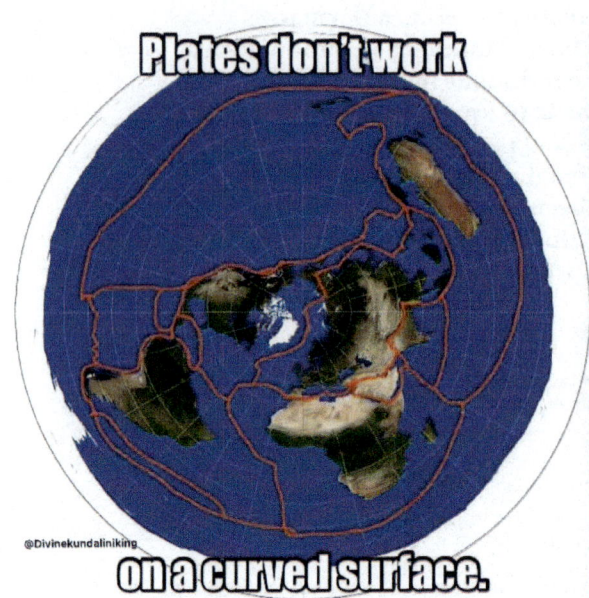

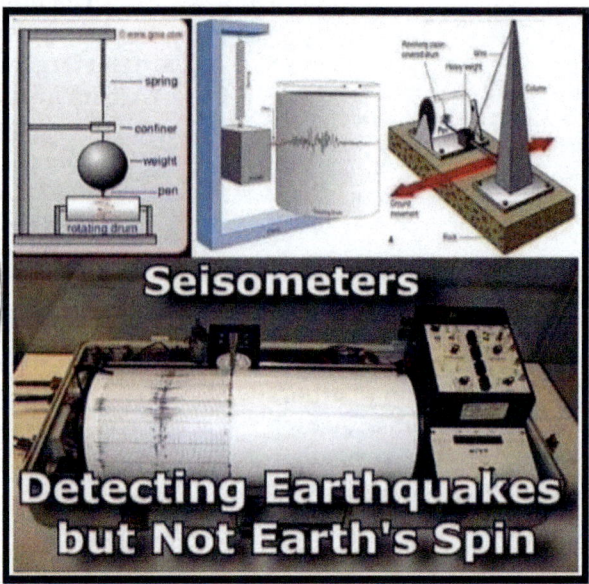

LIGHTHOUSES

"When you control opinion, as corporate America controls opinion in the United States by owning the media, you can make the masses believe almost anything you want, and guide them as you please." Gore Vidal

The distance at which lighthouses can be seen at sea entirely debunks the curvature math that we are given to calculate the idea that we are living on a huge ball. Ships being able to see lighthouses at different angles and distances tells us the sea is flat

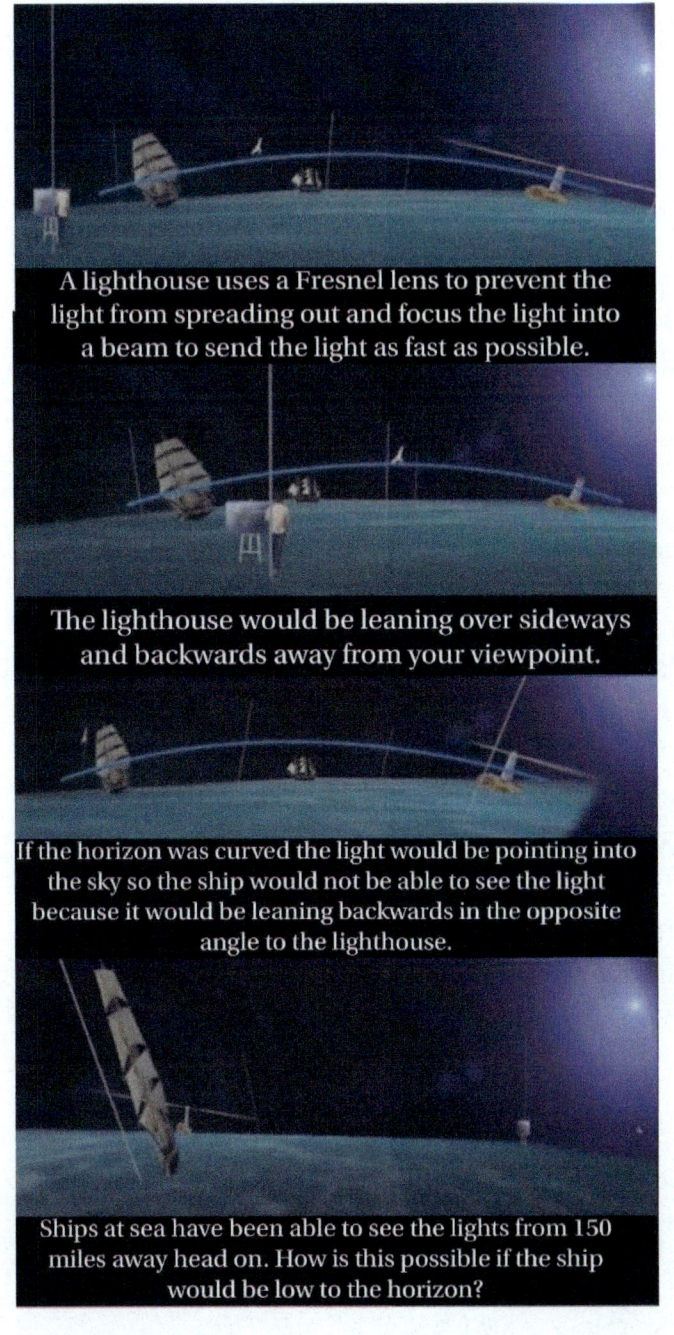

Not only can lighthouses be seen at distances that they shouldn't but life jackets as well. Some life jackets have light beacons on them. The cheaper ones can be seen up to 3 miles, that's 6 feet of missing curvature. There's another light beacon that can be seen up to 10 nautical miles, which is 11.5 miles. That's 88.16 feet of missing curvature.

Here's an article talking about the best equipment, from Boatingmag.com:

"This patented floating device activates with a twist of its Fresnel lens, emitting an SOS signal reportedly visible as far as 10 nautical miles. It satisfies Coast Guard signal carriage requirements, but only for recreational boats and only when accompanied with a day-signal orange flag — which is included in each package. The latter eliminates the need to carry flammable, toxic chemical-fire or smoke flares."

A lighthouse uses a Fresnel lens to prevent the light from spreading out and focus the light into a beam to send the light as fast as possible.

The lighthouse would be leaning over sideways and backwards away from your viewpoint.

If the horizon was curved the light would be pointing into the sky so the ship would not be able to see the light because it would be leaning backwards in the opposite angle to the lighthouse.

Ships at sea have been able to see the lights from 150 miles away head on. How is this possible if the ship would be low to the horizon?

A bright, long-burning life-jacket light.
Courtesy Amazon

The Statue of Liberty stands 326 feet above sea level; on a clear day it has been seen 60 miles away. How when, according to the globe theory, it should be 2074 feet below the horizon after you take away the 326 feet. The globular math has been thoroughly debunked in so many ways, this is but one.

I've worked on boats and have seen lighthouses too many miles away for the quoted curvature of our questionable ball earth. There's a lot of examples of this one way but I'll just share a few. You'll get the point.

A great book: "The lighthouse of the world." Get the book and do the math. Water is FLAT thus Earth is FLAT!

The following is from "The Bible versus Science," by J. C. Akester, Hull:
"A lighthouse on the Isle of Wight in England, 180 feet high (St. Catherine's), has recently been fitted with an electric light of such penetrating power (7,000,000 candles) that it can be seen 42 miles. At that distance, according to modern science, the vessel would be 996 feet below the horizon line of sight. The Cape L'Agulhas lighthouse in South Africa is 33 feet high, 238 feet above sea level, and can be seen for over 50 miles."

Extract from a letter written by a passenger on board the "Iberia" Orient Line, R.M.S.— "At noon on Thursday, 27th of September, we were 169 miles from Port Said; by the ship's log, our rate of steaming was 324 miles in 24 hours. At 12 p.m., we were alongside the lighthouse at Port Said, it having become visible at 7.30 when it was about 58 miles away. It is an ordinary tower, about as high as the tower at Springhead (60 feet), lit by electricity." According to modern science, the vessel would be 2,182 feet below the horizon.

Extract from "Manx Sun" July 24th, 1894. "The weather of late has been very fine. It was a splendid sight, on Sunday evening, to see the land in Ayr, and Cumberland, so clear that houses could be seen with the naked eye; and the smoke from Whitehaven, and other towns, could be seen very distinctly. Ramsey Bay appeared as if it was enclosed by the surrounding land, from Black Coombe to the Point of Ayr, Welney light being seen distinctly, distance 45 miles."

The BLACK SWAN
It's impossible to see through the curvature of the ocean so this is yet another physical fact that has debunked the quoted, but not proven, measurement of curvature.

RAILROAD, BRIDGES AND CANALS
"Here we have on one hand our government making resolutions or order respecting the construction of Railways on a datum horizontal line, on the principle that the Earth is a Stationary Plane, and, on the other hand, subsidizing the Astronomical Society and Board Schools which teach that it is a Whirling Ball." Author David Warsaw Scott

In the building of canals, railroads, bridges and tunnels, the surveyors, engineers and architects never have to factor in the curvature, as the datum line from which surveys are made IS ALWAYS A HORIZONTAL LINE.

If any acquiring minds wanted to know, they should call upon the surveyors to prove that he allows the necessary amount for curvature. The 'scientists' at the observatories should do this, instead of repeating to tourists, like parrots, but they wouldn't dare, because the allowance for invisible curvature is never made.

Here's what some engineers had to say regarding supposed curvature:

1) "It is customary in Railway and Canal constructions for all levels to be referred to a datum which is nominally horizontal, and is so shown on all sections. It is not the practice in laying out Public Works to make allowance for the curvature of the earth."—Manchester Ship Canal Co., Engineer's Office, 19th February, 1892.

2) In the Birmingham Weekly Mercury, of 15th February, 1890, "Surveyor" writes as follows:

"All our locomotives are designed to run on what may be regarded as TRUE LEVELS or FLATS. There are, of course, partial inclines or gradients here and there, but they are always accurately defined and must be carefully traversed. But anything approaching to eight inches in the mile, increasing as the square of the distance, COULD NOT BE WORKED BY ANY ENGINE THAT WAS EVER, YET CONSTRUCTED. Taking one station with another all over England and Scotland, it may be stated that all the platforms are ON THE SAME RELATIVE LEVEL. The distance between the Eastern and Western coasts of England may be set down as 300 miles. If the prescribed curvature was indeed as represented, the central stations at Rugby or Warwick ought to be close upon three miles higher than a chord drawn from the two extremities. If such was the case there is not a driver or stoker within the Kingdom that would be found to take charge of the train......"

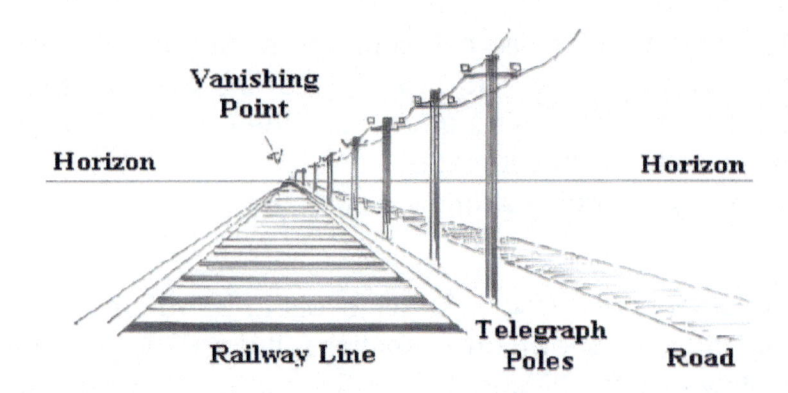

3) Engineer, W. Winckler was published in the Earth Review regarding the Earth's supposed curvature, stating:

"As an engineer of many years standing, I saw that this absurd allowance is only permitted in school books. No engineer would dream of allowing anything of the kind. I have projected many miles of railways and many more of canals and the allowance has not even been thought of, much less allowed for. This allowance for curvature means this - that it is 8" for the first mile of a canal, and increasing at the ratio by the square of the distance in miles; thus a small navigable canal for boats, say 30 miles long, will have, by the above rule an allowance for curvature of 600 feet. Think of that and then please credit engineers as not being quite such fools. Nothing of the sort is allowed. We no more think of allowing 600 feet for a line of 30 miles of railway or canal, than of wasting our time trying to square the circle."

The London and Northwestern railroad forms a line 180 miles between London and Liverpool. Its highest point is midway at Birmingham Station at 240 feet above sea level. At 180 miles it should have an arc at the center point in Birmingham Station about 21,600 feet above London and Liverpool. It does not.

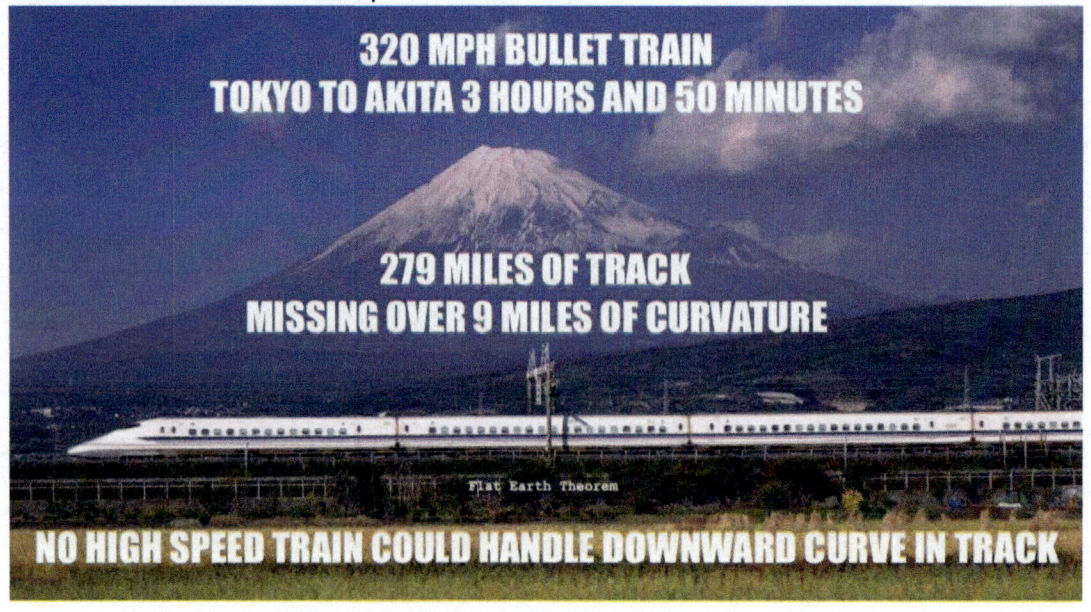

The Zetetic Method

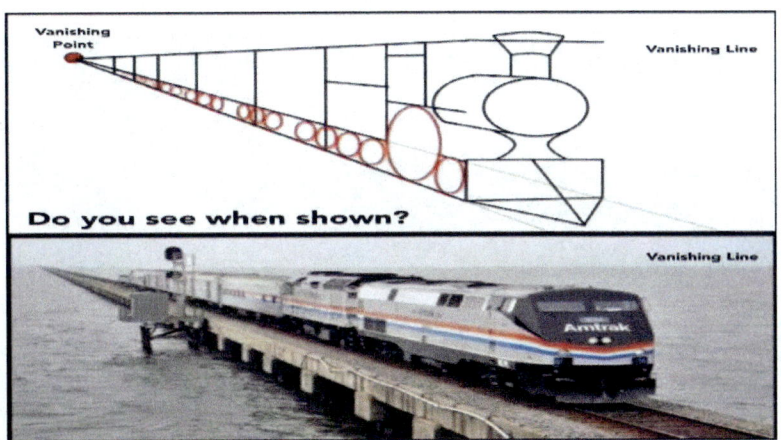

Lake Pontchartrain bridge

When discussing flat earth with people they often bring a picture of the Lake Pontchartrain Bridge to the conversation as proof of the globe. Once again people's ignorance of the laws of perspective come into play. Let's have a better look at it shall we.

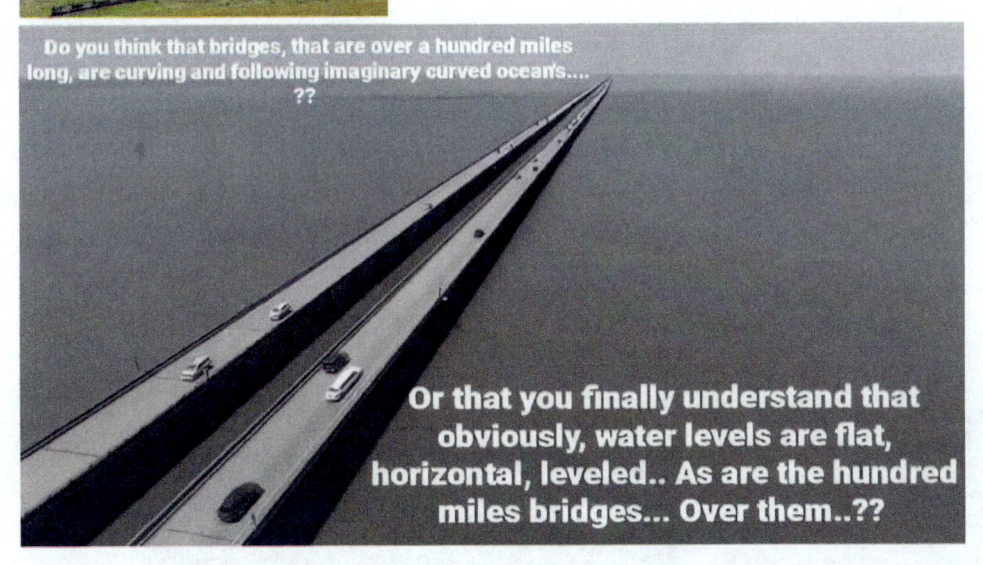

The Pontchartrain bridge is about 24 miles long, that's 384 feet of curvature. However the curvature in the background is far too much compared with the flat foreground and this would represent a small earth. Viewing the bridge or anything at length on a flat surface from certain angles and height will appear to curve. Don't let this illusion trick you, we must look at things from all angles if we want to learn the truth of the matter.

60

The Zetetic Method

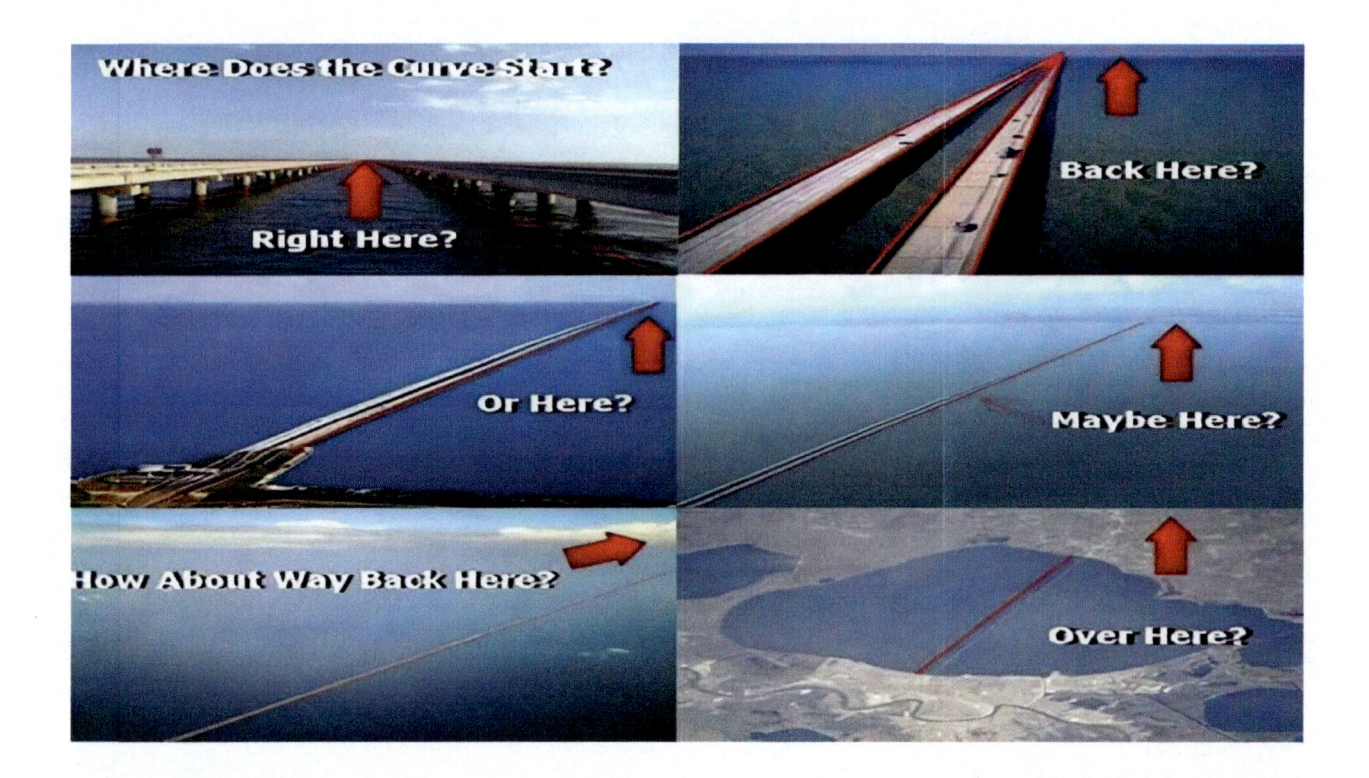

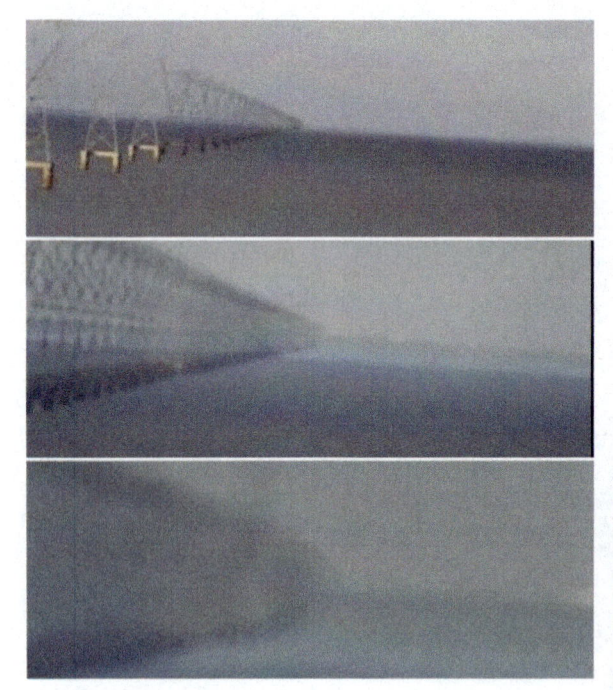

The curvature that 'appears' in the photo is a visual phenomenon and not a physical reality. You can zoom in and see that it's not curving or hiding behind curved water.

Once again, ignorance of the laws of perspective and how vision works, is not proof of any globe.

If you zoom in you can see the shore and water line. This zooming in can work all over the Earth, thus showing no curvature, only flatness.

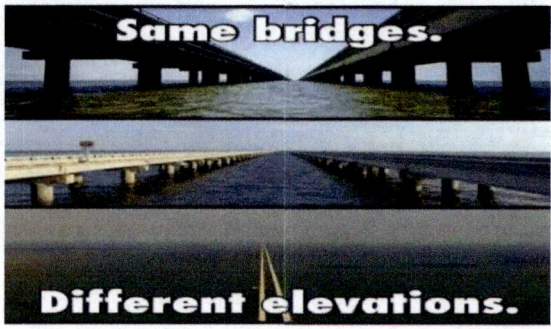

61

The Zetetic Method

THE LAKE PONTCHARTRAIN CAUSEWAY METAIRIE, LA

23.87 MILES LONG
380 FEET OF MISSING CURVATURE

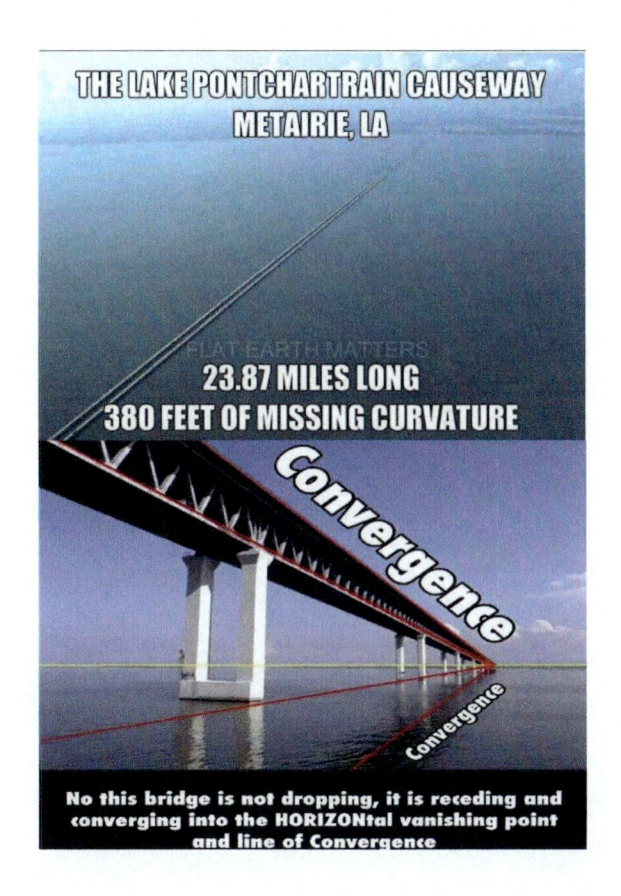

Convergence

No this bridge is not dropping, it is receding and converging into the HORIZONtal vanishing point and line of Convergence

Bridges are not designed with "Earth's curvature" calculated, nor railroads nor canal. Beliefs doesn't change this.

Globers have said this is proof of earth's curvature. How big is earth again?

Lake Pontchartrain power lines demonstrating the curvature of the Earth

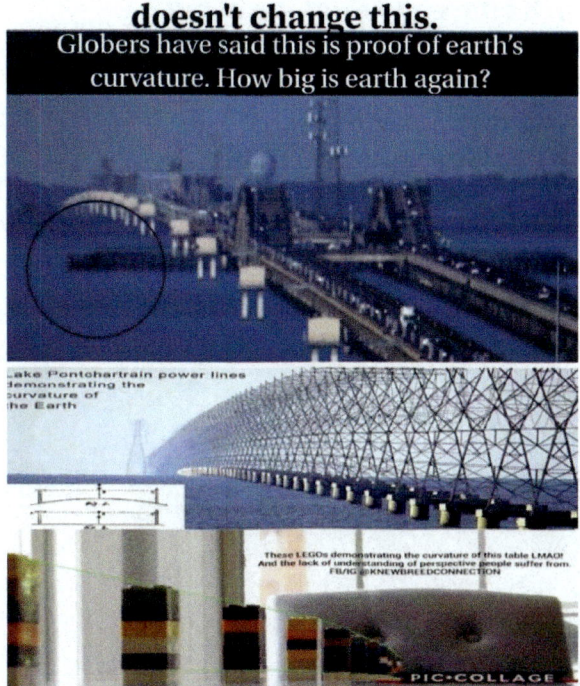

These LEGOs demonstrating the curvature of this table LMAO! And the lack of understanding of perspective people suffer from. FB/IG @KNEWBREEDCONNECTION

SURVEYORS, ENGINEERS, AND ARCHITECTS NEVER FACTOR IN THE SUPPOSED CURVATURE OF THE EARTH INTO THEIR PROJECTS.

EARTH IS FLAT! RESEARCH IT!

THE SUEZ CANAL IS 100 MILES LONG WITH ZERO CURVATURE. IF EARTH WAS A BALL, THERE SHOULD BE A 6,669 FT DROP FROM ONE END OF THE CANAL TO THE OTHER. BUT THE CANAL HAS NO LOCKS BECAUSE THE TERRAIN THROUGH WHICH IT PASSES IS FLAT.

A long bridge, on a ball, must be longer on the top then the bottom. But the pillars are parallel and the supposed earth curvature is not figured into the design. Lasers and spirit levels are used to make sure the bridge is flat and level. The spirit level is used to determine a horizontal line. A horizontal line is at right angles to a vertical. It is a level line.

Some bridges are up to 102 miles long. That's 6936 feet of missing curvature over water, which is 70% of the earth. If earth was a ball of claimed size, then why is this the case?

62

The Zetetic Method

People keep showing me the first picture saying it's proof of Earth's curvature. All it really proves is that they're not putting much effort into thinking about their view from ground vs view from above. The two must be compared to come up with an educated conclusion. There is no curvature.

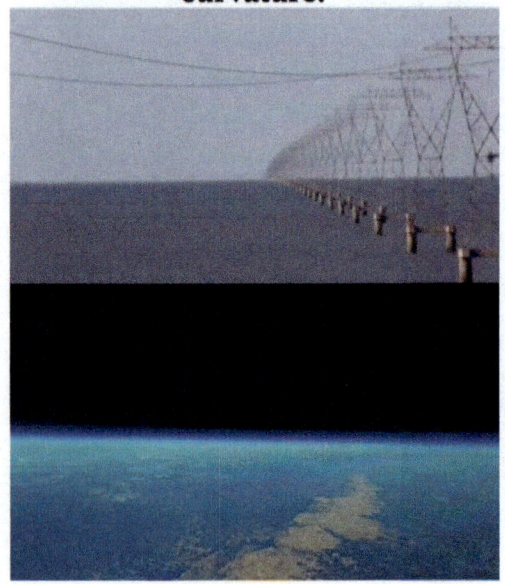

The BLACK SWAN

Once again the 8" per square mile is debunked. If it actually existed, it would be calculated into the construction of railroads, bridges, tunnels and canals, would it not?

We have a horizon line that refuses to drop downward, we have bodies of water that don't curve, Great Plains who are pretending they're not on a ball and now we have structures all over the "ball earth" that's designed for a flat plane. How odd.

AERONAUTICS

"Then, if Copernicus founded the present system, he founded upon nothing. He had nothing to base upon. He either never heard of, or could not detect one of these abstrusities. All his logic is represented in his reasoning upon this earth's rotundity: that this earth is round, because of a general tendency to sphericity, manifesting, for instance, in fruits and in drops of water—showing that he must have been unaware not only of abstrusities, but of icicles and bananas and oysters." Author Charles Fort

The French King XIV Witnessing Flight. HubPages

AERONAUTICS

Aeronauts are scientists who used to do scientific experiments on the atmosphere for weather forecasts and other reasons. This was in the 1700s, 1800s and even the 1900s. The highest manned balloon was 113,000 feet into the stratosphere. Now I've recently seen three video footage of unmanned balloons at 121,000feet. As expected, flat and at eye level.

As the balloon or plane or helicopter ascends, the earth beneath us seems to sink or recede while the horizon line 'appears' to slowly rise with us as far as the eye can see, the earth and sky appearing to meet. Oh what the two must talk about. :)

If the Earth were indeed a ball then the highest point would be under them and the lowest point would be the horizon. But that is indeed NOT the case.

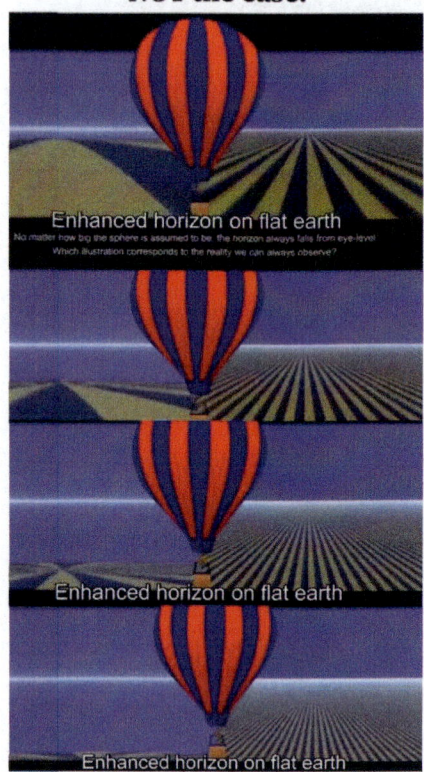

If the earth was a ball, the aeronaut would be one of the biggest supporters. The highest part of the surface of the globe would be directly under the balloon, and the sides would very gradually curve downward in every direction. However the horizon line still remains at eye level and 'appears' higher than the ground below the balloon car. This is impossible if the earth were a ball with a downward curvature, but is exactly what you'd expect on an extended plane.

The popular testimony of aeronauts is entirely against this globular assumption. I'll share some recorded testimonies here but you or I don't have to take anyone's word for it by any means. I've been on a plane, helicopter and skydiving and can testify to this physical reality they speak of.

I've taken these testimonials from the book Zetetic Cosmogony by Thomas Winship: "The London journal of 18th July, 1857, says:
1) "The chief peculiarity of the view from a balloon at a considerable elevation was the altitude of the horizon, which remained practically on a level with the eye at an elevation of two miles, causing the surface of the earth to appear concave instead of convex, and to recede during the rapid ascent, whilst the horizon and the balloon seemed to be stationary."

2) J. Glaisher, F.R.S., in his work, "Travels in the Air," states: "On looking over the top of the car, the horizon appeared to be on a level with the eye, and taking a grand view of the whole visible area beneath, I was struck with its great regularity; all was dwarfed to one plane; it seemed too flat, too even, apparently artificial." In his accounts of his ascents in the air, M Camilla Flammarion states: "The earth appeared as one immense plane richly decorated with ever-varied colours; hills and valleys are all passed over without being able to distinguish any undulation in the immense plane."

3) Mr. Elliott, an American aeronaut, says: "I don't know that I ever hinted heretofore that the aeronaut may well be the most skeptical man about the rotundity of the earth. Philosophy forces the truth upon us; but the view of the earth from the elevation of a balloon is that of an immense terrestrial basin, the deeper part of which is directly under one's feet.—Zetetic Astronomy. Page 37.

4) "In March, 1897, I met M. Victor Emanuel, and asked him to give me an idea of the shape of the earth as seen from a balloon. He informed me that, instead of the earth declining from the view on either side, and the higher part being under the car, as is popularly supposed, it was the exact opposite; the lowest part, like a huge basin, being immediately under the car, and the horizon on all sides rising to the level of the eye. This, he admitted, was exactly what should be the appearance of a plane viewed from a balloon. It is almost needless to say that a globe would present a totally different appearance, the highest part being directly under the car." "

If the world were truly a spinning ball we wouldn't have to take someone's word for it. There wouldn't be a flat earth awakening right now.

The aeronaut and the airPLANE passenger can see for themselves that the earth is a flat enormous plane and not a giant ball with downward curvature. This observable proof shows us a concave surface, which is exactly what you would expect from a level plane, it's the nature of level surfaces of great distances, to appear to rise to a level of the eye of the observer.

As high as the aeronauts rose the horizon went with them, and still today on a plane which can go even higher and furthermore upwards on a unmanned balloon which has gone over 121,000 feet, the horizon LINE still remains at eye level and remains a flat line from left to right, which is twice as far then straight ahead. Where then is the downward curvature that a ball earth requires? Do we really need NASA'S word for what we live on? No! Physical reality debunks their claims.

An old article had Auguste Piccard saying, when asked about the shape of the Earth, that it looked like a flat disk with upturned edges. Wikipedia however has since changed his claim. Just like with Tesla saying Earth was a realm, a Tesla coil, but his book said globe over and over again. He said earth is a Tesla coil and a Tesla coil is usually flat but I have seen ball ones. When I read his book the term globe made no sense for what he was talking about. Once more history has been rewritten to suit the narrative. Here's the Wikipedia extract:

"On 27 May 1931, Auguste Piccard and Paul Kipfer took off from Augsburg, Germany in a hydrogen balloon,[3] and reached a record altitude of 15,781 m (51,775 ft; 9.806 mi) (FAI Record File Number 10634). During this flight, they became the first human beings to enter the stratosphere,[4] and were able to gather substantial data on the upper atmosphere, as well as measure cosmic rays.[2] Piccard and Kipfer are widely considered the first people to visually observe the curvature of the earth."

This is what they said but where's the curvature when even higher up?

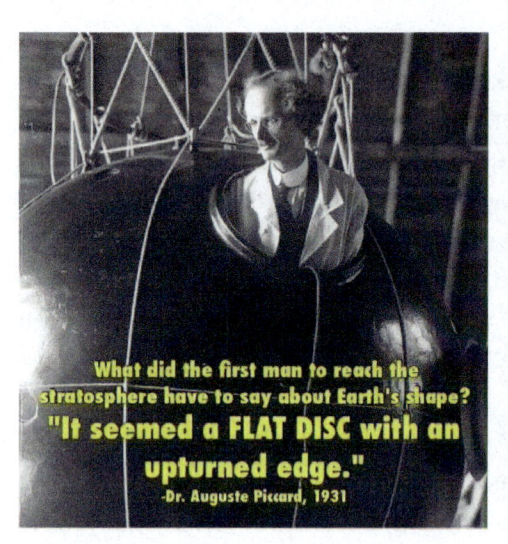

The BLACK SWAN

If we lived on a ball, the horizon line HAS to gradually drop downward as you ascend. Doesn't matter how big the ball is, you should be able to see more land but you should have to tilt downwards to see it, not straight ahead. The reason I keep hammering this point in, is because it's the point that woke me up to flat earth. Like water, it's a physical based fact. It's reality in its raw form. It can't be manipulated with math or any other kind of assumptions. It simply is what it is.

If you can disprove this BLACK SWAN then have at it. I have proven it for myself. Once again "Earth's curvature" has been debunked.

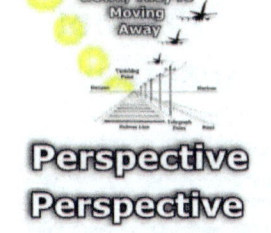

THE LAWS OF PERSPECTIVE

"Like a poor animal tied to a stake in the center of a meadow, where it can only feed in a limited circle, the theoretical philosopher is tethered to his premises, enslaved by his own assumptions, and however great his talent, his influence, his opportunities, he can only rob his fellow men of their intellectual freedom and independence, and convert them into slaves like him-self." Author Dr. Samuel Rowbotham

BILL NYE THE PSEUDO-SCIENCE GUY

Bill Nye "The Science Guy" as he calls himself, made the absurd statement that if the earth was flat you could see across the ocean to some other continent. It seems that common sense is not a guarantee or common trait for clowns (I mean "scientists") or the common man for that matter, because people say this to me ALL THE TIME!

But that is the whole point of the heliocentric globe model; to take, from the populace, any ability or drive to have independent critical thinking.

The Zetetic Method

    This half-witted fake scientist doesn't understand the laws of perspective very much. And not only does the laws of perspective take this fool out, but there are other reasons you can't see that far.

    Sometimes when the weather is bad the horizon line isn't that far off, other times when it is clearer it's way off. The horizon is not moving with the weather, it's your visibility that's changing. It depends on the atmosphere. But no matter how clear it is, we cannot see to infinity. The weather channel tells us our visibility everyday. My point is, you not being able to see things in the distance is based on a lot of things.

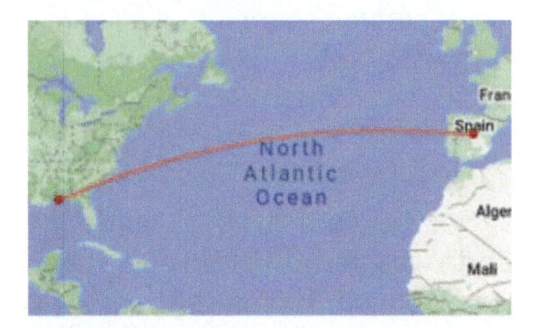

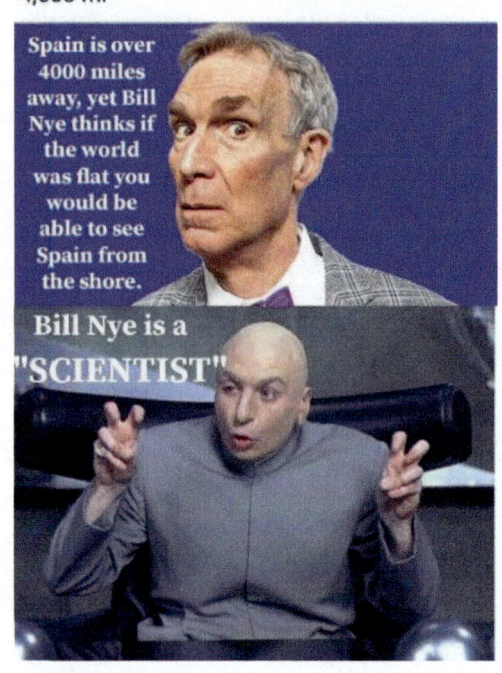

    Our sense of hearing is limited. Isn't our sense of vision also limited? Of course it is and the laws of perspective explains this limitation. Let us proceed to examine these laws.

THE LAWS OF PERSPECTIVE

Everything within our field of vision as far as the light is concerned is explained by divergence. The sky does not meet the Earth as it appears 5 or so miles out nor does the sky wrap around the Earth. You can fly all over the earth and prove this.

Right and left lines running parallel with each other will appear to approach in the distance. Examples would be railroad tracks. The surface of the Earth and sky run parallel with each other as well. Like the railroad tracks, the earth and sky appear to meet in the distance, like so: . ==============================>>]

If you put your face down to one of the rails and look between the tracks, you will see the two rails 'appear' to meet in the near distance, if you then move your face to the middle of the two rails, the distance at which they 'appear' to meet will have lengthen a bit. The same happens with the ground and sky. The higher you leave the ground the further you can see, but the horizon line will still remain at eye level. The sky does not wrap around any ball. It just keeps going.

A simple plane ride will show you the sky is NOT wrapped around a ball earth, nor are the railroad tracks meeting in the distance, nor is the sun going behind a curved ocean. Observable provable.

A plane will fly flat and level, until it runs out of gas, creating one parallel line. The ground/horizon is always a flat line that remains at eye level, thus proving no downward curvature, this creates a second parallel line. As the plane/sun (one parallel line) flies away from you it will appear to be going towards the horizon line (the other parallel line).

When you watch a plane leave you it will appear to be going downward as it leaves you. But the person in the next state will see the plane coming towards them and looks as if it's rising as it's approaching. But if you were on that plane you will see that it's flying flat and level. That's the laws of perspective.

Parallel lines never meet. How can anything be parallel with the Earth if it's a downward curving sphere? You can fly flat all you want and never leave earth at an upwards angle, nor make for invisible curvature. You will never witness any curvature the sun is supposedly going behind. The masses don't agree with this though, they believe just the opposite in fact. Not due to their observation or experience, but because they have faith in a ball earth and "established scientist" that the government has put into place to represent their propaganda. They believe that plump lines at any part of the Earth are at right angles to the horizon.

The appearance of rising, peaking and setting is due to the common law of perspective where tall objects appear high overhead when nearby, but at a distance gradually lower towards the vanishing point.

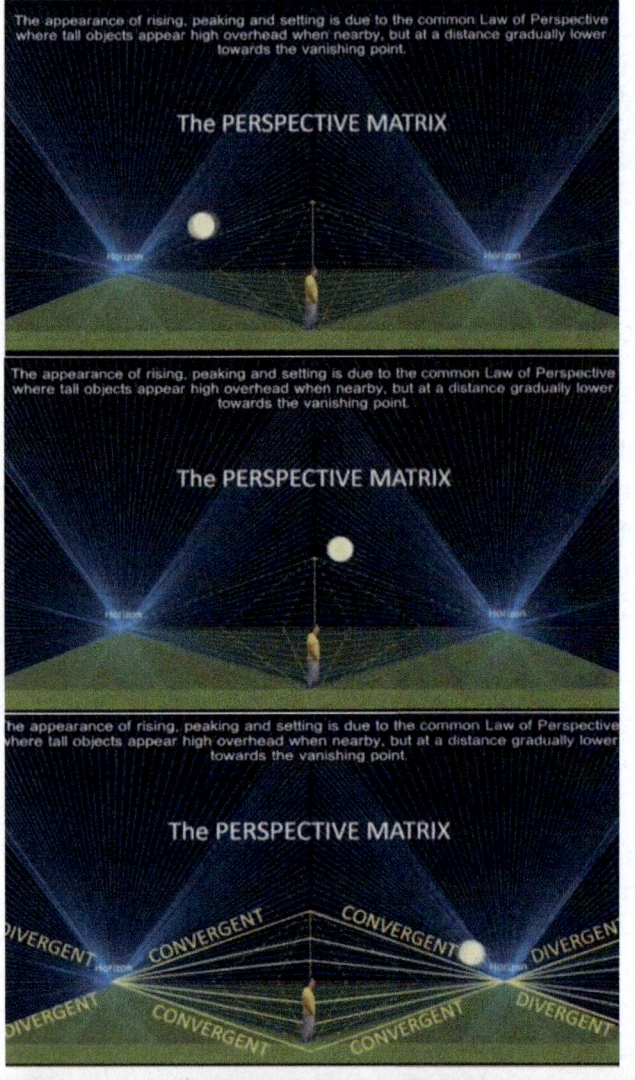

Don't let other people's claims change your mind about what reality is. They can't change the truth, only your perception of it.

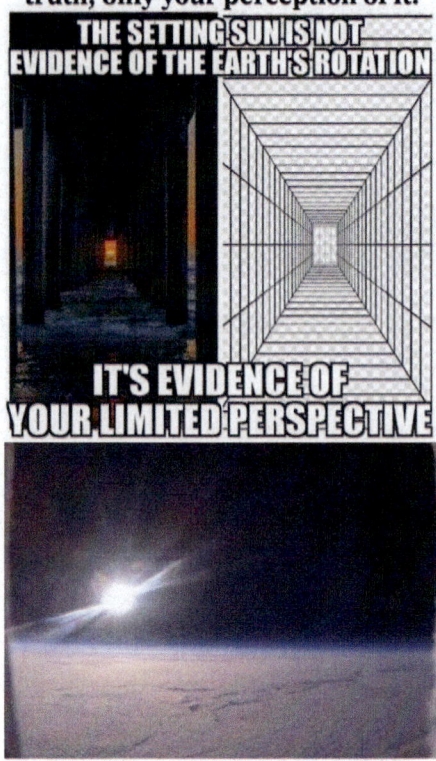

In "Some Unrecognized Laws of Nature," by I. Singer and L.H. Berens: "To the man who conceived the earth as a flat expanse nothing could be more conclusive than that plumb lines were strictly parallel……But notwithstanding such direct and positive evidence, the student of to-day disbelieves this conclusion, and that not because he has any direct evidence to the contrary, but because it conflicts with the now "established fact" that our earth is a sphere. His evidence is not due to direct observation, but is circumstantial depending on a concatenation of inferences."

FITTING 14 FEET INTO 8 INCHES

If you're on a flat street a mile long, containing a row of streetlights, you will notice, from where you stand at one end, the lights gradually decline to the ground, the last one appearing to be on the ground, furthermore and the last light would disappear altogether. Now according to the Astronomers there is 8" worth of curvature within that mile. The average streetlight poles are 9 to 14 feet tall, therefore 8" could not account for the depression of the lights going downward.

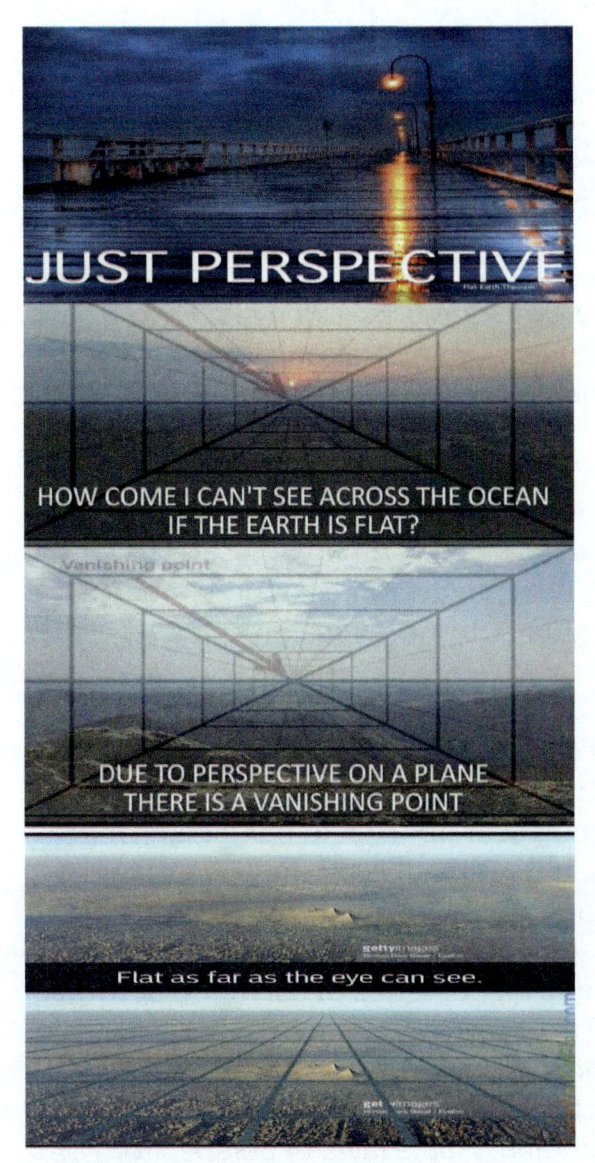

If you're standing at the end of a long row of streetlights, you will notice the furthest one looks the lowest and the closest one looks the highest. But if you walk towards the furthest one, it will appear to get higher yet the one you were just at seems to get lower. But they're all the same distance. This goes for everything on a flat surface.

Astronomers say that the North Star Polaris can't be seen past the equator (it can actually be seen 20 degrees past the equator) due to curvature. But, like the streetlights, the further we increase our distance from ANY object the more it appears to sink into the horizon and disappear. This disappearance can happen on a flat surface as is proven. It's called the vanishing point. When you get to the vanishing point for Polaris, this point will be the same distance all the way around it. This fact doesn't add curvature.

There are plenty of videos of ships and shorelines of cities that disappeared bottom first being brought back. If the city was disappearing over downward curvature as you were leaving it, the buildings would appear to be slanted back, but instead they are always upright.

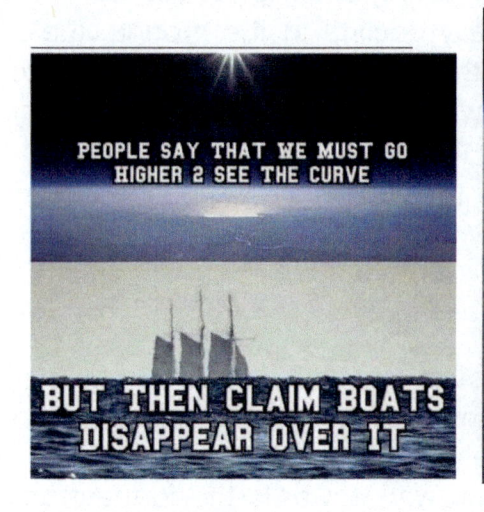

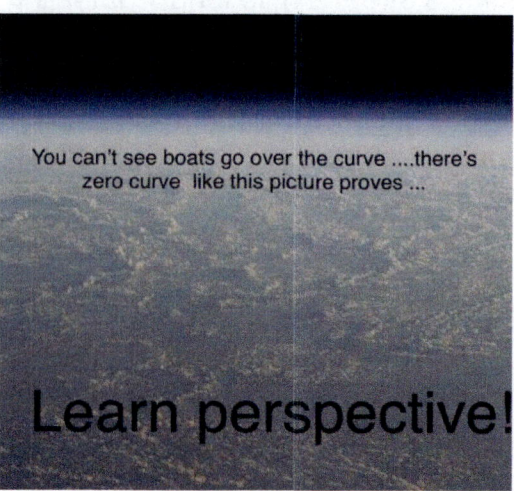

Regular cameras do not see through water. However, cameras, like eyes, have a limit. Eventually the object will still disappear bottom first through a zoomed camera. Because there's not a more powerful camera available doesn't mean there's a ball of ocean out there.

Your eyes can see 3 to 5 miles straight ahead at sea level. You can see twice that distance from left to right. Therefore, if I can see a ship disappear over the supposed curvature straight ahead then I should be able to see twice the amount of curvature from left to right correct? But we see no such thing. Either we live on a rolling pin or it's the laws of perspective. Where's the ocean's curvature on a plane if you can see it on the beach?

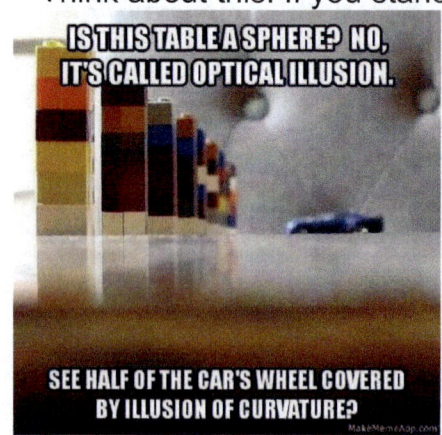

Think about this. If you stand on the beach and see, let's say 5 miles out in front of you, a ship appears to go behind curvature but you see NO curvature whatsoever from left to right; then what about the person that is standing on the beach 5 miles away from you but is turned half-way towards you? If that person's left to right is YOUR straight ahead does, he not see the same 'appearance of curvature between him and you? Yet he sees NO curvature whatsoever from his left to right which is YOUR straight ahead 'curvature.' This shows that it's not curvature your ship is going behind, but the simple laws of perspective.

LAWS OF PERSPECTIVE EXPERIMENT

Put your eyes level with a long table. Longer than a coffee table. The reason you have to have your eyes level with the table is because you are using a small scale. On a really long scale, like a long flat street or Earth for instance, you can rise above the surface.

When your eyes are level with the table you should see a straight line. If you see any of the table top then you're above the table. You need to be flush with the table top and see a straight line. Now get someone to put a salt shaker in front of you with an arch closer to you to represent the clouds. Make sure the top of the salt shaker is higher than the arch. Now they can slowly move the shaker back. The bottom will disappear until the shaker is gone, if the table's long enough, and the top of the shaker will be lower than the "clouds."

The shaker will appear to lower itself or to go behind curvature. But the table is flat. On a long flat road the tires will disappear before the bottom of the car.

An airport where you can stand still and let someone walk away from you. Their feet will disappear first then their legs, then torso, etc. EVERYTHING does this, including the sun, moon, plane and sky.

A fellow flat earther said: "Of course, the dimensions of the hallway remain constant for its entire length; the floor does not actually rise, the ceiling does not actually sink, nor do the walls actually close in; but to the human eye everything is perceived this way."

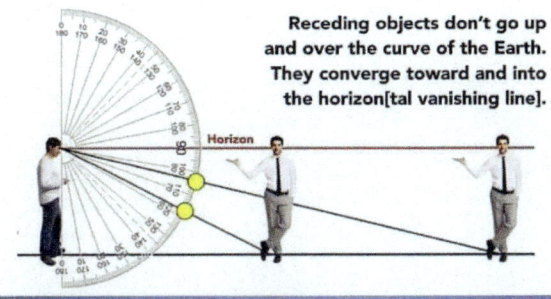

Similarly, when the Sun, Moon, airplanes or clouds appear to sink towards the horizon as they move away from us, they are not actually losing altitude and slowly approaching sea-level or going around curvature. They are in fact maintaining the same altitude except they are moving away from you and so the law of perspective makes them appear to sink."

SUNSET IN NEW YORK TO LA

If the sun sets in NY it has yet to set in LA or Hawaii. You can fly from NY to LA and see zero curvature, a horizon line at eye level and the plane will fly flat and level the entire way. You can then fly to Hawaii over a flat ocean at eye level. There's zero curvature for the sun to go behind.

Again, when you watch a plane or the sun leave you it will appear to be going down as it leaves you. But the person in the next state will see the plane/sun coming toward them and looks as if it's rising as it's approaching. But if you were ON that plane you will see that it's flying flat and level.

All these things are observable. You have no reason at all to believe just the opposite of what your senses tell you. It's simply the Laws of perspective not curvature.

"The conspiracy forest is a maze. In the maze, there are lots of trees with lots of hanging fruits. In the center of the maze there's the flat earth tree. There's a door on that tree. That's the door to the Rabbit hole." Author Gabrielle Henriet

I don't mean to carry on about the laws of perspective but it is very important to understand in order to break out of this indoctrination that they have humanity in. People need to see that NOTHING is going behind any curvature because there is no such thing.

Looks can be deceiving. People think the sun is going behind curvature. Everything moving away from you will appear to be getting lower. But a simple plane ride will debunk this illusion. The law of perspective is not just for paintings.

STORY TIME

I ripped this cute little story off from a great book titled "Zetetic Cosmogony" by Thomas Winship. Which he took from another book I'm reading now called The Earth an Irregular Plane By WILLIAM THOMAS WISEMAN:

"When a youth, I stood upon the Dover shore of the English Channel, and was told to watch a departing ship. "See! There she goes; down, down, down! The hull has disappeared! She is out of sight! Now, my boy, you have had an ocular demonstration that the world is round, and SEEING IS BELIEVING." I walked up to an "old salt" who had a telescope, and said: "Can you see that big ship through your glass that's gone down the Channel, and is now out of sight?" "Yes, my son. Look!" The big ship immediately came into view again, as I peered through the sailor's glass! "Why! He told me the earth was round, because that ship I can now see had turned down over the horizon!"   "Aha! aha! sonny, I know they all say it! Now, I have been all over the world, but I never believed it. But, then, I have no learning, only my senses to rely upon, and I say " SEEING IS BELIEVING."

The BLACK SWAN

The Laws of Perspective coupled with long distance photography proves that it's not curvature that the ship, sun, clouds, ____(place any object in blank) is going behind but rather it's the vanishing point. If your ship was going behind curvature, a high-power camera could not bring it back. Plus the ship would be slanted. If the ship is behind enough of a downward curvature of water to hide half of it, then the ship should appear to be slanted to the viewer from far away. But it is not, it is vertical, as always, to any viewer. Like this city here.

I think if more people realize this, they would snap out of the globe propaganda a lot more quickly.

Well, I hope we've covered enough of curvature, or the lack of rather, to help you see the Earth is indeed not a ball but a flat plane just as we see it. For me, anyway, it's enough but in the words of Pinhead, "Enough is a myth." Let's carry on shall we.

Sailing over a ball using flat earth math

"Earth is flat. You can only get elevation angle from a flat plane; you cannot get an elevation angle measurement from a sphere earth. It's game over. Elevation angle measurement proves flat earth."   Flat earth activist and debater Nathan Oakley

"The Margaret Todd" Bar Harbor, Maine

I worked on this boat, The Margaret Todd, in 1999 and loved it so much I wanted to take the opportunity to publish it here. It's the first four mast schooner to sail in New England waters in half a century. It does sailing trips out of Bar Harbor, Maine at Downeast Windjammer Cruises.

SEXTANT AND PLANE TRIGONOMETRY

If the world were a ball, then spherical trigonometry would be the go-to when navigating around it, but instead plane trigonometry is the popular winner. Why?

On YouTube I watched tons of videos of sailors with sextant and navigation training and they all used plane trigonometry only. One said that using spherical trigonometry can cause you to be out of reckoning. Why? If the earth was indeed a ball, wouldn't you need to be in conformity to its figure? If the ocean is on a globular earth, why are there no rules for calculations on that basis?

The Zetetic Method

ALL OF THESE DEVICES
TELESCOPE, PLUMB BOB, PLANISPHERE, THERMOMETER, CAMERA P900, LEVEL, LASER, SEXTANT, GEODETIC, ASTROLABE, SUNDIAL, PASCAL VASES, GYROSCOPE, THEODOLITE, COMPASS
PROVE THE EARTH IS FLAT

In plane trigonometry, you navigate from A to B with the calculations on the assumption that it's flat. I've had sailors tell me it's flat in small distances so they do small points from A to B, etc. I inquired 'why not use spherical trigonometry for longer distances instead,' and never get a real answer.

If you take your boat from point A horizon to point B horizon, with the measurements of flat and then from point B to C with a measurement of flat, and you keep going all over the world with this measuring system then you live on a flat plane sailing over a flat ocean mate, or a polygon earth. It's just that simple.

The datum line is always a horizontal line and thus spherical calculations are not made. Most navigators that I've talked to don't even fully understand spherical trigonometry. One, who made a crack on flat earthers, told me he just chooses to use plane trigonometry on his videos because it's simpler and that he usually uses spherical trigonometry. I ask him to give an example of a little spherical trigonometry. And he could not. I told him he couldn't simply because he doesn't use it, and to my delight, another sailor stepped in and agreed. Plane sailing is sailing on a plane and there is not the remotest chance of proving convexity from it.

A triangle is defined as "a plane figure with three STRAIGHT sides and three angles." Therefore, triangulation would be impossible across a curved surface.

In December, 1897, Captain Slocum sailed around this curve less ball on board "Spray." He said he had sailed his boat 33,000 miles by plane sailing. That's a LONG voyage, using a method that's for a plane surface, for 33,000 miles, and yet the world is a globe?

If the plane triangle is what we have to deal with, and such is the case, the base of the triangle would be a straight line—the ocean. That all triangulation used in sea navigation is plane proves that the sea is a plane.

In "A Primer of Navigation," by A. T. Flagg, M.A.: "Plane Sailing. —When a ship sails for a short distance on one course, the earth is regarded as a plane or level surface......The results obtained by this assumption, although not absolutely correct, are near enough in practice."

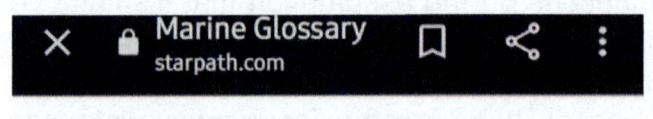

Marine Glossary — starpath.com

arpath online classroom || Celestial Navigation Glossary || Glossary Index || Ho

A B C D E F G H I J K L M N O P Q R S T U V W X Y Z

Circle of Equal Altitude

Any circle of points on the earth's surface that is equal distance from the geographical position (GP) of a celestial body at a precise moment of time. All observers located anywhere on this circle would measure the same sextant height of the body at that moment. The center of the circle is the GP of the body, the radius of the circle is the zenith distance (z). The Ho they would observe is Ho = 90° - z. When taking the sights, the observers would all be looking toward the body in the center of the circle, which means some would be looking north, others, south or west, etc.. If the body were 60° high, the zenith distance would be 30°, which means the distance to the GP would be 30° x (60 miles/1°), or 1,800 miles. The LOPs used in celestial navigation are short segments of the circumference of this circle, which we approximate as straight lines.

Here's a comment from a flat earther I thought nailed it pretty good: "The sun's distance was calculated (not measured) by observing the transit of Venus across the sun. Assuming the radius of Venus was equal to the radius of earth. The radius of earth was calculated (not measured) by triangulation (using elevation angles which require planar geometry) and assuming the sun's rays hit the earth in parallel rays (never been observed). Parallax measurements also require flat surfaces for triangulation.

If you first assume the surface of earth is curved because it's spherical, then use angles and planar geometry to prove the earth is a sphere, you are assuming the consequence of the very thing you are trying to prove. You are also using Euclidean geometry to prove the sphere that can only be proven using non-Euclidean spherical geometry."

"Plane sailing, the system of navigation now adopted, is sailing a ship, or making the arithmetical calculations for so doing, on the assumption that THE EARTH IS PERFECTLY FLAT." "Navigation in Theory and Practice " by Professor Evers, LLD (Globe believers and their assumptions)

I'm not going to spend any time on Great circle sailing but this: Great circle sailing is on the principle that the shortest distance between two points is the arc of the great circle between them. But physical reality shows us that the shortest distance between any two points is a straight line. If you look at the Great Circle sailing on a globe map you will see the arc, if you look at it on a flat earth map, you will see a straight line. The shortest distance between two points is what? A straight line. Prove me wrong!

The Zetetic Method

People claim that the great circle arc in plane flying saves on distance. They make this claim because the southern to northern routes they take only makes sense on a flat earth map. If you draw their "great circle arc" routes on a flat earth map, it makes perfect sense. It makes a straight line, which is the shortest distance between to objects.

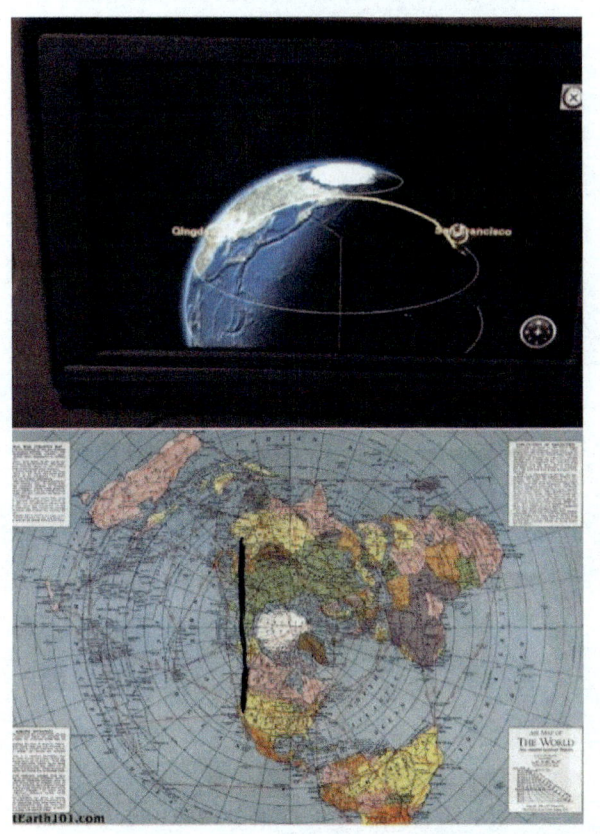

Look here to see what I'm saying. On this flight, like all other flights, the plane flies flat and level. When has anybody noticed such curvature? The bottom picture seems more legit and explains why your plane fly's flat and level.

Without any real proof, tell us how they find that the earth is not flat, but a globe. What is the evidence of it? Where can it be obtained? If we see, in physical reality, that the earth is flat then tell us how can WE prove that it is not? Do we really need to take someone's word for such a huge claim? If the earth seems to be what it is not, then we can't trust our own senses, and if we can't trust our own senses then are we no better than the brute and must give in to authoritarians.

This great circle arch also goes for airPLANE flights. Let's talk about those in the next chapter shall we.

CHAPTER 2
MAPS/FLIGHTS

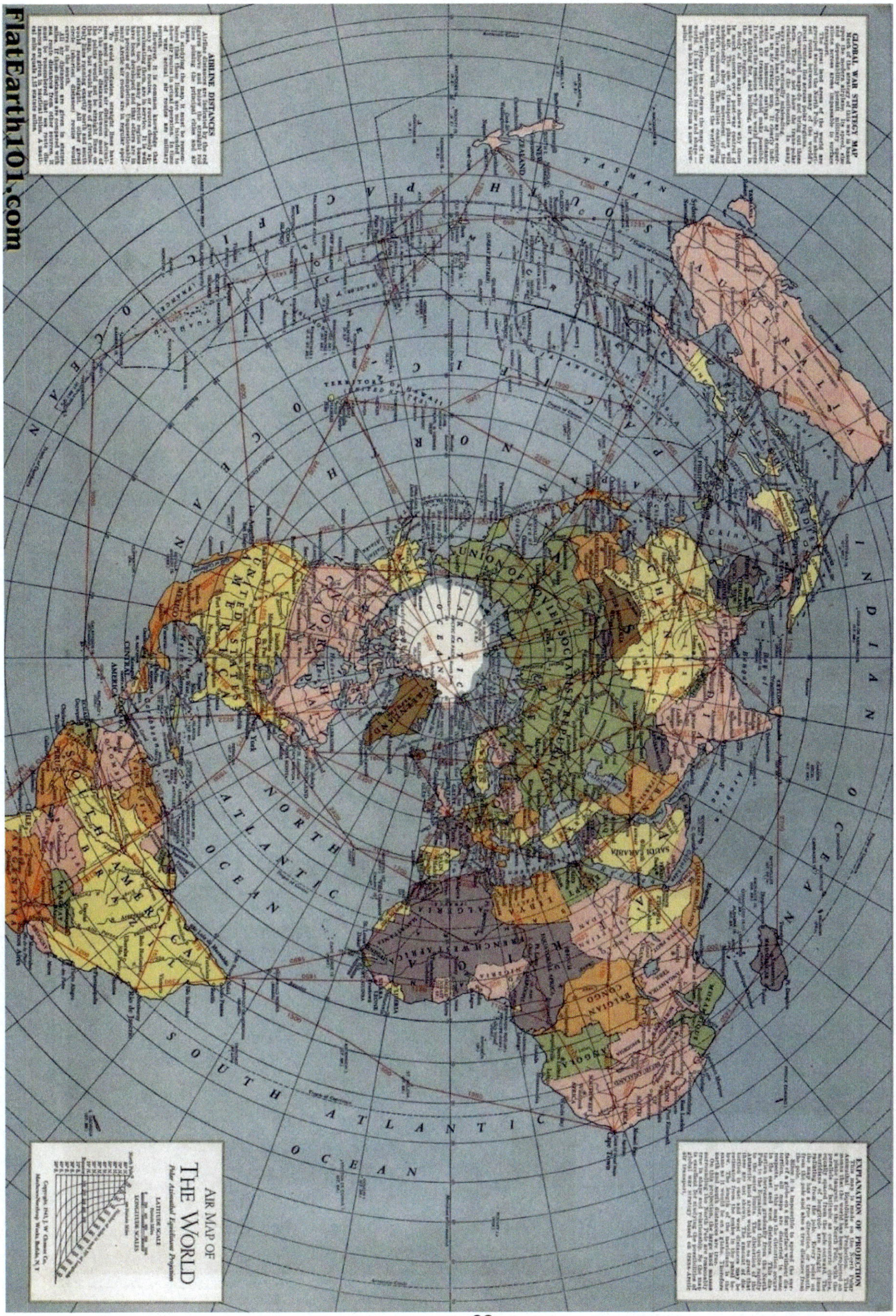
FlatEarth101.com
AIR MAP OF THE WORLD
NORTH ATLANTIC OCEAN
SOUTH ATLANTIC OCEAN
NORTH PACIFIC OCEAN
SOUTH PACIFIC OCEAN
INDIAN OCEAN
ARCTIC OCEAN
AUSTRALIA
SOUTH AMERICA
NORTH AMERICA
UNITED STATES
UNION OF SOVIET SOCIALIST REPUBLICS
CHINA
INDIA
SAUDI ARABIA
ALGERIA
FRENCH WEST AFRICA
BELGIAN CONGO
ANGOLA
GLOBAL WAR STRATEGY MAP
EXPLANATION OF PROJECTION
AIRLINE DISTANCES

"We are more gullible and superstitious today than we were in the Middle Ages, and an example of modern credulity is the widespread belief that the Earth is round. The average man can advance not a single reason for thinking that the Earth is round. He merely swallows this theory because there is something about it that appeals to the twentieth century mentality." Irish playwright, critic, polemicist and political activist George Bernard Shaw

THE FLAT EARTH MAP

People always seem to point to the sky when trying to prove a curved earth, but when they can't prove it pointing above OR below, they'll take a hit at the Flat Earth Map. If the earth were a globe, then all ships would be best fitted with a globe in the wheelhouse. I would think that that would be the best equipment for the navigator to take with him. But of course, that's not the case. So, let's have a look at said maps.

Here's what the Yale library said about Gleason's map. Some have said Gleason believed in a globe but his book says otherwise. False claims don't change reality now does it?

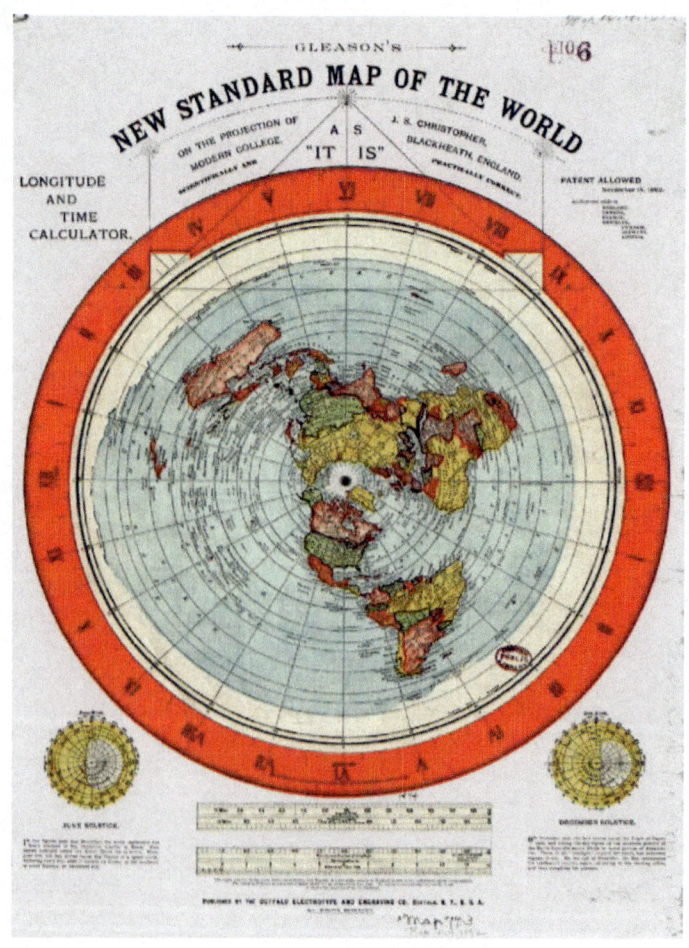

The Zetetic Method

The Gleason world map was used by explorers, sailors and the military for years with no problem. In 1893 Alex Gleason, the map maker and flat earther (as many were flat earthers back then), wrote a great book titled "Is the Bible from Heaven and Is the Earth a Globe." He traveled all over the world to make his map accurate.

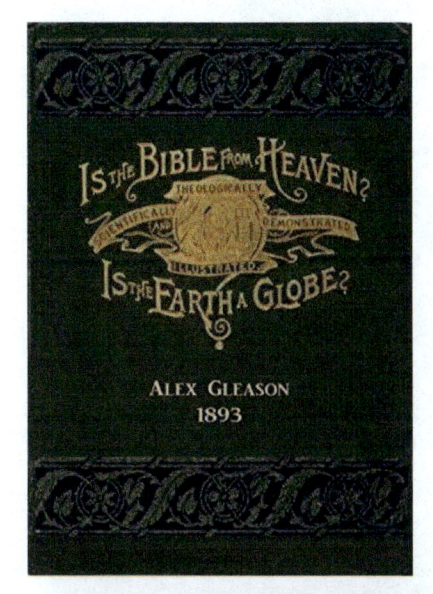

Globe Earth believers I talk to always say the flat Earth map is wrong and not a working map. That's odd because it's good enough for the Yale University review I posted just now. It's good enough for the United Nations. It's good enough for the World Health Organization. It's good enough to be on-board Airforce One. It's good enough to be in JFKs Situation Room. It was good enough before the whirling ball model was conned into people's heads.

Look at these government agencies and their logos. These are only a few, there are others as well. Truth in plain sight.

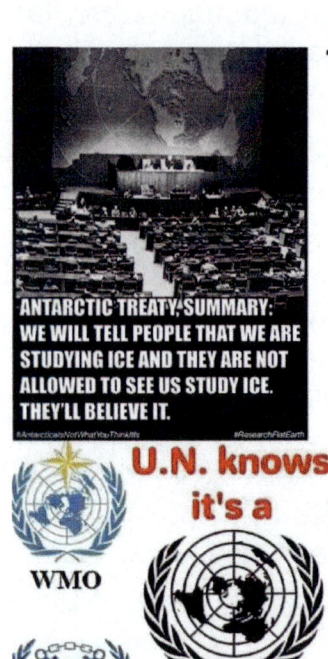

The Zetetic Method

The flat earth map is and have been used sense maps exist. The claim that the flat earth map is not good enough is only that, a claim, with no merits.

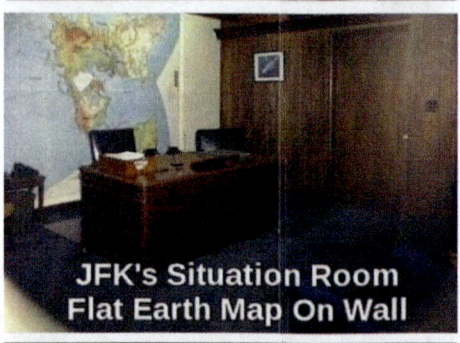

JFK's Situation Room
Flat Earth Map On Wall

85

ALL BUT ONE SCALE

Maps have scales for different things, also a compass, contour lines, dates, coordinates bearing legends, etc. etc. The one thing maps don't have is a scale of convexity or a method to calculate the distance before the natural curvature of the earth blocks two points from each other that the contour lines fail to show or ignore. Why not, it has all these other details? Point to point locations should, at a ratio of straight line distance vs curved indirect line distance, become out of calibration over long distances.

If the curvature scale math was on the map and people started calculating it, people might start to notice that it's simply not there.

Map Topography uses Contour lines
At school in Geography, Manuel Map Topography is based on a flat non-curved surface using contour height lines for point-to-point line of sight and side view Topography with distance, height, scale and showing gradients and water level.

The azimuthal equidistant projection is an azimuthal map projection. It has the useful properties that all points on the map are at proportionally correct distances from the center point, and that all points on the map are at the correct azimuth from the center point. Wikipedia

While maps and their scales may change. The contour lines depicting hills, slopes and mountains range heights and their steepness all play part of the landscape. The scales show distance and enable one to use angles and directions and even coordinates. All these fundamental tools are all flat and are placed and read on flat surfaces.

The United States Geological Survey (USGS), called this map an azimuthal map and is considered to be accurate in displaying continents and oceans. Useful for showing airline distances from the center point of projection.

So how are globe defenders saying the map doesn't work? Here's why, BECAUSE THEY HAVE NO PROOF OF THEIR OWN! A failed attempt at discrediting is not proof, it's just sad.On a side note, Mark Fonstad P.H. D., William Pugatch and Brandon Vogt P.H.D used data from the USGS to determine that, on scale, the state of Kansas is literally flatter than a pancake.

Map Projections, United States Geological Surve,
tp://egsc.usgs.gov/isb//pubs/MapProjections/projections.html

SOUTHERN FLIGHTS GO NORTH

When flying in the Southern Hemisphere to another continent in the Southern Hemisphere, you have to fly through the northern hemisphere. All southern flights fly north. All northern flights can be done on a flat earth or globe, it's the southern flights that exposes the lie. But no one really thinks of it. Why would they if they have no reason to.

Look at this flight from Sydney, Australia to Santiago, Chili. Now on the globe map, the flight is straight across. The map on one airline showed the flight path, on the globe map, to be straight across, but look at the ticket, these stops are nowhere on the route they showed, it makes no sense on the globe map and perfect sense on a flat earth map. I'll post a picture where I draw the route on both maps. Which one makes more sense? Here's the ticket.

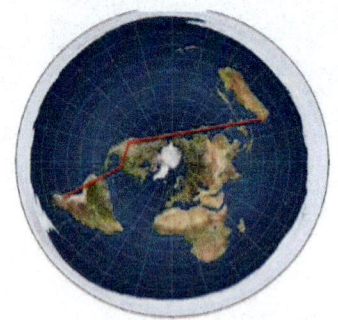

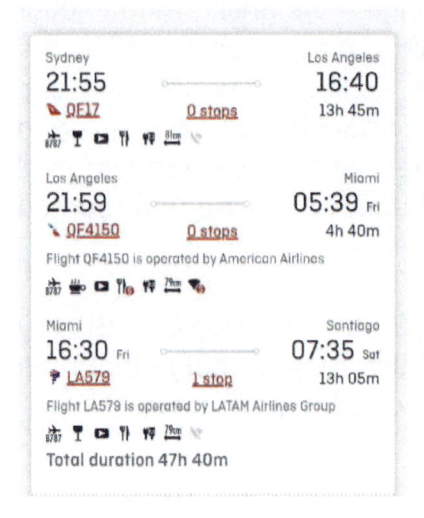

Flight plans are calculated with the Gleason flat earth map. The flight attendant and the sales rep only know their job. The pilots set their headings they're given and follow it. It's when there are emergency landings when the truth surfaces. Let's have a look at some shall we.

The Zetetic Method

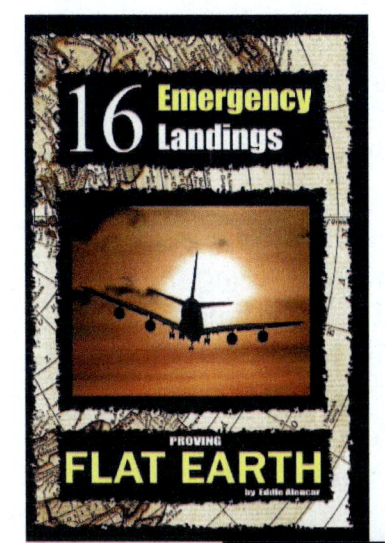

Emergency landings on a globe map vs a flat map

There's a great book called "16 Emergency Landings that Prove a Flat Earth" by Eddie Alencar. You can buy it on lulu.com.

A lady went into labor on a flight from Hong Kong to LA and they had to make an emergency landing in Alaska. Problem is that an emergency landing made zero sense on a globe. The GPS on the back of seats of the plane showed them over Hawaii. I have talked to flat earthers online who said that this is what made them start researching the earth possibly being flat. I'll post just a few of those emergency landings here for you.

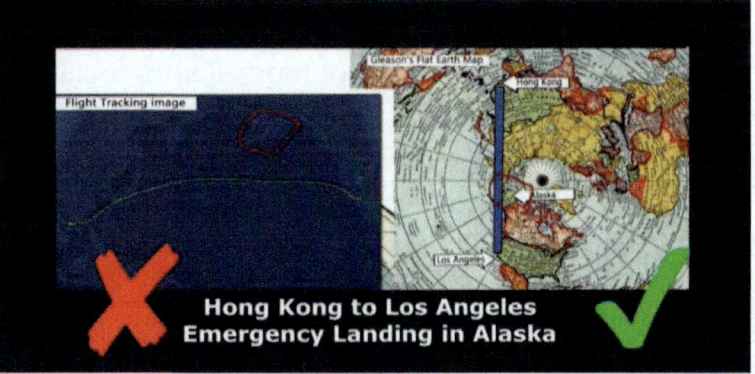

Hong Kong to Los Angeles
Emergency Landing in Alaska

To me, the "flat earth map" is starting to make more sense because why did we fly over Greenland? My flight to Egypt was from Houston to ATL up over Greenland to Rome to Cairo... Look like all those points really go in a straight line

https://bit.ly/FLAT_EARTH_MAP

A teenager from Saudi Arabia fell in coma aboard Qatar Airways flight QR725 which departed from Chicago towards Doha. After the teenager fell into a coma, the captain decided to make an emergency landing. Where the plane landed is where the argument Flat Earth versus Globe earth started. The plane landed in Moscow.

Chicago to Doha
Emergency Landing in Moscow

88

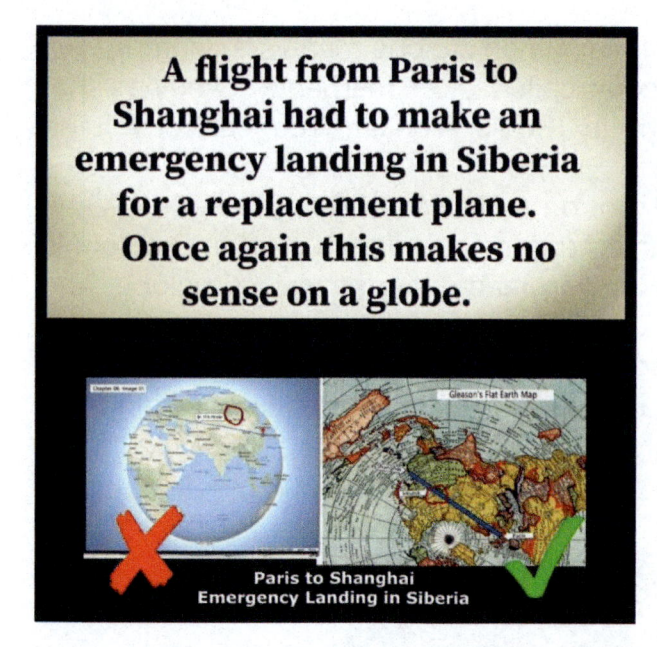

The Zetetic Method

A flight from Paris to Shanghai had to make an emergency landing in Siberia for a replacement plane. Once again this makes no sense on a globe.

Paris to Shanghai
Emergency Landing in Siberia

When I first started researching flat earth I looked into a flight from Japan to South California, and the Google map picture on the airline website showed a red line with a little plane on it going over Hawaii to get to LA. Well I thought that scored a point for the globe, but something kept telling me to check the reviews. I did and bingo. People were asking why they were flying near Alaska and Russia. That makes zero sense on a globe and perfect sense on a flat earth. So why the Google map image with the misdirection on it?

Here's some more emergency landings, plus southern flights making refueling stops in the northern hemisphere. Please look at them well with the intent to understand and see through the lie that we have been given. This, coupled with the lack of curvature is more physical proof that the world is not a ball but instead a flat plane just as we see it.

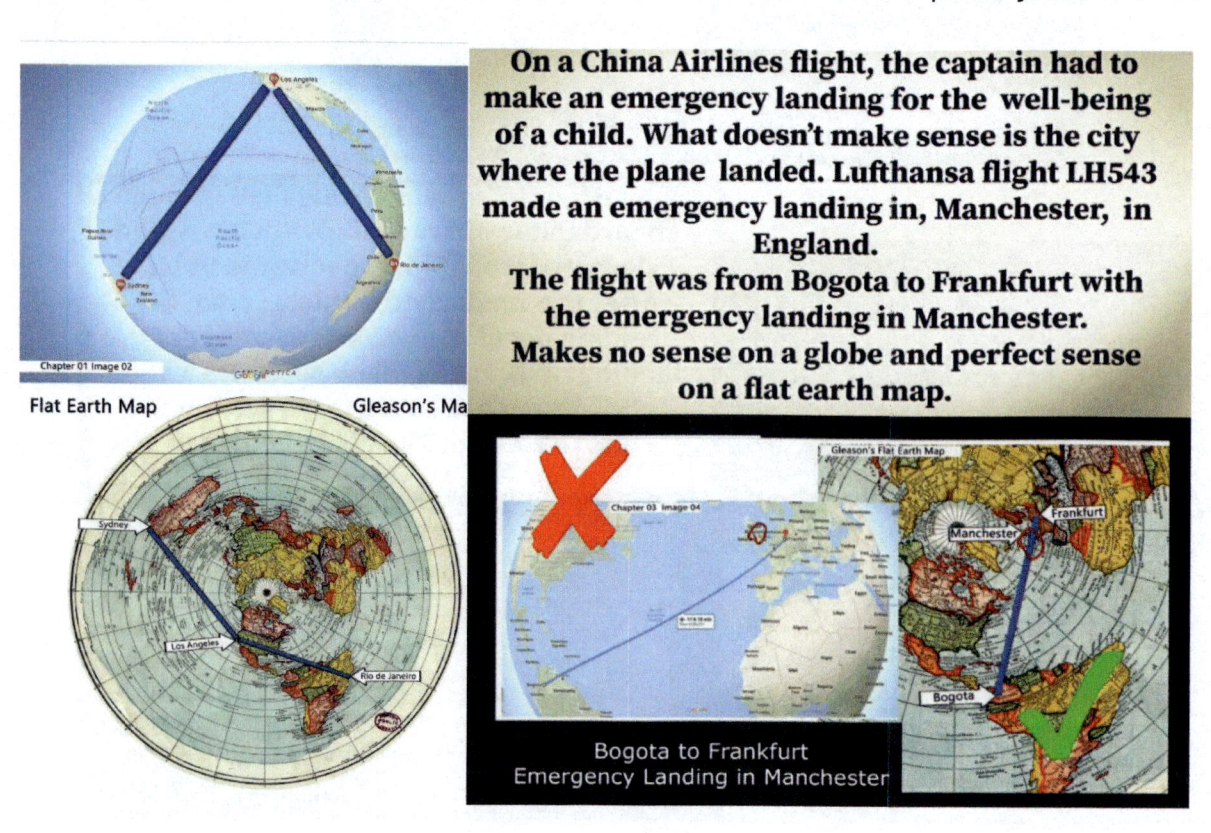

Flat Earth Map   Gleason's Map

On a China Airlines flight, the captain had to make an emergency landing for the well-being of a child. What doesn't make sense is the city where the plane landed. Lufthansa flight LH543 made an emergency landing in, Manchester, in England.
The flight was from Bogota to Frankfurt with the emergency landing in Manchester.
Makes no sense on a globe and perfect sense on a flat earth map.

Bogota to Frankfurt
Emergency Landing in Manchester

89

The Zetetic Method

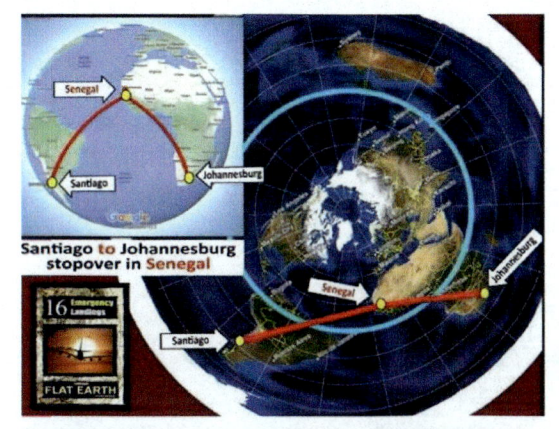

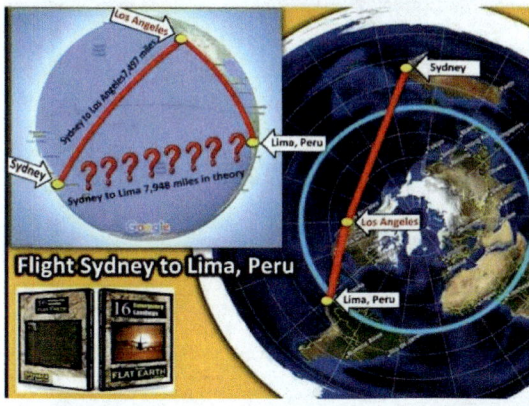

"If Earth was a ball, and Antarctica was too cold to fly over, the only logical way to fly from Sydney to Santiago would be a straight shot over the Pacific staying in the Southern hemisphere the entire way. Refueling could be done in New Zealand or other Southern hemisphere destinations along the way if necessary. In fact, however, Santiago-Sydney flights go into the Northern hemisphere making stop-overs at LAX and other North American airports before continuing back down to the Southern hemisphere. Such ridiculously wayward detours make no sense on the globe but make perfect sense and form nearly straight lines when shown on a flat Earth map." Eric Dubay 200 proofs Earth not a Spinning Ball.

On a globe, Johannesburg, South Africa to Perth, Australia should be a straight flight over the Indian Ocean with stops for refueling in Mauritius or Madagascar if needed. But as physical evidence would have it, most Johannesburg to Perth flights make their stops either in Dubai, Hong Kong or Malaysia, which make no sense on a globe, but makes perfect sense when mapped out on a flat Earth.

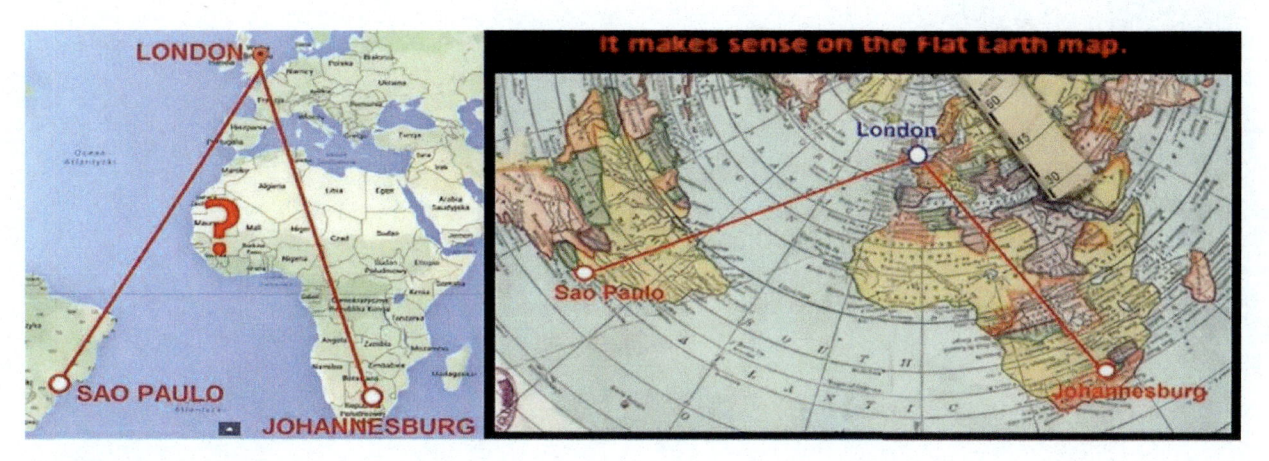

"On a ball-Earth Johannesburg, South Africa to Sao Paolo, Brazil should be a quick straight shot along the 25th Southern latitude, but instead nearly every flight makes a refueling stop at the 50th degree North latitude in London first! The only reason such a ridiculous stop-over works in reality is because the Earth is flat."   Ibid

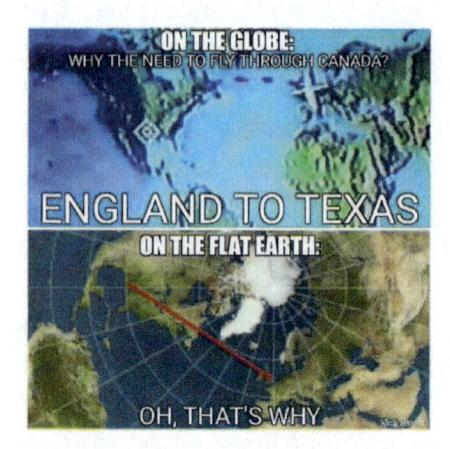

Look what Google map shows us versus the reality of it. They tell you what to think when you look at something with your eyes.

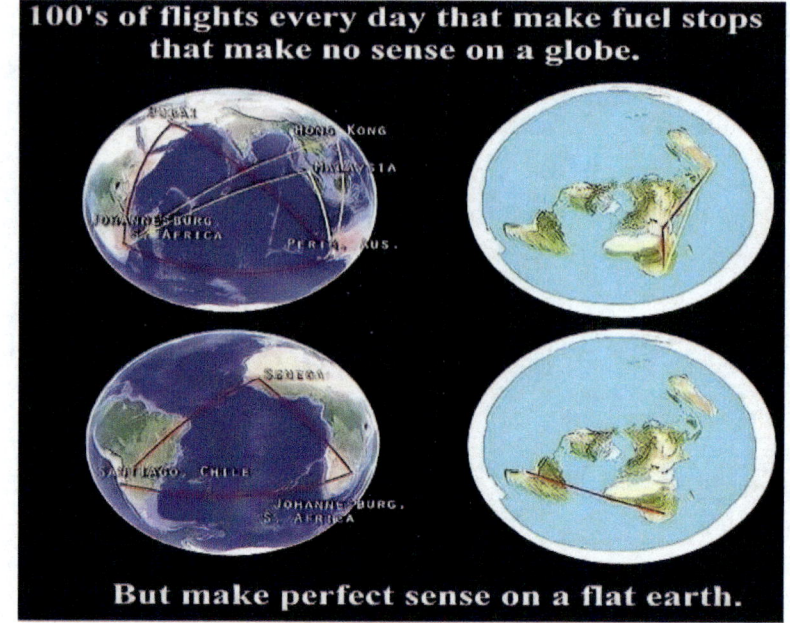

The flight from England to Texas goes through Canada. Why does this flight go through Canada to get to Texas? On a globe one can draw a straight line/path from England to Texas which does not touch Canada, however the flat earth map the straight line does indeed go through Canada.

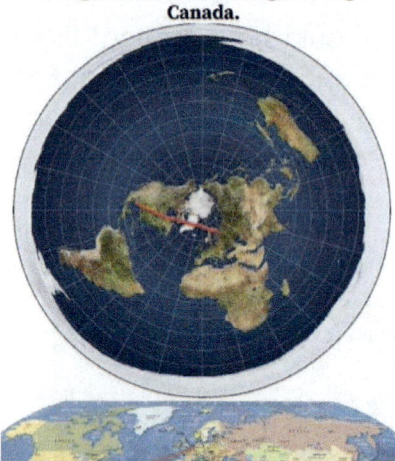

FLY TO CHINA ON A BALL

In the USA, people think that China is under their feet on the other side of a gigantic ball. They can jump on a plane and fly over a flat ocean while viewing an horizon line still at eye level the entire time. Then get off the plane in China and think that the USA is on the other side of the ball. This is what indoctrination does to otherwise smart people.

The plane would have to make a descent for curvature of 180° in a little over 10 hours depending on which flight you booked.

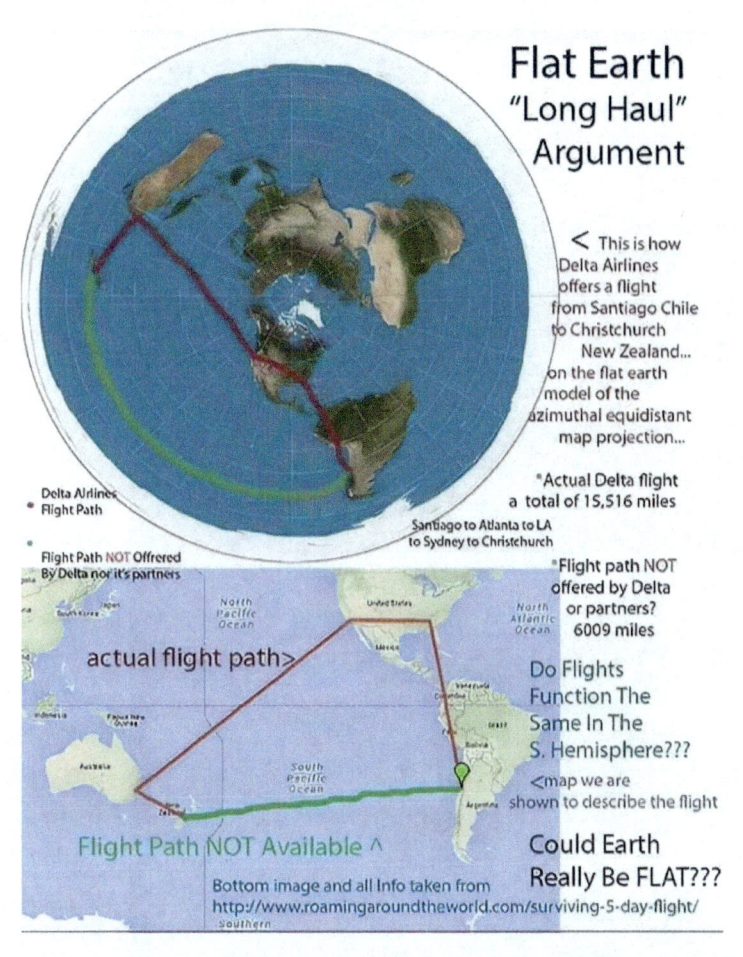

This view is all over the world. What solid physical proof do we have of a ball earth.

The Zetetic Method

Be deceived by no pilot. "Great Circle Routes" are nothing but shortcuts through the lines of latitudes. Lines of Latitude are the true "Great Circle" and the "Routes" in it refer to the shortcuts through the lines of latitude. You will never see a flight between two points at the Equator arcing south. They always arc NORTH because that is the shortest path between these two points. Arcing south would mean a longer route since earth spreads out on the outer side of the Equator.

You don't notice any such descent however, only during landings. A flat and level plane ride would be impossible if the airPLANE has to account for curvature. An airplane traveling at 500 mph would have to account for curvature or turn itself into a spaceship very soon.

You have no reason to believe you're flying to the flip side of a ball. If you were flying around a ball you'd notice. The fact that they tell us that we wouldn't notice is hilarious. If they never told you the earth was a spinning wobbling flying ball you'd never think it was.

You can fly across or around the earth like you would your neighborhood, either way you'll fly flat and level the entire time. Since the North Pole and Antarctica are guarded "no-fly" zones, no ships or planes have ever been known to circumnavigate the Earth in North/South directions. The only kind of circumnavigation which could not happen on a flat-Earth is North/Southbound, which is likely the very reason for the heavily-enforced flight restrictions.

The higher the plane goes on a ball the further the flight. Correct? So does plane flight plans calculate this, I wonder. It's an honest question.

The Zetetic Method

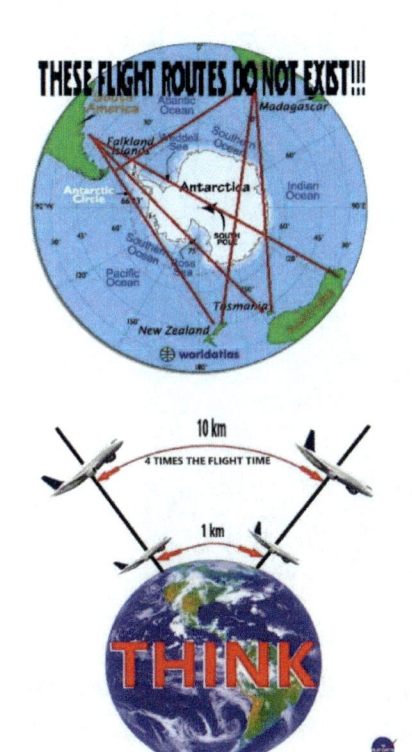

DON'T WORRY, THE PLANE'S NOT GOING DOWN ON YOU

Darrel Marble, a guy researching flat earth and doing his own experiments, took a spirit level on a plane flight from North Carolina to Seattle, to see if the plane compensated for the alleged curvature of the earth, he time-lapse video recorded the experiment. It only moved on take off and landings just as we sensed it. That's close to 5 miles of missing curvature. It was done again with a level on an app with the same results. You can also use a compass to detect anomalies in the flight path, and use the Protractor360 app to see if the plane is dipping. I want to see some ball earthers do the same experiments.

A pilot uses the horizon line to assure the plane flies level. When visibility is low the pilot uses an artificial horizon. The plane could not fly flat, as the spirit level showed, if the horizon line dropped due to curvature. The horizon line also would not remain at eye level no matter what height the plane is. Observable and provable.

Altitude indicator / Artificial horizon

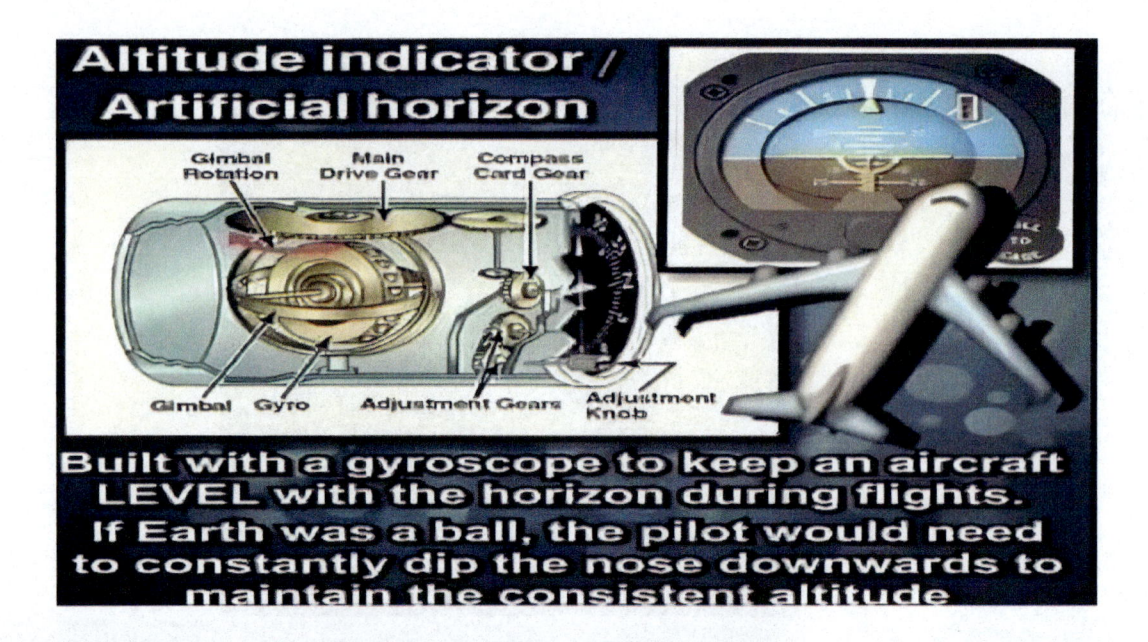

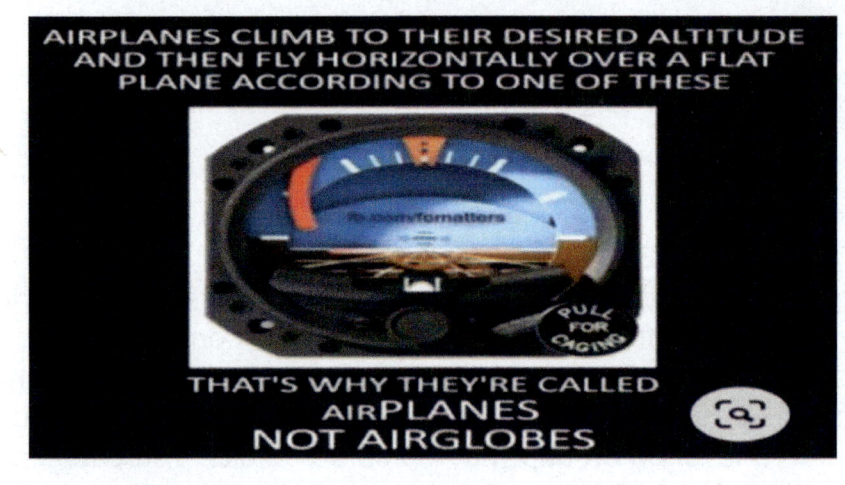

Built with a gyroscope to keep an aircraft LEVEL with the horizon during flights. If Earth was a ball, the pilot would need to constantly dip the nose downwards to maintain the consistent altitude

AIRPLANES CLIMB TO THEIR DESIRED ALTITUDE AND THEN FLY HORIZONTALLY OVER A FLAT PLANE ACCORDING TO ONE OF THESE

THAT'S WHY THEY'RE CALLED AirPLANES NOT AIRGLOBES

When you leave the airport, you'll notice you're flat and level, then you climb to scary heights and you'll notice the plane leveling off and flying flat and straight. Now at what point do you notice yourself flying sideways from where you started off? And if you're flying "around" the world, at what point did you start flying upside down as compared to where you started from? Did you notice any of this or did everything seem to stay the same, flat and level? Why exactly do you believe you're flying around a ball?

AGAIN!!!! How can you fly "around the world" to, let's say Australia, and you and the entire plane, go from flat and level to sideways and then upside down from where you started, in about 12 hours, and you don't even notice? Let's keep it real. You don't see or feel any such nonsense, you see and feel a stationary flat plane. PERIOD!

The Zetetic Method

DID YOU KNOW?
IF THE EARTH CURVED AT 8" X MILES² THEN A PLANE TRAVELING 500mph WOULD HAVE TO DESCEND 2,789ft. PER MINUTE TO MAINTAIN ALTITUDE. THIS IS NOT THE CASE AS PLANES FLY FLAT & LEVEL.

Meanwhile in Australia

The point I'm getting at here is that we experience a flat earth flight yet still believe that we live on a ball. We have no real reason to believe we just flew around a freaking ball. We have simply handed over our thought process to the elite government, its puppet scientists and the mainstream media. If you have done this then you have no room to complain about the current affairs of what's happening. It's the masses that buy the fraudulent product that keeps it around. A lie cannot change the truth, only your perception of it.

Look at this page from a flight Manuel. The pilot handbook says "assume a flat and stationary earth." If the pilot was flying an airPLANE over a whirling flying ball, why would they assume it's a flat stationary plane while training? It's simple, BECAUSE IT'S A FLAT STATIONARY PLANE! They have to assume a flat stationary earth because that's the only way it'll work in reality. Pilots do not have to account for curvature because it does not exist in reality. No part of a pilot's job requires the earth to be a ball.

Flight Dynamics Summary

1. Introduction

In this summary we examine the flight dynamics of aircraft. But before we do that, we must examine some basic ideas necessary to explore the secrets of flight dynamics.

1.1 Basic concepts

1.1.1 Controlling an airplane

To control an aircraft, control surfaces are generally used. Examples are elevators, flaps and spoilers. When dealing with control surfaces, we can make a distinction between primary and secondary flight control surfaces. When **primary control surfaces** fail, the whole aircraft becomes uncontrollable. (Examples are elevators, ailerons and rudders.) However, when **secondary control surfaces** fail, the aircraft is just a bit harder to control. (Examples are flaps and trim tabs.)

The whole system that is necessary to control the aircraft is called the **control system**. When a control system provides direct feedback to the pilot, it is called a **reversible system**. (For example, when using a mechanical control system, the pilot feels forces on his stick.) If there is no direct feedback, then we have an **irreversible system**. (An example is a fly-by-wire system.)

1.1.2 Making assumptions

In this summary, we want to describe the flight dynamics with equations. This is, however, very difficult. To simplify it a bit, we have to make some simplifying assumptions. We assume that ...

- There is a **flat Earth**. (The Earth's curvature is zero.)
- There is a **non-rotating Earth**. (No Coriolis accelerations and such are present.)
- The aircraft has **constant mass**.
- The aircraft is a **rigid body**.
- The aircraft is **symmetric**.
- There are no **rotating masses**, like turbines. (Gyroscopic effects can be ignored.)
- There is **constant wind**. (So we ignore turbulence and gusts.)

1.2 Reference frames

1.2.1 Reference frame types

To describe the position and behavior of an aircraft, we need a **reference frame** (RF). There are several reference frames. Which one is most convenient to use depends on the circumstances. We will examine a few.

FLAT EARTH AUTHOR'S
CONVERSATION WITH PROFESSOR ABOUT A FLIGHT

Here's an insert from Edward Hendrie's book "The Sphere of Influence," where he talks about his email discussion with three professors. One professor sent him a picture of the device on the back of the plane's seat, showing his plane route. And ask this question I'm quoting. Edward Hendrie answered with the route on a flat earth map with the explanation. Here's the route the professor was talking about, and the device on the seat.

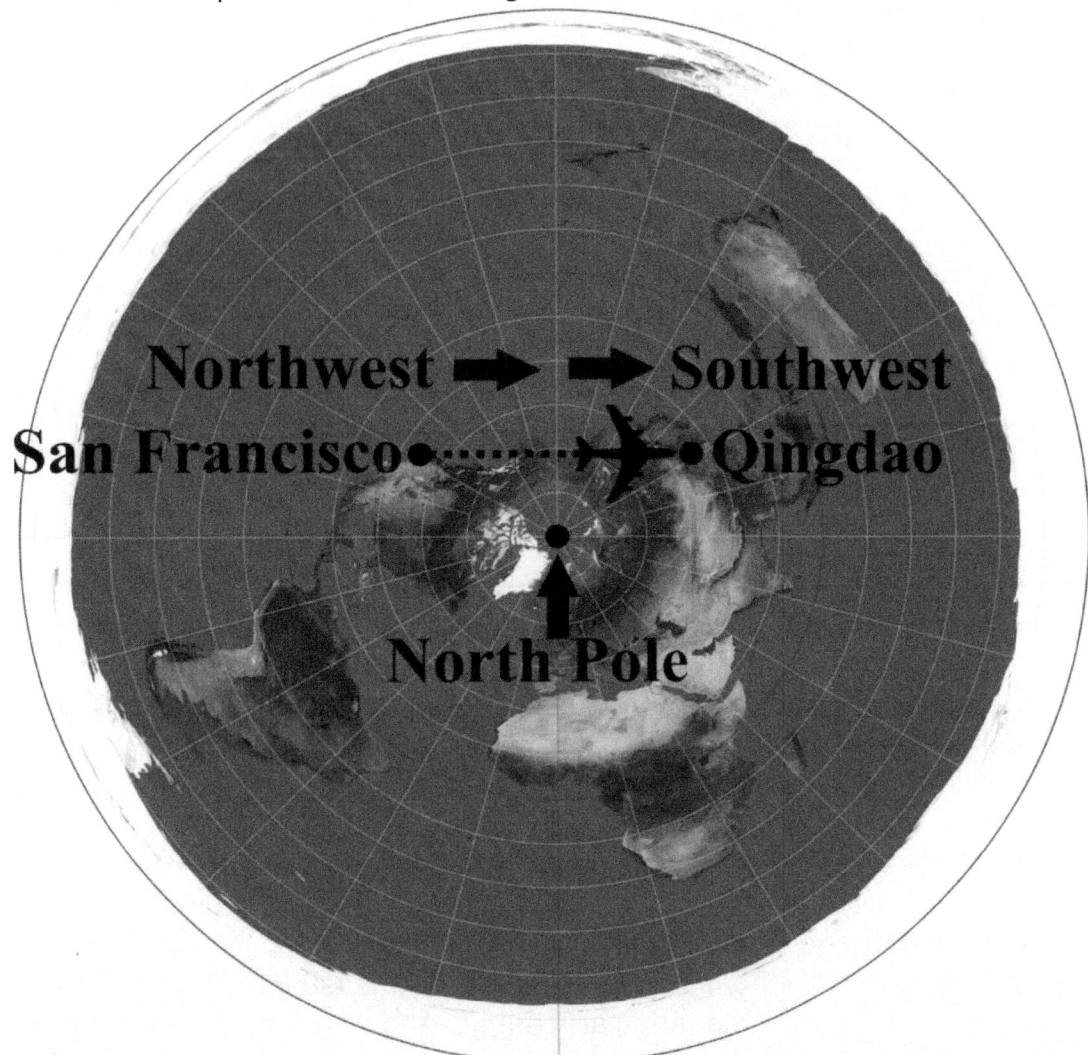

The flight path taken by the airline from San Francisco toward Qingdao can be seen to be a straight line on the flat earth. On that straight flight path, the plane starts out in a northwest bound direction and that straight path direction slowly becomes southwest bound. That happens because the plane is passing the North Directional Pole. At the beginning of the flight, the plane is traveling northwest toward the North Pole, but once it passes the North Pole it is traveling southwest away from the North Pole.

This was the picture of the device on the back of his airplane seat.

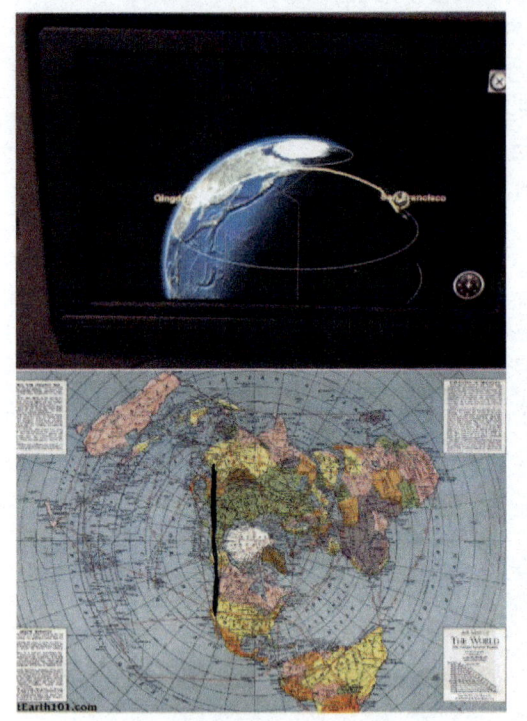

Professor: "Also, I watched the display and looked out the cabin window periodically. It was my observation that we flew North to China until we went over the pole and then we were flying South to China. On a flat Earth, how is it possible to be flying North and then South to the same destination?"

"Edward Hendrie: "The professor is, quite simply, afraid to be objective and honest with the facts. He knows that his academic career is at stake.
He has come to love big brother. He submissively accepts all the pablum coming out of academia, because he is afraid not to. He is ruled by fear. He is part and parcel of the problem in universities today, which are turning out obedient sycophants who cannot think for themselves." "That would put him on record questioning the legitimacy of the heliocentric model."

As you see from this picture of the route they are discussing, once you get past the Northern area you are headed south again. No ball needed. How could the professor not see this? Being a teacher doesn't mean you're smart. It just means they found someone who can't figure out the lies, thus will willfully spread them. There's a lot of dumb kids around, I wouldn't brag about being a teacher.

GYROSCOPE

Gyroscopes are designed to keep instruments and the plane level not constantly dipping over a curve. It sets itself on the runway which is level. It would do just the opposite of what it was designed to do if the plane had to dip to make any curve that we can't even see. The gyroscope artificial horizon line. Gyroscopes measure angular movement and the spinning mechanism resists angular change showing an angular difference in movement. Airplanes use these for the artificial Horizon. The horizon would roll backwards if traveling over a ball and proves that they don't fly upside down in Australia.

Here's what a pilot said in an interview about gyroscopes:
"So a gyroscope is critical as it's the eyes of a pilot when visibility is nothing or being greatly impaired. As a device, it has no circuitry, no uplink to ground control, or anything remotely digital to it in its purest form. It does its job of showing where a level plane orientation is, even if the plane is doing barrel rolls.
At no time does a gyroscope account for earth curvature and bend down in order to orchestrate the plane's navigational equipment to keep nosing the plane down every five

minutes to account for earth curvature. Proof for a non-planetary environment doesn't get any more definitive than this and if you can't see the basic mathematical logic being involved here, then you need to get new eyes, because yours are so full of lies as to keep you from ever believing in the truth even if it smacked you in the head and said. "Look!"
"

Same flat earth pilot pointed out:
"When the aircraft turns right as in the example on the right the white line is held parallel to the surface of the Earth by the internal gyroscope and the yellow lines remain parallel to the aircraft's wings.

If we divide 360 degrees of Earth's rotation by 24 hours we get 15 degrees of rotation per hour. That's a '15 degree tilt' every single hour. What good is a gyroscope-driven attitude indicator that remains level (or rigid) when the Earth is rotating, or 'tilting' 15 degrees every hour? On a rotating Earth the gyroscopic compass will show the aircraft in a constant left turn at a rate of 15 degrees per hour even though it is not moving and the view from the cockpit is not changing! Proof for an extended plane instead of a ball earth doesn't get any more definitive than this."

You, like a lot of pilots, are assuming curvature. The pilot in the interview was a ball earth til a friend had him research flat earth. A flat earther asked another pilot about this and the pilot said it was the gyroscope. That it was hooked up to the computers, etc. The flat earther called the gyroscope manufacturer and they said the gyroscope was completely mechanical. It keeps the instruments level when turning, descending, etc. It doesn't make the plane account for curvature. It even sets itself on the runway which is level.

Another pilot turned flat earther said the same thing and that no pilot questions this because there's no reason to. But now he has and sees it.

I had a great conversation with a fellow pilot flat earther and this was his take on pilots (excuse his French): "Lloyd Hunt this shit right here... simplifying assumptions... they just CANNOT read past what the f&#k this means. You cannot calculate SHIT to use in practice based on fantasy numbers. A model must be DEMONSTRABLE,
REPEATABLE AND MEASURABLE. If it is using unreal assumptions, they only work in simulations... and have no real life application...

But pilots use these DAILY and train for years on SIMULATIONS inside DIGITAL models. All using those same parameters, FLAT MOTIONLESS PLANE. But talk to them, they swear they understand aerodynamics, when they do not."

French physicist Georges Sagnac carried out a laser gyroscope experiment using a series of mirrors on a table. He was able to detect the rotation of his table as he rotated it, but unable to detect any motion when the device he built was at rest on an allegedly moving Earth.

Another experiment by Albert Michelson and Edward Morley in which the mirrors were arranged in such a way as to detect not angular or rotational motion but linear motion produced the same results; no motion of the Earth was detected.

The BLACK SWAN

1. All southern flights fly north.
2. Those emergency Landings only make sense on a flat earth.
3. So we can only fly east and west, which is the ONLY way to fly around the world on a flat earth.
4. So we have no North and South circumnavigation because of no fly zones for Antarctica mainland and the Arctic North Pole.
5. So we have no observable curvature whatsoever. It's starting to sound like a flat stationary greenhouse doesn't it?

CHAPTER 3
ANTARTICA

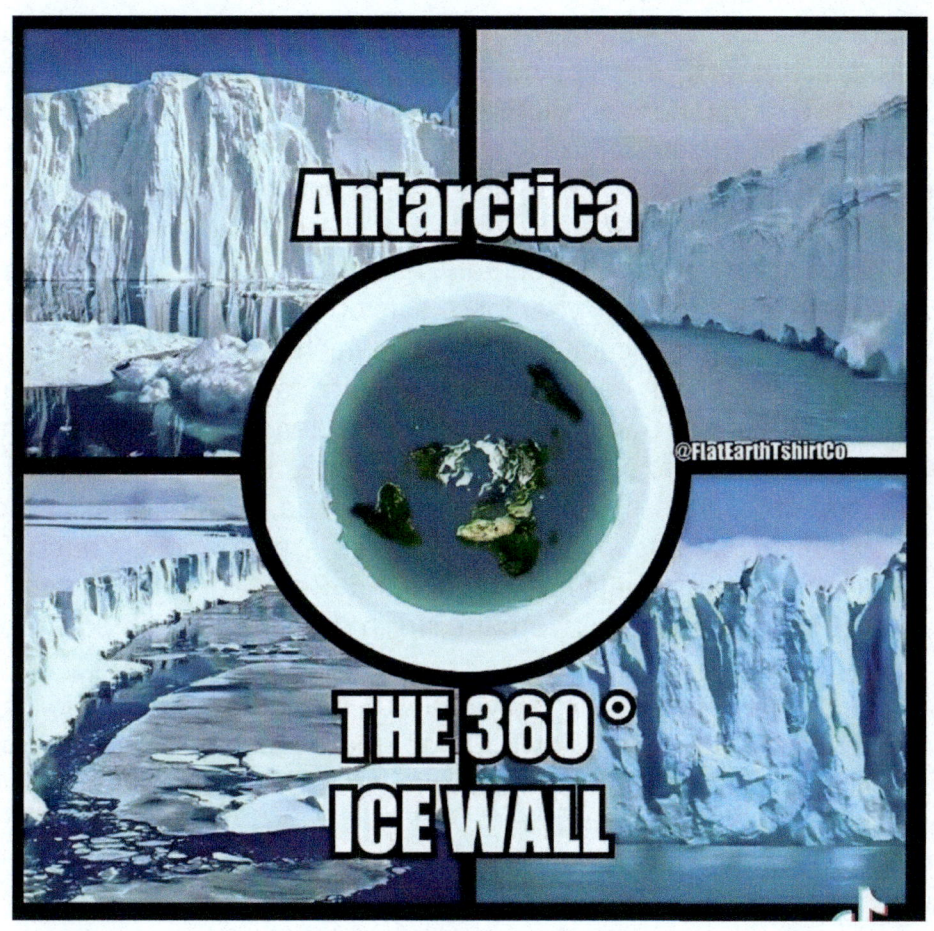

"The Antarctic is the coldest place on Earth yet it is closest to, and surrounded by, the warmest places on Earth; South America, South Africa, Australia and New Zealand. This makes no sense whatsoever if Antarctica is closest to the Sun for six months out of the year in a heliocentric model." Artist Rick Potvin

"The bigger the lie, the more inclined people will be to believe it." Adolf Hitler

"History is a set of lies that people have agreed upon." - Napoleon Bonaparte

ANTARCTICA

Why would governments, that are at war, sign a treaty for Antarctica, a treaty somehow never broken despite track records of broken treaties. All this for some ICE? Seriously? It looks like there is something there that draws powerful governments. Somehow I'm thinking it's not ice but something we know nothing of.

Why a treaty? The government inflicts man made diseases, kills innocent lives in the Middle East for profit, and they're worried about PENGUINs and some FREAKING ICE? Wake up!!! But more on the treaty later.

During Operation High Jump, Admiral Byrd had USS Mount Olympus under his command, aircraft carrier USS Philippine Sea, 13 US Navy support ships, six helicopters, six flying boats, two seaplanes, and fifteen other aircraft. And the number of personnel reached 4000. Doesn't this seem like it's too much gear and people for an exploration mission, especially when we are talking about an uninhabited continent of ice?

Antarctica, "discovered" in the 19th century, is one of the driest hostile places on earth and it's covered in ice and snow all year long. This uniformity of temperature in Antarctica partly accounts for the great accumulation of ice which is formed, not on account of the great severity of the winter, but because there is practically no summer to melt it.

One would think that if the earth was a globe, the same amount of summer heat and winter cold, should be experienced at the same latitudes North and South of the Equator. The same general conditions should exist. But instead the opposite is the reality and disproves the whirling ball assumption and the sun's size and distance. The contrast between places at the same latitudes North and South of the Equator, is a strong argument against the globe model where the North pole AND South pole receive 24 hour sunlight.

Other than man's interference, the snow and ice has been reported to never melt. Up north in the Arctic, as far as we're allowed to go, there's plant life and animals basting in the sun, but not at Antarctica, it's a wasteland of ice with no rain. Antarctica is an eternal winter. Why, if it gets a 24 hour sun too?

There are many recorded journeys around Antarctica throughout history that don't match the mileage of the globe theory. The average recorded traveling around Antarctica was between 58-62,000 miles, with stops for the winter. All say there's no break in the ice to go around, that it just keeps going. Hmmm! Seems odd, seeing as the circumference of Antarctica, according to the globe model, is around 9900 miles.

The journeyman always writes about the two months of complete darkness but never about the phenomenon of a 24 hour sun. You would think that this would be chronicle worthy as well.

Geography. The circumference of the Antarctic Circle is roughly **16,000 kilometres (9,900 mi)**. The area south of the Circle is about 20,000,000 km² (7,700,000 sq mi) and covers roughly 4% of Earth's surface. Most of the continent of Antarctica is within the Antarctic Circle.

W https://en.m.wikipedia.org › wiki
Antarctic Circle - Wikipedia

CROSSING ANTARCTICA

If you want to cross the mainland Antarctica you have to go to the government website to do it. They've made it impossible. Please go on Antartica.gov and try to apply for it. Read all the rules and regulations. You can however cross the peninsula with permission. They have 4 "South Poles" set up for tourists photo opportunities. They have said that these Poles are NOT actually the true south pole. So when you hear someone say they hiked to the south pole, tell them this author is laughing at them because there's only one proven pole, and it's the North pole and they won't be hiking there either. Asked them which south pole? LMAO

But as for the mainland you have to get permission from every country and pay for each. Even if every country says yes, you can still be turned away at the "gate."

A fellow flat earther named Taboo Conspiracy recorded himself going on there and looking through the rules and regulations. They've made it impossible. One ball earther, in a lengthy flat earth vs globe earth discussion, sent me, what he thought was the Antarctica guides til I sent him a link to the real one, I never heard back from him.

You have to bag your poop. Think of how many 1000s of miles that is. Don't want to leave poop on the ice I guess. But you can cut down a tree from the Amazon rainforest.

You can carry a sled but no sled dogs. Which makes no sense. So many others, all for the environment. I guess it's a danger to all that ice.

Recently a sailor named Jarle Andhoy, was held at gunpoint, fined and later imprisoned for attempting to enter territory in Antarctica that is off limits under the International, military enforced Antarctica Treaty. Maybe he wanted some of that precious ice. Another modern explorer went missing. Hmm!

The Zetetic Method

Anyway, there's a whole list of ridiculousness. What are they hiding over there? More ice or a firmament that's keeping this greenhouse going? What's this blue sky ice/glass I've heard about? Hmm. Could it have anything to do with this?

Why are they not protecting the Amazon rainforest?

No one sails around the world in a straight line but a series of straight lines. And once again there are no around the world trips north and south. There is a No-fly Zone over both Poles. All southern flights fly north. Airlines have said it's too cold for the engines. But what about space flight, and the military flying to the base, and the tourist spot on the peninsula?

Now they're changing their claim and saying "there are no fly zones but they have no reason to fly over it." Why not, it's a much shorter route? Why the change in claims? Flat earthers got them on the fences. Lol

People always ask me for proof of the ice wall. Not sure what they think Antarctica is covered in but here are some pictures of Antarctica though.

105

CAPTAIN COOK DONE WENT TO FAR

I got this from a great book by William Carpenter but I've read Captain Cook's book as well and find his adventures very interesting. There were many other explorers that had similar stories. I think Cook's book has changed from the original, based on his experiences, but that's just my opinion, I'm sure no one would change history like that, right?

["Captain Cook's journeys are not exactly hidden but his accounts of what he experienced is hidden. In 1773 Captain Cook became the first modern explorer known to have breached the Antarctic circle and reached the ice barrier. This expedition offered an exciting chance to find proof of either the flat or globe Earth models because Captain Cook intended to sail completely around Antarctica looking for inlets through the ice-wall. If the Earth was indeed a globe 25,000 miles in equatorial circumference as the heliocentrists claimed, then a complete circumnavigation of Antarctica would be approximately 12,000 miles, and if the Earth was flat with Antarctica surrounding the entire circumference, a complete circumnavigation of Antarctica would have to take over 50,000 miles. During three voyages lasting three years and eight days, Captain Cook and crew sailed a total of 60,000 miles along the Antarctic coastline, never once finding an inlet or path through or beyond the massive glacial wall! Captain Cook wrote: "The ice extended east and west far beyond the reach of our sight, while the southern half of the horizon was illuminated by rays of light which were reflected from the ice to a considerable height.

His comments that he wrote are not mentioned in schools. It is a good question to ask why? With all the lies and fraudulent actions by the space agencies along with a lot of evidence coming to light suggesting the Earth is flat one might be led to believe that the powers that be are hiding the true shape of the Earth.

If the truth about what Captain Cook's said about his journey's was taught in schools along with other truths then we wouldn't have all this misinformation that is spread like the other answers that were made to your question. So that leads me to believe that is the reason why the truth is hidden."

"Yes, but we can circumnavigate the South easily enough,' is often said by those who don't know, The British Ship Challenger recently completed the circuit of the Southern region - indirectly, to be sure - but she was three years about it, and traversed nearly 69,000 miles - a stretch long enough to have taken her six times round on the globular hypothesis." William Carpenter, "100 Proofs the Earth is Not a Globe."]

If the Earth were indeed a globe, as the elite would have us believe, then the southern hemisphere would be the same circumference as the northern. But Cook's journey makes no sense on a globe, even with his zigzagging for foul weather, but makes perfect sense on a flat earth.

THE 24 HOUR SUN

I've watched three videos with the "Antarctica" 24 hour sun off YouTube and Antarctica.gov and they are proven fake. On one video they inserted the words North, South, East and West as the directions changed as the camera panned around. Where they screwed up was in their layering of this fake video, they put the layer with the word North and the word West on it behind the mountain layer. A small part of the N and T was behind the mountain layer. The original video should only be one flat layer with no way behind the mountains. Plus the sun looked sooo fake. I have the same sun brush in my Photoshop digital painting software. I do digital art for a hobby and have made this mistake before. BUSTED!!!

On another video the video started with the sun coming from behind a mountain then as it circled it started going down but went behind the same mountain then came around again. So what was the issue with this? When it came around again the cloud formation restarted as it was from the beginning because it was a loop video from Artic. LMAO

The third video was also from the Arctic but claimed to be otherwise. And it was titled "Take that flat earthers." You only have to research both bases to see the difference.

When I emailed them asking why they would claim that that's Antarctica when it's clearly Arctic, the video was taken down but I got no response. HA! And these are scientists???

Another video had the "24-hour sun" going around twice but the second time the only difference was the clouds were removed. The steam cloud that looked like it was coming from the sun and the flash were still there and exactly the same. The bottom picture is "24 hours later" during this supposedly "24-hour sun" video from Antarctica. But it's the same with just the clouds removed. Why fake it? WHY!?!?

The Zetetic Method

Fake 24hour sun in Antarctica video exposed.

The words NORTH and WEST are both behind the mountain layer. The original video should be flat with no layers. Fake! The sun is a photoshop brush. I actually have one on my Photoshop.

24 hours later

108

The Zetetic Method

Here's the link to Taboo Conspiracy's video. He's really good at debunking these videos. https://youtu.be/aDjr5RG59lc

My chef, a globe believer, years ago spent three years in Antarctica feeding the scientist. He said there was never a 24 hour sun like he thought there would be nor could he ever leave the base, which he found odd because there was nothing but ice as far as the eye could see. He said not only could you not leave the base but you could not question the guards or anyone else about it.

I wasn't a flat earther at the time and didn't think much about what he said, but now it makes sense. I did get to see the 24 hour sun in Alaska though, making its way around the North star Polaris.

I don't have to debunk all of the Antarctica 24 hour sun videos to know that if it was real you wouldn't have to fake any. Let's get that straight the Midnight Sun only exists in the North. This is why they keep faking videos. Why fake it if it's real. There should be tons of real footage.

HOW DO WE HAVE ALL THAT ICE?

How can Antarctica have 10,000 feet of snow and an ice belt over 1000 feet thick, and remain one of the coldest places on Earth year round all while closest to the sun for six months and 3 million miles closer during the elliptical orbit? Furthermore, how can the closest continents, Australia, South Africa and South America, exist around the coldest place on Earth, Antarctica, and are consistently the warmest places on Earth?

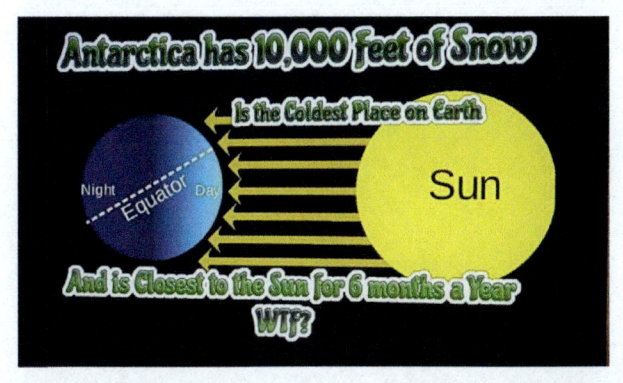

When a cloud covers the sun it instantly gets cooler, at night the sun is a full diameter of earth from us; yet Antarctica is only half diameter of earth from the sun on the equator. However Antarctica remains a frozen wasteland of ice. On the globe earth this makes zero sense, yet it is observable reality, unlike curvature. On a flat earth it makes perfect sense, as Antarctica is an ice wall that forms the outer circle surrounding Earth and the sun is smaller and local. (More on the sun later) Real pictures, videos, and an ice-wall everywhere south and no curvature proves this.

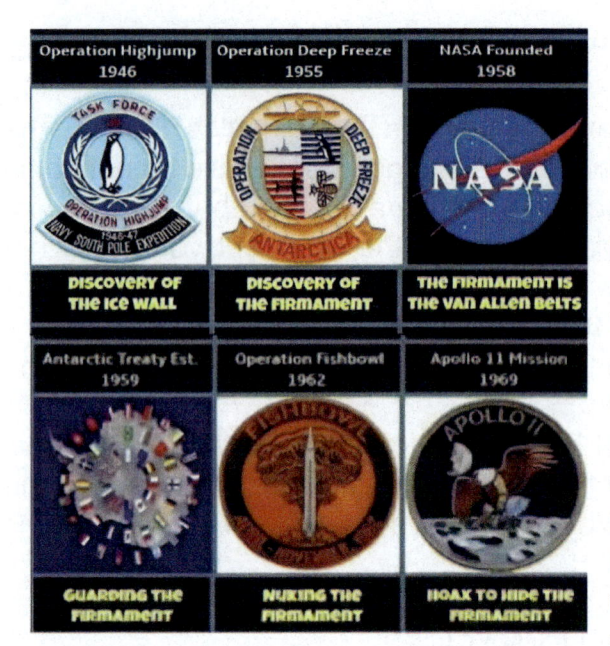

THE ONE UNBREAKABLE TREATY

There's a world treaty for Antarctica signed by 53 countries now. You can go to Antartica.gov and see for yourself. It's a treaty that has never been broken (With a white man that is saying something)

When the treaty was put together they were supposed to protect the environment. (You know all that ice) But they started shooting missiles in the sky up there. (Research Operation Highjump and Operation Fishbowl in the Antarctic) The U.S. and the Soviet Union, who were quite the enemies, agree to these treaty terms. I wonder how quickly and with how much debate. Must be some good ice for warring countries to make agreements over and stop independent exploration, wouldn't you say?

You can hike across the peninsula (with permission) and take the tours but not on the mainland. Only military, scientists and crew are allowed there. You know because of all that ice. Notice the dates here.

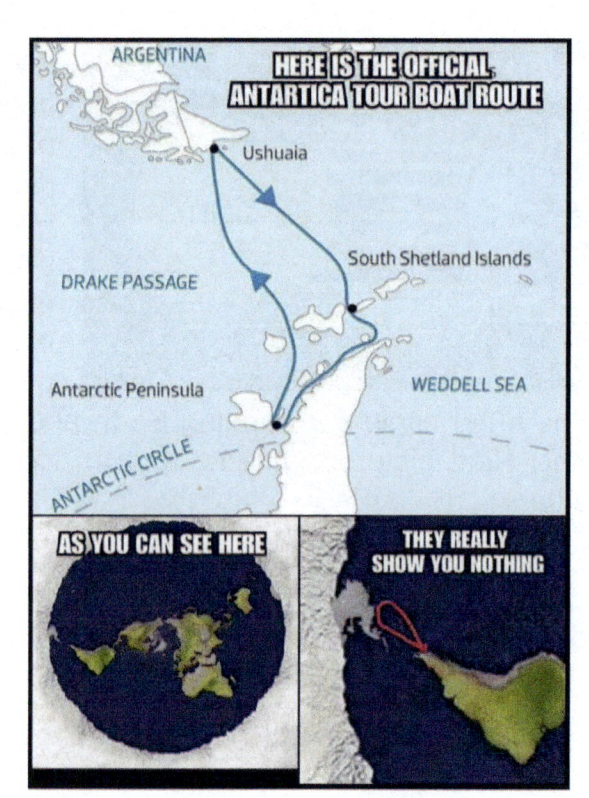

From Isaac Walker's book "The Breadth of the Earth": "The Antarctic treaty was officially enforced in June of 1961. The final operation to the Antarctic happened in 1956. NASA was formed in 1958. The Antarctic treaty was enforced in 1961. Sounds shady to me.

Shortly after these events unfold the United States and Russia begin operations where they are blowing up high altitude nuclear bombs. Operation Dominic was a series of 31 high altitude nuclear explosions with a 38.1 megaton total yield conducted in 1962 by the United States in the Pacific. A missile called Thor was used to lift nuclear warheads into near space and this operation was called Operation Fishbowl. Let me say that again... OPERATION FISHBOWL. Operation Fishbowl was part of Operation Dominic. The name Dominic means "of the Lord". Was the military of the United States of America purposely sending nuclear warheads into high altitude to test the "fishbowl of the Lord"?"

Sending nuclear missiles into the sky in Antarctica is one way to melt all that ice all those countries signed a treaty to protect. Researching all of these events truly put things in perspective for me. What are they keeping from us? Keeping all that ice to themselves? Get real!!! We deserve a cup of that too.

Commercial flights have said their engines can not handle the cold of Antarctica. If engines can handle space travel then Antarctica shouldn't be a problem. Also there's that no fly zone to keep all that ice safe. Also, what of the scientists flying back and forth, their engines can handle it? Hmmm

Why can't we explore Antarctica? We can and are destroying the Amazon rainforest but Antarctica is off limits for exploring; only the peninsula tours and hikes? Does that seem odd to you dear reader? Are you starting to question things yet?

The BLACK SWAN

1. The proof of the ice wall surrounding a flat earth is that there's no curvature as physical reality has shown and everywhere you go south you hit the Antarctic ice wall. Don't you love physical based evidence?

2. Antarctica IS a frozen wasteland whereas the Arctic is absolutely NOT. This major difference makes no sense on a ball with uniform rotation and a 24 hour sun in Antarctica.

3. Somehow countries, including the ones at war, agreeing to protect all that ice but not the Amazon rainforest is proof in itself that something fishy is going on with Operation Fishbowl/Dominic in Antarctica. We do live in a greenhouse; the enclosure has to be somewhere.

If it's too cold for plane engines then what about this helicopter's engine?

CHAPTER 4
THE ABOVE SITUATION

ASSUMPTIONS IN THE SKY KEEP ON TURNING

"Were the succession of stars endless, then the background of the sky would present us a uniform luminosity, since there could exist absolutely no point, in all the background, at which would not exist a star."   Edgar Allen Poe

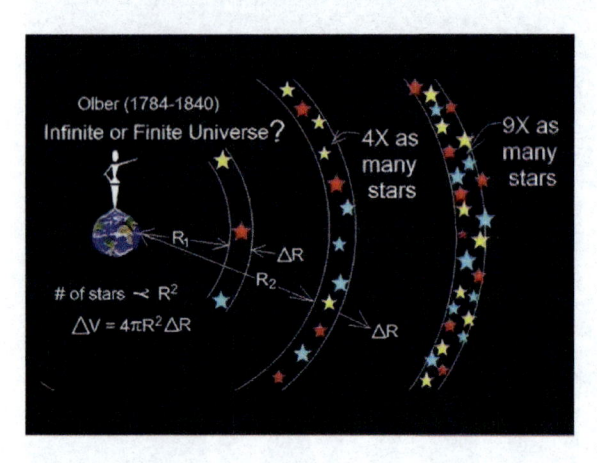

There are situations in the sky that we flat earthers can't explain, but that problem is in the area of celestial lights above us, it has nothing to do with the flat stationary plane below us. Whatever is happening up there does not make this earth/water plane warp into a ball and start whirling around and flying. There's a lot we haven't learned, we're just now discovering that we've been lied to, and we are still learning the truth of reality, now that the blinders are off, but we still have further to go. We Zetetics are open to receive further facts, but not to deny those already obtained.

If you want to trust the science community, you have to have faith in the outrageous numbers in the speed of....well pretty much everything. Earth spinning, flying, sun flying around the Milky Way, etc., etc., etc. The numbers they boost of Earth, sun and galaxy moving are 1000mph, 66,500mph, 500,000 mph, 1.3 million mph (remember the numbers may vary if you look the claims up. Different science websites have different number claims because that's how Pseudo-science works when you don't go off proven facts) These are numbers no human can relate to, and so we are stuck with faith and acceptance.

People often send me pictures of their night sky as proof of the whirling ball theory; it is not. When they do I ask them how exactly is it proof? And how can you prove any such great distances that are quoted? What method could possibly be used to measure something light-years away or even millions of miles? There's never an answer because there is none. It's all assumptions that's riding off a belief system. Prove me wrong.

And how fast is the Milky Way Galaxy moving? The speed turns out to be an astounding **1.3 million miles per hour** (2.1 million km/hr)! We are moving roughly in the direction on the sky that is defined by the constellations of Leo and Virgo.

https://nightsky.jpl.nasa.gov › ...   [PDF]

How Fast Are You Moving When You Are Sitting Still?

The Zetetic Method

They have no clue as to what they're looking at, just their beliefs. Which is useless as far as knowledge goes, isn't it? Their picture of the night sky tells them nothing as far as this subject goes.

What they call "Science" is a show, a scientific vaudeville if you will, of faith in assumptions and speculations and unproven claims. They tell us tales that can't be observed or proven. We believe them because we trust them. We accept these claims so we can have belief and not have to spend time thinking on such matters. We have hypotheses; we don't call them explanations; we've discarded explanations with belief in hypotheses or whatever they choose to say. It's my observation that a great deal of 'scientific' literature must be accepted with faith because no proof is provided.

Most of the people, and Astronomers alike, I talk to about flat earth will point to the sky, never the earth unless they're talking about a ship that's not appearing slanted while going over a downward curve, but remaining vertical instead. (Not leaning as it goes behind a downward curve. How odd huh?)

I believe the reason for this is because anything that's happening in the sky can be built on assumptions and speculations and harder to disprove. However, the physical earth is a different matter, isn't it? Either there's curvature or there's not. And the case of physical evidence shows that there's not. So, no matter what the celestial lights in the sky are doing, it cannot in any way affect or determine the shape of the earth. The celestial lights and the solid earth below are two different subjects. Below proves flat while above proves no wobbling and flying. People should question the legitimacy of arguments which cannot be tested by experiments, and which is entirely based upon hypothesis.

People point to the celestial lights in the sky and say 'if they're 'planets' then we are too,' this is a complete error in judgment based on a couple of assumptions.

A basketball is equal to another basketball, but it is not equal to the quart; the quart is a different matter altogether. An elephant has ears the same as you but that doesn't make it a human. It is an assumption to look at lights in the sky and believe they're terrestrial 'planets' like they claim; it's also an assumption to believe you're standing on a 'planet' because you believe a celestial light is one. They took the word 'plane' and added a T and sold it. All planets appear to be lights. They don't even look like terra firma. Other than a mirror or metal, when has matter reflected like this? They haven't given any physical proof of otherwise. Prove me wrong.

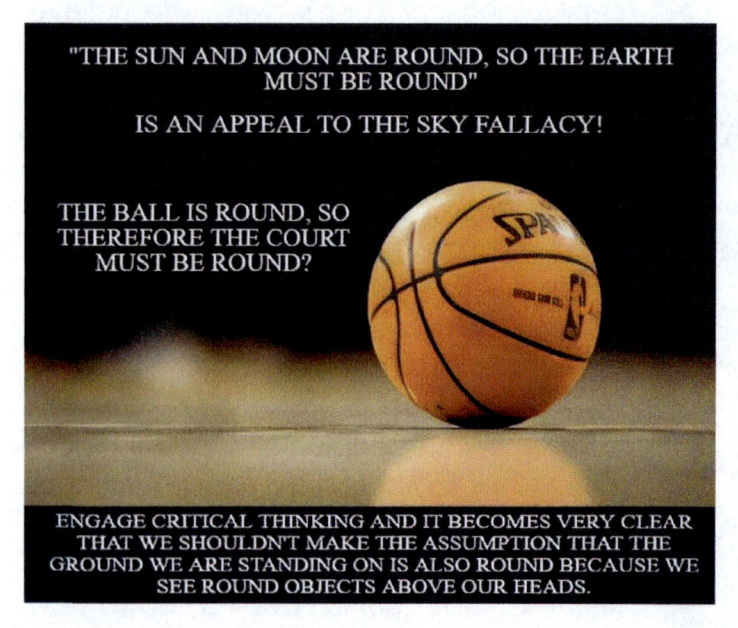

As far as Earth's shape goes, it is not of primary importance of what the lights are doing but we will now look at some of the claims our bought and paid for puppet Pseudo-scientist are making, involving the celestial lights, and run them through the Zetetic Method and see what physical reality can make of it all.

IS IT WRITTEN IN THE STARS

If we're wobbling and spinning at 1000mph, flying around the sun at 66,600mph and around the Milky Way at 500,000mph and leaving the Big Bang at 670,000,000mph then how have the constellations always had the same pattern and on the same course every night and the North Star Polaris NEVER moving from it's position at all? They would ALL have to be moving in unison with this spinning wobbling flying ball. The chances of that are the same chances of a monkey typing Shakespeare on a typewriter. But they all rotate around Polaris together as though they were connected.

With rates of speed which no man is able to grasp, and with the inhabitants, standing in every direction, some hanging upside down according to others location, you would think there would be overwhelming physical evidence. But, like me at the beginning of my research, you'd be wrong. There's no star displacement or change in their relative position. No movement felt at all. Nothing. Zero. Just an authoritarian word for it, nothing more.

The movement of earth is not proven thus not based on truth. It's a theory to explain away the movement of stars that is observable and has been tested and proven to be true.

Another observable physical fact a flat earther pointed out in a discussion I was following: "Take Orion. The stars are all supposed to be at different distances. And yet while traveling at 1/2 million mph every minute of every day for 1000s of years there is no deviation. For example, one of the stars on his belt moving. Closer stars will appear to move quickly while stars farther away will move slower. After 1000s of years nothing has changed. And it goes in a perfect circle and comes back to the same spot every year. That is impossible by the globe model. The distance factor is not science. The distances vary. There would be movement in some, more movement in others, and in some, very little movement. No movement means you have been programmed."

All of the following and not the first tread of physical evidence: "Briefly, modern astronomical teaching affirms that the world we live on is a globe, which rotates, revolves, and spins away in space at brain-reeling rates of speed; that the sun is a million and a-half times the size of the earth-globe, and nearly a hundred million miles distant from it; that the moon is about a quarter the size of the earth; that it receives all its light from the sun, and is thus only a reflector, and not a giver, of light; that it attracts the body of the earth and thus causes the tides; that the stars are worlds and suns, some of them equal in importance to our own sun himself, and others vastly his superior; that these worlds, inhabited by sentient beings, are without number and occupy space boundless in extent and illimitable in duration; the whole of these interlaced bodies being subject to, and supported by, universal gravitation, the foundation and father of the whole fabric." Thomas Winship

The Skyview app is an app that shows you what stars you are looking at and the location of where they should be. If the Earth was indeed wobbling and flying in three different directions and the universe was/is expanding, then how could the app possibly do its job? The app would be useless if all of this was happening. How could our ancestors map out the stars and predict their locations for 1000s of years if all of this was true as well? I should say that what we call knowledge is ignorance surrounded by laughter.

You see how the stars can be seen clearly, and, with a decent camera, you can take outstanding pictures. How is this possible? If the Earth were spinning at a 1000 miles per hour, flying in three different directions at three unimaginable speeds, all you would see is a nasty blur, of which you could not discern almost anything or get any clear pictures. Just think what you would get if you tried to take a picture, while riding in a car, that goes at 150 miles an hour or even 100 miles an hour. It's not just the 1000mph spinning we have to consider, there's many other movements and crazy speeds. 66,600 mph around the sun and even faster around the Milky Way and then EVEN FASTER moving away from the Big Bang. Not only do we not feel it but the camera doesn't catch any of it. Do we believe this or are we just accepting it? It's almost as if we were stationary, just as we sense it.

We've seen stars moving around Polaris in the night sky all our lives, that is except for Polaris, which stays put. Many of these other stars are supposedly further than Polaris yet they appear to move. So am I supposed to believe that the 25,000 mile distance of the spin of Earth is enough to make stars appear to move around Polaris but the 186,000 miles journey across space from June to December has no relative effect on viewing Polaris?

Again and again their theories have been challenged and exposed with pure reality, but the majority, who trust the authoritarian appointed scientists, accepted the popular belief. Its popularity is no argument for the accuracy of the theory.

"For Polaris to be seen from the Southern hemisphere of a globular Earth, the observer would have to be somehow looking "through the globe," and miles of land and sea would have to be transparent. Polaris can be seen, however, up to over 20 degrees South latitude." Eric Dubay "200 proofs the earth is not a spinning ball"

Astronomers will point to the sky and look at star trails and all the celestial lights' movement around Polaris, and then make the claim that it's us doing the rotation and not the lights. This extraordinary claim is accepted without any bit of evidence. There's no movement felt nor star parallax, just acceptance.

The North Star Polaris and the constellations are never out of sync. If we were wobbling and flying in three different directions, the night sky would be a blur of light and not just dots and time-lapse perfect circles. Scientists say we don't have star parallax because they're too far away, the fact that we have star circles proves differently. We have one but can't have the other? They just make up anything. There's always an excuse why we can't prove the claims for ourselves.

The truth of the matter.

When I went to the McDonald Observatory, the employee said that all their data comes from NASA and is put into calculation with what they see. Which means, when they look, someone else tells them what to believe in and what to think when they view these celestial lights.

A few examples of this is you looking at a ship disappearing bottom first while some half-wit is telling you it's because you're standing on a ball, or you feel hotter as the sun gets a little closer and some parrot is in your ear telling you the sun is 93,000,000 miles away. The theory is continuously passed down as fact and believed as so. But the masses acceptance of this claim does NOT make it a fact.

THE CASE OF THE MISSING STAR PARALLAX

All stars rotate around Polaris which is stationed directly above the North Pole. Their course never changes. You can take time-lapse pictures of these star trails all year long and see perfect circles. All these stars, constellations, Polaris and "gas clouds" would have to be moving in unison with the ball earth as it wobbles and flies in three different directions simultaneously.

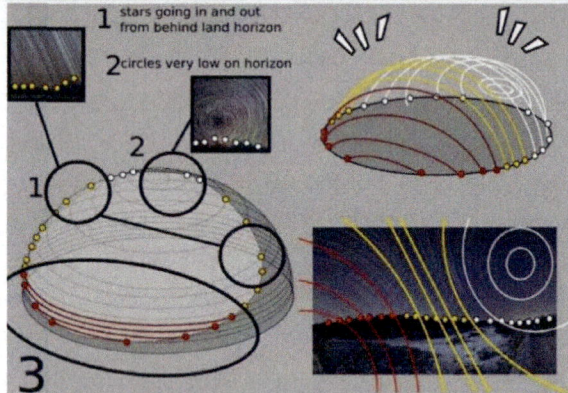

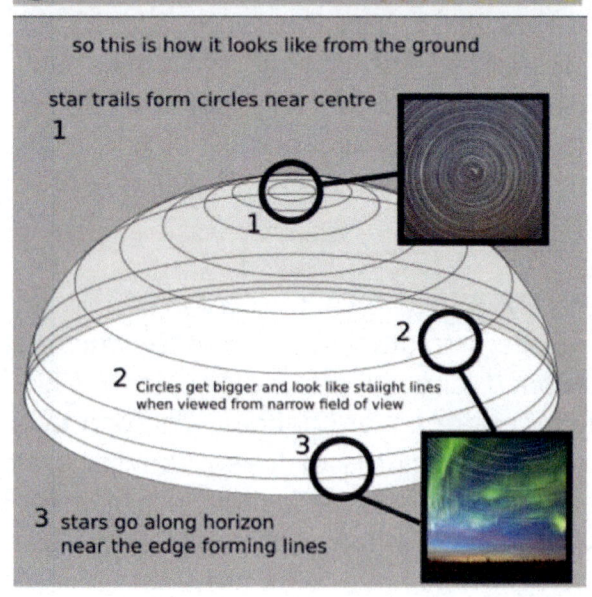

Eric Dubay puts it better than I ever could: "If Earth were a ball, the Southern Cross and other Southern constellations would all be visible at the same time from every longitude on the same latitude as is the case in the North with Polaris and its surrounding constellations. Ursa Major/Minor and many others can be seen from every Northern meridian simultaneously whereas in the South, constellations like the Southern Cross cannot. This proves the Southern hemisphere is not "turned under" as in the ball-Earth model, but simply stretching further outwards away from the Northern center-point as in the flat Earth model.

Sigma Octantis is claimed to be a Southern central pole star similar to Polaris, around which the Southern hemisphere stars all rotate around the opposite direction. Unlike Polaris, however, Sigma Octantis can NOT be seen simultaneously from every point along the same latitude, it is NOT central but allegedly 1 degree off-center, it is NOT motionless, and in fact cannot be seen at all using publicly available telescopes! There is legitimate speculation regarding whether Sigma Octantis even exists. Either way, the direction in which stars move overhead is based on perspective and the exact direction you're facing, not which hemisphere you are in."

The Zetetic Method

People claim the star trails go in a different direction in the southern hemisphere then the northern. But it's all perspective, like the different seating at a race track. Take a pencil out in front of you and start spinning it to the right. Keep spinning it and then move the pencil behind you. It will now be spinning left even though you didn't change anything but your perspective.

As one flat earther scientist/author put it "If the Earth revolved around the Sun, the change in relative position of the stars after 6 months of orbital motion could not fail to be seen. He argued that the stars should seem to separate as we approach and come together as we recede. In actual fact, however, after 190,000,000 miles of supposed orbit around the Sun, not a single inch of parallax can be detected in the stars, proving we have not moved at all."

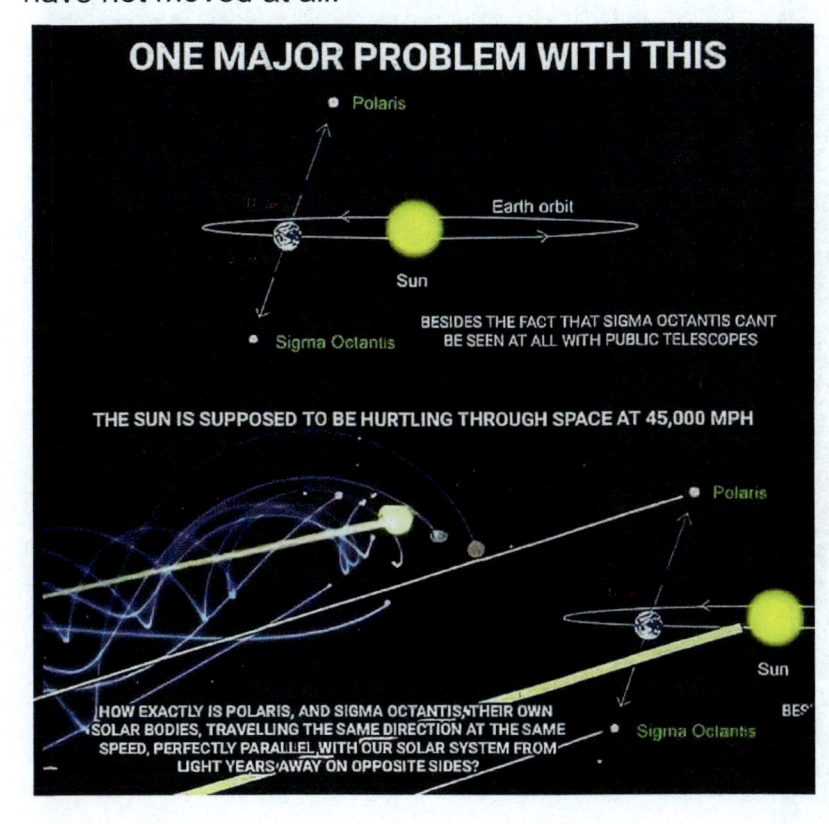

Time-lapse photos should show streaks across the sky, not perfect circles all year long. How is it not if we're on a whirling wobbling ball? This is a physical fact based on observable reality. No belief is required. Look at this picture and the question it presents.

They say we can predict eclipses and celestial events because of the globe model, but our ancestors had no problem knowing the earth is flat. Our ancestors have been mapping these stars, eclipses and other predictions, for thousands of years even before NASA started announcing it like

122

The Zetetic Method

they were the first to do so. And our ancestors did it based on a flat Earth cosmology.

Eclipses and other celestial happenings are recurring events, therefore predictable. It doesn't prove Earth is a whirling ball, but proves it's flat instead.

If the stars and solar system is traveling and expanding, as is the claim, all while we're traveling in three different directions, then shouldn't the stars and constellations be in a different location after 3,554 years? Yet the Egyptians saw and recorded the same constellations we see today, 3,554 years ago, and did so with the stars from trillion of miles away from our current location in space? Hmm. The Egyptians were not the only ancient astronomers who produced star charts.

Unlike most people today, thanks to our indoctrination system, the Ancients were not ignorant of what they lived on and not barbarians but intelligent people who built pyramids and made star charts. They sailed all over the world using stars. Polar coordinates would never work on spinning anything. Shooting an azimuth and then traveling a distance along the original azimuth and expecting to arrive at the desired destination would be less than probable. Navigation would be hit and miss and not reliable.

But not the people of today, we believe that we're talking monkeys on a spinning wobbling flying ball with invisible curvature. We've been duped and duped good. But the awakenings are happening, so there's that.

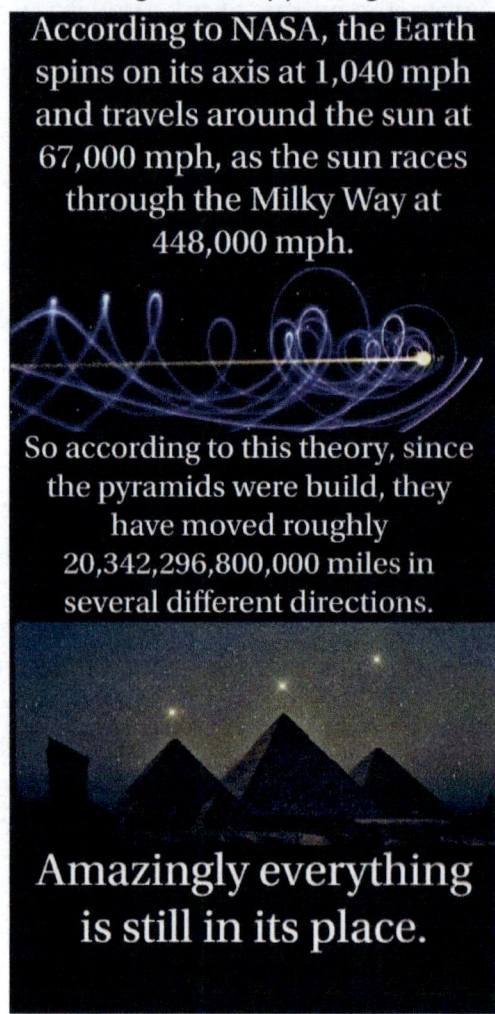

According to NASA, the Earth spins on its axis at 1,040 mph and travels around the sun at 67,000 mph, as the sun races through the Milky Way at 448,000 mph.

So according to this theory, since the pyramids were build, they have moved roughly 20,342,296,800,000 miles in several different directions.

Amazingly everything is still in its place.

Why have sailors used the same stars to navigate the oceans for thousands of years?

BECAUSE THEIR POSITIONS NEVER CHANGE

The Zetetic Method

Let's look at solar-motion. Astronomers, for some entertaining reasoning, decided that the whole solar system is supposedly moving, at a rate of about 13 miles a second from the region of Sirius to a point near Vega. Oh what proof of this is there I wonder.

If the earth has been traveling, as part of the solar system, from Sirius, toward Vega, in 2,000 years this earth has traveled 819,936,000,000 miles. This should be enough to change the constellations one would think. Or, as one book I read said, "Put a dent in the old Great Dipper or make the Dragon move." But not a star in the heavens has changed more than doubtful since the stars were cataloged 2,000 years ago by Hipparchus. There's no orbital parallax. The constellations are as the ancients have mapped them. All we see is perfect circles around Polaris, the North Star.

That awkward moment when you see lights rotating above your head, and you think it means that you're moving

How could the constellations be the same throughout history if we're wobbling and flying in three different directions and the universe is expanding all that time and the stars are at vastly different distances? The thought is ridiculous. They travel around Polaris over a flat plane just as we see it. Basic observation destroys the wobbling flying ball theory.

The Nikon P1000 has a monstrous 4K 125X optical zoom and a flat earth weapon and can disprove the given supposed curvature, especially on the water. It also can give you a better view of the stars that can only happen if they weren't light years away.

Many 'scientists' and their followers will claim the North star not being seen past the equator is proof of a ball earth. The North Star, like any other celestial light, is subject to the laws of perspective. The further you travel away from the North Star the more it appears to get closer to the horizon line. From every part of the equator, you can see the pole star, the Great Bear and many other

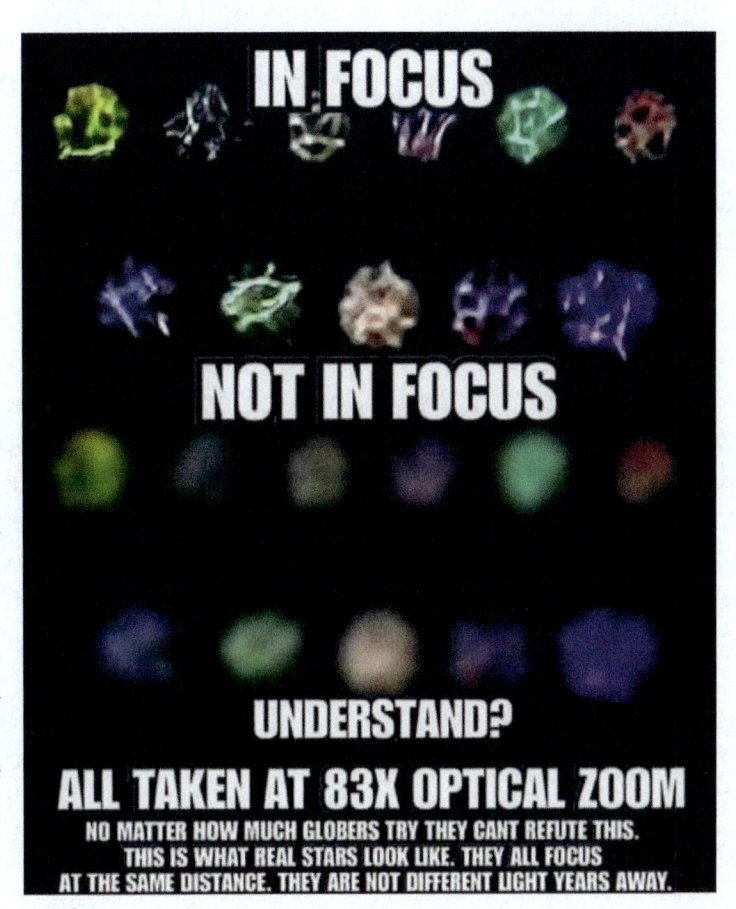

IN FOCUS

NOT IN FOCUS

UNDERSTAND?

ALL TAKEN AT 83X OPTICAL ZOOM

NO MATTER HOW MUCH GLOBERS TRY THEY CANT REFUTE THIS. THIS IS WHAT REAL STARS LOOK LIKE. THEY ALL FOCUS AT THE SAME DISTANCE. THEY ARE NOT DIFFERENT LIGHT YEARS AWAY.

124

constellations in the northern regions, but you cannot see the Southern Cross or the Sigma Octantis, which should be visible if there was a south pole. Back in the 1800s, there were explorers that said they didn't believe it even existed because it was not seen as it should be. I've never been there so I can't say, but it doesn't wrap this great plane, we live on, around a ball. And that's that.

Heliocentrism. The belief that 8 planets and 146 moons can revolve along with innumerable asteroids and comets around a star which is traveling half a million miles per hour around a galactic center...

#YouGottaHaveFaith

Astronomers are always making up claims without any provable science to back them up. Scientists will always make up new hypotheses to explain what they can't explain. They'll report these hypotheses as though they've already been proven. An example would be dark matter. John Reed covers this nicely in his book "Your Science Teacher Is Wrong and How You Can Prove It":

"However, the only evidence for dark matter is the fact that galaxies, as the scientific community describes them, cannot exist without it! Dark matter is an extraordinarily convenient fabrication; you can make all of it you need, stuff it in the gaps between stars, and voila! It provides exactly the right amount of missing gravity and it's so undetectable you can say it's there without ever having to prove it! Without a doubt, there is no religion requiring more blind (and blinding) faith than Scientism."

Another example: The astronomers like to tell the masses of just what gasses are burning in an unimaginably remote star, but have no way of knowing such claims or testing them, therefore they'll skim over such a claim with no real details on how this "knowledge" was obtained. You have to have faith. But more on what stars are, or rather might be, a little later.

To test whether the North star Polaris is moving or not, find it in your window. Now circle exactly where it's at and mark the exact spot YOU'RE standing in. Everything has to be EXACT.

Now throughout the change of seasons, if the seasons were created by a 23.3° wobbling, the North Star should move slightly. Spoiler alert, it does not. Despite the wobble and flying in three different directions simultaneously, it does not. You can also take time-lapse star trail pictures all throughout the year and see perfect star trail circles with no star parallax. All these experiments show that it's the lights, except the north star which is not moving, circling around us, and NOT this gigantic world with all its massive amounts of land, oceans and its stock.

If our distance from the sun is 93,000,000 miles, and its orbit is nearly circular, then it follows that in mid-winter, it is 186 million miles distant from where it was in mid-summer. If the earth has traveled such an enormous distance in order to make the base line 186 million, all the stars will necessarily have shifted in relative position. The closest ones more so than the farthest ones. But what difference is there? No difference at all. The constellations are always the same as Polaris, the North star. The Big Dipper remains a giant kitchen utensil.

If we were wobbling and flying in three different directions simultaneously then the stars wouldn't be perfect circles but instead, squiggly lines. I'm sorry if I'm repeating myself, but this is so obvious but unnoticed. So I'm drilling it. :)

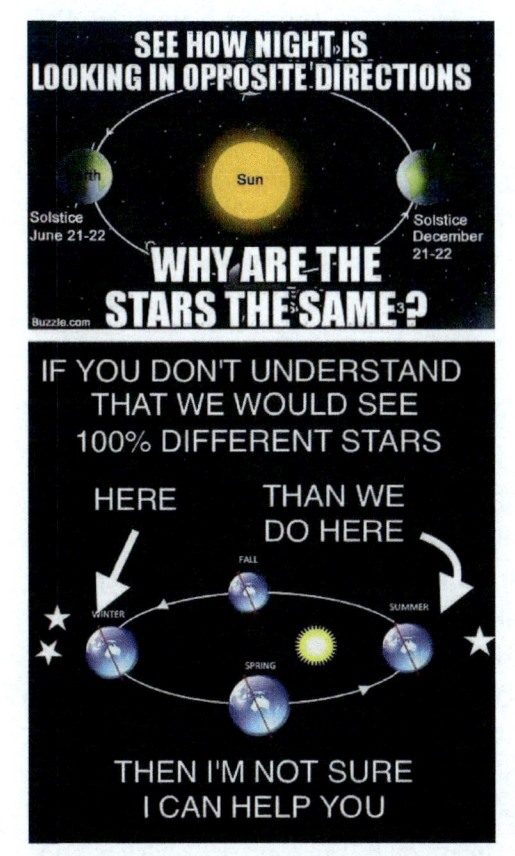

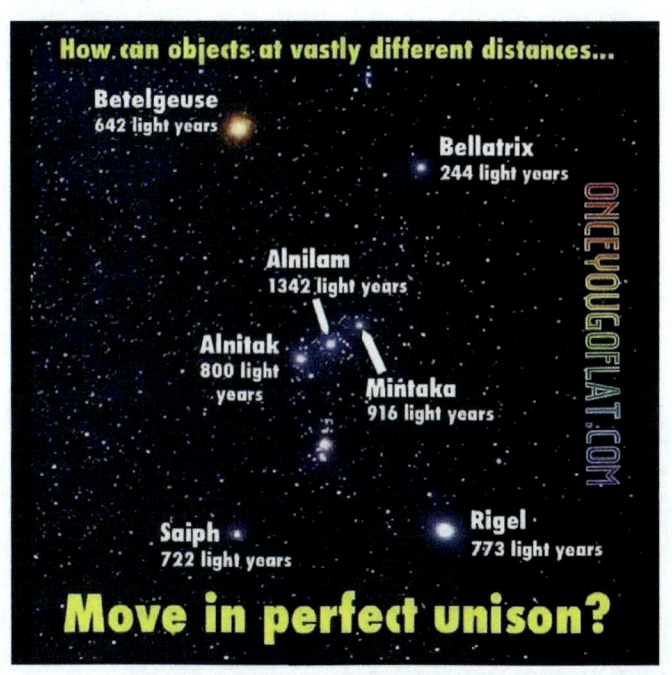

With observation, we can see there's no vastly different distances between stars. How can the stars maintain a relative observable position to each other if they are such different distances from each other and the Earth is wobbling and flying in three different directions? The closest stars should change position more so than the furthest stars. It shows the Earth is not moving and it's the mesh of stars that is moving as a whole around the Earth. The Ancients knew it and it was recorded in the bible writings.

Scientists tell us that the stars are just too far away to notice any movement. How convenient. Once again, there's always an excuse why we can't prove. How exactly does one measure something lights years away? They took countless guesses before they even settled on the distance of the sun. Pseudo-science. Prove me wrong.

The distance of stars is guess work indeed. One scientist concluded that the distance for the star Cygni was 60 billion, while another scientist guessed at 40 billion. Only a 20 billion mile difference. Hmmmm. Sense accuracy doesn't mean anything in Scientism, let me have a crack at it; I say it's 152 billion. I like to go big or go home. If you're going to tell a lie, tell a big enough one, where people will assume that you would NEVER!!! tell such an enormous fib, and assume that it MUST BE TRUE.

"The bigger the lie, the more inclined people will be to believe it." Adolf Hitler

As Thomas Winship talks about, to what degree can triangulation be relied upon? To a degree in measuring the height of a building, or in the little distances of a surveyor's survey. Their mathematical principle of triangulation they have taken from the surveyors, to whom it's serviceable.

That, by triangulation, there is not an astronomer in the world who can tell the distance of a thing only five miles away. According to Humboldt the Height of Mauna Loa is 18,410 feet, according to Captain Cook- 16,611, according to Marchand- 13,761, all according to triangulation.

You might say that there are no such fixed points in the sky. Why not, because astronomers say that there are none? The North Star is fixed, the stars rotating around the North star are fixed in their rotation. All observable, we have seen nothing but a fixed point and paths.

Tycho Brahe famously argued against the heliocentric theory in his time, positing that if the Earth revolved around the Sun, the change in relative position of the stars after 6 months orbital motion could not fail to be seen. He argued that the stars should seem to separate as we approach and come together as we recede. In actual fact, however, after 190,000,000 miles of supposed orbit around the Sun, not a single inch of parallax can be detected in the stars, proving we have not moved at all.

But there is something else that is implied with their statements. Scientism priests pretend that the science of astronomy represents all that is most accurate, and to go against it is blasphemous, as flat earthers are learning right now. This makes their claims semi-religious in human thought, and is therefore authoritative. If they're not providing physical evidence for their claims, and they are not, then it shows they're relying on their authority that the masses have bestowed upon them, and not by reasoning or facts. This is what priests, who don't use real science to back their claims, do. But we'll get to that later.

Not all scientists push the same narrative though. Tycho Brabe's model has the Earth stationary and the 'universe' revolving over it. The 5 celestial lights ('planets') revolving around the sun over a stationary Earth. His system did not violate the laws of physics or Bible scripture.

Which is more likely, this massive Earth with all its content is wobbling spinning and flying with all the atmospheric gasses, stars, planets, gas clouds, etc., etc. are all flying in unison in three different directions, OR the celestial lights in the sky are moving around the fixed point of the North star Polaris in their own fixed path just as we see it? Let's keep it real and logical folks, shall we?

"It is found by observation that the stars come to the meridian about four minutes earlier every twenty-four hours than the sun, taking the solar time as the standard. This makes

120 minutes every thirty days, and twenty-four hours in the year. Hence all the constellations have passed before or in advance of the sun in that time. This is the simple fact as observed in nature, but the theory of rotundity and motion on axes and in an orbit has no place for it. Visible truth must be ignored, because this theory stands in the way, and prevents its votaries from understanding it." Book Earth Not a Globe!" by Samuel Rowbotham

People often point to the sky to decide on what they're standing on. This makes no sense because a lightbulb is pear shaped but the floor is not. While you look at the sky, watch the clouds slowly drift by, Pseudo-scientist are claiming they are moving faster than the speed of sound with the spin of the earth, while moving with the speed of lighting around the sun and unimaginable speeds around the Milky Way, but the clouds don't seem to know any difference; they just drift lazily by, as if the claims were nothing but that, claims.

When you look through a telescope you see a flat light disk. You have to run your telescope through NASA's software on a computer to get the lights you're looking at to look anything like the "planets" that they tell you you're looking at. In Other words CGI images.

A glober (globe believer) who studies stars, for a hobby, told me the software adds different things like colored clouds to represent different gasses and details in the planets. He said all raw pictures show nothing but a light disk. And hear he was showing and bragging to me about these beautiful CGI images he collected. That's what brainwashing does to you. A very kind man loving his cartoons.

If you think your telescope is all powerful, here's how you can prove yourself wrong. Take your telescope and point it to a neighboring light. You'll quickly see that it's not that powerful. A lot of cameras are WAY more powerful. Point it to the ocean, however, and you'll see further than earth's supposed curvature would allow. On a globe, no matter how powerful the telescope/binoculars, only a certain distance can be seen, as the curvature of the globe would prevent a telescope from seeing round it, and of course, you can't see through it.

But, when weather conditions allow, objects at distances beyond to what the quoted curvature would allow, are visible with the assistance of a scope of some sorts. It's safe to say the "8 inches per square mile" is debunked.

Just like curvature, you've never seen, with your own eyes or a pure telescope, a "planet" the way they show you. You only see a celestial light. There has to be software involved. A court of law does not accept software manipulated images as proof of anything, so why should you? If your provable reality is different then what the scientists say, then they're not going off facts and therefore you should disregard the hearsay.

FLAT EARTH IN COURT

A flat earther name Zen Gracie offered $5000 dollars to anyone who could prove the whirling ball theory. One glober made a computer program of what the Earth is supposed to be doing and presented it, Mr. Gracie refused to give him the money and it was taken to court. The judge sided with Mr. Gracie that CGI and computer programming is not considered evidence. The glober decided to get a lawyer for a higher court and then turned around and dropped it. Hmmm. His lawyer probably advised that I'm sure.

So what then of NASA's fake photos? They couldn't be used as evidence either. But more on those later, I've jumped subjects here. Sorry.

To spin or not to spin

People say we don't feel the movement because the movement is constant. Once again there's always an excuse why we can't prove. Scientists have said "it's just like not being able to feel it on a train or a car because of the constant movement." This is true in a straight line motion. The whirling ball theory has us in three different circular motions. So why are these "scientists" comparing the two?

This is called not knowing physics. (Or rather them counting on YOU not knowing and comparing) Uniform circular motion is constant acceleration. Anything moving in a circle wants to keep moving forward, but it can't, instead it's continuously swung in a circle. Which is acceleration. Hence Uniform circular motion is constant acceleration. Put that train or car on a constant curve.

A fly in a car traveling at 70 mph, flying from the back seat to the front seat; was the fly flying over 70 mph? No, it's a sealed container. This does not compare with the wobbling spinning flying open ball earth. The atmosphere in the train or car is physically forced to travel with the car, unlike the atmosphere on ball Earth. And they're both going in one straight line motion. The two should not be compared.

One claim from globe 'scientists' is that we don't feel Earth's alleged 1000mph spin because it takes 24 hours therefore extremely slow compared with the enormous size, and they compared it to a merry-go-round taking 24 hours to go fully around; but then Neil Degrasse Tyson says if the Earth stopped its spin it would be devastating and destroy most living on it. Hmmm! They seem to compare things to Earth except when it's NOT in their favor, for if you stop the merry-go-round, nobody on it would die. Just like they say you're not high enough to see the curvature but then claim you can see it at sea level. They seem to move the goal post don't they, to match their claims.

Also not only is the earth supposedly spinning, but it's also, supposedly, flying around the sun at 66,600mph (or whatever different quoted speeds the different science websites have come up with) and flying even faster around the Milky Way. All while being shot out in a straight line by the allegedly Big Bang at another unimaginable speed. And let's not forget while all this is happening, it's wobbling.

So that's THREE different Uniform circular motions going on plus a wobble to boot. And here they are comparing it to a car that has one straight line motion.

Looking at all the physical based evidence in reality, I've come to the conclusion that we are not spinning, wobbling, and flying around. If you can prove that we are, please inform me and do so with physical based evidence. Can anybody prove, without going off astronomical hypothesis, that the earth is a wobbling spinning and flying ball? There have been plenty who have tried.

Here is a list of scientists who attempted to prove the rotation or movement of the Earth throughout history: Sir George Biddel Airy1871- failed. Michelson-Morley1887- failed. Trouton-Noble1901-1903-failed. Nordmeyer-Bucherer1903-failed. Michelson-Gale-Pearson1925-failed. Rudolf Tomaschek1925-1926-failed. Chase1926-1927- failed. Hayden1994- failed. The Sagnac Effect1913-failed. Albert Einstein with the theory of relativity-failed.

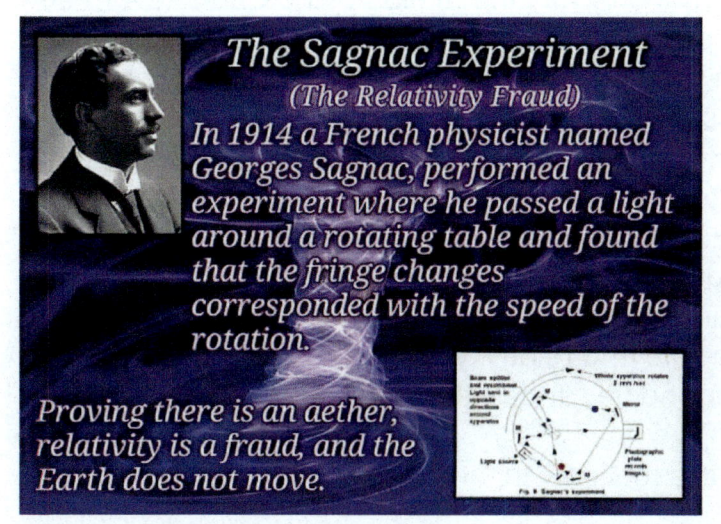

The Sagnac Experiment
(The Relativity Fraud)
In 1914 a French physicist named Georges Sagnac, performed an experiment where he passed a light around a rotating table and found that the fringe changes corresponded with the speed of the rotation.

Proving there is an aether, relativity is a fraud, and the Earth does not move.

This hilarious bit comes from the book "Terra Firma: The Earth not a Planet" by David Wardlaw Scott:

"Their calculations on celestial things are so preposterous and vague that "no fella" can understand them; just look at the following tit-bits of Modern Astronomic Science—

The Sun's distance from the Earth is reckoned to be about 92,000,000 miles.

The Sun is larger than the Earth 1,240,000 times. 58,000 Suns would be required to equal the cubic contents of the Star Vega. Struve tells us that light from Stars of the ninth magnitude, traveling with the velocity of 12,000,000 miles per minute, would require to travel space for 586 years before reaching this world of ours!

The late Mr. Proctor said—"I think a moderate estimate of the age of the Earth would be 500,000,000 years. The weight of the Earth, according to the same authority, is 6,000,000,000,000,000,000,000 tons!

And so on ad nauseam.

Now what confidence can any man place in a science which gives promissory notes of such extravagance as these? They are simply bankrupt bills, not worth the paper on which they are written. And yet, strange to say, many foolish people endorse them as if they were good, the reason being that they are too lazy to think for themselves, and, to their own sad cost, accept the bogus notes as if they had been issued by a Rothschild."

Also from the same works of Scott:

"Copernicus wrote—"It is not necessary that hypotheses be true or even probable; it is sufficient that they lead to results of calculation which agree with calculation. . . . Neither let any one, as far as hypotheses are concerned, expect anything certain from Astronomy, since that science can afford nothing of the kind, lest in case he should adopt for truth things feigned for another purpose, he should leave the science more foolish than when he came. . . . The hypothesis of the terrestrial motion was nothing but an hypothesis, valuable only so far as it explained phenomena not considered with reference to absolute truth or falsehood."

If you seek truth, drop your opinions.

CORIOLIS EFFECT

Flat earther: "Can you prove the earth spins."

Glober: "The best that I can do for you is flush the toilet."

Allen Daves put it nicely: "Most people who accept that the Earth is in motion believe it is a proven fact. They do not realize that not only has the motion of the Earth never been proven, but by the constructs of modern physics and cosmology cannot be proven. Again, even modern cosmology does not claim to be able to prove that the Earth is in motion. In fact the very best argument for Earth's motion is based on pure 'modesty' not logic, observation and experience. If anyone could prove the Earth's motion, that someone would become more famous than Einstein, Hawking and others. They may all be fools but even they would not make such an ignorant claim to proof of Earth's motions, and those who do so don't realize just how ignorant of physics they really are! Before folks go demonstrating how ignorant they are, they should consider:

1. The relationship between Mach's principle and relativity.
2. The relationship between Gravity and Inertia, and Gravity and Acceleration (and the paradoxes that exist).
3. Relativity does not claim to prove Earth's motions, in fact it 'dictates' the ridiculous idea that motion cannot be proven, period.
4. Relativity proposes motion, it does not nor can it claim to disprove that the Earth is the center of the universe!
5. Only those who are ignorant of physics attempt to make arguments based on weather patterns, ballistic trajectories, geosynchronous satellites, and Foucault's pendulums for evidence of Earth's motions! For all those 'geniuses' out there, not even Einstein would claim such stupidity."

"In physics, the Coriolis force is an inertial or fictitious force that acts on objects in motion within a frame of reference that rotates with respect to an inertial frame. In a reference frame with clockwise rotation, the force acts to the left of the motion of the object." Wikipedia

Copernicus and his great exponent Sir Isaac Newton, confessed that their system of a revolving Earth was only a possibility, and could not be proved by facts. Let's have a closer look at it shall we.

As one flat earther posted:

"And what is said to occur at the Equator, still water? (Coriolis effect) The Coriolis Effect cannot be replicated in a laboratory yet we are told that it occurs. When sailing south do we suddenly see a change in the way the water goes down the sink? No! Because, once again, the scientists tell us that size matters and only can be measured on the ocean of Earth. All effects of force one way or another occur by 1) the design of the bowl or sphere, 2) the power of liquid flow and 3) the direction from which the liquid enters the medium. Waterfalls would thus spiral perpendicular to the direction of motion, according to science, yet never do, thus disproving the Coriolis Effect theory."

DON'T AIM AT THE DEER OR YOU'LL MISS???

Neil DeGrasse Tyson and Joe Rogan on Joe's podcast said that long range shooters have to account for the Coriolis effect. So according to Scientism priest Neil Tyson, sniper bullets can travel so far that the globe's rotation will move the target out of the bullet's path, so shooters have to adjust their aim accordingly.

This goes against the other globe model's scientists claim that everything, including the atmosphere, is spinning with the Earth so we don't feel it. There's a blunt contradiction here.

So, according to this claim, if you're aiming at a deer three miles away, you have to aim a foot to its left so that the Earth will actually spin and move the animal into the path of your bullet. If you don't do this, then the Earth's spin will save the animal. And this is, they say, what snipers know.

Snipers do NOT account for curvature or Coriolis effect. That is just ridiculous. Try and find the adjustment in the Marine Corps Sniper manual. It's not there for a reason! If the Coriolis effect is so important why doesn't the army sniper handbook say anything about it?

It's just Windage and elevation. Windage is for the round to travel against the wind direction... Kind of like a curveball in baseball... Elevation is when you raise the rear sight to tilt the rifle upward so that a round travels further down range... Kind of like a Hail Mary pass in Football.

The Zetetic Method

Please explain then what is the exact Coriolis Calculation for each of these 3 shooters, whom are all spinning at different speeds and facing different directions!

- 0 km/hr
- 830 km/hr
- 1,275 km/hr
- 1,550 km/hr
- 1,650 km/hr
- 1,550 km/hr
- 1,275 km/hr

Direction of Earth's alleged spin

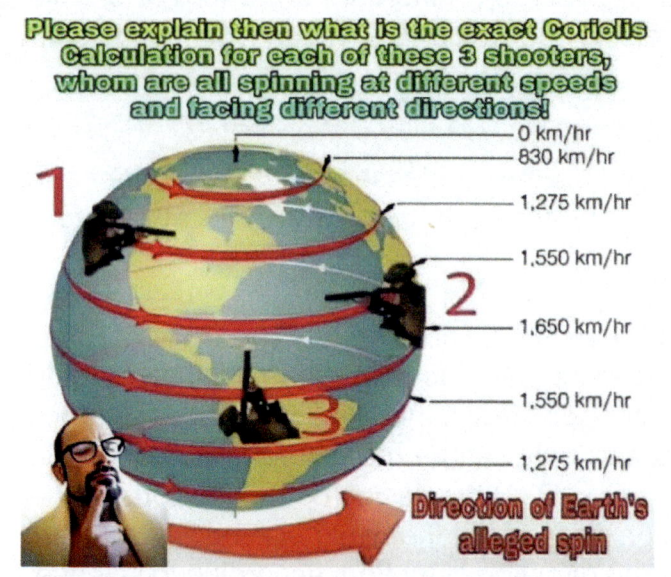

So, let's analyze the Coriolis effect on bullets, if there is any effect at all. If I were to shoot a bullet north or south, according to the Coriolis Effect, I would miss the target by a couple of hundred meters, since the earth is spinning around its axis at a 1000 miles per hour, but this does not happen at all, regardless of which altitude you shoot that bullet. This is reality and the facts are registered in the Army ballistic tables and you can check the facts for yourself.

What happens if I shoot near the poles, will my calculations be different then they would be at the equator? Is anybody calculating this when they shoot? Anybody? I was always told that you aimed AT the target, not ahead of it.

There shouldn't be a need for any flat earth books, one should only have to listen to these so-called scientists, with a thinking head, to be driven away from the globe model and back to reality.

Planes (which go a further distance than bullets ever have), hot air balloons, skydivers, and other moving objects in the sky don't have to account for the Coriolis effect. Not even once has the movement of the earth been calculated or even noticed, and that's because it is stationary. I once skydived and did not take into consideration the speed of Earth's rotation when trying to hit the target. Why would the earth not move under these things yet move under a pendulum and bullet? No one has made this adjustment. The ridiculousness in this claim is the only real thing about it.

If the earth is spinning under a bullet, a helicopter should be able to just hover and let the earth move west, correct? But such silliness doesn't happen because the earth doesn't rotate under a helicopter, bullet or anything else. Please prove me wrong.

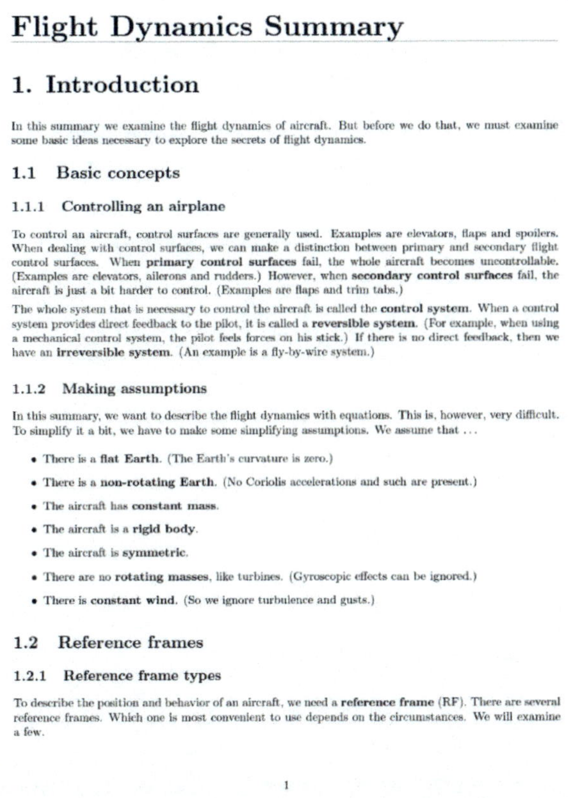

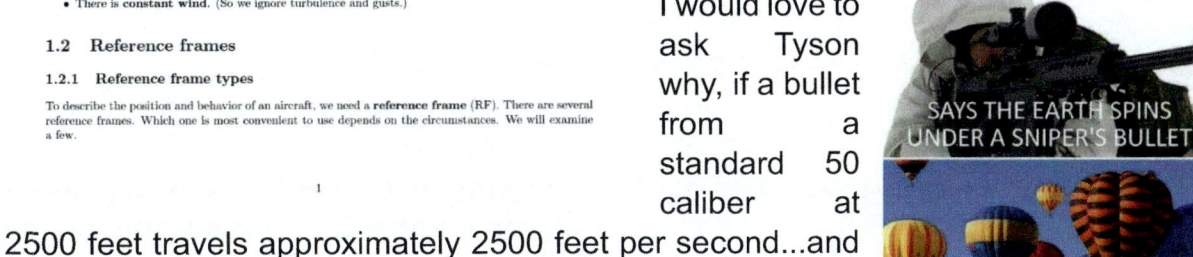

> **Flight Dynamics Summary**
>
> **1. Introduction**
>
> In this summary we examine the flight dynamics of aircraft. But before we do that, we must examine some basic ideas necessary to explore the secrets of flight dynamics.
>
> **1.1 Basic concepts**
>
> **1.1.1 Controlling an airplane**
>
> To control an aircraft, control surfaces are generally used. Examples are elevators, flaps and spoilers. When dealing with control surfaces, we can make a distinction between primary and secondary flight control surfaces. When **primary control surfaces** fail, the whole aircraft becomes uncontrollable. (Examples are elevators, ailerons and rudders.) However, when **secondary control surfaces** fail, the aircraft is just a bit harder to control. (Examples are flaps and trim tabs.)
>
> The whole system that is necessary to control the aircraft is called the **control system**. When a control system provides direct feedback to the pilot, it is called a **reversible system**. (For example, when using a mechanical control system, the pilot feels forces on his stick.) If there is no direct feedback, then we have an **irreversible system**. (An example is a fly-by-wire system.)
>
> **1.1.2 Making assumptions**
>
> In this summary, we want to describe the flight dynamics with equations. This is, however, very difficult. To simplify it a bit, we have to make some simplifying assumptions. We assume that ...
>
> - There is a **flat Earth**. (The Earth's curvature is zero.)
> - There is a **non-rotating Earth**. (No Coriolis accelerations and such are present.)
> - The aircraft has **constant mass**.
> - The aircraft is a **rigid body**.
> - The aircraft is **symmetric**.
> - There are no **rotating masses**, like turbines. (Gyroscopic effects can be ignored.)
> - There is **constant wind**. (So we ignore turbulence and gusts.)
>
> **1.2 Reference frames**
>
> **1.2.1 Reference frame types**
>
> To describe the position and behavior of an aircraft, we need a **reference frame** (RF). There are several reference frames. Which one is most convenient to use depends on the circumstances. We will examine a few.

The flight dynamics handbook for pilots says pilots need to ASSUME they are flying over a flat stationary Earth, WHY? If they're flying over a spinning wobbling flying ball shouldn't they consider that? That must just be for bullets. Ridiculous! Or maybe they're talking about the magic bullets used on JFK.

You can find and download this manual online, but I'll share the screenshot I took of it once again.

How does a plane that takes off in Alaska that is spinning at 400 mph land on the equator that is spinning over 1000 mph?

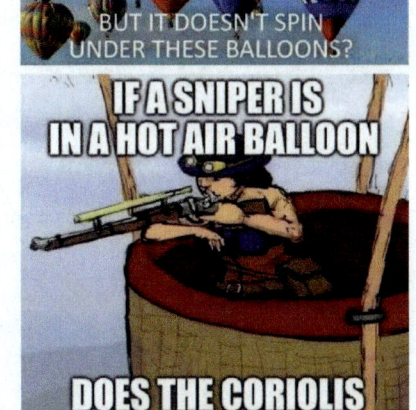

I would love to ask Tyson why, if a bullet from a standard 50 caliber at 2500 feet travels approximately 2500 feet per second...and the earth rotates at 1/4 mile per second, why don't snipers have to account for that 1000+ feet of spin while the bullet travels through the air?

Riddle me this: If a sniper is shooting from a hot-air balloon does the Coriolis effect come into play? LMAO! See how ridiculous these claims are?

To contradict themselves they also say everything spins with the earth by way of gravity and what's in motion stays in motion with the Earth.

The following from the National Geographic is an example of the modern explanation of the Coriolis effect that is supposed to be manifested on earth, but is, in fact, completely absent. Let's pretend you're standing at the Equator and you want to throw a ball to your friend in the middle of North America. If you throw the ball in a straight line, it will appear to land to the right of your friend because he's moving slower and has not caught up. Now let's pretend you're standing at the North Pole. When you throw the ball to your friend, it will again appear to land to the right of him. But this time, it's because he's moving faster than you are and has moved ahead of the ball. Oh what rubbish that no one has experienced, just believed.

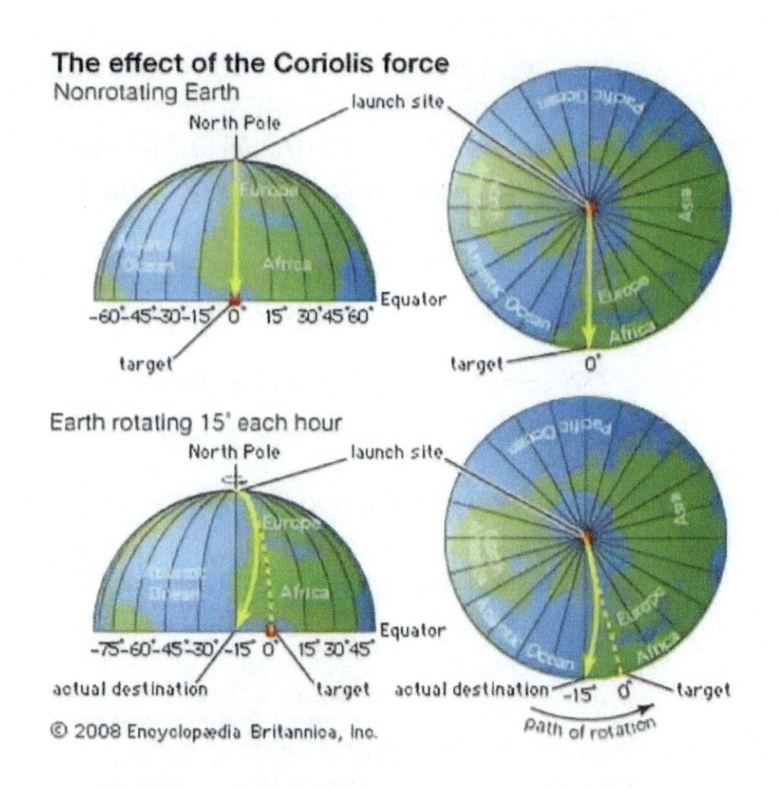

The effect of the Coriolis force

Nonrotating Earth
[diagram: North Pole, launch site, target at Equator 0°, with longitude markings -60° -45° -30° -15° 0° 15° 30° 45° 60°]

Earth rotating 15° each hour
[diagram: North Pole, launch site, actual destination, target, with longitude markings -75° -60° -45° -30° -15° 0° 15° 30° 45°]

© 2008 Encyclopædia Britannica, Inc.

[right-side diagrams showing Pacific Ocean, Asia, Europe, Africa, Atlantic Ocean with path of rotation]

Imagine a 747 is sitting on a conveyor belt, as wide and long as a runway. The conveyor belt is designed to exactly match the speed of the wheels, moving in the opposite direction.

Can the plane take off?

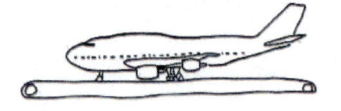

Does coriolis effect affect snipers?

The Coriolis Effect is **the idea that the Earth's rotation can influence the preciseness of your shot, moving the target away from the bullet as it heads towards it.** To avoid these influences, extreme long distance shooters should try and make the proper adjustments. Apr 7, 2022

https://www.laxrange.com › explain...

Coriolis Effect: What Is It & How Does It Effect Your Shooting

Pilots make no accommodations or calculations whatsoever for the Coriolis effect because there is none because the earth is not spinning.

Airline flight times don't change from LA to New York versus New York to LA. At a rotation of 1000mph one would think there would be quite the difference, but no there is no difference. And how would a plane land on a moving runway?

If aircrafts are presumed to fly with the atmosphere that is rotating with the spinning earth then why not bullets or the pendulum? Are they all like magic JFK bullets?

Look at what part of this article says below here, "The Coriolis effect is the "idea" that the Earth's rotation......" hmmm the wording says it all doesn't it.

The Zetetic Method

If the Earth is spinning at the equator at about 1000 mph and there's supposedly around 750mph spin difference in speeds from poles to equator. How does a plane flying North or South from the equator not have to adjust to this massive speed differential? How can it not be affected? Wouldn't people, living at the equator, feel a difference spinning a 1/3 of the speed less when at the poles? How can a plane traveling E-W, or W-E, land on a runway that runs N-S? If Tyson is telling me that we all spin with the earth including the Velcro air, yet a long range bullet does not, then I'll have to see the receipt on that claim.

In the air for seconds. Affected by Earth's spin.

In the air for hours. Not affected by Earth's spin.

Some Australians say the sink goes in one direction and the toilet in another. It's simply the design and the direction the water started, not the spin of the Earth that nobody feels or senses whatsoever. Which one requires more faith and assumptions?

My proof that the Earth doesn't move

And your proof that it does

The Earth is not moving under a plane or anything else. Let's rethink these claims within our indoctrination. The globe spins on theory, the flat earth rests on facts.

. The BLACK SWAN

The Coriolis effect is yet another claim that has no backing. If it was so, the sniper military handbook would have it and the Earth would spin under everything else. It's ridiculous to even entertain the idea that the Earth spins under a bullet but not a plane. The claim debunks itself.

The Coriolis effect is not calculated or evident in any profession or everyday use. It's totally debunked in all observable reality. Can you provide proof that's not hearsay or an assumption but instead based on physical reality that the Earth is spinning? If it's not based on physical facts and reasoning, then it's based on authority.

THE REVOLVING PENDULUM OR THE REVOLVING EARTH

"If you find from your own experience that something is a fact and it contradicts what some authority has written down, then you must abandon the authority and base your reasoning on your own findings." - Leonardo Da Vinci

The pendulum was made to prove the earth was spinning and rotating, but it doesn't move, you have to start it. If it was based on what it's claimed then it should start on its own. Correct? And sometimes it would move in the other direction and had to be corrected. Foucault pendulums are almost always driven by a motor, and not reliable when permitted to swing freely. 'The behavior of the pendulum actually depends on the initial force it swings out and the ball-and-socket used with most-ready facilitates circular motion over any other.' The supposed rotation of the earth has nothing to do and is irrelevant to the pendulum's swing. If the supposed constant rotation of the Earth affected pendulums in any way, there would be no need to manually start pendulums in motion. In a court of law it would be thrown out as evidence.

Sometimes it would swing in the wrong direction and sometimes not at all. A lot of scientists rejected it. When I made a comment on Smithsonian magazine.com about their pendulum article it was deleted. Truth fears no investigation. PERIOD

The heavier the ball, the more rapidly it will deviate. So the greater the weight of the ball the slower the vibration of the pendulum. How would it even work on the side of the ball earth?

The Comptes Rindus de l'Academie Francaise magazine published an article about experiments done with the pendulum: "
1. That the laws of Galileo are not quite exact as to the vibration
2. That the explanation of the retardation of the pendulum on the equator by the decrease of the force of attraction of the earth is evidently false;
3. That even the universally accepted laws of the gravitation of bodies are not sufficiently exact; and
4. That, in general, the means employed toward discovering the laws of nature with the help of calculations is not only being proved unreliable, but it serves but the more to darken the truth."

If the pendulum wasn't taken seriously by a lot of scientists then why is it still around? Is it because of who's funding science maybe?

Many people think the pendulum is proof that the earth is spinning. But if the Earth was spinning under the pendulum it would also spin under a helicopter, balloon and a plane, but it doesn't. The Earth is not moving under a pendulum, it's the device moving. Why would anyone think it was this entire gigantic world with its massive oceans and stock moving instead of the device itself? Is there no logic in the world? You can see the device moving but you can't feel the Earth moving, SO WHY EVEN ENTERTAIN THE IDEA?

The Zetetic Method

Water in a glass on a table is a motion indicator. The slightest movement and the water shows it. The Earth provides zero movement.

"Whilst we sit drinking our cup of tea or coffee the world is supposedly rotating at 1039 mph at the equator, whizzing around the sun at 66,500mph, hurtling towards Lyra at 20,000mph, revolving around the center of the Milky Way at 500,000mph and merrily moving at God knows what velocity as a consequence of the Big Bang. And not even a hint of a ripple on the surface of our tea, yet tap the table lightly with your finger and....." Dr. Neville T. Jones

Foucault's pendulum was a failed experiment which proved nothing but how easy it is for pseudo-science to deceive the malleable masses. The pendulum proves nothing but that.

In short, the sun, moon, and stars are actually doing precisely what everyone throughout all history has seen them do. We do not believe what our eyes tell us because we have been taught a counterfeit system which demands that we believe what has never been confirmed by observation or experiment. That counterfeit system demands that the Earth rotate on an 'axis' every 24 hours at a speed of over 1000 MPH at the equator. No one has ever, ever seen or felt such movement (nor seen or felt the 67,000MPH speed of the Earth's alleged orbit around the sun or its 500,000 MPH alleged speed around a galaxy or its retreat from an alleged 'Big Bang' at over 670,000,000 MPH!). Remember, no experiment has ever shown the earth to be moving." Marshall Hall

The pendulum can't be relied on and the Earth rotates under nothing, just as reality proves.

METEORITES

People often tell me that meteorites, meteor showers, shooting stars or whatever, are all proof of the Earth being a ball. So with this frame of mind, if something on my ceiling falls into my room, it's proof my house is a ball? Correct? I didn't think so. Let's have a look at meteorites, etc. shall we.

In all reality though, it doesn't matter as far as the shape of the Earth goes. But physical reality proves they lied about the shape of the Earth therefore, everything else involving it crumbles as well.

They tell you you're headed into a Meteor shower, so you mosey on outside to have a lookie, but when you get out there, you see that they're coming in all different directions. And at only slightly different speeds and angles, but never straight down it seems.

I won't pretend to know what's going on but I see that it's not what they say it is. What exactly is happening up there and why do they feel we shouldn't know?

If this ball O here heads into a 'meteor' shower like this ::,':;::..';:::;:::, how can they enter from all directions?

The Zetetic Method

Furthermore, the Earth, supposedly but unproven, orbits around the sun counterclockwise at 66,600 mph, yet there are 'meteors' coming from the same direction counter-clockwise around the sun, which means the meteor has to catch up to the Earth, then over take it, and then you see your "shooting star."

Then you have the 'meteor' that comes in the opposite direction of the Earth's orbit around the sun, which means it's set on a collision course with Earth. Yet you see the "shooting star" that's pretty much the same as the other, just a different direction. Shouldn't they be noticeably different seeing as how they're coming from opposite directions, one from opposite the Earth's orbit around the sun, and the other somehow faster then the Earth's orbit so as to catch up with the Earth. And yet there's never a straight dead on hit.

Then there's the "shooting star" that comes from the very same direction of the sun itself. Now how did that get there? Shouldn't the sun's powerful gravitational pull bring that meteor into itself? How did it get past or through the sun? Do you see what I'm saying?

These two images are just examples but factual. What a meteor showers should look like if it's what they say it is.

But this is what it looks like instead. Coming in all different directions. This shows that we're not flying into a shower but something is definitely happening.

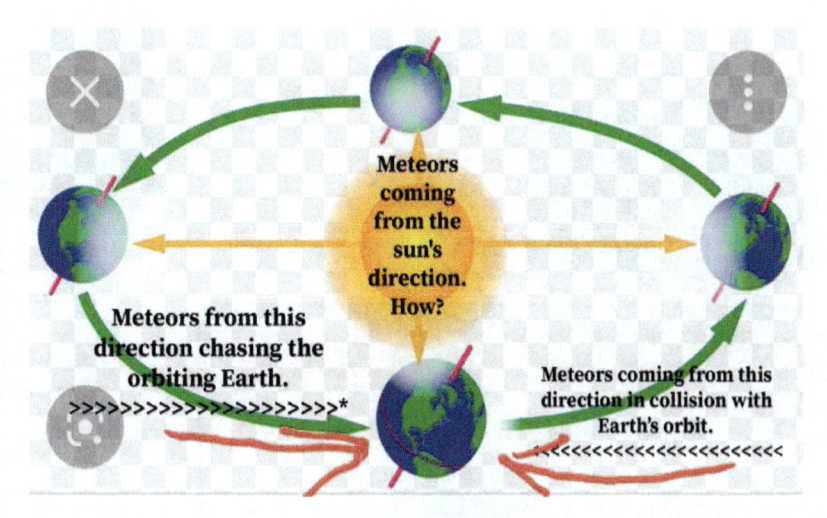

As far as craters go, there are plenty of reasons craters can and do exist. A rock traveling through space is one hell of an assumption though, and no rock to find. The meteorites that are claimed to fall are just that, claims. These rocks are made from the same material as Earth, so how do we know it came from anywhere but. Some speculation going on there. I'll have to see the receipt on those as well.

The Zetetic Method

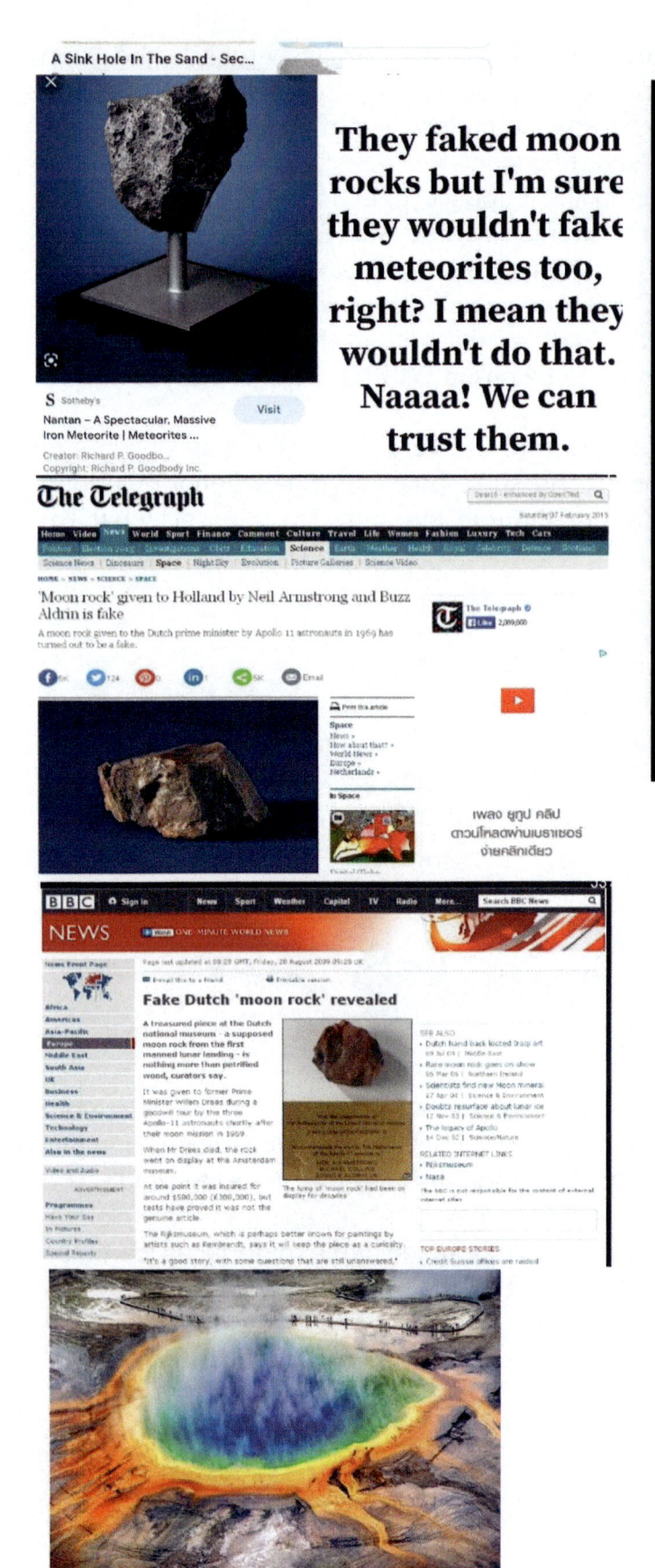

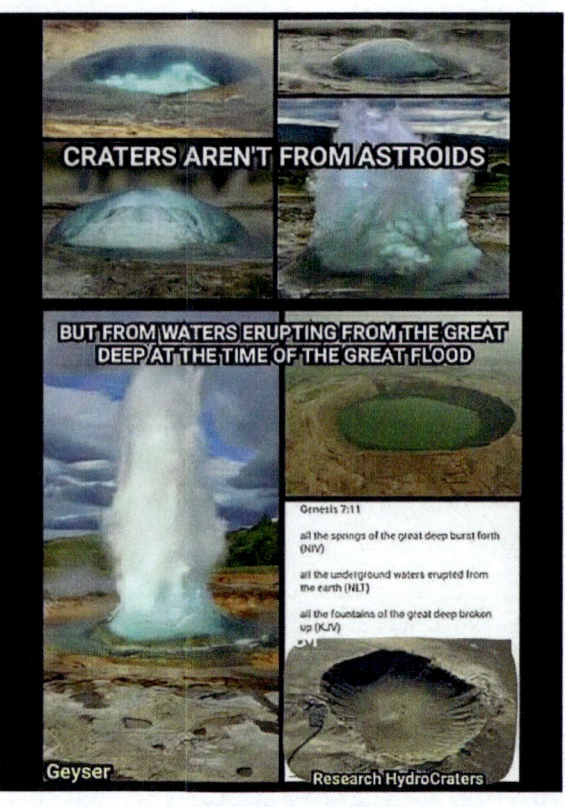

They faked moon rocks but I'm sure they wouldn't fake meteorites too, right? I mean they wouldn't do that. Naaaa! We can trust them.

CRATERS AREN'T FROM ASTROIDS BUT FROM WATERS ERUPTING FROM THE GREAT DEEP AT THE TIME OF THE GREAT FLOOD

Genesis 7:11
all the springs of the great deep burst forth (NIV)
all the underground waters erupted from the earth (NLT)
all the fountains of the great deep broken up (KJV)

Geyser — Research HydroCraters

An **explosion crater** is a type of crater formed when material is ejected from the surface of the ground by an explosive event at or immediately above or below the surface.

Crater created by the Sedan shallow underground nuclear test explosion

141

What if our future history books show these craters as meteor hits even though there are nuclear testing grounds? Would our government lie about history? Hmm

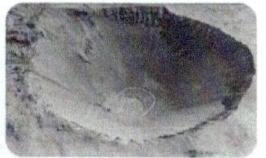

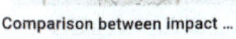

BACK TO THE STARS, LIGHTS OR BALLS OF BURNING GAS

What are stars exactly? How can anyone possibly know the answer to such a question? But our Pseudo-scientist will spin you a web, won't they? I don't buy the burning gasses, etc. theory in the least. Burning for all these billions of years. Another claim that can't be proven, observed or recreated, with their gas balls creating gravity. What tackle would this be for this gas gravity? More faith needed here yet again.

Here are three guesses from our beloved scientists that cannot be proven. They of course have no way of knowing any of this. Prove me wrong.

I won't pretend to know what stars are made of or look you in the face and spin you a ridiculous web and expect you to go by my "authority" that doesn't actually exist. We see lights in the sky, and that is that. We see them rotating around Polaris and that is that. And we see the constellations the bible talks about. But what we DON'T know is what they are made of, we have to take the government's word for that, don't we? But they wouldn't lie about such a thing, right?

Stars form from an accumulation of gas and dust, which collapses due to gravity and starts to form stars. The process of star formation takes around a million years from the time the initial gas cloud starts to collapse until the star is created and shines like the Sun. Jul 4, 2019

https://kids.frontiersin.org › articles
How Do Stars Form? - Frontiers for Young Minds

National Geographic
www.nationalgeographic.com

Stars—facts and information

Mar 20, 2019 — Stars are huge celestial bodies made mostly of hydrogen and helium that produce light and heat from the churning nuclear forges inside their ...

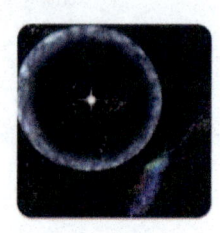

A star is an astronomical object comprising a luminous spheroid of plasma held together by its gravity. The nearest star to Earth is the Sun. Many other stars are visible to the naked eye at night, but their immense distances from Earth make them appear as fixed points of light. Wikipedia

I've read books from the 1800s that talk about metal balls falling from the sky, but no one ever gets smashed by them. This is also still happening today in modern times; nothing has changed. I'm not saying these are stars, but I'm not saying they're not either. ;)

THE SUN
"The fool on the hill
Sees the sun going down
And the eyes in his head
See the world spinning round"
The Beatles "Fool on the Hill"

THE SUN'S NOT GOING DOWN ON ME
The theory of the solar system maintains that the sun rotates around the Milky Way while comparatively motionless to us because we, supposedly, rotate around it. Seems like one of those things you have to prove when you say it. However observable physical reality

testifies against this delusion/lie. No one has ever felt or seen the earth whirling and wobbling through space at the unimaginable speeds that we've been quoted and believed.

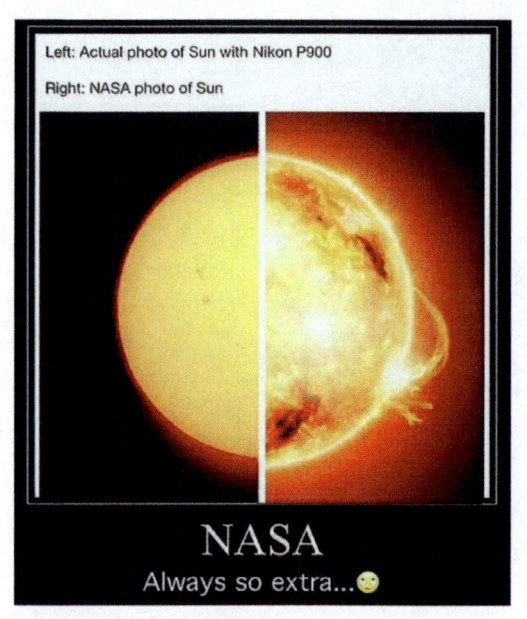

Everyone who is not blind, can see the sun move across the sky. Even the blind man can feel its warmth increase as it gets closer, then decreases as it leaves him behind.

If you drive a stake into the ground at a location where it's exposed to the sun all day, and mark the end of the shadow every quarter of an hour, you will find the marks form a elongated curve, showing the sun is moving across a stationary earth and hooks northwest at 'sunset.' Did you feel any movement during the day? No.

Now take time-lapse star trail pictures and you'll see no stellar parallax at all. Just perfect circles. Did you feel any movement during that time? No. Then why do YOU believe we are spinning, wobbling and flying in three different directions simultaneously? Why? Could it be faith in the scientism priest?

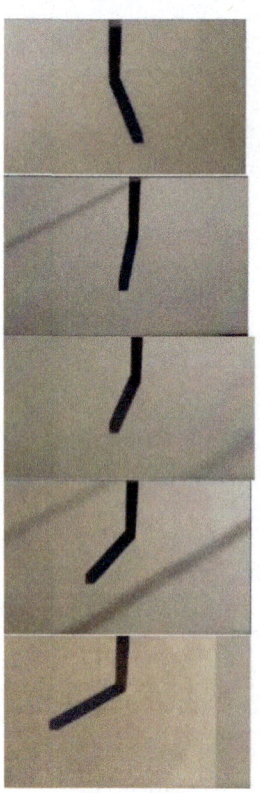

Take a stick and insert it into the ground. Follow the movement of the stick's shadow throughout the day. That's another way to follow the sun's movement. Did YOU feel any movement? NO.

We see the sun moving across the sky but feel no movement, so why believe that we're doing so?

"Against the Oval Earth man, the first card I can play is the analogy of the sun and moon. The Oval Earth man promptly answers that I don't know, by my own observation, that those bodies are spherical. I only know that they are round, and they may perfectly well be flat discs. I have no answer to that one. Besides, he goes on, what reason have I for thinking that the earth must be the same shape as the sun and moon? I can't answer that one either."   George Orwell

The sun: far or near

Why exactly do we believe the sun is 93,000,000 miles away? It can't be visual because the sun appears proportionately less and the same size as the moon. It can't be the heat/cool reaction from it because it's cooler when it's away from us and hottest when it's directly above us, which points to it being small and local. So why do we believe otherwise? It's a legit question.

Everything points to a smaller and local sun. Once again, if the sun is 93,000,000 miles away the North pole and South pole would have similar climates. But instead, Antarctica is a desolate wasteland of ice whereas the Arctic has animals, plant life and natives.

If the sun was 93,000,000 miles away, why is it hottest at noon when the sun is directly above you. It appears and feels closest to you. As it moves away it takes its light and warmth with it. As the sun moves away from you, it gets darker and cooler. This is the behavior of an object that approaches you and then passes by and then recedes, as it would on a flat level earth with a smaller and more local sun. Doesn't seem 93,000,000 miles away, does it?

If the earth were a sphere and the sun was such a great size then it would stay light out until the sun was completely around the curvature and then it would start turning dark. Why would light travel 93 million miles then start withholding its light before disappearing from the sky? Instead, as the sun moves away, it gets darker, even when the sun is in full view. You can look outside and prove this. No faith necessary.

People tell me the sun appearing larger during sunset and sunrise is another proof of the globe. When I ask how exactly, I get no answer because curvature wouldn't make the sun larger, would it?

The sun appears to be larger during the sunrise and sunsets. This is due to atmospheric magnification. A filter on your camera will cut the glare out. There are videos with the filter showing a smaller sun setting. It would not shrink this much if it was 93,000,000 miles away. There's no need to assume it's going behind any curvature that somehow flattens out when you're on a plane and enlarges the sun. How would the enlarged sun work on a ball earth I ask them. No answer.

Also, if you'll notice, the sun hooks to the right as it sets. This is due to its rotation around the North star Polaris. When I was in Alaska, I watched the 24-hour sun circle around the North star. (On and off throughout the day) Set up an experiment. Set your camera up, on a tripod, to film the sunset. Then take your film and draw a straight line where the sun is supposed to be setting, and then play the video. It crosses your line as it hooks to the right as it makes its rotation. Everyone on both coasts, or anywhere, can get the same results.

We see the sun moving and we see it hook to the right as it makes it's way around the North star Polaris. No movement felt or star parallax seen to show that it's us moving. So why believe that it is? Authoritarian's claims does not change reality.

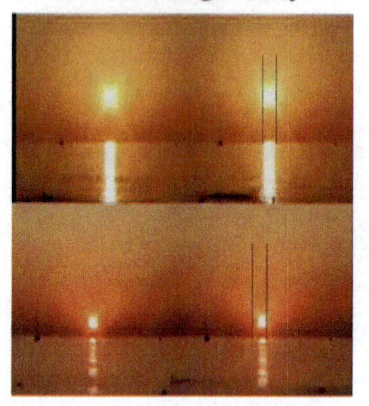

    NASA has said the sun is composed of layers made up almost entirely of hydrogen and helium. Now how could they possibly know what the sun's made of when it's supposedly 93,000,000 miles away? When asked how it can burn in space with zero oxygen, they say it makes its own. Give me a break. How would they know or test this claim? What instruments were used? What scientific method with "peer review" was used? If you can't test or recreate something then how is it considered scientific? And more importantly why do we blindly believe them when they have no merits due to exposed lies?

    People tell me that "if the sun was local, it would get hotter instead of colder the higher you went up." Well, the same goes for the globe model if the sun were a burning ball of gas like the globe model teaches, the closer you got the hotter you'd get. But I see no evidence of a burning ball of gas, do you? Do the real pictures look like a burning ball of gas to you?

    The ground is very dense and the lower gasses have more density than the upper gasses. More dense objects would be better heat conductors, correct? If you stand in 100° heat you will be ok, but if you put your hand on a rock that's 100° it hurts, then if you put your hand on the denser metal that's 100° it will burn you. If you went higher the air would be thinner with less density gasses thus cooler. A rock in direct sunlight is hotter in lower elevation then a rock in direct sunlight in higher elevation.

    A gas fire would get hotter the closer you get. The sun simply heats up molecules. The lower gasses conduct heat and transfer it to the denser matter. The air heats up before the ground does. The higher gasses, being less dense, don't heat up the mountain top as well as lower, denser, gasses do. Observable provable. Once again, no faith needed.

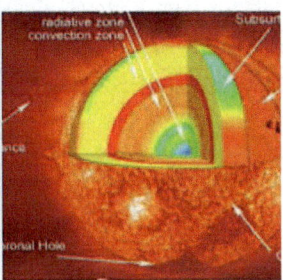

The Sun is **the star at the center of the Solar System**. It is a nearly perfect ball of hot plasma, heated to incandescence by nuclear fusion reactions in its core, radiating the energy mainly as light, ultraviolet, and infrared radiation. It is the most important source of energy for life on Earth.

W   https://en.m.wikipedia.org › wiki

Bogus claims of 'science,' built upon nothing but speculations, have always been around. Look at this article and think of how we don't see this in today's magazines, even though the reasoning that is given here still stands true. In the magazine "The Future," in 1892 it states: "Astronomers are very fond of boasting of the wonderful exactness of their science, and that it is based on the principles of incontrovertible mathematics; and of ridiculing astrology as a pseudo-science. The exactness belongs to practical and not theoretical astronomy. For example, when the writer learnt the principles of astronomy at school, he was taught that the Sun was exactly 95 million miles from the earth; now-a-days astronomers say that this was an error, and that the Sun is only 92 million miles distant. Newton made the Sun's distance to be 28 million miles, Kepler made it 12 million, Martin 81, and Mayer 104 million! Dr. Woodhouse, who was professor of astronomy at Cambridge about fifty years ago, was so candid as to admit the weakness of the Newtonian speculations. Woodhouse wrote: 'However perfect our theory, and however simply and satisfactorily the Newtonian hypothesis may seem to us to account for all the celestial phenomena, yet we are here compelled to admit the astounding truth that if our premises be disputed and our facts challenged, the whole range of astronomy does not contain the proofs of its own accuracy."

If the sun's rays had traveled 93,000,000 miles to get here, how could it be simultaneously burning up in the Sahara Desert and some 1000s of miles further a frozen wasteland of ice. Australia and Antarctica would be more like. If this was the case then when the sun is hitting the other side of the whirling ball night time would be a lot colder while the days burned up. The absurdity of this is the only thing real about it.

People often say to me "But on a flat earth it would be daylight everywhere." They are mixing up both models with this statement. This way of thinking comes from the assumption that the sun is 93,000,000 miles away and 1.3 million times bigger than the earth. But why do we assume this when we see and feel otherwise? It's small and local. The proof is observable and you can feel it.

The sun should not light up the whole flat earth and we should not see the sun all the time. It takes its light and warmth with it as it moves along. A light is only strong as its brilliancy. A street light doesn't light up the whole neighborhood just like a night light doesn't light up the whole room. The closer you get to the bulbs the warmer it is. Correct?

People assume scientists have figured out how far the sun is. They can't decide on a lot of things. One example would be the age of the Earth. Somewhere between 20 million and 400 million years ago. How is that scientific? The word "about" is used a lot in science. A way out is what it is. Let's have a look at their guesses.

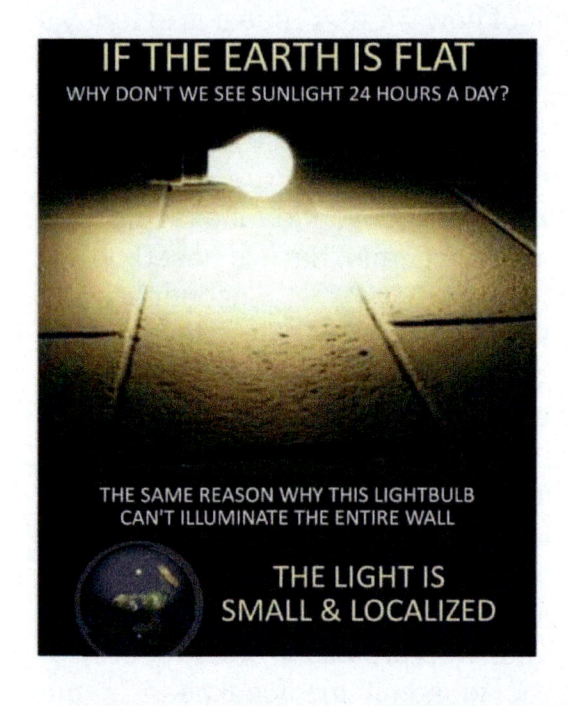

SUN'S DISTANCE
Copernicus- 3,391,2000 miles away
Johannes Kepler- 12,376,800 miles away
Benjamin Martin- 81 and 82 million miles
Thomas Dilworth-93,726,900 miles away
John Hind stated positively 95,298,260 miles
Benjamin Gould- 96 million miles away
Christian Mayer- 104 million miles away

"It matters not whether reckon it 28 or 54 million miles distant for either would do just as well." Isaac Newton

How is THAT science? If scientists went off facts this comedy wouldn't exist.

When you see the sun/moon in the sky and all those clouds, where are the most lid clouds located? Around the sun/moon, correct? Would this happen if the sun is 93,000,000 miles away? If the sun was 93,000,000 miles the sun's rays would come in parallel, not at an angle. There's zero proof the sun is 93,000,000 miles away and observable proof it's local therefore smaller. Think about it.

If the sun's distance is wrong then the size would be wrong as well, correct? The theory just starts to crumble at this point, as if it already hasn't.

LMAO I love this quote by Thomas Winship: "If you are a modest person, go in for a few millions; but if you wish to be "very scientific" and to be "mathematically certain" of your figures, then I advise you to make your choice somewhere about a hundred million. You will at least have plenty of "space" to retreat into, should the next calculation be against the figures of your choice. You can always add a few millions to "keep up with the times," or take off as many as may be required to adjust the distance to the "very latest" accurate column of figures. Talk about ridicule, the whole of modern astronomy is like a farcical comedy—full of surprises. One never knows what monstrous or ludicrous absurdity may come forth next."

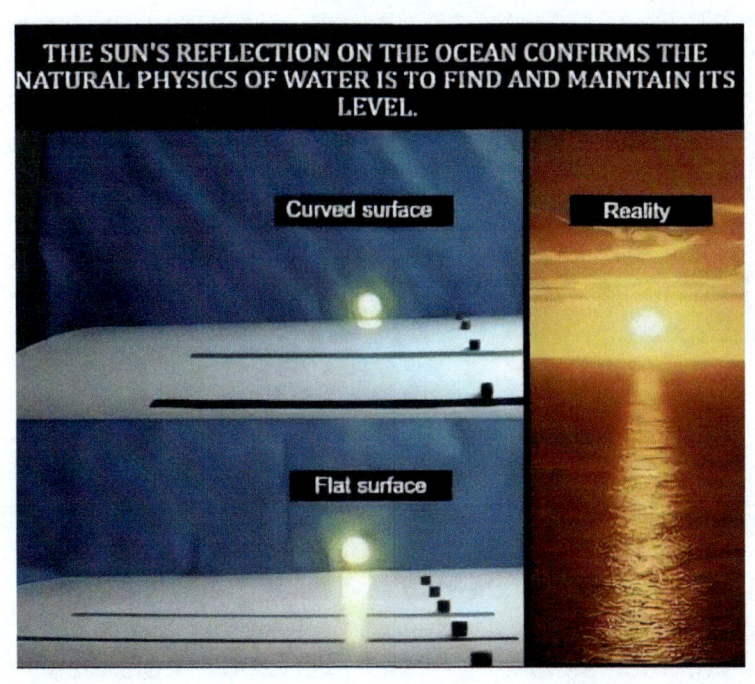

Is there ANY evidence to support what they call evidence? Remember you CAN'T measure any distance without a measuring rod. Whether it be a tape measure or foot in front of foot or laser (which doesn't go far without dissipating). Some measured it with plane trigonometry and came up with the sun and moon being around 3000 miles away. Hmmm! I'm not at that level yet, so I won't preach on it. As I've said before, how far can we trust plane trigonometry?

How does math work without guesswork? There's no way for them to know it's 93,000,000 miles away. But they tell you that anyway, don't they? Sun spots on the clouds and ocean proves a local sun. And a sun streak across the ocean proves the ocean is not curved.

We believe what we're told and not what we see. Example being the sun and the moon appear to be the same size, unless someone tells you that the sun appears small because it's far and huge, and that the moon is relatively smaller and closer, therefore appears the same size, you would think they were the same size. They tell you the sun is the perfect distance from Earth to appear the exact same size as the moon and for the temperature to be perfect for us. Give me a break!

Scientists actually preach that the sun and moon looking the same size and being a perfect fit for eclipses is a coincidence. It's like taking two new different color pencils from a pack and saying they're being alike is a coincidence.

Both rotate around the North Star. The sun's rotation is faster and thus they overlap causing the occasional eclipse.

You see two equally sized equidistant circles tracing similar paths at similar speeds and reflecting on water in the same manner, yet you believe one is hundreds of times larger and farther away than the other. Why and based on what evidence?

"The ball-Earth model claims the Sun is precisely 400 times larger than the Moon and 400 times further away from Earth making them "falsely" appear exactly the same size. Once again, the ball model asks us to accept as coincidence something that cannot be explained other than by natural design. The Sun and the Moon occupy the same amount of space in the sky and have been measured with sextants to be of equal size and equal distance, so claiming otherwise is against our eyes, experience, experiments and common sense." Eric Dubay's "200 Proofs the Earth is not a Spinning Ball."

If you observe carefully and really think about it, you'd understand how easy it is to keep someone mentally blind while his eyes are wide open. It's their belief system working and not their thought process.

The Zetetic Method

This is a serious question. We observe the sun move across the sky everyday while feeling no movement. Can you prove it does not do what is observed, or just tell me about things you believe? Until you do, you have no real reason to believe it does not move across the sky. You are simply dealing in faith.

We see the moon moving and acknowledge it, why not the sun? They both seem to be doing the same things, as far as motion goes. Can you possibly prove the sun is not moving as we observe it doing, but that it's us that's flying around it?

The BLACK SWAN

1) The variety of GUESSES does away with any credibility to the ones staking the claim of the distance of the sun and moon. There's no proof WHATSOEVER in the claims made with distance or substance that the sun would be made of. Even the pictures are a joke. If it's not based on physical facts and reasoning, then it's based on authority. Here's some real pictures of the sun and a fake one.

Real pictures of Earth taken by real people.

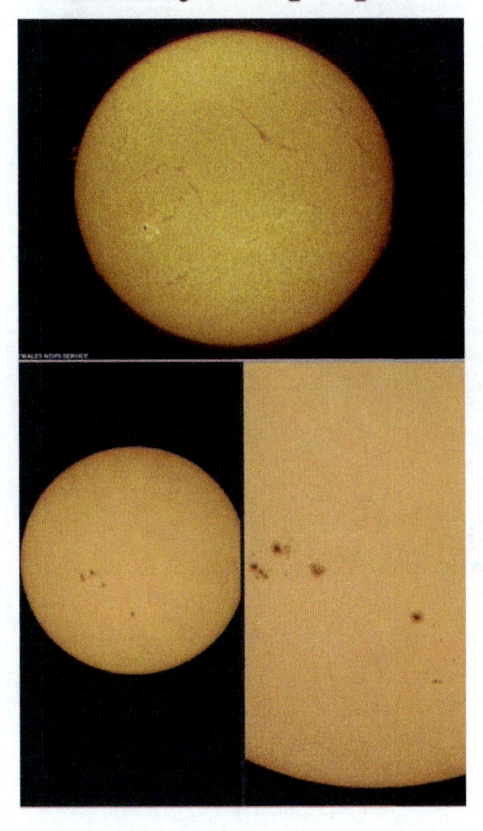

2) It's quite simple. It's hotter when the Sun is closer to you and colder when the Sun is farther away. Just like a regular heating bulb, not 93,000,000 miles away. In the morning it's cool but as the sun gets closer it warms up, then hottest at noon, directly above you. As it leaves it cools back down and starts getting dark before the sun even leaves your sight. The sun is smaller, closer and rotates above us. The physical proof is everywhere.

MOON HAPPENINGS

"Again, the Earth, with a supposed diameter of 8,000 miles, is said to revolve around the Sun, with the velocity of about 1100 miles per minute; the Moon being reckoned to have a diameter of 2,200 miles, and to go round the Earth at the rate of 180 miles per minute, thus, according to calculation, the Eclipse of the Moon, by the shadow of the Earth passing it, should not take four minutes, whereas the usual time occupied by a Lunar Eclipse is generally about two hours, and it has been known to have been extended to four." Author David Wardlaw Scott

"The moon is not a rock. The moon is a plasma phenomenon. A cosmic plasma." Scientist R. Foster

THE MOON: CHEESE OR LIGHT BULB?

According to current science the moon was once a piece of molten rock fractured off from the earth. How though? What physical evidence do they have to back up this extraordinary claim? Did this happen to other planets as well? How about the 'planets' with two moons? How about the gas 'planet', how did that moon break off? Seems like one of those things you have to prove when you say it. What are the chances of the moon having its proper orbit to tell the months and appear the same size as the sun? The ridiculousness of the theory is the only thing real about it. If you seriously question it, it falls apart.

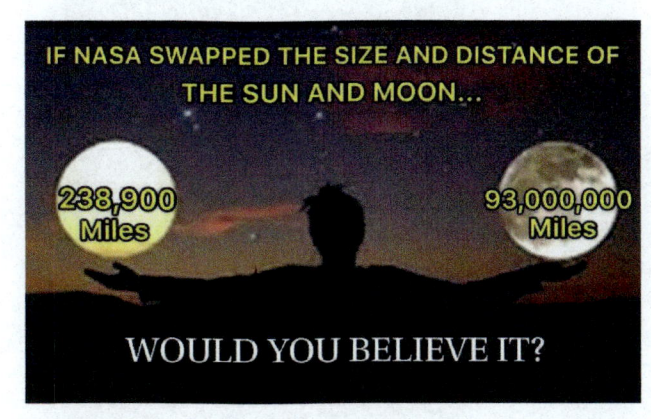

The moon we're told is 238,855 miles away. The crater Tycho, we're told, is 53 miles wide. We can see Tycho with our naked eyes. We can also see a stretch of 300 to 500 miles on a plane which is ONLY 35,000 or more feet up, depending on which plane you take and weather. This makes no sense. Our eyes follow the law of perspective, which makes things appear smaller the further they move away from us. If you can see a stretch of hundreds of miles just 35,000 feet up then it's impossible to see a 53 mile stretch 238,855 miles away. Think about it, the laws of perspective would have none of it. They claim you can fit all these "planets" between the moon and Earth, yet we're supposed to see a 53-mile-wide crater?

The Zetetic Method

Astronomers make the assumption when talking about our moon: "Every one of the thousands of stars that can be seen with the unaided eye, is enormously larger than our satellite (moon)."

How would they know this? How does one measure light years? Is it going off assumptions? Can any of it be proven, or is this yet another authoritarian saying so?

Again, look at the moon and clouds. Where are the most lid clouds located? Around the moon. Just like the sun, the moon is local and not 238,855 miles away. There's no proof for one and observable proof for the other.

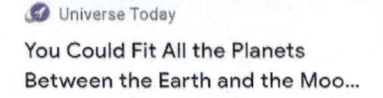

Take your telescope or high-powered camera and look at a mountain a few miles away, you'll notice it's not THAT powerful, but look at the detail. Now take the same telescope or camera and look at the moon; does it look like it's over 280,000 miles away? Look at the details and compare. You went from zooming a few miles away, to 280,000 miles away. Think about it. It's like saying your camera can zoom 238,000 miles away and see the details of the "craters." You can however point it level to Earth and see further than the supposed curvature would allow.

Are we sure the moon's 238,000 miles away? Is there solid proof for this claim?

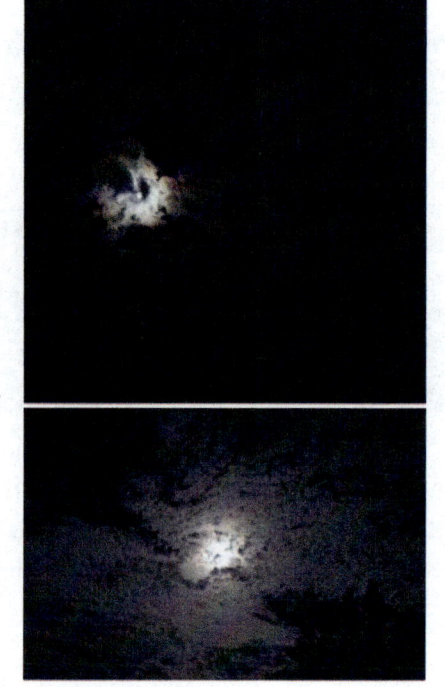

So, the moon is rotating on its axis, yet we never see the backside? Are we supposed to believe it's rotating perfectly with the rotation of the earth for us not to see the backside? What are the chances? Call me skeptical, but NO.

"An unalterable rotational velocity thru all phases of planetary evolution is manifestly impossible. The truth is, the so-called "axial rotation" of the moon is a phenomenon deceptive alike to the eye and mind and devoid of physical meaning. The moon does rotate, not on its own, but about an axis passing thru the center of the earth, the true and only one." Nikola Tesla

The Zetetic Method

CRATERS

Moon craters are circular. What are the odds that every meteor impact happened at a 90º angle, while spinning and flying through space in three different directions simultaneously? If the same side is always facing us how can meteors cause these perfect circles on that side? They would have to go THROUGH the Earth. None of the craters on the earth side of the moon appear as streaks across the lunar surface or in any way indicate they were created by asteroids or meteorites striking the moon's surface at an angle.

MOON BEING A REFLECTOR

Look at a full moon. Does it look like a reflecting sphere? The moon does not reflect like a sphere in the least. The lid part of the moon lights up equally. Especially on a full moon. It seems more self-luminescent with phases.

Reflectors are either flat (where angles are involved) or concave, but never a convex (sphere). A convex surface cannot concentrate and reflect light. But concave surfaces can be a reflector and are used as such, where angles are not involved.

If the moon is reflecting the sun and the sun is 93,000,000 miles away and the moon is only 238,000 miles away then how can we have a full moon during the day when it's near the sun in the sky? The sun is 93,000,000 miles behind the moon. Even at an angle it doesn't work.

Hold a ball up in front of someone and then a light source much further away from them and you and see if that person sees a fully lid ball with the lighting coming from the side or behind the ball. Common sense tells you they won't.

How bright would a reflected light source have to be in order to light the tops of clouds from 237,000 miles away?

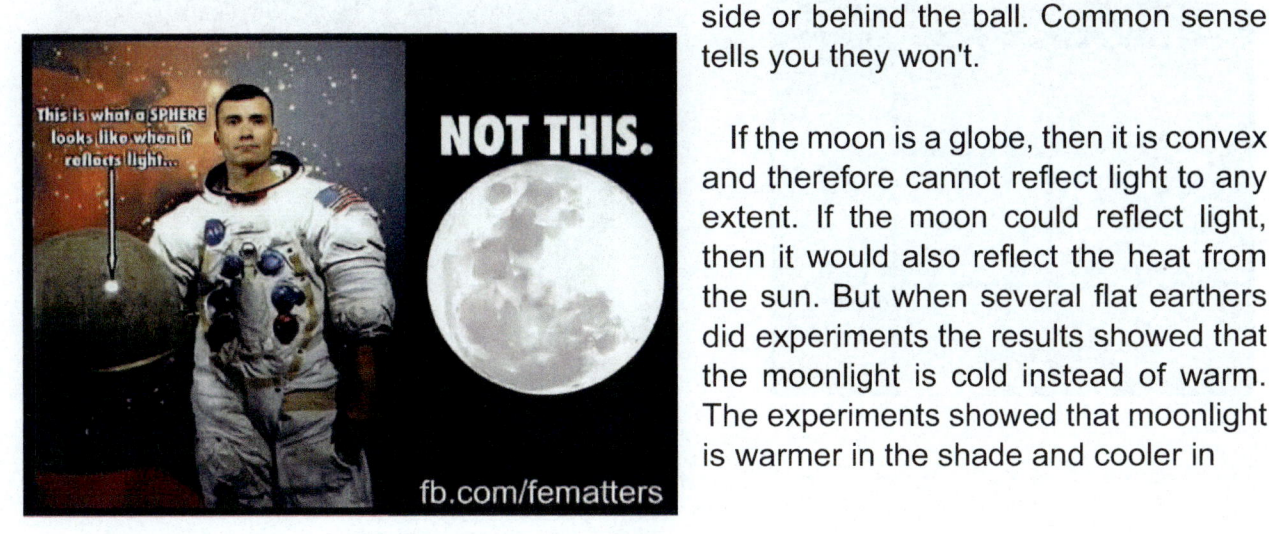

Apparently not very bright at all!

If the moon is a globe, then it is convex and therefore cannot reflect light to any extent. If the moon could reflect light, then it would also reflect the heat from the sun. But when several flat earthers did experiments the results showed that the moonlight is cold instead of warm. The experiments showed that moonlight is warmer in the shade and cooler in

This is what a SPHERE looks like when it reflects light...

NOT THIS.

fb.com/fematters

direct moonlight. This is not how a reflector works. Also, the sun is orange and heat-causing, the Moon is pale and cold.

In an article "Lectures on Chemistry," (before Big Brother took over such things) it is said: "The light of the moon, though concentrated by the most powerful burning glass, is incapable of raising the temperature of the most delicate thermometer."
"The moon's rays, when concentrated, actually reduce the temperature upon a thermometer by more than 8°. That soft silvery light, so unlike sunlight, or gaslight, or any other kind of light seen upon the earth."

When light and heat are received by a reflector, light and heat are reflected, as anyone reading this may prove for themselves, by testing the claim. If you reflect a red light the reflection of it is red. Test this and you will find that reflectors reflect just what they receive.
Moonlight and sunlight have totally different properties. Sunlight is hotter in direct sunlight and cooler in the shade. It also has preservative properties. Moonlight on the other hand is cooler in direct moonlight and warmer in the shade. It also is cool, damp, putrefying and septic. This is not how a reflector works. The sunlight acts as a preservative while the moonlight creates combustion and decay. If you hang fish up to dry in the sun, they will be preserved, but if exposed to the moon, will be putrid in one night. The same applies to fruits, etc. The light from the moon cannot be of the same nature as that of the sun. Furthermore showing, that the moon shines by its own light, thus has its own phases.

Moonlight and sunlight have totally different properties. Sunlight is hotter in direct sunlight and cooler in the shade. It also has preservative properties.
Moonlight on the otherhand is cooler in direct moonlight and warmer in the shade. It also is cool, damp, putrefying and septic.
This not how a reflector works. The sunlight acts as a preservative while the moonlight creates combustion and decay.

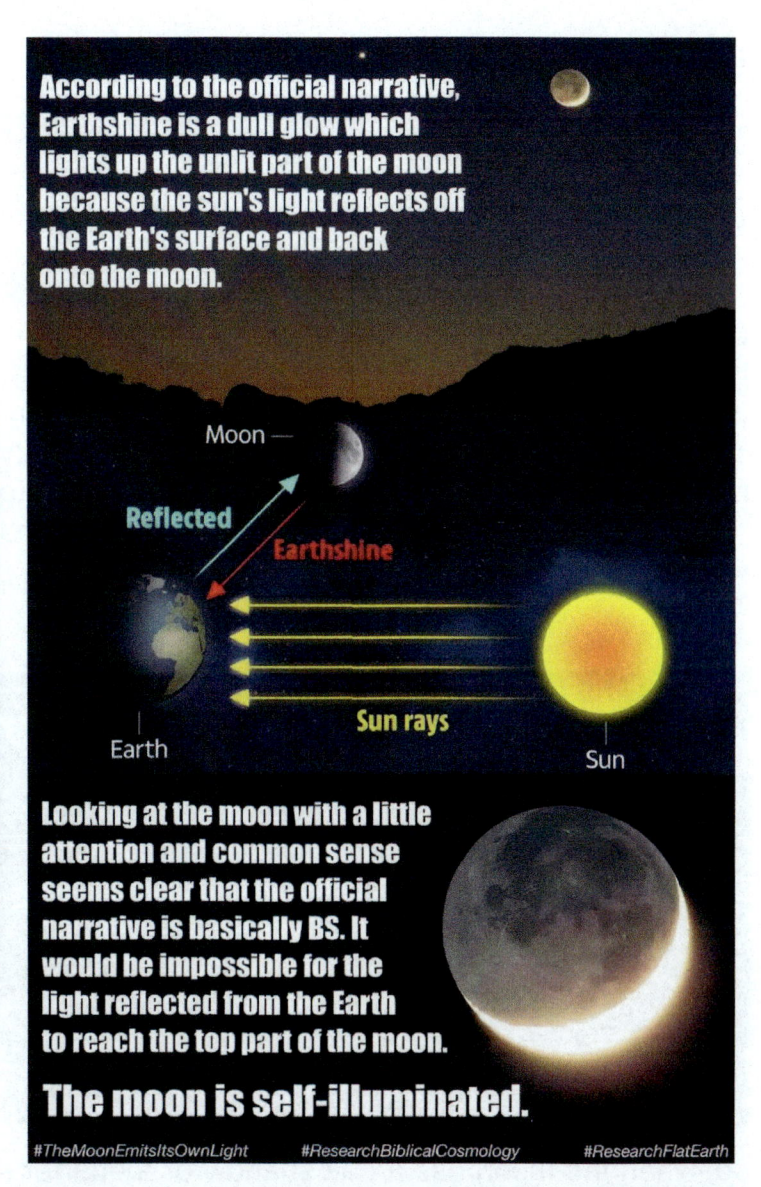

According to the official narrative, Earthshine is a dull glow which lights up the unlit part of the moon because the sun's light reflects off the Earth's surface and back onto the moon.

Looking at the moon with a little attention and common sense seems clear that the official narrative is basically BS. It would be impossible for the light reflected from the Earth to reach the top part of the moon.

The moon is self-illuminated.

#TheMoonEmitsItsOwnLight   #ResearchBiblicalCosmology   #ResearchFlatEarth

Notice how the light falls on the surface of the sphere. The entire sphere is illuminated but there is a distinct spot where a small portion of the surface of the sphere appears much brighter than the rest of the sphere.

If you move to the left or right of the sphere you will see the bright spot change positions on the sphere. In moving, the portion of the sphere angled to reflect the most light from the light into your eyes changes, thus causing the bright spot to appear to move to another location. Another person in a different part of the room will see their own bright spot in a different location.

A reflecting flat surface has no distinct bright spot, it's evenly illuminated by the light source? A dead ball of rock and dust is not reflecting the light from a massive ball of fire.

MOON PHASES

The round earth theory explaining the phases has nothing to do with the earth's shadow. It simply states that the moon is a sphere. So, the angle of the sun to the moon creates the phases. We know this isn't true because we can see that the angles are impossible. The moon is often directly across the sky and directly in the path of the sun yet the moon is not full. Sometimes it is full but the sun is not in front of the moon but off to the side at "93,000,000" miles away. So, the moon phases must be something other than what we were taught.

When the moon is full on the western horizon and, at the same time, the sun is up on the eastern horizon, that can make sense on a globe or flat earth because the sun is fully hitting the moon. However, wait a few days or so, when the moon has a half shadow or a quarter shadow while the sun is still directly across from it. How is the moon not fully lid when the sun is directly hitting from across the way? Yet only half or quarter is lid.

Now this picture here is not what I just mentioned. It's something else and explains itself. To see what I just mentioned above, simply wait till the moon is full during the day when it's in the west and then sun in the east, then look at it every day and you will see the phase that makes no sense going by the globe model.

TIDES BUT NOTHING ELSE

"If the moon lifted up the water, it is evident that near the land, the water would be drawn away and low instead of high tide. Again, the velocity and path of the moon are uniform, and it follows that if she exerted any influence on the earth, that influence could only be a uniform influence. But the tides are not uniform. At Port Natal the rise and fall is about 6 feet, while at Beira, about 600 miles up the coast, the rise and fall is 26 feet. This effectively settles the matter that the moon has no influence on the tides....In inland lakes, there are no tides; which also proves that the moon cannot attract either the earth or water to cause tides." Thomas Winship (Zetetic Cosmogony)

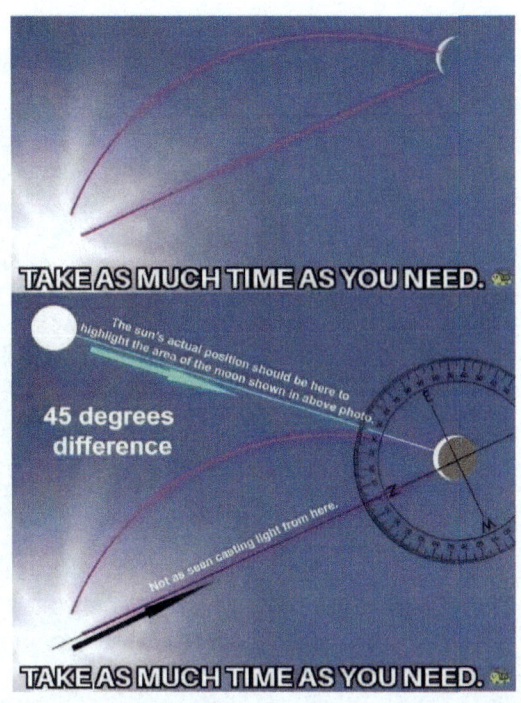

Not sure what causes tides. Scientists have admitted that the ocean expands when heated. Explorers reported gigantic whirlpools near the north pole (when you could go to these certain places that is), sucking in, then pushing out for periods of time.

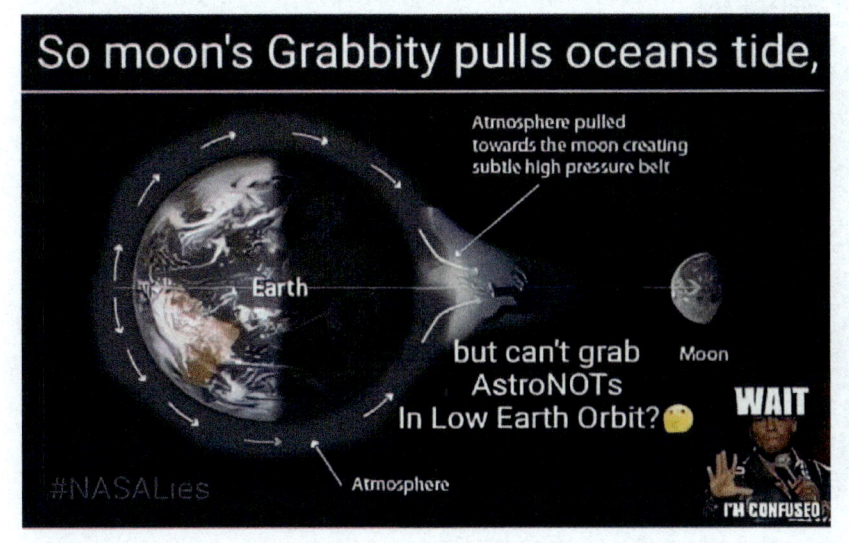

Also, if the sun has a magnetic field, then it would exert itself on salt water. This could be one reason as to why there is no high tide or low tide in freshwater lakes and ponds. Scientists have said that lakes do have tides but are too small to tell. There's always an excuse why we can't prove their claims, have you noticed that? Only lakes near and connected to the ocean have tides, and it's the ocean that causes it, not the lakes. Either way it doesn't make this plane warp into a ball. All of the ocean is ONE body of water.

The moon doesn't cause the tides. Tides are local and probably have more to do with the sun (smaller and more local) than moon. Salt water is highly magnetic. If the sun is electromagnetic. Tides do not respond concurrently across the earth's surface. Any tide table will show this. Also, if the moon caused tides, then the equator would have the highest tides, but instead it's Canada.

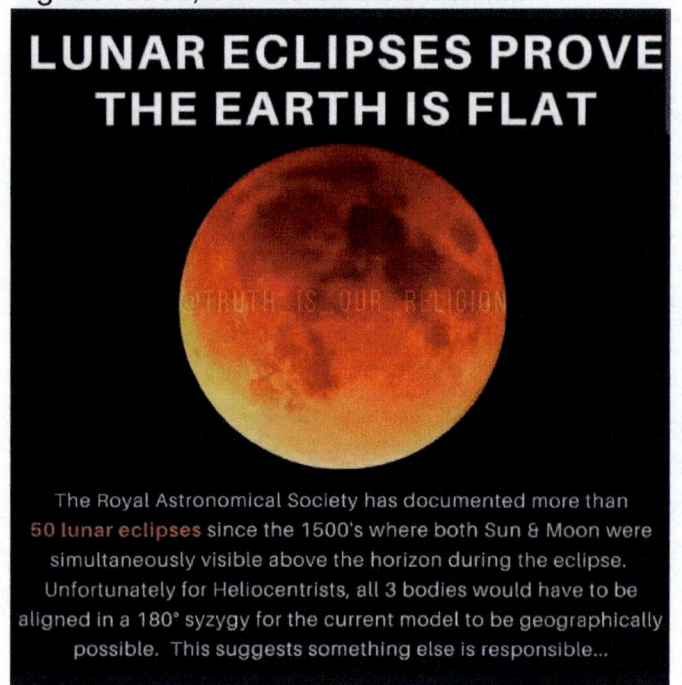

LUNAR ECLIPSES PROVE THE EARTH IS FLAT

The Royal Astronomical Society has documented more than **50 lunar eclipses** since the 1500's where both Sun & Moon were simultaneously visible above the horizon during the eclipse. Unfortunately for Heliocentrists, all 3 bodies would have to be aligned in a 180° syzygy for the current model to be geographically possible. This suggests something else is responsible...

How can the moon pull the massive oceans but not lakes, clouds or gasses from the atmosphere? Why not astronauts and satellites out of orbit? Only gigantic oceans? If the earth's gravitational pull is stronger than the moon's, how can the moon, which is said to be 238,000 miles away, pull the tides, which are located here on Earth's surface, further from the earth's core, where gravity would be much stronger? It is the weaker force, correct? So, they're saying the weaker force is overcoming the stronger force.

IF YOU THINK IT'S JUST A COINCIDENCE
THE SUN IS "400 TIMES FARTHER"
AND THE MOON IS "400 TIMES SMALLER"
SO THEY "APPEAR" THE SAME SIZE

AND THE MOON IS
"ORBITING AND SPINNING PERFECTLY IN SYNC
SO THE SAME SIDE ALWAYS FACES EARTH"

YOU NEED TO START THINKING FOR YOURSELF

LUNAR ECLIPSES
According to Astronomers, for a lunar eclipse to happen, it requires that the earth should be exactly midway between sun and moon to cause the shadow on the moon. Thus, the sun and moon would be opposite each other with earth in-between. The argument they have, says the curved shadow proves the earth is a sphere. Let's have a better look at this claim and compare it with physical based evidence and see if it matches reality.

Lunar eclipse has happened with the sun and moon in the sky at the same time throughout history. This is called a selenelion. The Royal Astronomy Society has recorded 50 of them.

Selenelion: when both Moon and Sun are visible above the horizon. Moon is setting in the West while Sun is rising in the East.

Taken January 31, 2018 in Chipley, Florida by Ron Hagberg

How is this lunar eclipse even possible according to Heliocentric theory?

In 2018 we had the eclipse at 5:30 am. The sun wasn't quite in view and the shadow came from the top of the moon on the opposite horizon then the sun. I enquired about this online and other people had seen it too. This debunks the claim that's it's the earth that's making the shadow. The fact that I don't know what it doesn't change this fact.

Some ancient cultures believe a second moon called Rahu exists and causes eclipses. In Sir John Herschel's book "Herschel's Astronomy," he admits, "Invisible moons exist in the firmament."

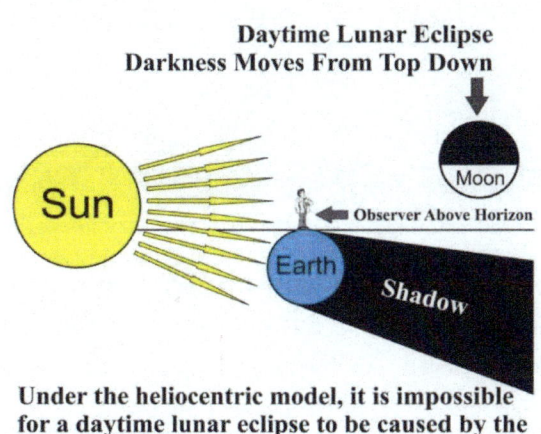

Daytime Lunar Eclipse Darkness Moves From Top Down

Under the heliocentric model, it is impossible for a daytime lunar eclipse to be caused by the earth's shadow.

So whatever causes phases and eclipses it's not what they say. I don't know much about Rahu so I don't "preach" it. But I know what I saw. This picture below is not from me but the same eclipse.

In 2018, I saw this eclipse around sunrise. The shadow came from the top left which makes it impossiball for the Earth to be the shadow. The mainstream media didn't cover that eclipse. Hmm why not, they cover others?

Another daytime lunar eclipse was on December 10, 2011. You can go on the website TimeandDate.com and see all the data for sun/moon-sets/sun/moon-rises from all across this great plane of ours, and see the data for what I'm saying here in this book. It will further prove that both the sun and moon were above the horizon during the lunar eclipse.

Also, the earth's shadow is much larger than the moon. Where have you seen an object's shadow smaller than the object? An object's shadow is always larger than the object. According to NASA the moon is 3474.3 km but the moon's shadow is 70 km in an eclipse. Why doesn't the shadow go right across the moon in the same general direction, as all the bodies involved continued in the same course as when the eclipse started?

THE FAILING GLOBE THEORY

Observation of Lunar Eclipses proves Earth does not cast a shadow on the Moon. On a Globe Earth, the shadow should be cast on the opposite side of the Moon, from bottom up, but what we see is top down.

Lunar Eclipse Jan. 31, 2018

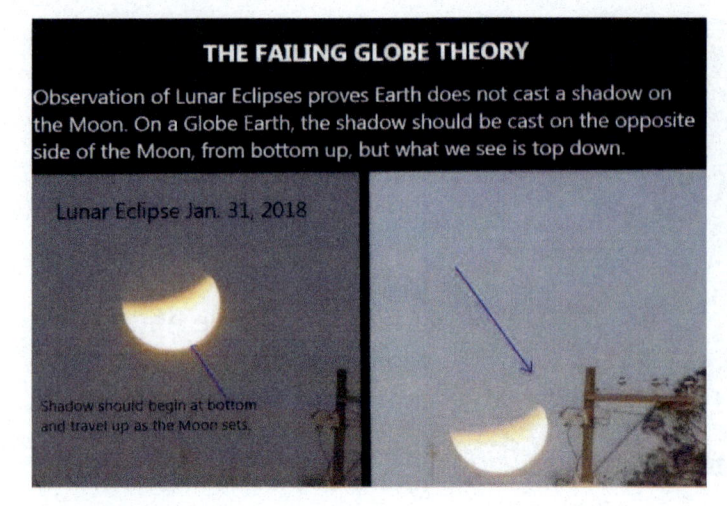

Shadow should begin at bottom and travel up as the Moon sets.

A daytime lunar eclipse excludes the earth from being the cause of the lunar eclipse. A daytime lunar eclipse is impossible under the heliocentric globe model.

Scientism priest 'fix' for this is atmospheric refraction, which causes astronomical objects to appear higher in the sky than they are in reality. Well if the sun is in your eye and lighting up the sky and so is the moon, then this explanation is a fail. Furthermore, the fact that the shadow for the daytime lunar eclipse starts from top to bottom does away with the light refraction explanation. Sometimes, like in the case here at Big Bend where I'm currently at, the sun is not quite up, yet enough on the horizon to prove my point 100%.

The table below is a restructure from Joe Rao, a writer for Space.com, and posted with his article. It shows the information for the sunrise and moonset times at different cities. Those cities both have the sun and moon above the horizon at the same time during the lunar eclipse on December 10, 2011.

Lunar eclipse on December 10, 2011 in Madison, Wisconsin.

Daytime Lunar Eclipse

City	Time Zone	Sunrise	Moonset	Percent Covered
Chicago	CST	7:05 a.m.	7:06 a.m.	28.9%
Dallas	CST	7:17 a.m	7:18 a.m.	45.4%
Winnipeg	CST	8:14 a.m.	8:17 a.m.	TOTAL
Denver	MST	7:08 a.m.	7:11 a.m.	TOTAL
Phoenix	MST	7:20 a.m.	7:23 a.m.	TOTAL
Helena	MST	8:00 a.m.	8:04 a.m.	*94.3%
Calgary	MST	8:27 a.m.	8:33 a.m.	*61.9%
Los Angeles	PST	6:46 a.m.	6:50 a.m.	TOTAL
San Francisco	PST	7:13 a.m.	7:17 a.m.	*81.1%
Portland	PST	7:38 a.m.	7:44 a.m.	*47.5%
Vancouver	PST	7:55 a.m.	8:01 a.m.	*24.2%

The Zetetic Method

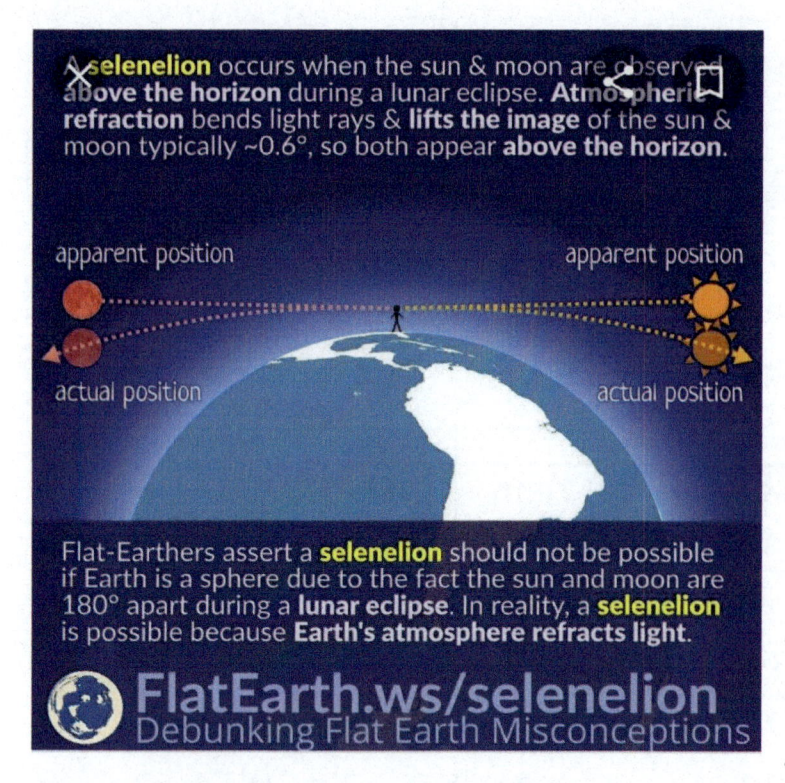

> A **selenelion** occurs when the sun & moon are observed **above the horizon** during a lunar eclipse. **Atmospheric refraction** bends light rays & **lifts the image** of the sun & moon typically ~0.6°, so both appear **above the horizon**.
>
> apparent position — apparent position
> actual position — actual position
>
> Flat-Earthers assert a **selenelion** should not be possible if Earth is a sphere due to the fact the sun and moon are 180° apart during a **lunar eclipse**. In reality, a **selenelion** is possible because **Earth's atmosphere refracts light**.
>
> FlatEarth.ws/selenelion
> Debunking Flat Earth Misconceptions

Look at this claim, from this website that says they debunk flat earth with their claims, but does no such thing.

Are we supposed to honestly believe that it's not the sun and moon we're actually seeing, but a refraction? Are they for real with this? That it's a mirage of source? What about the shadow coming from the top? Why doesn't this happen all the time, us seeing the sun and moon but it's not really them? BAHAHA! Oh what silliness. This is one of those claims that you should have to prove when you make it, but of course there's no way you can. So, once again, we rely on authority. Just a cartoon as their proof. Why not show a picture of the actual thing like I did? Look at the pictures I posted of the moon; does it look like a freaking mirage? If it was refraction then the real moon and sun would be coming up pretty soon, but it already has. The reality of this and the shadow coming from the top debunks this clowning website's claim.

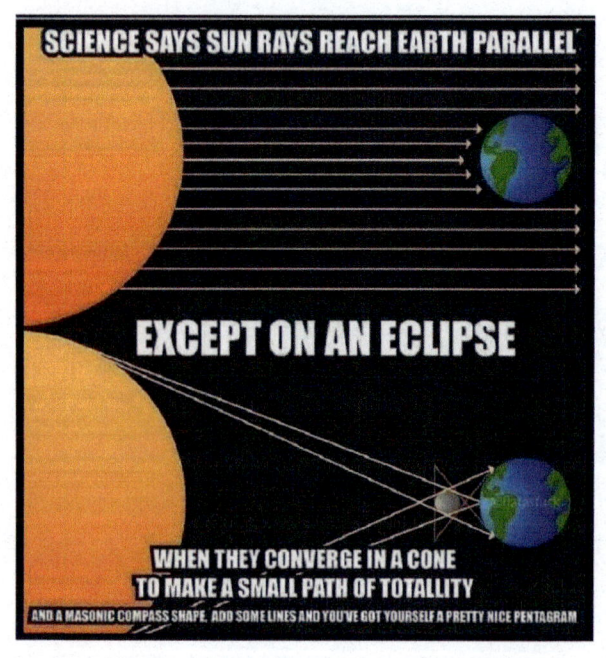

> SCIENCE SAYS SUN RAYS REACH EARTH PARALLEL
>
> EXCEPT ON AN ECLIPSE
>
> WHEN THEY CONVERGE IN A CONE TO MAKE A SMALL PATH OF TOTALITY
> AND A MASONIC COMPASS SHAPE. ADD SOME LINES AND YOU'VE GOT YOURSELF A PRETTY NICE PENTAGRAM

If it was atmospheric refraction then it would happen more than just on the selenelion eclipse. If the earth, being in-between the sun and moon, is what causes the eclipses, and the earth is, supposedly, traveling at 1,100 miles per minute and the moon itself is traveling 180 miles per minute, then how long would it take the chicken to cross the road during the eclipse? Hmmm

The bottom line is that the earth's shadow does not cause a lunar eclipse, and the daytime lunar eclipses on December 10, 2011 and the one in 2018 are proof of that fact, not counting the recorded 50 other times. It is not the shadow of the earth causing the lunar eclipse, so that's one leg for the proof of heliocentrism knocked out. The fact that we don't know for sure of what creates this, doesn't mean we should make stupid claims and pretend, nor does it wrap this plane around a whirling ball.

Assuming curvature doesn't add curvature. Also assuming that a ball is the only way to see something flipped is absurd and also doesn't add curvature.

Most things can happen in different ways so never assume claimers have the correct way.

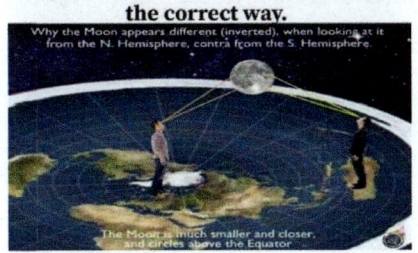

THE FLIPPING MOON

Some people claim that the moon viewed one way in the southern hemisphere and another in the northern hemisphere proves the earth is a ball. This is a result of low effort thinking. The same can happen for a flat earth. There's also the same claim for the stars. But if the stars are millions of miles or light years away then they would look the same at that distance. The fact that they do appear 'flipped' shows that they're not light years away, but much closer. You can put a picture on the ceiling and stand in one spot while someone else stands in a different spot and sees a different angle. See, thinking works.

SEXTANT CALCULATIONS

I'm trying to learn how to use a sextant but it's definitely a hard one to master. I don't trust any math at a great distance but then I'm not sure on the workings of this. A sailor on YouTube did this experiment, using a sextant, and came up with the same as this author here, Thomas Winship: "Both the distance and size of most of the objects in the heavens may be measured with a high degree of accuracy. It only requires to be known that the object is vertical to a certain part of the world at a certain time, when the observer must take a position—which could be ascertained by previous experiment—where the angular distance of the object is 45°. A base line measured from that position to the point at which the object was vertical at the moment of observation, will be the same length as the distance of the object from the earth's surface. Size, except in the case of very small stars, may be as easily determined. Let the instrument with which the angular distance was taken be graduated to degrees, minutes and seconds, the minutes and seconds corresponding to miles and sixtieths of miles on the earth's surface. Having carefully adjusted the instrument, bring the image of the lower limb of the object to be measured down to the horizon, and note the reading on the instrument. Now bring the upper limb in contact with the horizon, and the difference of the reading will be the diameter of the object. It would, of course, require a very finely adjusted instrument, and one graduated to say the one hundredth part of a second to measure some of the smaller stars."

Instead of the diameter of the moon being 2,160 miles, it is, by the above process, found to be about 32 nautical miles in diameter.

January 31 lunar eclipse
earthsky.org

Lunar Eclipse Jan 31,...
fs.aminus3.com

THE BLACK SWAN
1) We see far too much detail for the moon to be at said distance. We can see 100s of miles at only 35,000 feet up, how can we possibly see a 53-mile crater at 238,855 miles away.
2) Moon doesn't reflect like a sphere nor does the moonlight have the same properties as the sunlight. Just the opposite in fact.
3) Moon "gravitational pull" seems to pull nothing but salt water, showing it's not a gravitational pull at all.
4) The craters on the side of the moon facing us would be impossible on the ball Earth model as how the Earth would be in the way.
5) A lunar eclipse on a ball Earth has the Earth, moon and the sun a perfect 180° alignment for it to occur, yet recorded over 50 times and now two more added in recent times, they both have been in the sky at the same time, with the shadow coming from the TOP. Reality can be ugly yet beautiful and also a wonderful teacher and debunker.

SEASONS
"An important scientific innovation rarely makes its way by gradually winning over and converting its opponents: it rarely happens that Saul becomes Paul. What does happen is that its opponents gradually die out and that the growing generation is familiarized with the idea from the beginning."   German theoretical physicist Max Planck

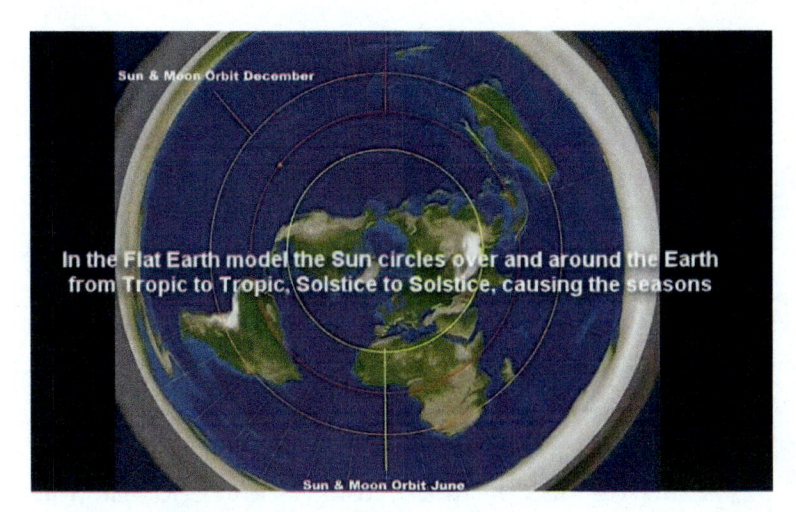

WHAT CAUSES SEASONS

With observation, you can see the sun rotates around the North star Polaris all year long. I started writing this book about 10 months or so ago. As I write this sentence right now, summer is three quarters over, the only difference other than temperature is the positioning of the sun. According to the globe model though, we have been doing quite a bit of wobbling for the seasonal change, but nothing has been felt or no star parallax seen and the North star Polaris is still in its same location, the only thing that has changed is the sun's position in it's rotation around Polaris.

During the summer, the sun is closest to Polaris on June 22nd, on the Tropic of Cancer, then it slowly rotates outwardly moving towards and over the equator and then outwardly more to the Tropic of Capricorn causing winter where it stays for three days, then starts back towards the North again.

The equator, being the center of the outermost rotation and inter most rotation throughout these observable movements, is, as a result, the warmest place year around. The sun moves faster in the Tropic of Capricorn causing short days, and slower as it gets closer to Polaris on the Tropic of Cancer causing longer days. It's quite simple. It's hotter when the Sun is closer and colder when the Sun is further away. When it's closest to you, it's summer but it'll be winter somewhere else because the suns further away from them, then it switches places. All of this is observable throughout the year. When it's summer in the USA the sun is closer to Polaris and it'll be winter in the south because the sun's is further away, if the sun had traveled 93,000,000 miles, then would such a little distance make THAT much of a difference? However, if the sun is smaller and local, distance would play a bigger factor.

The strength of flat earth is in its simplicity and its observation. You don't need to be an indoctrinated "genius" to understand flat earth reality.

Some globers have a problem with the thought of the sun speeding up, even though it's observable, but they don't have a problem when the globe theory calls for the equator to have to move faster than the poles, even with the earth moving at a constant rate.

I've said this before and I'll say it again because this is what we are observing, and very important. Picture the face of a clock, with the minute hand circling its rotation around the center, the part of the hand closest to the center moving slower than the outer most pointy end which actually has more surface to cover on its rotation but still does so in the 60-minute time limit, just like the sun in its 24-hour southern and northern rotations. The pointy end of the clock's hand/sun during winter moves faster than the inner end of the hand/sun during the summer, all in a 24-hour time limit.

All of this causes time zones and seasons. The moon rotates around Polaris as well but slower in its rotation then the sun, about 25 hours, thus overlapping eventually.

The nearer the sun gets to the Pole star the earlier it rises, the higher it reaches at noon, and the later it sets; and the further it gets from the Pole Star the later it rises, the lower it appears at noon, and the earlier it sets.

The daily rotation around the earth causes the alternations of day and night; while the northern and southern rotation causes the seasons. ALL of this is observable and provable. You can't say the same for the wobble, spinning and flying, can you? Go ahead and tell me what you believe.

What I just said is purely observable and no assumptions needed. One only has to get past their assumptions to see the truth in plain sight.

A good experiment from the book "Terra Firma" by David Wardlaw Scott: "The Path of the Sun is Concentric, expanding and contracting daily for six months alternately. This is easily proved by fixing a rod, say at noon on the 21st of December, so that, on looking along it, the line of vision will touch the lower edge of the Sun. This line of sight will continue for several days pretty much the same, but, on the ninth or tenth day, it will be found that the rod will have to be moved considerably toward the zenith, in order to touch the lower edge of the Sun, and every day afterwards it will have to be raised till the 22nd of June. Then there will be little change for a few days as before, but day by day afterwards the rod will have to be lowered till the 21st of December, when the Sun is farthest from the Northern Centre, and it is dark there. This expansion and contraction of the Sun's path continues every year, and is termed the Northern and Southern Declination, and should demonstrate to Modern Astronomers the absurdity of calling the

World a Planet, as it remains stationary while the Sun continues circling round the heavens."

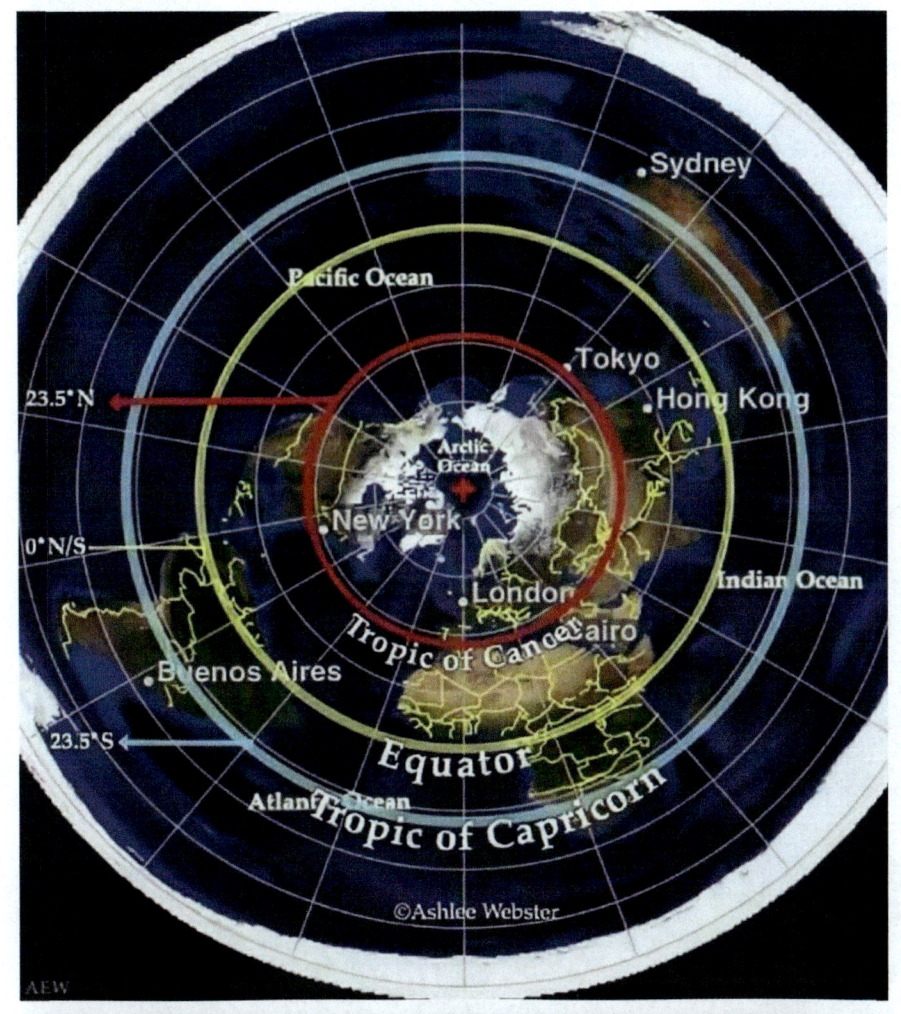

The globe model has the sun 91,400,000 miles away in January when it's actually winter, and farthest from the Sun, 94,500,000 miles in July when it's actually summer throughout most of the Earth. They tell you this is caused by the wobble of the earth and its elliptical, or slightly oval-shaped orbit. But how, when Polaris never moved nor any star parallax? The only thing that moved was the position of the sun and moon. So why should we believe it?

When the earth is nearest the sun there should be summer in both northern and southern latitudes, and when it is farthest from the sun there should be winter all over the earth at the same time, because <u>the entire earth would be farthest from the sun,</u> not just part of it. Just like it being hottest at noon when the sun is directly above us. The evidence for a smaller and more local sun is there for the noticing.

It's impossible to account for the seasons on the assumption that the earth is a whirling ball, and that it rotates around the sun. They tell us just the opposite of what it truly is, a smaller more local sun rotates around Polaris above a flat plane.

170

There is a hole in the Georgia Guide Stones that is fixed on Polaris. This shows that the star does not move. Two motions of the Globe model are disproved. Spinning rotation would not work as the world is supposedly tilted and you are not looking upward but diagonally. Revolving motion of seasons showing the sun moving up and down with summer and winter while the star Polaris remains stationary through the Guide stones hole. Or you can set up a mark on your window, locking onto the North star Polaris, and see if it moves all year. Make sure your feet are also locked in the same position every time to get a more accurate reading. Be honest in your experiments otherwise why do them?

A spherical earth, as we're told, is on an axis of 23.4 (66.6). It revolves around the sun 365 days, changing its position of direct sunlight. Only problem is that if the sun's rays can travel 93M miles, the mere circumference of the earth wouldn't have THAT much effect on temperature, should be tropical everywhere, not desert, ice world and tropical.

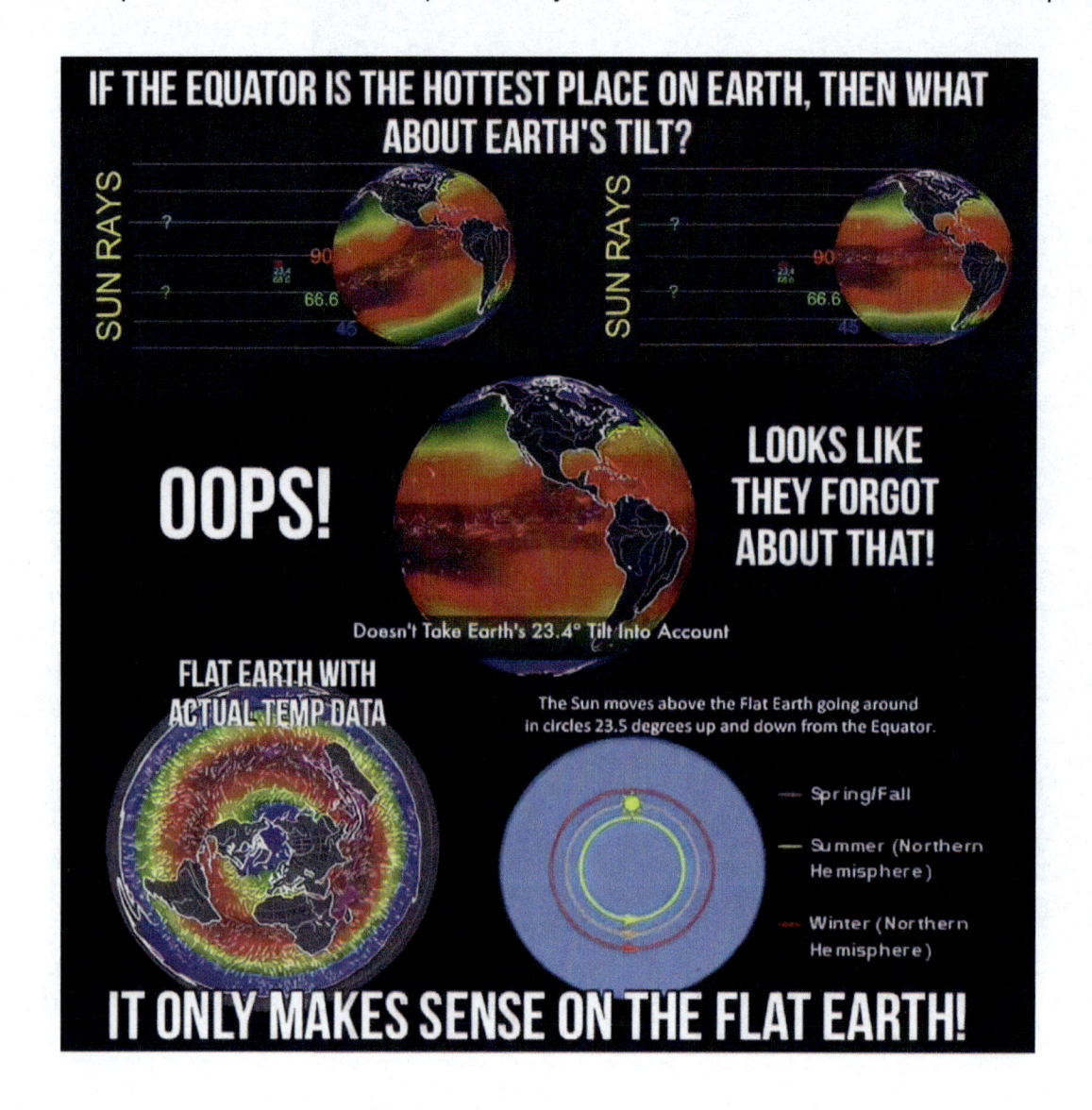

The Zetetic Method

Eric Dubay asked a great question. "How does the system of gravitation account for the seasonal variations in the lengths of days and nights if the earth rotates at a uniform speed in twenty-four hours?"

Common sense tells us that if the Earth were actually a ball spinning daily with uniform speed around the sun, there should be exactly 12 hours days and 12-hour nights everywhere all year round. The great variety in length of days and nights throughout the year all over Earth (shortest day of the year vs longest day in equinox) testifies to the fact that we do not live on a spinning ball Earth and the sun is not 93,000,000 miles away, rather smaller and local.

Observable rotations causing seasons:

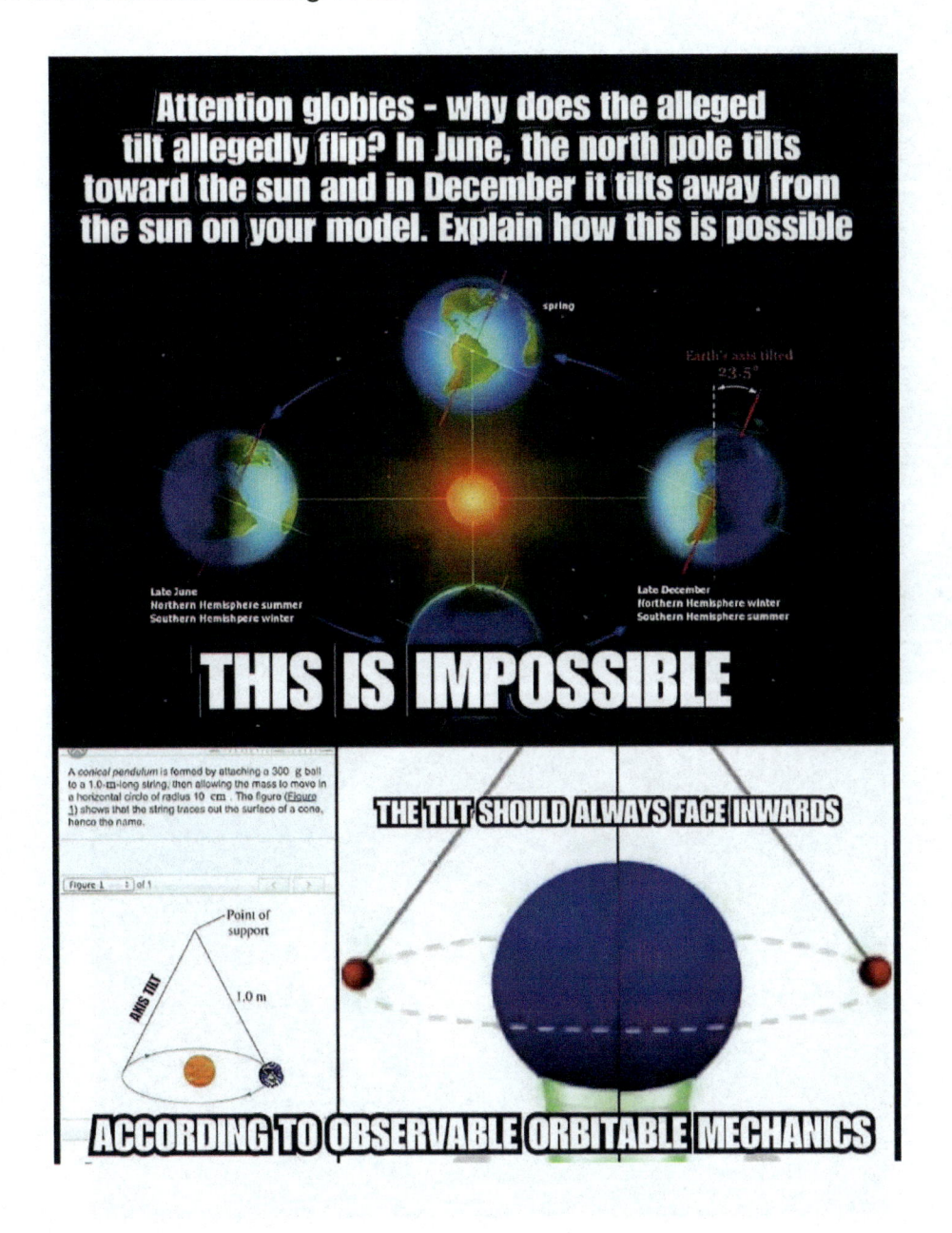

173

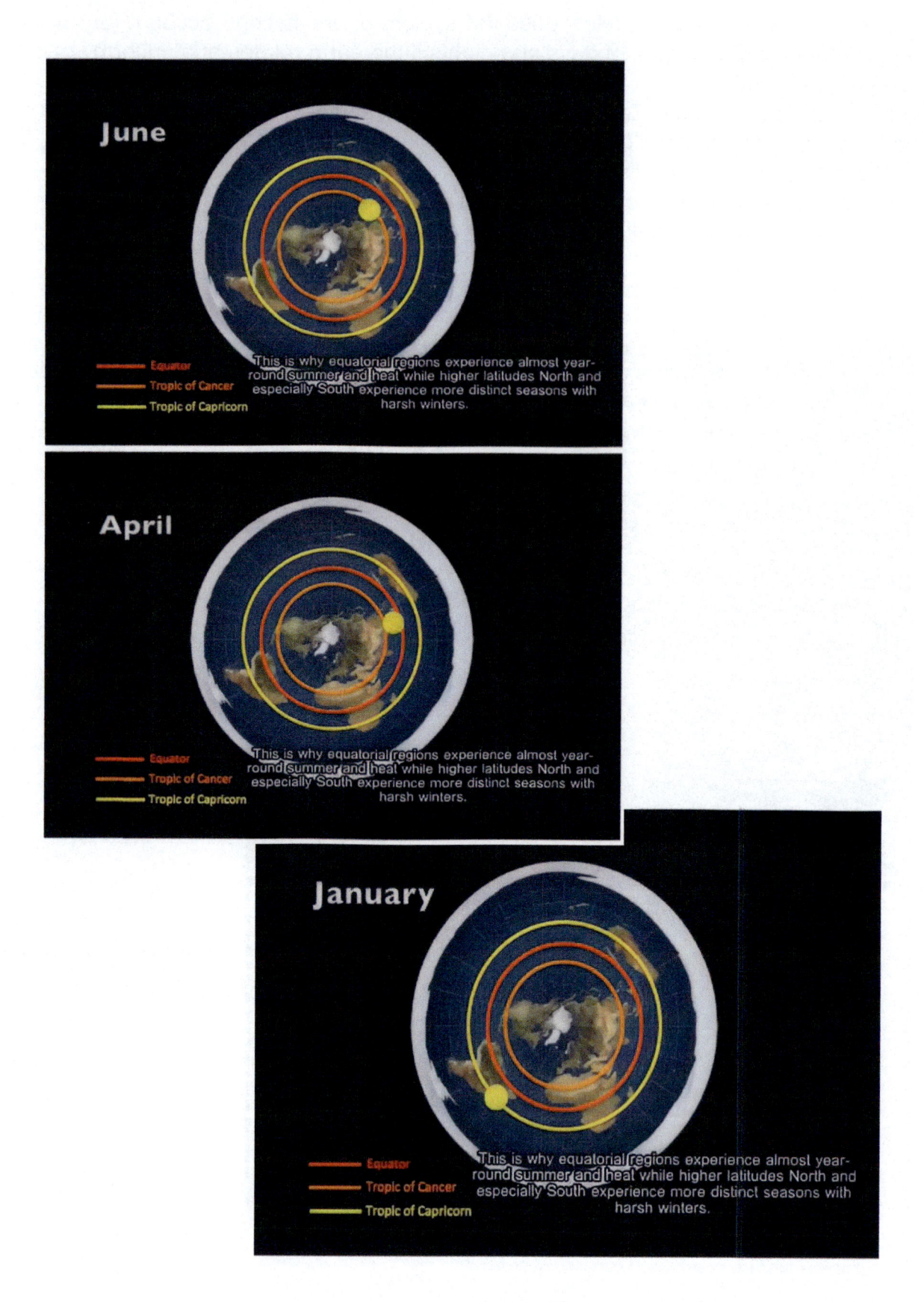

The Zetetic Method

March

Equator
Tropic of Cancer
Tropic of Capricorn

This is why equatorial regions experience almost year-round summer and heat while higher latitudes North and especially South experience more distinct seasons with harsh winters.

July

Equator
Tropic of Cancer
Tropic of Capricorn

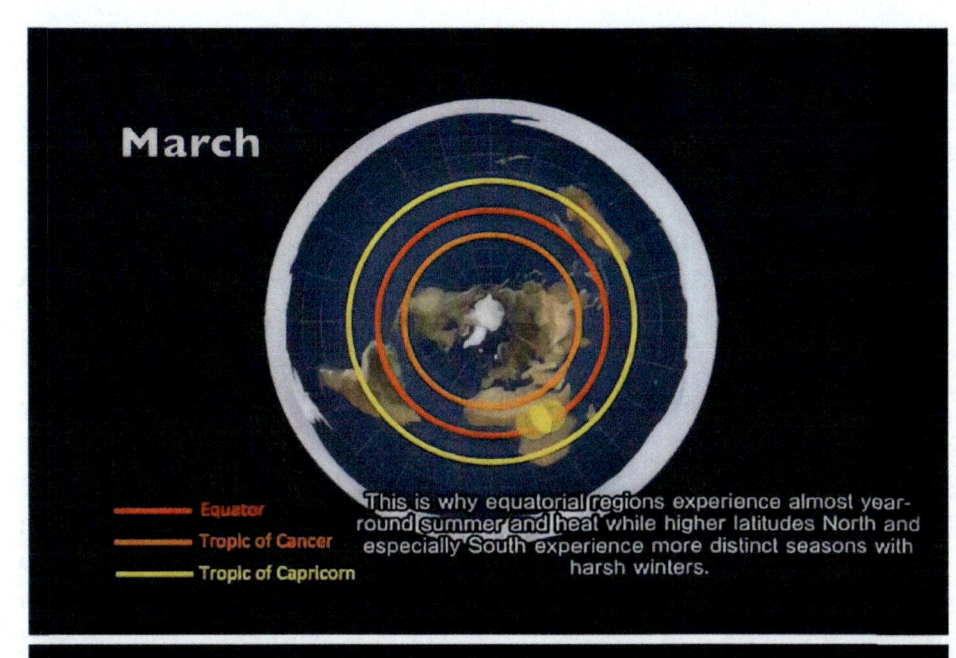

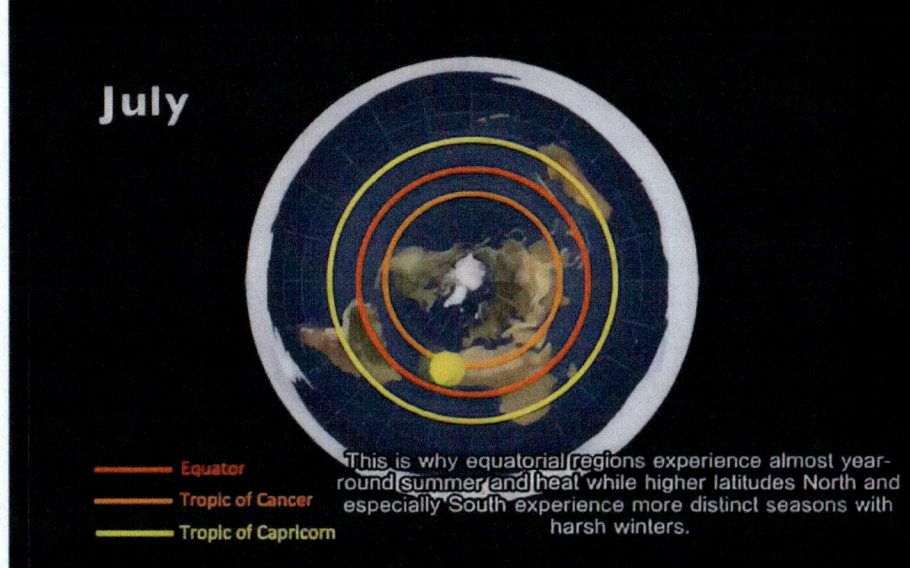

This is why equatorial regions experience almost year-round summer and heat while higher latitudes North and especially South experience more distinct seasons with harsh winters.

On the FE model, with a much closer sun, the sunlight spreads out its rays like a spot light, with the most intense heat being directly below, and less as you travel farther away. The sun is on a circuit between and on the Tropic of Capricorn and Tropic of Cancer for 365 days. This in and out movement causes the temperature change thus giving us seasons. Then you also have to include the jet streams of heat and cold. Our level Earth has so many climates which keeps our balance in this huge terrarium.

174

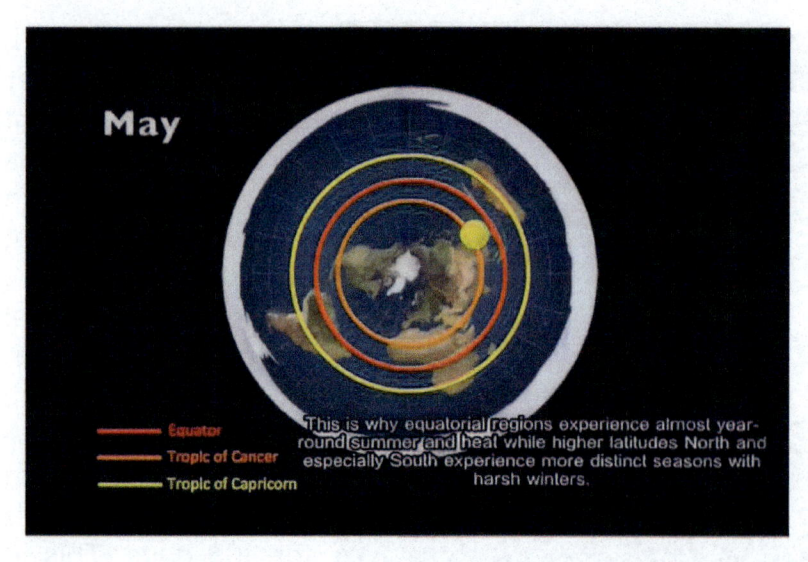

How can the equator be the warmest part of the whirling ball if the ball is tilted? The equator should be at a different location.

This statement by Thomas Winship is very much observable throughout the year, whereas there's no movement felt or sensed in any way: "The earth is a stretched-out structure, which diverges from the central north in all directions towards the south. The equator, being midway between the north center and the southern circumference, divides the course of the sun into north and south declination. The longest circle around the world which the sun makes, is when it has reached its greatest southern declination. Gradually going northwards the circle is contracted. In about three months after the southern extremity of its path has been reached, the sun makes a circle around the equator. Still pursuing a northerly course as it goes around and above the world, in another three months the greatest northern declination is reached, when the sun again begins to go towards the south. In northern latitudes, when the sun is going north, it rises earlier each day, is higher at noon and sets later; while in southern latitudes at the same time, the sun as a matter of course rises later, reaches a lesser altitude at noon and sets earlier. In northern latitudes during the southern summer, say from September to December, the sun rises later each day, is lower at noon and sets earlier; while in the south it rises earlier, reaches a higher altitude at noon, and sets later each day. The fact of the alternation of the seasons flatly contradicts the Newtonian delusion that the earth revolves in an orbit around the sun. "

The analemma

"In astronomy, an analemma, Greek for "support," is a diagram showing the deviation of the Sun from its mean motion in the sky, as viewed from a fixed location on the Earth." ~Wikipedia

Ball earthers have told me that this analemma is a proof of the globe. Is it though? When I ask how, they never have an answer. Let's have a closer look at this shall we.

Now with that in mind, think of this next picture that I'll post here and why it says what it says.

An analemma is an image that shows the changing position of the sun in the sky throughout the year. It is achieved by taking pictures from the same spot at the same time of day over 12 months. (Image: Giuseppe Donatiello)

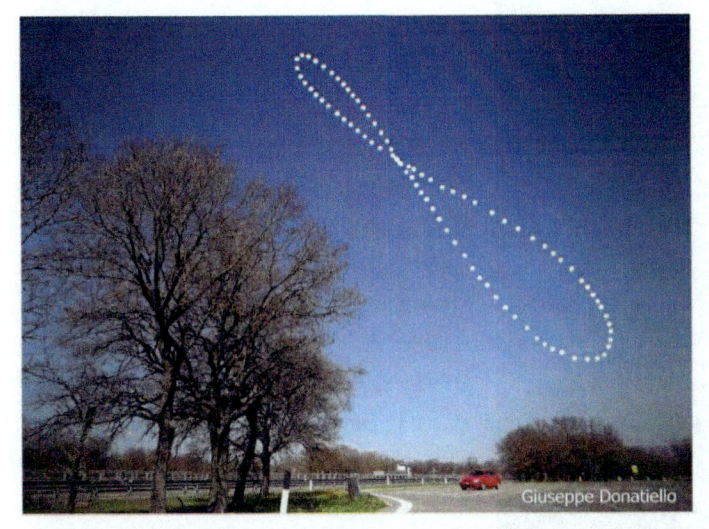

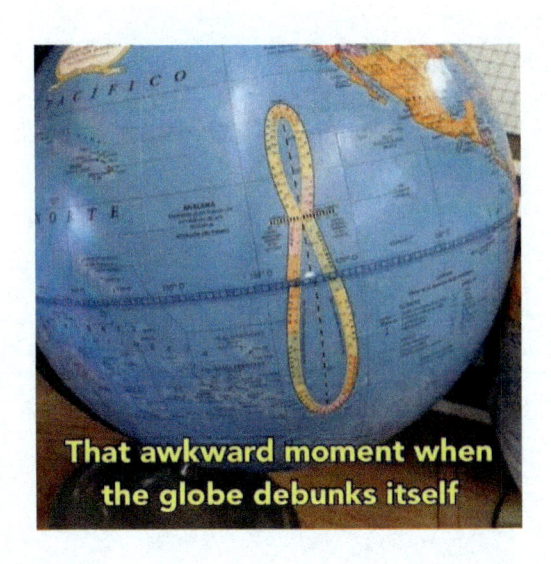

Now why would it say that the globe here debunks itself? Look at this figure 8 here, it represents the positioning of the sun at the same time all year. Now remember, during the summer in the north, the sun rotates closer to the north star Polaris and then makes its way south for the winter. This is all observable and no need for assumptions.

If the Earth were a sphere, the northern latitudes and the southern latitudes would be the same, but here it shows that the sun takes a much larger loop around the southern latitudes then the northern latitudes.

On the flat earth model, however, it makes perfect sense. Physical reality always makes more sense than unprovable assumptions. With the sun going around the southern latitudes on our provable flat earth, the sun would have a much larger distance to cover, thus a larger loop in the figure 8. The sun picks up speed causing shorter days yet still cover longer distances within the 24 hour time period.

Some say the figure eight is created by the earth's tilt. But why is the Analemma wider on the bottom and smaller on top if Earth is a round nearly uniform ball? Some say that it's caused by the elliptical, or slightly oval-shaped orbit of Earth around the sun. But observable physical reality shows that the only thing that changed positioning was the sun. If we change that amount of distance there would be star parallax and the North star Polaris would be off, but no such thing is the case, the only thing that changed positioning was the sun, just as we see it. They can't change reality, only your perception of it.

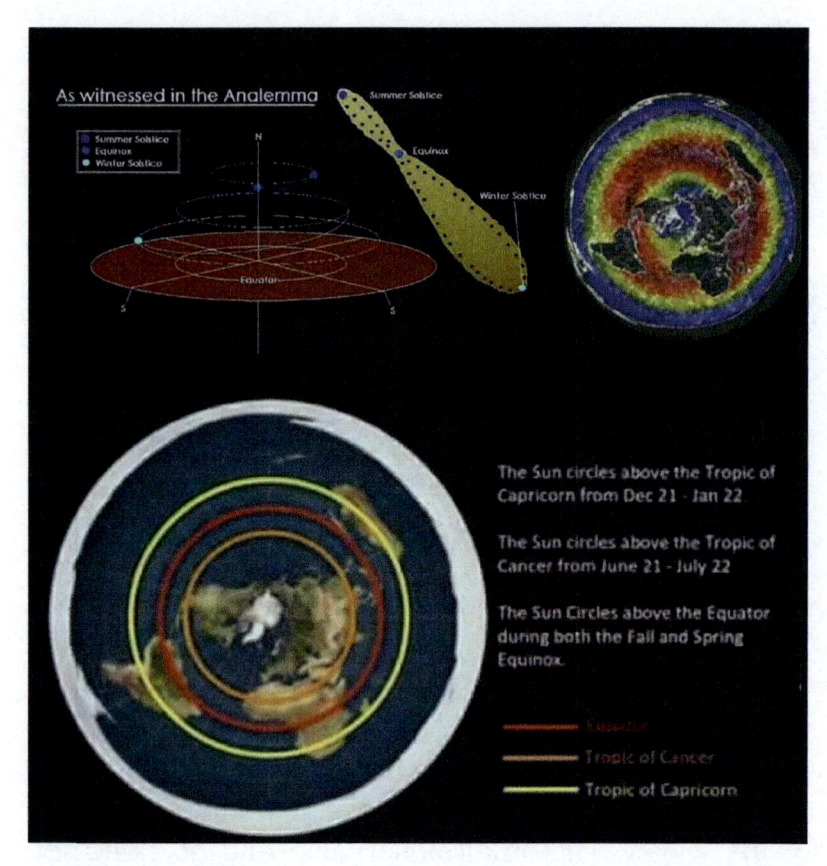

And if the earth were truly a sphere, the southern Antarctica weather would be more similar to the northern Arctic weather. But it's far from it. This, coupled with the fact that there's no movement in the north star Polaris nor star parallax, is more observable to prove the earth is a flat motionless plane. It's the sun that's moving, just as we see it. There's no need to take anyone's word for it. It's right there. Look at this picture below and picture what I'm talking about and you'll see it.

I love the way Gabrielle Henriete puts it: "It can be said, in this connection, that in the case of a science which should be based exclusively on observation and not on speculation such as astronomy, the evidence of the senses is the only factor upon which conclusions can, and must be, based. This method of investigation by means of the senses is neither primitive nor naive, as has been suggested; it is used in all existing sciences, except in occult research, where invisible phenomena are described as real, and exactly, it may be remarked, as in the case of the gravitation system. If the planets can be seen revolving round the earth, it is for the decisive factor that they do revolve in such a way. It is asserted that this is not so, and it is maintained that the earth and the planets revolve around the sun."

The Zetetic Method

Analemma proves that the Earth is Flat

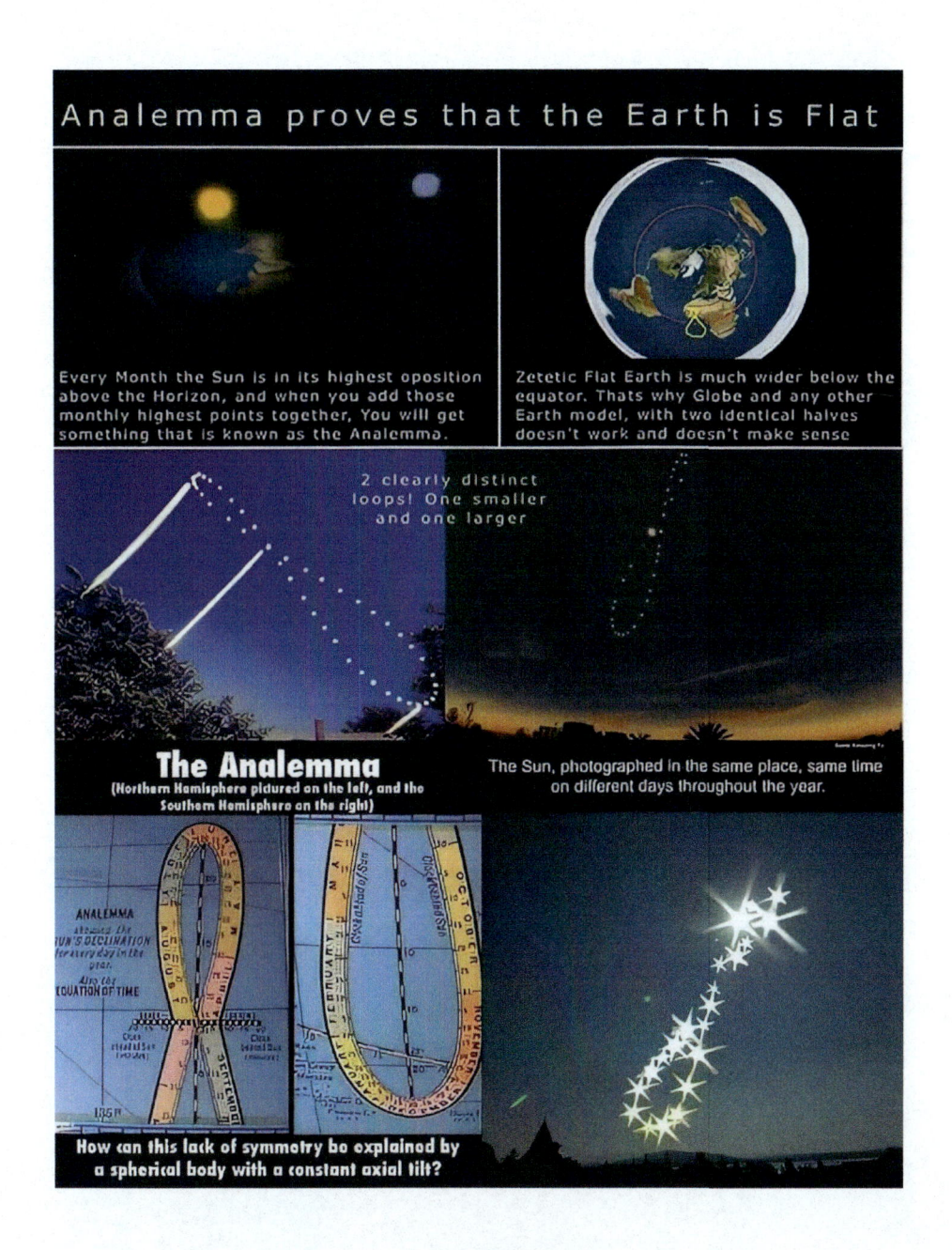

Every Month the Sun is in its highest oposition above the Horizon, and when you add those monthly highest points together, You will get something that is known as the Analemma.

Zetetic Flat Earth is much wider below the equator. Thats why Globe and any other Earth model, with two identical halves doesn't work and doesn't make sense

2 clearly distinct loops! One smaller and one larger

The Analemma
(Northern Hemisphere pictured on the left, and the Southern Hemisphere on the right)

The Sun, photographed in the same place, same time on different days throughout the year.

How can this lack of symmetry be explained by a spherical body with a constant axial tilt?

The BLACK SWAN

1) The sun acts as a smaller and local light source, not 93,000,000 miles away. Why ignore what it's doing and believe otherwise?

2) There's no North star movement nor any star parallax nor any movement felt, only the sun's observable movement, therefore there's no reason to believe we're spinning, wobbling and flying for seasons to happen. You believing so is a choice based on authoritarian claims.

The strength of flat earth is in its simplicity. You don't need to be a genius to understand reality, which is a flat motionless Earth.

CHAPTER 5
GRAVITY

"In a letter to Dr. Bentley, Feb. 25th, 1692, Newton says "That gravitation should be innate and inherent in matter, so that one body can act upon another at a distance—is to me SO GREAT AN ABSURDITY, that I believe no man who has, in philosophical matters, a competent faculty of thinking, can ever fall into it."
https:///pages/books/3537/sir-isaac-newton/four-letters-from-sir-isaac-newton-to-doctor-bentley-containing-some-arguments-in-proof-of-a-deity

To Fall or to Settle

Since we have shown, through physical reality, the earth is a stationary plane, we are able to examine Sir Isaac Newton's laws of gravitation without mental hang-ups on curvature.

Gravity, like the system of Astronomy and the whirling globe, is largely based upon claims incapable of proof. "Newton's three laws are three articles of faith." No one's questions gravity but when you seriously question it, you'll find it's not proven at all, just assumed, for the purpose of making the flying ball theory work. This "great discovery" of which astronomers are so proud is absolutely non-existent. When gravity's action is explained, it's the same as density and buoyancy with a medium.

"What Is Gravity? | NASA Space Place – NASA Science for Kids days:
"Earth's gravity comes from all its mass. All its mass makes a combined gravitational pull on all the mass in your body. That's what gives you weight. And if you were on a planet with less mass than Earth, you would weigh less than you do here."
https://spaceplace.nasa.gov

Now, with that above claim in mind, let's look at this other globe claim: It is claimed that an experiment, where a feather and a bowling ball are dropped at the same time in a vacuum, and land at the same time, proves gravity. But does it? Let's look at it shall we.

If gravity pulls by the amount of mass an object has, then how can the feather fall at the same rate as the bowling ball? The bowling ball has much more mass for the gravitational pull to affect than the feather, thus the bowling ball should land first.

Now on the flat earth model, it's density and buoyancy acting according to its medium, air. If you take away the medium, everything will settle at the same rate. Proving that nothing is being pulled according to the amount of mass it has. Otherwise, the bowling ball would fall first.

As one flat earther pointed out "Air has some resistance which affects a feather falling. All you've done is completely remove all resistance, so of course the feathers will drop to the nearest place of resistance at the same rate as anything else. Try parachuting in a vacuum and see how that works out for you."

If the bowling ball is receiving more pull because of mass, how can the feather fall at the SAME rate?

Gigazine
Will the feather fall at the same speed as the iron ball without ...
Visit

Look at this elephant swimming shamelessly naked in the lake, is the water stronger than gravity or is it simply buoyancy with nothing actually being pulled?

You can go swimming and pull a piece of floating wood and make it go under water. THAT is what happens when you actually have a pulling force working. Still think the elephant's getting pulled down?

If the Earth's gravitational pull pulls and holds the massive oceans down, then we should be crushed with such a force, how could a fish possibly swim in such a packed force? How could a butterfly flit across the field? It's simple, nothing's being pulled. There's no such force but instead a settling. No experiments have shown greater objects attracting smaller objects and/or making them orbit.

Any objects placed in denser mediums rise up while objects placed in less dense mediums sink downward.

"To fit with the heliocentric model which has no up or down, Newton instead claimed objects are attracted to large masses and fall towards the center. Not a single experiment in history, however, has shown an object massive enough to, by virtue of its mass alone, cause other smaller masses to be attracted to it as Newton claims "gravity" does with Earth, the Sun, Moon, Stars and Planets." Eric Dubay's "200 prove the Earth is not a spinning ball."

Why is science accepted as facts when the whole basis of it is theory. Why can't we question these "scientific facts," without ridicule, if they're true? What's the harm in challenging these theories constantly? People defend these claims like it's their God.

"Unfortunately what our learned astronomers advance as theories, our college and school professors teach us as facts." Dr. T. E. Reed

Universal Gravity is a theory, not a fact, regarding the natural law of attraction. This material should be approached with an open mind, studied carefully, and critically considered. The Universal Theory of Gravity is often taught in schools as a fact, when in fact it is not even a good theory.

https://ncse.ngo › gravity-its-only-th...
Gravity: It's Only a Theory | National Center for Science Education

Having a few objects attracting each other is one thing, but when there are countless millions of objects, celestial and terrestrial, all struggling to attract each other at the same time, while some are moving, is absurd and an impossibility to live in. Think of the confusion.

Sir Isaac Newton doesn't even attempt to give one proof of the truth of gravitation; with him it is only supposition and assumptions from beginning to end. If you can't prove that such a mess exists then why believe it does. Things settling to levels of density and buoyancy; observable, testable, and provable.

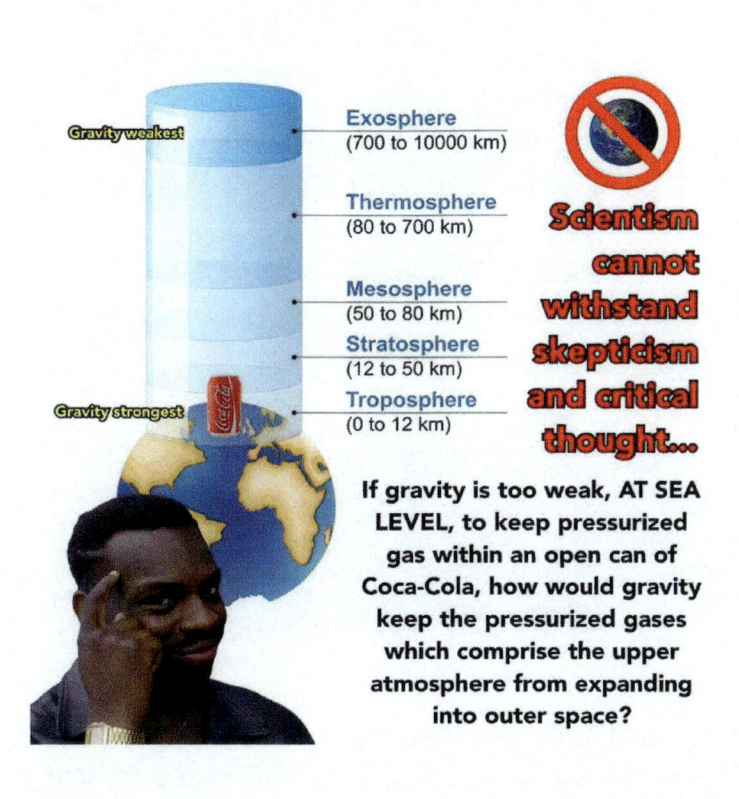

Gravity weakest — Exosphere (700 to 10000 km)
Thermosphere (80 to 700 km)
Mesosphere (50 to 80 km)
Stratosphere (12 to 50 km)
Gravity strongest — Troposphere (0 to 12 km)

Scientism cannot withstand skepticism and critical thought...

If gravity is too weak, AT SEA LEVEL, to keep pressurized gas within an open can of Coca-Cola, how would gravity keep the pressurized gases which comprise the upper atmosphere from expanding into outer space?

LAMP OIL — PING PONG BALL
RUBBING ALCOHOL
VEGETABLE OIL — SODA CAP
WATER — BEADS
DISH SOAP — CHERRY TOMATO
MILK
100% MAPLE SYRUP — DIE
CORN SYRUP — POPCORN KERNEL
HONEY — BOLT

When you question the theory of gravity deeper, they give you explanations that no one can understand much less prove, that way you rely on them to get your 'information.' This is how they cover up and conceal everything, by making it too complicated. This is on purpose; they know full well you will just believe them because they are "educated" and are in the "know."

The Zetetic Method

But flat earth is very simple, observable and you can see for yourself that it's true, IF you don't let the globe indoctrination get in your way. Listen when I tell you that the truth is always simple. But first we have to think for ourselves with a skeptical mind.

HOW DOES ONE PULL GAS

One flat earther put this nicely: "On a calm day a little fluffy cloud hangs in the sky about 3 miles high and below is a 10 ton block of concrete and they spin in sync together at 1000mph, that's not all because 50 miles above them is a helium balloon which 'gravity can't hold down and that too spins in sync with the 10 ton concrete block and the little fluffy cloud, it's truly amazing, it's magical stuff."

How can the upper atmosphere be moving with the Earth, same as the lower atmosphere, when gravity is supposedly stronger closer to the Earth? Gravity would have less effect on the upper atmosphere.

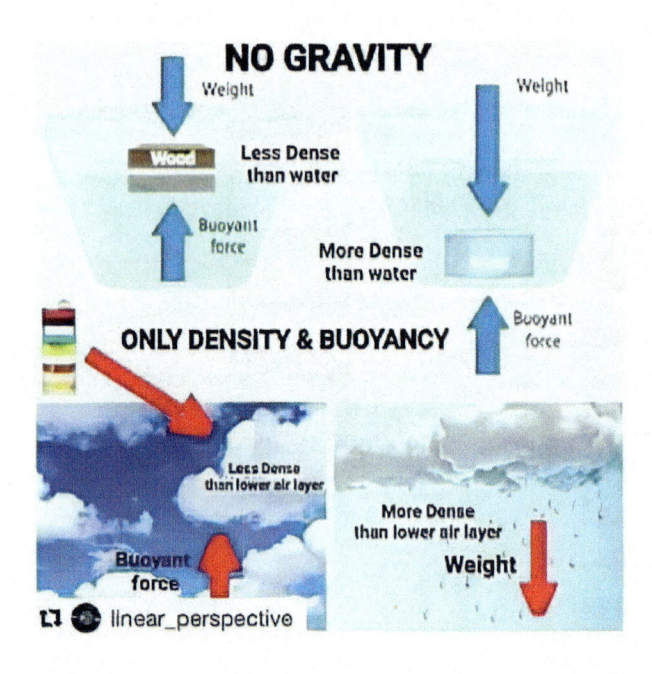

The higher you ascend on a spinning ball Earth, the faster you have to go to keep up with the lower ground. Only if physically attached to the Earth can this happen, like the tip of the hand on a clock with more distance to cover, to make its complete rotation, then the end that's nearer the center, that has a shorter distance, yet same time in rotation. The hand's tip and end are both physically connected. The atmosphere however is not physically attached to anything and moves freely about in all directions.

The sun however has an observed uniform path towards Polaris (slower with longer days) and away from Polaris (faster with shorter days) causing seasons. The sun moves as though it was moving up and down on a 24 hour hand on a giant clock that is this world. You can tell the time of month by the moon, the time of day and year by the sun and directions by the stars. We are living on a giant timepiece as our ancestors and the bible have described. Could this be the sun's "track" the book of Enoch was talking about?

Gravity does not work on millions of pounds worth of rain in the clouds? Gravity is simply a theory to explain buoyancy and density. If it was based on mass then how could gravity pull and hold gas?

This was a great point made by a flat earther I was talking to: "Without a natural phenomena to test a dependent variable, you cannot add in an independent variable to prove the hypothesis. In this case the experiment to validate that there is a force called gravity, which makes mass attract mass would depend on a natural phenomena whereby mass attracts mass. Apples falling does not mean that the mass of the apple was attracted by the earth, only that the apple was heavier than air therefore it displaced the less dense medium and fell due to having no other support. If one wants to become an expert at inventing imaginary forces, then I suggest you go to a university where they devote their time to maintaining such imaginary beliefs, from other foolish scientists in that disciplic succession of mudhas."

Exactly how massive does an object have to be before you and I can observe the object having an effect on smaller masses around it? Can you recreate it?

If this can't be answered and can't be demonstrated, then all there is is faith in the indoctrination given to us by the ruling class.

I've talked to hundreds of globe believers, and 100% of them continuously use gravity to "explain" away things they can't explain. A few examples are:
1. How does the high pressure system of Earth exists next to the low pressure system of space/vacuum; they'll say "gravity."
2. How does trillions of gallons of water stick to a ball; gravity they'll say.
3. How does a rock the quarter size of Earth float above your head; gravity once more.
4. What keeps you sticking to a ball....gravity.
5. What makes things orbit around the same ball.....gravity.
6. How does a airplane follow the curvature of Earth while it is flying at an attitude, they will tell you gravity. If the plane's engineering is making the plane overcome gravity with air lift then how is gravity causing the plane to make the curvature?
7. ....tides.....gravity.

Gravity is the claim they use to explain everything that is completely illogical and defies reality, nature and common sense; like someone standing on the bottom of a ball. And when asked to prove such a claim, they'll drop something or offer a math equation that's complicated so you'll assume it must be correct. I've had globe believers do this to me, and when I ask them to explain and prove their math, they never can. EVER! This is Scientism in a nutshell. It sounds scientific and complex but in reality, it's not scientific at all.

Without gravity the ball theory cannot exist; nor can the Big Bang Theory, etc. Gravity relies on two other unproven theories, Dark Matter and The Theory of Relatively, to exist. The black hole is yet another unproven theory that needs gravity to even entertain its silliness.

Without gravity, no one stands upside down, according to someone else's perspective, on a ball. Without gravity, the sun would have to be the one moving and not us, just as we see it. Without gravity the wobbling ball can't be lived on while spinning and flying in three different directions at unimaginable speeds.

It's the glue that keeps the globe theory together, and yet it's unprovable. All people can do is drop something and call it PROOF. Literally that's exactly what they have done many times in our conversations.

You have three theories that go off each other, and they all are needed for the Big Bang Theory to even be thought of. What a load of garbage that goes against everything that we actually observe and experience. Think about ALL of it, the whole Big Bang, etc. and ask yourself why do I believe this while I'm experiencing otherwise.

If the "Big Bang" produced hydrogen and some helium, how did the other 105 elements of the periodic table evolve? How did these elements come together, all over the universe, to make all these stars and planets and moons after being shattered about from the Big Bang? Like throwing chemicals and dust into the air and creating things.

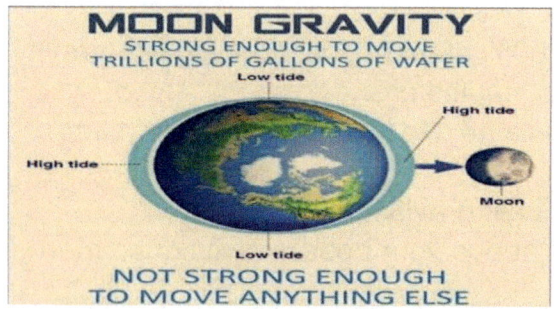

Saying that motions are produced by material attraction is absurd and demands proof. It is not in the nature of matter to attract anything but instead be passive; saying matter has such power of attraction is an illusion and requires a belief system. What tests are done to prove this theory that defies common sense?

The attraction of gravitation is said to be stronger at the surface of the earth than at a distance from it. Is it so? So the earth's gravitational pull is strong enough to hold the moon, which is further away in a circular orbit, so it won't be flung in a straight line away from us, but weak enough to let us, right here on the ground where gravity is strongest, to walk around easily enough? How kind. One would think we would be crushed by such a strong force.

The Zetetic Method

Outside the Earth there's little to no gravity, yet the moon is held by Earth's gravity; do you see anything wrong here? There's two opposite claims there. How can gravity skip over other things to get to the moon? Either there's gravity past Earth or there's not. Once again, they move the goal post to fit their claims.

Meanwhile in Australia

MEANWHILE ... AT THE EQUATOR ON THE GLOBE

TIME= a concept used for measurement
SPACE= literally nothing

You can not warp or curve nothing or a concept. Quit falling for stupid claims. Wake up!

"Yet, how can gravitation increase to hold at the backside of a tilted Earth of 23.5 degrees, yet not even be measured on the largest lakes in the world? The moon has 1/6 the gravitational pull of the Earth, yet it moves our oceans up and down, twice each day and actually changes the shape of a mass 4X greater than itself from 238,000 miles away. This is achieved despite the greater Earth's pull and the even greater gravitational pull by the Sun some 93 million miles away that locks in both the Earth and moon in his orbit." Eric Dubay

If the moon's gravitational force is powerful enough to affect earth's tides from 238,000 miles away, why is the moon's gravity not strong enough to pull all satellites and space junk out of orbit? Why not our lovely feather? (oh no wait, the feather has just as much of Earth's pull as the bowling ball, never mind) Why doesn't the Earth itself pull astronauts out of orbit? The Scientism priests' answer to this is 'it's because of the speed, 17,000mph, of the satellites'; they answered this with yet another thing that can't be proven, thus you get, once again, no solid proof, just trust in the establishment. Let's continue with this clown show.

If the sun is pulling with such power at the earth and other 'planets', and the 'planets' are orbiting at different speeds, then why don't some get pulled into the sun and some don't? If the sun has a gravitational pull much stronger than the Earth's, how come the sun doesn't pull the moon out of its orbit from around the weaker Earth?

If the sun's gravitational pull is keeping the Earth in orbit and from flying away, then how is the earth still spinning? If the equator is the outermost section, then the greatest pull would be at the equator and the Earth would eventually slow down in its spin. Like taking a string tied to a ball and swinging it. Gravity is the string.

In the gravitation theory between all the bodies in the universe, there is a connecting link which keeps the body that attracts attached to the body that is attracted. This connecting link is the string. The Earth would, at points, be spinning against the sun and other attracting forces and would eventually, sooner than later, stop.

The other theoretical attracting forces I'm talking about, that is supposedly pulling on the Earth, which would cause resistance to Earth's spin other then the sun's pull, are the moon's slight pull, the black hole's enormous pull and plus all that dark matter, that no one can see or feel or prove, causing resistance.

What about when the sun and moon are both lined up on the same side of the Earth, shouldn't that slow down the spin to an eventual stop? They seem to forget the movement of the oceans, the flowing of rivers and the changes in our atmosphere. All these are resistance as well.

Plus, as Thomas Winship, whom made me think of the spin while bringing up another point, has said: "The "ball and string" device sets forth that the "body" that attracts is not only connected with the "body" attracted, but that the former IS THE MOTIVE POWER OF THE LATTER—that the sun is the power which compels the earth to revolve round it, even as the motive power of the ball is the exertion of the hand of the operator. Without the connecting link the earth would fall (according to the astronomers) in a rectilinear path forever. But what these wise men do not see, and which is a necessary part of the theory, as represented by the ball and string idea, is that the motive power also must come from the sun. Without this motive power and the connecting link, the whole of the theory falls to pieces. THERE IS NO MOTIVE POWER IN THE SUN TO CAUSE THE EARTH TO REVOLVE AROUND IT, AND THERE IS NO CONNECTING LINK BETWEEN THE SUN AND THE EARTH TO KEEP THE LATTER IN ITS POSITION, consequently the theory of universal gravitation has no existence in fact. "He who cannot reason is a fool; he who will not reason is a bigot; he who dares not reason is a coward; but he who can and dares to reason is a MAN."

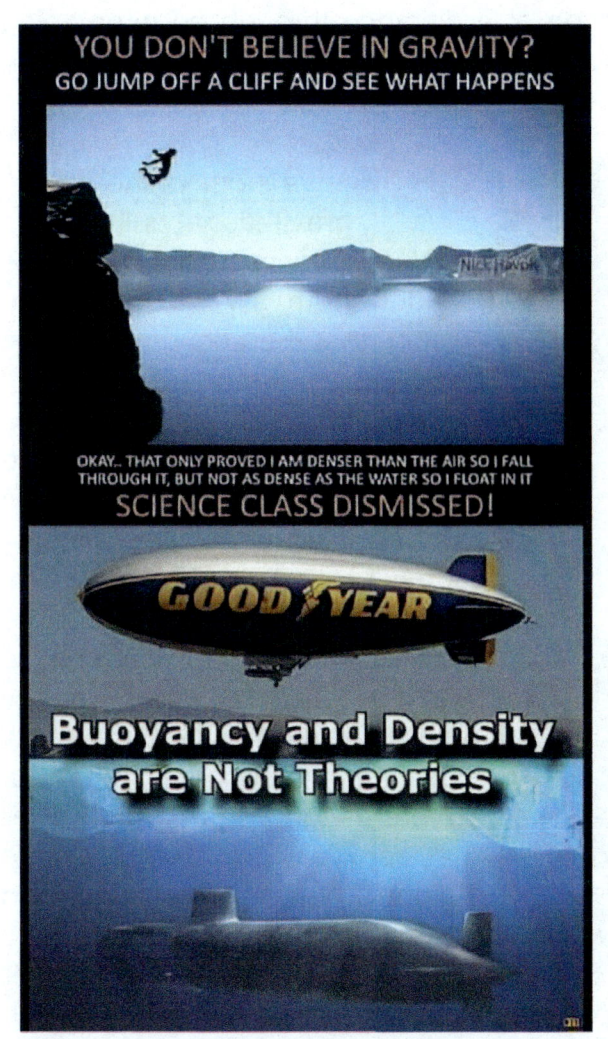

If the sun's gravitational pull retain the Earth in its orbit when nearest the sun, then when the earth arrived at its elliptical path farthest from the sun, the gravitational pull would be incapable of preventing the Earth from flying off into space in a straight line forever, unless the gravitational pull was greatly increased.

Then there's vice versa. If the sun's gravitational pull were just sufficient enough to keep the Earth in its rotation path when farthest from the sun and not rushing off into space, then the gravitational pull would be greatest when closest to the sun, unless the gravitational force is decreased, or the Earth would be pulled into the sun. Is there a counterbalancing focus to prevent such a horrible ending? It is impossible to make a ball tied to the hand with a string revolve in an elliptical path, circular motion only being possible, with no spinning.

Why believe such an utterly impossible theory when we can feel no movement and observe the sun moving around us and not the other way around? No assumptions nor faith needed. All observable. All simple.

This "universal law" of science has never been proven or observed. Eric Dubay puts it nicely: "This magnetic-like attraction of massive objects gravity is purported to have can be found nowhere in the natural world. There is no example in nature of a massive sphere or any other shaped-object which by virtue of its mass alone causes smaller objects to stick to or orbit around it! There is nothing on Earth massive enough that it can be shown to cause even a dust-bunny to stick to or orbit around it! Try spinning a wet tennis ball or any other spherical object with smaller things placed on its surface and you will find that everything falls or flies off, and nothing sticks to or orbits it. To claim the existence of a physical "law" without a single practical evidential example is hearsay, not science."

Gravity, attraction and statements like 'You're not big enough to see curvature,' or 'it's too slow to feel the spin wobble and flying.' These are claims said to explain facts when, in reality, they've explained nothing at all. There's always an excuse why we can't prove.

Even Newton himself felt doubt about attraction at a distance through an intervening vacuum. Saying it was the weak point in his system. They never mentioned THAT in school.

The vacuum vs the gravitational pull

When I was a kid the claim was made, from NASA on tell-a-vision, that the vacuum of space was the strongest vacuum known to man. Now, like the Great Wall of China being the only man made structure that can be seen in space claim, NASA doesn't say that anymore. Hmmm

If empty space creates a vacuum because all the empty space seeks to be filled then how can our atmosphere, made of layers of lighter gas and heavier gas coexist with this empty space without being in an enclosed environment?

If gravity can't stop these lighter gasses from floating up then how can they stop them in the upper atmosphere? How can gravity pull the same gasses along with the spin if it couldn't hold them to begin with? How can our atmosphere be made of layers of lighter gas and heavier gas and all spin with the Earth simultaneously?

Gravity is not dragging the clouds to the ground anymore than the atmosphere is being controlled by gravity. Nor is black smoke being pulled to the ground. It only stays within its level of density. Seems like it's density instead of gravity and in an enclosed environment. And a weather system depending on pressure and accumulation works in an enclosed environment. At what altitude does atmospheric drag start to let go of me, and how do I re-enter once I'm not locked into earth orbit anymore?

If I can create a vacuum in my weak lungs and suck water from the surface of the Earth, then how can the vacuum of space not draw in our atmosphere? Someone told me once that it does, and that's why the upper atmosphere is thinner than the lower atmosphere. This is called an assumption and it makes no sense, seeing as how the atmosphere at the top of the mountain is thinner yet I weigh the same as on the bottom of the same mountain. A pound of helium and a pound of weight are the same but one remains at its level of density in the upper atmosphere while the other at its level at the bottom. Or an anvil floating in mercury. Gasses, like liquid, separate according to its level of density. If the vacuum of space was drawing in the atmosphere at the top, it wouldn't stop at the upper atmosphere, it would go all the way to the ground. Furthermore there wouldn't be an upper atmosphere and this place would be unlivable.

Solarsystem.nasa.gov says: "Comets orbit the Sun just like planets and asteroids do, except a comet usually has a very elongated orbit. As the comet gets closer to the Sun, some of the ice starts to melt and boil off, along with particles of dust. These particles and gasses make a cloud around the nucleus, called a coma."

Actually, gravity is the weakest of the four fundamental forces. Ordered from strongest to weakest, the forces are 1) the strong nuclear force, 2) the electromagnetic force, 3) the weak nuclear force, and 4) gravity.
May 22, 2013

WT https://wtamu.edu › 2013/05/22 › w...

Why is gravity the strongest force?

Comets supposedly obey the gravitational pull of the sun yet there seems to be a singular power pulling the tail away from the sun. It seems the Comet's tail is almost always found to be streaming in an opposite direction from the sun. Is this a failure of the laws of gravitation, which is said to be universal? More unproven claims from NASA that observable reality lies rest too.

"But just imagine, if you have the bump of imagination, a great sea-earth globe-more sea than land—whizzing away one thousand times faster than an express train, and by some imaginary " stick-phast " called " Gravitation " we are lashed to this ball, like a man tied to a great flywheel. The idea is preposterous, unnatural and wicked!" LMAO! I can't remember which book I got that from.

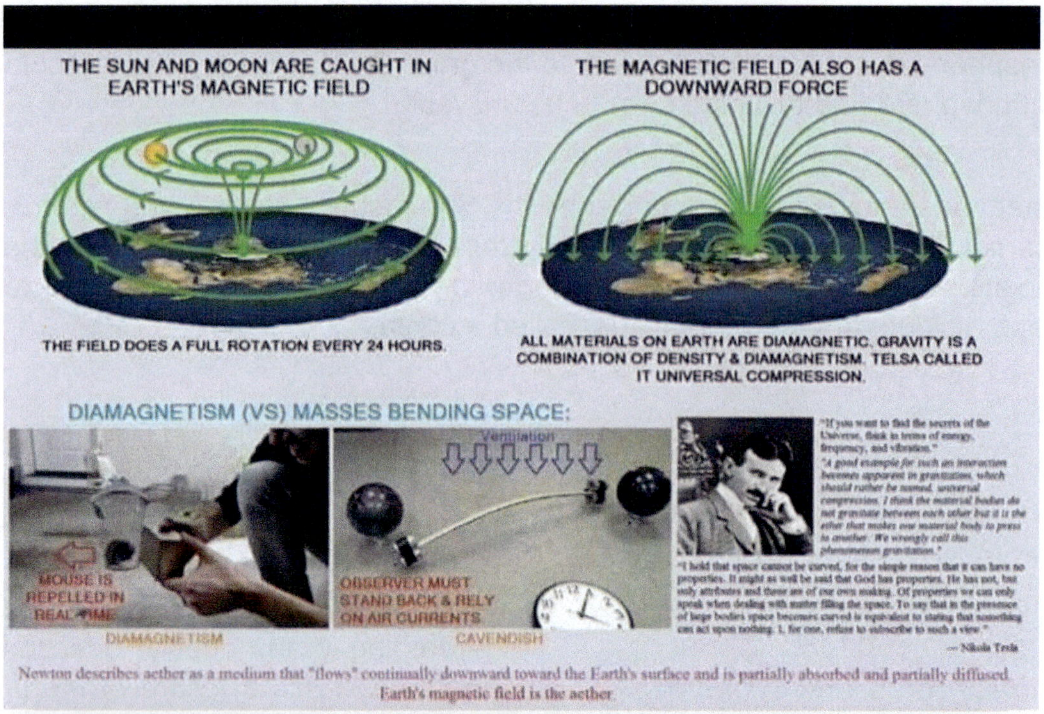

Your INABILITY to GRASP SCIENCE is not a VALID ARGUMENT against it!

How many laws and claims are they going to MAKE UP as problems arrive that debunk their theories?   Examples:
1) If the earth is a ball then people will fall off so they created the unproven law of gravity;   2) oh but then if the ball earth is spinning things will fling off and people will weigh far lesser at the equator due to centrifugal force (centrifugal force is a proven claim), so in comes centripetal force to counter the centrifugal force. If you're swinging on a merry-go-round there's centrifugal force to fling you off but no such centripetal force. You can't prove "centripetal force" is keeping centrifugal force from happening, just like you can't prove the earth is a spinning ball. If you can't prove the law then it's not a law, it's an assumption. What you CAN prove is things with more density than air will fall below air and a spinning ball has centrifugal force.
3) As author T.J. Hegland explains this one: "In typical reverse-engineered fashion, trying to explain away the midnight sun, problematic Arctic/Antarctic phenomenon, and the fact that Polaris (the North star) can be seen approximately 23.5 degrees south of the Arctic, desperate heliocentrists in the late 19th century again modified their theory to say the ball Earth actually tilts back 23.5 degrees on its vertical axis, thus explain away many problems in one swoop! If it simply tilted the same direction constantly, however, this would still not explain the phenomenon because after 6 months of supposed orbit motion around the sun, any amount of forward tilt would be perfectly opposite backward, thus negating their alleged explanation for Arctic/Antarctica irregularities."

Gravity was needed for the heliocentric globe earth model to even be considered. How else would people not feel the centrifugal force and fly off the ball? If you want people to believe they can stand on the bottom of this curve less ball then there has to be a force that holds them here. On a level stationary earth there is no centrifugal force delt because there's no movement or standing on a ball. Everything would be just as we see it is now, in reality.

The sun should rise and set at the same hours. One should think about this before stating that the Earth has a movement of uniform rotation. How does the system of gravitation account for the seasonal variations/daylight saving time, in the lengths of days and nights if the Earth rotates at a uniform speed in 24 hours and the sun is 93,000,000 miles away lighting up half the ball Earth at a time?

"If there were proof in the theory of a ball earth, then we might welcome such a law as gravitation, because we are not like flies, able to stick on to a whirling ball. It would be necessary for such a force to exist and could be proven to do so, if the earth was a ball with any axial motion. We would need gravity to stick to the bottom of the whirling wobbling ball, but somehow or other WE ALL are always on the top. People everywhere cannot be on the top too. Yet everyone appears to be on top of the whirling ball. Why? Because they are on top but on a flat motionless plane." Not sure.

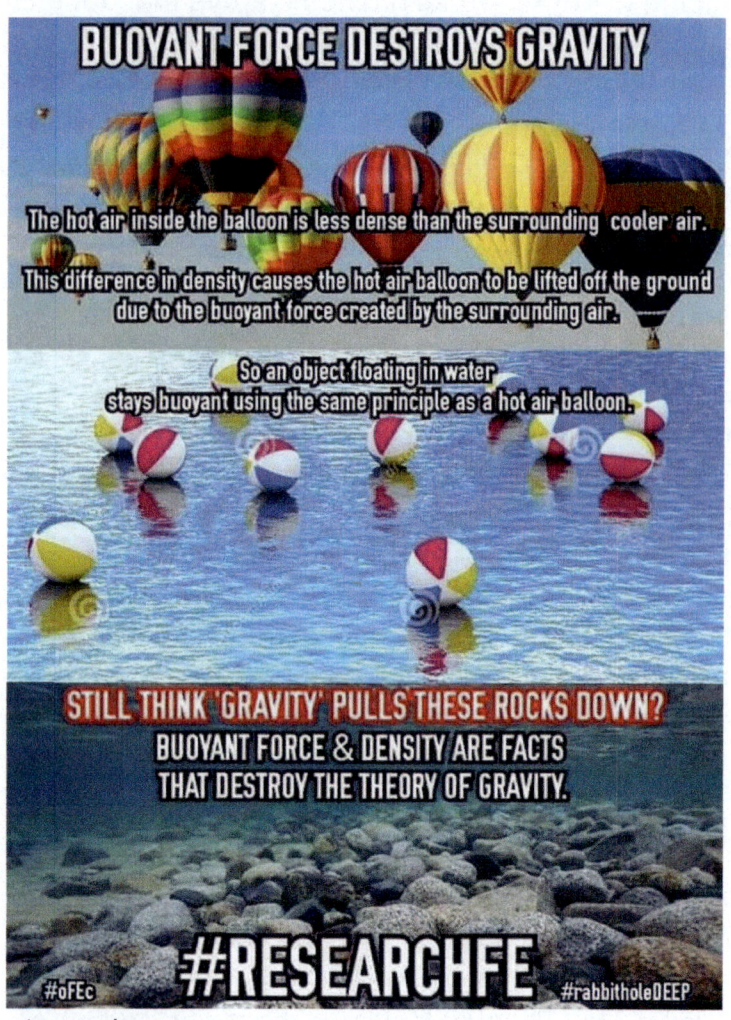

We can take a flat and level jet flight all the way across this 'ball' and somehow still believe we are curving 180° to the other side. This faith based belief is due to indoctrination, not evidence.

Is no one able to explain the actual cause and workings of this mystery? Can someone prove something definite and solid about it or are we taking gravity, like curvature, as yet another hearsay 'fact'?

We don't feel any such attraction/pull from any objects nor see any such thing. We believe because we're told so. We do, however, see objects settling according to their level of density, like different oils or different soils in a jar. No belief necessary.

Bodies by their own weight will either fall/settle or rise, until they have found their equilibrium. Newton's apple fell to the ground because it was heavier than the atmosphere.

"It may be boldly asked where can the man be found, possessing the extraordinary gifts of Newton, who could suffer himself to be deluded by such a hocus-pocus, if he had not in the first instance willfully deceived himself? Only those who know the strength of self-deception, and the extent to which it sometimes trenches on dishonesty, are in a condition to explain the conduct of Newton and of Newton's school. To support his unnatural theory Newton heaps fiction upon fiction, seeking to dazzle where he cannot convince. In whatever way or manner may have occurred this business, I must still say that I curse this modern theory of Cosmogony, and hope that perchance there may appear, in due time, some young scientist of genius, who will pick up courage enough to upset this universally disseminated delirium of lunatics. Someday someone will write a pathology of experimental physics and bring to light all those swindles which subvert our reason, beguile our judgment and, what is worse, stand in the way of any practical progress. The phenomena must be freed once and for all from their grim torture chamber of empiricism, mechanism, and dogmatism; they must be brought before the jury of man's common sense." Johann Wolfgang Von Goethe, a German Poet and Philosopher (1749-1832)

It is easy to disprove gravity as being the force that keeps us stuck to the earth, for the simple fact that air can be lifted by mechanically creating empty space. We are told that gravity prevents diffusing into empty Space. But when we create an empty space here closer to earth, the air diffuses into it. Even though gravity is supposed to be stronger closer to earth.

How is it that a constant downward force, created by the earth's mass, can pull an air molecule away from the vacuum of space at high altitude, but at earth's surface, where it's stronger, air immediately fills a vacuum and gravity is powerless to prevent it diffusing into empty space? With gravity a vacuum lift would never work, because the constant downward force of gravity would pull the air molecules away from empty space and towards earth's surface.

WHAT YOU CAN PROVE

So we have a spinning wobbling flying ball that has things rotating around it and all other "planets" spinning around a ball of gas that's spinning around a galaxy that's also spinning around a black hole that's being shot out by a Big Bang.

Out of all of that, the ONLY thing you can actually prove is that things fall. You can't measure gravity, only the rate of fall. Pretending it's being pulled by the earth does not count as proof. As physical reality shows us, nothing is being pulled but instead settles.

Astrophysicist Neil Degrasse Tyson was trying to debunk flat earth on a talk show and said "as far as gravity goes," and holds out the microphone and then drops it and walks away. The low effort thinking audience loved it and started clapping. The reason Tyson just dropped the microphone and walked away, is because that's all he truly had. But he proves absolutely nothing. I could execute the exact same tactic and say it was settling, and walked off.

So what's pulling us down you ask, nothing really. Nothing is pulling us down. Why would there have to be, answer that. Down is down, up is up. Prove me wrong. Density is all that is required to make an object fall. If the object is less dense than the air around it, it rises.

You assume that things would float away if not for gravity. But you've never seen this in nature. Who says that that is what is the nature of things? Is helium anti-gravity?

The only time you've ever seen this is when NASA showed you on their videos while they floated around on their harness. You believe the rest based on what you're told but not proven or personally experienced or seen. Ask yourself why they would wear necklaces in zero gravity. With it floating around getting tangled in things and in their faces. One such time the necklace disappeared into the astronauts' neck. Awkward!

It's for show. To aww people. And it works. But you've never seen this in nature. Ever! So you HAVE to take NASA's word for objects floating away because of the absence of gravity.

We're told that gravity is uniform world wide. If you weigh 200lbs, you'll weigh 200lbs everywhere. But if the equator is where the centrifugal force is the strongest because we're a spinning ball then how can you weigh 200lbs in Canada, away from the equator, and still weigh 200lbs at the equator? That doesn't make any sense. How can you weigh 200lbs at the North Pole?

If gravity is pulling to keep us from being flung off at the strongest point of centrifugal force, then we shouldn't weigh the same where there's no centrifugal force. And shouldn't all the water be at the equator where the centrifugal force is strongest? Reality doesn't match what we're told in the least.

When I ask for proof that objects attract other objects by way of mass, I am told that every mass has a pull but the earth's pull overwhelms smaller objects on earth because earth is so big compared, so that's why you're not pulled to the wall when you walk by one. The only time I've been pulled to the wall was when I was drunk.

But when you ask for an experiment proving gravity, then they'll do the Cavendish experiment to try and prove gravity. How???? How, if earth's pull makes other objects pull obsolete? How can the two objects attract each other? This is a contradiction. You can't have both.

The Zetetic Method

Seems more similar to attraction created by a static charge. How can mass, in and of itself, possibly create a pulling effect? Electro magnetism can, though, and is easily observed and replicated on any scale.

When I first started researching flat earth, I went on YouTube and was looking at cavendish experiments to try and find proof of the theory of gravity. I got a compressed extremely long video, originally it was 13 hours, of two objects just sitting there on a pivot. The whole point of the experiment was to prove that objects attract each other thus proving gravity. At the end of the video the objects finally started moving towards each other and then bounced off each other and stopped. Hmmm odd. LMAO

The globe-believers in the comment section were even making fun of it. I asked in the comment section "Why did it take so long and then bounce and stop? And why don't they attract each other on the ISS videos? One would think they would stick to the walls. Where's the centrifugal force on the ISS and the supposed attraction?" I got two notifications of likes and then my comment was gone. Try the experiment yourself. It doesn't happen in reality. Too much fraud in people's experiments. They don't care about the truth, they just want to look like they're "right."

A flat earther was talking with a glober and I copied this comment from him. Worth thinking about in my opinion: "Gravity is nothing more than density and buoyancy reacting to its medium (air/water/helium) in an electromagnetic environment. Gravity and magnetism are one of the same, like steam and ice are both hydrogen monoxide, only the coherence is different. Gravity is a spell that substitutes itself for electromagnetism. The whole ecosystem is electric Positive/negative. Everything has electromagnetic properties. Electromagnetism can be witnessed on a quantum level right down to protons electrons and atoms which are all bound by magnetism.

Gravity on the other hand is Non detectable on a quantum level let alone in the world we experience. And gravity is a poorly constructed substitute for covering up electromagnetics."

How can the moon maintain its speed and circular rotation around the earth, when its rotation puts it between the sun and earth. The sun's gravitational pull is much stronger than earth's and the moon's, so wouldn't the sun pull the moon out of its circular rotation or at least affect the speed?

If the earth's gravitational pull is so strong it can hold the moon and satellites in their orbit then how can things float around on NASA's videos? Hmmm

Can anyone prove massive objects attract other objects? If a theory is unobservable and can't be proven, then it should be disregarded. This should not be a faith based belief.

In order for gravity to be proven you have to prove it's there and to do that you have to show what happens when it's not there. And you simply can't. You have to take the word of someone who has already lied to you. Which is what you're doing.

"Gravity is completely different from the other forces described by the standard model. When you do some calculations about small gravitational interactions, you get stupid answers. The math simply doesn't work." Mark Jackson, Theoretical Physicist

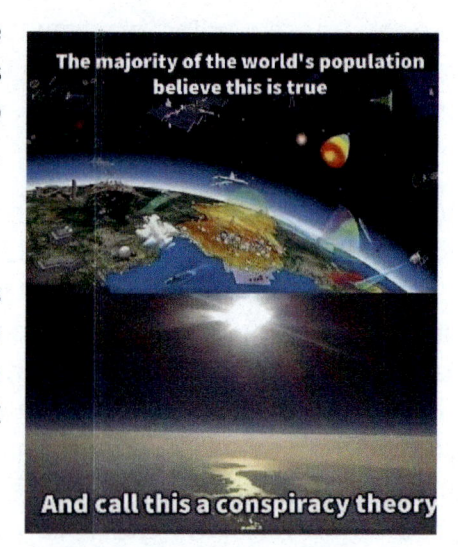

Dear Theoretical Gravity
1. How does an inanimate object, earth, execute the action of pulling? And why?
2. At what point are we weightless as we ascend? Is it gradually or suddenly?
3. If the gravitational pull is strongest towards earth's core then would I weigh more if I hiked down into a cave?
4. Do I weigh less on a plane than in my living room?
5. So the bigger the object the more powerful the pull? So if I created an object too big it would start to pull things? How? What gives the mass this power? What is the pulling tackle?
6. If the plane's engineering is making the plane "overcome" gravity with lift, then how is gravity causing the plane to make the curvature?
7. How can the atmosphere, which is made up of gasses with different levels of density, spin with the earth at the same rate? The higher altitude gasses have a lower density yet they have to spin faster to keep up with the lower atmosphere and ground of the ball earth, but gravity has a weaker hold on it.

""Ah!" say our Astronomers, "you must not trust your own senses, but believe what our system demands!""

Things settle in nature according to its level of density and buoyancy. There's no proof of any downward pull whatsoever. I can't prove things are being pulled down but I can prove that they're not.

If you pull a helium balloon it will come down because it's being pulled, but if you stop pulling it, it will continue on its journey to find its level of density amongst the surrounding gasses, showing that it was never being pulled in the first place, til I pulled it.

Can anyone show me an experiment where a constant force picks and chooses only the larger objects and not the lesser density smaller ones? To pull the larger and not the smaller is absurd and does not fit reality. If the mass of the Earth causes a gravitational pull that can pull the oceans and hold them, then it should also do the same for a helium balloon, but IT DOESN'T, because nothing is being pulled by any force. Everything seeks its level of density and buoyancy. There is an up and there is a down in nature. Simple, observable and provable.

So Sir Isaac Newton eventually concluded, from an apple falling to the ground by its own proper weight, that atoms millions of miles apart, stars and all other celestial lights can pull each other without tackle but by merely "Natural Law." What is the theory based on exactly, things falling? Lights rotating around the North star?

Our ruling class scientists say that the universal law affirms that everybody in the universe attracts every other body, with a force which varies inversely as the square of the distance. If this is so, I would like to know what is the nature of the pulling tackle. Is it solid, liquid or gaseous? Can no one tell what gravitation is? The only thing they know and can measure is the rate of fall.

From the proceedings of the Royal Institution of Great Britain,1895. C. Vernon Boys, F.R.S., A.R.S.M., M.R.I., in his paper, "The Newtonian Constant of Gravitation," says "It is a mysterious power which NO MAN CAN EXPLAIN. OF ITS PROPAGATION THROUGH SPACE ALL MEN ARE IGNORANT."

This is an honest and authoritative confession of Astronomical ignorance of their theories' position.

Professor W. B. Carpenter, in his paper published in Modern Review, 1890 (This is before the government took over science financially and making it authoritarian 'must believe') "Nature and Law," says " We have no proof, and in the nature of things can never get one, of the ASSUMPTION of the attractive force exerted by the earth, or by any of the bodies of the solar system, upon other bodies at a distance. . . . The doctrine of universal gravitation then is A PURE ASSUMPTION."

When Michael Morley, a fellow scientist who set out to prove the earth was rotating, actually proved it was the stars that rotated and not earth. So Einstein then came up with the theory of special relativity to explain away the experiment. A mathematical equation built on assumptions to explain away an actual experiment. How is this science?

"Einstein's relatively work is a magnificent mathematical garb which fascinates, dazzles and makes people blind to the underlying errors. The theory is like a beggar clothed in purple in whom ignorant people take for a king...it's exponents are brilliant men but they are metaphysicists rather than scientists." Nikola Tesla

If gravity is mass attracting mass then how can Jupiter's magical gravity be, supposedly, 2.5x stronger than that of earth? IT'S MADE OF GAS! How about a 'black hole?' (If you believe in that whack job of a theory)

When you question the theory of gravity it falls apart. Just like everything else in the globe theory. People need to start questioning the theory and question the "answers" they'll give you.

Strong enough to hold oceans but gentle enough to allow the fish to swim unchallenged by the packed water, all while a butterfly flies its flight. Sounds like things aren't getting pulled down but settling down to its level of density. The proof is in the actions of reality.

How can gravity make things stick to earth while others then orbit around it? Has this been proven or recreated or just believed?

If we can not prove that mass or gas or the nothingness of a blackhole, can attract/pull anything without any chain, rope or magnetic attraction or any pulling tackle whatsoever between two objects, then why do we believe that this is happening? What physical based evidence are we going off of? A microphone dropping?

In the words of Sir R. Ball, "The law of gravitation, THE GREATEST DISCOVERY that science has yet witnessed."

Scientism says "The law of gravitation announces that everybody in the universe attracts every other body with a force which varies inversely with the square of the distance." The same group of Pseudo-scientists say "Gravitation is the force which keeps the planets in their orbits."

Neither of these contradicting statements can be recreated. The theory is ridiculous and can not be proven. And I understand why. How can we ever have real proof of the assumption of 'the attractive force exerted by the earth or any of the 'bodies' of the solar system upon other bodies at a distance?' How can you test or prove that bodies, light years away, or any great distance for that matter, are attracting anything or what's it even made of? From a telescope? Negative.

If it's a universal law then its existence should be easy to prove. The idea of universal attraction is hearsay and based on nothing, it is an absurd theory foisted upon the non-questioning masses. The doctrine of universal gravitation is a pure assumption and the proof is that the physical reality around us is showing otherwise.

There is zero proof of this attraction whatsoever. This false science fooled all of us into believing the opposite of what is natural and true. Newton won his fame, and the people lost their senses.

"Mortals, like moths, are often caught by glare, And folly wins success where Seraphs might despair."

"If the law of gravitation ever failed to be true, even to the smallest extent, for that period, the calculations of the Astronomer have no application." Professor T.H. Huxley in "Science and Culture."

"Let Reason, Fact, and Learning die, But spare us Newton's grand Astronomy."
(Not sure where I got two of those quotes)

This is an insert from the Encyclopedia Britannica on gravity. A contradiction and unscientific statement: "gravity, also called gravitation, in mechanics, the universal force of attraction acting between all matter. It is by far the weakest known force in nature and thus plays no role in determining the internal properties of everyday matter. On the other hand, through its long reach and universal action, it controls the trajectories of bodies in the solar system and elsewhere in the universe and the structures and evolution of stars, galaxies, and the whole cosmos."

Gravity supposedly brings things down to Earth yet makes things orbit Earth yet keeps celestial bodies in their place and keeps them from falling into each other while keeping them from drifting apart. All of this is unprovable, unobservable and plain ole silly; yet it's told as a scientific fact. One has to use their imagination and desire to believe it. And believing in this requires FAITH!

'Gravity' doesn't curve the horizon line does it. 'Gravity' doesn't make all this land and water, with all its mountains and lakes and oceans with all its stock, spin, wobble and fly around does it? NO it does not! There's no proof, only belief in such claims. No curvature, no ball, thus no need for gravity.

The BLACK SWAN

It's easy to prove objects and gasses settle according to their density and buoyancy, but you can't prove that objects with any kind of mass attract another object of mass. All

The Zetetic Method

you can prove is that things fall. You also can't prove that things float away when gravity is not there. I challenge you to do so.

Can you prove or demonstrate an object executing the action of pulling another object by way of using its own mass? Can you show an experiment in which one object orbits the main object while the main object pulls another object to it keeping it still? Can you prove in any way that the main object is orbiting yet another object with zero effect on the other orbiting object? If not then I rest my case.

CHAPTER 6
THE FIRMAMENT

"Here is a fish swimming around comfortably and (he thinks) unobtrusively, flicking here and there amongst the kelp and the plankton. Draw away for the long view and there's the kicker: It's a goldfish bowl." Stephen King

THE FIRMAMENT OR OPEN SPACE

The astronomers say that the planets keep moving, and that a whole system does not run down because space is empty, and there is absolutely nothing to stop the moving bodies, no friction. Astronomers say this in their claims until something else requires explanation, then they tell a different story. They say there's space dust and debris. They tell of millions of tons of meteoric dust and meteors that fall from space to this earth, every year. A story of an absolute vacancy that is enormously occupied. Something that is so, except when it isn't so. LMAO

Why do they not include this in their mathematical calculations?

Astronomers and their indoctrinated victims repeat the claim that the atmosphere moves with the earth because there's no resistance in space. But this is a contradiction to the globular theory because the wobbling spinning flying ball theory has all kinds of resistance happening. Like I mentioned in the chapter of gravity, there's the sun's theorical pull, the moon's theoretical pull, the black hole's theorical pull, the ether and all that Dark Matter that people are pretending is hanging around.

A high altitude kite experiment was done at Boston from the Blue Hill Observatory, it was the highest a kite has ever reached. A height of 10,016 feet above sea level. The wind was blowing from the west at 5000 feet while at the ground it was blowing from the south.

If the earth is a spinning ball, then everything within the atmosphere would be subject to this movement, however, you have winds closest to the earth blowing in all kinds of different directions at different places sometimes the opposite of the supposed spin and sometimes with it (even though it's closer to the earth's core, which, supposedly, has a stronger pull) In the mid-atmosphere the same and the upper atmosphere, once again the same.

How could there be two different directions of wind at a distance of only 5000 feet if the spinning theory was close to being true? The earth's spin itself would cause some friction. If you spin a top and the rotation of the top causes the air within its sphere of rotation to go all one way. Earth being at rest should come to mind here.

The Zetetic Method

If these gravitational pulls have an effect on earth then it should also have effect on earth's atmosphere. But instead earth's atmosphere is moving in all different directions and speeds simultaneously all across this great plane of ours. The upper atmosphere is moving in all different directions all across the world and so is the lower atmosphere. (I repeat myself a lot in this book, did you notice? And I mean to.)

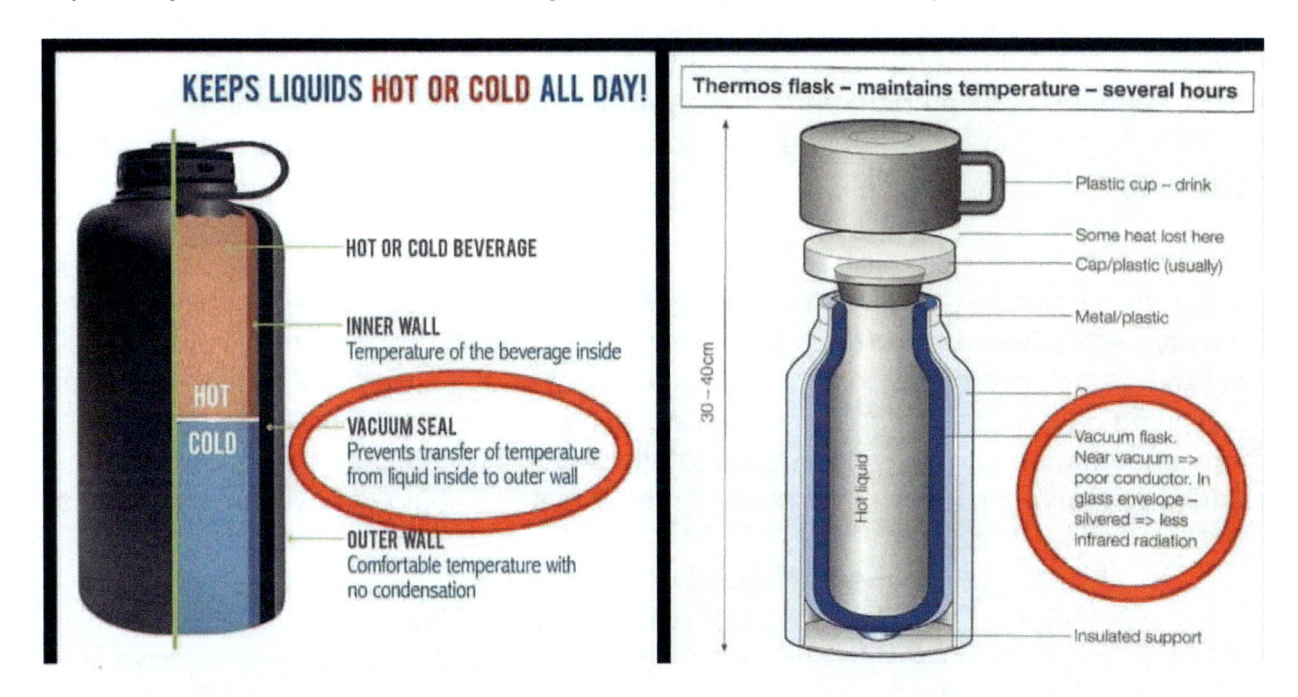

Some people misrepresent the flat earth model, sometimes on purpose and sometimes due to ignorance of the subject or simply to make fun of it. Example would be a teacher telling kids that "you can sail around the earth because it's a globe. If the earth were flat you'd sail right off the edge." And the kids laugh. 20 years later, they're still laughing.

I have people that are arguing with me about flat earth, telling me that I need to go back to fifth grade. That's THEIR problem right there, they're thinking like they did in fifth grade. They're regurgitating hearsay and expecting a "good job" said to them, but instead I'm correcting them. They've been taught to do this since kindergarten, to repeat, repeat, repeat.

The government funded scientists tell us that the atmosphere is moving along, by way of gravity, with the Earth which is said to be spinning at 1000 mph and wobbling and flying.

When asked about this, these so-called government appointed 'scientists' compare a moving train or car with earth, this is ridiculous and very unscientific. Let's have a look at it shall we. I've mentioned this before but hang in there with me please. We live in an enclosed greenhouse, and to expose this we really need to think about absurdities of the globe earth claims.

The Zetetic Method

The claim is that "we don't feel earth movement because the atmosphere and everything on it is moving with the Earth, like traveling in a car or train, you don't feel the movement because you're traveling with the vehicle."

But the vehicle is not only traveling in a straight line motion instead of a circular motion like I mentioned before, but also the atmosphere IN the vehicle needs a solid barrier to move with the vehicle, a barrier which Earth is said not to have. Physical reality shows the atmosphere ON the earth is not bound to the Earth, therefore would not travel with the Earth. It moves in all different directions simultaneously, at different speeds. So comparing the Earth with a straight line vehicle is unscientific and exposes the non-thinking puppet scientists.

Sometimes the upper clouds are moving in a different direction and speed than the lower clouds. It's like they're moving on their own accord over a stationary enclosed earth.

If gravity can't stop a light breeze then how can it stop the wind from blowing off this ball? I have yet to see any demonstration, experiment or any solid proof that we are living on a spinning ball, with spinning air and water, with no centrifugal force.

There's nothing about reality that says the atmosphere is clinging to a spinning ball. If you think you can prove it does then contact me on Flatearthlogic.net. Would love to hear it.

AIR PRESSURE AND GAS
GRADIENT IN OUR ATMOSPHERE

We live in a greenhouse. Greenhouses have to be enclosed. Can you prove that greenhouses do not need to be enclosed and can survive the openness of SPACE?

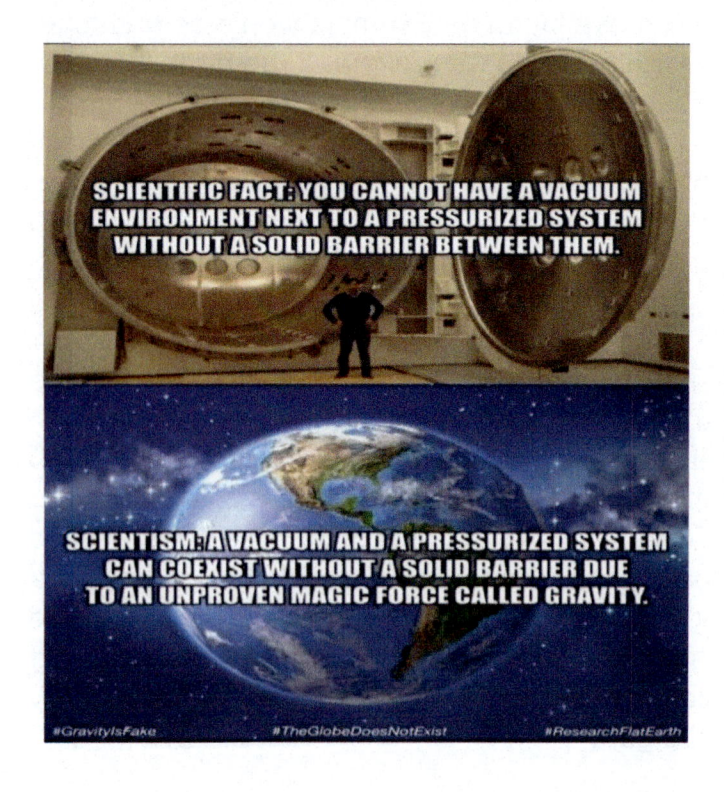

"Facts do not cease to exist because they are ignored."

-Aldous Huxley

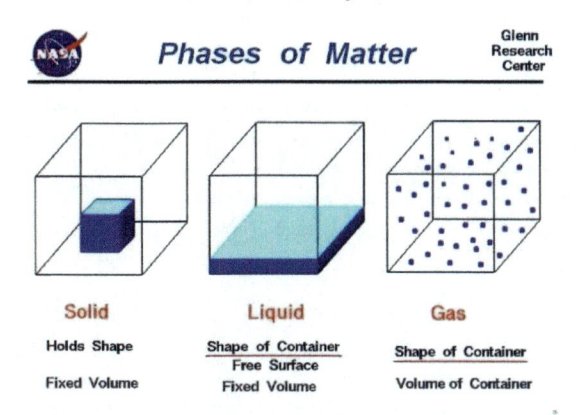

People have said to me that the upper atmosphere, being thinner with less pressure then the lower atmosphere, is proof of the globe model because the vacuum of space pulls the gas out which means no firmament. Let's have a look at that shall we.

If this was the case then why would the vacuum stop there, why not go to the ground? High density gasses settle to the bottom thus pushing lower density gasses upwards; this causes your pressure gradient, not the vacuum of space. Elementary dear Watson.

The gas with less density than air rises above air so atmospheric pressure is thinner the higher you go. The more dense gasses settle at the bottom, like propane, which makes it more dangerous, thus the pressure in the lower atmosphere is greater.

To prove this go climb a mountain and see how much harder it is to breathe. All of this creates a pressure gradient. If the more density gasses are held more by gravity then the lesser density gasses then how can gravity account for all the gasses spinning with the Earth together? How can the wind have less mass and keep up with the spin?

Like oils in a jar, the gasses separate according to density levels, creating a gradient. And, like oils in a jar, they need a container to do so.

Like I said before, NASA once claimed that the vacuum of space was stronger then any vacuum a man could make; they have been called on this BS, and have sense quit claiming this and now claiming that the vacuum isn't actually a vacuum at all. LMAO

If you can take a plunger and create a vacuum and pick up a small table then the 'vacuum' of space should do away with our atmosphere. But no such thing exists because there is no 'space', or at least not like what we're told.

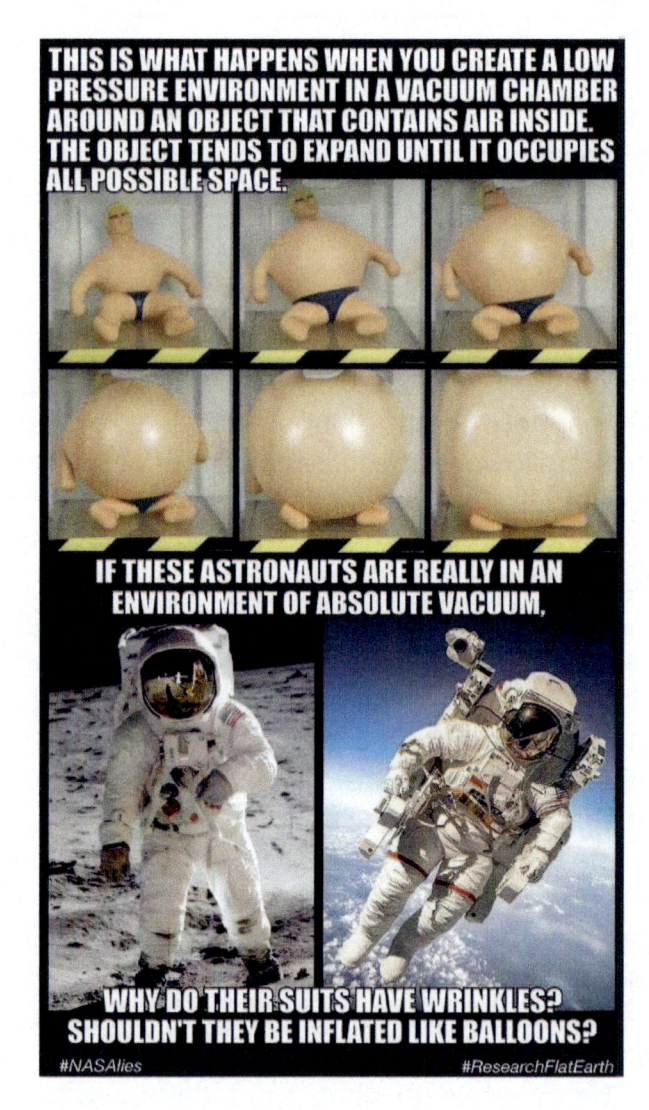

The Zetetic Method

Scientists claim the atmospheric pressure on Earth is around 14.7 pounds-per-square inch or 14psi. A vacuum of space has zero psi. How do we magically go from 14 psi to 0 psi is unexplained by physicists?

We live in a giant ecosystem. A big green house with a pressurized environment. It MUST be enclosed for the greenhouse to work. We have a weather system depending on pressure and accumulation. We have layers of gasses light to heavy that keep the earth habitable, it needs to be enclosed.

Does thunder ever sound like it's echoing? I believe so, but off what? It's a legit question. If it was the atmosphere then everything would be echoing. When you bang two pans together or shout, it would echo right back to you in this more dense atmosphere that you're standing in right now. But the thunder is in a less dense atmosphere yet it echoes and your sounds do not. A cave echo's because it's surrounded by a solid barrier.

Let's look at the gegenschein, caused by the close proximity of the sun, is a round patch of light in the sky. It seems to be reflected sunlight, at night, because it keeps position about the opposite of the sun. But reflected sunlight off what exactly? Look at the gegenschein, it has no parallax. And if it was dust that was reflecting the sunlight it would change as you move your position, but it does not.

Tesla and Mosley supposedly 'proved' the existence of an ether (firmament maybe?). If the earth were rotating then the lower atmosphere would rotate with the earth, being the closest to the earth thus having the most gravitational pull, however the upper atmosphere, with less gravity effect, would gain friction from the ether, and thus have an opposite motion or slower one. The upper atmosphere moving opposite of the lower atmosphere would cause an upset in the mid-atmosphere.

But as luck would have it, none of this is happening in the least. The entire atmosphere is moving in all directions simultaneously, at different speeds, some not at all, caused by winds and temperature pressures; there are increases and decreases. Once again physical reality is destroying false claims everywhere. We must pay attention and the truth will reveal itself.

Why don't the winds and upper atmosphere follow the laws of inertia? If gravity doesn't have that good of hold on the upper atmospheric gas, such as helium, then why doesn't it keep going straight as the ball spins, or go off into the vacuum of space?

I've had people tell me the Ham radio was a proof of the globe. When I question how, they tell me the Ham radio bounces off the upper atmosphere and bounces till it gets to the other side of the whirling ball. This is ridiculous and holds no logic. Why would the signal go through the more dense lower atmosphere just to bounce off the thinner upper atmosphere? Why would it not bounce off the wind or the lower atmosphere? Has all logic left the world? The denser atmosphere=no problem, the thinner less dense atmosphere=annnnd it bounces. LMAO

Wouldn't it make more sense that the signal bounces off the firmament and spreads out to all the antennas that were designed for the device? The Ham radio also uses towers and satellite balloons.

Gegenschein

Gegenschein is a faintly bright spot in the night sky centered at the antisolar point. The backscatter of sunlight by interplanetary dust causes this optical phenomenon, also called counterglow.

W More at Wikipedia

W https://en.wikipedia.org › wiki › Gegenschein

Gegenschein - Wikipedia

Gegenschein is distinguished from zodiacal light by its high angle of reflection of the incident sunlight on the dust particles. It forms a slightly brighter elliptical spot directly opposite the Sun within the dimmer band of zodiacal light. The intensity of the **gegenschein** is relatively enhanced because each dust particle is seen at full phase.

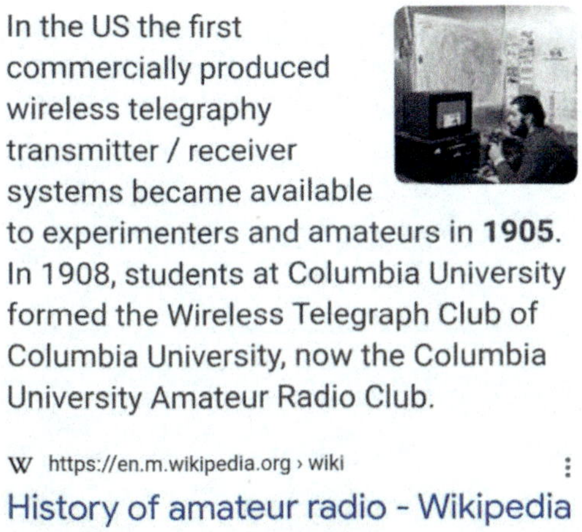

The Zetetic Method

In the US the first commercially produced wireless telegraphy transmitter / receiver systems became available to experimenters and amateurs in **1905**. In 1908, students at Columbia University formed the Wireless Telegraph Club of Columbia University, now the Columbia University Amateur Radio Club.

W https://en.m.wikipedia.org › wiki
History of amateur radio - Wikipedia

If earth is spinning faster than the speed of sound and wobbling and flying unimaginable speeds, then WHY does physical based reality, show us living on a stationary greenhouse? How could our atmosphere possibly not be affected by all of this. Is there no solid physical proof of a spinning wobbling flying open ball? Acceptance is not knowledge.

"Only the existence of a field of force can account for the motions of the bodies as observed, and its assumption dispenses with space curvature. All literature on this subject is futile and destined to oblivion. So are all attempts to explain the workings of the universe without recognizing the existence of the ether and the indispensable function it plays in the phenomena." Nikola Tesla

The Black Swan

The fact that you can't have a greenhouse and a pressurized system without a container and the fact that we see the same stars revolving around at the same speed tells me they're connected. Prove me wrong, otherwise these observable facts are a black swan.

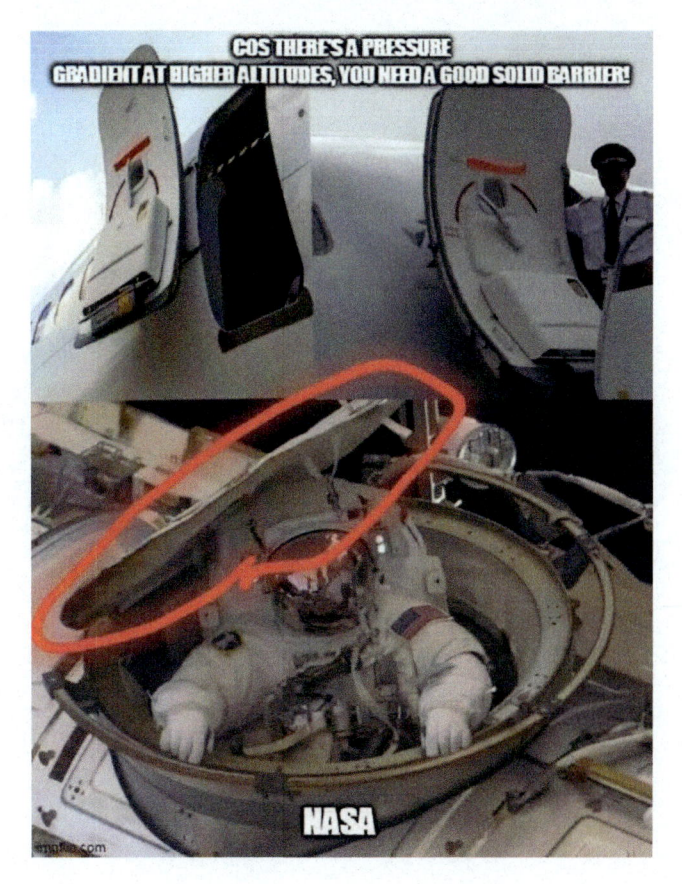

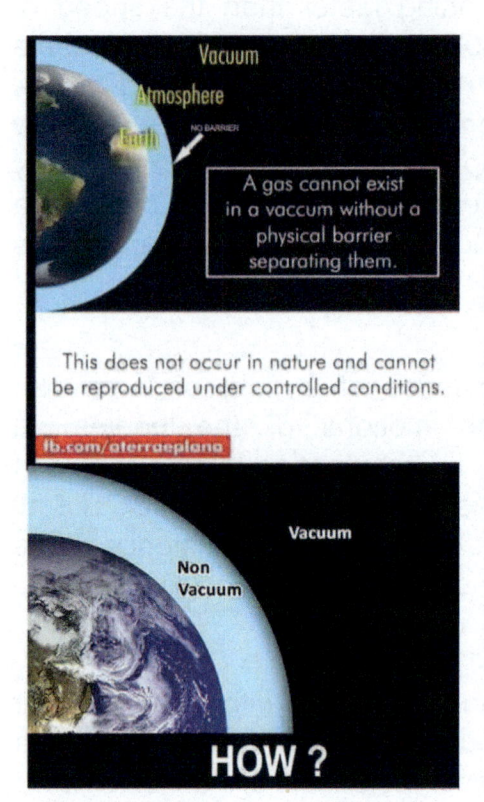

Vacuum / Atmosphere / Earth — NO BARRIER

A gas cannot exist in a vaccum without a physical barrier separating them.

This does not occur in nature and cannot be reproduced under controlled conditions.

fb.com/aterraeplana

Vacuum / Non Vacuum

HOW ?

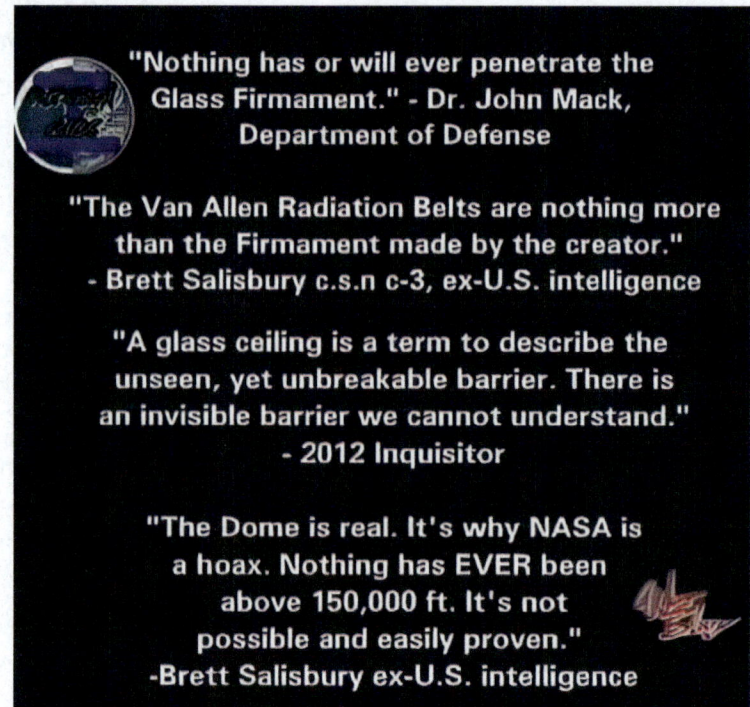

"Nothing has or will ever penetrate the Glass Firmament." - Dr. John Mack, Department of Defense

"The Van Allen Radiation Belts are nothing more than the Firmament made by the creator."
- Brett Salisbury c.s.n c-3, ex-U.S. intelligence

"A glass ceiling is a term to describe the unseen, yet unbreakable barrier. There is an invisible barrier we cannot understand."
- 2012 Inquisitor

"The Dome is real. It's why NASA is a hoax. Nothing has EVER been above 150,000 ft. It's not possible and easily proven."
-Brett Salisbury ex-U.S. intelligence

CHAPTER 7

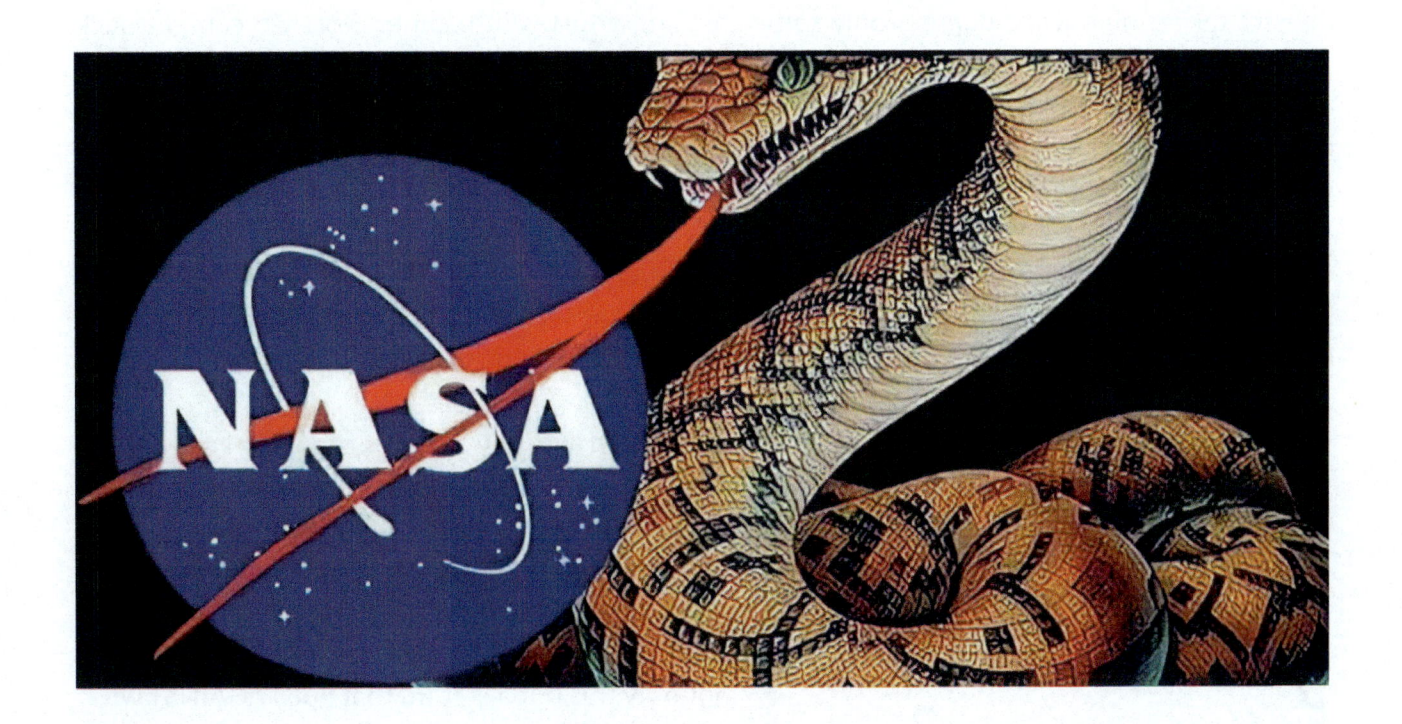

The Zetetic Method

"For the scientist who has lived by his faith in the power of reason, the story ends like a bad dream. He has scaled the mountain of ignorance; he is about to conquer the highest peak; as he pulls himself over the final rock, he is greeted by a band of theologians who have been sitting there for centuries." Robert Jastrow-Founding director NASA

"The high priests of scientism need no proof of their claims because they are smarter than you." Author Isaac Walker (I'm taking this out of context to use the phrase, Isaac Walter goes on to debunk the said high priests in his book)

LET'S GET THAT OL BRAIN ON THE RIGHT TRACK

If you live with this mindset, that scientists are smarter than you, then you will assume that you don't understand what they're saying because you're not intelligent enough and therefore it MUST be true. In reality, however, what they are saying has nothing to do with reality and thus is absurd, which is probably why you can't understand it. But with this mindset of "you're not intelligent enough", they will have you believing ANYTHING they want you to.

Anybody in good mental health, educated (or what passes as educated), rich, poor, homeless, etc., can figure out reality. It doesn't take a high IQ or degree, only some thinking effort. With some effort we can get back what we've lost, which is knowledge of where we live and, possibly, who we really are.

Someone once said to me that because the government lies to you doesn't mean scientists will. First of all, doctors, judges, lawyers, scientists, politicians, etc. etc. can be bought. Second, NASA'S website is NASA.GOV. Hello!!!

What's happening now, in this world, is hypothetical science is having a run-in with the truth. Like Thomas Winship said, "Its relation to truth is as darkness to light. Science has as much chance in a collision with TRUTH as a rotten ship would have in a collision with an ice clad."

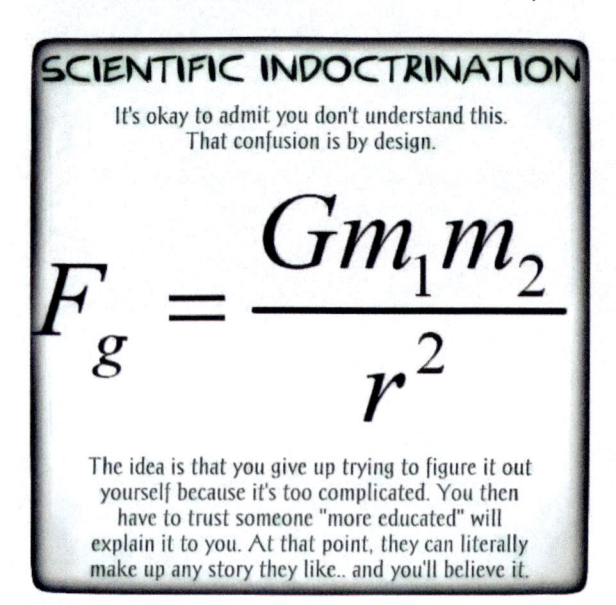

SCIENTIFIC INDOCTRINATION

It's okay to admit you don't understand this. That confusion is by design.

$$F_g = \frac{Gm_1m_2}{r^2}$$

The idea is that you give up trying to figure it out yourself because it's too complicated. You then have to trust someone "more educated" will explain it to you. At that point, they can literally make up any story they like.. and you'll believe it.

How can we rely on a "system of knowledge" that's built upon assumptions? Wouldn't that make it a system of self-proclaimed truth, instead of facts? We are taught a counterfeit system that requires us to believe in what has never been confirmed by observation or experiments. And not only this but a system that goes AGAINST what we observe and can prove.

If people do not understand the ridiculousness of these impossible theories that's being smeared in their ears, they cannot help and will assume it's for more educated men to deal with these things; and thus hand all power of thinking and investigating over to the 'authorities' who wanted it in the first place. If the kid doesn't question the magicians, he'll grow up ignorant, thinking 'these people are marvelous,' and never know they're just con-artists who have gained control of your beliefs.

TRUST

"But when it comes to institutional lying, as in propaganda, people are rendered defenseless by their own blind trust. The trust people place in the propagandists and the filtered reality it presents is largely a product of habit, tradition, and naivety." Can't remember.

The idea here, in this chapter, is to expose chinks in the globe-believers armour that is NASA, by exposing NASA for the liars and deceivers they are. To let globe-believers know that going to NASA for your 'proof' does not help create a valid argument, but instead, shows their lack of self-proving. Take them off what they assume to be an intellectual high ground. NASA has no merits.

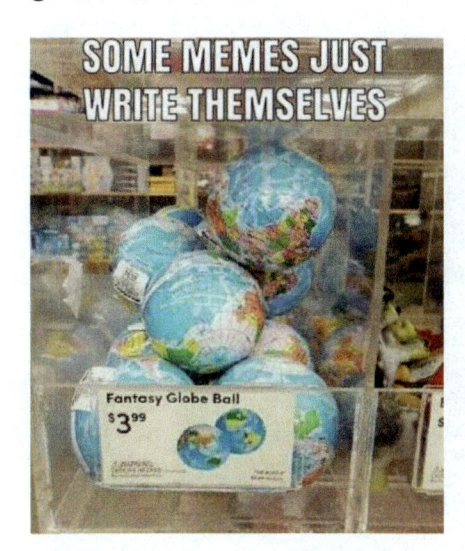

Most of what people believe today comes from government sponsored science fiction movies presented as news. These inconsistencies, that people have accepted into their minds, have been unchallenged for the most part. But now flat earthers are challenging it. My object is to expose these and allow people to experience the cognitive dissonance which comes with having a delusion shattered. By using logic, reasoning and common sense to question the theories and the answers that are given, you will not be easily fooled. We will see if NASA's credibility is ruined when their "work" is questioned with the Zetetic method.

"When you control opinion, as corporate America controls opinions in the United States by owning the media, you can make the masses believe almost anything you want, and guide them as you please."   Gore Vidal

Things That Make You Go Hmmm

People constantly show me NASA's videos as proof of the whirling ball Earth. I can't share videos in book form, otherwise I'd show you. These screenshots I took of the videos don't do them justice. But let's go ahead and talk about them shall we. Here's 18 things that make you go hmmm:

The Zetetic Method

1. Where is the centrifugal force on the ISS videos? A bullet goes around 1700 mph and the ISS goes 17,000mph in a circular motion. Circular motion creates constant acceleration. Whatever is moving wants to continue forward but instead is forced in circles, causing constant acceleration. There should be some hella centrifugal force.

2) How did one astronaut almost fall when flipping?
3) One astronaut's arm disappeared before he "floated" into another room.
4) One object appeared out of thin air for the astronaut to grab. For some reason she kept looking forward. Why would you do that? Why not pay attention to what you're doing?

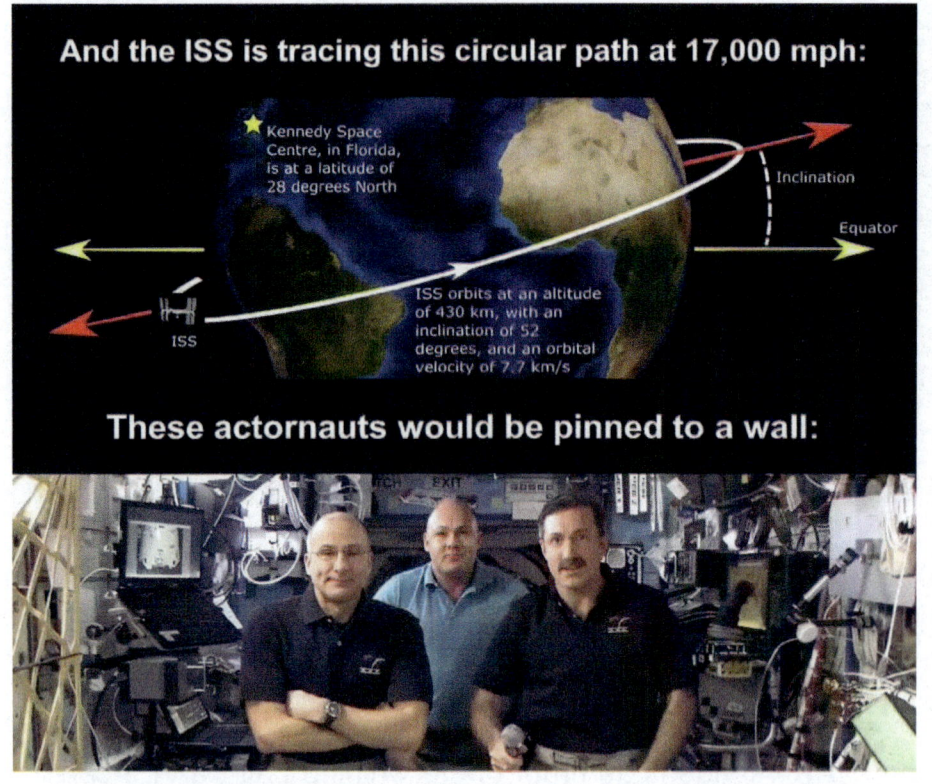

5) And as one flat earth comment I read said: "Yet not one report ever of any astronaut ever being hit, much less killed by any of the millions of space debris, nor even more than minor damage to any of the thousands of satellites said to be in continual orbit over the decades. (According to NASA, they have a tracking system that allows for 'Debris Avoidance Maneuvers' called D.A.M.")
6) One astronaut dropped a screw.
7) One astronaut dropped something but caught it quickly. Then turned away awkwardly.

215

The Zetetic Method

8) Twice an astronaut's necklace disappears into his neck. Furthermore, why would you wear a necklace with all that horrible wiring done on the ISS? Accident waiting to happen.
9) Another astronaut, in a live ISS phone interview, accidentally said where they were.
10) One astronaut almost drowned.
11) Neil deGrasse Tyson says the earth is more pear shaped yet NASA keeps showing perfect spheres.
12) And my personal favorite. There are six videos with moths flying around in the background. Space moth I presume. We have the right to know about these alien moths. How about some disclosure on those space moth NASA?
13) One astronaut seen in the background with his harness not photo shopped out. Opps! Another astronaut grabs his invisible harness to steady himself after flipping.
14) One astronaut was grabbing stuff that was "floating" around and grabbing something that wasn't there and put "it" away. It seems the computer graphic guy forgot to add something.
15) One astronaut's head goes magically through the wall. OUCH!

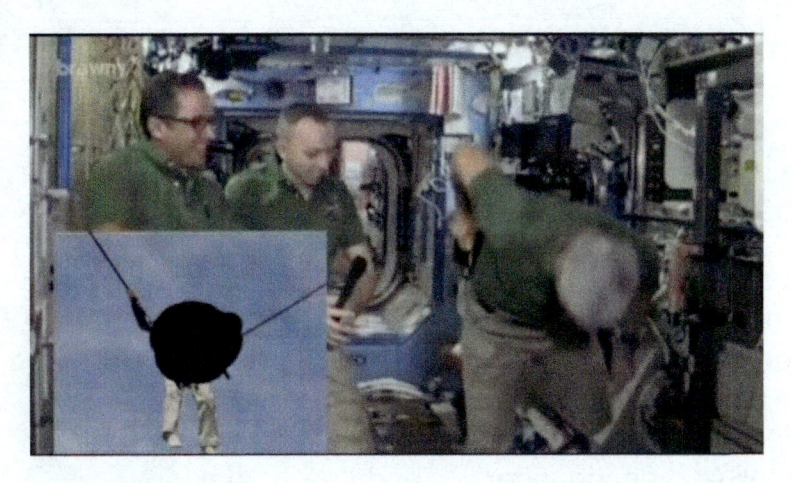

This teddy bear appears out of nowhere, and oddly enough, instead of looking at it she keeps looking at something in front of her. Every now and then she glances at it.

The Zetetic Method

NASA'S post production artist forgot to add what this astronaut was supposed to grab and put away. So he was left empty handed. BUSTED!

16) Something was floating behind the astronaut, then the camera cut to a close up of something the astronaut was talking about, then back to the regular view, when it came back the other object was sitting on a table. Hmmm

17) One astronaut grabs another astronaut's invisible harness.

18) The astronauts were playing a game with the condiments at their lunch table, catching them as they floated away. The computer graphic guy forgot about the ketchup all of a sudden and it stayed put.

19) BONUS 19: George Bush senior visits NASA headquarters and in the background, you can see them faking a video. The astronaut is in front of the blue screen playing with a green ball. On the next screen however, he's on the ISS and that green ball is now a floating ball of water.

Some things that make you go hmmm indeed.

217

The Zetetic Method

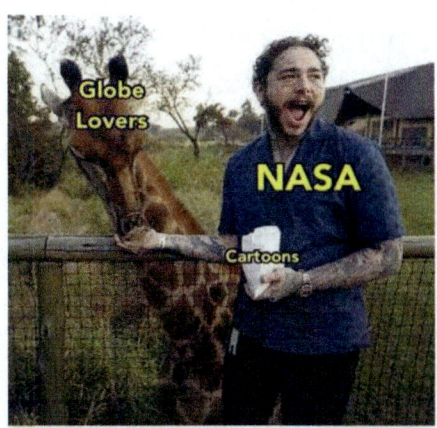

"There are two ways to be fooled. One is to believe what isn't true,. The other is to refuse to believe what is true."
Philosopher and Scholar Soren Kierkegaard

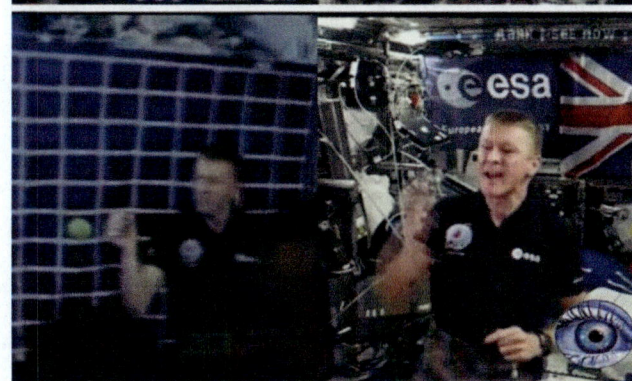

Is he pulling on a invisible harness or getting fresh with that astronaut.

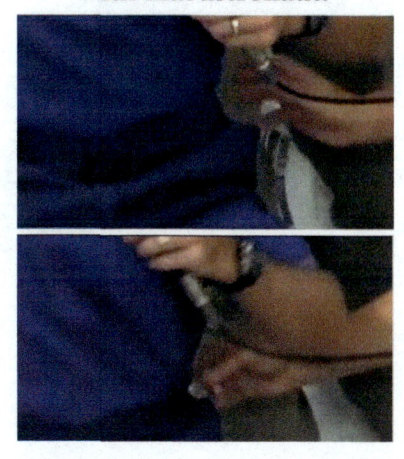

THAT AFTER MOON LANDING GLOW
Look at these astronauts after the moon landing. What do they look like to you? Doesn't look like someone who just made history do they?

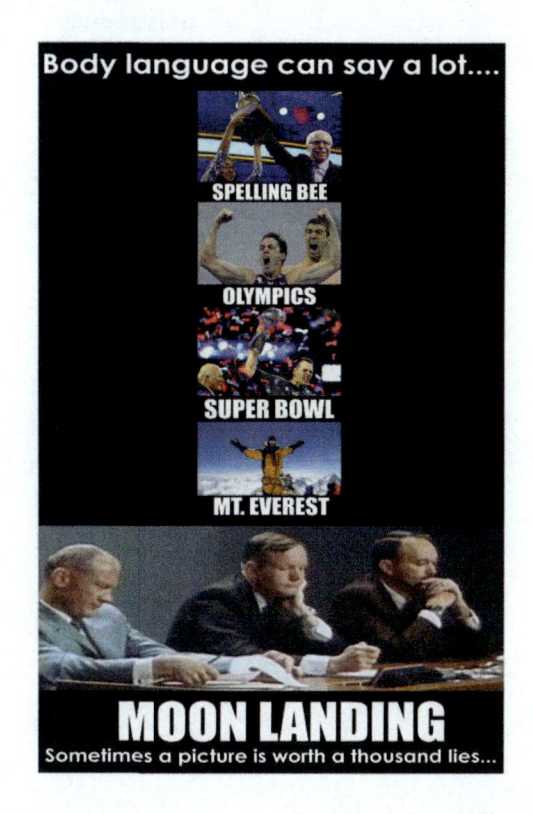

218

The Zetetic Method

FILM DIRECTOR STANLEY KUBRICK MEETING WITH NASA IN 1965
- Donald Slayton (NASA astronaut)
- Unknown
- Stanley Kubrick
- Frederick Ordway III (NASA adviser)
- Arthur C. Clarke (Sci-Fi Author)
- George Mueller (Senior Administrator, Apollo project)

They go on through the years contradicting themselves and each other. You can't trust NASA. You must know this. If you are falsifying facts to reach conclusions then you are not a scientific organization. NASA, therefore, is not scientific.

Notice they don't timestamp their videos. If they did we could go and research the weather patterns of that time period and prove them wrong. Correct?

Moon Dust Could Be a Problem for Future Lunar Explorers
By Leonard David published October 21, 2019
Lunar dust is abrasive and gets into everything.

Well well well, another blunt lie. Not only is dust not on the lunar module footsie, but there's no crater from the landing either. The thrust wasn't enough to disturb all that abrasive dust I guess.

Things that make you go hmm...
Average american adult men (1976): 172.2 pounds
Total mass of the LM: 33,296 lb.
Plus 2 average adult men: 33,640 lb

Awkward

If you speed up NASA's videos of the moon landing, to twice the speed, they're moving normally. They simply slowed it down to make it look like low gravity.

I love the part where he's yanked up by the cord he's hooked up to when the other astronaut is trying to help him up. You can't beat that comedy. Or where the lightning bouncing off said cord as he walks around.

And NASA was worried that the power engines would make a hole when landing; it didn't even disturb the dirt. The landing gear's gold tin foil pads don't even have dust on them. Not only did the moon landing not kick up dust, but the engine would have made a lot of noise, yet you can clearly hear Armstrong talking.

During the Apollo 17 moon mission you can clearly hear an astronaut hitting something with a hammer, how? In a vacuum of space there's no medium for sound waves to travel.

People have tried experiments and combustion engines don't work in a vacuum. One guy has a video I saw where he "does it" but it was not a vacuum. Flat earthers smashed him in the comment section. He said "I'm going to create a vacuum," then he got out his duct tape. LMAO

Here's a comment someone made that makes perfect sense:

"Do you even understand the Bernalillo principle of gasses? Be like the firearm hose whipping around once the water leaves the nozzle it hits AIR. What does the air do? It causes the water to push against itself, in doing so it starts to move. Whipping around. If it was a vacuum there is no air so no resistance to push against. On top of having no oxygen to burn fuel you need your own supply and that is way too much to carry. The biggest misconception is that a jet blast will move anything they like to use Newton's law of motion but you also need to be in an environment that allows all the fundamentals to play out."

So, what does a rocket push off of to travel exactly? Let's narrow it down, it's not earth, water or air. What's the fulcrum point then for the rocket to push off of?

In 2013 an astronaut almost drowned while he was supposedly in space. How can one drown in the vacuum of space? NASA has now fitted space suits with snorkels. Fox News reported: "After a spacewalking astronaut nearly drowned in his helmet in July, NASA has a plan to protect its crew when they venture into the vacuum of space this weekend: snorkels and absorbent towels. ..."

"Some smart engineers on the ground said, hey, this looks like a snorkel you'd use for scuba diving," explained Allison Bolinger, NASA's lead U.S. spacewalk officer."

Hashtag bubbles in space. There're videos of the astronauts in "space" and you can catch a bubble coming out of their suit or in the background. Steve Blakey discovered, while watching an official NASA International Space Station video, in the reflection, a scuba diver wearing a tank swimming around in the background. WTF? Enough with this! It's not science, it's an IQ test. And for NASA's next trick they're gonna "gotcha nose "

The only thing consistent with NASA is inconsistency. Luca Parmitano even almost drowned when water started filling up his helmet while allegedly on a "space-walk".

There are plenty of videos of astronauts having bubbles floating around. Go on Twitter and Hashtag 'Bubblesinspace.' Something tells me they're not in space but in NASA's training pool.

"If you never tell a lie then you never have to play dumb." Red Hot Chili Peppers

The Zetetic Method

"Open your eyes and see the lies right in front of you. Open your mind so your ears aren't just ornamentation."   Rocky Pinard

People, globers and flat earthers alike, are waking up to this proven truth. We're copying NASA's videos and see bubbles float upward from the helmets and from off camera.

When asked about this Astronaut Mark Kelly said it was paint chips. It was obviously not and if it was, why would they shoot upwards?
hashtag #bubblesinspace

Is this a secret club sign we aren't in on?

When a flat earther, at a conference, asked astronaut Mark Kelly why there are bubbles in space coming out of helmets, etc., Kelly played dumb and said he didn't know what he was talking about, then he said it was paint chips they get taken off because of the harsh environment. What harsh environment? All that nothingness? Or maybe all that dark matter is banging stuff around up there. What the flat earther should have asked was why do the 'paint chips' go upward. But instead security led him out. Why? Truth fears no investigation. A man can't ask a real question? What if a kid would have asked, what then? Would he have gotten snagged by the ear and led out?

Now they're claiming that we can't get past the van Allen belts, which is between us and the moon. I guess the astronauts didn't know about this then and got extremely lucky going there and coming back safely. Hmmm! If we're not told the Bering Sea is dangerous, can we make it across safely without incident?

At first, we can pass the Van Allen Belt then we can't get pass them and now it's not a problem; how often and when and why do they open and close and strengthen and weaken? Scientists can't seem to make up their mind and contradict each other when you question them.

Apollo 11 missing tapes

From Wikipedia, the free encyclopedia

The **Apollo 11 missing tapes** were those that were recorded from Apollo 11's slow-scan television (SSTV) telecast in its raw format on telemetry data tape at the time of the first Moon landing in 1969 and subsequently lost. The data tapes were used to record all transmitted data (video as well as telemetry) for backup.

THIS.........this is just shrugged off? Really?

Another odd consequence that would raise suspicions with every logical person, is the fact that NASA "lost" all the telemetry data and destroyed the technology that allowed us to travel to the moon. Now I can't lose any paper at my job without a fuss being put up over it, but

Here's another contradiction from NASA. They can't show us a clear picture of the gear we supposedly left on the moon over 60 years ago, that's when we had the high-tech technology to go there, but they showed us stunning pictures of Pluto, a planet or whatever it's called today, that's around 3 billion miles from Earth.

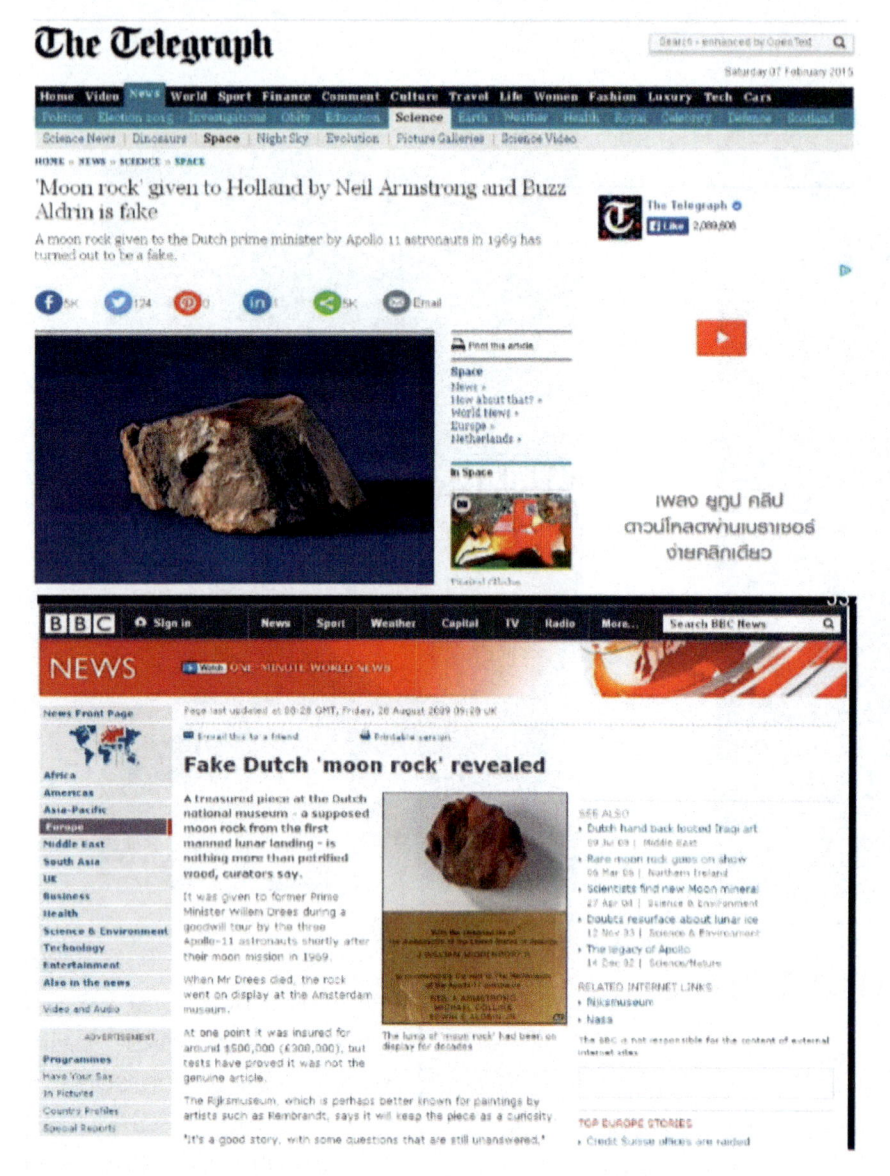

Moon Rocks or Old Kindling Wood

Seven "moon" rocks were given to world leaders and museums. Years later, in 2009, a few young scientists from Free University of Amsterdam, wanted to hold them. So the former Prime Minister Drees agreed. When they got to have a closer look and tested them, they found out that it was actually petrified wood from the United States. Suddenly the moon rocks were removed off the shelf of the museums. Hmmm

Here's a fun article for the family.

ASTRONAUTEN BIJ KONINGIN

October 9, 1969, news article appearing in *Nieuwsblad van het Noorden*, with a picture documenting the Apollo 11 astronauts' meeting with Queen Juliana of the Netherlands, at which time they gave her two gifts, one of which was a moon rock. Left to right in the picture: Queen Juliana, Prince Bernard, Collins, Aldrin, Armstrong, and Prince Claus. The last sentence of the article, translated into English, states: "When the astronauts arrived at the palace, the Queen received a replica of the message the astronauts left on the moon and a piece of moon rock." A similar moon rock, which was given to the former Dutch Prime Minister during the astronauts' visit that day, was determined in 2009 to be fake; it proved to be petrified wood. The moon rock given to the queen, conveniently "disappeared" before it too could be proven to be fake.

De Amerikaanse astronauten Neil Armstrong, Michael Collins en Edwin Aldrin hebben vandaag een bliksembezoek aan ons land gebracht. Om tien uur landden ze op Schiphol (met een der vliegtuigen van president Nixon) en om drie uur vanmiddag vertrokken ze weer. In deze paar uren zijn ze op het koninklijk paleis op de Dam in Amsterdam ontvangen door de Koningin en in een rondvaartboot naar het RAI-congrescentrum gevaren, waar zij voor 1400 genodigden een film van hun maanreis vertoonden, en de tentoonstelling „Maanvaart 69" openden. Bij de ontvangst in het paleis kreeg de Koningin een replica van de boodschappen die de astronauten op de maan achterlieten en een stukje maansteen.

The Zetetic Method

PICTURES VS IMAGES

"Beware of false knowledge. It's more dangerous than ignorance." George Bernard Shaw

NASA uses the term "image" when showing their shots of space and Earth. If you think any pictures, you see are even real from space, stick a quarter in your ass because you played yourself. We'll be looking at those here in this sub-chapter. But first let's see what the definition of an image is shall we.

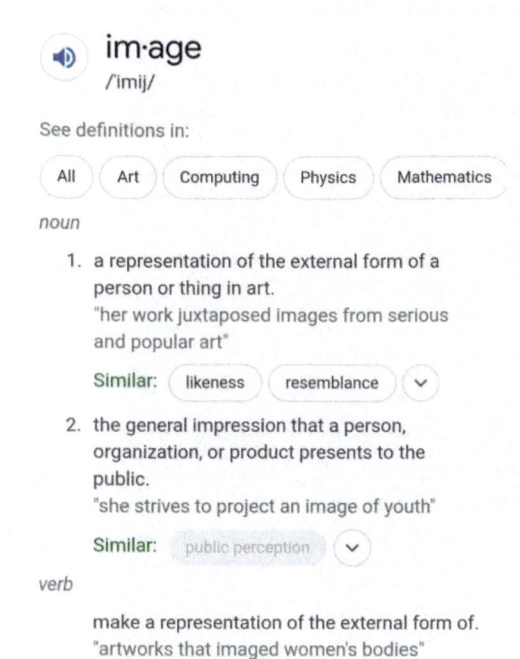

im·age
/ˈimij/

See definitions in:
All | Art | Computing | Physics | Mathematics

noun
1. a representation of the external form of a person or thing in art.
   "her work juxtaposed images from serious and popular art"
   Similar: likeness, resemblance
2. the general impression that a person, organization, or product presents to the public.
   "she strives to project an image of youth"
   Similar: public perception

verb
make a representation of the external form of.
"artworks that imaged women's bodies"

Notice the definition uses the words representation and impression. This means it's not a raw picture, it's been manipulated. And now let's start looking at what stunning images NASA brings to the table.

Look at these pictures of the rocket. Do you see anything odd? (The video is much more helpful here but these screenshots of the video will have to do) The earth is filmed, at high altitude, with a wide-angle lens camera which makes it curve and flip flop around, and the rocket is actually in a studio. If you'll notice, the rocket and equipment is not flip flopping yet it's in the same shot. How can the background have the flip flop effect but not the foreground? This is proof that it's done with a green screen with the earth footage added.

Now in this first picture you'll notice the strap and cable are affected by the gopro. First, they bend with the lens and affect them fixed when the lens effect is corrected. This doesn't happen on NASA videos. Only the earth flip flops and bends. One is real, the other is in front of a green screen.

Why use a gopro cam to begin with if there's already earth curvature? What happens when you use a gopro cam on an actual ball earth I wonder. Why do people send me these videos saying it's proof of Earth's curvature, then when I point out the earth is flip flopping, they tell me it's because of a gopro cam? Which means they're admitting it's NOT actually earth's curvature but a lens effect, so why did they say it was proof of ANYTHING? How are they not understanding that?

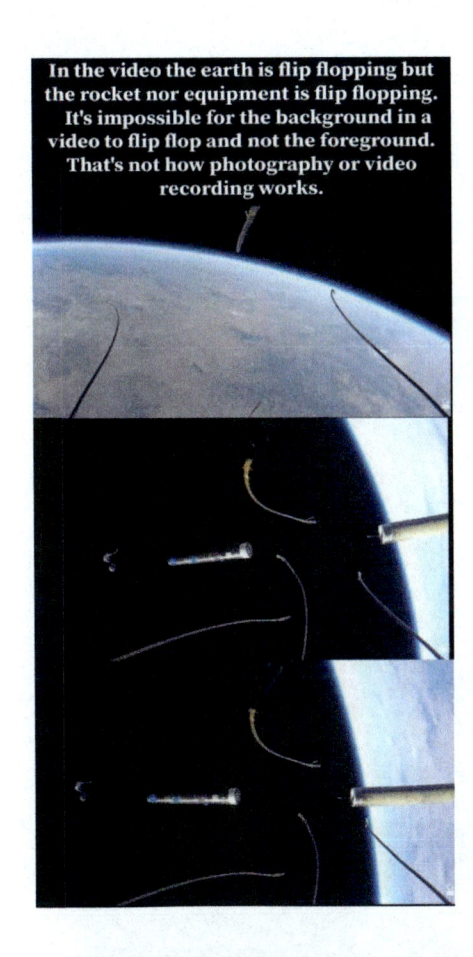

In the video the earth is flip flopping but the rocket nor equipment is flip flopping. It's impossible for the background in a video to flip flop and not the foreground. That's not how photography or video recording works.

SAME EXACT CLOUDS
1978   2017
AND DIFFERENT AMERICA
2012

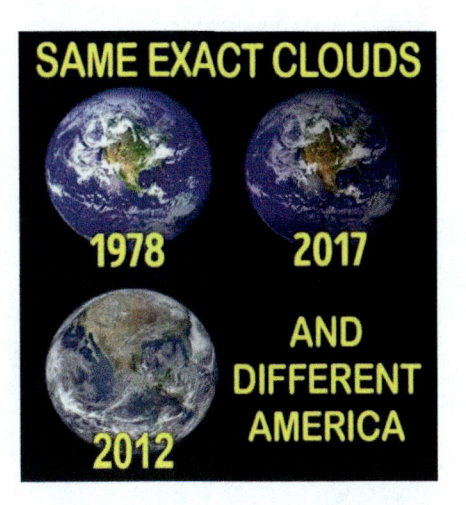

Just like the covid cases, if you have real curvature of your own, you don't have to create any.

The man in this Blue Origin "space" video said "we can see the curvature of the Earth" then it flattens out. Of course later, as they land, you can see it again. LMAO

The Zetetic Method

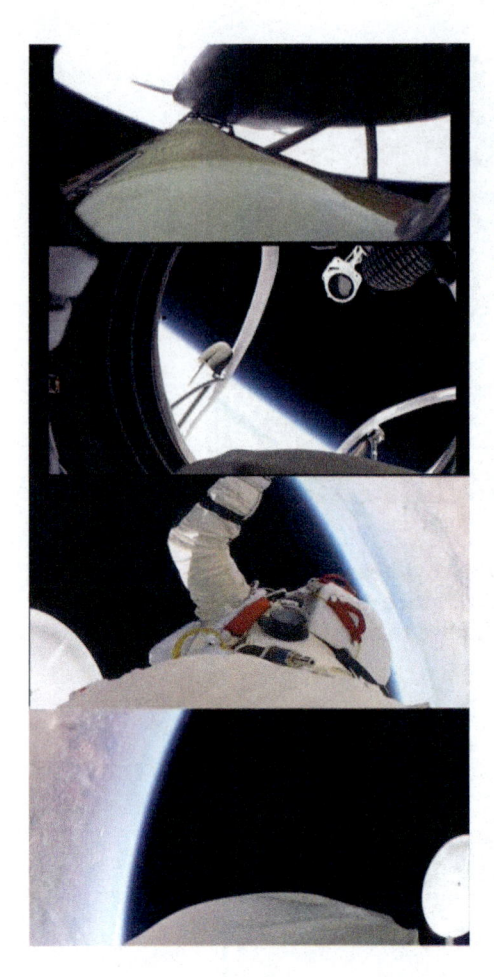

Look at these ball earth pictures. Have you ever seen earth from a plane? The atmosphere from a plane makes earth look hazy and blueish, and you're only 35,000 feet up. Now look at these pictures and see the details at almost 300 miles up.

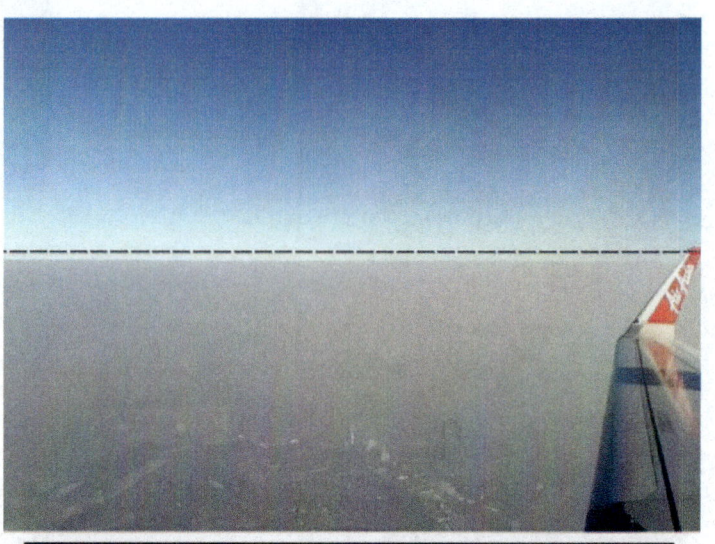

In one video the Earth was flip flopping through the window behind the astronaut but the window was not affected. How can that be? Simple, the Earth is filmed and added to the capsule scene.

In the videos of earth rotating, they will have the same cloud formation throughout, yet in the physical reality that we actually live in, the clouds disburse and change and even disappear as well as form and move with wind currents.

These images were of a time-lapse video of the rotation of the earth from NASA. Unfortunately, I can't show videos in a book but here are some screen shots. The clouds never moved or dissipated the whole time. Unlike what we observe in reality.

I've had people to tell me that the flat earth movement is a psy-op by the government to separate people.

The ones saying that haven't researched flat earth.

Even a government offical said it was a psy-op. Trying to get people off it.

It's not fake pictures that proves flat earth, it's no curvature that does that.

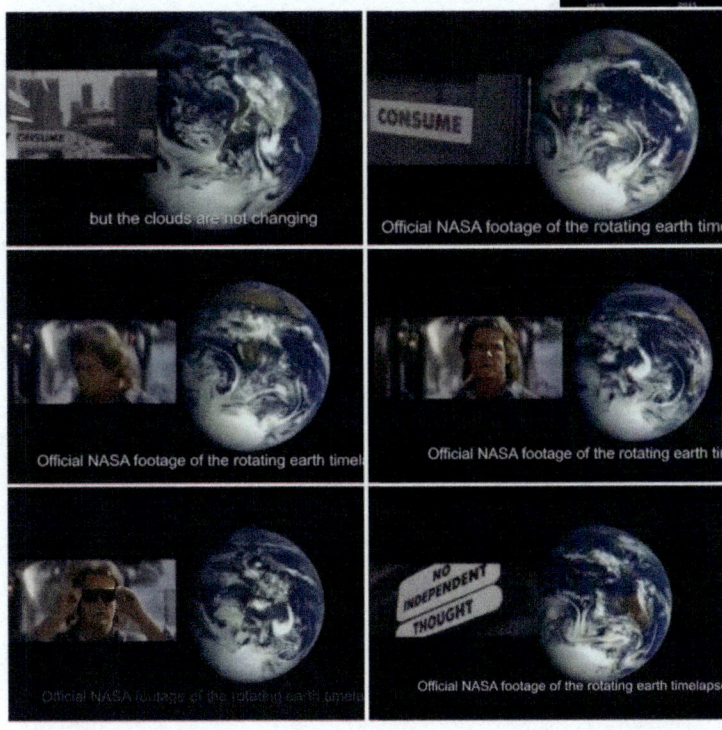

Look at these ISS pictures. The ISS is said to be traveling at 17,500mph. The average bullet only travels at 1700 mph. So, where's the motion blur? How can this image be crystal clear? And the foreground and background are both in focus at the same time. Hmmm

They will claim they use long exposure; how can you use long exposure on a 1000mph spinning ball that's also whirling at unimaginable speeds in three different directions through space? Yet there's never any motion blur in their "photos." Long exposure my ass. I guess the world stops for NASA'S picture taking.

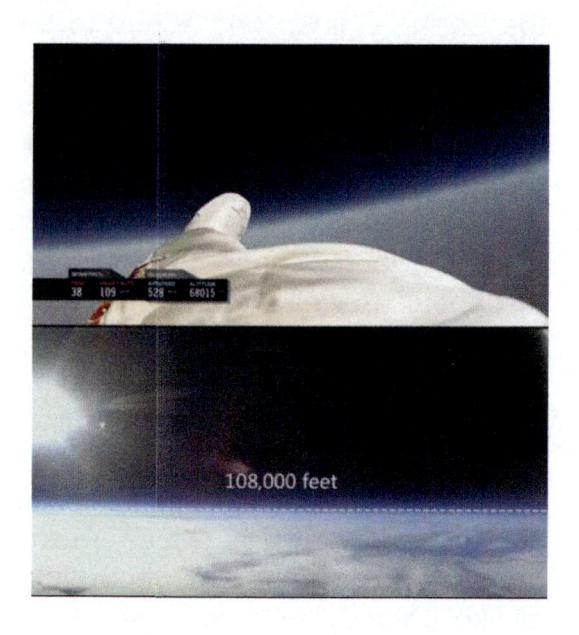

NASA has admitted that these pictures are fake. They had to, they were caught. CGI seems to be the stable for their proof and thus belief system. A fellow flat earther recorded himself going on NASA's website and taking images and putting them on Photoshop and proving them fake. One picture even had the word SEX in the clouds. And the clone tool was used on the clouds. This video made its way around the internet and NASA then released a video stating that they have to compress images from different satellites to get a full picture of earth.

Robert Simmon, NASA's data Visualizer and Designer created the famous Blue Marble image of Earth and said "It's Photo shopped because it has to be." He even said he paints in the clouds and decides what color the atmosphere should be.

At the same time NASA's video was released to combat the flat earthers, Obama said that they just released a full photo of earth from space. How rich in comedy.

Robert Simmon, NASA's data Visualizer and Designer said it was hard creating a flat map of the Earth's surface, then he used the same map that's been around since the 1500s. Does anybody else find that hilarious?

In a 2012 interview for an article for NASA, Simmon explains the following: "The last time anyone took a photograph from above low Earth orbit that showed an entire hemisphere (one side of a globe) was in 1972 during Apollo 17. NASA's Earth Observing System (EOS) satellites were designed to give a check-up of Earth's health. By 2002, we finally had enough data to make a snapshot of the entire Earth. So, we did. The hard part was creating a flat map of the Earth's surface with four months of satellite data. Reto Stockli, now at the Swiss Federal Office of Meteorology and Climatology, did much of this work. Then we wrapped the flat map around a ball. My part was integrating the surface, clouds, and oceans to match people's expectations of how Earth looks from space. That ball became the famous Blue Marble. I was happy with it but had no idea how widespread it would become. We never thought it would become an icon. I certainly never thought that I would become "Mr. Blue Marble." " LMAO!!!

The Zetetic Method

Let's look at a few of the images shall we. He put Buzz in the video, and he doesn't look too happy. Lol!

Taken right off NASA'S website and shown to be CGI images.

Before the video from NASA came out admitting that their images were fake, Robert Sungenis, Ph. D., in an attempt to prove flat earthers wrong, tried to say the clouds were natural and the wind current made them look like they had been duplicated. How awkward is that! LMAO!

Matthew Boylan, a former NASA Operation Graphic Manager, states he was hired to create planets, etc. for NASA, even showing how he did some of them. He has sense quit and is exposing them for lying about the Heliocentric globe model.

Boylan shows evidence in a time-lapse video showing the clouds remaining static without changing their form or position during the rotation as we witness in real life. He has stated that all the images from Hubble are a hoax.

Now don't get me wrong, fake pictures and fraudulent videos from NASA doesn't prove flat earth, it proves that these "established" scientists are actually puppet Pseudo-scientist used for propaganda and covering up something. You even have puppet Pseudo-scientist of the past, like Galileo. Anybody with a high-powered zoom camera can debunk him. It's no curvature that proves the earth is flat. If it's not based on physical facts and reasoning, then it's based on authority.

Here's some fake images to look at while you believe. Look at this sloppy Photoshop clean up job.

The Zetetic Method

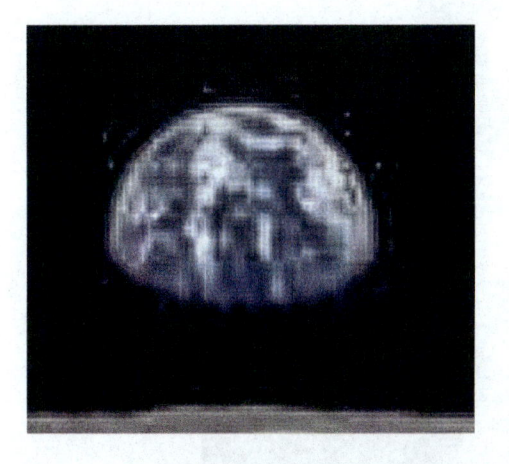

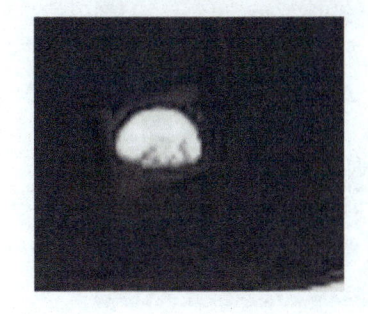

232

Science Of The Universe's Post
Astronaut Bruce McCandless II floats untethered away from the safety of the space shuttle, with nothing but his Manned Maneuvering Unit keeping him alive. The first person in history to do so.
Credit: NASA
Lies and fraudulent evidence everywhere At what point do people just STOP and say "no more?" Seems like one lie would be enough but there are many.
CORRECTIONS
SPLIT TONE
BLUR
VIGNETTE
Clarity
Sharpen

Are we being manipulated so we can be controlled easier?
Amateur balloon footage Real
From movie GRAVITY fake
ISS footage Real or fake???
NASA
FAQ: The International Space Station 2022 Transition Plan |...
Visit

NASA JUST POSTED THIS...
IT'S CGI

"There are three classes of people: those who see. Those who see when they are shown. Those who do not see."
-Leonardo da Vinci

Welcome to Earth's grid. Can you find your porch light?

How bad is your lie, when your own evidence can be held against you?

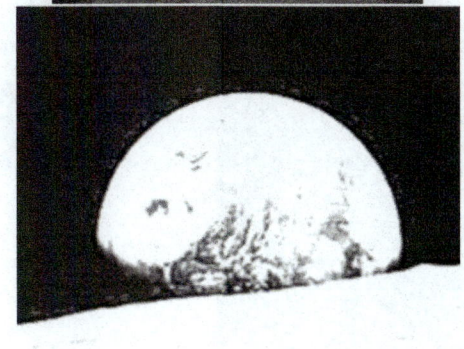

Computer shows that earth is pasted into photo!

Buzz don't look to happy with all this research going on.

In the world of Photoshop and video manipulation, we call this "lazy clean up."

The Zetetic Method

PHOTOSHOP CLONE TOOL REPLICATING CLOUDS

10 / 12

There should be a shadow from the moon on this picture. The artist forgot about that.

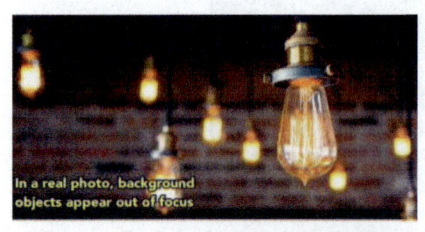

THERE SHOULD BE AN ECLIPSE HERE

DIRECTION OF SUNLIGHT

In a real photo, background objects appear out of focus

How can both be in focus? The truth is in the details.

CNET
Track Elon Musk's Tesla in space with site that uses NASA data -...
Visit

Images may be subject to copyright. Learn More

Thomas had never seen such bullshit before

235

The Zetetic Method

If objects attract each other by some gravitational force that mass has then why do objects on the Space Station float freely about? Shouldn't the objects be clinging to each other or the sides of the ship? And again, where's the centrifugal force? But wait, in this photo not all things float away. Must be a pocket of gravity.

The televised Red Bull persecute jump on the left and NASA floating on the right.

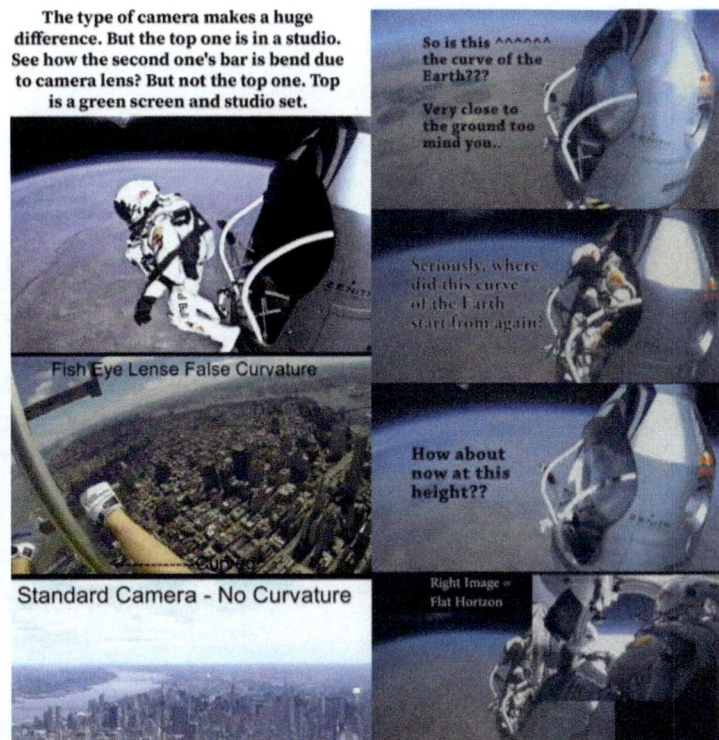

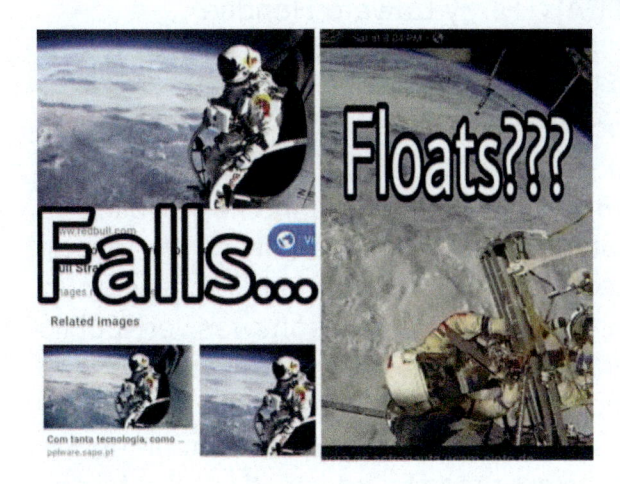

The International Space Station's nine-person crew of Expedition 60 poses in "space band" shirts in this photo shared by European Space Agency astronaut Luca Parmitano (upside down) on Sept. 30, 2019. The shirts say "Kryk Chayky" (Cry of the Seagull in Russian).

The type of camera makes a huge difference. But the top one is in a studio. See how the second one's bar is bend due to camera lens? But not the top one. Top is a green screen and studio set.

When I was a kid NASA said that the Great Wall of China is the only man-made structure that could be seen from space. Someone called them on it and they have since withdrawn that statement. So why did they make it in the first place? To aww you into believing.

The Great Wall width differs in different sections.

They are about 10 meters (33 feet) high on average, **7 - 8 meters (23 - 26 feet) wide at the bottom, and 4 - 5 meters (13 - 16 feet) wide at the top of the wall**. Aug 9, 2019

https://www.travelchinaguide.com › ...

How Wide Is the Great Wall of China? - Averagely 4-5 Meters

Here's the issue with their statement. The Great Wall of China is only around 20 feet wide.

Length doesn't matter at an overhead view if you can't see 20 feet from almost 300 miles away. You can barely see a football field from 35,000 feet up. Another issue is interstates are wider so how could the Great Wall possibly be the only man-made structure?

They lie to dazzle you, like a magician, to believe their utter bullshit. But they can't change reality. They can only change your perception of reality.

Think about these measurements as you think about NASA's claim and their picture, the lower one. You cannot see something around 20 feet wide from 100s of miles away. Ridiculous!

WHEN TELLING THE TRUTH CAN GET YOU KILLED

It seems that NASA, a ventriloquist, doesn't need a dummy that speaks for itself. Here's an extracted from the book "THE GREATEST LIE ON EARTH" by Edward Hendrie

"O'Leary was not just any astronaut; he was a NASA astronaut in the 1960s and served as a science advisor during the Apollo moon missions.

Brian O'Leary's claim that the moon landing astronauts would have told him if the Apollo missions were faked is incredible for yet another reason. He was fully aware that all astronauts know what would happen to them if they were to let that secret out. For example, Gus Grissom was very public about his view that the chances were slim of NASA meeting the Apollo mission requirements.

Shortly before Grissom died, he hung a large lemon on the Apollo space capsule as the press looked on, thus graphically

NASA - China's Wall Less Great in View from Space

indicating his opinion of the space capsule. Grissom, along with fellow astronauts Ed White and Roger Chaffee, was shortly thereafter immolated inside a test capsule when it burst into flames as it sat on the launch pad during a test. During the test, and before the fire, there was a communication failure. Grissom is recorded saying at that time: "How are we going to get to the moon when we can't communicate between two buildings?" Grissom's opinion that the Apollo mission was doomed to failure was based upon his close study and examination of the mission rocket and other equipment. He took detailed notes and wrote reports about his findings. The day Grissom died on the launch pad, FBI Agents burst into Grissom's home and seized all of his records. Grissom's wife reports that those records were never returned. The fire on the launch pad took place on 27 January 1967, at 6:30 p.m. The FBI search took place in the evening of January 27th, immediately after Grissom died. Someone was ready to give the order to conduct the search as soon as it was determined that Grissom was dead. That suggests governmental foreknowledge of the launch pad fire.

The younger [Scott] Grissom had his suspicions in the 1960s but wasn't able to prove foul play until the 1990s when he was granted access to the charred Apollo 1 capsule. Rooting around the instrumentation, he found a "fabricated metal plate" behind a switch on one of the instrument panels that controlled the source of the capsule's electrical power. Its placement behind that switch, he said, was clearly an act of sabotage. It ensured that when any crew member toggled that switch there would be a spark. That spark would have been enough to start the fire that killed the crew.

A McDonnell-Douglas engineer, Clark MacDonald, backed Scott Grissom's story. In his own accident investigation, he identified an electrical short brought on by a changeover to battery power as the reason for the fire. But NASA destroyed his report, he said." I have agonized for 31 years about revealing the truth but I didn't want to hurt NASA's image or cause trouble," MacDonald told the paper. "But I can't let one more day go by without the truth being known."

James Irwin, the Apollo 15 Command Module Pilot, by the grace of God, became a Christian and was giving his Christian testimony in Nashville, Tennessee. At that time, he met a fellow Christian, Lee Gelvani, who had almost convinced James Irwin to confess to the moon landing hoax. Irwin suspiciously died the day before he was expected to confess to the hoax."

As you can see, it can cost you everything to be right when everybody's wrong.

The Zetetic Method

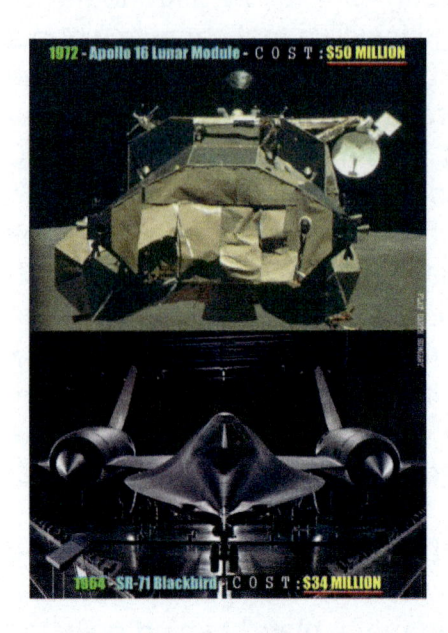

If you are having a bad day and you aren't feeling very smart remember most of your family and "friends" believe this trash can landed on the moon.....

Who would inspected this and signed off on it for space travel?

Don Pettit, a NASA astronaut, stated at a Space Museum conference "I'd go back to the moon in a nanosecond. The problem is that we don't have the technology to do that anymore. We used to, but we destroyed that technology. And it's painful to build it back again."

Painful to build back technology from 1959? Really? Oh well, scrap it and let's use this new shity technology and go to Mars. A clown show indeed.

If you're wondering about the video tapes don't bother. The official report from NASA states: "The 45 Apollo 11 tapes were degaussed, recertified, and reused to satisfy a NASA-wide shortage of one-inch tapes more than a decade later. NASA's M-22 recordings of the Apollo 11 moonwalk are likely gone forever."

So 45 tapes of this historical event are gone. The only thing that's left is the televised versions. Hmmm how convenient.

Wikipedia: "The researchers discovered that the tapes containing the raw unprocessed Apollo 11 SSTV signal were erased and reused by NASA in the early 1980s. It is claimed this was according to NASA's procedures because they were facing a major data tape shortage at that time."

Check out the documentary "A Funny Thing Happened on the Way to the Moon." It's showing on YouTube. Busting NASA's balls.

"The scientists of today think deeply instead of clearly. One must be sane to think clearly, but you can think deeply and be quite insane." Nikola Tesla

In 1975 author Bill Kaysing was giving a radio interview about the moon landing being fake when suddenly they went off the air. It seemed a helicopter dropped a bomb on the radio stations' tower. The police offered Kaysing protection after the incident.

Author John Andrew Reed said it best, "We cannot expect a community whose business is endorsing supposed facts by offering its perceived credibility as its only proof.

Once the industry of science has accepted an unchallengeable truth, and consequently becomes heavily vested in that belief, it can no longer accept contradictory information at face value.

This is especially true if that organization belongs to a government which has previously violated the public trust in one way or another at some point in its history. Fool me once, shame on you. Fool me twice... you know the rest."

Astronomers claim it goes in this order. They'll say anything about the latest celestial scandals that sounds enticing to ahh and ooh their unwitting audience, who will flock to it, opening up the indoctrination books to see it written down as if that's proof of anything. They'll look at CGI images and green screen videos and pretend they're researching. Not actually thinking about the theory but accepting and then believing and then defending the unproven claims that have no merits.

Here's some more NASA fallacies

Have a closer look at more unobservable unproven illogical fallacies that are presented to us. How did the station get going faster than the speed of a bullet at 17,000mph? How would the shuttle stop? How does fuel work in zero gravity with it floating around? How much oxygen has to be carried for this floating fuel? How about other oxygen needs? When you open the lunar module to get in and out you have to replace all that oxygen, plus enough air for the trip to the moon and back.

How can two of those backpacks and suits fit in there with that small space and through that small hatch, plus three clowns, I mean astronauts and the camera man that filmed Armstrong stepping off?

Where is the footage of them getting out with those big backpacks on, that's big as the doors? That would have been comical. Having to put on all that equipment in that small space, that's film worthy for such a huge event. If all this footage disappeared in the 1980s, why not show it all that time they did have it? Hmm! And where's the room for the air tanks? Think of that. Again, all that air rushing out to the vacuum of space has to be replaced, plus the amount of oxygen needed for the drops of fuel, floating about.

The Zetetic Method

These pictures made some good points I thought, so I shared them. Wouldn't putting your hair in a bun be safer than hairspray.

242

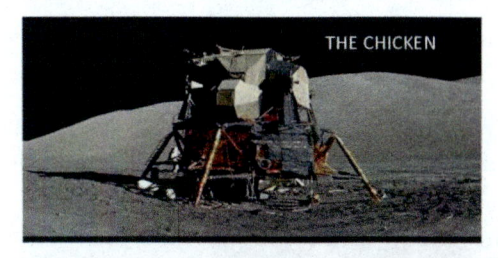

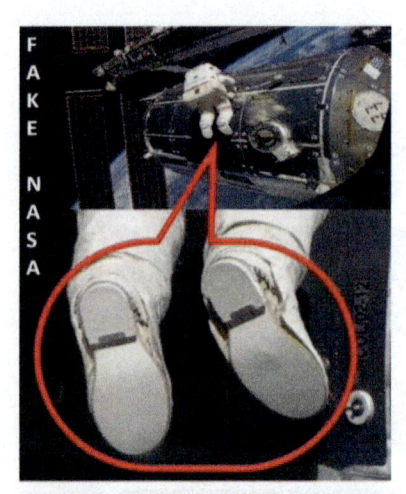

In some of the ISS photos there's green reflections; off what exactly? It wouldn't be a green screen because that would make them fake, wouldn't it? Wonder what it's from.

The Zetetic Method

Why is it that in 1969 there was 0 second delay when Nixon talked to astronauts on the moon with his desk phone hooked to a radio but now there is around 11 second delay? The problem with faking stuff is you have to be consistent; NASA is not.

The putting together of the moon rovers were not videotaped or photographed. Such a 460 lbs. untested in space creation, would be worthy of video recording, wouldn't it? And how would they fit that in the Lunar module?

Author J. Gillespie says, in his "Triumph of Philosophy," "I can challenge any astronomer in Great Britain on any point in theoretical astronomy, and prove that the present theory is a regular burlesque, A HOAX and A SWINDLE. If it is a sin to tell a lie, what must be the doom of men who teach generation after generation one of the most glaring and degraded falsehoods ever laid before mankind."

What confidence and trust can we have in these so-called 'scientists' when they deliberately reject physical reality and their own senses?

You have to take NASA's word for far too much for my taste. Their track record is absolutely horrible and filled with fraud and lies. Let's look at some of the claims we have to rely on NASA to even entertain.

1) Ocean wrapped around this Earth instead of stretched out upon it.
2) Curvature period. You have never seen it on the ground or on a plane or from the high-altitude balloon footage, only on NASA videos. Curvature would be the #1 proof for a ball Earth, and NASA is the only one showing it to you.
3) Gravity; you need NASA to even entertain the idea that an object would float away if not for gravity. You've never seen anything of the sort except on NASA videos, except of course when the astronauts accidentally drop something. Ha!
4) "Planets" being anything but celestial lights. You've never seen "planets" the way you believe they are, you simply believe they are
terrestrial globes because of fake images shown to you by NASA.

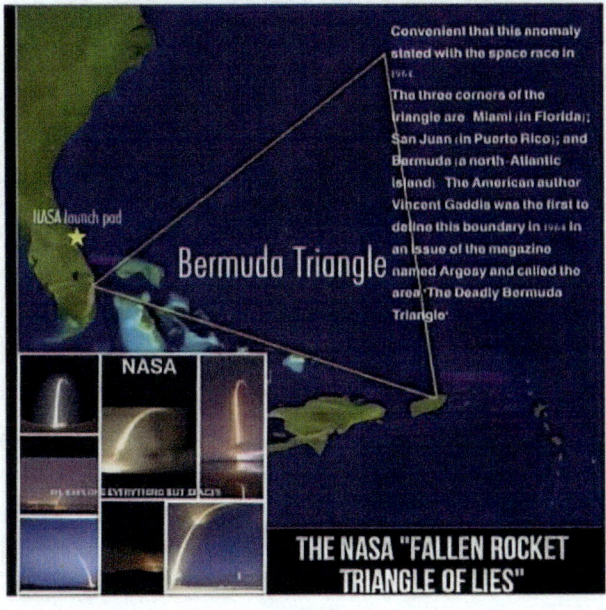

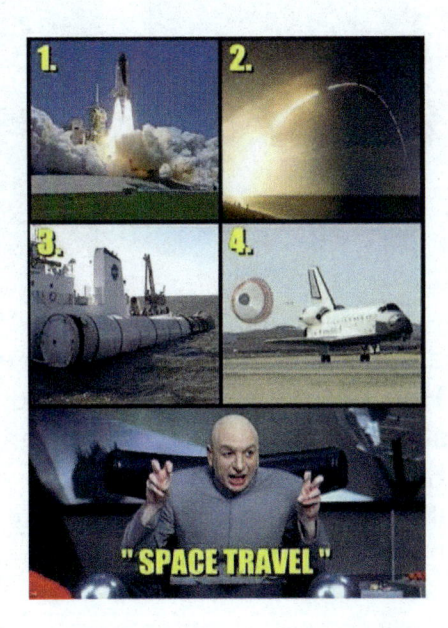

The Zetetic Method

The bottom picture of Neil Tyson on the left is manipulated. Why not have some fun with the clown, huh?

Puesdo-scientist Neil Degrasse Tyson catching hell from flat earthers. Not all of the masses comply.

They have made quite a bit of stories about the lost ships and planes of the Bermuda Triangle. Seems like someone doesn't want people going there. I wonder why not. There's a video I can no longer find that has NASA removing the rocket from the ocean with the boat shown on the last page, with the NASA logo on the side. So many videos that were out there I should have saved but did not because I had just started looking into this flat earth thing. I wish I had.

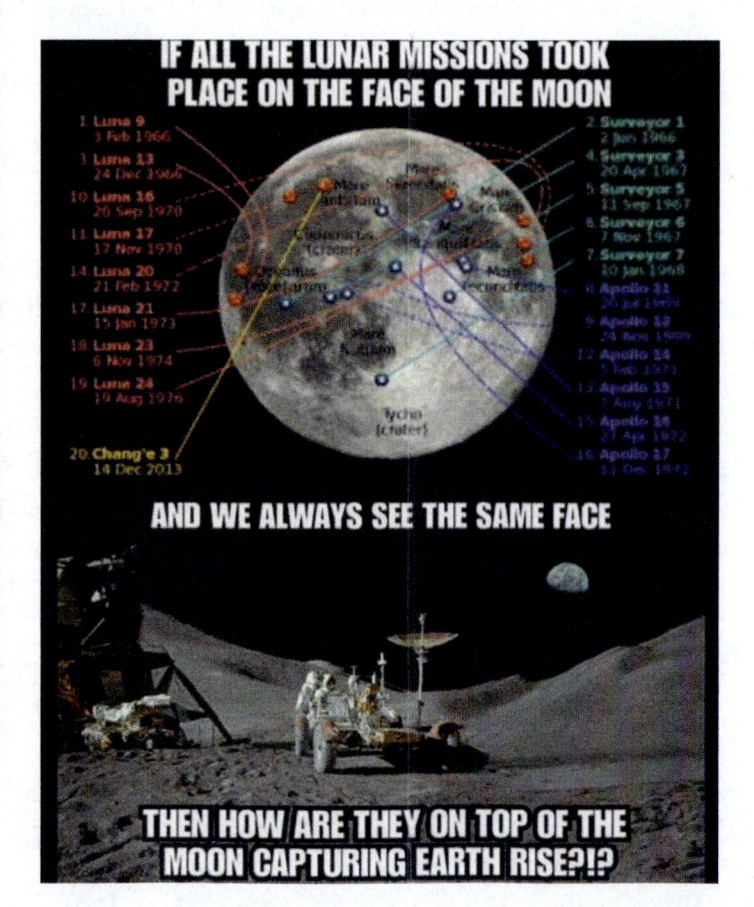

We always only see one side of the moon. If NASA landed in the places, they say they did, then the earth would be directly above their head not on the horizon. The truth is in the details. How do you know we landed on the moon when there is footage showing the astronauts staging photographs of the Earth as though they were in a film studio instead of a vessel hurtling through space.

And now they tell us the moon is rusting! WTF!

245

The Zetetic Method

Even globe believers have stated that flat earthers have made them see that NASA is indeed lying about a lot of things. So where is NASA'S billions of dollars being funneled back into?

The tarp covering the circus clown tent is coming undone and starting to blow away.

WHAT ABOUT OTHER SPACE AGENCIES?
People often say to me "It's not just NASA, it's also other space agencies." Well, if NASA is proven wrong and lying then what does that say about the other space agencies? Look at this covid scam. All governments worldwide, and those who didn't play the covid game suddenly died. Hmmm

Perhaps the other space agencies, in China, Japan, India, and Russia, etc., are all subsidiaries of NASA maybe. They make the same claims, use Photoshop pictures like NASA, the logos are similar and they say the earth is a wobbling spinning flying ball, which is unproven with physical facts.

Let's not forget the Antarctic treaty signed by 53 countries now. (You know to protect all that ice while shooting missiles at the sky) The space agencies are from those countries. The United Nations. United means together.

Not long-ago China claimed to have released a "picture" of earth from the dark side of the moon from one of their satellites said to be orbiting the moon. I copied said picture and put it on Photoshop and proved it fake. I went back to the comment section and told everyone what to do to prove it fake.

246

The Zetetic Method

The picture disappeared and came back later that day and it was done better and cleaned up. (It's good to know something about Photoshop) However you could still zoom in and see that it was fake.

There are other ways to debunk the picture. The earth was crystal clear with detail. How, when it's over 280,000 miles away. A plane ride has the earth's land all hazy and blueish. So how can a picture over 280,000 miles away have such detail? Also the moon itself was crystal clear. How can the moon and the earth both be crystal clear with detail? Not including all the movement that's going on; the satellite moving, the moon flying, the earth flying.... hmmm

Another thing that makes me suspicious about this claim is the satellite orbiting the moon. How can it orbit the moon with the Earth's gravitational pull on it and the sun's, both being way stronger than the moons? What would the speed of the satellite have to be at and how in the world would they get at that speed at THAT location?

Seems like one of those things you have to prove when you say it. Let's have a look at the picture I'm talking about and other space agencies images of Earth.

The Zetetic Method

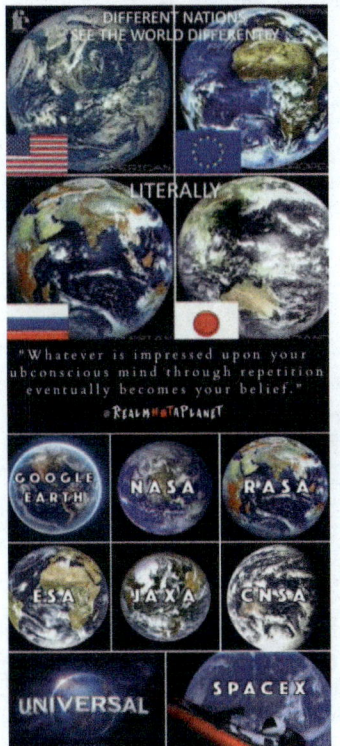

The Zetetic Method

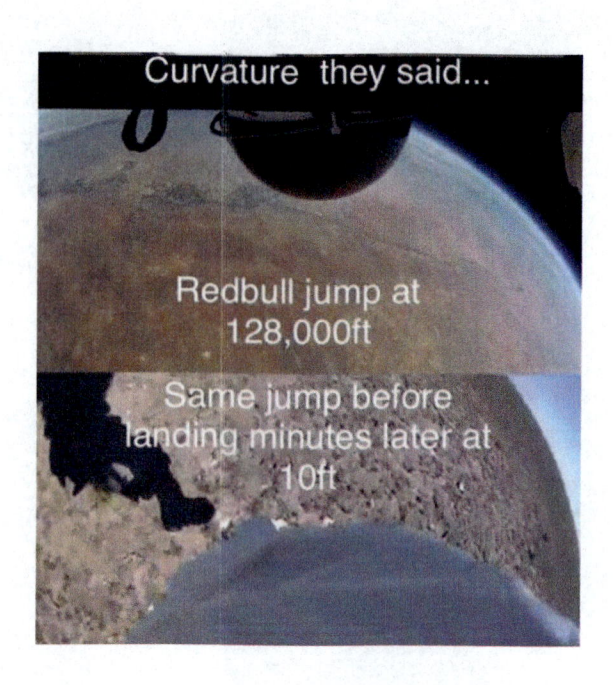

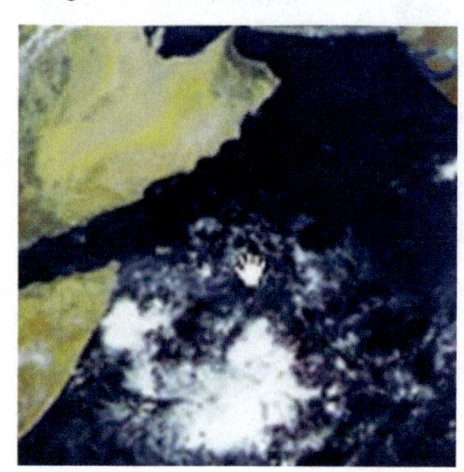

249

Next time they tell you your luggage is too heavy, show them that. Lol!

Look at these next pictures. One has a microphone going into the astronaut's neck. Another has bubbles coming from the ISS (the video is far better). Another has a glass of water that doesn't seem to float around. Instead it stays put all flat like.(Lazy water!)
Another has the light bouncing off the cable. And finally, another one has the CGI cliché with the solar panels disappearing and reappearing on the satellite

250

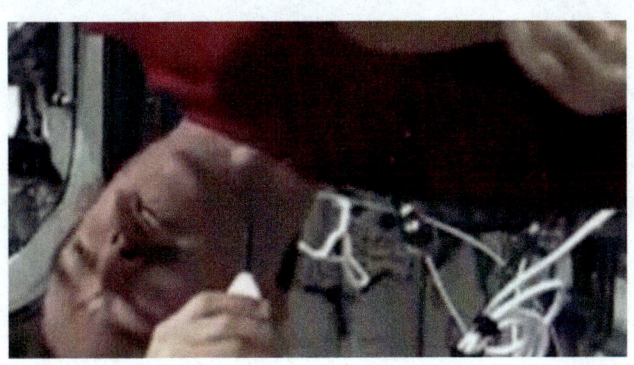

The Zetetic Method

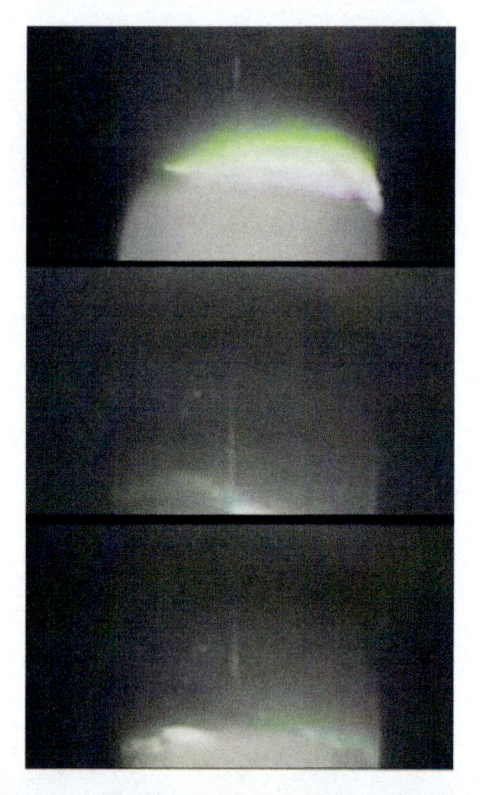

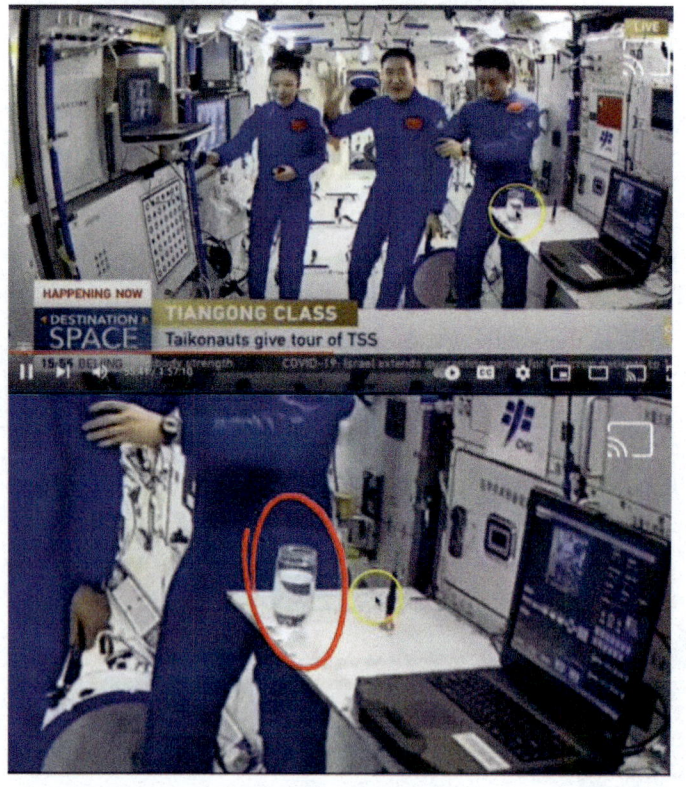

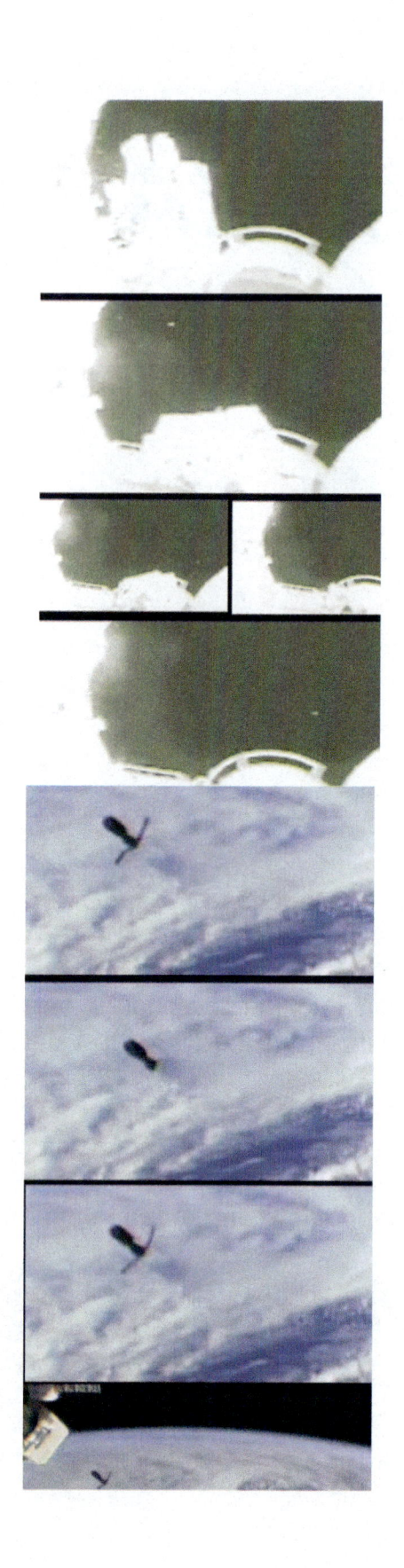

251

HONEST AND NOBLE CONFESSIONS

) Dr. Woodhouse, formerly Professor of Astronomy at Cambridge— "When we consider what the advocates of the Earth's stationary and central position can account for, and explain the celestial phenomena as accurately to their own thinking as we can ours, in addition to which they have the evidence of their, senses and Scripture and facts in their favor, which we have not; it is not without a show of reason that they maintain the superiority of their system. However perfect our theory may appear in our own estimation, and however simply and satisfactorily the Newtonian hypotheses may seem to us to account for all the celestial phenomena, yet we are here compelled to admit the astounding truth, IF OUR PREMISES BE DISPUTED AND OUR FACTS CHALLENGED, THE WHOLE RANGE OF ASTRONOMY DOES NOT CONTAIN THE PROOFS OF ITS OWN ACCURACY."

) From the book "The Cause of an Ice Age" by Sir R. Ball: "I have found it necessary to ASSUME the existence of several ice ages."

) Sarah Palin once said you could see Russia from Alaska, she was ridiculed for it. LMAO! On the globe model, at 55 miles away, that would put Russia at 2016 feet below earth's supposed invisible curvature.

) William Cooper, Former US Navy Intelligence "Exploration of the moon stopped because it was impossible to continue the hoax without being discovered. And of course, they ran out of pre-filmed episodes. No man has ever ascended much higher than 300 miles, if that high, above the Earth's surface. At or under that altitude the astronauts are beneath the radiation of the Van Allen Belt and the Van Allen Belt shields them from the extreme radiation which permeates space. No man has ever orbited, landed on, or walked upon the moon in any publicly known space program. If man has ever truly been to the moon it has been done in secret and with a far different technology. The tremendous radiation encountered in the Van Allen Belt, solar radiation, cosmic radiation, Solar flares, temperature control, and many other problems connected with space travel prevent living organisms from leaving our atmosphere with our known level of technology. Any intelligent high school student with a basic physics book can prove NASA faked the Apollo moon landings. If you doubt this please explain how the astronauts walked upon the moons moon's surface enclosed in a space suit in full sunlight absorbing a minimum of 265 degrees of heat surrounded by a vacuum... and that is not even taking into consideration any effects of cosmic radiation, Solar flares, micrometeorites, etc. NASA tells us the moon has no atmosphere and that the astronauts were surrounded by the vacuum of space."

Allen Daves "If the Government or NASA had said to you that the Earth is stationary, imagine that. And then imagine we are trying to convince people that 'no, no it's not stationary, it's moving forward at 32 times rifle bullet speed and spinning at 1,000 miles per hour.' We would be laughed at! We would have so many people telling us 'you are crazy, the Earth is not moving!' We would be ridiculed for having no scientific backing for this convoluted moving Earth theory. And not only that but then people would say, 'oh then how do you explain a fixed, calm atmosphere and the Sun's observable movement, how do you explain that?' Imagine saying to people, 'no, no, the atmosphere is moving also but is somehow magically Velcro to the moving-Earth. The reason is not simply because the Earth is stationary.' So what we are actually doing is what makes sense. We are saying that the moving-Earth theory is nonsense. The stationary-Earth theory makes sense and we are being ridiculed. You've got to picture it being the other way around to realize just how RIDICULOUS this situation is."

The BLACK SWAN
1. NASA's "photos" are proven, and admitted, to only be images, which is not actually a photo. This means no real pictures of Earth from space. CGI images are not allowed in court as evidence so images from NASA are not evidence to any thinking person either.
2. NASA's videos are full of things that prove them fraudulent. No centrifugal force, astronauts dropping things, grabbing invisible things, some things float some things don't, some things float sometimes but not always, etc. etc.
3. They contradict each other and make up distances and make up their own "facts." Those are not scientific methods. This shows they CAN'T BE TRUSTED!
4. People in upper levels of NASA, that don't go with the narrative, seem to have shorter lives.
5. NASA lost the moon landing tapes. You'd have to be quite a nit-wit to believe this claim.

CHAPTER 8
SATELLITES

SATELLITES

"Children are taught in their geography books, when too young to apprehend aright the meaning of such things, that the world is a great globe revolving around the sun, and the story is repeated continuously, year by year, till they reach maturity, at which time they generally become so absorbed in other matters as to be indifferent as to whether the teaching be true or not, and, as they hear of nobody contradicting it, they presume that it must be the correct thing, if not to believe at least to receive it as a fact. They thus tacitly give their assent to a theory which, if it had first been presented to them at what are called 'years of discretion,' they would at once have rejected. The consequences of evil-teaching, whether in religion or in science, are far more disastrous than is generally supposed, especially in a luxurious laissez-faire age like our own. The intellect becomes weakened and the conscience seared." David Wardlaw Scott, Terra Firma: The Earth not a Planet Proved from Scripture, Reason, and Fact

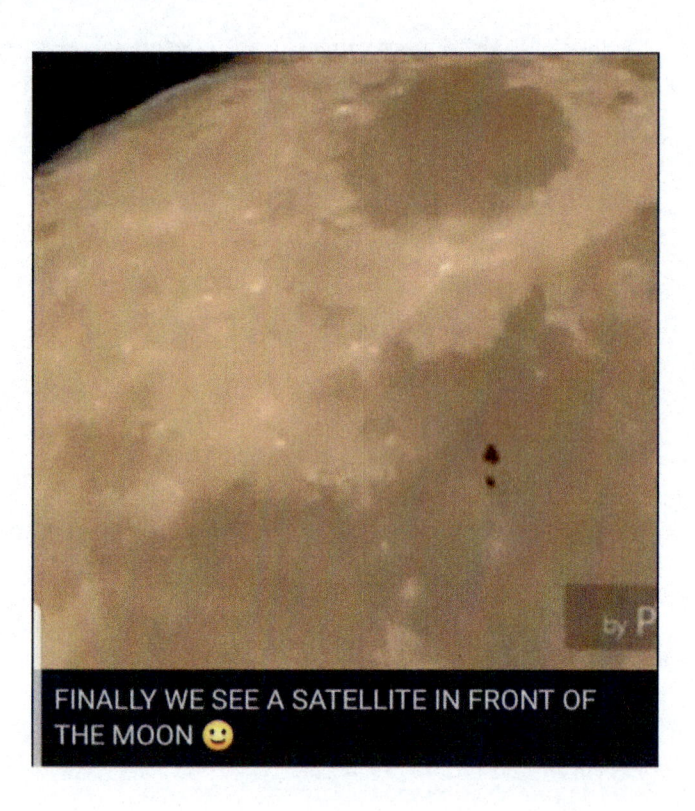

LOOK HOW COOL NASA IS

THEY TOOK A PIC OF THE THING TAKING PICS

In 1981 CIA Director William Casey stated "We'll know our disinformation program is a success when everything the American public believes is false."

FINALLY WE SEE A SATELLITE IN FRONT OF THE MOON 😀

These satellites drones that we see at night are in the jet stream. If you watch them you will see them blow a little off course, then straighten up again. They are all over the world. NASA has a phone number on the side to call and they retrieve them. YouTube satellite crashes. People film them.

Are we really seeing these satellites at said distances? People say you can see satellites from here on the ground but yet you don't see them in space videos. Why not, they're up there next to thousands of them, right?

Remember things appear smaller and smaller the further they move away from us. If the ISS and satellites are about the same size and shape as a plane, that you can barely see at 35,000 feet, then how can we see them at these distances they claim, like 300 miles? They can't even agree on how many are in space orbiting this ridiculous ball. Let's have a look at these claimed distances.

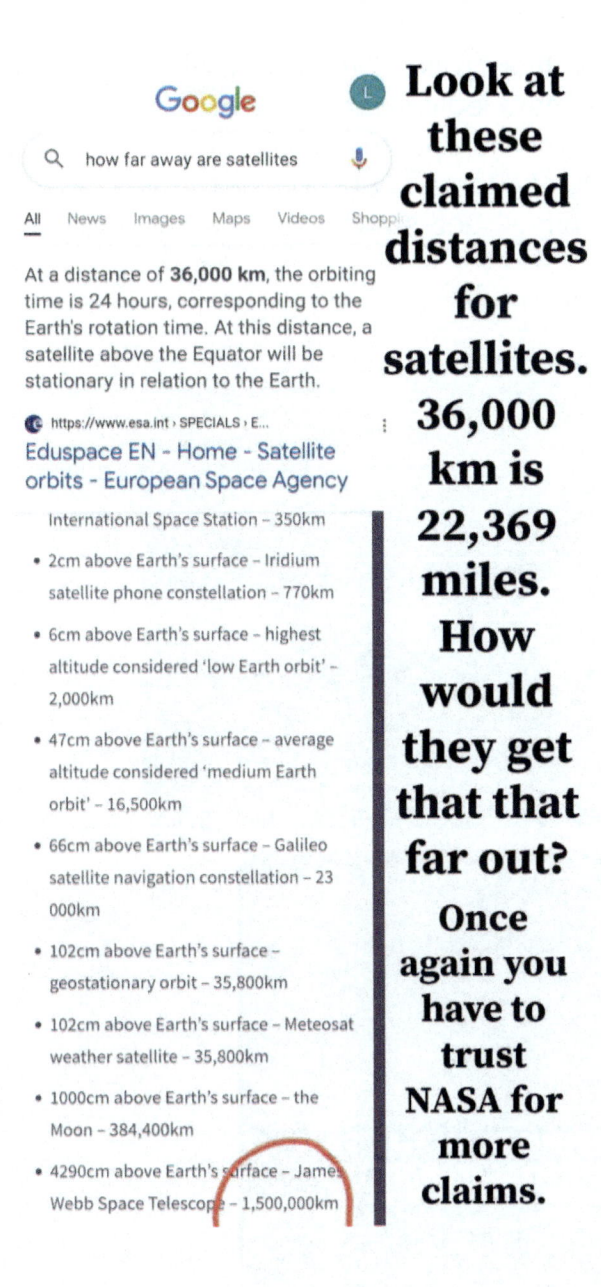

Look at these claimed distances for satellites. 36,000 km is 22,369 miles. How would they get that that far out? Once again you have to trust NASA for more claims.

Google — how far away are satellites

At a distance of **36,000 km**, the orbiting time is 24 hours, corresponding to the Earth's rotation time. At this distance, a satellite above the Equator will be stationary in relation to the Earth.

https://www.esa.int › SPECIALS › E...
Eduspace EN - Home - Satellite orbits - European Space Agency

- International Space Station – 350km
- 2cm above Earth's surface – Iridium satellite phone constellation – 770km
- 6cm above Earth's surface – highest altitude considered 'low Earth orbit' – 2,000km
- 47cm above Earth's surface – average altitude considered 'medium Earth orbit' – 16,500km
- 66cm above Earth's surface – Galileo satellite navigation constellation – 23 000km
- 102cm above Earth's surface – geostationary orbit – 35,800km
- 102cm above Earth's surface – Meteosat weather satellite – 35,800km
- 1000cm above Earth's surface – the Moon – 384,400km
- 4290cm above Earth's surface – James Webb Space Telescope – 1,500,000km

SPACE SATELLITE FALLS INTO BACKYARD
SAGINAW COUNTY

People film these crashes. They're on YouTube. NASA has a phone# on there for people to call so they can retrieve them.

The space station is not much bigger than a 747 plane. If we can barely see a 747 plane at 35,000 feet then wouldn't it be IMPOSSIBLE to see the space station at almost 300 miles up? Satellites are about the size of a Volkswagen van, which you can barely see a few miles away, so how can we possibly see it at the given distances?

Look at this drone from NASA, at the bottom. Which is more logical, the top satellites at quoted distances or the bottom, which you can see with your eyes? Remember how our eyes vision works, things get smaller and smaller till it's gone.

Let logic be your guide.

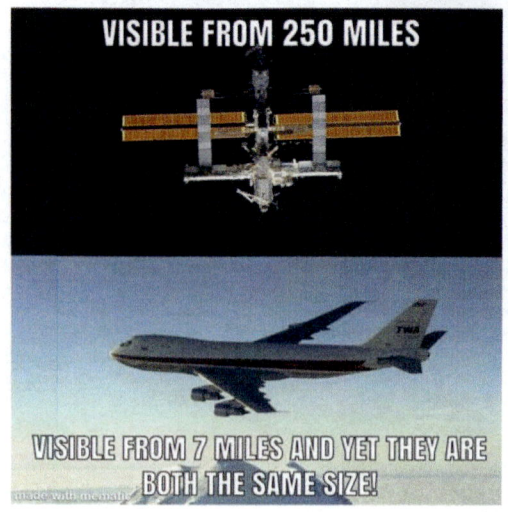

257

The Zetetic Method

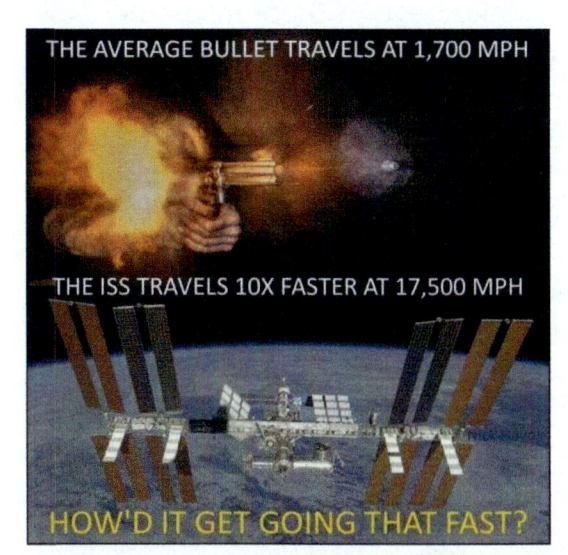

Satellite picture experiment: take a picture of a car moving and see the motion blur and think of a Satellite going 7,000mph. How can the pictures be THAT clear? Where's the motion blur? How can pictures from the ISS, that is said to be going 17,000mph be so clear without any motion blur? Fix a telescope on a plane. Can you imagine it going 17,000mph? And people say they follow the ISS with their telescope.

"If satellites existed, you wouldn't need an airplane for pictures." Dr. James Mae Department of Defense

The Zetetic Method

How can you see them from the ground with your naked eye 100s of miles up? Now you CAN see them but are they 100s of miles up, or are they closer and in the atmosphere on balloons and drones?

Look at the sizes of satellites compared to vehicles. Now look at the second picture of a vehicle probably barely a mile away. See how small it is? Are you sure you can see it 100s of miles away? If claims don't match physical reality then you have to drop one of them. Which one seems more logical to drop?

Is it really in the vacuum void of endless space where God's non-existence or is it within our atmosphere, closer where we can actually see it.

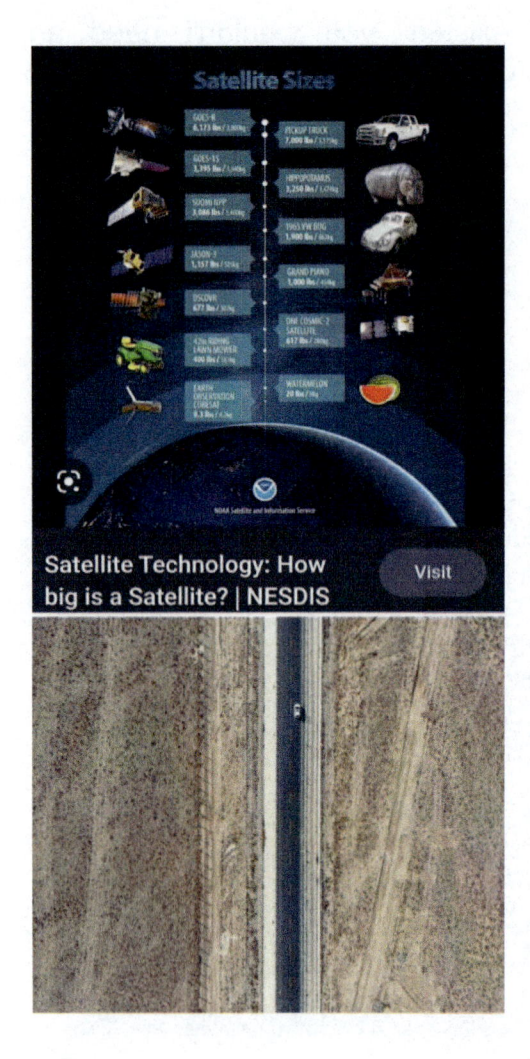

This guy at work told me that Elon Musk's Starlink satellite service has 1000s of satellites in space, and that you have to point the dish at the equator because that's where the satellites orbit so the southern hemisphere and the northern hemisphere can both have this super fast satellite internet. On a ball earth this makes perfect sense doesn't it? Well let's see what the physical evidence shows us shall we.

On a flat earth the best place to put your balloon satellites is in the central North. The North pole is the fixed center of our flat stationary earth and would be the ideal place because it's the closest place to all locations at once, dead center.

Apparently this guy has done zero research and made up some of his own assumptions. The Starlink website clearly states that people in the northern hemisphere must point their dishes North. It did not say anything about the southern hemisphere at all. And not everyone has service. You have to put in your location on their website to see if you have service in your area. You might have service but someone a hundred miles or so down the line doesn't. WHY NOT? If there are 1000s of satellites in space for this starlink, or even just a few, then why can't everyone have service?

Satellite balloons, drones, cables and towers have been used for a very long time and are still being used. They just updated it. (The government has far better technology than you and I. By time you get it, they're done with it.) If it truly went off Satellites in space, as the website claimed, then everyone should have this service. But that's clearly not the case. However as the business grows more towers and satellite balloons will be in operation just like any other business. All globe believers have to go off of is assumptions. Look and think clearly, and you'll see what's going on.

So-called satellite phones have been found to have reception problems in third world countries and other rural areas with very few towers. If the earth were a ball with 3000 or 4000 satellites surrounding, such dead spots should not regularly occur in any rural countryside areas. Why even have cell phones any more, wouldn't SAT phones be the best way to go? How can it lock on a satellite that's going 17,000mph and while we're spinning at 1000 mph?

GPS is another "satellite" device that goes out in rural areas. It downloads your location ahead of time so when it does go out, it's still good to go to a certain extent. But why bother if there are that many satellites orbiting? One reason could be you can fix a broken cable or cell tower. Once a satellite is broken it is disabled.

NASA issues satellite image of storm battered USA, Ne...

Not only are there satellite balloons and satellite drones but also SAT buoys. These, like towers, use triangulation to cover more area. If communications, GPS and the Starlink service went off Satellites then there should be no "dead spots" whatsoever. Yet there are. Why does your GPS have to download the maps, locations, etc. so you won't miss out when you're in a dead spot? <u>Have you ever seen the "pictures" of the USA from space? You can see almost the whole country, so why are there dead spots?</u> If Starlink is going off satellites, then everyone could use it, but it's not so, everyone can't.

The Zetetic Method

You have spots with no service and spots where you have service, this means they are fixed stationary spots which means towers not flying satellites. Think about it.

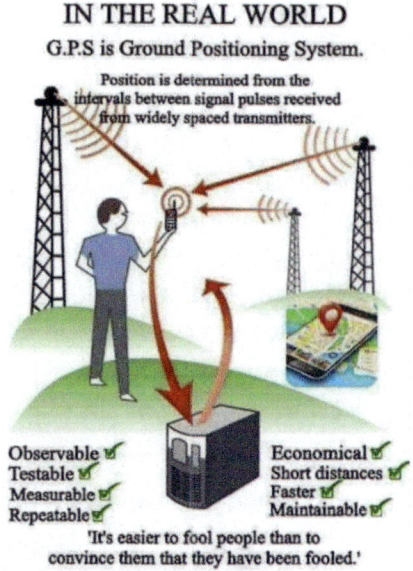

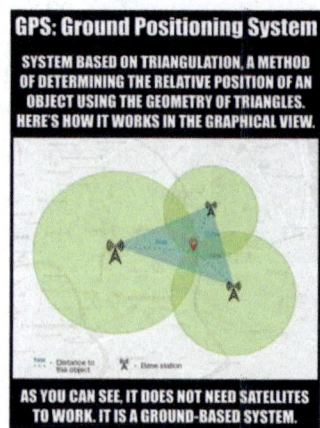

I've seen these for myself, satellites orbiting a whirling ball is not necessary or provable. Why have these with satellite in space.

In rural areas and rural countries, SAT phones and GPS has known not to work. No towers. GPS will download your map and destination and keep using it without service for a good distance

261

Freemason science-fiction writer Arthur C. Clarke wrote about satellites a decade or so before they were claimed to be a fact orbiting in space. He put this idea in everyone's mind so they'd believe it when it was later claimed. They still use this method today with movies and tell-a-vision shows with their programming. Before these "space" satellites were claimed, there were radios, television, and navigation systems like LORAN and DECCA out there doing the job using only ground-based technologies and balloons for all communications. Why would Google use balloons and cables with 1000s of Satellites out there. How could a balloon survive in the vacuum of space and with all the temperature changes as it rotates closer to the sun then further?

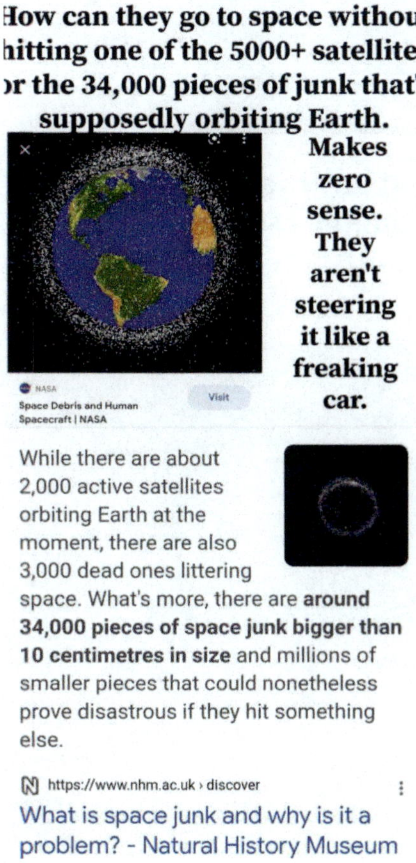

How can they go to space without hitting one of the 5000+ satellites or the 34,000 pieces of junk that's supposedly orbiting Earth. Makes zero sense. They aren't steering it like a freaking car.

While there are about 2,000 active satellites orbiting Earth at the moment, there are also 3,000 dead ones littering space. What's more, there are **around 34,000 pieces of space junk bigger than 10 centimetres in size** and millions of smaller pieces that could nonetheless prove disastrous if they hit something else.

https://www.nhm.ac.uk › discover
What is space junk and why is it a problem? - Natural History Museum

So, all this debris is orbiting earth (but not seen on the space videos). How does debris keep its trajectory? When hit, it would have exploded in all directions. Therefore losing its momentum. Thus it would immediately fall to earth. Think about it.

"The Hubble telescope is credited with finding thousands of exoplanets, or Earth-like planets. This is an amazing feat by the tiny micro radio waves that must go through space dust, comet tails, time and space warp gravitons, and the mass rocks in the asteroid belts, without so much as a deviation, or a wave interference, to accurately capture and record such precise measurements. The current physical distance we are told of our galaxy's width and breadth, measured solely by infrared microwave and radio frequency beams, is just over 46 billion light years, according to NASA. If we take their numbers and measure in terms we can be familiar with, we get a number of 276,000,000,000,000,000,000,000 miles away! Just trust the science we are told, yet we can lose a radio signal in our car while just driving around." Author James Lee

Google Satellite Cables

Google has spent billions on underwater satellites cables. Why bother?

All satellites dishes point at a 90º angle. In the city you'll notice one side of the city's dishes points in one direction the other side points in the other direction. All towards the tower. Well, if they were picking up their signal from moving satellites, then why isn't your antenna moving with the satellite? How does it pick up the signal, when the satellite is on the other side of the ball earth, then? Don't get me wrong there are satellites out there but not in space.

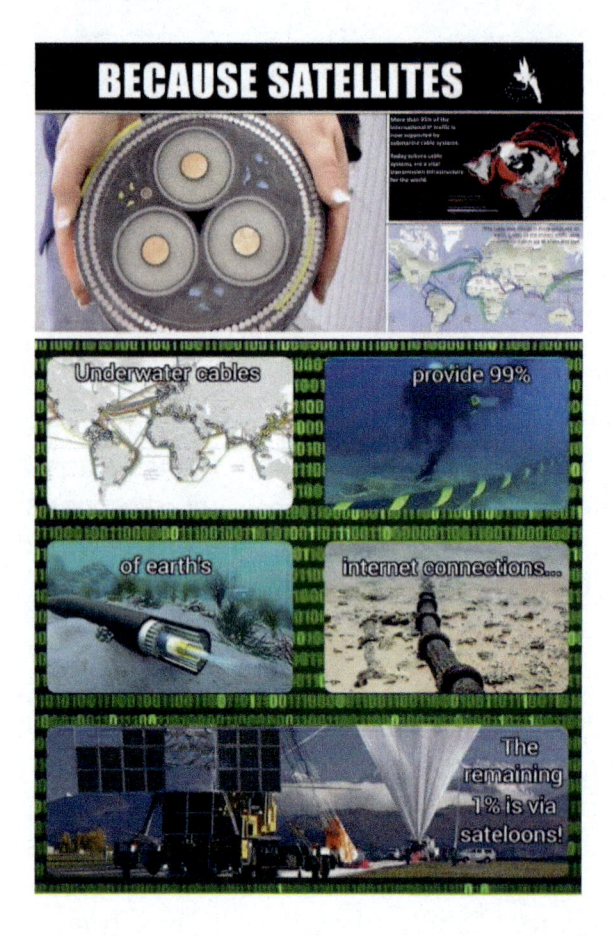

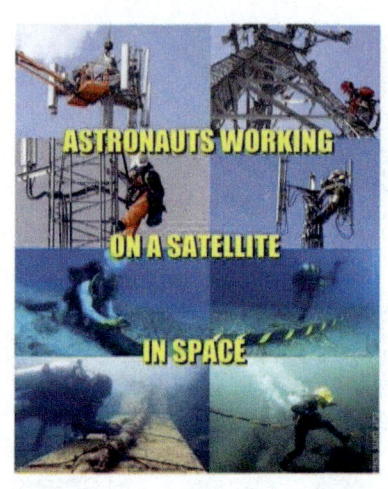

No headline will ever bring me as much joy as this.

The Zetetic Method

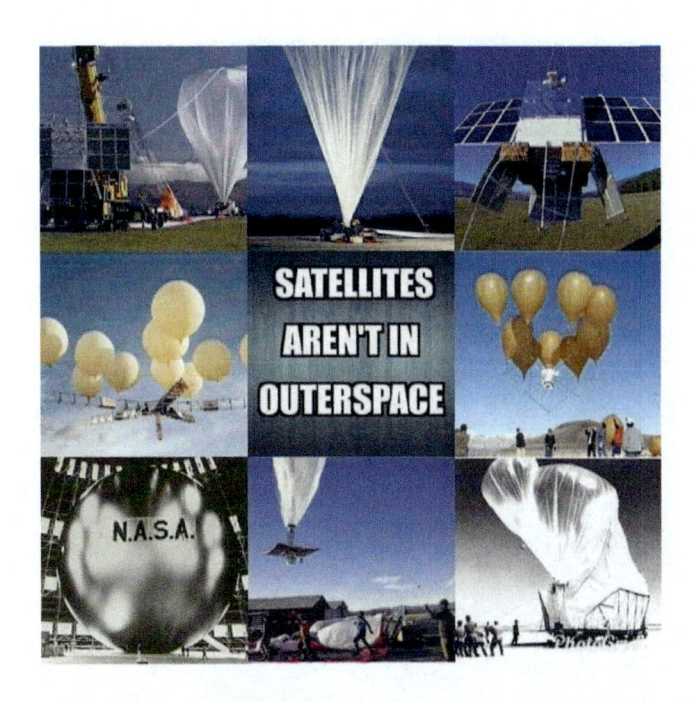

The Zetetic Method

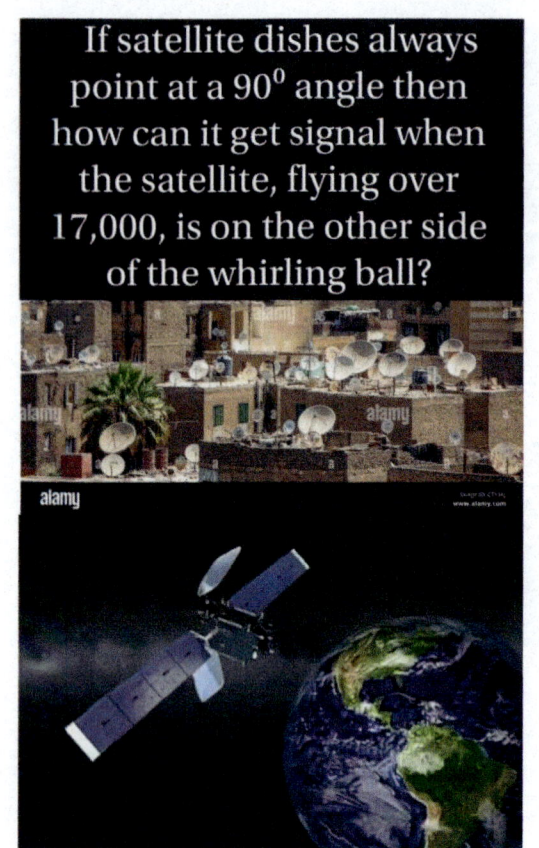

If satellite dishes always point at a 90⁰ angle then how can it get signal when the satellite, flying over 17,000, is on the other side of the whirling ball?

NASA says a satellite requires a speed of 17,450 miles per hour in order to maintain a low Earth orbit. Your satellite antenna stays in a fixed position. How does it follow these satellites?

A few years ago we got a local news announcement that you could see the ISS fly through the sky during the daytime in Big Bend, Texas. And sure enough there it was, you could see it with your naked eyes.

Everyone started joking with me about it, but the joke was on them for not thinking things through. You can't see a 747 plane from almost 300 miles up. Plus it's daylight and blue skies were behind it. Low effort thinking does not create a point.

Are we the highest conscious being here or not?

So what are we seeing making its way across the sky? Hmmm good question. I, and 3 others I've talked to, have seen one light hit a star and take a 90⁰ turn and never slowed down. What's going on up there that they're not telling us about? I don't think it's the balloons or drones (more about those up next) that's turning at a 90⁰ angle without slowing down.

Satellite Balloon

NASA is the biggest helium consumer in the world. One has to wonder why. Let's have a look at it shall we.

NASA almost killed some people when they were releasing one and the wind caught it and dragged it across the parking lot for NASA employees. It made the local news and NASA said there were expensive telescopes, etc. attached. Why go through all that trouble if there are 1000s of satellites orbiting this whirling ball? Now look at this satellite crashing here, it's not any bigger than the truck. Still think you can see it 100s of miles away. How do satellites work in space with the dramatic constant change in temperatures? How do the astronauts deal with these huge changes as well?

The Zetetic Method

The biggest consumer of helium is NASA, using annually almost 75 million cubic feet, followed by the USA Department of Defense, which uses a significant quantity to cool liquid hydrogen and oxygen for rocket fuel.

http://www.issuesmagazine.com.au › ...
Helium: Is the Party Really Over? - Issues Magazine

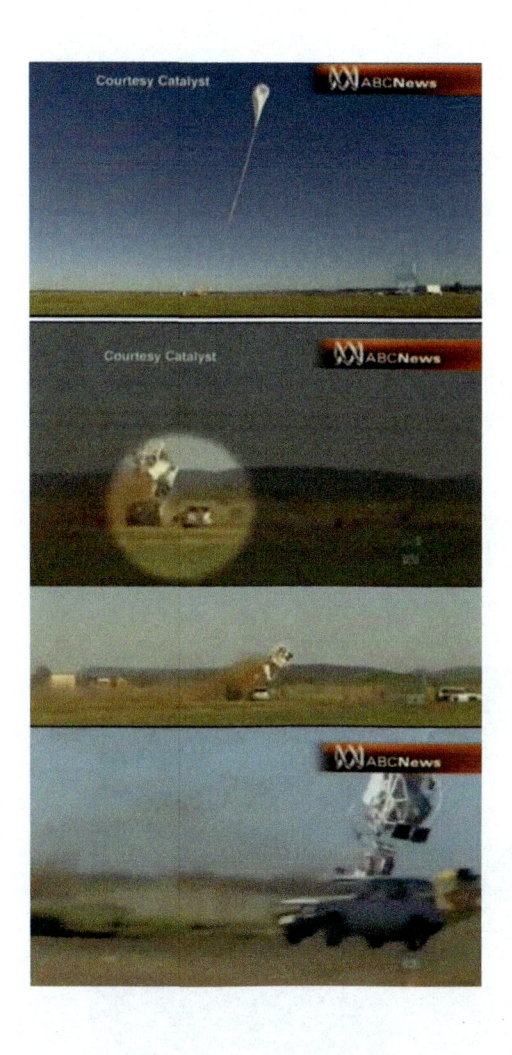

If you go to NASA'S website to track the ISS, you'll see that it's all over the place, zigzagging. It goes over the more developed countries. If you trace its path on a flat earth map it creates a circle. Which makes more sense?

LMAO: "To fanciful minds and theoretical speculators, the so-called 'science' of modern astronomy furnishes a field, unsurpassed in any science for the unrestrained license of the imagination, and the building up of a complicated conjuration of absurdities such as to overawe the simpleton and make him gape with wonder; to deceive even those who truly believe their assumptions to be facts."   Thomas Winship, Zetetic Cosmogony.

The Zetetic Method

Am I suppose to believe that these extreme temperature differences dealt to the ISS over and over and over again, doesn't destroy it OR it's passengers?

When the ISS faces the sun, the (external) temperature it experiences is around 250 degrees Fahrenheit (121 Degrees Celsius). On the other hand, when it's on the side when our planet completely blocks out the sun, the thermometers plummet to minus 250 degrees Fahrenheit (-157 degrees Celsius).

You can go on NASA'S website and see the ISS tracking, it makes no sense on a ball earth and perfect sense on a flat stationary earth. If you can see the ISS in the sky, and you can, then it's not 300 miles away. It's said to be the same size as a 747 plane, which is barely visible at 35,000 feet.

Notice it's tracked over the most developed countries. which makes more sense, circling or zigzaging?

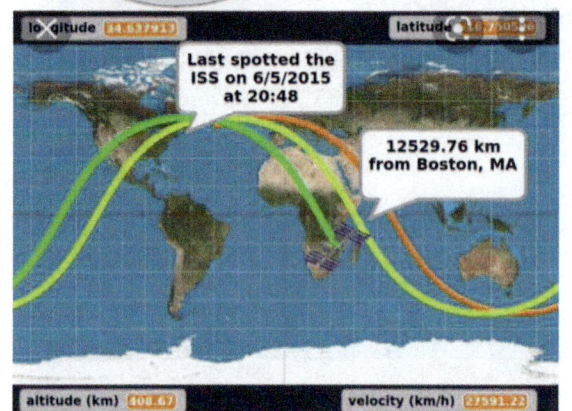

Scratch ISS Tracker Extension

ALL THIS TO PUSH A RADIO SIGNAL A DISTANCE OF 300 MILES THROUGH ATMOSPHERE

A SIMPLE BATTERY FROM 1960 TO PUSH A SIGNAL 240,000 MILES, AND ONCE IT HITS THE EARTH, THROUGH 500 MILES OF ATMOSPHERE

THE BLACK SWAN

$85,000,000 NASA plane with telescopes and other equipment on-board. Why when there's 1000s upon 1000s of satellites.

1. You can not see an object some 100s of miles away if you can barely see it 35,000 feet away.
2. If satellites were in space there wouldn't be dead spots everywhere and satellite dishes wouldn't have to point in a fixed direction towards a tower. That means the service is in a FIXED location. Google wouldn't be spending billions on internet and satellite cables and helium.

Perhaps this plane is bouncing signals off something. Firmament maybe, or a satellite shooting past at 17,000 mph.

CHAPTER 8.5

GOVERNMENT DOCUMENTS SAYING FLAT EARTH

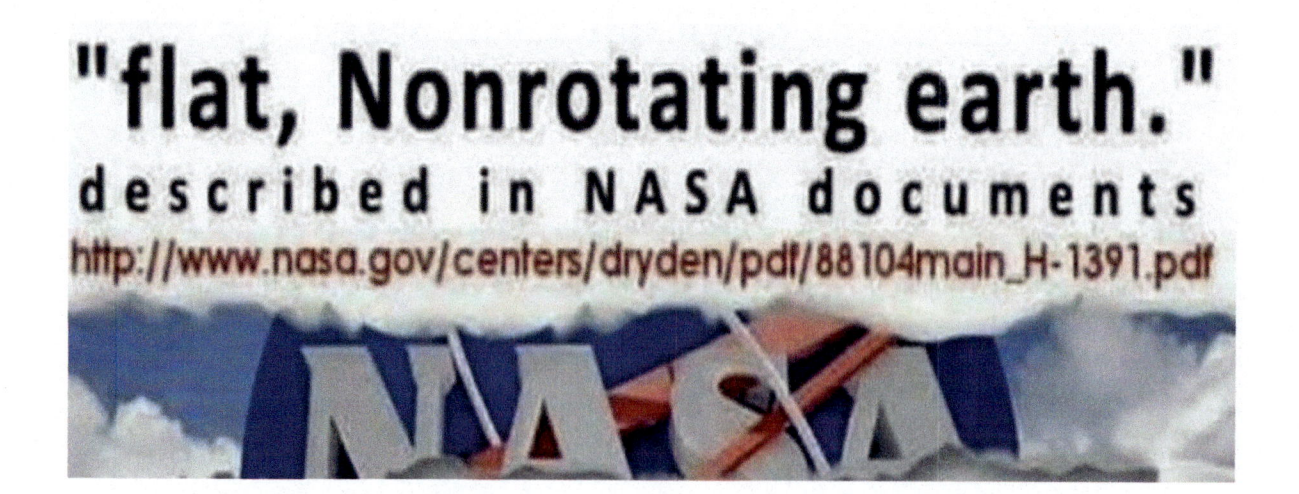

"flat, Nonrotating earth."
described in NASA documents
http://www.nasa.gov/centers/dryden/pdf/88104main_H-1391.pdf

I found a video here (https://youtu.be/ny9-5AXaAl4) about 44 government documents that said the Earth was flat. There was also a link to a website (https://greatmountainpublishing.com/2022/05/11/official-government-documents-verify-that-the-earth-is-flat/) that had a link to each government website with the documents. I went to each one and looked over it and saw the truth with my own eyes. Now, I never at that point thought that I'd be writing a book on the subject or I would have taken a screenshot of each one. But I did not and now I'm kicking myself over and over again.

I was very excited about this chapter until I tried to go on the government websites again to do my own screen shots but here's what I found instead for each site. You see the government site and you see it's now locked.

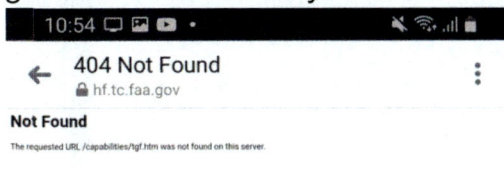

So now I had to go through the video to get theirs. I did not get all of them, only a few for you to get my point. I beg of you to watch the video, because he talks more about each one. Well worth the time spent. At the end of this chapter some contradictions are shown.

The government did announce that it would be taking the sites down and it did just that. But why? Truth fears no investigation!!!

These documents come from all over and from different military branches and NASA. First there will be the screenshot of the beginning of the article to know what subject they're discussing, then the flat earth claim. Why assume a flat non-rotating earth when training and calculating when we live on a whirling ball earth? Doesn't make sense, unless that is, you live on a flat non-rotating earth.

Let's begin shall we. (All the blue writing, red underlining and the flat earth symbol, but <u>not the NASA</u> symbol is added)

If this aircraft is flying at 2193 mph, then that means in 1 hour it has to account for 3,206,166 feet of curvature, so why are they calculating and training under an assumption of a flat non-rotating earth?

Lockheed SR-71 Blackbird / Top speed

2,193 mph

The DPS equations of motion use four assumptions that simplify the program while maintaining its fidelity for most maneuvers and applications: point-mass modeling, nonturbulent atmosphere, zero side forces, and <u>a nonrotating Earth</u>. The primary advantages of us-

The Zetetic Method

"APPROVED FOR RELEASE: 06/15/2000   CIA-RDP86-00513R001343720008-3

49-12-15/16

Dissertations Defended in the Scientific Council of the Institute of Physics of the Earth, Institute of Physics of the Atmosphere and Institute of Applied Geophysics, Ac.Sc. USSR during the First Semester of 1957.

near-sun halo and also from the sun on a surface perpendicular to these rays. The dissertation contains **a certain formula** of the brightness of the sky, taking into consideration only the brightness of the first order and derived on the assumption of a "flat" Earth and giving some conclusions derived on the basis of this formula. For a certain coefficient of transparency of the atmosphere, the brightness of the sky at any point is represented by derivation of two functions of which one is the function **of the diffusion of** light and the other is a function of the zenith distances of the sun and of the observed point of the sky. On changing of the zenith distances of the sun z from 90 to 0°, the brightness of the sky on the almucantar of the sun increases first, reaching a maximum for a certain value of z, and then decreases. A method is also proposed of determining the brightness of the clear daylight sky at any point based on measuring the brightness along the almucantar of the sun and of 5-6 points of the firmament located at various zenith distances. This method permits determination

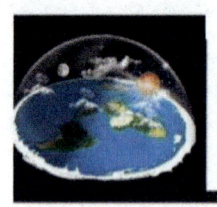

Card 7/21

Page 20 of 100

Government Admits Flat Earth: Doc #2

ARMY RESEARCH LABORATORY

Propagation of Electromagnetic Fields Over Flat Earth

Joseph R. Miletta

Title: Propagation of Electromagnetic Fields Over Flat Earth

Author: Joseph R. Miletta

URL: https://www.arl.army.mil/arlreports/2001/ARL-TR-2352.pdf

ARL-TR-2352

February 2001

Government Admits Flat Earth: Doc #30

Army Research Laboratory

Beacon Position and Attitude Navigation Aided by a Magnetometer

by Xu Ma and Gonzalo R. Arce

Title: Beacon Position and Attitude Navigation Aided by a Magnetometer

Author: Xu Ma and Gonzalo R. Arce

URL: https://www.arl.army.mil/arlreports/2010/ARL-CR-650.pdf

ARL-CR-650   June 2010

2.1 Coordinate Systems

The motion of an object is usually described by rigid body equations of motion derived from Newton's laws (29). This section summarizes and notates three kinds of coordinate systems. The first is the Earth-fixed coordinate system, which is fixed to the Earth with <u>a flat Earth assumption</u>. Denote **X**, **Y**, and **Z** as the unit vectors pointing in the directions of the X, Y, and Z axes, respectively. Without loss of generality, the X, Y, and Z axes point to forward, right, and down, respectively. The second is the body-fixed coordinate system, with three unit vectors $\mathbf{X_b}$,

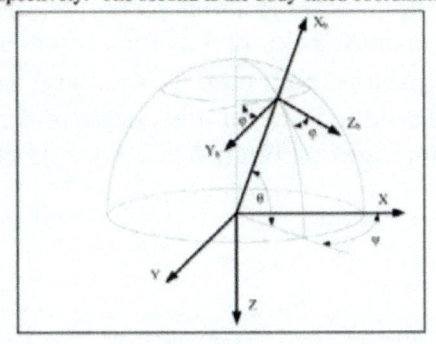

Figure 1. Earth- and body-fixed coordinate systems and the Euler angle rotations.

Doc #30: Page 11 of 31

Government Admits Flat Earth: Doc #31

ARMY RESEARCH LABORATORY

Automatic Target Acquisition of the DEMO III Program

by Sandor Der, Alex Chan, Gary Stolovy, Michael Lander, and Matthew Thielke

Title: Automatic Target Acquisition of the DEMO III Program
Author: Sandor Der, Alex Chan, Gary Stolovy, Michael Lander, and Matthew Thielke
URL: http://www.arl.army.mil/arlreports/2002/ARL-TR-2683.pdf

ARL-TR-2683

August 200[2]

of tolerance. For example, in some scenarios, it is assumed that the range is known to within a meter from a laser range finder or a digital map. In other scenarios, only the range to the center of the field-of-view and the depression angle is known so that a flat earth approximation provides the best estimate. Many algorithms, both model-based and learning-based, either require accurate range information or compensate for inaccurate information by attempting to detect targets at a number of different ranges within the tolerance of the range. Because many

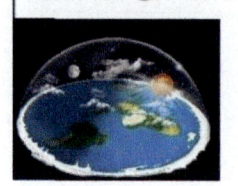

Government Admits Flat Earth: Doc #38

The Pennsylvania State University
Graduate School
College of Engineering

A DISCUSSION OF METHODS OF REAL-TIME AIRPLANE FLIGHT SIMULATION

Title: A Discussion of Methods of Real-Time Airplane Flight Simulation

Authors: Carl Banks

URL: http://citeseerx.ist.psu.edu/viewdoc/download?doi=10.1.1.510.7499&rep=rep1&type=pdf

A paper in
Aerospace Engineering
by
Carl Banks

Flat-Earth Coordinates. In many flight simulators, global navigation is not important. For example, the range of flight could be limited to a small area, or the simulator might not care about the airplane's location.

In such cases, it is appropriate to model the Earth as a plane half-space rather than an oblate spheroid. Then, the simulator need not worry about how the local horizontal plane changes as the airplane flies around the Earth. This simplifies the bookkeeping in the simulator considerably.

The flat-Earth coordinate system is a Cartesian system, which originates at the surface. The z-axis points vertically down, the x-axis points north, and the y-axis points east.

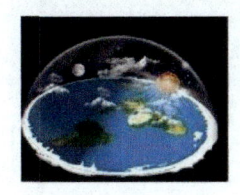

Doc #38: Page 11 of 50

Government Admits Flat Earth: Doc #44

FM 6-40
MCWP 3-16.4

Tactics, Techniques, and Procedures for the Field Artillery Manual Cannon Gunnery

Title: Tactics, Techniques, and Procedures for the field Artillery Manual Cannon Gunnery

URL: https://www.marines.mil/Portals/1/Publications/mcwp3_16_4.pdf

U.S. Marine Corps

Here there's a condication. Talks about the rotating earth but not when apply it in real life, then it's assumed flat and non-rotating. Hmmm

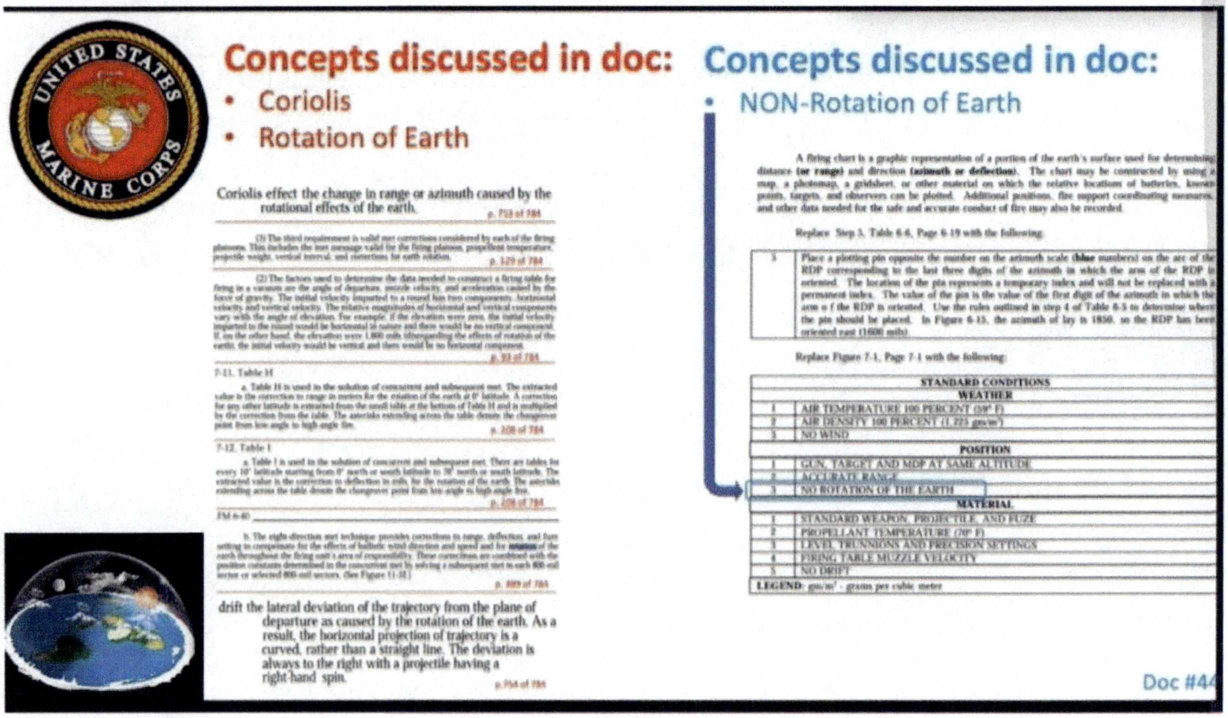

Concepts discussed in doc:
- Coriolis
- Rotation of Earth

Coriolis effect the change in range or azimuth caused by the rotational effects of the earth.

drift the lateral deviation of the trajectory from the plane of departure as caused by the rotation of the earth. As a result, the horizontal projection of trajectory is a curved, rather than a straight line. The deviation is always to the right with a projectile having a right-hand spin.

Concepts discussed in doc:
- NON-Rotation of Earth

STANDARD CONDITIONS
- AIR TEMPERATURE 100 PERCENT
- AIR DENSITY 100 PERCENT
- NO WIND
- GUN, TARGET AND MDP AT SAME ALTITUDE
- ACCURATE RANGE
- **NO ROTATION OF THE EARTH**
- STANDARD WEAPON, PROJECTILE, AND FUZE
- PROPELLANT TEMPERATURE (70° F)
- LEVEL TRUNNIONS AND PRECISION SETTINGS
- FIRING TABLE MUZZLE VELOCITY
- NO DRIFT

Doc #44

The Zetetic Method

39th Annual Precise Time and Time Interval (PTTI) Meeting

mapping functions. Two are rough approaches, namely a simple plane troposphere (assuming a flat Earth) and the straight "line of sight" through the spherical troposphere shell [14]. While these two functions result in too large or too small values, respectively, we use for the path length computation the mapping function as reported by Niell (equation 4 in [15]). The results for all three mapping functions for different elevation angles at a fixed troposphere height (11 km) is shown in Fig. 6 (right).

Doc #25: Page 6 of 12

Government Admits Flat Earth: Doc #27

ARMY RESEARCH LABORATORY

User Manual for the Microsoft Window Edition of the Scanning Fast-Field Program (WSCAFFIP) Version 3.0

by John M. Noble

Title: User Manual for the Microsoft Window Edition of the Scanning Fast-Field Program (WSCAFFIP) Version 3.0
Author: John M. Noble
URL: https://www.arl.army.mil/arlreports/2003/ARL-TR-2696.pdf

ARL-TR-2696

January 2003

Government Admits Flat Earth: Doc #21

UNPUBLISHED PRELIMINARY DATA

NsG-304

ATMOSPHERIC OSCILLATIONS

by A. J. Lineberger and H. D. Edwards

Georgia Tech Project A-652-001

Contract No. AF19(628)-393

GPO PRICE $ _____
OTS PRICE(S) $ _____
Hard copy (HC) 2.00
Microfiche (MF) .50

Title: Atmospheric Oscillations
Author: A. J. Lineberger and H. D. Edwards
URL: https://ntrs.nasa.gov/archive/nasa/casi.ntrs.nasa.gov/19650015408.pdf

A model frequently used is that of a flat, nonrotating earth. The temperature is assumed either to be constant, to increase or decrease monotonically with altitude, or to be stratified. Gravity is usually considered to be constant. Density and pressure are usually considered to vary exponentially with altitude.

The most one can profitably simplify the problem is to consider an isothermal atmosphere, plane level surfaces, and a nonrotating earth. This case has been handled by Eckart [1960], Lamb [1932], and Hines [1960]. The simplification is

Doc #21: Page 13 of 34

16. Abstract

An interactive FORTRAN program that provides the user with a powerful and flexible tool for the linearization of aircraft aerodynamic models is documented in this report. The program LINEAR numerically determines a linear system model using nonlinear equations of motion and a user-supplied linear or nonlinear aerodynamic model. The nonlinear equations of motion used are six-degree-of-freedom equations with <u>stationary atmosphere and flat, nonrotating earth assumptions</u>. The system model determined by LINEAR consists of matrices for both the state and observation equations. The program has been designed to allow easy selection and definition of the state, control, and observation variables to be used in a particular model.

17. Key Words (Suggested by Author(s))	18. Distribution Statement
Aircraft model Computer program Control law design Linearization	Unclassified — Unlimited Subject category 66

19. Security Classif. (of this report)	20. Security Classif. (of this page)	21. No. of pages	22. Price
Unclassified	Unclassified	124	A06

NASA FORM 1626 OCT 86

For sale by the National Technical Information Service, Springfield, Virginia 22161

NASA-Langley, 1988

Doc #14: Page 126 of 126

AIRCRAFT LANDING MODEL

1. Equations of Motion

The two-dimensional model for aircraft motion presented in this section follows the general form developed by Frost [12]. It accounts for both vertical and horizontal mean wind components having both time and spatial variations.

The aircraft trajectory model employed in this study was derived based on the following assumptions:

a) <u>The earth is flat and non-rotating.</u>

Doc #18: Page 14 of 93

Problem Statement

The example problem is a fixed-time problem in which it is required to determine the thrust-attitude program of a single-stage rocket vehicle starting from rest and going to specified terminal conditions of altitude and vertical velocity which will maximize the final horizontal velocity. The idealizing assumptions made are the following:

(1) A point-mass vehicle
(2) A flat, nonrotating earth
(3) A constant-gravity field, $g = 9.8$ m/sec^2 (32.2 ft/sec^2)
(4) Constant thrust and mass-loss rate
(5) A nonlifting body in a nonvarying atmosphere with a constant drag parameter $K_D = \frac{1}{2}\rho C_D S$, where S is the frontal surface area.

Doc #11: Page 14 of 43

Government Admits Flat Earth: Doc #12

NASA TN D-645

EXTRA COPY

TECHNICAL NOTE
D-645

CALCULATION OF WIND COMPENSATION FOR LAUNCHING
OF UNGUIDED ROCKETS

By Robert L. James, Jr., and Ronald J. Harris

Langley Research Center

Title: Calculation of Wind Compensation for Launching of Unguided Rockets

Author: Robert L. James, Jr., and Ronald J. Harris

URL: https://ntrs.nasa.gov/archive/nasa/casi.ntrs.nasa.gov/20040008097.pdf

1. Introduction

Effective military or law-enforcement applications of high-power microwave (HPM) systems in which the HPM system and the target system are on or near the ground or water require that the microwave power density on target be maximized. The power density at the target for a given source will depend on the destructive and constructive scattering of the fields as they propagate to the target. Antenna design for an HPM system includes addressing the following questions about field polarization: Should the fields the transmitting antenna produces be vertically, horizontally, or circularly polarized? Which polarization maximizes the power density on target? (The question of which polarization best couples to the target is beyond the scope of this report.) While this report does not completely answer these questions, it addresses the interaction of the radiated electromagnetic fields with earth ground. It is assumed that the transmitting antenna and the target (or receiver) are located above, but near the surface of a flat idealized earth (constant permittivity, ε, and conductivity, σ) ground. First an ideal vertical dipole (oriented along the z-axis perpendicular to the ground plane) is addressed. The horizontal dipole (parallel to the ground plane) follows.

Doc #2: Page 7 of 35

Figure 6. Comparison of principal fields from an ideal dipole oriented perpendicular and horizontal to a homogeneous flat earth. In each case, dipole is placed 2 m above ground plane and observer or target is 1000 m down range: (a) sea water, (b) wet earth, (c) dry earth, (d) lake water, and (e) dry sand.

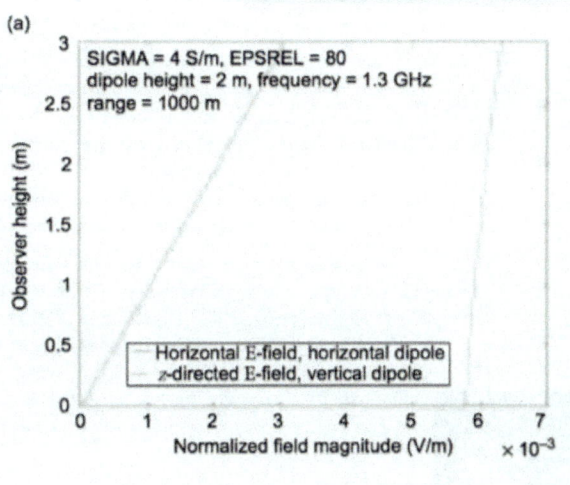

Doc #2: Page 17 of 35

280

Government Admits Flat Earth: Doc #7

NASA Reference Publication 1207

August 1988

Title: Derivation and Definition of a Linear Aircraft Model

Author: Eugene L. Duke, Robert F. Antoniewicz, and Keith D. Krambeer

URL: https://www.nasa.gov/centers/dryden/pdf/88104main_H-1391.pdf

Derivation and Definition of a Linear Aircraft Model

Eugene L. Duke,
Robert F. Antoniewicz,
and Keith D. Krambeer

INTRODUCTION

The need for linear models of aircraft for the analysis of vehicle dynamics and control law design is well known. These models are widely used, not only for computer applications but also for quick approximations and desk calculations. Whereas the use of these models is well understood and well documented, their derivation is not. The lack of documentation and, occasionally, understanding of the derivation of linear models is a hindrance to communication, training, and application.

This report details the development of the linear model of a rigid aircraft of constant mass, flying over a flat, nonrotating earth. This model consists of a state equation and an observation (or measurement) equation. The system equations have been broadly formulated to accommodate a wide variety of applications. The linear state equation is derived from the nonlinear six-degree-of-freedom equations of motion. The linear observation equation is derived from a collection of nonlinear equations representing state variables, time derivatives of state variables, control inputs, and flightpath, air data, and other parameters. The linear model is developed about a nominal trajectory that is general.

Whereas it is common to assume symmetric aerodynamics and mass distribution, or a straight and level trajectory, or both (Clancy, 1975; Dommasch and others, 1967; Etkin, 1972; McRuer and others, 1973; Northrop Aircraft, 1952; Thelander, 1965), these assumptions limit the generality of the linear model. The principal contribution of this report is a solution of the general problem of deriving a linear model of a rigid aircraft without making these simplifying assumptions. By defining the initial conditions (of the nominal trajectory) for straight and level flight and setting the asymmetric aerodynamic and inertia terms to zero, one can easily obtain the more traditional linear models from the linear model derived in this report.

D.2 Evaluation of the Derivatives of the Time Derivatives of the State Variables

The generalized derivatives of the time derivatives of the state variables are defined in appendix C, equations (C-1) to (C-15). In this section, these generalized derivatives are evaluated in terms of the stability and control derivatives, primative terms, and the state, time derivative of state, and control variables. In this section, the notation $\partial(\dot{x}_i)/\partial x_i$ is used to represent the more correct notation $\partial f_i/\partial x_j$ that is employed in the discussion at the beginning of section 3. This notation is used because there is no convenient notation available to express these quantities clearly—particularly not the usual notation employed in flight mechanics texts such as Etkin (1972) and McRuer and others (1973). The notation that defines quantities such as $L_p = \partial(\dot{p})/\partial p$ and $M_q = \partial(\dot{q})/\partial q$ is misleading in this context because the definitions of those terms (such as L_p, M_q) are based on assumptions of symmetric mass distributions, symmetric aerodynamics, and straight and level flight, and additionally do not include derivatives with respect to atmospheric quantities.

Doc #7: Page 55 of 102

---

16. Abstract

This report documents the derivation and definition of a linear aircraft model for a rigid aircraft of constant mass flying over a flat, nonrotating earth. The derivation makes no assumptions of reference trajectory or vehicle symmetry. The linear system equations are derived and evaluated along a general trajectory and include both aircraft dynamics and observation variables.

17. Key Words (Suggested by Author(s))	18. Distribution Statement
Aircraft models Flight controls Flight dynamics Linear models	Unclassified — Unlimited Subject category 08

19. Security Classif. (of this report)	20. Security Classif. (of this page)	21. No. of pages	22. Price
Unclassified	Unclassified	108	A06

NASA FORM 1626 OCT 86

For sale by the National Technical Information Service, Springfield, VA 22161-2171.

NASA-Langley, 1986

Doc #7: Page 102 of 102

The Zetetic Method

REPORT DOCUMENTATION PAGE			Form Approved OMB No. 0704-0188
Public reporting burden for this collection of information is estimated to average 1 hour per response, including the time for reviewing instructions, searching existing data sources, gathering and maintaining the data needed, and completing and reviewing the collection of information. Send comments regarding this burden estimate or any other aspect of this collection of information, including suggestions for reducing this burden, to Washington Headquarters Services, Directorate for Information Operations and Reports, 1215 Jefferson Davis Highway, Suite 1204, Arlington, VA 22202-4302, and to the Office of Management and Budget, Paperwork Reduction Project (0704-0188), Washington, DC 20503.			
1. AGENCY USE ONLY (Leave blank)	2. REPORT DATE February 2001	3. REPORT TYPE AND DATES COVERED Summary, Oct 99 to Sept 00	
4. TITLE AND SUBTITLE Propagation of Electromagnetic Fields Over Flat Earth			5. FUNDING NUMBERS DA PR: AH94 PE: 62705A
6. AUTHOR(S) Joseph R. Miletta			
7. PERFORMING ORGANIZATION NAME(S) AND ADDRESS(ES) U.S. Army Research Laboratory Attn: AMSRL-SE-DS email: jmiletta@arl.army.mil 2800 Powder Mill Road Adelphi, MD 20783-1197			8. PERFORMING ORGANIZATION REPORT NUMBER ARL-TR-2352
9. SPONSORING/MONITORING AGENCY NAME(S) AND ADDRESS(ES) U.S. Army Research Laboratory 2800 Powder Mill Road Adelphi, MD 20783-1197			10. SPONSORING/MONITORING AGENCY REPORT NUMBER

Doc #2: Page 35 of 35

Government Admits Flat Earth: Doc #3

ARMY RESEARCH LABORATORY

Title: An Energy Budget Model to Calculate the Low Atmosphere Profiles of Effective Sound Speed at Night

Author: Arnold Tunick

URL: https://www.arl.army.mil/arlreports/2003/ARL-MR-563.pdf

An Energy Budget Model to Calculate the Low Atmosphere Profiles of Effective Sound Speed at Night

by Arnold Tunick

ARL-MR-563   May 2003

> Lockheed SR-71 Blackbird / Top speed
>
> **2,193 mph** 
>
> The DPS equations of motion use four assumptions that simplify the program while maintaining its fidelity for most maneuvers and applications: point-mass modeling, nonturbulent atmosphere, zero side forces, and a <u>nonrotating Earth</u>. The primary advantages of us-

> "APPROVED FOR RELEASE: 06/15/2000   CIA-RDP86-00513R001343720008-3
>
> 49-12-15/16
> Dissertations Defended in the Scientific Council of the Institute of Physics of the Earth, Institute of Physics of the Atmosphere and Institute of Applied Geophysics, Ac.Sc. USSR during the First Semester of 1957.
>
> Ye.V. Pyaskovskaya-Fesenkova - <u>Investigation of the Scattering of Light in the Earth's Atmosphere</u> (Issledovaniye rasseyaniya sveta v zemnoy atmosfere) - Doctor dissertation. Opponents: Doctor of Physico-Mathematical Sciences Ye.S. Kuznetsov, Doctor of Physico-Mathematical Sciences S.M. Polozkov, Doctor of Physico-Mathematical Sciences G.B. Rozenberg, Doctor of Physico-Mathematical Sciences I.S. Shklovskiy. March 23, 1957. The dissertation represents the result of many years of study of the clear, daytime sky. The observations were carried out in twelve locations at various altitudes above the sea, various climatic, meteorological and synoptic conditions. The observations were carried out mainly during high-transparency of the atmosphere in the visual range of the spectrum in the absence of a snow cover. In the investigations two instruments, designed by V.G. Fesenkov were used; one of these was a visual photometer of the daytime sky intended for measuring the <u>brightness of the firmament</u>; the other was a photo-
> Card6/21 electric halo photometer for determining the brightness from 
>
> Page 19 of 100

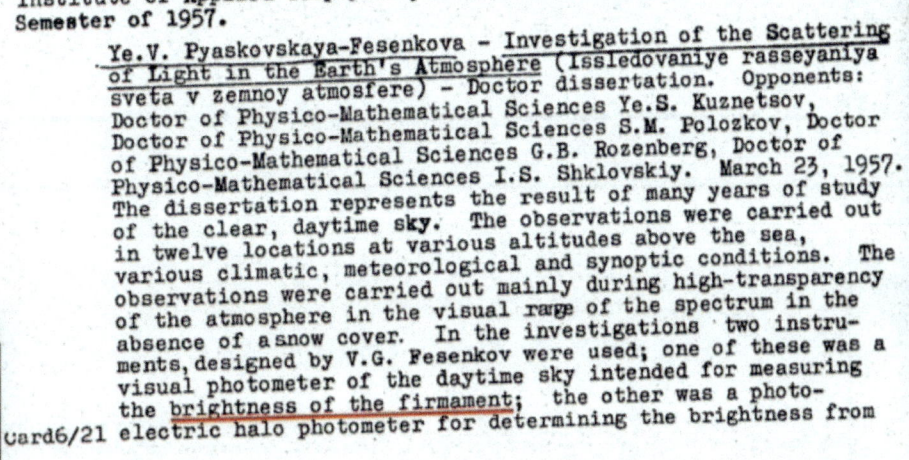

D.2 Evaluation of the Derivatives of the Time Derivatives of the State Variables

The generalized derivatives of the time derivatives of the state variables are defined in appendix C, equations (C-1) to (C-15). In this section, these generalized derivatives are evaluated in terms of the stability and control derivatives, primative terms, and the state, time derivative of state, and control variables. In this section, the notation $\partial(\dot{x}_i)/\partial x_i$ is used to represent the more correct notation $\partial f_i/\partial x_j$ that is employed in the discussion at the beginning of section 3. This notation is used because there is no convenient notation available to express these quantities clearly—particularly not the usual notation employed in flight mechanics texts such as Etkin (1972) and McRuer and others (1973). The notation that defines quantities such as $L_p = \partial(\dot{p})/\partial p$ and $M_q = \partial(\dot{q})/\partial q$ is misleading in this context because the definitions of those terms (such as L_p, M_q) are based on assumptions of symmetric mass distributions, symmetric aerodynamics, and straight and level flight, and additionally do not include derivatives with respect to atmospheric quantities.

---

16. Abstract

This report documents the derivation and definition of a linear aircraft model for a rigid aircraft of constant mass flying over a flat, nonrotating earth. The derivation makes no assumptions of reference trajectory or vehicle symmetry. The linear system equations are derived and evaluated along a general trajectory and include both aircraft dynamics and observation variables.

17. Key Words (Suggested by Author(s))	18. Distribution Statement
Aircraft models Flight controls Flight dynamics Linear models	Unclassified — Unlimited Subject category 08

19. Security Classif. (of this report)	20. Security Classif. (of this page)	21. No. of pages	22. Price
Unclassified	Unclassified	108	A06

NASA FORM 1626 OCT 86
For sale by the National Technical Information Service, Springfield, VA 22161-2171.

NASA-Langley, 1988

Government Admits Flat Earth: Doc #41

TC 3-09.81

Field Artillery Manual Cannon Gunnery

APRIL 2016

DISTRIBUTION RESTRICTION: Approved for public release; distribution is unlimited.
*This publication supersedes TC 3-09.81/MCWP 3-16.4, dated 1 March 2016.

Headquarters, Department of the Army

Title: Field Artillery Manual Cannon Gunnery

URL: https://armypubs.army.mil/epubs/DR_pubs/DR_a/pdf/web/tc3_09x81.pdf

STANDARD CONDITIONS	
WEATHER	
1	AIR TEMPERATURE 100 PERCENT
2	AIR DENSITY 100 PERCENT
3	NO WIND
POSITION	
1	GUN, TARGET AND MDP AT SAME ALTITUDE
2	ACCURATE RANGE
3	NO ROTATION OF THE EARTH
MATERIAL	
1	STANDARD WEAPON, PROJECTILE, AND FUZE
2	PROPELLANT TEMPERATURE (70° F)
3	LEVEL TRUNNIONS AND PRECISION SETTINGS
4	FIRING TABLE MUZZLE VELOCITY
5	NO DRIFT

Figure 7-1. Standard Conditions.

Doc #41: Page 175 of 664

Concept discussed in doc:
- Azimuth

aka "FLAT", no curvature

Doc #4

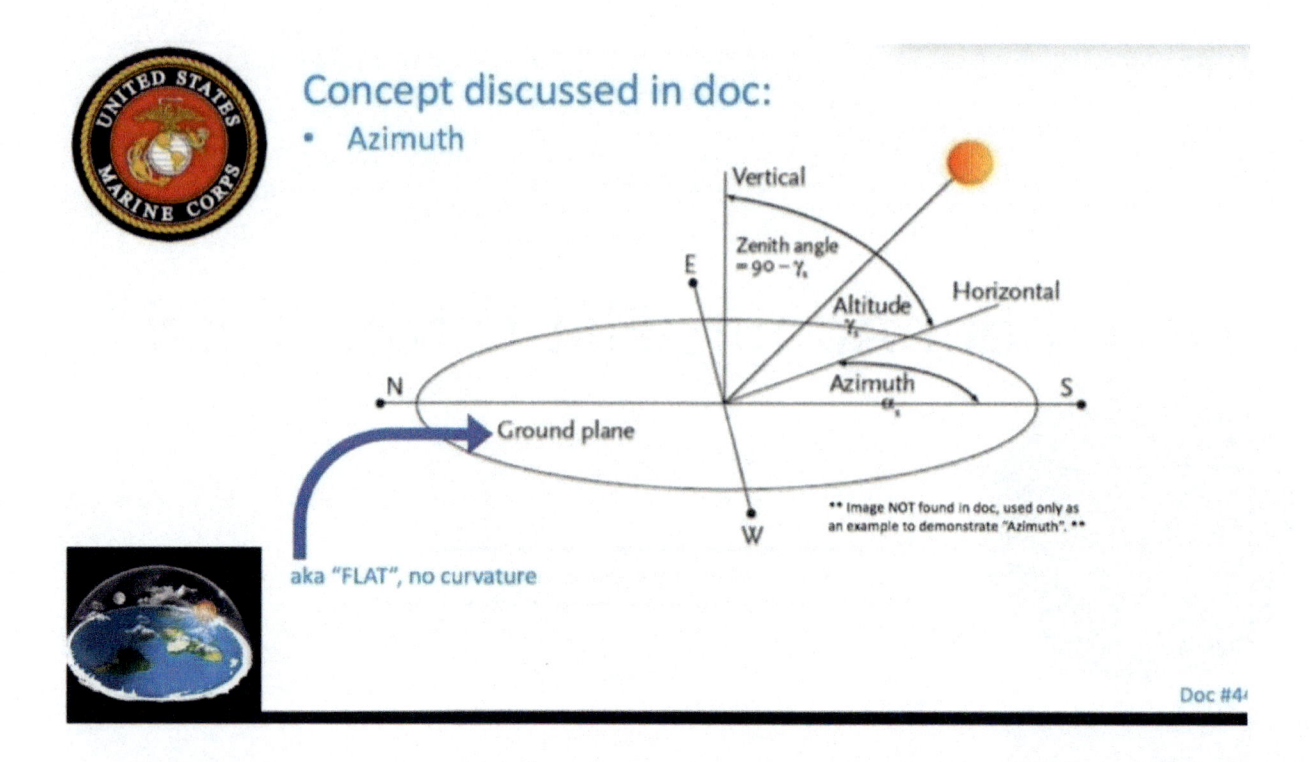

Earth is flat and our top government knows it. It's only us that's not "in the know". But if we use our heads we can't be fooled so easily.

The Zetetic Method

I have cut this chapter short, eliminating a lot of documents to keep this book at a decent size. The point of this chapter is to show you that calculating a ball makes no sense but it seems calculating a flat stationary earth is more sensible method. Plan to fly a high-speed jet over a wobbling spinning flying ball while calculating a flat stationary earth. Seems legit

Government Admits Flat Earth: Doc #21

UNPUBLISHED PRELIMINARY DATA

NsG-304

ATMOSPHERIC OSCILLATIONS

by A. J. Lineberger and H. D. Edwards

Georgia Tech Project A-652-001

Contract No. AF19(628)-393

GPO PRICE $ _____
OTS PRICE(S) $ _____
Hard copy (HC) 2.00
Microfiche (MF) .50

Title: Atmospheric Oscillations
Author: A. J. Lineberger and H. D. Edwards
URL: https://ntrs.nasa.gov/archive/nasa/casi.ntrs.nasa.gov/19650015408.pdf

A model frequently used is that of a flat, nonrotating earth. The temperature is assumed either to be constant, to increase or decrease monotonically with altitude, or to be stratified. Gravity is usually considered to be constant. Density and pressure are usually considered to vary exponentially with altitude.

The most one can profitably simplify the problem is to consider an isothermal atmosphere, plane level surfaces, and a nonrotating earth. This case has been handled by Eckart [1960], Lamb [1932], and Hines [1960]. The simplification is

Doc #21: Page 13 of 34

Chapter 9
DISINFORMATION AGENTS

Disinformation Agent or Truth Seekers

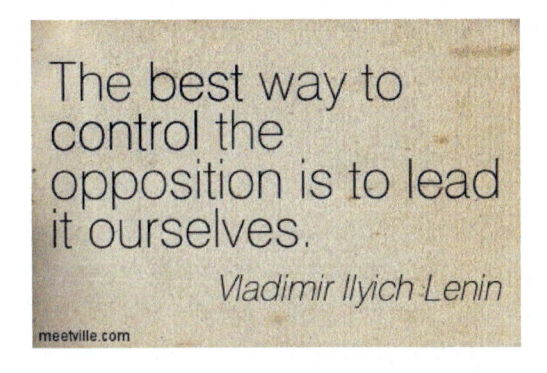

> The best way to control the opposition is to lead it ourselves.
> — Vladimir Ilyich Lenin

"Is it possible to deliver men from the spell and sorcery of 'great names?' If only a fable or lie is called scientific, and fathered by a writer reputed a 'great man,' how many thousands believe at once without proof? Is it not as hard to turn men from the worship of their fellow-worms. The scientific favorites of newspaper scribblers are larded over with flattery until the reputation of greatness is attained; and to argue against pet scientific fictions is only to provoke silly jesting or astonishment at the presumption of daring to differ from the scientific slave-drivers. Will any of their slaves of science dare be free, or use their common-sense?" So true, I wish I could remember where I got it from.

I have many quotes to share if you've noticed. This one I like a lot; it tells exactly how our "Scientists" are packaged. They're put on mainstream media and TV shows and built as characters and people buy what they say without a second thought. Like Neil Degrasse Tyson and Bill Nye "The Science Guy." One an actor, the other a comedian, given degrees and packaged as scientists, they make ridiculous claims with no real science backing, and yet people take out their mental wallets and buy it.

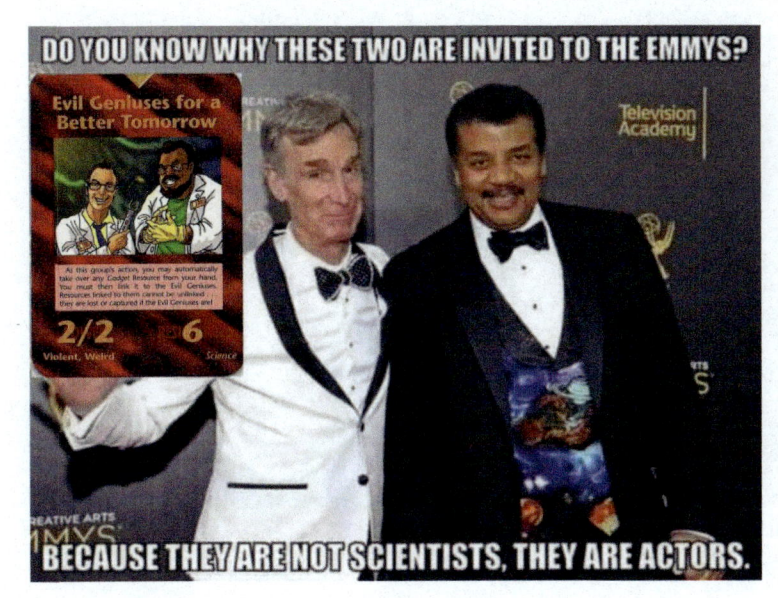

If the government and its puppet Pseudo-scientists were so confident in their ball Earth model, then why don't they think it would stand up to scrutiny, why the big fuss that they're making about flat earthers? Why censor us even worse than 9/11 truthers? Why not censor hollow earthers and Bigfoot people and alien claimers? Why the heavy censoring for flat earthers? Why won't Neil Degrasse Tyson debate flat earth truther Eric Dubay? Need I say more? And the world still awaits real gravity and bendy water experiments.

The way the government and its pseudo-scientist have acted towards flat earthers is a red flag in itself. People don't think the government would lie on this scale. There are people who believe the governments are shape shifting lizard aliens or are hiding such things. There are so many conspiracy theories like this out there it's insane. The government never disputed or said anything.

There are people who believe the earth to be hollow with a hidden civilization inside. The government never disputed that. There's always "leaked" info spilling out pointing towards aliens and hollow earth, etc. Does this have anything to do with the fake alien invasion called Project Blue Beam? Look at that clown show up for a good laugh.

Think about it, ET= extraterrestrial which means extra-terrestrial. Extra people that live on Earth. If aliens were so secretive then why the books and TV shows. They're pre-programming your mind to accept and believe when it comes.

But anyway back to the subject at hand, they don't argue against these conspiracy theories at all but when the flat earth awakening starts happening, they start making comments and trying to discredit us, making fun and completely lying about us. Hmmm

Everywhere you look on TV and movies the globe is shown now more than before. So many times it's mentioned out of the blue. Even globe believers have said this. Suddenly NASA and SpaceX are releasing missions right and left. They even said there's a helicopter on Mars. I'm not even going to get into that.

Look at these people here, they're discussing the elite controller's Pseudo-scientists' activities.

"Group of thirty-five heads" by Louis Leopold Boilly

The Zetetic Method

THAT MOMENT WHEN YOU THOUGHT YOU SAW A UFO

BUT THEN YOU REALIZE ITS JUST YOUR SNEAKY LYING GOVERNMENT

Before I researched flat earth, I was into researching aliens. All the "whistleblower" books. But something seems off and fishy. One whistle blowing author said that he saw what he saw but now he thinks that it was a man who did it and it was done for him and the other soldiers to see.

Another man who said he was abducted by aliens said it was more like a military base, and the aliens seem to not be able to move their hands, with it's long fingers, correctly and their head moved more like a mask. Very interesting indeed.

WHY THE LIE

People need to get past the why and look at the evidence. Evidence shows you that we're not on a whirling rock with an air bubble around it that's flying through the vacuum of space. Why is a good question, but first let's learn what is!

People ask me all the time "what difference does it make whether it's flat or a ball, how does it change my life," this is insanity in my opinion. Are they a brute or animal, someone who cares nothing about where they come from, who they are and why they're here or even the shape of their world, as long as they have food and movies? Only globe believers ask such questions; I have yet to talk to a flat earther who says such small minded things.

Some people have a problem seeing reality simply because it points to a Creator. That, in my opinion, is just sad and at the same time comical. It's like hearing someone get upset when you tell them they're more advanced than any computer and computers don't grow on trees or come together in a hurricane.

Some people don't like to think they could be fooled on such a grand level. That's an ego problem and maturity growth is obviously needed. And some people are simply emotionally attached to the concept of a ball earth. I find that to be just as pathetic. I already knew I couldn't prove ball earth when I believed in it, so it only took a few solid physical facts of flat earth to make me drop the ball earth theory like the bad joke that it is.

If people feel insignificant and nothing but a speck of dust, they will accept anything and, instead of looking within, they will turn to someone for guidance; aka Big Brother government. They will forget that they're the highest conscious being on this plane, we are the only creature here that's called a being. They will hand their thought processing to someone else, thus lowering their consciousness and becoming a being of servitude. This has happened to humanity, and now they're easy to control.

Another reason could have to do with the bible. Anyone who knows what the Bible says knows exactly what I'm talking about. The elite government has tried THEIR BEST to turn people away from God, why? You could say because religion causes war, but so do atheists. War is fought for power and control now.

Another reason for the lie could be a test from God. Again, anyone familiar with the Bible will know what I'm talking about. Is God testing us to separate the wheat from the tare? It's a good question.

Either way, when people feel insignificant and nothing but a speck of dust they are much easier to control. When they find out that they're on a designed flat stationary ecosystem and they are the highest conscious being in it for a reason other than corporation slavery and greed, then the elite will lose power. The house of cards will fall. A mass awakening is the only thing that will make this happen. Let's look at some of the people trying to stop this from happening. There are many but we'll only talk about a few. Let's do that shall we.

Not sure who the artist is here but I love it. This is not for people who disagree but for people who trash talk me and other flat earthers without putting any effort into thinking about the subject. You are the perfect sheep.

TRUTH FEARS NO INVESTIGATION!!!

Neil DeGrasse Tyson continues to talk nonsense about flat earthers, even goes on tour doing so, but when Eric Dubay, an educated author and flat earth activist, challenges him to a live debate, Tyson says we shouldn't give flat earthers the time of day and refused. TRUTH FEARS NO INVESTIGATION!!! Flat earthers are begging you to investigate because we know things aren't adding up to reality. Flat Earthers fears no investigation because it's the truth.

NASA and "scientist" even went on TV and said that flat earth was "dangerous misinformation" and "It's not good to think the earth is flat." How? And why is believing in hollow earth ok? Because you can prove the earth is flat, stationary and enclosed. You can't prove swat about hollow earth. Or does it have anything to do with the fake alien invasion coming soon perhaps? Congress mentions something about UFOs and they're spotted everywhere now. Hmmm

"A subject or system that will not bear discussion is doomed." Lord Beaconsfield

With flat earthers, the Scientism priest can't be characterized as a heresy. By doing so would reveal the religious nature (faith based) of this entire deception of the heliocentric globe model. So, the heresy of a flat and stationary earth must be dealt with in a different way. Instead of being called a heresy, we are called lunatics, science deniers and

The Zetetic Method

uneducated morons, and are ridiculed, scorned and discredited by fake flat earthers posing as real flat earthers making ridiculous claims. What we're never dealt is hard evidence to support a whirling ball earth. Only hearsay and the theory repeated in mathematical form.

Our "education system" has taught us and our kids to believe what we've been taught but not to question what we've been taught. Only certain questions are encouraged. If you question the theories deeper it will fall about. You have been trained, not educated.

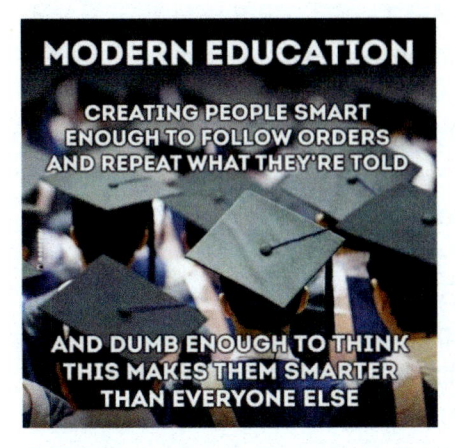

One flat earther, on a podcast, interviewed an astronomer that's been on Ted Talks and tours. She thought he was someone else and did not realize he was a flat earther. When his questions turn from normal stupid questions that most numbnuts sheople like to ask, into real questions, she starts to fumble in her words and deflect the questions and talk around them. Started saying gravity gravity gravity to explain things that defy nature. She even made the statement that maybe we didn't go to the moon, and then chuckled. When taken to the task, the "educated" fall on their faces. I've talked to many that brag about their degree, and then I watch them crumble when I question them. They can only repeat indoctrination, anything beyond that exposes the lie. When the astronomer found out he was a flat earther she got mad and said that he had better not release the interview and then she walked out. Why? Truth fears no investigation! Of course, he released it, he's about spreading truth not hiding truth. Let's talk about people who DON'T do this.

Disinformation Agents

A disinformation agent is a person who is there, posing as a truther for whatever movement, to spread BS and discredit real truthers who are trying to wake you. To make the dumb down masses laugh at the cause. Example would be the small set up group that stormed the White House with their earpiece in their ear listening for instructions. Regular people like you and I, recorded them. Wow!

There are a few fake flat earthers out there that spread disinformation and lies. There's a "documentary" on Netflix that's posing as a flat earth documentary, IT IS NOT. It's called "Behind The Curve," where they do experiments to prove the earth is flat. They don't show either experiment but claim that both experiments were a fail. This "documentary" is there to discredit us and make people laugh at us. And it works.

One "flat earther" on a National Geographic show started jumping up and down and saying he wanted to see the curvature under his feet. This clown is what flat earthers call 'a shill.' He's there to discredit us and make us look foolish.

After the "flat earther" announced that the test failed he said quietly, to another "flat earther", in front of the camera "keep this confidential." Then said that if this other test fails, I don't know what we'll do. Then the camera goes to the other experiment and they announce it as a failure. But they showed neither experiment. Hmmm! Does that seem odd to you? Can you not see the tricky? Even some globe believers have said this, but most throw it in our faces.

When I talk to people about flat earth, they throw this documentary in my face. When I ask for a timestamp on when they actually showed the experiment, I never get one, because they never did. Like the gyroscope experiment, they skimmed over it. The idiot posing as a flat earther just held it and said it failed. He said a neighbor bought the gyroscope for $20,000. LMAO!! So, $20,000 and they did not even show the experiment, just said it failed? Really? Yet people are always throwing the Netflix documentary in my face, as if it had actual proof in it. Are they not thinking while watching?

If someone points a laser to the sky and it shows some movement, but we feel no movement, then wouldn't it be more logical to say it is the lights in the sky moving and not us? But no flat earther on the "documentary" said this.

If you don't THINK about what's going on in your life and just keep with the childhood habit of accepting things, then you'll always be easily fooled and controlled.

In the second picture here, the guy on the left is the "Bob the flat earther" who was holding the gyroscope saying it failed thus proving the movement of the Earth. OH the web we weave. I wrote to him and he never wrote back. And they never showed the laser experiment they say failed, so we're left taking their word for it. And we know where that can lead us, don't we? But here's a laser experiment that succeeded and was shown on a real flat earth video on my YouTube channel.

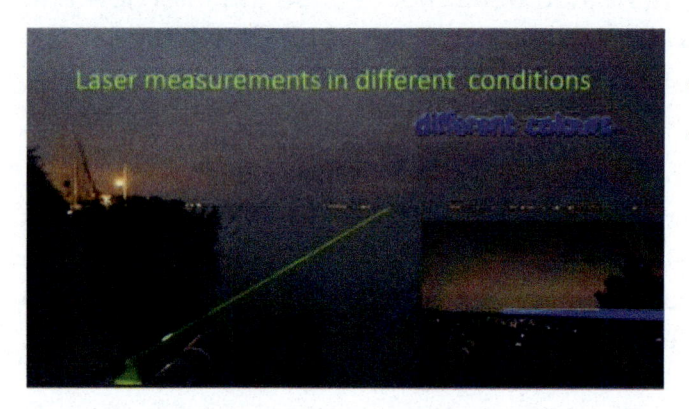

Here's some real laser experiments. Watch the Netflix "documentary" and compare.

The Zetetic Method

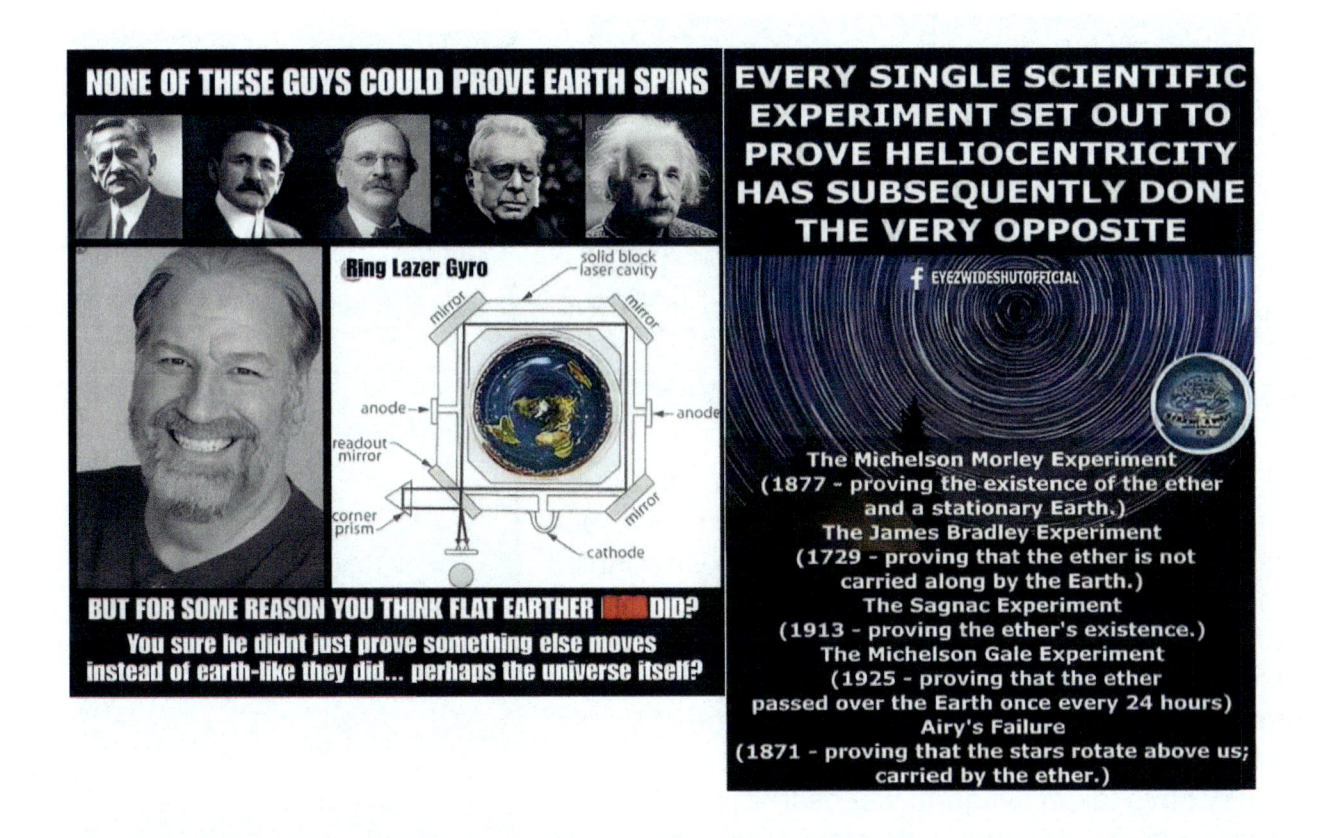

National Geographic released a video with an experiment showing a boat with a layered flag going slightly "behind" a curve of water. One of the "flat earthers" that was there started jumping up and down yelling "But I want to see the curvature under my feet." (Something like that) They did that so people will laugh at flat earthers. Why do that if it's not true to begin with?

A real flat earther, like myself, would have simply pointed out the observable fact that the horizon line is behind the boat along with the distant shore. Thus, debunking the whole experiment. LMAO!

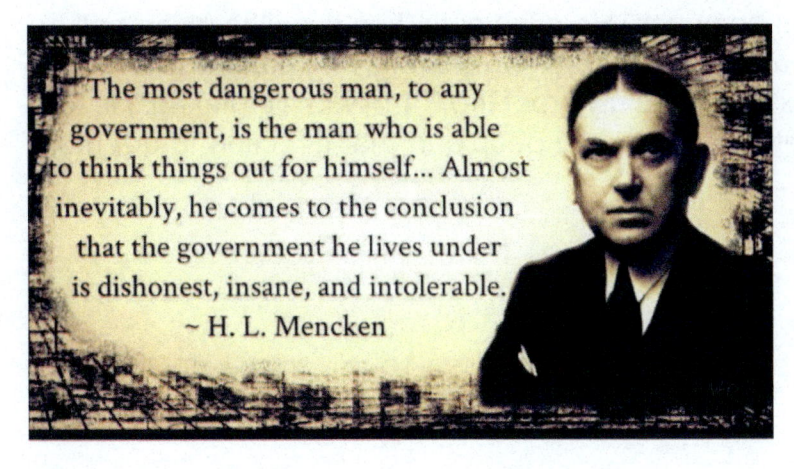

And Neil Degrasse Tyson has already said, that the curvature is not visible til you get to over 128,000 feet (which it's not visible then either as a weather balloon has shown).

The Zetetic Method

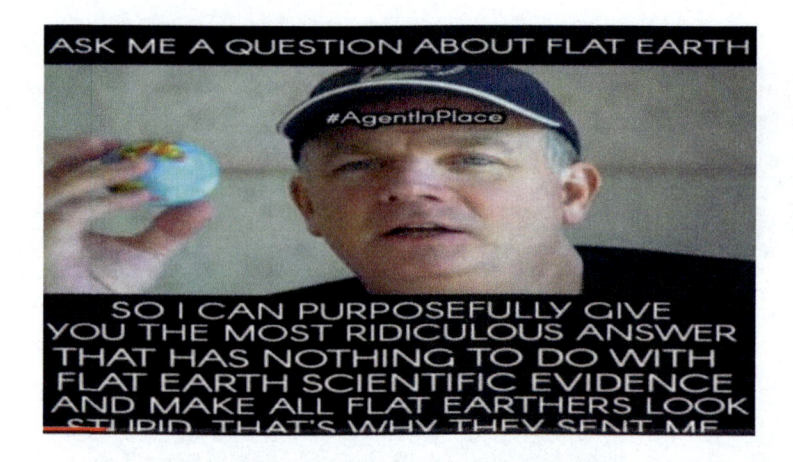

How can you see this flag, at sea level, start to go over curvature that's not even apparent till 128,000 feet? How can the physical horizon line be way behind the boat if the boat's going over the curvature hiding part of the flag? Makes no sense. Also you should be able to see double the curvature from left to right then straight ahead. But none was shown. None of the flat earth shills said any of this. NONE!

They have taken flat earth videos from the YouTube search engine and have deleted 1000s of videos where flat earthers are doing experiments proving the earth is flat. But they're releasing a documentary? That shows me it's not legit. You don't cover up proof then release a real documentary.

Another is Mark Sargent. He's been on the news, talk shows and Netflix spreading nonsense and making outrageous claims. And he tells everyone to go to HIS site to research flat earth. His YouTube channel popped up out of nowhere, full of videos. He seems to be there to discredit us. He does an excellent job at it. He mixes truth with lies, which is why he's put on talk shows and such. He constantly has this little globe ball he shows the camera, subconsciously reinforcing the globe while giving ridiculous answers to questions. Saying that ancient text was the only proof the Earth wasn't rotating. He tells people he's of the Flat Earth Society, thus sending people in that direction to get more disinformation.

The Zetetic Method

This kind of discrediting agent was done before in the 70s against flat earthers until people found out the guy was working for the government then he simply stopped and someone else started.

There's also the Flat Earth Society making horrible claims.

People like this might be slowing down the awakening but they're not stopping it by any means. But people are constantly bringing him up to me in our discussions. But his discrediting doesn't add curvature, does it? It doesn't turn this observable flat plane into a whirling ball, does it?

When I first woke up to flat earth, I heard Obama and John Kelly tell bold face lies about flat earthers. It's one of the things that made me realize what an information war is all about.

Freemason hand signs from Mark Sargent and Neil deGrasse Tyson.

Nothing to see here, just a few Freemansons showing their Masonic hand signs. Mark Sargent is the one on the right. He called himself the leader of the flat earth community. That's a no for me. No one leads me.

Neil De Grasse Tyson and Mark Sargent throwing up Masonic hand signs
#ShillingLikeVillans

Oh, what a tangled web we weave.

"It's a big club and we aren't in it." George Carlin

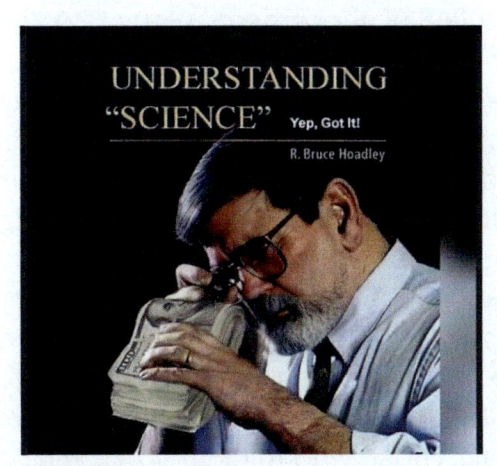

The fact that the USA scientist aren't questioning and showing real experiments like Brazilians are, says something about the hold the government has on our scientists. To lose all sense of decency and value of data, but to be agreeable; but to be like everybody else, and intend to turn our agreeableness into profit. One scientist said that the conversations they have backstage is a lot different than the one they have at the podium. Mind you it wasn't about flat earth but you get my point. One said they have financial handcuffs on. Hmmm

Why don't TV personalities say something for the flat earth? Some did, Mike Tyson, Norman MacDonald, author T.J. Hagard (who set out to write a book to debunk the flat earth but ended up becoming one instead), some famous basketball players, a few football players and a few others did. There were a few that did and caught backlash for it and retracted their statements, so I won't mention them. Good, that exposes the system even more. And a retired CIA agent which is now dead.

You don't have to know history to see the government is evil and crooked. If the government doesn't want you to research to know something THEN YOU NEED TO KNOW THAT SOMETHING! If the government is trying to discredit something THEN THAT SOMETHING SHOULD BE LISTENED TO!

"Believe none of what you hear and half of what you see." Edgar Allen Poe

Lead Developer At Google Earth Believes Earth Is Flat

"Everything in this world is theory. From black holes to the roundness of the earth."

"After years of diligent study and intent work I have concluded there is no way the world can be spherical. Given how our data at Google has never matched up to NASA's data, and given how modern technology simply cannot measure the magnitude of such a planet, we can never really be guaranteed the earth is spherical. The truth is, this idea is so ingrained in our culture that no one questions it. Well, I'm questioning it."

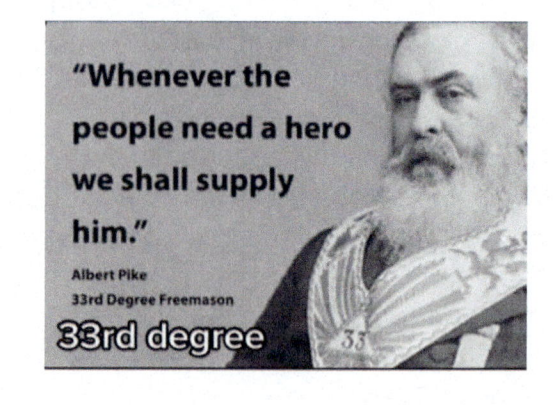

"Whenever the people need a hero we shall supply him."

Albert Pike
33rd Degree Freemason

33rd degree

One such TV personality that has come out is Michael Tellinger, also the author of "Slave Species of God?" and "Temples of the African Gods." A flat earther emailed him some flat earth material and this is what he had to say on a podcast:

"After many months of research, I still cannot find any scientifically accepted proof of a physical nature, that the Earth is moving through space – and that it actually is a ball. Everything I held dear and as an unshakable truth has been shaken to its core and stripped of all credibility. It is clearer than ever before that everything we have been told is a lie, and the most important teachings have been strategically omitted by our education system – whose objective is to create a future labor force to keep the money monster alive – and not to teach us to think and give us real skills. This Flat Earth could be the biggest lie of them all. Those who think that this will go away soon have a big surprise coming. We have to discard most of NASA's imagery as part of the LIE – which is one of the first disturbing things everyone finds when entering this realm of research. My most recent research into the relationship between sound, magnetism and electricity clearly shows that all the physical manifestations of shape and matter and the magnetic fields are the same TOROIDAL shapes that are proposed for the sub-atomic model of the electron AND the magnetic fields of the Earth and even the model of the galaxies that seem to spew forth matter at its galactic equator of the gigantic TORUS shaped galaxy. My breakthrough discovery is that the evidence suggests that the land or Earth itself follows this DOUBLE TORUS model and the land which we have been told is a ball – is actually the FLAT Accretion disk emerging at the center of the Earth

Torus Magnetic field. All North – South Magnetic alignments and everything else that has been attributed to a ball Earth can be explained even better with a FLAT Earth model. Like a giant RING Magnet with all the expected magnetic fields around it and inside it. This also accounts for the so-called DOME and hollow Earth theory or Agartha, magnetic drift, processional wobble, Aurora Borealis, and so many more global mysteries. Everything can be explained by simply re-evaluating the magnetic fields around the Earth and the full shape they hold. For those that thought the Flat Earth Theory is a bunch of ignorant nonsense devised to confuse humanity and not worthy of debate, have a growing scientific mountain of evidence to deal with. I look forward to seeing how this research evolves. As so many others have done – I have also done my own experiments with the curvature of the Earth and I found to my surprise that THERE IS NO CURVATURE. No matter how hard I looked. And if there is no curvature, there is only one conclusion we can reach. The Earth's surface is flat. If the weather man can show Chicago from Michigan City some 40 odd miles across Lake Michigan, that should be enough proof that there is no curvature. At that distance Chicago should be about 1060 feet below the horizon. And so the new exciting journey begins – sifting through layers upon layers of deception and lies. The only thing I have to hold on to is my sanity, sense of humor and an open mind." (This would work very well with the salt water oceans)

Why don't Joe Rogan or Alex Jones (with his pushing the alien agenda), who has a huge audience and is very outspoken about NASA and other conspiracy theories on both their famous podcasts, ask real questions like "Can someone prove, without using NASA, that the ocean is wrapped around a ball? Someone please explain to me how curvature is determined in math but long-distance photography debunks it? Why is there a formula but no measurement for it?"
I always liked Joe Rogan, but he was against the moon landing until Neil Degrasse Tyson showed up on his podcast, then he suddenly was playing a different tune. He's always talking trash about flat earthers now. Famous people have a leash. The New World Order Sucklings!

"Ridicule is their primary weapon, a weapon they have built over time, and now, they use it with the utmost viciousness, attacking everything and everyone, who dares to oppose their theories. That's all they have, no facts, no proof, or anything of that sort, and they attack continuously, so they can stay in power. They're using the same old principle, divide and conquer, and now, they've added ridicule to the process." Robbie Davidson on scientism and its priests.

The Flat Earth Society
The Flat Earth Society was created in the 1970s by Luo Ferrari as a disinformation campaign. It is controlled opposition to discredit the real flat earthers who were/are trying to wake the sleeping masses, and they do a good job of it too. Making false claims, such

as that the Earth is constantly moving upward and that's why everything sticks to it. They once said their ship had been lost over the edge. They said they were clinging to a rock so as not to fall off. They even went around on talks shows, etc. showing said rock and making ridiculous claims. One thing they don't do is give people real physical proof.

This is pushed into the search engines and people see it and instantly get turned off. People constantly bring up the Flat Earth Society and their claims when I'm trying to have a serious discussion with them. Then they assume the flat earthers have failed and I'm just in denial about it. If they would only listen and think, they could break out of this tricky situation. I have gone on this site and was disgusted by it. The information war is real.

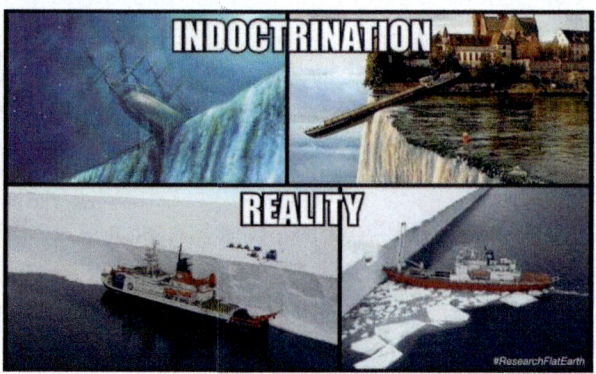

A LYING GOVERNMENT?? WHAT???

Flat earthers wrote the government asking for disclosure on flat earth. Obama announced this and said "I do not have time for the Flat Earth Society." The sheople audience laughed and cheered. But the Flat Earth Society is not the one who wrote him. He wanted the masses to hear this and then go to the Flat Earth Society's website and have a good laugh and then move on with their lives. He also said that flat earthers wanted us to continue using oil instead of natural energy. That the government wanted to move forward while flat earthers wanted to stay behind. This is another BOLD FACE LIE. What flat earther said this??? And, get this, while he was saying this, the government was kicking American natives off their land to run oil pipelines through and pollute their water. Oh! What a false narrative.

John Kelly, his target audience was the religious people, said that "flat earthers don't believe in the Great Flood because the water would fall off the edge." This is pure nonsense, as there's plenty of physical evidence of a great flood and a firmament for this greenhouse. Ancient accounts from all across the world also talked of the great flood. How would a great flood work on a ball earth? Where would the extra water come from and then go? The dumbed down audience never thought of that. Where would all that extra water come from and then go? From the void of endless space? But never mind logic, they clapped like stupid seals anyway.

TRUTH does not mind being questioned.

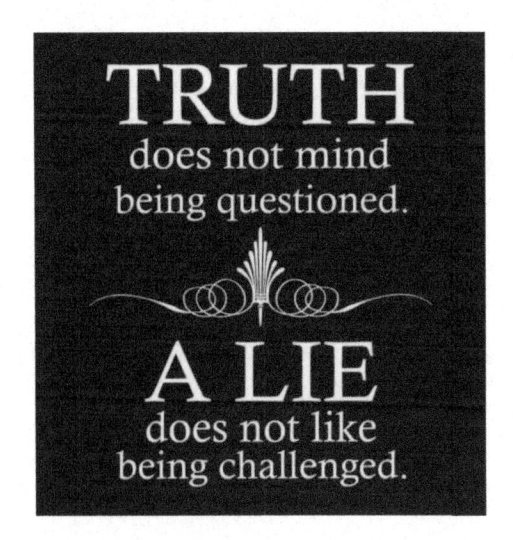

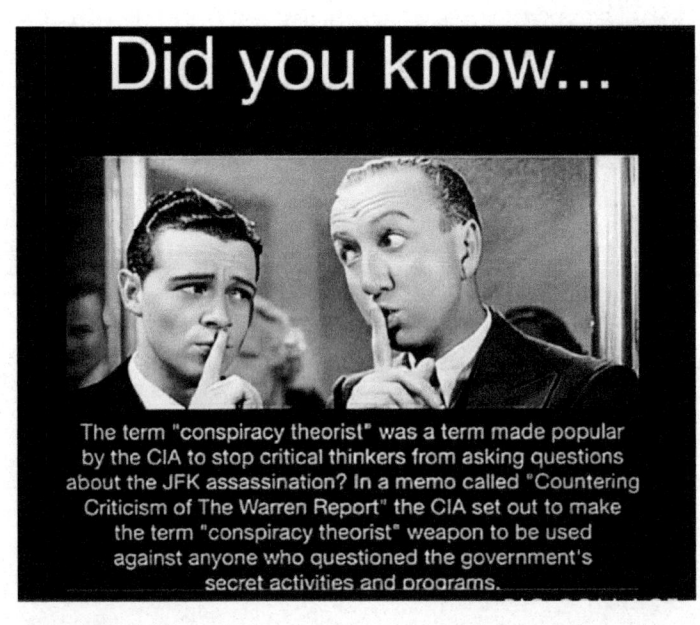

A LIE does not like being challenged.

Did you know...

The term "conspiracy theorist" was a term made popular by the CIA to stop critical thinkers from asking questions about the JFK assassination? In a memo called "Countering Criticism of The Warren Report" the CIA set out to make the term "conspiracy theorist" weapon to be used against anyone who questioned the government's secret activities and programs.

"In our dream we have limitless resources, and the people yield themselves with perfect docility to our molding hand. The present educational conventions fade from our minds; and, unhampered by tradition, we work our own good will upon a grateful and responsive rural folk. We shall not try to make these people or any of their children into philosophers or men of learning or of science. We are not to raise up among them authors, orators, poets, or men of letters. We shall not search for embryo great artists, painters, musicians. Nor will we cherish even the humbler ambition to raise up from among them lawyers, doctors, preachers, statesmen, of whom we now have ample supply." Rev. Frederick T. Gates, Business Advisor to John D. Rockefeller Sr., who founded the US General Education Board in 1903

BOOK BURNING

There's still book burning going on in our 'evolved' 'civilized' world. Modern day book burning is called censorship. People are spoon fed their 'information' through school, news, church and even entertainment outlets. They are told what to think and are taught to assume all other information is false. They are not taught to double check and run the claims through serious thinking. They turn their heads at modern day book burning unless it's something they disagree with, because they have no need for it in their opinion.

Rock group "Mr. Matty Moses" said it best in their album "Conventional Education":
"To many people use to spoon-fed learning,
Which is why they ain't worried about the modern day book burning.
 Boot lickers come quick for their controllers
Barking up the wrong tree for the leach holders.
 Yawl got jokes when it comes to schooling on YouTube,
Because you prefer your info censored, don't you?"

Here are some articles headlines that show censorship and science being controlled. Remember truth fears no investigation.

"An Indiana Physics professor was censored for discussing intelligent design in class."

"College cancels class on evolution debate after 'Free thought' group threatens disruption." (Why not debate them if your theory is correct?)

"The EPA is accused of withholding important scientific data from Congress."

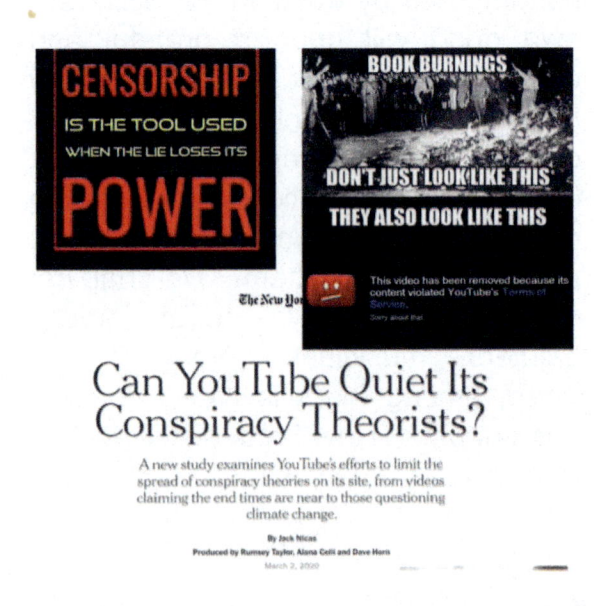

The only way to learn the truth should not be in the hands of a handful of people, especially the ones that rely on the government for funding. If you question them or their theories or the direction they may be taking you in, you'll be ridiculed by them and the dumb down masses and censored online. Your "BOOKS" will be burned.

I saw a video where the spokesperson for YouTube actually bragged about its successful censorship of flat earth and 9/11 videos.

When I first started researching flat earth in 2016, there were flat earth videos everywhere, providing experiments and provable information. Now you will get none of this, just disinformation. A lot more videos are there but not in the search engine. So, you won't find them unless someone shares the links, which I'll be doing at the end if this book has many good videos. I hope you check them out.

Eric Dubay has woken up millions to flat earth, including myself. His website and YouTube channel has been deleted a few times. I find it odd that they can delete his websites yet child porn sites seem to linger.

The Zetetic Method

In January of 2015 there were 50,000 results for flat earth on YouTube, in 2016 there were 12,000,000 results.

> For years it has been a highly effective megaphone for conspiracy theorists, and YouTube, owned and run by Google, has admitted as much. In January 2019, YouTube said it would limit the spread of videos "that could misinform users in harmful ways."
>
> One year later, YouTube recommends conspiracy theories far less than before. But its progress has been uneven and it continues to advance certain types of fabrications, according to a new study from researchers at University of California, Berkeley.
>
> YouTube's efforts to curb conspiracy theories pose a major test of Silicon Valley's ability to combat misinformation, particularly ahead of this year's elections. The study, which examined eight million recommendations over 15 months, provides one of the clearest pictures yet of that fight, and the mixed findings show how challenging the issue remains for tech companies like Google, Facebook and Twitter.
>
> The researchers found that YouTube has nearly eradicated some conspiracy theories from its recommendations, including claims that the earth is flat and that the U.S. government carried out the Sept. 11 terrorist attacks, two falsehoods the company identified as targets last year. In June, YouTube said the amount of time people spent watching such videos from its recommendations had dropped by 50 percent.

Governments worldwide are struggling to contain a new virus that could have a huge impact on billions of lives worldwide.

The virus has been named:

TRUTH

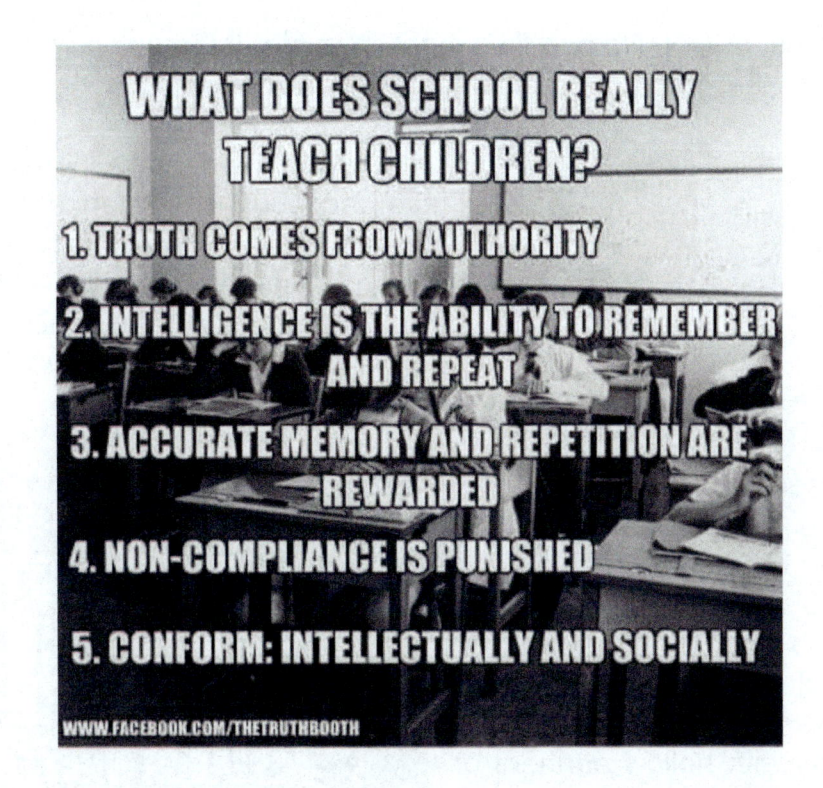

WHAT DOES SCHOOL REALLY TEACH CHILDREN?

1. TRUTH COMES FROM AUTHORITY
2. INTELLIGENCE IS THE ABILITY TO REMEMBER AND REPEAT
3. ACCURATE MEMORY AND REPETITION ARE REWARDED
4. NON-COMPLIANCE IS PUNISHED
5. CONFORM: INTELLECTUALLY AND SOCIALLY

WWW.FACEBOOK.COM/THETRUTHBOOTH

I'm not asking you to take MY word for anything. I've provided plenty of physical evidence. Look into it, though they've made it almost impossible to research flat earth without a lot of disinformation getting in the way. But if we use the Zetetic method they can't change our perception. The war is spiritual, not physical. You have to give consent to be fooled. You remember that.

Try to debunk what I say with physical based facts. I've said it many times and I'll say it again, truth fears no investigation. Period. Their desperation shows that flat earthers got them on the ropes. GOOD! It's about time somebody did.

Here's some comments from the mouth of the world's best known elite puppets:

) "If I say that the world is round and somebody else says it's flat. That's worth reporting. But you might also want to report on a bunch of scientific evidence that seems to support the notion that the world is round." —Barack Obama

) "Sixty years ago, when the Russians beat us into space. We didn't deny Sputnik was up there. We didn't argue about science or shrink our research and development budget. We built a space program almost overnight and twelve years later we were walking on the moon." — Barack Obama

(Sputnik was almost the size of a basketball and was also claimed to be seen in space from Earth. Ridiculous!)

) "I fly a lot, and I mean a lot. No one flies more than me. If the world was round, believe me I would know it!" — 45th US President, Donald Trump

The Sputnik 1 satellite was a **58.0 cm-diameter** aluminum sphere that carried four whip-like antennas that were 2.4-2.9 m long. The antennas looked like long "whiskers" pointing to one side.

https://nssdc.gsfc.nasa.gov › nmc

Russian Satellite Sputnik 1 - NASA - NSSDCA - Spacecraft - Details

) "And we need, as responsible leaders, to take account of science --- not some cockamamie ideological hypothetical, but science. And we need to make sure that those members of the Flat Earth Society are on the wrong side of history." US Secretary of State John Kerry

The BLACK SWANS

When they can no longer control you, they will try to control how others see you. They're doing this with fake flat earthers. They didn't do this with hollow earthers or Bigfoot and people who believe the governments are lizard people. If it's not true then why even pay attention to flat earthers? There's a huge awakening going on, are people dumbing down or waking up? Only those who have something to hide will work relentlessly to censor those who speak truth. This is a red flag in itself.

To ball earthers that refuse to even listen

If you can't let go of the ball then here's 10 easy ways to prove earth is a globe that you can try at home. (This is literally what I deal with when talking to most people about flat earth)
1. Stop thinking, other people have done that for you.
2. Have faith and belief, because NASA and the government said so and would never lie.
3. Look at CGI images, videos and digital media because they cannot be faked.
4. Say gravity out loud proudly when faced with questions about your unnatural claims.
5. Imagine you're a super monkey flying through space at over a million miles per hour, stuck to the outside of a spinning space rock that was the result of literally nothing exploding for no reason, despite this never being part of your human experience and with zero evidence.
6. Look at spherical things and assume the earth must be spherical as well. Ignore that there's no earth's curvature that you witness.
7. Find a flat earther and call them a flattard.
8. Don't research flat earth.
9. Don't ask me about flat earth, and if you do, ignore me and what I've said.
10. Watch the entire Star Wars anthology and pretend, deep in your
heart, that it is real.

The Illuminati card game and Hollywood truths

The Illuminati rituals
"The further a society drifts from the truth, the more it will hate those that speak it." George Orwell

"People laugh but the flat earthers know something." Steve Jackson

Freemason have many rituals, but my favorite is, they tell you what they're going to do. They do this in all sorts of ways. They do this by telling you straight, and controlled opposition, they'll let things "leak out" and "whistle blowers", etc. When conspiracy theorists are proven correct some people say that conspiracy theorists keep calling it and are correct. It's not that they're "calling it" or anything, they're not prophets, they're just paying attention. No need to take my word for what I say, everything's there, if people just pay attention. We'll look at movies and shows later but let's start with having a look at The Illuminati Card game and trading cards made by known Freemanson Steve Jackson who said "People laugh, but the flat earthers know something." Read this gem:

Illuminati
Card game

Illuminati is a card game made by Steve Jackson Games, inspired by the 1975 book, The Illuminatus! Trilogy, by Robert Anton Wilson and Robert Shea. The game has ominous secret societies competing with each other to control the world through various means, including legal, illegal, and even mystical.
Wikipedia

Check each of these cards out from the Illuminati game and trading cards from the 90s, which often foretold what was to come. They simply told more truth than the media ever did. Freemason Steve Jackson, keeping up the Freemanson's ritual of telling you what they're going to do and keeping the truth in plain sight.

Flat earthers strike gold indeed.

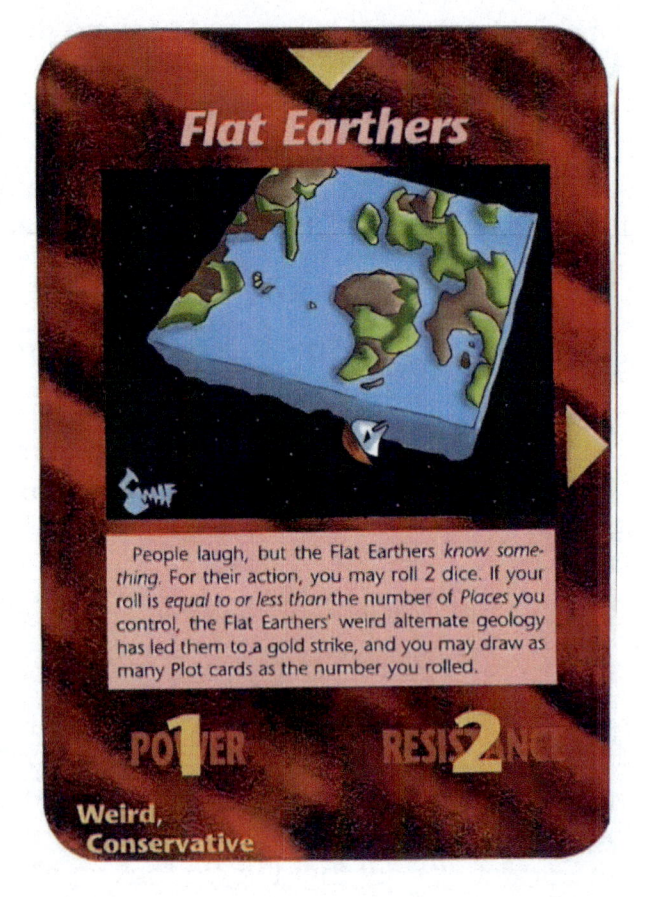

Notice what's written on the door. "Ministry of truth." And then you have the History book in the garbage. So, we don't really KNOW anything about history. Just a lot of lies. And the transgender agenda and White House storming, all told to us.

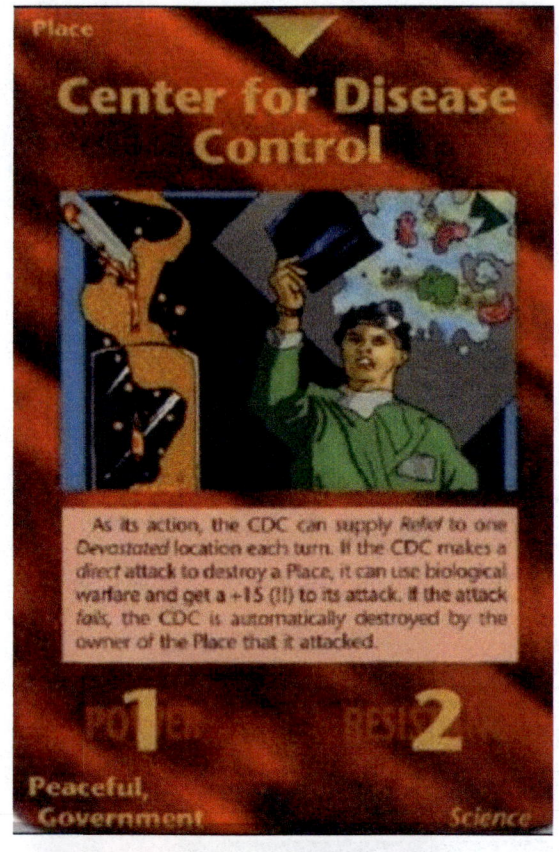

Who's the real terrorist being talked about here?

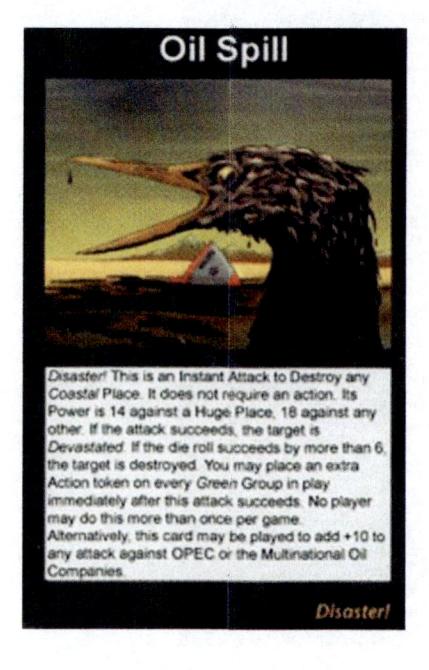

Notice what this one says if gun control succeeds. "Increase the power of all violent governments..."

And here's another from The Simpsons telling of the White House going to be stormed.

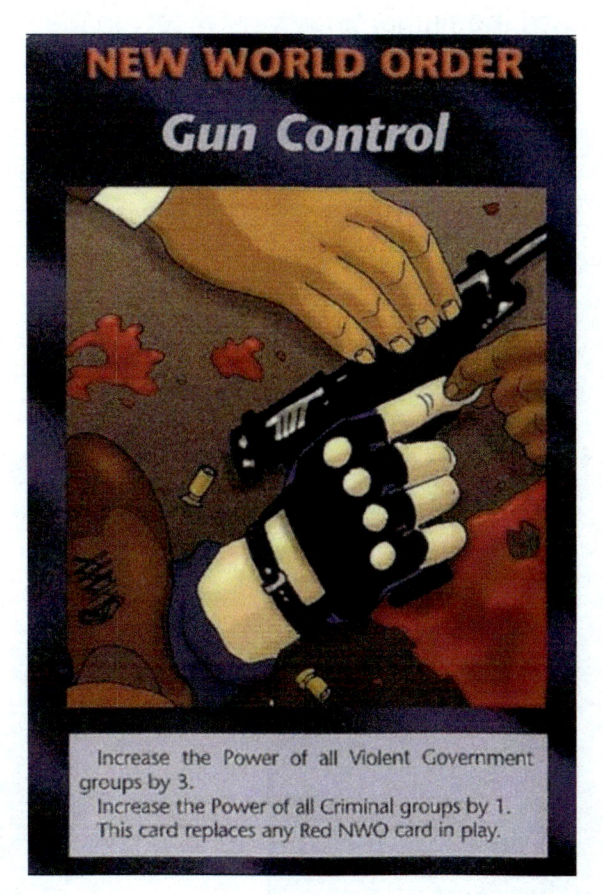

There are many more but we'll move on.

Hillary Clinton said "It may be hard to see tonight, but we are all standing under a glass ceiling right now." Then again on a different day, "We weren't able to shatter that highest hardest glass ceiling this time but thanks to you, it's got about 8 million cracks in it." (Perhaps here, she's talking about our tax paying money used to bomb it in Operation Fishbowl. Who knows) And again, "I know, I know, we still have not shattered that highest and hardest glass ceiling, but someday someone will. And hopefully sooner than we might think right now." Gee, interesting choice of words there. Isn't there a better way to explain something?

The Zetetic Method

Other rituals are numerology and symbolism. A guy who goes by the handle of RVTruth breaks down the numerology very nicely in his videos. He goes through false flag events and exposes it very well. I used to think the man was crazy until I started researching flat earth. False flags have numerology all over them. Truth in plain sight indeed.

Titles held by the pope:

Vicar of Christ, in latin = Vicarivs filii dei
In roman numerals

V ... 5	F ... 0	D ... 500
I ... 1	I ... 1	E ... 0
C ... 100	L ... 50	I ... 1
A ... 0	I ... 1	---
R ... 0	I ... 1	501
I ... 1	---	
V ... 5	53	
S ... 0		

112 + 53 + 501 = 666

Vicar of the court, in latin = Lvdovicvs

L V D O V I C V S
50 + 5 + 500 + 0 + 5 + 1 + 100 + 5 + 0 = 666

holy light of god, in latin = sancta lvx dei

S ... 0	L ... 50	D ... 500
A ... 0	V ... 5	E ... 0
N ... 0	X ... 10	I ... 1
C ... 100	---	---
T ... 0	65	501
A ... 0		

100 + 65 + 501 = 666

Clergy captain, in latin = Dux cleri

D V X C L E R I
500 + 5 + 10 + 100 + 50 + 0 + 0 + 5 = 666

King of roman priests,
in latin = rex latinvs sacerdos

R ... 0	L ... 50	S ... 0
E ... 0	A ... 0	A ... 0
X ... 10	T ... 0	C ... 100
---	I ... 1	E ... 0
10	N ... 0	R ... 0
	V ... 5	D ... 500
	S ... 0	O ... 0
	---	S ... 0
	56	---
		600

10 + 56 + 600 = 666

MASSES BE LIKE:

"It's just conspiracy theory."

IT'S A BIG CLUB

AND YOU AIN'T IN IT!

311

The Zetetic Method

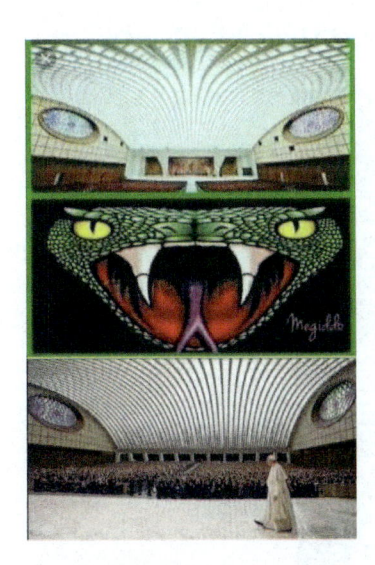

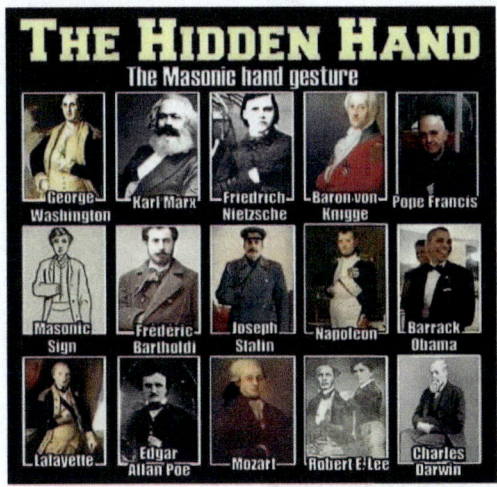

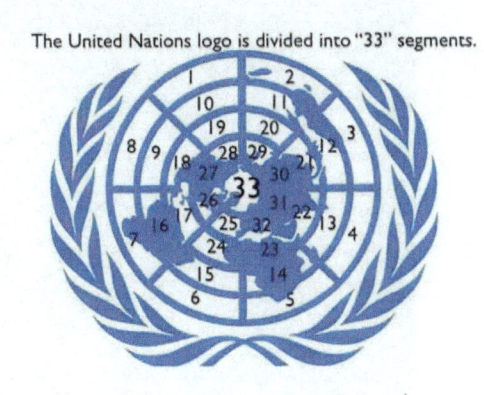

312

The Zetetic Method

Truth in Hollywood
"Space is the final frontier but it's made in a Hollywood basement." Red Hot Chili Peppers

The Zetetic Method

If one pays attention, you can learn a lot from Hollyweird. But for this book we'll stick to flat earth stuff, mostly. The job of the entertainment world is to get your mind ready and accept the world that is about to be presented to you, and to tell you what they're going to do, and showcase symbolism and numerology. How else would they do it?

You name a big event that has happened and I bet you it was shown before it happened. They have movies and shows with pandemics in them right and left then, guess what happens, a pandemic pops up. Hmmm. Remember that, with all the alien invasion entertainment showing.

In many movies and TV shows they've either hinted or plain out said the Earth is flat. In a few movies and shows they have flat earth maps in the background. One show had a pin with a flat earth map on it holding up a globe map. One said out of the blue that "It's like the deep south pole, if there was one. But there isn't, though." Hmmm

In the movie The Truman Show (Tru-man Show) produced by one of the elite, a Rothschild, has flat earth all over the place. There was a video breaking the whole movie down, showing symbolism everywhere, but it was taken down.

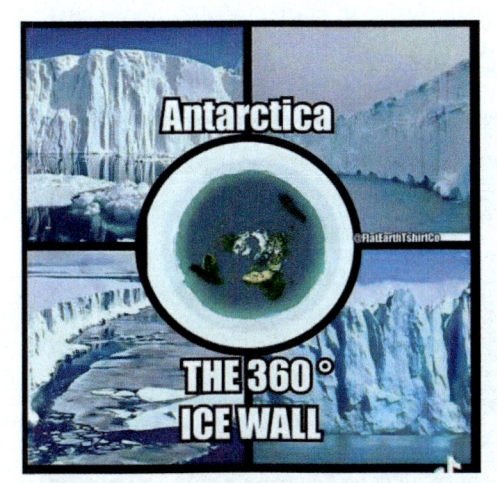

In the movie, the tell-a-vision programming helps Truman to accept his false world. In a deleted scene, Truman paints a picture of a world of snow and ice and says "Personally, I think the unconquered south face is the only one worth scaling. It's a 20,000-foot sheer wall of ice....."

Later on, he sails, (south if you're looking at the flat earth model in front of Christof), and finds the firmament of his fake world and is no longer trapped. He is awake and aware.

In another movie, a character says "Go to the dark isle, beyond the ice." In that movie the answer to the truth is beyond the ice. Towards the very end of the Truman Show, one character says "he's gone," (talking about Truman) and the character is right next to a globe with a hole busted in it. Then at the very end Truman breaks through the firmament leaving a hole.

Here's a few snapshots from the Truman Show. I'd also like to take the time to thank ODDTV for his hard work and dedication to truth and waking people up. I used a lot of his shots for this. I highly recommend his YouTube channel under the same name. People are waking up everywhere and taking on the battle of this information war.

The Zetetic Method

This character below left is Christof who runs the Truman Show in the movie, his station is located on the moon. In an interview, when asked why the main character, Truman, didn't figure out where he lived at, Christof said "We Accept The Reality Of The World With Which We're Presented. It's As Simple As That."

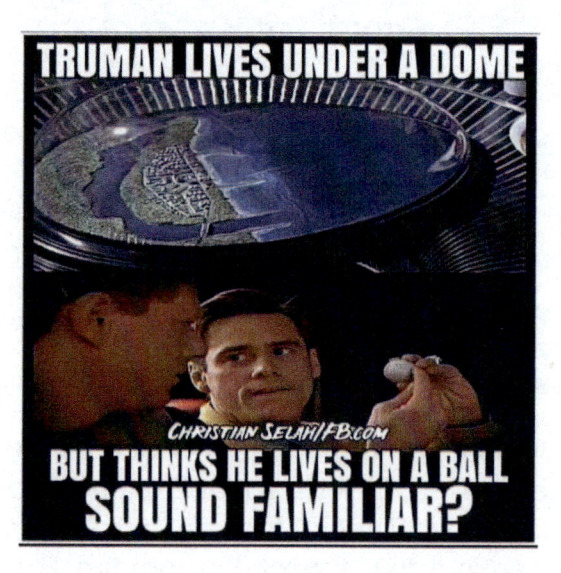

A model of Truman's world, covered in its own firmament, is in front of Christof (Christ-off). On the talk show he's on the sign has "The Truman Show" with the globe on it.

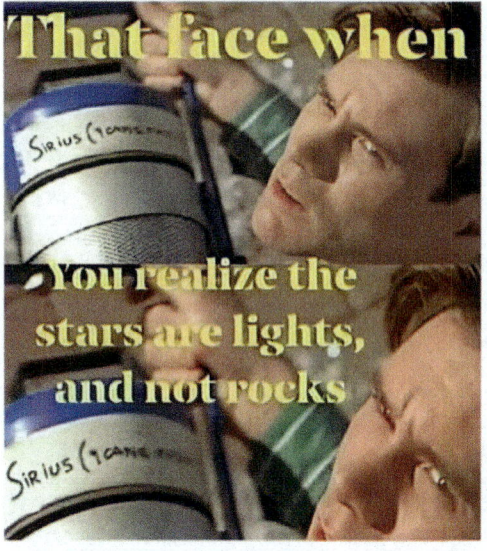

"Things are not what they seem to be and that's what this show is about." Matt Groningen, The Simpsons creator.

The Simpsons, which has quite a few flat earth and fake moon landing hints, among other conspiracy theories that have come true, had one character hitting a baseball up in the sky and breaking the glass firmament, filling the stadium with the ocean from above. While the commentator is saying "And the ball shatters the sky, bring the ocean itself down into the stadium. Oh Simpson just broke this dreams reality wide open."

The Zetetic Method

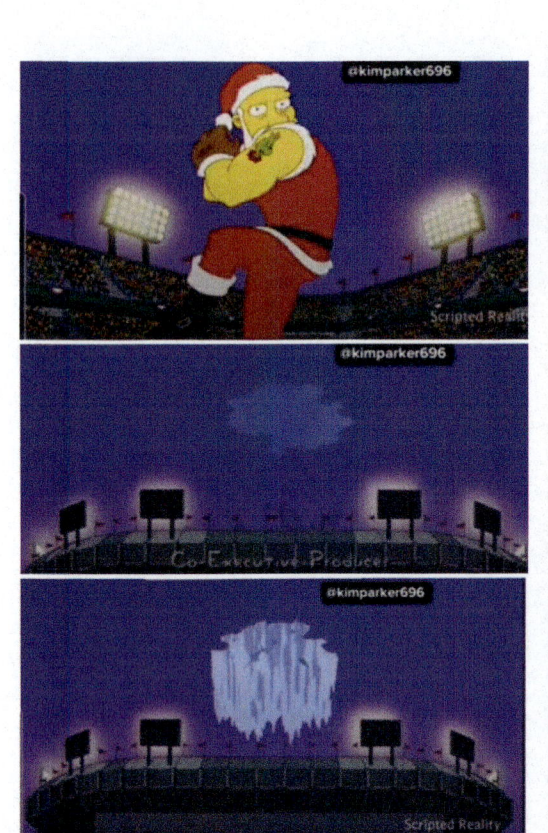

SCAM indeed

The Zetetic Method

In this scene below, one character says "this area is filled with books about pretend people." Then the other character says " That's right this is the fiction section. Fiction means it's a made up story." While she says this she points to the globe and rocket.

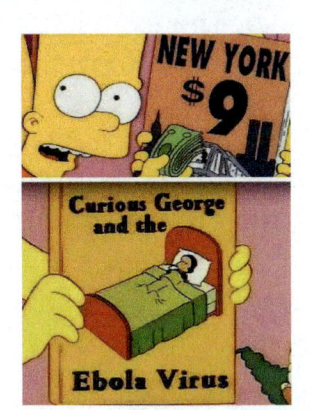

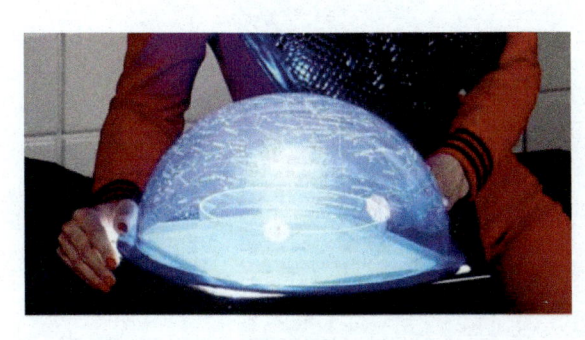

In case you haven't heard this song, Sweet Dreams, you're missing out. Don't get me wrong, the song is not about flat earth but maybe the hidden message is there.?

The device on the left is almost the exact model on the flat earth.

There are many more movies, shows and music videos and lyrics but I'm only mentioning a few. In Back To The Future here below us, there's a flat earth map clock:

318

The Zetetic Method

The TV show "Fear of the Walking Dead" has another flat earth map clock with an airPLANE on it. A craft that flies in the air over a plane. Play on words there. Truth in plain sight.

In the movie "Image Dragon" there's a shot of the man's eye. The eye is that of the flat earth map. Why put that there? Subliminal messages perhaps, who knows. Symbolism with the all-seeing eye with the flat earth in its sights.

In the TV show Dinosaurs, one character says the Earth is not flat but round like an orange. Another character holds an orange up to be seen. A numerology calculator shows 33, a Freemanson numerology. Many might not think much about this, but if you start looking into numerology, you'll see it in certain events. Like the ones created for gun control laws. They leave their mark.

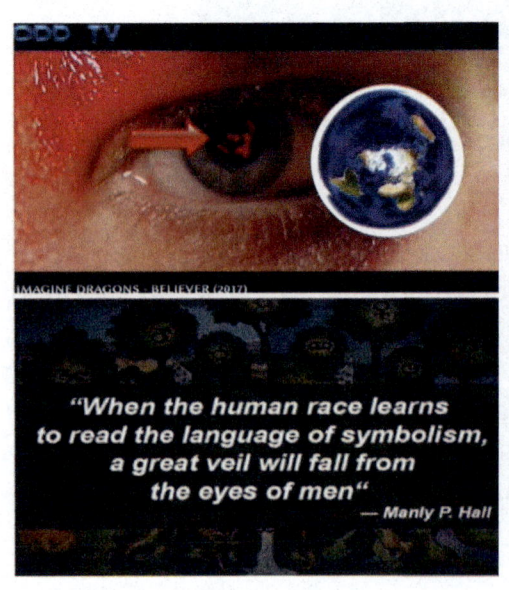

"When the human race learns to read the language of symbolism, a great veil will fall from the eyes of men"
— Manly P. Hall

319

The Zetetic Method

In the James Bond movie "Diamonds Are Forever" Bond, James Bond is on the run and bursts through the set of the fake moon landing. There are tons of movies and shows talking about the fake moon landing. This book isn't big enough for all that.

Any truther knows about Stanley Kubrick and the fake moon landing. He has hinted in his movies to the truth of the matter. One such movie was The Shining by Stephen King. The room number of the haunted hotel is the studio the moon landing was supposedly viewed at. Danny, in the film, is wearing an Apollo shirt. Notice the floor in the picture as well. The film company called "Illumination Entertainment" uses this room number and floor in their film as well as the fake moon landing truth in plain sight scenes.

In the movie "A Few Good Men" one character says you can't handle the truth, then he goes on to say "We live in a world with walls, and those walls have to be guarded by men with guns." Antarctica treaty anyone?

320

The Zetetic Method

In the movie "Moonwalkers" there is more truth in plain sight. I recommend this one too. It's literally about a man faking the moon landing.

In the movie "The Sword and the Stone" the wizard shows a silly version of the flat earth map and says it's evil and then shows the globe and says it's time to clear the way for new ideas. Hmmm. The dumbing down of humanity is what the new idea ends up being.

In the movie "Mars Attack" the Agent is walking on a flat earth while displaying and walking towards the globe map. Truth in Hollywood indeed.

The Zetetic Method

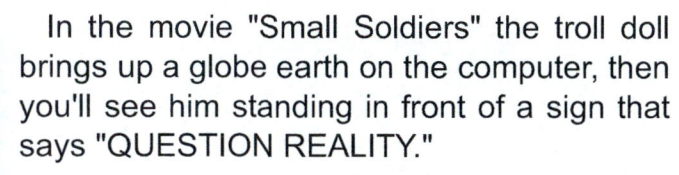

In the movie "Small Soldiers" the troll doll brings up a globe earth on the computer, then you'll see him standing in front of a sign that says "QUESTION REALITY."

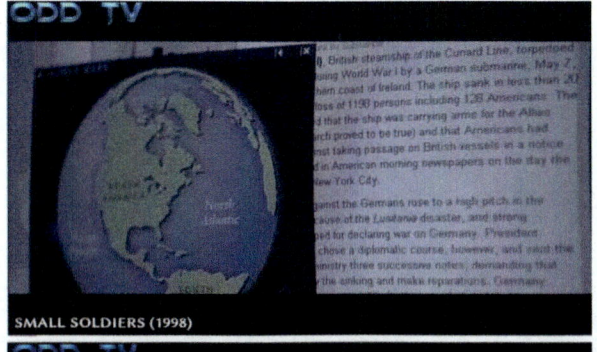

In these two different movies the flat earth map is in the background. In one it's right next to the globe.

Here's some symbols showing the truth in your face. They brainwash you while showing you the truth. Mockery at its finest. On the eye chart and chalkboard it tells you what to research. Then we have the all seeing eye and 666.

For those of you who say this is not evidence for a flat stationary earth, you are absolutely correct, and I never said it was. There's plenty of physical evidence for that. This chapter is about them telling you things in ways you don't catch it. And they do. Any self-respecting conspiracy theorist knows exactly what I'm talking about. Symbolism, numerology and telling you the plans. I don't need movies or shows to tell me the truth of reality. But some people do. Nor do I need an authoritarian to tell me what I'm living on or what to think. Here's some false flag funnies for you, and other things that make you go hmmm.

Just noticing a few ODD things...

1. **Where's any trail of blood whatsoever?** If this person had stopped bleeding, wouldn't he be passed-out by now?
2. **BOTH legs blown-off and he doesn't look to be in pain** *or in shock.* Also, who'd they steal the wheelchair from?
3. **The "victim" is double-amputee disabled Army Vet.** by the name of: **Lt. Nicholas Vogt,** Army, 25th Infantry Div.

Boston Marathon Bomb Victim is actually Nick Vogt, former US Army officer who lost his legs in Kandahar Afghanistan with the 1st Stryker Brig 25th Infantry Divison in Nov. 2011. There is more going on here than the media will tell!

Chilling photos show blood soaked survivors emerging from the Linwood Mosque just minutes after Brenton Harrison Tarrant allegedly opened fire

Why was the same girl at so many massacres/terrors?
Aurora • Boston • Brussels • Sandy Hook • Manchester • Paris • Parkland
100% FACIAL RECOGNITION MATCH
Who sent her? Are the same people behind these terrors?

The Zetetic Method

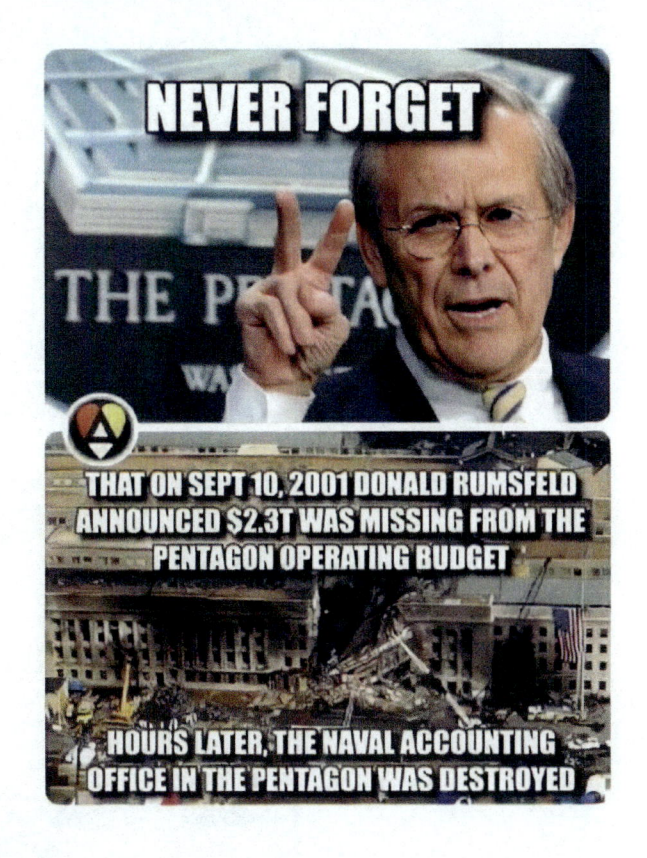

Crisis actor taking a phone break.

The Zetetic Method

MEET LUCKY LARRY

FB/IG: CONNECTING CONSCIOUSNESS

JUST MONTHS BEFORE 9/11, LARRY SILVERSTEIN BOUGHT THE WORLD TRADE CENTER'S LEASE AND THEN TOOK OUT AN INSURANCE PLAN WHICH 'FORTUITOUSLY' COVERED TERRORISM. AFTER 9/11, LARRY TOOK THE INSURANCE COMPANY TO COURT, CLAIMING HE SHOULD BE PAID DOUBLE BECAUSE THERE WERE 2 ATTACKS. FB/IG: CONNECTING CONSCIOUSNESS

HE WON, AND WAS AWARDED $4,550,000,000

THE TRUTH IS NO LONGER HIDDEN

NOW PEOPLE HIDE FROM THE TRUTH

Truth will always be truth, regardless of lack of understanding, disbelief or ignorance.
— W. Clement Stone

The Zetetic Method

CHAPTER 10
RIDICULOUS CLAIMS

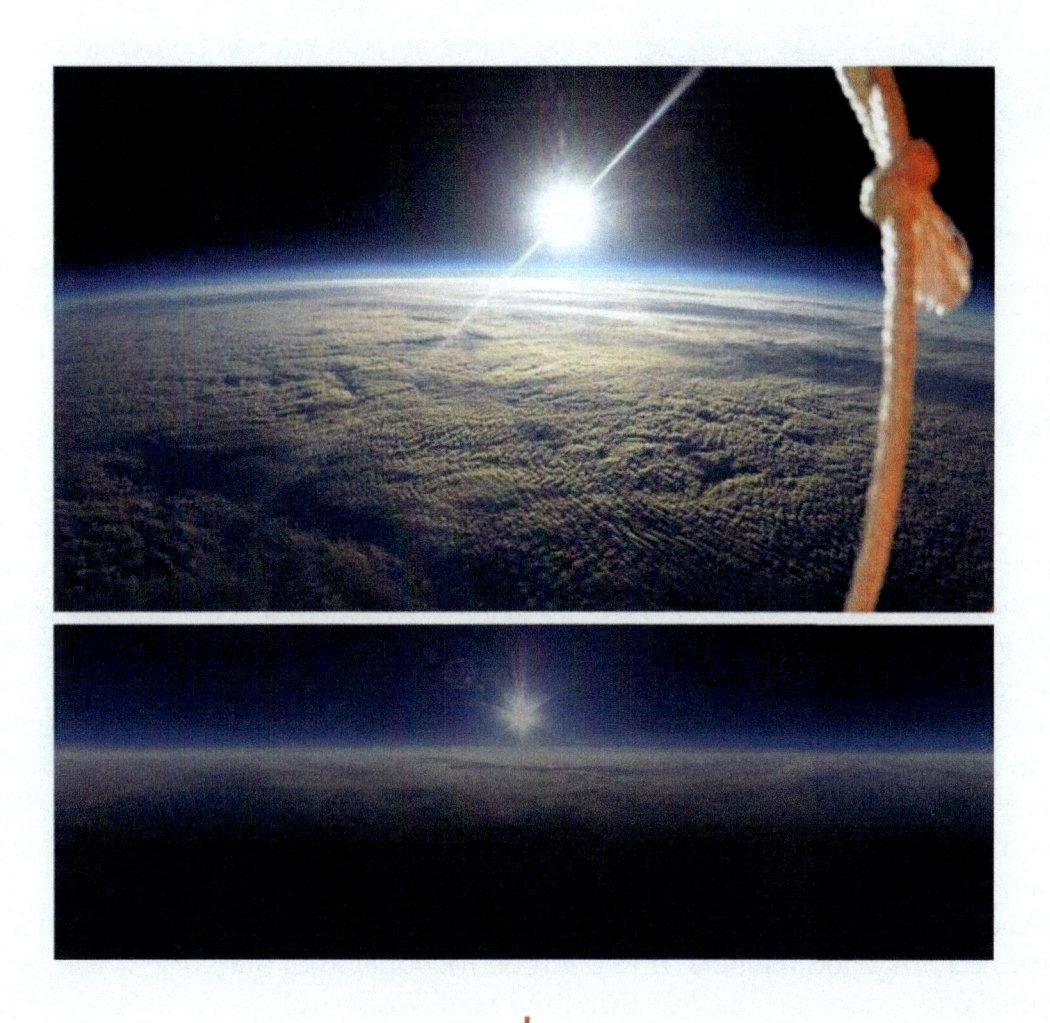

326

"Oh mortal man, is there anything you cannot be made to believe."   Adam Weishaupt

CALCULATED ASSUMPTIONS OVER EXPERIMENTS

Why are we taking calculations built on assumptions instead of experiments? I know it goes against everything we've been taught as a child but we've been taught to ignore our senses. We have a calculation that says the earth has 8" per square mile of curvature. Yet experiments of long distance photography, the blank down the beach, water test, horizon test and laser test have all debunked that so many times. So why still believe it?

We have the calculations of Earth's wobble and flying, yet we have experiments showing no parallax, and no North star location displacement, yet it's still believed. Why?

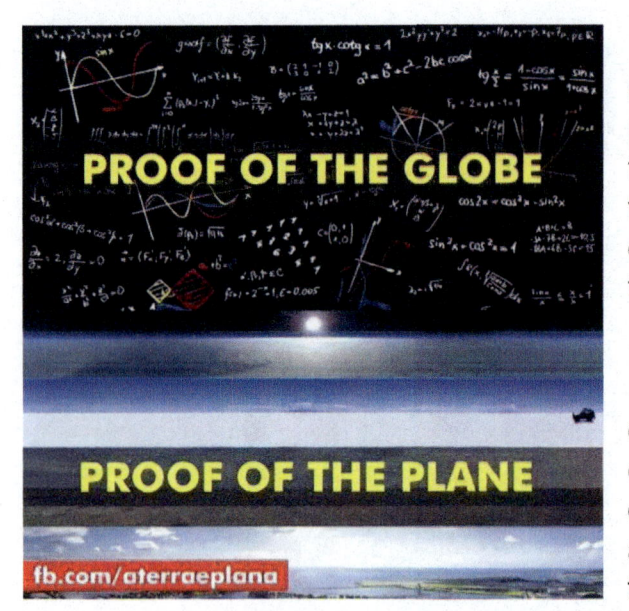

How can there be a formula for curvature but none established? In a court of law, if we can't prove it then it doesn't exist. If not testable then how is it scientific? I've said this a few times in this book: If we can't prove the theory or prove the said "proof" of the theory, then we take it on as authoritarian.

AGAIN: "If you find from your own experience that something is a fact and it contradicts what some authority has written down, then you must abandon the authority and base your reasoning on your own findings."   Leonardo Da Vinci

Members of scientism came up with all sorts of untested and unproven ideas and claims, built off assumptions, and preached them to be universal truths, and we accepted them without evidence with no shred of doubt. A real education system would have people actually thinking about what's being said to them, and not just accepting it. But then, once again, a ventriloquist has no use for a dummy that speaks for himself, does it?

When these theories came out we could barely look at the sky with some decent telescopes, let alone test anything, and yet, it was accepted. We have high powered zoom cameras now that debunk the given curvature anytime it's used. And flat earthers are doing just that with these cameras and putting out scores of videos. By all rights we should've seen that it doesn't match reality.

Why should we accept an education system in our schools and universities that include theoretical science preached as facts, and a forced recognition of a theory, which, when thoroughly questioned, doesn't hold up? Can anyone tell me why?

The Zetetic Method

People are so conditioned to regurgitate what they have been told by authoritarians, and believing in it without verification, that they have become intellectually lazy. Accepting instead of figuring things out is the norm. I like science that's provable and can be questioned. What we called "science" has been taken over and is now from the government, is just propaganda that we dare not question or be called science deniers.

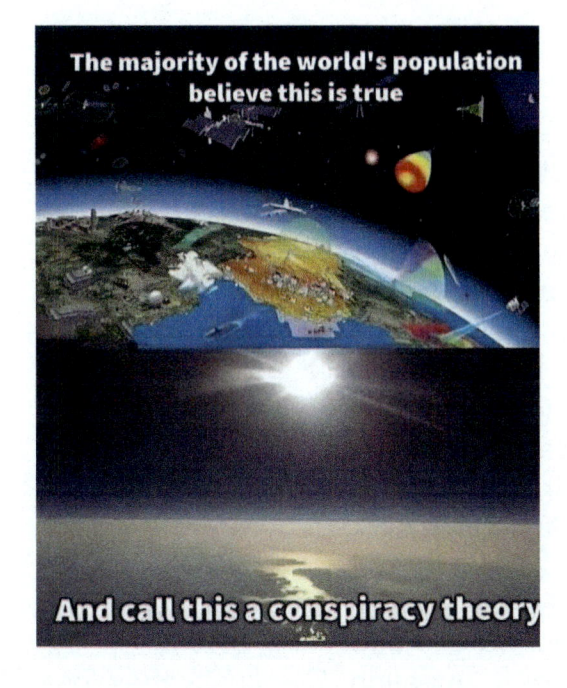

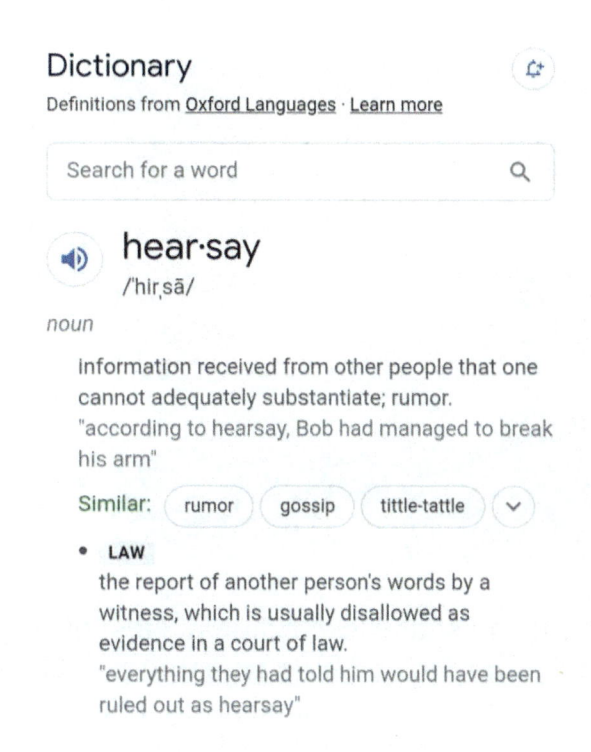

Before we get to some of the ridiculous claims that hold no merit, let's look at some examples of hearsay, so you can see where I'm coming from. I get these all the time when talking to people, repeated claims as though THAT is proof enough. Perhaps it is for the sheep but not for this goat here.

Hearsay is not evidence. We must fall on reality as evidence. Hearsay is people telling you the ocean is wrapped around a ball while you stand there looking at the flatness of it all. One is proven the other is hearsay. Hearsay is when you're told the world is whirling around all crazy like, while you balance your house of cards like it's not moving. One is proven, the other is hearsay. You're standing there enjoying a northern breeze while watching the cloud float towards the east and some half-wit is telling you the atmosphere is spinning with the Earth. One is proven to be the opposite while the other is hearsay. Impossible to have both, I like to go for the reality one.

Imagine someone telling you that you live on a spinning wobbling flying ball that's flying around a light that's flying around a black hole that's flying through the endless void of nothingness, because it was shot out by a Big Bang (not a regular bang mind you, but a BIG Bang) but you don't see any curvature or feel and see any such movement and can

The Zetetic Method

never, in any way, prove this oversized bang that hasn't happened again sense, and that rain cooled down the earth so we could evolve; where did all that rain water come from one has to wonders. Imagine someone telling you all of this, would you believe them? Oh no wait someone did. Do you? Why? Extraordinary claims should require extraordinary evidence. Unproven claims don't prove unproven claims. People's emotional attachment to the theory does not change this.

Some claims they've made in the past that were stated as fact have changed over time, which makes me wonder why it was stated as fact to begin with. As our lives go on, we should listen to these make believe 'scientists' and check to see if their narrative changes from what you remember them being. Example would be, they're now claiming the moon is within the Earth atmosphere. Also, they claimed dreams lasted only a split second, now they're saying just the opposite. Why state it in the first place?

Unlike most adults, children at least question the answers to questions, at least up to a certain age before being taught to just OBEY and not to question. Eventually they lose this superb act and just start regurgitating what they're told without questions. Very few children's deeper level of common sense when it comes to everyday reality, makes it out of the "education" system.

These theoretical claims here have been accepted because they have not been questioned thoroughly. Until now that is.

"Once a generation has been sold such a gradually reinforced lie from country to country, school by school, and across the entire world over decades, the very next generation will believe it as accepted truth without question or investigation. This is how the universal heliocentric lie was sold over the past generations." Can't remember who said that, but it's proven true, doesn't even need a generation, as this covid scam has proven.

Let's look at some of these claims shall we.

Ridiculous Claims

) On Astrophysicist Neil de Grasse Tyson's podcast his co-host asked him what gravity was, let's see how that went shall we.

Co-host Leighann Lord "What is gravity?"

Neil Tyson. "I have no idea. Okay, next question." Then, he explained "Here's the difference. We can describe gravity; we can say what it does to other things. We can measure it, we can predict with it, but when you start asking, like, what it is? I don't know."

The Zetetic Method

Leighann Lord then asks, "So I accidentally asked a deeper question than I meant to?" Tyson says "No, no, you were meant to ask deep questions in life. So...in an Einstein-ian answer, we'd say gravity is the curvature of space and time, and that objects will follow the curvature of space-time and we interpret that as a force of gravity. That's probably the best answer I can give to a 'What is gravity?' question."

The claim here is that space and time are curved and warped. And they call flat earthers crazy. Space and time have no properties thus cannot be curved or warped. The co-host should have asked deeper questions. I bet if it was me that conversation would have gone much differently.

SPACE is literally the absence of substance. It's not solid, liquid or gaseous. It can't bend or warp. Prove me wrong PLEASE!

TIME is a concept used for measurement. It's also not solid, liquid or gaseous. It can't be changed in any way. A minute is always a minute. Prove me wrong PLEASE.

This is utter nonsense. Fabric is physical material that can be woven, warped, curved, etc.
Space is just the opposite of all of that. You can't do anything with it, it's quite literally nothing.
And time is a concept, you have to be a special kind of stupid to by this "science" claim.
"Einstein can be credited as the man who saved Scientism from science." Author John Andrew Reed

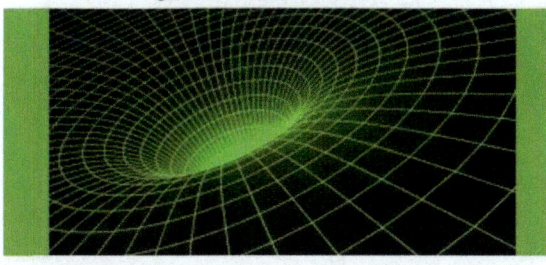

The only thing measured is the rate of fall, not any gravitational pull. Everything going downward here on Earth is described as density and buoyancy, they just stamped "gravity" on it. Just like everything that involves the laws of perspective, they've stamped "curvature" on it. They see the moon circling and say gravity. Everything else they claim going on up there is one assumption/claim after another. If you believe these ridiculous claims from this guy but can't prove him, then he is your priest.

The biggest lesson from Einstein's general theory of relativity is that space itself isn't a flat, unchanging, absolute entity. Rather **it's woven together, along with time, into a single fabric: spacetime**. This fabric is continuous, smooth, and gets curved and deformed by the presence of matter and energy.
Jul 22, 2017

https://www.forbes.com › 2017/07/22
Ask Ethan: Could The Fabric Of Spacetime Be Defective? - Forbes

They're now claim moon is within Earth's atmosphere. But their calculations before were spot on, despite not knowing at the time that the Moon is in Earths atmosphere? LMAO
More like straight outa Photoshop here.

The Moon is inside Earth's atmosphere, European researchers say. Observations made by the SOHO spacecraft over 20 years ago lead to a new discovery. The Earth has a hydrogen envelope as part of its outer atmosphere called the geocorona. The geocorona stretches well past the Moon, reveals a study.
Feb 24, 2019

https://bigthink.com › hard-science

If my body is attracting anything then why am I using my hands? Why can't I prove this claim? Why do I repel women? Never mind.

Google — time and space warped

Large objects such as the Sun and planets aren't the only masses that warp the fabric of space-time. **Anything with mass—including your body—bends this four-dimensional cosmic grid**. The warp, in turn, creates the effect of gravity, redirecting the path of objects that travel into it.

https://www.amnh.org › gravity › y...
You Bend Space-Time! | AMNH

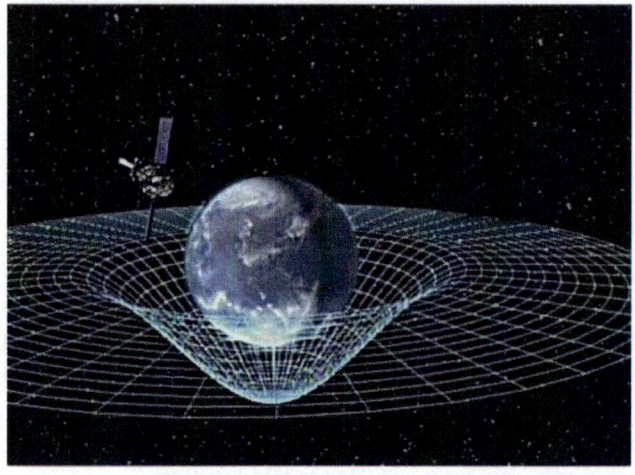

"I hold that space cannot be curved, for the simple reason that it can have no properties. It might as well be said that God has properties. He has not, but only attributes and these are of our own making. Of properties, we can only speak when dealing with matter filling the space. To say that in the presence of large bodies space becomes curved is equivalent to stating that something can act upon nothing. I, for one, refuse to subscribe to such a view." Nikola Tesla

) Now they're claiming they have built a telescope that can see from London to New York, which is 3,459 miles away. So that's 7,976,454 feet of missing curvature.

) Another claim I'm always hearing is that time zones and seasons couldn't happen on a flat earth and can only happen on a globe. This is ridiculous and really hasn't been thought through in the least. Time zones and seasons are both created by nothing more than the positioning of the sun according to where you are, it has nothing to do with curvature. This is pure elementary dear Watson. I have no doubt, the individuals making this claim, that I hear more often than not, pushed themselves to the head of the line to get 'the jab'.

The amazing telescope that lets you see New York from London's Tower Bridge

By Paul Harris for the Daily Mail

） People often say that they see the earth's curvature through the plane window. Windows in planes and jets are made curved to match the fuselage to handle the high speeds and pressure. Jets are curved even more so, so the earth looks even more curved. People mistake this curve for horizontal curvature, but the horizon is still a flat line when viewed without manipulation. Like curved lenses, curved windows also have an effect when looking through. If it was earth's curvature that you were viewing, the curvature would not change with the type of window you look through.

If this really was Earth's curvature then how long would it take to fly around it? The Earth wouldn't be that much bigger then the plane. We must think when we look.

You can stick your face to the window and see the flatness of earth. Or you can look at the window next to you and see it's flat again. Or you can look straight ahead as far as you can, and see the earth continues and then pretend that we live on a rolling pin. Just have fun with your imagination. Call it science. If the earth's curvature was that much at the edges of each side of your window at 35,000 feet up, then it wouldn't take you long to fly around the world, would it? And notice too, the horizon LINE still at eye level, same as it was at the airport. So much for downward curvature. Personal beliefs need to be put aside and then, only then, can reality be seen.

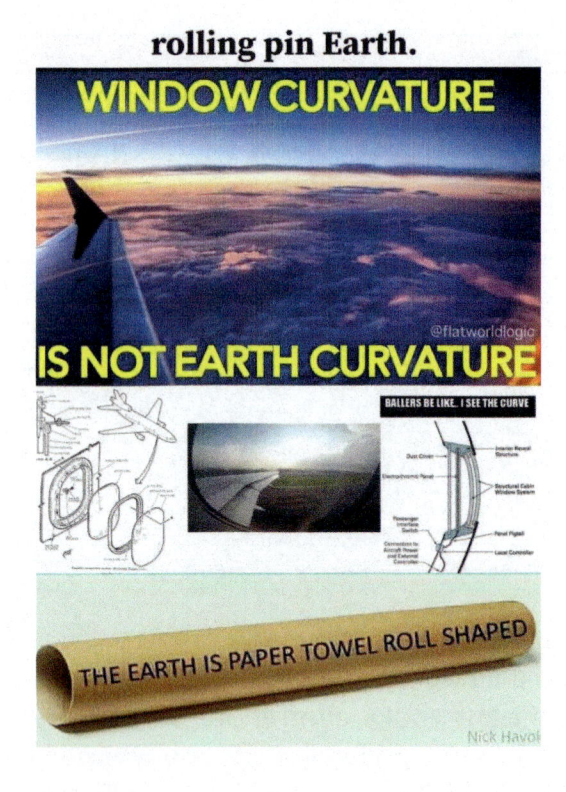

) Even though the deepest mine in the world is only a few thousand feet down and the farthest man has ever dug is 8 miles, the geologists will still make the assertions that they know what underlies the crust, of this curve less ball, to a depth of 4,000 miles and even the core itself.

And the public and repeating teachers (who unknowingly spread the globe properganda and false history to our kids with good intentions) will believe this as though the claiming 'scientists' have actually been down there, making a personal inspection and favoring the world with the result of their research.

As one flat earther put it: "To come up with a theory, then pretend that that theory is a discovery is ridiculous and not scientific in the least. Furthermore, a theory explained with suppositions is not explained at all. Their claims must be rejected as purely an assumption and incapable of proof. This makes the entire heliocentric ball Earth model taught in schools showing this supposed crust, outer-mantle, inner-mantle, outer-core and inner-core layers, are all going off assumptions and speculation as we have never penetrated beyond 8 miles."

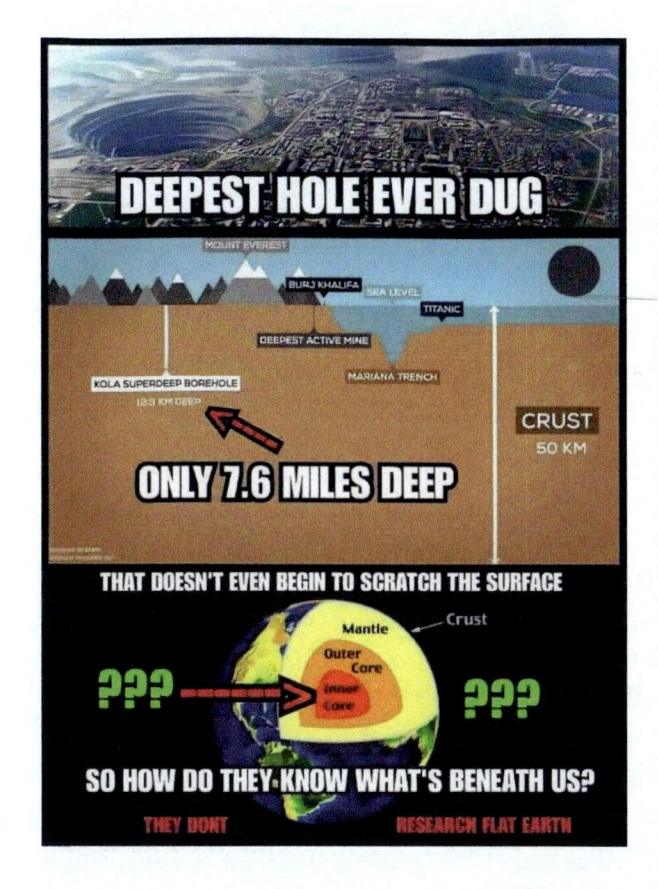

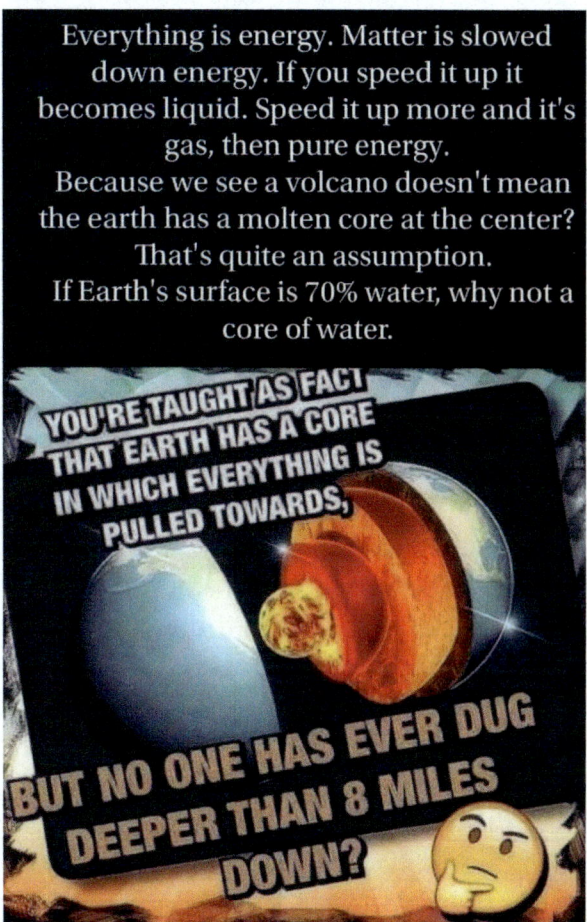

The Zetetic Method

) One claim/assumption is that you can only sail/fly around the world on a globe. I love when people say "I've flown all over the world, trust me it's a ball." This is laughable and completely ignorant. That's the equivalent of me saying that you can only walk around your neighborhood if it's a globe.

The earth has been circumnavigated, at a time when people actually knew the earth to be flat and the world hadn't been deceived yet, many times. No one was assuming the world was a wobbling ball while sailing around it.

If I can walk around my neighborhood or city or country and they are all flat(ish), then I can sail around the earth. It's the exact same concept. Sailing or flying around the world does not prove a ball earth.

Running around your neighborhood doesn't make it a sphere.

The Zetetic Method

This goes in line with people claiming Columbus proved globe earth by sailing around the world. How ignorant is this statement? First of all, Columbus didn't sail around the entire world, but it's irrelevant even if he did, because sailing in a circle doesn't cause a flat curve less plane to warp into a ball, does it? As long as you are using the magnetic north pole as a reference point, which is always the cast, the world would not have to be a globe to go around the land masses.

) People tell me, in my flat earth discussions, that "astronomers can predict eclipses, etc., because they know the earth is a globe." This claim is ridiculous and false. Predictions of eclipses, etc. have been happening for all recorded time, even before people were dumbed down and were actually aware of the earth being flat. For thousands of years the Chinese have predicted various solar and lunar eclipses before the globular theory was thought of, which means the shape of earth for these predictions is unimportant.

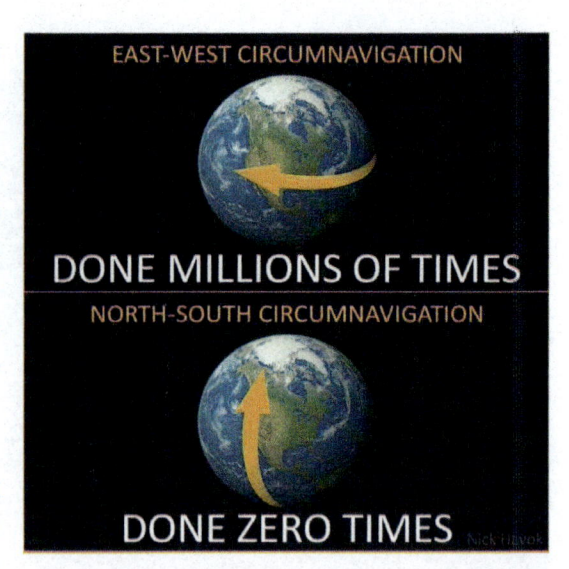

These predictions are made because the celestial lights go on cycles; it simply means that they've been happening throughout time. It doesn't mean the earth is a spinning wobbling flying ball. Just the opposite in fact. If the earth was such a whirling ball that's flying in three different directions throughout the 'expanding universe', then wouldn't it be harder to predict these things because everything would be in a different place?

The Egyptians predicted eclipses and knew the sun rotated around the earth. Because the eclipses, etc. have no connection with the shape of the earth and are not calculated on such, but on well-known cycles. Astronomy is strictly a science of observation. Scientism priests use math and people's trust in the mathematicians to throw dust in their eyes so they won't see absurdness when shown to them, and then they demand respect for such actions.

Sir R. Ball, in his "Story of the Heavens." he informs us: "If we observe all the eclipses in a period of eighteen years, or nineteen years, then we can predict, with at least an approximation to the truth, all the future eclipses for many years. It is only necessary to recollect that in 6585 1/2 days after one eclipse a nearly similar eclipse follows. For instance, a beautiful eclipse of the moon occurred on the 5th of December, 1881. If we count back 6585 days from that date, or, that is, 18 years and 11 days, we come to November 24th, 1863, and a similar eclipse of the moon took place then......It was this rule which enabled the ancient astronomers to predict the occurrence of eclipses, at a time when the motions of the moon were not understood nearly so well as we now know them."

It's simple, cycles is not curvature, thus the shape of the Earth is irrelevant in this manner.

) Neil Degrasse Tyson claimed that you can see the sunset longer on top of a tall building, it was proof of Earth's curvature; this is absurd and easily disproved. What Tyson did not mention was that the horizon line will still remain at eye level on top of said building or plane or high altitude balloon or whatever, which means THERE IS NO DOWNWARD CURVATURE! Fly west with a flat level flight, then email Tyson and tell him there's no downward curvature and that he's full of it. If people think the sun is going down, then they also have to believe that receding objects are literally shrinking in size.

You can not see the sun go behind the curvature more so on a tall building like Neil Degrasse Tyson claims, because there IS NO curvature. If there's none this far up then there's none on a tall building.

Before you Judge Neil deGrasse Tyson, walk a mile in his shoes

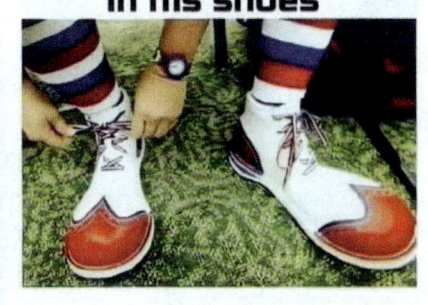

Someone mentioned to me, when I showed him the video where the picture (screen shot) below came from, the Earth's curvature was on the right of the picture; but in the video, as the camera pans to the right it shows to be flat. A lens effect is a desperate attempt at some kind of proof for ball Earth, but it debunks itself easily enough.

) Another false claim is that "physics proves globe earth." So, if we see a chalkboard full of equations next to a stack of fake pictures and at the same time, we observe plenty of physical evidence and real pictures that debunk the math that's built on assumptions, should we disregard the reality-based evidence and go with equations? What logic is this?

Here a statement that has been proven many times over with long distance photography, railroads, bridges, etc.

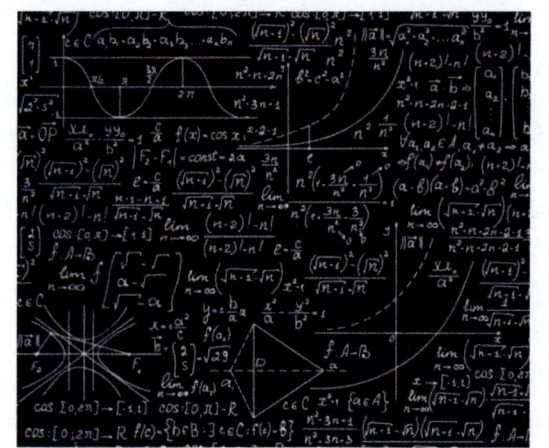

"Today's scientists have substituted mathematics for experiments, and they wander off through equation after equation, and eventually build a structure which has no relation to reality."
- Nikola Tesla

) It's been claimed that people age slower in space. Well now there's yet another claim with zero evidence. I'll have to see the receipt on that one. A year is a year no matter where you're at. Body ages due to genetics and design. That CAN be proven, the other CAN NOT.

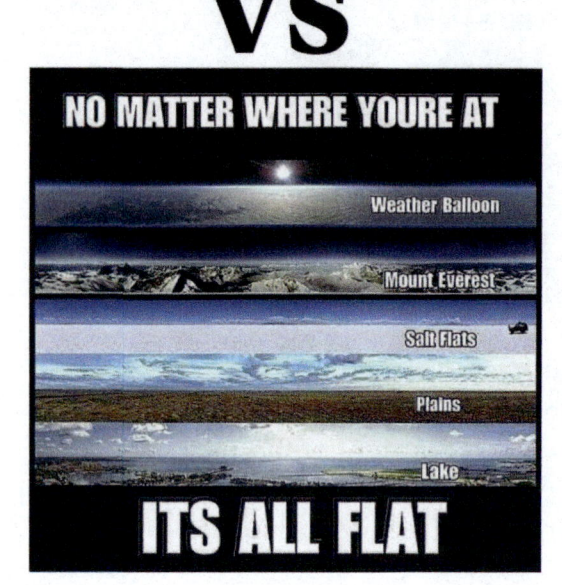

) People believe there's a car orbiting in space. The original live video of the launch for Elon Musk's Tesla car was recorded and dissected by flat earthers everywhere. On a very quick glitch, and a freeze frame exposed it for being in a studio.

Elon Musk's car is said to still be orbiting the Solar System and you can track this fairy tale if you like and believe in what you're tracking. But how did it get out of Earth's gravitational pull and that far out? Shouldn't it be orbiting Earth right now like the moon, satellites, ISS, all that junk? Why does it get to float freely about but nothing else does? Such nonsense is put out there for low effort thinkers, of which there are many.

It has been almost exactly four years since Elon Musk launched his Tesla Roadster into space on SpaceX's Falcon Heavy rocket. It is now more than 234 million miles (**377 million km**) from Earth and is actually closer to Mars. Feb 20, 2022

https://www.carscoops.com › 2022/02

Elon Musk's Tesla Roadster Has Traveled Almost 2 Billion Miles In ...

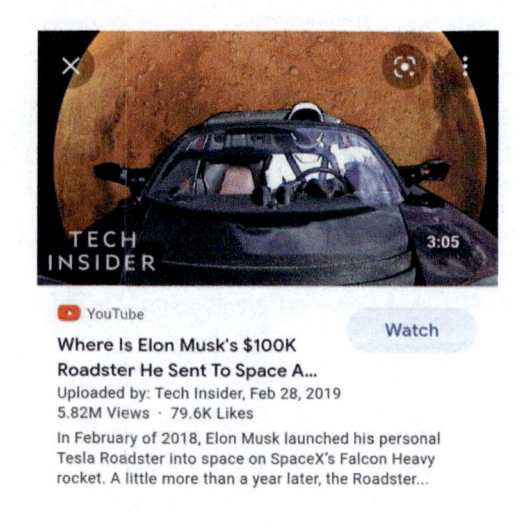

Where Is Elon Musk's $100K Roadster He Sent To Space A...
Uploaded by: Tech Insider, Feb 28, 2019
5.82M Views · 79.6K Likes
In February of 2018, Elon Musk launched his personal Tesla Roadster into space on SpaceX's Falcon Heavy rocket. A little more than a year later, the Roadster...

The Zetetic Method

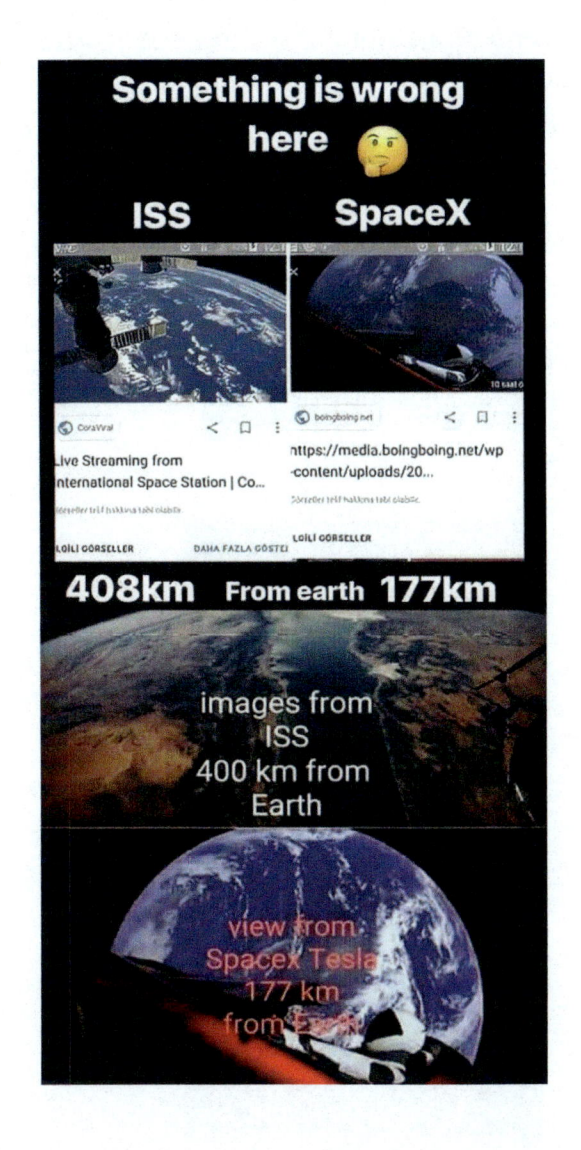

Elon Musk had a live feed for a rocket launch one time. The camera kept going between the spectators and the ground shot from the rocket, (why don't they have the camera filming upwards so we can see space coming? Hmmm), anyway, the camera went to the spectators, who were watching the rocket level out but still fired up, but when the camera shot came back to the camera ON the rocket which showed the rocket was already in space orbiting Earth. How can both be true? And how can the camera not burn up when leaving the atmosphere, is that just for entry?

So as the rocket's orbiting the Earth, the Earth starts to flip flop around. I asked in the live chat room how the Earth flip flopped in the video shot but the rocket did not flip flop while in the same shot. How can one be affected by the wide angle lens yet the other is not affected, it's in the same frame. It proves it's in a studio in front of a green screen. They do the same in movies. I was kicked out of the live chat. People started to question what I was saying.

So, then I went to the ISS live feed, where I came right onto the chat room and announced that I was here to see Elon Musk's rocket that was just launched. The ISS was over Africa but it was daytime there, how when it's daytime here in the USA? I questioned this and about the location of Elon Musk's rocket and was instantly kicked out. WHY???? TRUTH FEARS NO INVESTIGATION!!!

One guy was tracking the ISS while watching the live feed and Hawaii was not where it was supposed to be. Hmm

) Neil Degrasse Tyson has made the claim that our Earth is somewhat pear shaped. Well, someone needs to get with and inform NASA's artist, because they're creating spheres for us to believe in.

) Some claim a drop of water proves an ocean can be wrapped around a ball. That is a desperate comparison. How does a water droplet compare with an entire ocean? The water droplet spherical shape is due to what's called SURFACE TENSION. Surface tension of the water is about 72 mN/m, that means it is about 1.2 mm drop, larger than that it breaks. Bodies of contained settled water are measured flat and level when undisturbed by wind or tide.

) Astronomers have claimed that they've taken an inventory of the planets, measured their distances, the shape of their orbits, and the positions of these orbits, their times of revolution and in some cases their weights. Well gee, I wanna see the CGI footage so I can believe it.

13 thousand, 170 billion trillion pounds

(Inside Science) -- Earth isn't even close to being the largest planet in our solar system, but it's also no lightweight, weighing in at a whopping **13 thousand, 170 billion trillion pounds**, or 13,170,000,000,000,000,000,000,000. Sep 7, 2021

https://astronomy.com › 2021/09

Video: How much does Earth weigh? - Astronomy Magazine

One cannot truly weigh even the earth that we are standing on. We don't even know the depth of every square mile of the oceans or unknown caves. How can one truly weigh the earth with that fact alone standing in the way? We have only dug 8 miles into the earth crust. And, no actual curvature to measure. Yet they have made the claim that the earth weighs 170 billion pounds. LMAO

And some of these 'planets' are claimed to be hundreds of millions of miles away. The Scientism priest made these claims over 100 years ago.

T. G. Ferguson, in the Earth Review September, 1894: "Let us now glance at their theories about the Planets....... Saturn's mean distance from the sun, as given in the 'Story of the Heavens,' is 884,000,000 miles, and the diameter 71,000 miles. Professor Lockyer gives its distance as 890,000,000 miles; a difference of 4,000,000 miles. Professor Olmstead gives Saturn's distance from the sun as 890,000,000 miles, and the diameter 79,000 miles. Others could be quoted equally at variance. WHERE, WE ASK, IS THE ACCURACY OF THIS 'MOST EXACT OF SCIENCES."

Please prove to me that the belief in this claim is not full-blown faith. Scientism is a false religion. The proof is everywhere. And they've taken the best of humanity.

) The claim that if the earth were flat you could see the sun 24 hours a day.
I get this claim a lot when talking to globe believers. This is a question from someone who has mixed models. In the globe model the sun is 93,000,000 miles away, thus the whole flat earth would indeed be lid. But on the flat earth model the sun is smaller and local. Like a street light that doesn't light up the whole street. The proof for this is the temperature in the morning vs noon vs the evening, it acts as a local sun, as was talked about earlier in this book. Another proof is that sunspots and clouds that are closest to the sun are lid the most. That is not how it should be if the sun is 93,000,000 miles away. Where's the proof of such a claim?

The Zetetic Method

I'M OFTEN ASKED BY GLOBE EARTHERS, "IF THE EARTH IS FLAT THEN WHY ISN'T IT DAYTIME ALL OVER THE WORLD AT THE SAME TIME"?

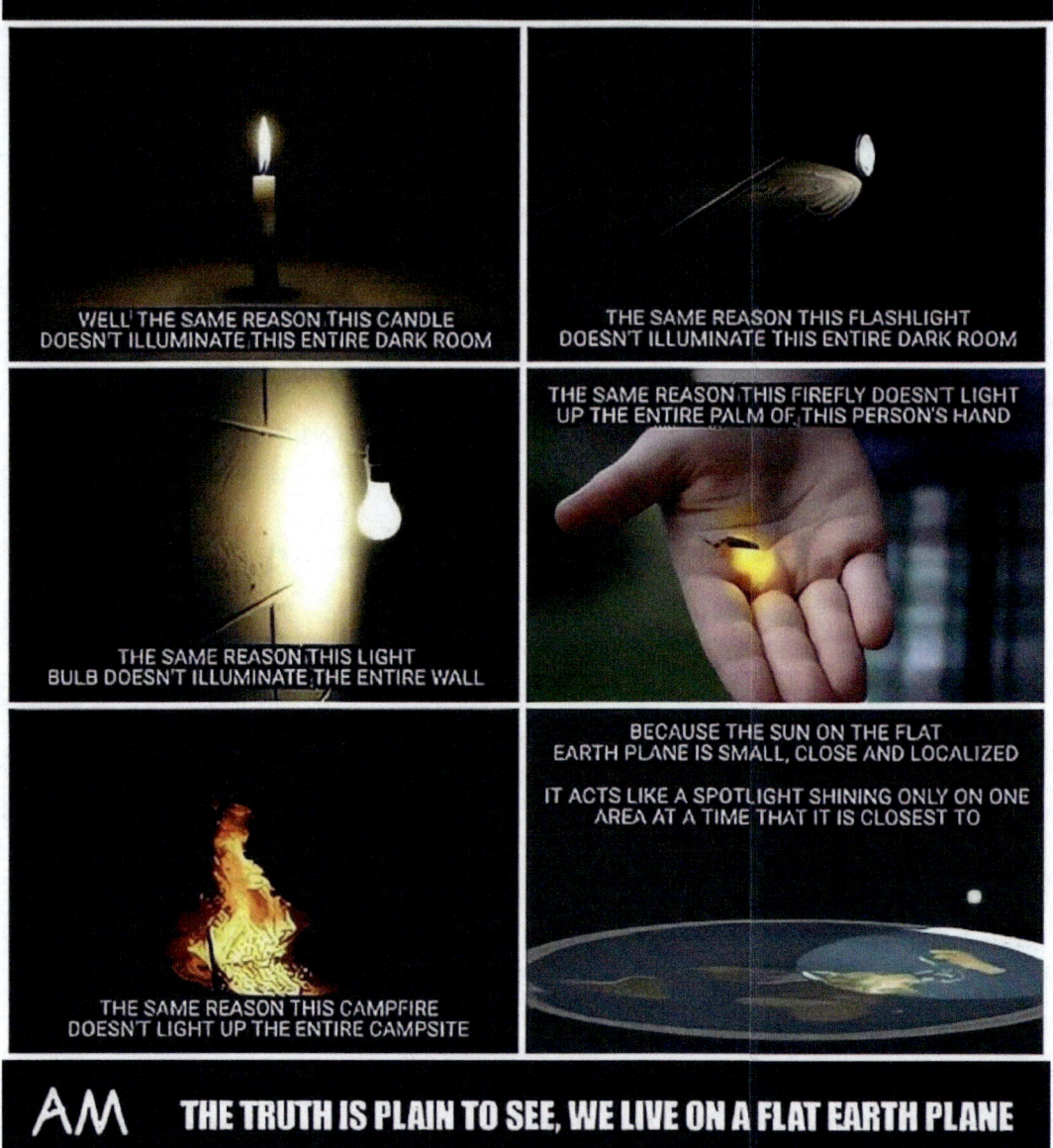

WELL THE SAME REASON THIS CANDLE DOESN'T ILLUMINATE THIS ENTIRE DARK ROOM

THE SAME REASON THIS FLASHLIGHT DOESN'T ILLUMINATE THIS ENTIRE DARK ROOM

THE SAME REASON THIS LIGHT BULB DOESN'T ILLUMINATE THE ENTIRE WALL

THE SAME REASON THIS FIREFLY DOESN'T LIGHT UP THE ENTIRE PALM OF THIS PERSON'S HAND

THE SAME REASON THIS CAMPFIRE DOESN'T LIGHT UP THE ENTIRE CAMPSITE

BECAUSE THE SUN ON THE FLAT EARTH PLANE IS SMALL, CLOSE AND LOCALIZED

IT ACTS LIKE A SPOTLIGHT SHINING ONLY ON ONE AREA AT A TIME THAT IT IS CLOSEST TO

AM THE TRUTH IS PLAIN TO SEE, WE LIVE ON A FLAT EARTH PLANE

) One claim made is that if the earth were flat, then the same constellations would be seen all over the earth at the same time. That the northern hemisphere would have the same constellations as the southern hemisphere. This is a strawman argument.

The heliocentric globe model has each of the star's trillions, or whatever, different light-years away, therefore you would see them north and south, all over the flat earth. But the geocentric flat earth model has the stars a lot closer and rotating around the North star Polaris. This is observable. They all rotate the same, thus they are connected.

The Zetetic Method

People believe because we see the moon right side up in the northern hemisphere and upside down when viewed from the southern hemisphere, that this is proof of the earth being a globe. Let's have a look at this shall we.

If you look at the street light from one side of it and I looked at it from the other side, would we both have the same view? No, our views would be flipped. This is NOT proof of a globe Earth, it's proof of not thinking about how it would work on both models, globe and flat.

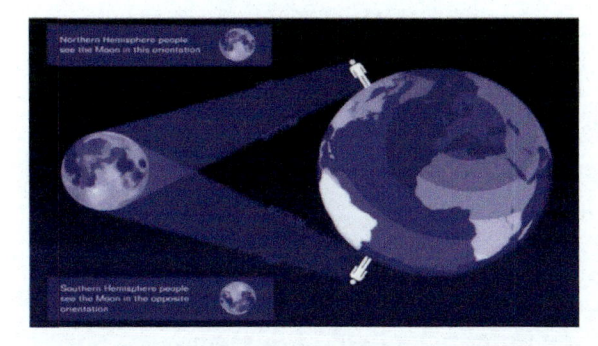

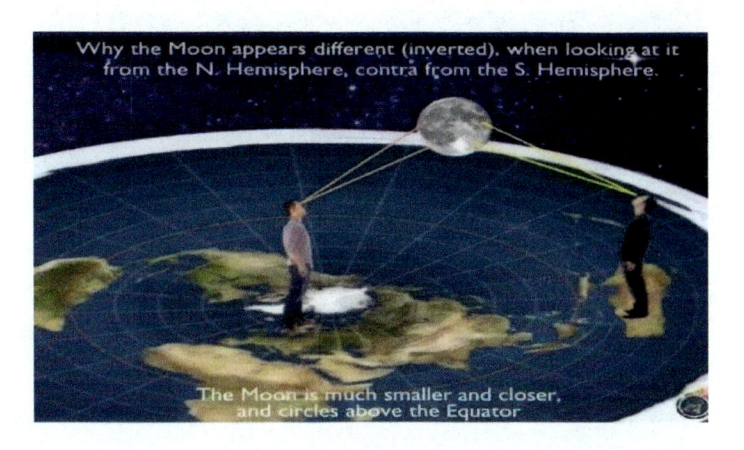

People try to combine the two models when assuming how a flat earth model works. They look at the flat earth model with globe earth claims. This comes from people being ignorant about the flat earth model and not really knowing what they're arguing against. The internet has made it very hard to research flat earth without getting nothing but garbage and discrediting claims, hence the reason I'm writing this book and my website, flatearthlogic.net.

But the physical reality of constellations and star trail circles does not support the 'light-years away' theory. As the Earth moves through space shouldn't the stars closer to us appear to move more than the more distant ones? Every night year after year the positions of the stars do not change in their rotation. Only the celestial lights, once called planets and once called "wandering stars," change position in relation to the rest of the stars.

If we were standing in a large building, and I was standing towards the middle and you were standing towards the end, then we both would see different spots on the ceiling, correct? The laws of perspective limit your vision. You can see a certain distance all the way around you. As you move across this great plane we live on, the sky view will change. This fact does not add curvature to said plane, only changes what's in your view.

The existence of light-years is not proven in the least, therefore the entire cosmology predicated upon the existence of light-years has been called into question. The whole model is a fabrication from assumptions and speculations, and does not match physical reality.

) The below claim: This screenshot I took when I Google "How did the Earth begin rotating," and this is what popped up. How could they even come up with such a laughable theory? There's no proof for such a claim. They can't even give us solid proof the Earth is spinning now, much less what it was doing "billions" of years ago. I ask them how they found this out and what instruments were used and what scientific method was used. Still waiting on an answer. If you can't test it then it's Pseudo-science.

The Zetetic Method

This is only part of the indoctrination they're teaching our kids, it's from the Children Museum website.
What proof is there of such a claim? Can the "proof" be proven? No man could possible know this. Kids go without questioning these claims and then grow up defending them.

How did the Earth begin rota...

All Videos Images News Maps Shoppi

According to scientists, 4.54 billion years ago, **an immense cloud of dust and hydrogen gas began to collapse, which caused the dust cloud to flatten and spin**. As it became flatter, the disk rotated faster and faster.

https://www.childrensmuseum.org › ...
Why Does the Earth Spin? | The Children's Museum of Indianapolis

) The Big Bang is just a Big Claim, nothing more. Whenever they create matter in the lab, anti-matter is equally created; but the universe does not have this equal measurement. So how can the Big Bang create a certain amount of matter but not anti-matter? Like evolution, time is the enemy of the Big Bang. Things fall apart as time goes, not get better and get more organized and have predictable order. This only happens if an outside intelligent force is interacting.

If everything is spinning because of the Big Bang then why are some "moons spinning in opposite directions" according to the globe theory? If the Big Bang happened then one would think that particles would be spreading outward not clump together and forming a perfectly designed time-piece and greenhouse. How can matter be created out of

The Zetetic Method

nothing? Where did all the information that life has programmed into it come from? Where did consciousness come from out of this Big Bang? A book is more than ink thrown onto wood made into paper, it has thoughts and information in it. Not only is the book designed but the data in it is thought about and delivered with a language that's learned.

The Big Band goes against the laws of thermodynamics. Things degrade over time and matter doesn't create itself and doesn't give itself consciousness either. Prove me wrong.

If I ask you how computers get here but you can't say mankind then what can you say? Everything you use is mankind designed with materials from Earth. And they're only dead things, no matter how good you think your phone is, it doesn't have the beautiful gift that is life. But I'm getting ahead of myself. More on all that later. This theory is not provable in the least nor can be recreated on a small scale, it's simply a theory based on, can we reasonably call it but" nothing at all"? Show me where I'm wrong and prove it.

) People claim that sunsets are proof that we live on a ball. I beg to differ. Ignorance of the laws of perspective does not add curvature. See CHAPTER 1 "Curvature/The Laws of Perspective".

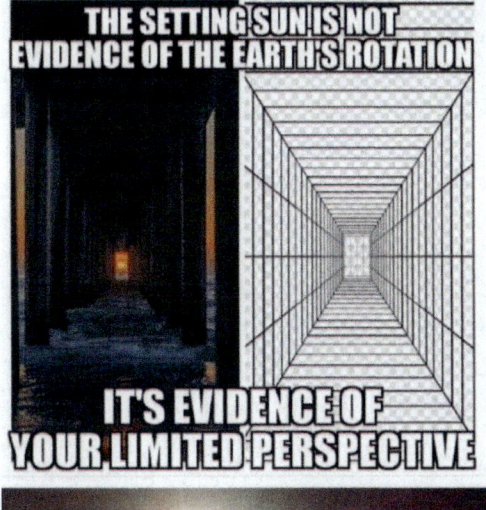

The Zetetic Method

) Another ridiculous claim from astrophysicist Neil Degrasse Tyson made that is supposed to be believed, even footballs are affected by the Earth's rotation. So, did the Bengals kicker forget to calculate this? Maybe it's a joke.

) A flat earther, and many others now, have sent unmanned balloons up with a non-gopro cam to the height of 121,000 feet. The horizon line was flat and remained at eye level, same as on ground level, which means it's not curving downward. Astrophysicist Neil Degrasse Tyson, trying to refute this flat earth reality proof, has made the claim that we're not high enough at 121,000 feet to see the curvature. But he also states we see ships going behind curvature at the beach.

You can bring them back into view with a telescopic lens. This is consistent with a level earth and the laws of perspective but due to converging planes and the limitations on how far the eye can actually see the ships will appear to disappear bottom first. This illusion, by any means, does not prove that we live on a ball.

If ships are going over the horizon, it means that the earth curves and the higher you go, the more pronounced that curve should be, correct? But when people tested this with high altitude balloon cams, they revealed a lack of any curvature or a lowered horizon line. If it curves enough to hide boats within a 5 or so miles, then with a view from five miles up, the earth's edge should start to curve, not stay flat and horizontal. You can't have both. It's one or the other. To be consistent with your beliefs you have to let go of the flat horizon at eye level or the ship going behind any kind of curvature. The logical choice would be the one that matches reality, and physical reality shows that there isn't any curvature.

Either let go of the idea that we're too small to see the curvature or you must let go of this claim that ships go over it. You either can perceive the curve or you can't.

) Here's a silly claim from R. Manning, Marquette, NASA Astrophysicist, that has no merit or any way to prove and is disproved, like others, with pure reality. There's always an excuse why we can't prove.

CLAIM: "Indeed, tides exist in all bodies of water, even one's bathtub, but are so infinitesimally small, as to be unmeasurable. Even on Lake Superior, the largest of the Great Lakes of North America, the tiny effect of a tide is overcome by the effect of barometric pressure and the phenomenon known as a seiche. There are no Tide Tables of the Great Lakes and seiche warnings are rarely broadcast, as most cause a variance of less than 50 cm. The effects of a seiche may be felt strongest in the Straits of Mackinac between Lakes Huron and Michigan."

) Many people I discuss flat earth with, when the theories they are defending starts to fall to pieces as I put them to the test with real questions, will start attacking me with silly claims about flat earth to discredit it or make them appear to be 'winning,' or just to throw the attention off, ignoring any physical facts I've brought up and focusing instead upon some ridiculous facet of a Flat Earth model nobody takes seriously.

Some examples of such foolish claims are "If the earth was flat the water would run off," "ships would fall off the edge," "I can't believe people think we live on a floating disk," "If the earth was a flat disk the shadow on the moon would be a line." I could go on and on. This is a deliberate form of deflection, allowing them to censor your message by conflating it with nonsense.

This is also the result of their ignorance of what they're arguing against. So WHY argue against it. Learn then argue if you disagree.

) Sir Robert Ball, in his book "Story of the Heavens," tells us that "We cannot pretend to know how many thousands of millions of years ago this epoch was, but we may be sure that earlier still the earth was even hotter, until at length we seem to see the temperature increase to a red heat, from a red heat we look back to a still earlier age when the earth was white hot, back again till we find the surface of our now solid globe was ACTUALLY MOLTEN."

I don't know about you but I'll have to see the receipt on that one. First of all you don't KNOW squat about what happened on "day one" and second "thousands of millions of years"? LMAO

Now how do we come across this 'knowledge' (and I use that term so loosely that it might fall off) that the

earth was a whirling mass of vapor? Based on what evidence does this claim rest on? Can this 'evidence' be proven?

Perhaps I will make my own assumption here and assume that this, like other assumptions from the scientism religion of astronomy, is based on nothing at all. Your imagination is left to fill in the blanks.

From the science magazine of its time "Modern Science and Modern Thought," we are told that "It is right, however, to state that ALL MATHEMATICAL CALCULATIONS OF TIME BASED ON THE ASSUMED RATE AT WHICH COSMIC MATTER COOLS INTO SUNS AND PLANETS, AND THESE INTO SOLID AND HABITABLE GLOBES, ARE IN THE HIGHEST DEGREE UNCERTAIN."

So, after all that theory pushing and school teaching, we are told that all these mathematical calculations are based on assumptions and in the highest degree uncertain? Why are they still teaching it in school? I rest my case.

) During discussions I demand logical consistency. This is very important. Many ball earth claims are ridiculous and if you apply them to the rest of the theory, you'll see that these same claims do not always apply consistently.

Scientists' will change and alter their theories at will, when need be, to match whatever new theory they are now feeding you, and they'll do so without even confessing their previous mistakes. And of course people won't even notice.

Example would be we are told that gravity keeps everything at a constant, so everything within the earth's atmosphere is spinning at a 1000mph eastward in unison and undetectable to those on earth. But then we're told the Coriolis effect has to be counted with bullets. If that was the case, a plane flying against the spin going westward should face a headwind of 1000 miles per hour, but of course that is not the case. While going against the spin of the earth isn't a factor for airplanes' flight times and gas mileage, space agencies apparently use it to their advantage.

A 2016 article on space.com titled 'How Fast Is Earth Moving?' describes the interesting phenomenon: "Space agencies love to take advantage of Earth's spin. If
they're sending humans to the International Space Station, for example, the preferred location to do so is close to the equator. That's why space shuttle missions used to launch from Florida. By doing so and launching in the same direction as Earth's spin, rockets get a speed boost to help them fly into space."

Another example would be that we're told we're too small to see the curvature and at 121,000 feet up that we're not high enough, then the same scientists will say that you can see the ship going over the curvature at sea-level.

Another example is that we're told that Earth's gravitational pull cancels out smaller objects' gravitational pull, but then we're told the Cavendish experiment proves objects attractive towards each other.

Another example is that we're told objects attract each other but on the ISS space station videos everything's 'floating' around. Shouldn't the objects be attracted to each other and the walls of the ISS?

With all the contradictions that exist in the industry of 'science' of Astronomy, it's a wonder anybody accepts a theory coming from such Pseudo-scientists. If they went off facts then how could there be any contradictions? Let's look at a few now.

1) Sir Isaac Newton, in his crazy ranting of unproven theories says "The sun is the center of the solar system and immovable."
Then Professor Herschel discovered that the sun was "not immovable."

2) They have absolutely no way of knowing anything about Mars' atmosphere but that doesn't stop them from claiming they do. In the Christian Million (San Jose) of 9th August, 1894, we find that "Mr. Norman Lockyer has been telling an interviewer that Mars is like us in many respects. IT HAS AN ATMOSPHERE LIKE OURS."
The Standard magazine of 18th August, 1894, says: "Professor Campbell, of the Lick Observatory, announces that he has demonstrated that MARS presents NO EVIDENCE OF HAVING AN ATMOSPHERE."

3) In Sir David Brewster's book, "More World than One," he tells us that the atmosphere extends for about 45 miles.
In Science Siftings magazine the claim is made: "We may infer that a few hundred miles embrace all the gaseous envelope of the globe." And in "Elementary Physiography," we have "The height of the atmosphere is not known with any certainty. There is probably no fixed limit to the atmosphere."

4) In Amèdée Guillemin S book "The Heavens: Handbook of Popular Astronomy," says that light travels at the rate of 192,000 miles a second. M. Leon Foucault says 184,000 miles; Sir R. Ball 180,000 miles; the Editor of Science Siftings says at first 186,000 miles, second time 196,000 miles. Then a writer in the English Mechanic who says: "I BELIEVE NO ONE NOW HOLDS THE VIEW THAT LIGHT ACTUALLY MOVES."

5) Sir R. Ball writes a book on "The Cause of an Ice Age." But he discredits the entire book by stating: "I have found it necessary to ASSUME the existence of several ice ages." Then later states: "In fact it might almost be said that the astronomical theory (of accounting for ice ages) must be necessarily true, as it is a strictly mathematical consequence FROM THE LAWS OF GRAVITATION."

Here he uses one theory to 'prove' yet another theory. The 'evidence' of the ice age can also be taken as 'evidence' of a great flood. The latter actually has more evidence than the former; but that's another book.
So where are they getting these ridiculous numbers and why are they preaching it in school? Can there be any truth in science which is not founded on assumptions, guess work and instead supported by 'facts' which have never existed outside the brains of their claimers/inventors?

6) The Big Bang, Bolton Davidheiser, Ph. D. "A Statement Concerning the Ministry of Dr. Hugh Ross"
"The Big Bang idea began with astronomer Georges Lemaitre.

According to Isaac Asimov, Lemaitre conceived this mass to be "no more than a few light-years in diameter." (at least 12 trillion miles). By 1965 that figure was reduced to 275 million miles, by 1972 to 71 million miles, by 1974 to 54 thousand miles, by 1983 to "a trillionth the diameter of a proton", and now, to nothing at all! A singularity!"

) It is claimed that once you leave Earth's atmosphere and enter space you become weightless. You can travel in any direction forever by a gentle pull or push.

Let's think about that for a moment. Completely weightless, which means no forces of gravity pulling you in any direction? You got that? Ok then let's continue.

They also tell us that Earth, weighing 170 billion tons, is locked into an orbit at speeds of 66,000 mph around the sun by way of the sun's gravitational pull. Then there's the moon's business with tides and its attraction to Earth. Does anybody else see anything wrong with that? So my question now is how can the astronauts be weightless in space while the massive Earth is being pulled at those speeds? How is it that the astronauts and satellites, etc. are not being pulled into the sun?

349

The Zetetic Method

How can you send a satellite all the way to Saturn and Mars to take photos and it doesn't get pulled into the sun by this massive force? How can the gravitational pull just skip over all these objects and select Earth to pull? Are satellites and astronauts not subject to the sun's gravitational pull? How can the sun not pull anything in space except for planets?

) Here's one more ridiculous claim. This is NASA'S "picture" of New Zealand from space. I'll just leave these two for you to gaze upon:

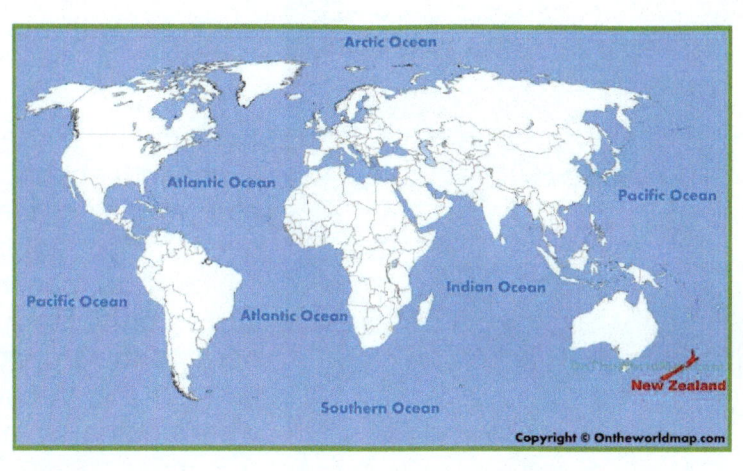

) Here's a list of quick claims that have no real backing or merit and can be proven wrong.
1) "Ships go over the curvature"--the P900 camera proves that it does not.
2) "Circumnavigation" --- only east to west is possible on a flat earth and that's all that's ever done, courtesy of no fly zones for the north and south 'poles.'
3) "Space" --- you can't have a vacuum next to a non vacuum atmosphere that depends on the pressure that it has without a barrier.
4) "Bendy oceans"--- large bodies of water don't and will never curve. Prove me wrong.
5) "Space travel" - rocket propulsion is impossible in a vacuum plus see #3.
6) "Everybody knows it's a globe" --- self proclaiming knowledge without evidence is not knowledge, being taught something and repeating it is not knowledge either. Parrots do this action as well. If you believe something because it's popular, then put a quarter in your ass crack because you're playing yourself, and cheating yourself from real knowledge.
7) "Solar system" - distances can't really be proven but lies about them have been proven. The assumption of terrestrial "planets" have not been proven, but their rotations around Polaris can be observed. What we observe is celestial lights in real life, and CGI on your computers and tell-a-vision. The solar system, as it is taught, is purely hypothetical. Prove me wrong with evidence not hearsay from NASA.

8) "Satellites"---- yes and no, refer to chapter 8 on satellites plus look into thermosphere, if the globe theory was true, satellites wouldn't last up there. Hmmm

9) "Dark matter, dark energy, quasars, black hole" --- hearsay, never been proven. If you can prove it I'm listening, but remember I don't go off your beliefs, I need evidence, like a court of law would. And I thought mass created gravity, so what's this black hole BS?

10) "Relativity" --- theoretical make believe created to get rid of nonsense created by the globe model. Works on paper with math built on assumptions but can't be shown or applied to real life.

11) "The Sun is the star at the center of the Solar System. It is a nearly perfect ball of hot plasma, heated to incandescence by nuclear fusion reactions in its core, radiating the energy mainly as light, ultraviolet, and infrared radiation."

Now how can they know what's happening in the sun's core? They don't even know what's happening here or the bottom of the ocean. How can anything burn in the vacuum they've claimed? Prove to me what's going on in the sun's core. I'll wait.

12)

13) "The sun (or hot ball of plasma and gas) makes things orbit around it and is much stronger than Earth's gravitational pull."

If objects are orbiting Earth, then that means that at some point in the orbit they have to be going in the opposite direction of the location of the sun, thus away from it. So how come the gravitational pull of the sun doesn't slow it down? It's supposedly MUCH stronger than Earth's gravitational pull.

If the sun's gravitational pull is THAT much powerful then Earth, then how come it doesn't pull the moon out of orbit when the moon is between the Earth and sun? It would be 280,000 miles closer to the sun.

Because the amount of gravity exerted by the sun is so much more than the Earth's gravitational pull, the Earth is forced into an orbit around the sun. The sun's gravity pulls the Earth toward it the same way it does to all the other planets in the solar system. Apr 23, 2018

https://sciencing.com › earth-rotates-...

Why the Earth Rotates Around the Sun - Sciencing

accepted there.

These are only a few ridiculous claims made by Pseudo-scientists and their followers. Physical reality proves that the Earth is flat, does not move and it's the sun that's moving above us and around the North star Polaris, just as we witness it every single day. People are not questioning these theories and claims because they are so busy being entertained and working.

So globe earthers feel free to disprove anything in this book, but please make sure it's not hearsay or CGI, take that silliness somewhere else, to your local "education institution" maybe. It's

P.S. I'll just leave these here:

If they're lying about ball earth, moonlanding and 9/11 what else are they lying about?

The Zetetic Method

WHEN I SAY "THEY'VE LIED ABOUT EVERYTHING" I TRULY MEAN "EVERYTHING!!!"

Everything you thought you knew is a lie!

Sincerely,
Stonehenge.

~R.W.Rock

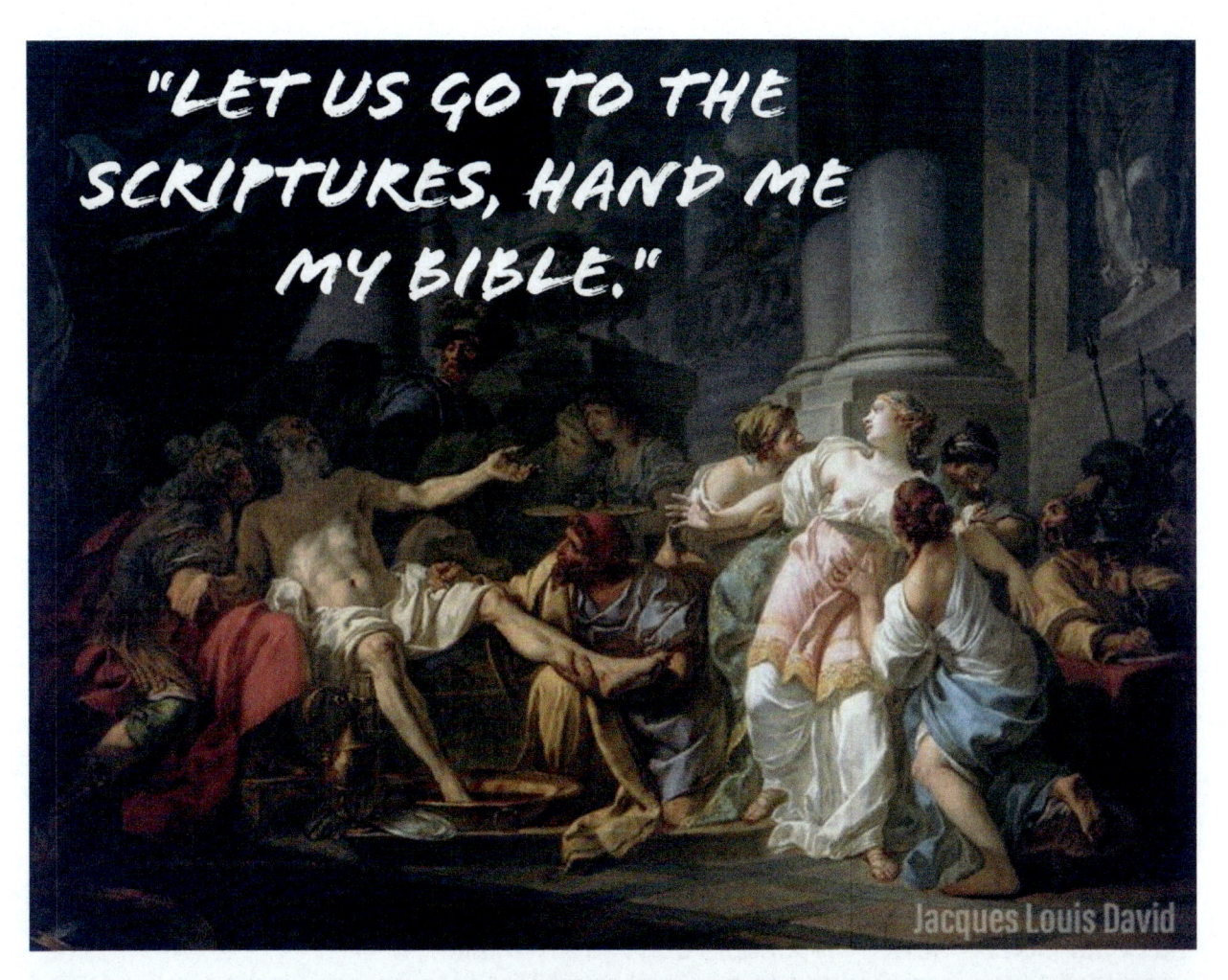

"LET US GO TO THE SCRIPTURES, HAND ME MY BIBLE."

— Jacques Louis David

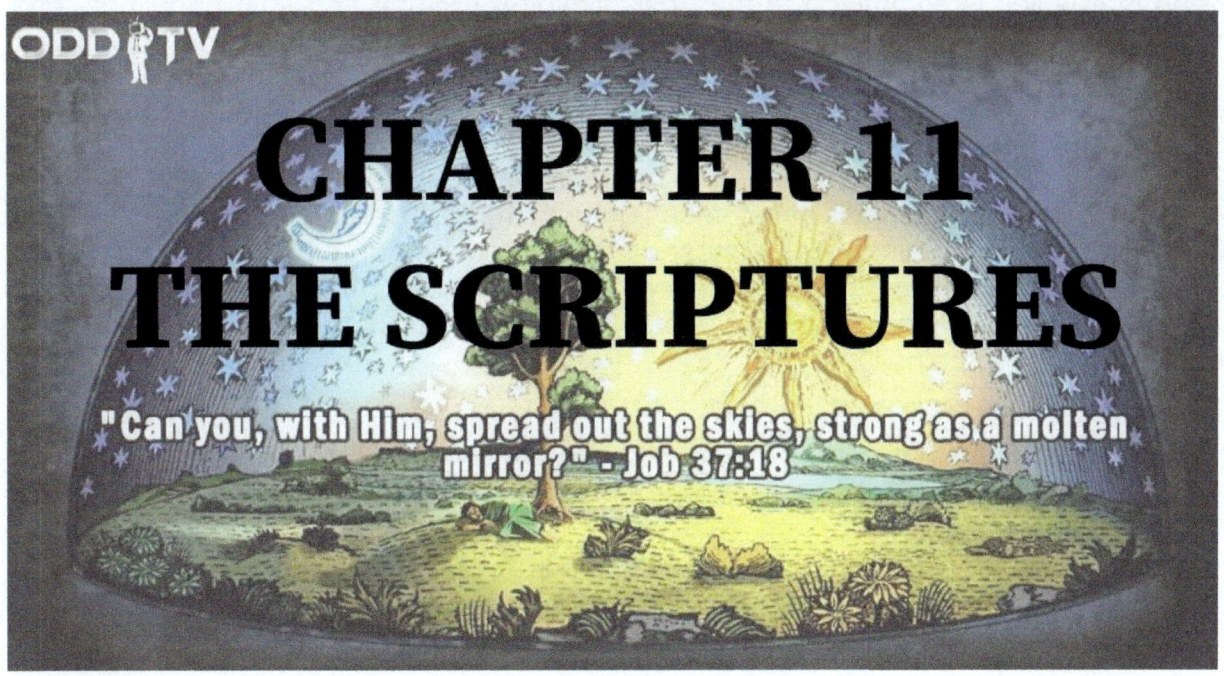

CHAPTER 11
THE SCRIPTURES

"Can you, with Him, spread out the skies, strong as a molten mirror?" - Job 37:18

"And ye shall know the truth, and the truth shall make you free." John 8:32

The Importance of a True Cosmogony.
1 Thessalonians 5:21 "Prove all things; hold fast that which is good."

And some GREAT advice that people don't seem to take:
"Keep that which is committed to thy trust, avoiding profane and vain babblings, and oppositions of science falsely so called: Which some professing have erred concerning the faith. Grace be with thee. Amen." 1 Timothy 6:20-21

The Bible, flat earth book or flying ball book
The globe theory is a religious belief based on faith masquerading as science. The Bible warns us of such happenings. Yet, almost all religions have not avoided the "opposition of science falsely so called;" it has embraced it and preaches it. It's simple in my opinion, that if man uses the senses that the Creator has given him, he gains knowledge; if he uses them not, he remains ignorant.

From Paine's "Age of Reason": "The two beliefs—modern astronomy and the Bible—cannot be held together in the same mind; he who thinks he believes both has thought very little of either."

The Zetetic Method

This book 100% does not endorse any religion whatsoever, it is clearly talking about the earth in regards to the Bible and in this chapter only. I'm not affiliated with any religion, and I disagree with the globe earth theory that they support, although they haven't always supported the globe theory. It was when the church started losing followers to the religion of scientism that the churches started claiming some of the same claims. They shouldn't have. Truth fears no investigation and shouldn't fear competition. This shows the head of churches never believed the Bible was the word of God to begin with, otherwise they wouldn't be changing its meaning. I don't know if it's the word of God or not but it's a flat earth book regardless of what my opinions are.

The globe model hasn't been around as long as we claim. A woman who is 102 years old said in an interview that when she was a kid, they were taught that the earth was flat in school but they changed it. But she still always thought it was flat. It was in schools in the 1920s. The globe claim goes back a lot further but didn't receive the push it has until then, as the elite takes control of more and more of our education system and science industry and changes it. There have been a few old people that have talked about this.

As far as a Creator goes, there are too many 'coincidences' in reality, when it comes to Earth and everything that's involved with it, showing that it's clearly by design. Reality shows that we live in a finely, logically designed timepiece. When I was an atheist, I ignored these things, but not anymore. Not at all.

"We speak of the "system" of the planets, and not of their "government": but in considering a store, for instance, and its management, we see that the words are interchangeable." Charles Fort

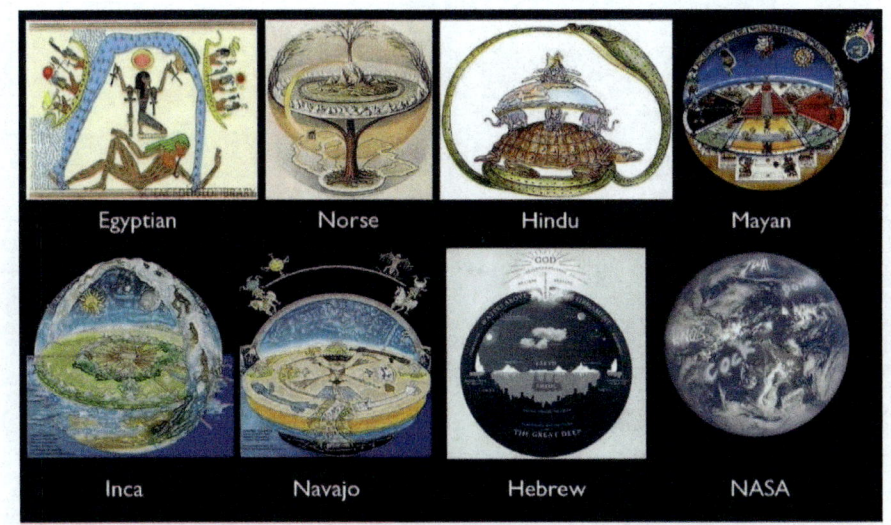

Claims

Some of the flat earthers say "the bible is one of the proofs of flat earth", whereas the bible is a flat earth book, it does not prove the earth is flat. The objective reality and true independently verifiable science supports a motionless level plane.

Water, horizon line that remains at eye level, long distance photography, greenhouse effect and star trails proves flat earth.

I will be using the King James Version for this chapter, seeing as that's the most popular version. Some people say the bible preaches globe earth. I disagree and we will be looking at some of the reasons why I disagree in this chapter.

The Zetetic Method

One of the two scriptures that they think support this, talks about God setting about the circle of the earth, but they seem to ignore the second part of the same scripture. Let's have a look at it shall we.

) Isaiah 40:20 "It is he that sitteth upon the circle of the earth, and the inhabitants thereof are as grasshoppers; that stretcheth out the heavens as a curtain, and spreadeth them out as a tent to dwell in:"

KING JAMES VERSION BIBLE

Isaiah 40:22
It is he that sitteth upon the CIRCLE of the earth, and the inhabitants thereof are as grasshopper; that strectcheth out the heavens as a curtain, and spreadeth them out as a TENT to dwell in:

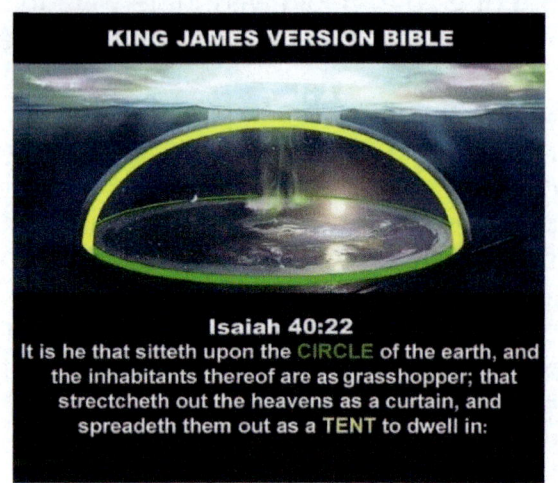

Now how does anybody get a spinning wobbling flying ball hurtling through the vacuum of endless space out of that? What scripture can you provide that supports that mind controlling propaganda? Let's look at it closer.

A circle is (Google)noun
• 1.a round plane figure whose boundary (the circumference) consists of points equidistant from a fixed point (the center). "draw a circle with a compass"

A sphere is (Google) noun1. a round solid figure, or its surface, with every point on its surface equidistant from its center.

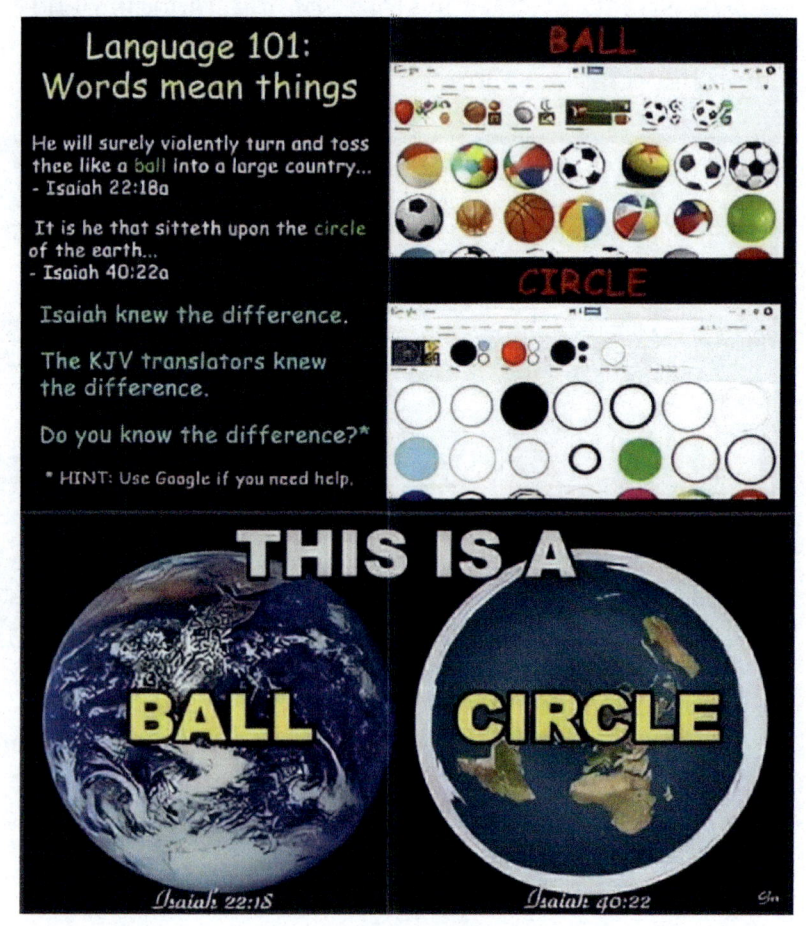

Circles are always flat-if you research The Elements of Design that is taught in all art colleges. Spheres are classified under "Forms" after "Shapes".

A circle and sphere/ball are two different things. One is three dimensional, the other is two. If we agree that a cylinder is not a circle, then we must agree that a ball is not a circle as well. The face of the cylinder is a circle. The circle of the cylinder is a flat circular face just like the circle of the earth.

Language 101: Words mean things

He will surely violently turn and toss thee like a ball into a large country...
- Isaiah 22:18a

It is he that sitteth upon the circle of the earth...
- Isaiah 40:22a

Isaiah knew the difference.

The KJV translators knew the difference.

Do you know the difference?*

* HINT: Use Google if you need help.

BALL

CIRCLE

THIS IS A BALL — Isaiah 22:18

CIRCLE — Isaiah 40:22

357

) Isaiah 22:18 "He will surely violently turn and toss thee like a ball into a large country: there shall thou die, and there the chariots of thy glory shall be the shame of thy lord's house."

Imagine, if you will, a teammate saying "hey pass me the circle." A plate can be a circle. No one confuses a ball for a circle, so why confuse a circle for a ball? Also notice the scripture says "the circle OF the earth." Think on that wording, OF. God is not sitting on a spinning ball. This scripture is a weak argument.

The other scripture they use is in Job 7, it says "He stretcheth out the north over the empty place, and hangeth the earth upon nothing."

But the Bible has already said the earth is stretched out on a foundation and made immovable. A house hangs upon nothing, it sets on a foundation. To hang means to suspend from above, but in Psalm 75:3 it mentions pillars, and countless other scriptures it mentions a foundation; therefore no need to hang upon anything.

) 1 Samuel 2:8: "For The Pillars of the Earth are the Lord's, and He has set the world upon them."
) Psalm 75:3 "The earth and all the inhabitants thereof are dissolved: I bear up the pillars of it. Selah."

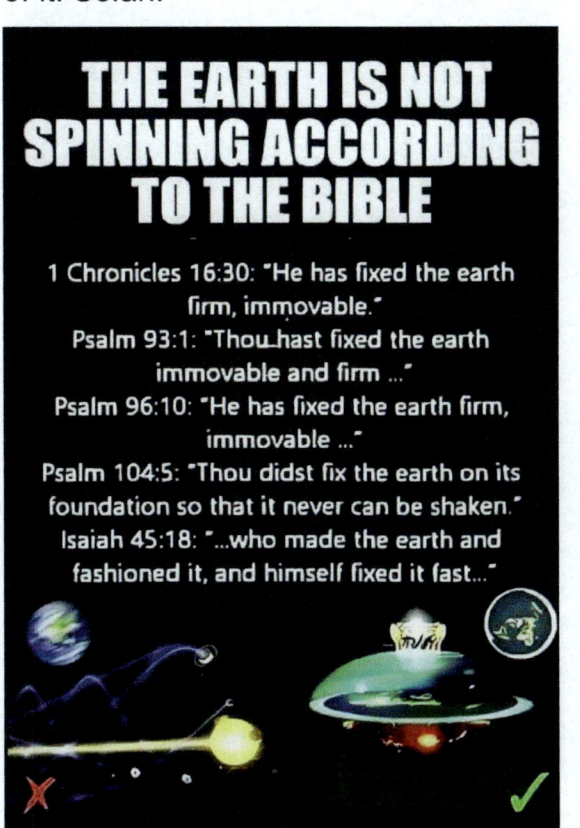

THE EARTH IS NOT SPINNING ACCORDING TO THE BIBLE

1 Chronicles 16:30: "He has fixed the earth firm, immovable."
Psalm 93:1: "Thou hast fixed the earth immovable and firm ..."
Psalm 96:10: "He has fixed the earth firm, immovable ..."
Psalm 104:5: "Thou didst fix the earth on its foundation so that it never can be shaken."
Isaiah 45:18: "...who made the earth and fashioned it, and himself fixed it fast..."

And what's this North bid? North star perhaps. After all, it is the only star that does not move. It is the center of it all. The only magnetic pole, all celestial lights revolve around it. Could it be God's throne of emerald? Who knows.

The Earth hangs upon nothing because it sets upon a foundation. We should use our senses when listening to "Scientists" and also when reading the bible.

It clearly states in the bible, that there is a difference between celestial bodies and terrestrial ones. We know that the Earth is a terrestrial one, not a celestial one as astronomers would have you believe. You can't prove we're a celestial ball whirling through space because we're not. Not because the bible says so, but because all evidence points against it. But here's the scripture all the same:

) 1 Corinthians 15 "40 There are also celestial bodies, and bodies terrestrial: but the glory of the celestial is one, and the glory of the terrestrial is another.

41 There is one glory of the sun, and another glory of the moon, and another glory of the stars: for one-star differeth from another star in glory."

Terrestrial bodies are land. The bible says in Genesis that land is called earth and the waters are called seas. Then you have the heavens, the two lights and the celestial bodies.

Who knows if there's more Earths "OUT THERE", I won't pretend to know, I'm just going off what we can see for ourselves.

) Job 11 "9 The measure thereof is longer than the earth, and broader than the sea."

How can it be longer than a ball? Either way the bible does not preach anything about the globe model. Try again.

SUN, THE GREATER LIGHT

If the earth was created on the first day, Genesis 1:1, and the sun on the fourth day, Genesis 1:14-19, then how could the earth be rotating around the sun? And the Bible never mentions anything about the earth spinning and wobbling on any axis.

The sun is said to be moving, not Earth. Where in the bible, does it say it's moving?

) Ecclesiastes 1:5 "5 The sun also ariseth, and the sun goeth down, and hasteth to his place where he arose."

has·ten
• be quick to do something.
"he hastened to refute the assertion"
• move or travel hurriedly.
"we hastened back to Paris"

) Psalm 19 "4 Their line is gone out through all the earth, and their words to the end of the world. In them hath he set a tabernacle for the sun,
5 Which is as a bridegroom coming out of his chamber, and rejoiceth as a strong man to run a race.
6 His going forth is from the end of heaven, and his circuit unto the ends of it: and there is nothing hidden from the heat thereof."

It also mentions the sun being the greater light for the day, but nothing about this gigantic earth, with all its water and stock spinning, wobbling and flying around this said light. The bible also clearly states that each "celestial orb", if you will, has its own light. Let's look at these scriptures.
A real picture of the sun.

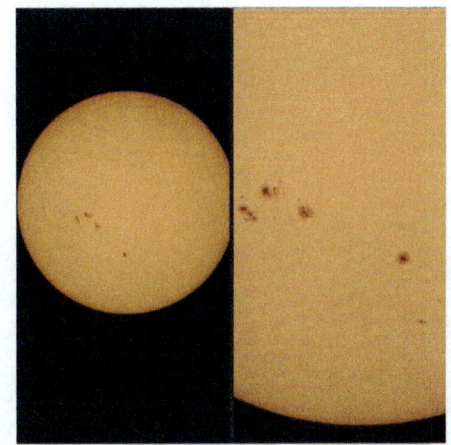

"God created the sun to light the world. Whoever heard of a light being made bigger than the place to be lighted? We never carry a room round the candle, but always the candle round the room."
- Ebenezer Breach

TRUTHER.ORG

) Matthew 24:29 "Immediately after the tribulation of those days shall the Sun be darkened, and the moon shall not give her light, and the stars shall fall from heaven, and the powers of the heavens shall be shaken."
) Psalms 136 "6 To him that stretched out the earth above the waters: for his mercy endureth for ever. 7 To him that made great lights: for his mercy endureth for ever: 8 The sun to rule by day: for his mercy endureth for ever: 9 The moon and stars to rule by night: for his mercy endureth for ever."

) Genesis 1:14-19 "14 And God said, Let there be lights IN the firmament of the heaven to divide the day from the night; and let them be for signs, and for seasons, and for days, and years:
15 And let them be for LIGHTS in the firmament of heaven to give light upon the earth: and it was so.
16 And God made two great lights; the greater light to rule the day, and the lesser light to rule the night: he made the stars also.
17 And God set them in the firmament of the heaven to give light upon the earth,
18 And to rule over the day and over the night, and to divide the light from the darkness: and God saw that it was good.
19 And the evening and the morning were the fourth day."
) Jeremiah 31 "35 Thus saith the Lord, which giveth the sun for a light by day, and the ordinances of the moon and of the stars for a light by night, which divideth the sea when the waves thereof roar; The Lord of hosts is his name:"

It's quite obvious the sun and moon are not what we're told according to the Bible. They have their own light properties and jobs, one is not the reflection of the other.

"No where in the Bible does God speak of a Globe that is whirling and turning with it's terrible load. But he did set the sun whirling in it's journey to run, to make to return to whence it had come.

If all christians we're anxious the truth to obtain, and would search in sincerity twould not be in vain, for the deeper they search it is sure and plain, they have to believe earth a straight level plane." - CHARLES MORSE

) Deuteronomy 33:14 "And precious fruits brought forth by the sun, and for the precious things put forth by the moon.
) Isaiah 60:19,20 "19 The sun shall be no more thy light by day; neither for brightness shall the moon give light unto thee: but the Lord shall be unto thee an everlasting light, and thy God thy glory. 20 Thy sun shall no more go down; neither shall thy moon withdraw itself: for the Lord shall be thine everlasting light, and the days of thy mourning shall be ended."

Also according to the bible, and observation, the stars are not massive balls of gas light years away. And how could they fall upon Earth? Is Revelation 6 the "shooting stars" we see?

) Revelation 6:12-14 "12 And I beheld when he had opened the sixth seal, and, lo, there was a great earthquake; and the sun became black as sackcloth of hair, and the moon became as blood; 13 And the stars of heaven fell unto the earth, even as a fig tree casteth her untimely figs, when she is shaken of a mighty wind. 14 And the heaven departed as a scroll when it was rolled together; and every mountain and island were moved out of their places." (Firmament anyone?)

) Revelation 8 "12 And the fourth angel sounded, and the third part of the sun was smitten, and the third part of the moon, and the third part of the stars; so as the third part of them was darkened, and the day shone not for a third part of it, and the night likewise.

GOD'S FLYING FOOTSTOOL?

Sense the bible mentions that He stretched out the earth and put on a foundation, before He made the sun, and then on the fourth day, made the sun, why doesn't it mention the earth warping into a ball and spinning on its alleged axis and started flying around the greater light that was made for the day? Why would He even need to do such a thing? Why has the bible not mentioned this transformation and motions?

More on the stars a little later though. It does mention 'stretched out' a few times though. Clearly the biblical earth is stationary with a structure that can be opened.

) Genesis 1:2 "God moved upon the face of the waters."
) Amos 9:6 "6 It is he that buildeth his stories in the heaven, and hath founded his troop in the earth; he that calleth for the waters of the sea, and poureth them out upon the face of the earth: The Lord is his name.

Water is proven flat, as the face of a clock is flat. Speaking of clock face:
Psalm 104:30 "Thou sendest forth thy spirit, they are created: and thou renewest the face of the earth."

You do not spread out a ball, you spread out something flat.
) Psalm 136:6 "To him that stretched out the earth above the waters: for his mercy endureth for ever."
) Isaiah 44 "24 Thus saith the LORD, thy redeemer, and he that formed thee from the womb, I am the LORD that maketh all things; that stretcheth forth the heavens alone; that spreadeth abroad the earth by myself. 25 That frustrateth the tokens of the liars, and maketh diviners mad; that turneth wise men backward, and maketh their knowledge foolish;"

Scientism claims the earth is spinning faster than the speed of sound as it orbits the sun 80 times faster than a bullet; all while the sun is hurtling through around the Milky Way more than 500 times faster than a bullet. And the Milky Way is not being lazy by any means either. Scientism has claimed it is racing through space at around 1000 times faster than the slow poke bullet.

The bible, however, paints a different picture, doesn't it?

) Chronicles 16:30 "Fear before him, all the earth: the world also shall be stable, that it be not moved."
) Psalm 104:5 "Who laid the foundations of the earth, that it should not be removed forever.
6 Thou coveredst it with the deep as with a garment: the waters stood above the mountains."
) Samuel 2:8: "For The Pillars of the Earth are the Lord's, and He has set the world upon them."
) Job 26. "10 He hath compassed
the waters with bounds, until the day and night come to an end. 11 The pillars of heaven tremble and are astonished at his reproof."
) Isaiah 44:24 Thus says the Lord, your Redeemer, who formed you from the womb: "I am the Lord, who made all things, who alone stretched out the heavens, who spread out the earth by myself,
) Psalm 93:1 "The LORD reigneth, he is clothed with majesty; the LORD is clothed with strength, wherewith he hath girded himself: the world also is stablished, that it cannot be moved."
) Isaiah 40: 21,22 "21 Have ye not known? have ye not heard? hath it not been told to you from the beginning? have ye not understood from the foundations of the earth?
22 It is he that sitteth upon the circle of the earth, and the inhabitants thereof are as grasshoppers; that stretcheth out the heavens as a curtain, and spreadeth them out as a tent to
dwell in"

How can God stretch out a ball? A curtain around a ball sounds like a comical mess. And further on the bible speaks of a line being stretched, but nothing of it being stretched around a whirling ball. That'd be a fun thing to try huh?

) Job 38 "4 Where wast thou when I laid the foundations of the earth? declare, if thou hast understanding.
5 Who hath laid the measures thereof, if thou knowest? or who hath stretched the line upon it?
6 Whereupon are the foundations thereof fastened? or who laid the
cornerstone thereof;
7 When the morning stars sang together, and all the sons of God shouted for joy?
8 Or who shut up the sea with doors, when it broke forth, as if it had issued out of the womb?"

God Stretched the Heavens

17 times the Bible declares that God stretched the heavens

2 Sam 22:10	Job 37:18	Isaiah 51:13
Psalm 18:9	Isaiah 40:22	Jeremiah 10:12
Psalm 104:2	Isaiah 42:5	Jeremiah 51:15
Psalm 144:5	Isaiah 44:24	Ezekiel 1:22
Job 9:8	Isaiah 45:12	Zechariah 12:1
Job 26:7	Isaiah 48:13	

- Isaiah 44:24 "This is what the LORD says— your Redeemer, who formed you in the womb: I am the LORD, who has made all things, who alone **stretched out the heavens**, who spread out the earth by myself,
- Isaiah 45:12 It is I who made the earth and created mankind upon it. My own hands **stretched out the heavens**; I marshaled their starry hosts.

) Job 38:18 "Hast thou perceive the breadth of the earth? declare if thou knowest it all."

) Psalm 104: 1-5 "Bless the LORD, O my soul. O LORD my God, thou art very great; thou art clothed with honour and majesty. Who coverest thyself with light as with a garment: who stretchest out the heavens like a curtain: Who layeth the beams of his chambers in the waters: who maketh the clouds his chariot: who walketh upon the wings of the wind: Who maketh his angels spirits; his ministers a flaming fire: Who laid the foundations of the earth, that it should not be removed for ever."

How many times must the bible say He laid down foundations, not twirled a ball? Huh? How many?

) Jeremiah 31:37 "Thus saith the LORD; If heaven above can be measured, and the foundations of the earth searched out beneath, I will also cast off all the seed of Israel for all that they have done, saith the LORD."
) Psalm 102:25 "Of old hast thou laid the foundation of the earth: and the heavens are the work of thy hands."
) Isaiah 48:13 "Mine hand also hath laid the foundation of the earth, and my right hand hath spanned the heavens: when I call unto them, they stand up together."

None of these speaks of a globular earth. None whatsoever. Here God claims to see the world's inhabitants and the heavens are above. What is above on a ball is underneath to someone else on a ball and yet sideways to someone else. How could He possibly do so on a ball when the inhabitants 'underneath' is out of view and upside down from His view? Do Australians get the blind side or is it the northern folks? :(

) Psalm 33:14 "From the place of his habitation he looketh upon all the inhabitants of the earth."

THE FIRMAMENT

) Ezekiel 1:22 "The likeness of the firmament above the heads of the living creatures was like the color of an awesome crystal, stretched out over their heads."

The bible also talks of a firmament and a sky of molten looking glass. This makes perfect sense seeing as how we're living in a perfect greenhouse. It never mentions the vacuum of space, which would not work with a greenhouse at all. It would be a piss poor design, would it not? There is space between earth and the molten looking glass but that doesn't change the ladder does it.

) Job 37:18 "Hast thou with him spread out the sky, which is strong, and as a molten looking glass?"
) Revelation 4:6 "And before the throne there was a sea of glass like unto crystal: and in the midst of the throne, and round about the throne, were four beasts full of eyes before and behind."
) Genesis 1:6 we read that "God said, Let there be a firmament in the midst of the waters, and let it divide the waters from the waters."
) Genesis 1 "20 And God said, Let the waters bring forth abundantly the moving creature that hath life, and fowl that may fly above the earth in the open firmament of heaven

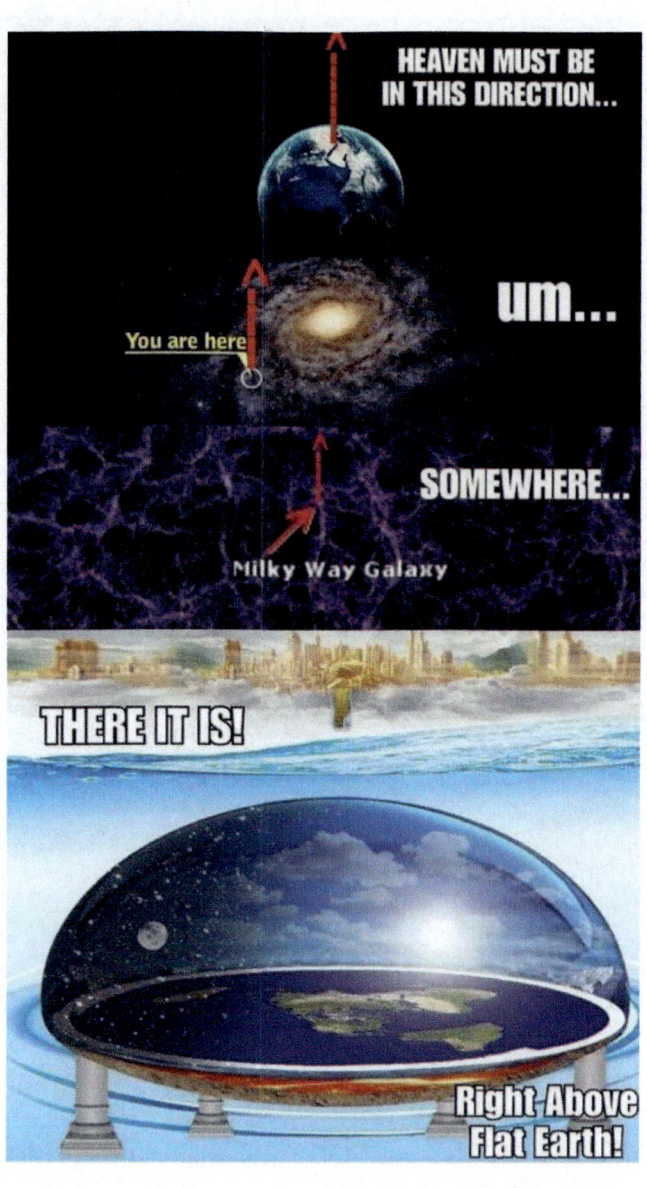

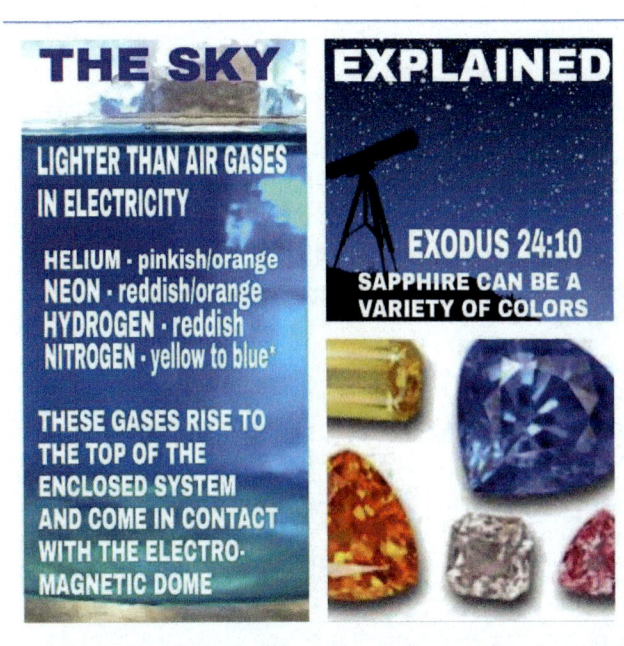

) Isaiah 34:4 "The host of heaven shall be dissolved, and the heavens shall be rolled together as a scroll, and all their host shall fall away as the leaf falleth from off the vine, and as a fading leaf of the fig-tree"
) Ezekiel 1:26 "And above the firmament that was over their heads was the likeness of a throne, as the appearance of a sapphire stone: and upon the likeness of the throne was the likeness as the appearance of a man above upon it."

The firmament canopy divides the waters, which means that there is water above the firmament in heaven.
) Psalms 148:4 "Praise him, ye heavens of heavens, and ye waters that are above the heavens."

How can heaven and Earth stand together if Earth is a whirling ball and heaven is nothing but space?
) Isaiah 48 "13 Mine hand also hath laid the foundation of the earth, and my right hand hath spanned the heavens: when I call unto them, they stand up together."

I was talking about the biblical "end times" with someone who was defending the 'globe bible' and they said to me "God will open up the heavens to allow space travel to other planets so the world won't be over populated when the new world paradise comes." The bible, however, says no such thing about planets or over population therefore the claim cannot be backed by scripture. The Bible does mention the heavens opening up however, but how can you open up nothing but empty space? I can't open up my yard but I can open up my house because it has a barrier. Sense the bible mentions the sky is that of a molten looking glass, that's a barrier indeed. Could the Milky Way be the opening perhaps? The ancient people thought so. Called it "The Great Rift."

The Bible does not mention anything about overpopulation but does mention no marriage, which might mean no reproduction, or are we to reproduce without marriage at that time? What's the sense in this? Is it the men that get this free ride? LOL! The bible says sex is for marriage and procreation. The bible does state the angels do not marry and we will be like the angel in this manner. Angels do not reproduce; they are not created the same way as us. And it does have it where you CAN leave Earth, just as you can now. Here, let me back up what I say, unlike some, with actual scripture.

Paradise scriptures:

) 2 Peter 3:13 "13 Nevertheless we, according to his promise, look for new heavens and a new earth, wherein dwelleth righteousness."

) Luke 23:43 "43 And Jesus said unto him, Verily I say unto thee, Today shalt thou be with me in paradise."

) Isaiah 65:17 "17 For, behold, I create new heavens and a new earth: and the former shall not be remembered, nor come into mind."

) Matthew 5:5 "5 Blessed are the meek: for they shall inherit the earth."

) Psalm 37:29 "29 The righteous shall inherit the land, and dwell therein for ever."

Heaven opens up--Genesis 7:11 "In the six hundredth year of Noah's life, in the second month, the seventeenth day of the month, the same day were all the fountains of the great deep broken up, and the windows of heaven were opened."

) Genesis 8:2,3 "The fountains also of the deep and the windows of heaven were stopped, and the rain from heaven was restrained"

Windows to what, open space or the enclosure to this greenhouse we obviously live in?

No marriage--Matthew 22:30 "30 For in the resurrection they neither marry, nor are given in marriage, but are as the angels of God in heaven."

) Luke 20:34-36 "34 And Jesus answering said unto them, The children of this world marry, and are given in marriage 35 But they which shall be accounted worthy to obtain that world, and the resurrection from the dead, neither marry, nor are given in marriage 36 Neither can they die any more: for they are equal unto the angels; and are the children of God, being the children of the resurrection."

Angels are all unique individual creations that were created but not by birth. Angels are not replicated or reproduced, they are formed individually. Humans rely on marriage and procreation in this world, but in the "New Earth", as the bible calls it, the meek inherit the Earth and we (Listen to me say "we", as if I'm meek. Lol!) are like angels. It says nothing about replenishing the Earth. And why would it, the wheat has already been harvested. (Mathew 23)

Leaving Earth-- Genesis 1:9,10 "9 And God said, Let the waters under the heaven be gathered together unto one place, and let the dry land appear: and it was so. 10 And God called the dry land Earth; and the gathering together of the waters called he Seas: and God saw that it was good."

Did you catch that? See, you CAN leave Earth. Hehe! The terrestrial bodies are the land masses.

The Zetetic Method

Where does it say we move to other planets? Where? Show me the scripture. People say these things but they never quote a scripture, because it doesn't exist. Prove me wrong.

Like the government puppet scientists, who claim the Earth is a whirling ball without any physical evidence to support such a claim, neither does any religion, who makes such a ridiculous claim, have any scriptures to back them up. So why bother claiming it? Doesn't evidence mean anything to anybody anymore?

The bible states that when God flooded the earth he opened the windows of heaven to let out some of the water that was above the firmament. How could this be with nothing but 'empty space' above? Where would all that water come from and then where would it all go afterwards? Could it be that the waters above the firmament were used as a reset? You can recreate this, flooding a container and then drain it. The flood happening on a whirling ball, in 'empty' space, is simply illogical. A sealed container however, with water above it, is completely logical and can be recreated.

Sense water is proven time and time again to be flat, this scripture makes a lot more sense. Job 11:9 "The measure thereof is longer than the earth, and broader than the sea."

Research Mudfloods, so much evidence of a great flood. Ancient buildings buried in mud. Windows and doors leading outside that's below ground level. Fossil buried with vegetation still in its mouth. Animals buried in groups, etc., etc.

Then when the flooding was over, He closed the windows of heaven and drained the waters of the deep. Where else would the water go?

) Genesis 8:2,3 "The fountains also of the deep and the windows of heaven were stopped, and the rain from heaven was restrained;

3 And the waters returned from off the earth continually: and after the end of the hundred and fifty days the waters were abated."

HEAVENS DOORS

Many claim the bible is full of myths, maybe, but all myths are based on some facts. Why repeat such things if people will think you're insane? People all over the world are telling the same stories without a news media to spread them. Here's one such "myth" here:

In the bible they tried to build the Tower of Babel to reach the heavens. It seems obvious that they did not think the Earth was an open flying ball in space. Quite a few times the bible mentions heaven having openings and being opened. Nothing about the vacuum of ending hostile space. Were they trying to reach an opening?

) Ezekiel 1:1 "Now it came about in the thirtieth year, on the fifth day of the fourth month, while I was by the river Chebar among the exiles, the heavens were opened and I saw visions of God."

) Revelations 4:1 "After these things I looked, and behold, a door standing open in heaven, and the first voice which I had heard, like the sound of a trumpet speaking with me, said, "Come up here, and I will show you what must take place after these things.""

) Revelation 19:11 "And I saw heaven opened, and behold, a white horse, and He who sat on it is called Faithful and True, and in righteousness He judges and wages war." This scripture is engraved on the tombstone of one of NASA'S founders Werhner Von Braun.

) Psalm 19:1 "The heavens declare the glory of God; and the firmament sheweth his handywork."

So, what of the ice wall that is proven to be there?
) Job 26:10 "He hath compassed the waters with bounds, until the day and night come to an end."
) Proverbs 8:29 29 When He assigned to the sea its limit, so that the waters would not transgress His command, When He marked out the foundations of the earth

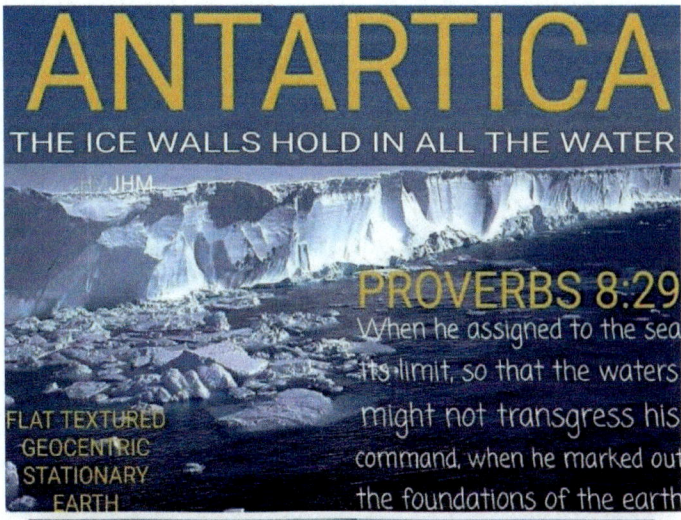

) Job 38:8 "8 Or who shut up the sea with doors, when it broke forth, as if it had issued out of the womb?
) Job 38:11 "11 Hitherto shalt thou come, but no further: and here shall thy proud waves be stayed?"

Ernest Shackleton, who "discovered" something in Antarctica that got it shut down and an unbroken 53 country treaty going, ship was named Nimrod. Nimrod was the man under whose rule the construction of the Tower of Babel was attempted. Coincidence or Freemason wording with truth in plain sight ritual being kept?

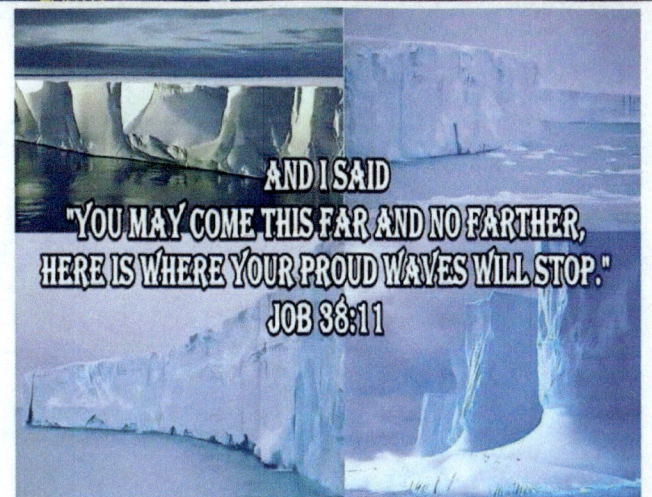

STARS

The bible states that in the end times the stars will fall to earth like figs from a tree. Now, going by the globular model, this would be impossible, with most of the stars being suns and enormous and millions of light years away. How can the stars fall from heaven when most are said to dwarf the sun? One star could engulf the earth, after it made its way from light years away, that is. How would they "FALL" to earth? Lucky, the priests of Scientism are lying about our reality and the bible.

) Revelation 6:13 "And the stars of heaven fell unto the earth, even as a fig tree casteth her untimely figs, when she is shaken by a mighty wind."

) Revelation 8:10 "And the third angel sounded, and there fell a great star from heaven, burning as a lamp, and it fell upon the third part of the rivers, and upon the fountains of waters,"
And the star is called wormwood: and the third part of the waters became wormwood; and many men died of the waters, because they were made bitter.

) Revelation 8:12 "And a fourth angel sounded, and the third part of the sun smitten, and the third part of the moon, and the third part of the stars; so as the third part of them darkened, and the dat shone not for a third part of it, and the night likewise."

) Isaiah 13:10 "For the stars of heaven and the constellations thereof shall not give their light: the sun shall be darkened in his going forth, and the moon shall not cause her light to shine."

How can anyone honestly believe that the stars forming constellations are by accident or big burning balls of gas that happen to be in that position? How would this work if stars were millions of miles or light years or whatever unprovable distance from each other?
In Matthew 24:29 Jesus said that the stars shall fall from heaven.
God took five times as long to make the earth as He did the heavenly bodies. Do these next scriptures sound like they're meaningless balls of gas light years away?
) Psalm 147:4 "He telleth the number of the stars; he calleth them all by their names."
) Job 38:31 "Canst thou bind the sweet influences of Pleiades?"
) Isaiah 13 "For the Stars of heaven and the constellations thereof will not give their light; the Sun shall he darkened in his going forth, and the Moon shall not cause her light to shine"

So what exactly is falling? Are these the shooting stars you see? Because we don't know doesn't turn this observably flat plane into a whirling ball. These balls have been reported falling since the 1800s. I've read science books written in that time era that talks about them, some with writing on them. Fascinating!
Again, how can random chaos create predictable order?

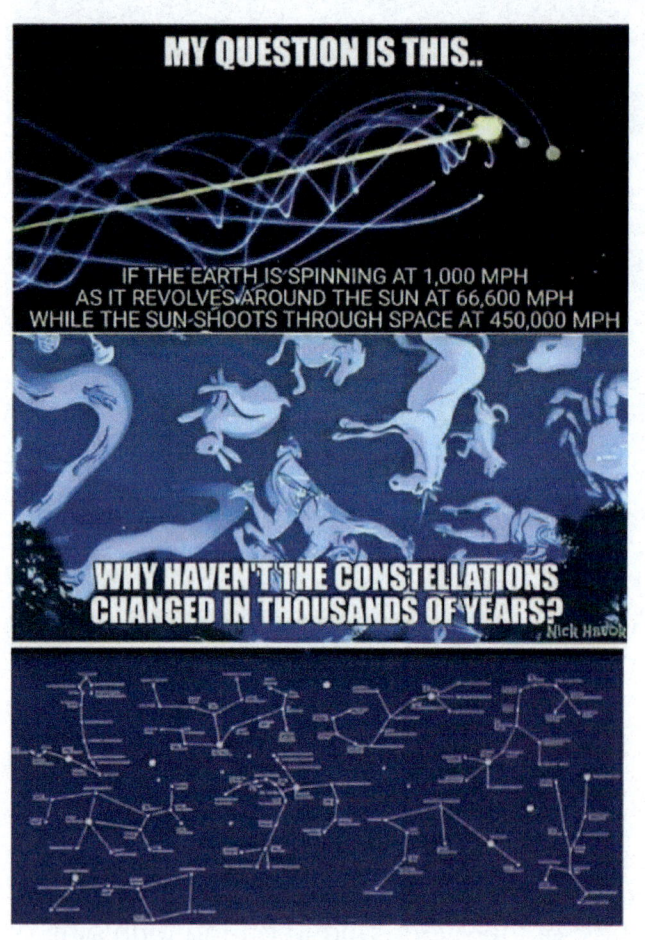

The bible says God has numbered and named the stars, but according to the globe model, 275 million stars per day are dying and that number is pretty much met by stars being born daily. Wow that's quite a number there. Should I even bother to ask for a receipt?

All these claims are unproven of course and I take none of it seriously. Extraordinary claims require extraordinary evidence. That goes for science and religion and the bible.

Modern astrophysics contradicts the Bible. The bible states God has finished his work of creation and rest on the seventh day, as reported in Genesis 2:1-2, but how is this possible if stars are still popping up in crazy numbers?

) Genesis 2:1-2 "Thus the heavens and the earth were finished, and all the host of them. And on the seventh day God ended his work which he had made; and he rested on the seventh day from all his work which he had made."

) Job 9:9 "9 Which maketh Arcturus, Orion, and Pleiades, and the chambers of the south."

) Job 38:31-33 "31 Canst thou bind the sweet influences of Pleiades, or lose the bands of Orion? 32 Canst thou bring forth Mazzaroth in his season? or canst thou guide Arcturus with his sons 33 Knowest thou the ordinances of heaven? canst thou set the dominion thereof in the earth?

"They are splendid lamps, placed in the canopy of the sky, to give light, instruction, and blessing to this world of ours, and we may be positively certain that, like the lamps of a city, they are very much smaller than the place they were made to illuminate." Author David Wardlaw Scott

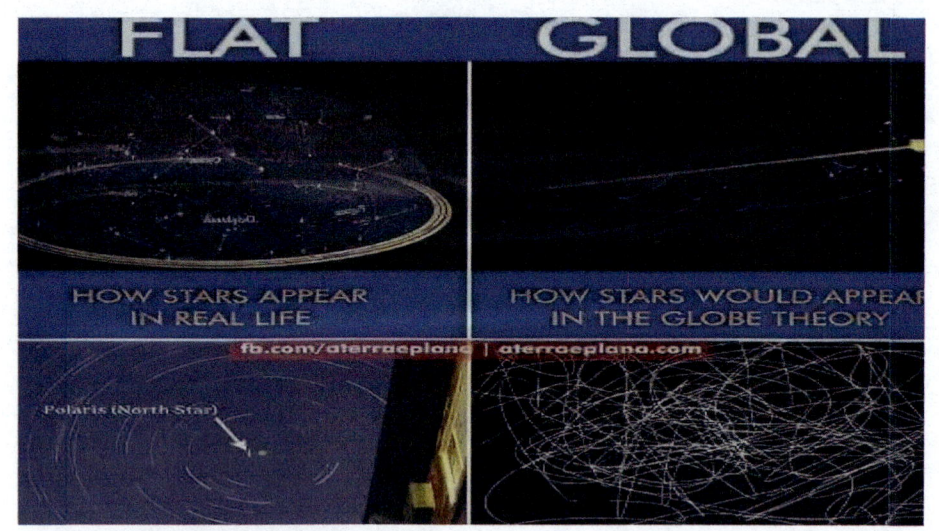

WHERE'S THE UP AND DOWN

In the ball earth model there is no TRUE up or down, only perception of where you are on the ball, but in reality, not only is there a up and a down but there's no curvature for any ball. Up is not a location 'above your head. If you're hanging "upside down," UP will still be located where it was before, only your head is changing. Hanging "upside down" does not make UP towards the ground.

We are taught just the opposite of what truly is. The bible has its ups and downs as well. How can heaven be above or Sheol beneath? Is the Earth engulfed in heaven so you can go up no matter where on the ball you are and still hit heaven? Hmmm

) Numbers 26:33 "So they, and all that pertained to them went down alive into Sheol"
) 2 Kings 2:11 "Elijah went up by a whirlwind into heaven"
) Psalm 139:8 "If I ascend up to heaven Thou art there; if I make my bed in Sheol, behold, Thou art there"
) Revelation 11:12 "And they heard a loud voice out of heaven saying—Come up hither; and they went up to heaven in the cloud, and their enemies beheld them"

In the book of Ecclesiastes Solomon uses the expression "under the Sun" no less than twenty-five times, bearing reference to the Earth. The bible mentions nothing of earth being a ball, whirling round the sun. On the globe model nothing is under the sun.

) Ecclesiastes 1:9 "The thing that hath been, it is that which shall be; and that which is done is that which shall be done: and there is no new thing under the sun."

There are many more that mention things happening under the sun, but you get the jest of what I'm saying.

) Job 22:14 "Thick clouds are a covering to him, that he seeth not; and he walketh in the circuit of heaven."
Google: Circuit— noun
a roughly circular line, route, or movement that starts and finishes at the same place. "I ran a circuit of the village"

Once again, on a ball, who's getting the blind eye here, Australia or Canada?

THE DAY THE SUN STOOD STILL
The bible believers, who also believe in the heliocentric globe theory, please explain why God commanded the sun to stand still, instead of the earth to stop spinning. If the sun did so, it would create chaos in the solar system of the very theory you believe.

Egypt — 1440 B.C
America — 2018 A.D
Ecclesiastes 1:9
What has been will be again, what has been done will be done again; there is nothing new under the sun.

If the earth suddenly stopped its wobbling spinning and flying there would be chaos for everyone on-board, as well. The oceans would cover hundreds of miles of dry land. However if the earth is indeed flat, and real evidence shows that it is so, then the sun is smaller, local and rotating above the earth, and stopping it wouldn't cause nearly as much chaos.

In the globe model, the sun and all that orbits around it, are rotating around the, ridiculously unproven black hole, of the Milky Way; which itself is sailing through an endless universe by way of being shot out by the Big Bang. There's no scientific proof of any such happenings nor any Bible scripture that says such a thing. God stopped the moon and the sun in its usual circuit over a stationary, flat earth.

) Joshua 10:12-14: "Then spake Joshua to the Lord in the day when the Lord delivered up the Amorites before the children of Israel; and he said in the sight of all Israel, 'Sun, stand thou still upon Gibeon; and thou, Moon, in the Valley of Ajalon,' AND THE SUN STOOD STILL, AND THE MOON STAYED, until the people had avenged themselves upon their enemies......So the sun stood still in the midst of heaven, and hasted not to go down about a whole day."

Physical reality has shown that the sun, moon and stars are inferior to the world we live on, and moves above earth, which remains at rest. The sun indeed is the greater light for the day and the moon indeed is the lesser light for the night. And have not the stars shown to be for signs and directions?

Reality has shown that the Scientism religion has not provided one physical proven fact, in astronomy, that has any solid foundation against the biblical earth. Instead they have proven themselves to be untrustworthy and thus have no merits. Even bible believers, in any religion, have been hoodwinked and misled by modern hypothetical 'science.'

Why did scientists name the planets after mythology Gods? How is that scientific? For what purpose? Why is science bringing religion into it if it's trying to debunk religion?

Why did the Pope, a man claiming to be a man of God, name his telescope L.U.C.I.F.E.R. (Large Binocular Telescope Near-infrared Utility with Camera and Integral Field Unit for Extragalactic Research) and later talks about aliens?

Pope Paul VI declared "The smoke of Satan has entered the sanctuary," then died a little later. That year, 1978, they had three different popes. Something is going on with them. After the Romans pillaged and burned the Great Libraries of Alexandria around 48 B.C., they have controlled most of our modern history.

What is this picture about? Uncover that thing and let everyone see!

The Pope is supposed to be about the Bible yet disregards it constantly. Here's one example of his sun worship. In Deuteronomy 5 "8 Thou shalt not make thee any graven image, or any likeness of any thing that is in heaven above, or that is in the earth beneath, or that is in the waters beneath the earth" Yet here we have sun worship. And what's that second picture all about? Hmmm

I'm not religious but what exactly is going on? Why are they obsessed with the serpent exactly? I don't believe in the devil but at the same time......

It's just a reptilian 'all seeing eye' .. nothing to make a fuss about 🙄

Not all religious people have been dumbed down though. There are flat earth preachers popping up everywhere. They're making videos and putting them online trying to wake people up. Recently one preacher woke up to flat earth and was kicked out of his church for showing it to his congregation from the bible and the real provable science to back it up; fortunately, there was a church of flat earthers who had gotten rid of there sleeping pastor, and both problems solved each others. Ahhh life has a way doesn't it?

Another preacher, Rev. John Wesley did not believe in the teachings of Scientism of astronomical school, though his followers did.: "The more I consider them, the more I doubt all systems of astronomy .... Even with regard to the distance of the sun from the earth, some affirm it to be only three, and others ninety million of miles."

I found this next statement by the Bishop of Peterborough to be very true in recent years. He says: "I have no fear whatsoever, that the Bible will be found, in the long run, to contain more science than all the theories of philosophers put together."

So unless you can show me in the bible where it says that the earth is a spinning wobbling flying ball hurtling through space, while orbiting the light that God made for the days, and the sun and stars are going to dwarf and kill us all, if the big black hole don't kill us first; unless you can show me these things in the bible then please stop saying the bible supports the globe model. Because it DOES NOT. If you think it does then show me the evidence that it does.

Someone said to me "when the Bible says that the earth is 'immovable,' it means it doesn't leave orbit."
The Bible actually mentions something about this big no no when it comes to ad-libbing the bible.
) Revelation 22:18-19 "For I testify unto every man that heareth the words of the prophecy of this book, If any man shall add unto these things, God shall add unto him the plagues that are written in this book:
19 And if any man shall take away from the words of the book of this prophecy, God shall take away his part out of the book of life, and out of the holy city, and from the things which are written in this book."

The Devil in the detail...

) 2 Timothy 4 "3 For the time will come when they will not endure sound doctrine; but after their own lusts shall they heap to themselves teachers, having itching ears; 4 And they shall turn away their ears from the truth, and shall be turned unto fables.

) Romans 1:22 "Professing themselves to be wise, they became fools."

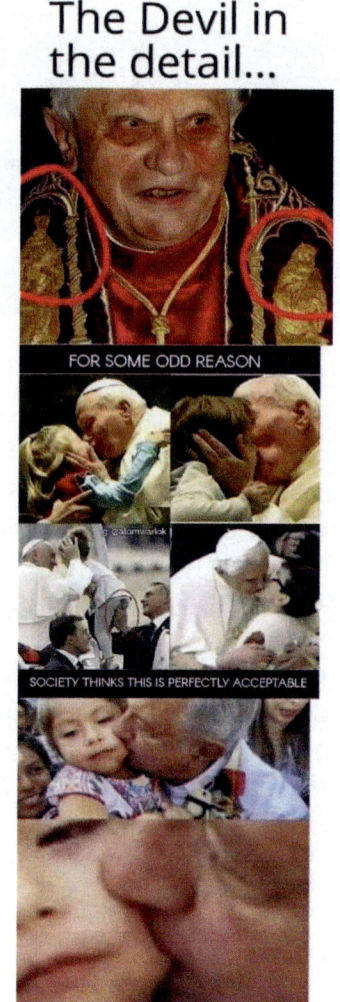

) Romans 3:2 "Let God be true but every man is a liar."

The Sumerians, Chaldeans, Babylonians, Egyptians, Ancient Hebrews, Greeks, Nordic Vikings, Ancient Chinese, Hindus and Buddhists all held the Geocentric model, that we were the center of this Universe, inside a vaulted dome, with water above and water below.

They did not teach, in any school, that Einstein nor any other government scientists ever proved the Big Bang Theory, but that it was written by Jesuit priest Father Georges Lamaitre who said he based his work on Einstein's theories. Now why would a Roman Catholic priest create the Big Bang Theory when they are supposed to preach creation. Seems like a fake priest that hijacked a religion. The Bible warns us of such happenings. The bible does not talk in a mysterious language or riddles about Earth, it talks plain and simple, and when understood, corresponds with the right reason and the observation of the world we live in.

The earth is proven, through physical based evidence, to be an extended stationary plane with the North pole and its star being the center of the sun's rotation. It is a proven fact that shuts down all the lies and deceptions that say otherwise. It's the Creator's truth that shows creation. No falsehoods spreaded by man's unclean mind can change this. And, if the heart be right with God, we may be sure that the mistakes of science will not shut the door of grace.

200+ FLAT EARTH Bible Verses

EARTH CREATED BEFORE THE SUN: Genesis 1:1-19

UNIVERSE IS COMPLETE: Genesis 2:1

EARTH MEASUREMENTS UNKNOWN: Job 38:4-5, Jeremiah 31:37, Proverbs 25:3

EARTH IS A DISK/CIRCLE, NOT A BALL: Isaiah 40:22, Job 38:13-14

EARTH MEASURED WITH A LINE, NOT A CURVE: Job 38:4-5

PATHS ARE STRAIGHT, NOT CURVED: 1 Samuel 6:12, Psalm 5:8, Psalm 27:11, Isaiah 40:3, Jeremiah 31:9, Matthew 3:3, Mark 1:3, Luke 3:4, John 1:23, Acts 16:11, Acts 21:1, Hebrews 12:13

WATERS ARE STRAIGHT, NOT CURVED: Job 37:10

EARTHQUAKES SHAKE EARTH, AND DOES NOT MOVE: 2 Samuel 22:8, Isaiah 13:13, Revelation 6:12-13

EARTH IS FIXED AND IMMOVABLE: Psalm 33:9, Psalm 93:1, Psalm 96:10, Psalm 104:5, Psalm 119:89-90, Isaiah 45:18, Zechariah 1:11, 1 Chronicles 16:30

"BE STILL, AND KNOW THAT I AM GOD": Psalm 46:10

EARTH HAS PILLARS, AND HANGS ON NOTHING: 1 Samuel 2:8, Job 9:6, Job 26:7, Psalm 75:3, 2 Peter 3:5

EARTH HAS A FACE (A GEOMETRICAL FLAT SURFACE): Genesis 1:29, Genesis 4:14, Genesis 6:1, Genesis 6:7, Genesis 7:3, Genesis 7:4, Genesis 8:9, Genesis 11:8, Genesis 11:9, Genesis 41:56, Exodus 32:12, Exodus 33:16, Numbers 12:3, Deuteronomy 6:15, Deuteronomy 7:6, 1 Samuel 20:15, 1 Kings 13:34, Job 37:12, Psalm 104:30, Jeremiah 25:26, Jeremiah 28:16, Ezekiel 34:6, Ezekiel 38:20, Ezekiel 39:14, Amos 9:6, Amos 9:8, Zechariah 5:3

WATERS HAVE A FACE (A GEOMETRICAL FLAT SURFACE): Genesis 1:2, Genesis 7:18, Job 38:30

EARTH HAS ENDS: Deuteronomy 28:49, Deuteronomy 28:64, Deuteronomy 33:17, 1 Samuel 2:10, Job 37:3, Job 38:13, Psalm 46:9, Psalm 48:10, Psalm 59:13, Psalm 61:2, Psalm 65:5, Psalm 67:7, Psalm 72:8, Psalm 98:3, Psalm 135:7, Proverbs 8:29, Proverbs 17:24, Proverbs 30:4, Isaiah 5:26, Isaiah 26:15, Isaiah 40:28, Isaiah 41:5, Isaiah 41:9, Isaiah 42:10, Isaiah 43:6, Isaiah 45:22, Isaiah 48:20, Isaiah 49:6, Isaiah 52:10, Jeremiah 10:13, Jeremiah 16:19, Jeremiah 25:31, Jeremiah 25:33, Jeremiah 51:16, Daniel 4:22, Micah 5:4, Zechariah 9:10, Acts 13:47

EARTH HAS CORNERS: Isaiah 11:12, Revelation 7:1

FIRMAMENT/DOME: Genesis 1:6-8, Genesis 1:14-18, Genesis 1:20, Genesis 7:11, Genesis 8:2, Job 37:18, Psalm 19:1, Psalm 150:1, Isaiah 40:22, Ezekiel 1:22-26, Ezekiel 10:1, Daniel 12:3

SUN MOVES, NOT THE EARTH: Genesis 15:12, Genesis 15:17, Genesis 19:23, Genesis 32:31, Exodus 17:12, Exodus 22:3, Exodus 22:26, Leviticus 22:7, Numbers 2:3, Numbers 21:11, Numbers 34:15, Deuteronomy 4:41, Deuteronomy 4:47, Deuteronomy 11:30, Deuteronomy 16:6, Deuteronomy 23:11, Deuteronomy 24:13, Deuteronomy 24:15, Joshua 1:15, Joshua 8:29, Joshua 10:27, Joshua 12:1, Joshua 13:5, Joshua 19:12, Joshua 19:27, Joshua 19:34, Judges 8:13, Judges 9:33, Judges 14:18, Judges 19:14, Judges 20:43, 2 Samuel 2:24, 2 Samuel 3:35, 2 Samuel 23:4, 1 Kings 22:36, 2 Chronicles 18:34, Psalm 50:1, Psalm 113:3, Ecclesiastes 1:5, Isaiah 41:25, Isaiah 45:6, Isaiah 59:19, Jeremiah 15:9, Daniel 6:14, Amos 8:9, Jonah 4:8, Micah 3:6, Nahum 3:17, Malachi 1:11, Matthew 5:45, Mark 16:2, Ephesians 4:26, James 1:11

SUN STOPS MOVING: Isaiah 60:20, Job 9:7, Joshua 10:12-14, Habakkuk 3:11

SUN MOVES BACKWARDS: 2 Kings 20:8-11

MOON HAS ITS OWN LIGHT: Genesis 1:16, Isaiah 13:10, Isaiah 30:26, Isaiah 60:19-20, Jeremiah 31:35, Matthew 24:29, Mark 13:24, Ezekiel 32:7, Revelation 21:23

HIGH ALTITUDE PERSPECTIVES: Daniel 4:11, Daniel 4:20, Matthew 4:8

EVERYONE SEES JESUS: Revelation 1:7

NEW JERUSALEM, THE HUGE CUBE: Revelation 21:15-17

"Breadth", spread out FLAT, of the Earth: Revelation 20:9

MATTHEWS BIBLE FROM 1537 SAYS "FLAT EARTH": 2 Samuel 11:11

CREATION WORSHIPPERS: Deuteronomy 4:19, Deuteronomy 17:3, 2 Kings 23:5, Jeremiah 8:2

GOD'S WORD IS ALWAYS FAITHFUL AND TRUE: Jeremiah 42:5, Revelation 3:14, Revelation 19:11, Revelation 21:5, Revelation 22:6

www.FlatEarthDoctrine.com

Flat Earth Qur'an

"If you accept the literal truth of every word of the Bible, then the Earth must be flat. The same is true for the Qur'an. Pronouncing the Earth round then means you're an atheist. In 1993, the supreme religious authority of Saudi Arabia, Sheik Abdel-Aziz Ibn Baaz, issued an edict, or fatwa, declaring that the world is flat. Anyone of the round persuasion does not believe in God and should be punished."   Carl Sagan

"The earth is flat. Whoever claims it is round is an atheist deserving of punishment."

Sheikh Al-Azeez bin Baaz, the supreme religious authority of Saudi Arabia, 1993

Seems that a lot of religions cherry pick their holy book when preaching it. Deny it all you want, it's still there. I don't care what your opinion is.

"Intelligent design is a modest position theologically and philosophically. It attributes the complexity and diversity of life to intelligence with the God of any religion, faith or philosophical system." William A. Dembski

The text, translation and commentary of this version of the Quran is by Abdullah Yusuf Ali. It is exactly as I copied and pasted from the Kindle version that I reread in research for this book. Let's begin shall we.

Qur'an 15:19 "And We have spread out (like a carpet); set thereon mountains firm and immovable; and produced therein all kinds of things in due balance."

Qur'an 20:53 "He Who has, made for you the earth like a carpet spread out; has enabled you to go about therein by roads (and channels); and has sent down water from the sky." With it we produced diverse pairs of plants each separate from the others.

Qur'an 43:10 (Yea, the same that) has made for you the earth (like a carpet) spread out, and has made for you roads (and channels) therein, in order that ye may find guidance (on the way);

Qur'an 50:7 And the earth- We have spread it out, and set thereon mountains standing firm, and produced therein every kind of beautiful growth (in pairs)-

Qur'an 51:48 And We have spread out the (spacious) earth: How excellently We do spread out!

Qur'an 71:19 "And Allah has made the earth for you as a carpet (spread out), Have We not made the earth as a wide expanse."

Surah al-Ghashiya 88:17 "Let them reflect on the camels, how they were created; and heaven, how it is raised aloft; and the mountains, how they are hoisted; and the earth, how it is spread out."

With the wording it depends on where you look, but the message is the same. Here's a link to Quran scriptures pertaining to this subject.
https://www.islamawakened.com/quran/71/19/#:~:text=%22Allah%20has%20laid%20the%20earth,you%20as%20a%20wide%20expanse.%22&text=%22And%20God%20made%20the%20land%20for%20you%20as%20a%20plain.%22&text=%22And%20God%20made%20the%20land%20for%20you%20a
s%20a%20plain.,-And%20Allah%20has

"Allah has laid the earth out for you as a wide expanse." "And God made the land for you as a plain." "And God made the land for you as a plain.

https://www.islamawakened.com › ...

Ayah Nuh (Noah) 71:19 - IslamAwakened

As someone pointed out to me: "Muslims pray in one direction towards Mecca but if the Earth were a globe they could pray in two directions and still be praying towards Mecca but NEVER does anyone purposely do this. They can only pray in one direction, because it's not a globe."

Realize the greatness of your mind
"If the Earth is the center of the Universe then the ideas of God creation and a purpose for human existence are resplendent, but if the Earth is just one of billions of planets revolving around billions of stars and billions of galaxies then the ideas of God creations and a specific purpose of for Earth and human existence become highly implausible." Eric Dubay, The Flat Earth Conspiracy

Minds are like parachutes. They work best when they are open. Don't let your own mind fool you or let your emotions decide things for you. Let the filter of logic, reasoning and common sense guide you. The eyes are useless when the mind is blind.

) 1 Corinthians 3 "18 Let no man deceive himself. If any man among you seemeth to be wise in this world, let him become a fool, that he may be wise. 19 For the wisdom of this world is foolishness with God. For it is written, He taketh the wise in their own craftiness."

The Zetetic Method

I highly recommend the book "Bible cosmology: The world according to the Bible and the ancients" by D. Haughey. You have to download it. It's not in book stores. Contact me through my site and I'll send you the link. He breaks the flat earth bible down nicely. Better than I ever could. However poorly I do it, the Bible and real observable provable science still points to a flat motionless plane that has been flooded. Prove me wrong by either.

"The first gulp from the glass of natural sciences will make you an atheist, but at the bottom of the glass God is waiting for you." Werner Heisenberg father of quantum physics

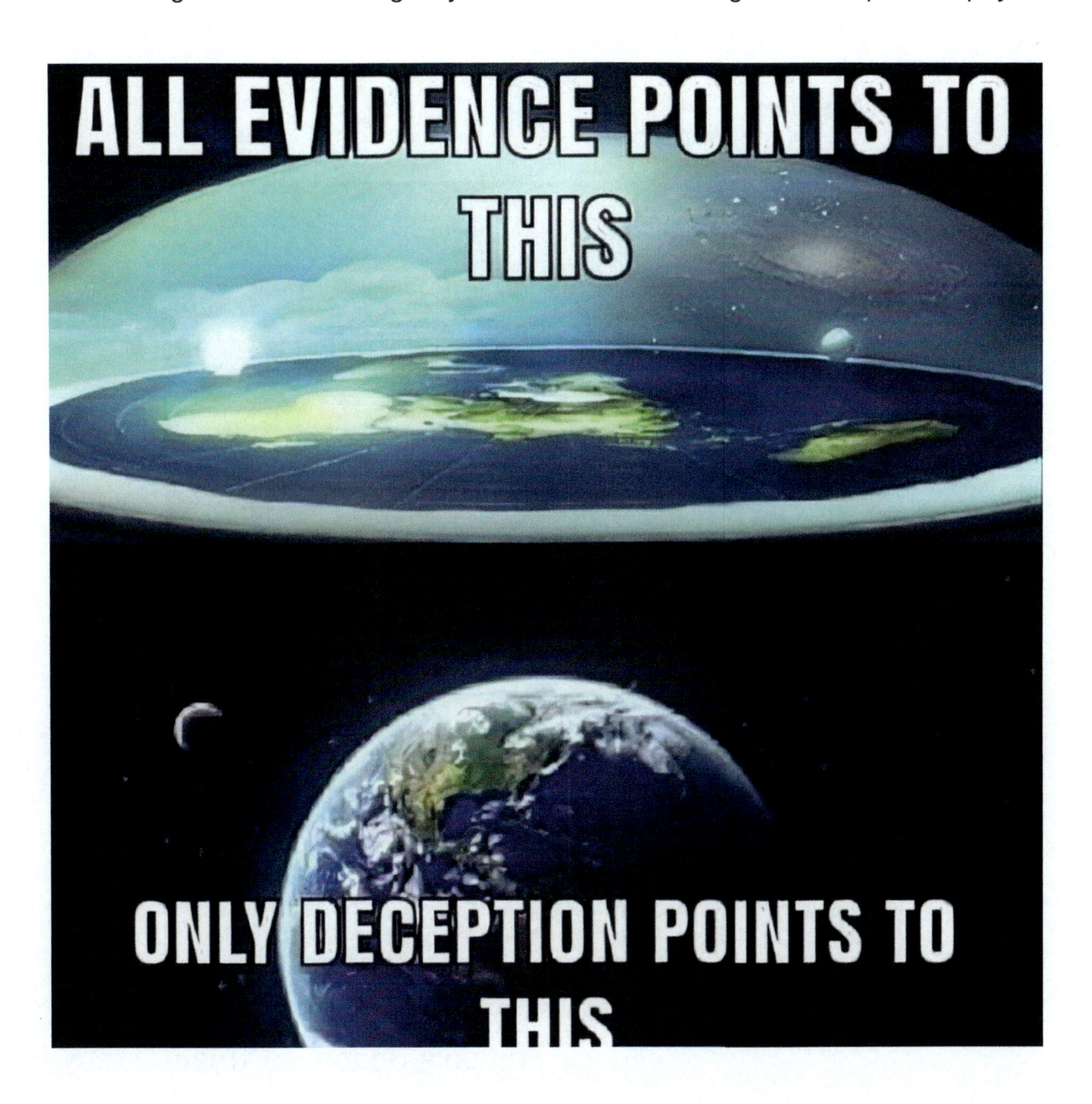

CHAPTER 12
COMMENTS AND ARGUMENTS

Francois-Benòit Hoffman

" The pole star hasn't moved an inch in millenia
while the other constellations all around turn perennial.
Group rotations perfect formations
never moving an inch from their relative locations."
        Eric Dubay's song "The Flat Earth Movement"

In this chapter I'm going to share different comments and arguments I've come across, from flat earthers, that I liked. There's many but here's just a few. Some make good points in my opinion, I hope you consider them.

There are parents speaking out at parents and teacher board meetings about the false globe science. One lady had a board set up showing solid proofs. I've seen a few videos where people are video recording the parents bringing their case to the board of education, the teachers making the students that are there leave so they won't hear it. One man brought a bunch of government documents saying the earth was flat and the education system was lying to our kids.

Another incident where a college student kept asking deeper questions concerning the globe model to his professor who couldn't answer so he stated that NASA said...and the students laughed.

The mainstream media has stated that flat earth was disrupting and dangerous to college and schools. A high school kid was sent to the principal's office for questioning the science teacher about the globe.

Armed with truth, a group of people have taken on the elite, waking up people and building an info army. Exposing lies and showing the truth. Here are some people that have awakened.

COMMENTS AND ARGUMENTS

))) "As a RF engineer we didn't account for" bent radio waves ", only straight ones.
If earth is round then none of the microwave link dishes should have worked. This is how I discovered we were being lied to."

))) "I typically say things and talk about things that I can prove. Nothing happens in a vacuum. No spark flame or fire can exist in a vacuum. I can prove these things therefore I believe them. Why else would you believe something?? The sun is a burning ball of gas, roflmao fairy tales."

))) "In 2005, I flew from Heathrow to Cape Town. I looked out the window and the stewardess kept asking me to shut the screen. I asked if it was annoying anyone, everyone around me said "no" in fact they were enjoying looking out.

This was when I noticed that the vastness of the earth was flatter than I had expected. No curve, no horizon line relative to the height. That piqued my interest and that's when I started to question the narrative.

On my return I purchased a ×200 telescope and had hours of fun. I went to Dover and zoomed in and could see France. If the world was round that would never have happened. I now live in The North West of England. I can do the same with the Isle of Man that is 40 miles away by sea. I set my scope up, I point it to the Isle of Man and guess what, I can see the beach.

The observable data is proof that the earth is either a magnitude bigger or flat.

If the world were round and at 9 miles the horizon disappears then at 40 miles the Isle of Man should not be visible to the naked eye as there will be 4 horizon points.

The globe theory fails under the most basic observational scientific inquiry.

Same way they won't let citizens explore Northern and Southern Poles. We are on a massive plane of the vastness and scale which is unimaginable to the current average muppet who believes narrative instead of observing one's own environment. Then again, they did have an injection without looking into the adverse effects....

Trust their science they said..... What is science if you remove the right to enquire, investigate, evaluate and observe? At this point it becomes purely Religious Dogma.

Trust the science....yeah, they gave you cigarettes= cancer, they gave you sugar= feeds cancer, they gave you 5G= gives you radiation sickness.They send you off to war whilst they make the money.

Have you woken up yet?"

))) "Whether or not the world really is flat or spherical, one thing I have learned in the journey of discovery is that MOST ballers (I'm talking upwards of the high 90% range) have very poor arguments for their beliefs. Pathetically poor in many cases. In fact, it's quite ironic really. They are the ones who claim Flat Earthers are morons/stupid/idiots and such. Yet, the vast majority of them still believe the shape of the Earth causes the phases of the moon and a host of other equally uninformed nonsense, like ships allegedly going over the curve - something easily debunked with a good zoom lens (definitely with the Nikon Coolpix P900). They will dogmatically hold to this idea of ships going over the curve in less than 5 miles, but then when you show them pics and video of perfectly flat horizon shots at WELL ABOVE 100,000 feet (and at eye-level), they'll claim it's because "you aren't high enough to see the curve" (while simultaneously claiming to have seen it from commercial airlines at below 40,000 feet). And Christians are even worse. They'll go ballistic about Isaiah 40:22, declaring that "circle" can't mean "disc" because it is a "two dimensional object"... therefore, they say, Isaiah meant to use the word in order to describe... a sphere (which is a 3D object). SMH. Honestly, it's enough to drive someone crazy... or into becoming a Flat Earther - which they would say is the same thing, but considering their exceptionally flawed logic skills, that's got to be the perfect example of the pot calling the kettle black." Rob Skiba

RIP Rob Skiba. A kind and honest individual seeking truth. Him and his experiments debunking the globe model are missed.

))) "Empirical Evidence versus unproven theories:
The Earth is Observably Flat and Motionless because of many things, but my favorite two nails in the supersonic speeding globe coffin is the circular rotation of the stars above and also airplane travel using gyroscopic navigation. The Earth is claimed to be in a super sonic 66.6 thousand mile per hour orbit around a hyper sonic Sun at some 500,000 mph, all while the galaxy is rocketing through infinite space over 1 Million miles per hour!! Astounding speeds that cannot even be conceived of, much less proven with empirical evidence! Not one person on Earth has a single credible experiment that proves these ludicrous speeds and astronomical distances. Regurgitating science fiction fantasies that were handed down by your government funded mainstream schooling system does NOT prove we are moving at all..

So we turn to the Scientific, and in fact the ZETETIC Method of discovery.. which is based on what is observed and asks the fundamental question WHY it is being Observed. All we know that we can all agree on, is that the stars ROTATE in perfect concentric circles above us. That is a Fact that only a blind person may not accept. In order to determine whether the stars are moving or the Earth is moving, we must look at the stars and constellations themselves and ask ourselves why they NEVER DEVIATE from their relative positions in the sky. Nothing changes at all, except the same rotation every single day around Polaris. This can only be explained with the Firmament, as the stars are shown to remain perfectly FIXED IN THEIR POSITIONS, while rotating in this fixed position above us..

Like spinning a massive cosmic umbrella over our heads, the stars show ZERO observed Parallax in the sky. Do you know what parallax is?

Parallax is what happens when a viewer is watching objects move in the distance.. and the objects appear to change their positions due to perspective and angle of view.

If you watched cars on a distant highway passing each other, although they are actually moving at the same speeds.. this is parallax. The cars that are further away APPEAR to go slower.. because they are further and take longer to come "around the loop" so to speak. The cars closer to you only appear to go around faster because you are closer to them. Same thing happens on an airplane watching the clouds around you. The clouds at a higher elevation are much closer to you, so they move faster than the clouds way lower.

The FACT that there is Zero Parallax observed in the stars above, is scientific empirical evidence that the stars are moving and not us.

How many experiments have you personally conducted?? Just repeating someone else's teachings and coming up with an interpretation is not enough. I have plenty of videos and blogs of my own personal observations and experiments. The Earth isn't moving, and the observation of the stars above prove it."

))) "At 35000 feet, standard commercial flight altitude you have about 230 miles of observable distance to the horizon which is over three degrees of spherical declination according to the Heliocentric model but we see no such curvature in sight at any angle since the earth is not shaped like a tube. The horizon is always flat and at eye level. There is a 2000 mile time lapse trip footage of a flight going from Spain to Turkey that was stitched together on Photoshop showing a constant flat horizon with no curvature for the duration of the flight. There is also footage of someone monitoring the wings flaps on a commercial flight showing no activity and therefore locked into place which indicates that the plane is constantly flying in a straight linear pattern parallel to the surface of the earth with no adjustments for the spherical curvature of the globe during the trip. Also logically on a sphere from any distance and altitude anything on the surface of the earth including natural things such as mountain ranges and man made thinking like structures would follow the spherical shape of the earth, nothing would be parallel to each other on the surface. The simplest undeniable evidence is the fact that on a sphere the higher you go the more the spherical horizon drops below all around you. That's physics that cannot be refuted period but what we observe instead is a constant eye level horizon regardless of altitude. My wife travels dozens of times across the US including Asia where she flies over Alaska and the North Pole from Los Angeles to get to Shanghai and I assure you that the horizon is always flat."

))) "Actually there is provable evidence that the earth can not be moving. It is in plain sight. Almost everyone knows where it is, just don't know how to use it. It is in Egypt and is a Pyramid. It has a very long tunnel built into it. If you go all the way in and then look back out you can always, night or day any hour, see the North Star. If the earth was moving in any way spinning or orbiting the sun this would not be possible. also proves that the axis of the globe idea does not tilt 23 degrees. This proof destroys all the globe theories in one shot. please do some research on these pyramids as they were not built to be the tombs of the kings of Egypt. They were made to remind us of the truth of our world. Check it out for yourself."

))) "Darwin writes a book about species. By what constitutes a species? He does not know. He even admitted the lack of evidence frustrated him. Despite the lack of solid evidence, missing links and all the fraudulent "evidence" that has come to light, the theory still persists.
  Newton "explains" his assumptions on all things in terms of gravitation. But what is gravitation? He doesn't really know or can prove it exists. All he can prove is that things fall. Despite the many fallacies his theory persists."

))) "Actually, if you believe in space, and believe we're on a ball of certain mass whizzing through space, then you'd have to accept that only planets specifically Earth size and mass can have water. Water comes in all three forms, solid (ice) liquid (water) and gas (vapor). The boiling point does not just depend on temperature alone, but mostly relies upon pressure. For example, it's said that the boiling point at the top of Mt Everest is about 93°C, but at sea-level, it's 100°C. Apparently deep underground it needs to be even hotter still.
  However, at room temperature, a beaker of water in a vacuum chamber starts to boil as the pressure of air is reduced to virtually zero. Since the globers claim that gravity determines air pressure, and it must be a specific volume of air unique to the earth, then to be an inhabitable planet with liquid water, the pressure must be almost identical to Earth's, plus the amount of atmospheric gasses. Plus then you'll require a similar "goldilocks zone" proximity to a star to have very similar temperatures. The odds of which,

from a random destructive massive big bang would be so astronomical... not to mention that we can't actually create or destroy water. We can alter its state, but ultimately it is fated to keep recycling back into one or another original state. Which means Earth had to have originated with all its water in the first place. Now again, because it relies upon pressure to remain stable, space couldn't have been a vacuum in the first place, because all our water would have boiled and dispersed into the void. Ergo, we've just destroyed the Big Bang model while realizing that Earth is quite unique, and cannot be in space.

Therefore, the rational conclusion any thinking person can conclude is that the Stationary Planar Earth is fixed at the bottom of the known universe."

))) Satellites inside Earth's atmosphere or outside Earth's atmosphere!?

The first possibility. If the satellites are inside the atmosphere, and the atmosphere is not more than 100 km .. then the satellite is subject to the Earth's gravity, so in order not to fall on the ground, it needs an engine that pushes it upwards against gravity like a helicopter until it stabilizes in its place

In this case, the satellite needs powerful batteries, jet engines, and huge energy to maintain this level, and solar energy is not enough for this purpose.

And if the solar energy was sufficient, they would have to change the batteries every once in a while! This is not what they do! We have never heard in our lives that a satellite has been landed for maintenance, and we have never heard that a maintenance team has been sent to repair the satellite in orbit! I do not know what is this super satellite that does not need any maintenance?!

The other possibility (rotation with the earth, until it is fixed in its position) here is to not forget that the speed of the earth's rotation is 1600 km / h, .. and this is faster than sound!! If the satellite wants to move with the Earth, it must be installed at a speed of 1600 km or more (because this speed is from the surface of the Earth and the higher it is, the higher the speed)

This is in addition to the fact that the satellite must rotate with the Earth's rotation around the sun. This is another movement that they should take care of!!!! The satellite must swim in space at the same speed as the Earth around the sun, because it is not subject to its gravity now.. If it slows down a little, it will move away from the Earth and get lost in space, because the Earth will not wait for it, but it will stay by any satellite.

Free your mind from the bluff....there are no satellites..just blimps and balloons.

))) "I believe its flat because of what my own common sense, human senses, and Nikon P900 tell me. And 15 years of experience in corporate America I can tell a bullshit story and a cover-up when I see one. And they are doubling down with the NASA cartoons and everything else they can reach for. But really what got me to change my mind about it and go "wooooah" was Eric Dubay's "200 proofs the earth is not a spinning ball."

And the fact that they have tried so hard to censor him and people like him. And the fact that Barack Obama said something to the effect of it's not OK to create your own facts (on Letterman's new show). Oh so you're telling me what I can and can't think now? And the fact that they're pushing so hard saying that flat earth is "dangerous misinformation."

And all of the social media sites censor it, All of the search engines are programmed to show results that ridicule it and us. That oughta tell you something. That they're hiding something reeeeal big. And that they are shitting bricks because of how many people are waking up. What a convenient time for a plandemic distraction. Look at how all of a sudden people that don't trust the government are eating out of its hand now. Please Quarantine us. Please give us your "vaccine." I digress.

I think the world would be a much better place if we took every cell phone, every iPad, and every computer, and just burned them all in a big pile. I mean hell, it would take away their main methods of controlling us wouldn't it?"

))) "The Globe model is possible only in mathematics. It is only possible in numbers because it was reverse engineered from the Geocentric model. It might be 'proven' through numbers, pixels and paper but will never be observable in reality.

Actually, we all see and sense the same things, but are indoctrinated to perceive them in a different way. For example, the sun and the moon appear almost the same size, unless someone tells you that the sun appears small because it's far and huge, and that the moon is relatively smaller and closer, therefore appears the same size. But, if you'd observe carefully and really think about it, you'd understand how easy it is to keep someone mentally blind while his eyes are wide open.

Some people assume Flat Earthers see the world as a disc, for the same reason they assume they live on a globe... Pictures.

The web is full of pictures of a flat disc in black space and stars, so we assume an edge. This is also why people want photos of the edge. They put so much trust in pixels, swallowing photos as valid proofs. They trust all photos, as long as the imagery comes from the government, who already designed our current world view, instead of actually exploring reality itself."

))) "Can someone point me to the manual in navigation that uses a Curved Adjacent Angle...or 3 circles of Equal Elevation on a curved surface??? Anyone?"

))) "Anyone read the history of astronomy physics? Talk about moving goal posts. Lol!

))) I've already proven the Earth is not the shape we are told... when flying from Sydney Australia to Johannesburg South Africa the only direction you could fly on a globe is west. When in fact you travel north for most of the way... I measured this with both a normal compass and phone compass at regular intervals along the 14 hour flight, and before the globists say its caused by all the metal in the plane the same does not happen in the northern hemisphere when travelling west ergo I proved this nearly a decade ago...

))) So a balloon makes its way from China 2023, across the globe it goes with no propulsion and no other country spots it, amazingly it makes its way unaided unchallenged to the USA... And you fucking idiots find flat earth a step to far 😵 .... The plane has got the IQ of a piss flap🫠 in medical stasis

))) "Ok on a globe there's not really an "UP" or a "DOWN"... It would be more "INTO" or "TOWARDS"... if there is a gravity on a globe it would be pulling you towards the core of the earth which is heat and metal,, but also the environment is super magnetic which would contradict gravity because magnetic force is easier to prove than gravity... How come nobody believes in electromagnetism over gravity??? It's a lot easier to believe when you consider what you're made of and basically everything you ingest has magnetic properties of sort in the way of minerals and even water and air have magnetic properties."

))) When talking about Einstein:
"He plotted mathematically a formula to fit an idea...theoretically and maybe mathematically yes but not practicality nor reality by means of observation and sheer mind blowing 1st hand accounted facts that say we are not on a spinning ball, not on your best day!"

))) (This was a review of a book that was desperately trying to debunk flat earth but failed. The reviewer pitied the ball earth author.)
"It's really quite sad and pathetic to see such feeble and cringe worthy attempts as this to "logically" prove that our world is a sphere or spheroid with everyone and everything up and down and all around the sides of it, all at different angles to each other, that spins 25,000 miles a day at faster than the speed of sound, and flies several million miles a day around a stationary Sun in the sky. Such bizarre, deranged and demented theories are not only unscientific and have no relationship with anything to do with real life, they represent nothing but the most monstrous and catastrophic cognitive and philosophical capitulation on the part of human beings, by far, in recorded history. Happily, this shocking and egregious blunder (which has of course been reinforced by diabolical, cruel, criminal and evil hoaxes) is nearing the expiry of its natural shelf life."

))) "Weight alone is the reason why you will fall. The acceleration towards the ground is due to the fact that we do have "up" and "down" contrary to the globe earth theory misconception. No need to introduce the theory of gravity into the equation. It is unnecessary and absurd. Let alone it cannot be detected or measured by any means whatsoever. It simply cannot be proven (among other scientific myths people blindly believe in)"
> https://medium.com/starts-with-a-bang/5-scientific-myths-you-probably-believe-about-the-universe-9a34597d7435

))) "The almanac shows that the moon, from last quarter to the new moon, is found that for part of one day, immediately before the new moon, the dark part of the moon is turned towards the sun. At the new moon the sun is still eastward of the moon, which is still illuminated on the western side."

))) "Remember when everyone finally admitted that pro wrestling was fake but the fans didn't care and kept pretending it was real anyways? This is where we're at with NASA now."

))) Part1 & 2

> Having served in the Marine Corps and spent at 2 years of my enlistment term at sea with the Navy, I concur. I was stationed on the barge Hercules in 1988 in the Persian Gulf. I was involved in operation praying mantis. I manned a 30 mm deck gun and kept watch over the ocean for surface contacts. Surface contacts that human eye couldn't see, but radar confirmed was there, could be seen using enhanced vision equipment such as Big Eyes. There is no earth curvature.
>
> I've been in Atlantic, the Pacific, the Indian Ocean, The Med, crossed the Suez Canal 4 times, did the shellback naval tradition and each time I'd stand top side and look at the vast water of the ocean that surrounded the ship, further than I can see. I wonder where the bend is in the midst of the patches?

> This water is flat. That water past it is flat. All water is flat. At what point does the bend appear? It's certainly not in the flattest water as far as I can see in all directions. They say refraction, but can't say at what mile that effect ends, either. Isn't it amazing that they can openly say that the Earth looks flat like we say, but it's still round, because light is bending the curve perfectly flat, just like the fe community is saying it looks.....riiiiiight. That's how indoctrinated they are. They can directly contradict themselves in this way and not even notice TO question it. By their logic, I should be able to zoom straight ahead, and see the back of my head, with a powerful enough zoom.

))) "Plants and Trees grow upwards. If the earth were spinning, the trees on the equator would lean eastwards to counter imaginary conflicting rotational forces being perpendicular to earth's surface. This however is not the case and is a living testament that the earth is not a spinning ball."

))) "The law which makes objects apparently diminishing in proportion to their distance from the observer does not affect luminous bodies; the brighter the light of the body the longer its bulk will remain unchanged in our sight, whereas an object but faintly lighted becomes invisible, as I have said, at a distance which exceeds its diameter 5,000 times. If the said law extended to luminous bodies, then a flame one inch wide could not be seen at the distance of 225 yards, whereas we know from experiment that the size of its apparent bulk does not change even when the candle is carried to a distance of several thousand yards. As the sunlight is extremely bright, the bulk of the sun must therefore seem unchangeable at an extremely long distance,

Vain have been all the efforts of the astronomers to find a central body whose force of attraction might account for the fact that these stars are kept within their orbits; and such a body must exist somewhere. This central body is our earth. May it not also explain the fact that the greater the accumulation of soil in the northern hemisphere the larger is the number of stars above?"

)))   )))

> quart chunk taken out and the ring diagram of the layers of earth with the magma core in the middle. He told us earth is 4 billion years old and the universe 12 billion years. The reason there's a magma core is because it's still so hot from the Big Bang and flying through space. I asked, what is the source of heat generation, causing such high degrees as to melt rock for 4-12 billion years. He didn't have an answer so he tried to humiliate me by saying in a very obnoxious tone "what do you want me to say, 'god' "? And on cue, the class laughs and the teacher rolls his eyes and moves on with the lecture. I genuinely always wondered that since like 5th grade when they first introduced that age old visual aid of the layer of inner earth. That woke me up to realize that these "smart" college teachers had no clue what they were

> Edit: Eric already mentioned this in the video but I didnt realise
> I came up with another fact...*A planet cannot maintain orbit infinitely without spiraling into the sun*. Here's why, the planet has no form of propellant keeping it to maintain its velocity, for e.g. if the planet has been acted upon (slowed down), it will lose velocity, it cannot regain that lost energy...Now what causes orbiting is "gravity", a force that acts as a pull on the planet constantly at every point around the sun, by the planet having to change direction it is losing its intitial energy, there is no constant force acting against the constant pull of gravity to maintain orbit. Its like saying a seat on a swing will swing back n forth forever without air resistance or friction, just with the use of gravity.

))) Someone left this message on one of Rob Skiba's videos:

"Get your mind ready .. I'm a retired Air Force Visual Information specialist, Historian, and retired Army Aviation, and a once practicing Christian. My great granddad was a 33-degree mason ..This planet is surprisingly not round, and does not rotate. I promise. I was pissed at first, and of course it's annoying to me to see how it's being delivered, but it needs to be said. Flat is a fact. I was surrounded by brilliant minds and pilots for over 24 years ... it's flat. I was a designer for satellites, and worked with a communications squadron for many years ... the planet is not a sphere, and satellites are not in orbit. Makes me sick. I was raised to believe I lived on a round rotating planet and it's simply untrue. The word is getting out, and the truth is stranger than fiction. Think dome. Take your time to understand why you were lied to, I myself will not tell you because it's right in front of you. Do the research yourself and keep an open mind. The discovery was made in the 1940s. These people are not delusional sad to say."

))) "Inevitably, the High Priests of whatever topic points a finger at the heretic who questions traditional beliefs. The heretic is looked upon with suspicion, and the people all think, "He must be a bad guy or else no one would have accused him of anything." The heretic is rejected ostensibly because of doctrine, but in reality, it was because he refused to join, and thus sanctioned their conspiracy. The doctrinal issues in question are not allowed to be questioned because truth is not their objective – rather, they seek power through cohesion. That is the way the educational system and government works."

))) "Top ten facts flat earthers had to teach globe believers by Flat Earth Hebrew.
1) No, you can not see forever. The atmospheric conditions, refraction of light, perspective, convergence, and your optics will determine where the horizon will be.
2) No, you can not fall off the edge. We have atmospheric pressure, so a dome is required for that to be possible.
3) No, we did not know the earth was a sphere for 2500 years. It was actually illegal to teach heliocentrism all the way up to the 1920's.
4) No, Columbus didn't think the earth was flat. Reading his diary, he found exactly what he was looking for. (Jerusalem/America)
5) Stop saying the other "planets " are spheres when you can only see it from one angle.(a circle isn't a sphere)
6) The shadow on the moon during an eclipse or moon phase isn't earth.
7) When NASA says they have an "image" or "picture" of earth or space, it does not mean they have a photo!
8) The waste of cash that is the Antarctic cruise ,won't prove the earth is a globe.
9) Einstein said "an optical experiment to prove earth's motion can't be found".
10) No ,flat earthers didn't get all their information on YouTube, if globies studied history then they'd know these things.(hundreds of flat earth books online and in libraries)"

))) "Here is where the globe theory falls down. If I stand on a beach and view a boat on the distant horizon I am at the highest point because the boat is going down over the horizon. But..for the people on the boat...they are at the highest point and I am going down over the horizon. BUT...you cannot have two objects at their highest point but each below each other...it's impossible. No matter where you are on globe earth you are in theory always at the highest point in relation to every other point on the globe because the round globe is always falling away from you, no matter how insignificant the measurement. But once again...it's impossible to walk down over the horizon and still remain at the highest point. remaining at the highest point in relation to all else is only possible on a flat surface."

))) "It is affirmed that the intensity of attraction increases with proximity, and vice-versâ. How, then, when the waters are drawn up by the moon from their bed, and away from the earth's attraction – which at that greater distance from the center is considerably diminished, while that of the moon is proportionately increased – is it possible that all the waters acted on should be prevented leaving the earth and flying away to the moon? If the moon has power of attraction sufficient to lift the waters of the earth at all, even a single inch from their deepest receptacles, where the earth's attraction is much the greater, there is nothing in the theory of attraction of gravitation to prevent her taking to herself all the waters which come within her influence. Let the smaller body once overcome the power of the larger, and the power of the smaller becomes greater than when it first operated, because the matter acted on is nearer to it. Proximity is greater, and therefore power is greater… How then can the waters of the ocean immediately underneath the moon flow towards the shores, and so cause a flood?"

)))

Dude, you said it perfectly, it's so hilarious these people that say the "atmosphere" is spinning with the earth (as an excuse for no one being able to scientifically show or prove any motion), have a 2year old's understanding of matter. I mean, A solid rock in space is spinning, and when it does, a layer of air, fucking AIR, which is NOT solid, magically spins completely in sync with it? WTF! Have you ever seen AIR?! it's uncontrollable it's nebulous it moves in all kinds of direction even in the molecular level let alone winds, and then it's supposedly so perfectly linked to the earth and spins so perfectly with it that from the perspective of a helicopter over the earth, it seems like there is zero movement, because the chopper is supposedly spinning with it, even though it's in the AIR!!! it's like, they ridicule religious people for believing in miracles and then they believe

)))

It is pretty simple
There are several insidious sub-objectives of the whole fabricated Space Program that these elitist globalist are bent on.

Truthers are exposing this scam not only because it is a hoax, but because it is the glamour, superiority, and high-profile

Bastardized science, nonsensicalized scientific media, and rascalized Agenda.

SCIENCE

that the elitist globalist would like you to believe to be real.

"If we can make the masses believe we have the science to take humans to Mars and back and one day colonize Mars, we can make them believe we have the science to do many things, no matter how nonsensical and bizzare they may sound. For example creating disasters and blame them on Aliens, asteroids, and even as teeny-weeny as viruses."
Space mission researcher

))) "A Great Lie expertly crafted and installed in our minds through social media and fictional historical narratives where to even question the official narrative of modern heliocentric theoretical science deems you crazy by a compliant and obedient society."

CHAPTER 13

DEAR FLAT EARTHERS

> **To all Flat Earthers**
> Whoever you are.
> Wherever you are.
>
> Know that you're not alone.
> Every day there are more and more enlightened souls
> who are waking up to the Globe lie
> and are going through the same experience.
>
> Stay STRONG and keep fighting for the truth.
>
> **Because Flat Earth is the TRUTH!**

By Kan Ev Art

Congratulations to all those that woke up to the real Tru-man show. And thanks to the info soldiers that woke them. Finally, soldiers who actually fought for our freedom.

I couldn't be more happier at the amount of people waking up to flat earth and other conspiracies. The awakening era is indeed here. I see so many new flat earthers in the comment section on forums, who are saying the fake plandemic brought them to research flat earth and other conspiracies. If they can lie about this, what else can they lie about? And they're finding that, at the bottom of the rabbit hole, is the flat earth. And thus the numbers are growing.

I have seen more trolls, however, than middle-earth on flat earth Facebook groups that I'm a part of, and I don't mind saying, I have argued with my share of them, when I question their flying whirling ball Earth, with it's bendy oceans, they seem to think that I'm not suppose to do that, nor am I supposed to question the answers they give. In response, they call me names and call me a science denier.

I love the way one flat earther, obviously tired of the abuse and narrow mindedness, has put it when a globe believer calls the flat earth 'retarded.' He says:

"Typical glober. Closed mindedness makes ignorance a guarantee. So let me get this straight, you think a spinning, wobbling, open atmosphere, non vacuum ball flying through an endless vacuum of hostile space in the Goldie Locks zone is perfectly sane but a flat unmoving plane is retarded?"   AND SCENE!!!! Beautifully said!

I totally get the way he feels. Globers have called us everything under the sun. They have been harsh and close minded and everything despicable to us. They've done everything but prove their case. When you resort to attacking the messenger and not the message, you have lost the 'debate.' I only attack to defend. They have cheated themselves out of knowledge.

I'm around people that know I'm a flat earther and will use the words 'globe and 'planet' as many times as they can when talking to me. Sometimes I see it's on purpose and sometimes I'm not sure. I'm really not sure what they think they're trying to do, it's definitely not proof of anything. If they're trying to get under my skin, they're not. I pity them more than anything. I look at them and want so badly to ask, 'can you prove the theory behind that word?' But I know they can't. So I suffer through their babbling, and dumb down the conversation and play pretend, like a knowledgeable kid listening to his friends talk about Santa Claus. Shaking his head to get along.

If anyone seriously wants to know the truth, the flat earth proof is available to those that wish to confirm it for themselves using their own observation, thought, reason, logic and common sense. The flat levelness of water meets them on every coast and lake shore. Every horizon line always at their eye level to greet them on every flight. Star parallax never screws up the sky with squiggly lines, only beautiful circles. The sun shares its warmth as it passes by on its observable daily route, then getting cool as it leaves.

Here are a couple of examples all can do for themselves as one flat earther put it in a forum:

1) Go to the beach or a mountain top with unobstructed views. On a clear day at Sea-level you can see some 10 miles scanning from side to side and about 3 to 5 miles straight ahead. Basic spherical geometry says we should see at least 66 feet of curvature with a cresting ocean front and center of your viewing. Go up to the mountain top and estimate how far you can see. Multiply miles x miles x 8 inches divided by 12 to get the curvature. Do you see a curvature anywhere?

2) As you increase in altitude in an aircraft or hot air balloon, the horizon line does not fall away from your vision. The Earth never falls away from your eye yet the ground rises to meet your eye's viewpoint proving Earth is not a globe but a flat plane…as observed from the aero- plane!

Arguments VS DEBATING

I see a lot of flat earthers, when people question them, say "Go do your own research." This tells people you have no idea how to answer their questions. And it sends them to the disinformation that's put out there waiting for them to come across. They will find propaganda and fake flat earthers spreading lies. The best thing to do is to learn the reality that is the flat earth model and how to question the globe model. (Write your arguments down in your notepad for copying and pasting to save time.) The ball earther has to see that his model that he believes in is theoretical and does not match reality. Questioning is the only thing that's going to bring them to understand that. We all have been there. When they discover they have zero physical evidence, then the awakening could begin.

One ball earther sent me the top picture as "proof" one time. Can you believe that? This is someone who has put no effort into thinking about what he's posting. Another flat earth added a sheep to it later on. Lol

One cannot debate about physical reality. You can discuss it but not debate it. There's a chance for a winner in a debate. Example would be debating which place to go out and eat. There's a chance for a winner. But contained bodies of water are flat and there's no debating it. You either can disprove it or not. Physical reality says it is. But I do use the word "debate" instead of discuss because it's the most used word in the topic, but I use it loosely.

The ultimate ignorance is the rejection of something you know nothing about, yet refuse to investigate. People will make you think they want an intelligent conversation but when tried, they leave out the intelligent part. If you tell them a solid fact and they deflect it without even trying to discuss it, call them on it, don't let it go. If they persist, tell them to fuck off, they're not there for an intelligent conversation. Don't waste your time.

It's hard to have a fruitful discussion with someone who believes just the opposite of what they themselves see? They refuse to listen, then it becomes a waste of time. Example:

FEer: "Water is flat, horizon never lowers and Polaris never moves." (Then you show then the video of the ship being brought back with a high zoom camera, and pictures from a plane ride with the camera NOT tilting downward to see the horizon and then you show them time-lapse pictures of perfect star trail circles)

Glober: "You have no proof of your claims."

A waste of time but very necessary all the same. For the deceiving to stop, it will take the masses to stop buying into it and wake up. Simple as that. I'm looking for people who'll listen and think about what's being said and look at the physical reality, and stop believing in the Powers That Be's "Established Scientist" claims without proof.

I've talked to a college professor and even a science magazine author, and they talked down to me like they're coming from a place of superior knowledge then me, but they are getting their information from their priesthood. How do I know this? I just stumped them with deeper questions. They prove it to me when they can't prove what their leader claims. And all they give me is a circular argument and I call them on it and they get angry. Here's an example of their types of arguments:

If Travis said "Lloyd, Tom killed Tony."
Lloyd: "Travis can you prove that?"

Travis: "Tom picked up a rock and knocked him in the head."
Lloyd: "But Travis I need you to prove that."
Travis: "I'll give you the math because math doesn't lie. Tom picked up a rock weighting (a number) and swung it at (a number) speed. That speed and weight creates this much force. (Equation) A human skull can only handle this much pressure per square inch (another number). The pressure of the force of the rock is greater than the skull can handle. (Equation)."

So then Lloyd does the math and sure enough it works out. The rock force is greater than the skull can handle per square inch.
Lloyd: "Can you prove it happened though?"
Tom: "You're a science denier. You don't understand math"

But has Travis actually PROVEN anything? No. His math is built on the assumption that the murder took place in the first place like he said. He hasn't proven two things here. That Tom is the murderer or perhaps self defense or that there was even a murder. Where's the physical evidence? Would this math stand in the court of law? No, then why should it for us?

A circular argument that goes nowhere but wastes plenty of time. NASA, astronomers, and globe believers do this constantly. They can't prove their "proof."

(As to not leave you hanging on my exciting story, come to find out, Tony wasn't murdered, but bent over to pick up a wooden nickel, and fell head first into a anvil that someone left laying around, and cracking his melon open completely, and thus died of covid)

So my first tactic is to deny their mindset of a 'intellectual higher ground' with questions and more questions. We stop and expose their flow of lies with questions. The right questions and the demands for proof have stumped professors, teachers and average Joe's alike. We seek the truth while they constantly re-establish their dogmas, force-feeding people into accepting what they believe to be intellectually honest and scientific when, in fact, is religious dogma from scientism.

Teachers believe and repeat the same as everyone else. Before teaching children, one should make sure the claims are true or you're just dumbing down the next generation. You're just becoming a deceiver and don't even realize it. The Powers That Be have turned us against our own perceptions so that we become tools and guardians for our own enslavers and work as our own prison wardens. That is, until we awaken to the liberating, matrix destroying truth of the Flat Earth.

I love when discussing flat earth vs whirling ball earth, a lot of them will give their credentials and various degrees they've accumulated and then wait for a reply. But for what kind of reply exactly? For you to summit perhaps? A job or degree means absolutely nothing if it doesn't prove the world's a whirling ball does it? It's a sign of authoritarian worship. In people's heads, a job or "education" makes them an authoritarian. But I've meant homeless people that's more attune with the world than they are. To me, it's a form of deflecting their baseless beliefs that they have no way of proving, and talking about something else. Pathetic!

That their pronouncement that things are so is to be taken as proof in and of itself. Ahh no. I would be a fool to think so. There are people with 10 years in higher education that can't sense BS when it's presented to them, yet there are high-school dropouts who can decode what the government is doing and break through the propaganda. There are Mensa members with the highest IQs in the world and millions of college graduates that ran to get a vaccine with no long term testing. I rest my case.

It's like they're saying "I'm better than you because I paid for extra indoctrination." LMAO! I might not be the sharpest tool in the shed and my spalling is absalutily allful but I'm aware that bodies of contained water are flat and have never been proven otherwise.

When you have a ball earther tell you their credentials, ask them "how does your job/education prove the shape of the earth? What part of your job requires that the earth HAS to be a globe?" OR "Good I was hoping to speak to someone educated like yourself, could you please prove the whirling ball model? Could you give me your observable physical proof that the school has given you?" And then grab some popcorn and watch them start repeating unproven claims as if that, in itself, is proof enough. Question their answers and watch them do it again, enjoy yourself :) have fun with it. Show them their job and "education" is irrelevant to this subject. Tell them they should spend their comment time proving their stance, not trying to impress with a useless resume.

"Here's my link"

When ball earthers share links to government puppet websites, go to the link they shared and ask them questions about it and ask for proof of each said claim. When they can't answer, ask them why did they share it then? If you share a link to flat earth material (I highly recommend you do, because it bi-passes the disinformation agents out there) be prepared to talk about it. LEARN THE FLAT EARTH MODEL. You can't argue it otherwise, right? This is why the Flat Earth discussion is so important to discuss and analyze.

I see many who can't answer questions because they don't know the model that well. Seeing reality enough to know that the earth is indeed flat is one thing, but to argue against someone, who's spitting out indoctrinated claims he worships, as proof is another. Know that observable physical REALITY defeats unproven claims, and makes that work for you. Remember if reality doesn't match what they have said then they haven't said anything.

My suggestion is to read many flat earth books and watch flat earth videos that ONLY have real proof in them. Otherwise disregard them. PERIOD. I'll leave a recommendation list at the end of this book. Research and learn different approaches and arguments. Flatearthlogic.net is my website that I compiled, what I consider to be, good videos full of proofs.

The ball earthers in the field of astronomy should be ashamed of themselves. They, of all people, should know better. They are either two things; 1) They are repeaters. They've regurgitated some BS and got good grades and now do jobs that require no such skill that requires them to know the shape of the earth and never even question it or are just to stupid to figure it out. Or 2) They are completely lying, which means they are upper management and are in the need to know group. They infiltrate the higher education system.

Most are in group one. I've talked to people at Observatories and they seem to be reading a script, but are quick to say 'we do this' and 'we do that.' But when I questioned one, he said they get their data from NASA on what they're viewing. Hmm

The globe theory requires collective belief to exist because it has no physical reality to back it up. And it needs a complicity of people to help hold it up. But the flat earth truth is a spellbreaker, a liberator, and a reformer. People from all walks of life are waking up. Every person who leaves this globe matrix of lies is one less source to preach it and instead debunk it.

SHOW ME THE MATH

Yet the truth of it AGAIN: "Today's scientists have substituted mathematics for experiments, and they wander off through equation after equation, and eventually build a structure which has no relation to reality." Nikola Tesla

Most ball earthers will bring up math as they go to, with the saying "math doesn't lie." They do this because there's absolutely no physical evidence to back up their religion, so they resort to something they consider to be solid. But is it? It will not curved a line or change a physical fact. They should do curvature and star parallax experiments instead of math built on pretend.

Both models are possible in mathematics since math is a language that allows you to calculate and manipulate values and numbers. It's a way to present things.

Math and photographic astronomy can be taken and claimed in any kind of way. You can show pictures, fake or real, and claim any kind of distance or size. Mathematician's will make all kinds of claims with no merits whatsoever. Other mathematicians can make just the opposite claims in this clown show we call "science." Math claims are authoritatively said by someone and authoritatively denied by someone else.

I'll quote author Charles Fort here: "Anybody who dreams of a mathematician's heaven had better reconsider, if, of its angels, there be more than one mathematician."

Pure mathematics is architecture, it has no place in astronomy. It's simply arbitrary, solely built on assumptions and speculations. Again, it will not curved a line or change a physical fact. Every number in an equation stands for something. Whatever that something is, it has to be proven or the math is worthless.

When I first became a flat earther and ball earthers brought up math, I got a little nervous, not knowing how to reply, ohhh but now I wish they would. The low effort thinkers.

Dear flat earthers, ask the ball earthers for this math:
) Give me the numbers for curved water.
) Give me the numbers for how the distance of the sun was found out without using assumptions.
) Give me the numbers for curved earth then research long distance photography and explain your findings.
) Give me the numbers for an horizon line that rises with you yet supposedly drops downward.
) Give me the numbers that explains how military sonar testing can cover 1000s of miles on a ball.
) Give me the numbers that answer why the earth spins under the pendulum but not the helicopter or plane, THAT IS when it spins in the correct direction.
) Give me numbers on the curvature that's supposed to be on 100 mile bridges and canals but is not.

So don't let math equations intimate you, just beg them to prove their math. They can't. Watch them look down at their big red shoes trying to figure out how.

People can change their mind

People can and are changing their minds. The numbers of flat earthers are proving that. We used to believe the Earth was a whirling ball before we snapped out of the belief system they had us in. I have a video on my YouTube account that shows scientists in Brazil doing experiments trying to prove the earth curved but instead proving the opposite. Scientists have changed their mind in the past as well. Here's a few examples:

Professor Herbert Dingle believed in the theory of relativity then he later realized that it was only supported by math built on assumptions not by scientific experiments.

He states "Not only are hypotheses held to contain the 'real truth'; it is now claimed that any (mathematical) hypothesis is necessarily true." "In the language of mathematics we can tell lies as well as truths, and within the scope of mathematics itself there is no possible way of telling one from the other." And this sums up the theory of relativity.

Other scientists did not go for it either: "Einstein's relativity work is a magnificent mathematical garb which fascinates, dazzles and makes people blind to the underlying errors. The theory is like a beggar clothed in purple in whom ignorant people take for a king...it's exponents are brilliant men but they are metaphysicists rather than scientists." Nikola Tesla

"Heretics were the good guys – the heroes who stood against all odds in confronting the powerful establishment. We have been taught to think negatively about heretics, but that was wrong. With the correct definition of "heresy," we can understand that it is NOT right to suppress independent thought. We should not support the establishment (any establishment) which suppresses the freedom of conscience. And we should be grateful to all the heretics who had the guts and moral courage to stand against this tyranny in the past." Unknown

All good lies have a sprinkle of truth, that is what makes a lie believable but a lie is a lie nonetheless. I suggest we let the NASA bedtime stories for the round earthers. We, the flat earthers, must do what we do best: Look at the evidence.

A lot of the books I recommend a little later are from scientists going against the establishment.

CHAPTER 14
EVOLUTION

The Evolution Of Blind Acceptance

"Out of the cradle, on to dry land here it is standing, atoms with consciousness, matter with curiosity," Richard Feynman American theoretical physicist

I wasn't going to write a chapter about evolution in this flat earth book but I decided to at least mention a few points on it. This chapter may not be about flat earth but both subjects point to a Creator and some huge deceptions.

These are not the bones you are looking for

Some say it's religious dogma to acknowledge God's existence? If that's so, as one scientist puts it, excluding God as a possibility seems no less dogmatic. A cake doesn't make itself. Going by evolution logic, you can't prove the cake was made if no one steps up and admits it. But you can put all the ingredients in a pile and the cake will never form, must less come alive. The proof of the cake being made is in front of you. No one walks into a room and sees a cake and says "Someone must have spilled a primordial soup and this delicious thing formed." That takes faith.

We have been bamboozled into believing that we are talking monkeys on a spinning wobbling flying ball without any evidence whatsoever provided. Now once again, when I say no evidence what I mean is actually proven evidence, something that doesn't require faith or fraud. So how about evolution? What's the solid evidence for evolution? Where and who does it come from? The reason I ask is because there has been some naughty business with evolution, same as the heliocentric globe model. Like the ball earth, if evolution is true, then there's no need to fake it.

They will find a few teeth and come up with a huge creature, with the sound effects and everything. Pseudo-science in its full form. If something is scientific, it is observable and testable and able to be repeated.

"We are told dogmatically that Evolution is an established fact; but we are never told who has established it, and by what means. We are told, often enough, that the doctrine is founded upon evidence, and that indeed this evidence 'is henceforward above all verification, as well as being immune from any subsequent contradiction by experience;' but we are left entirely in the dark on the crucial question wherein, precisely, this evidence consists." Robert E. Smith, a member of the western Missouri affiliate of the American Civil Liberties Union

If evolution was a fact, there would have to be missing links for humans and all other creatures. And there are claims of missing links found you might say. How exciting huh? Let's have a look at some "scientists" and their "found" fossils shall we. (Remember, I'm not saying I don't trust science, it's the assumptions that are mixed in with it by biased scientists, I don't trust. The theory of evolution is based on several faulty premises which

The Zetetic Method

are clearly contradicted by observation and common sense. Like one scientist said "Evolution implies chaos and meaninglessness. Creation implies order and value.")

) Let's look at the Piltdown man. Scientists held up this skull with the big jaw bone claiming it was proof of Darwinism. They put it in a museum and started teaching it in public schools. 40 years down the road independent scientists got a hold of it to find it was the skull of a man and jaw of an orangutan dipped in chemicals to age it and the teeth were filed. Obviously done by someone intelligent.

The great Piltdown hoax

A straight out hoax by scientists pushing evolution. Scientists went and looked into his other "evidence" and found 38 clear hoaxes. The web we weave.

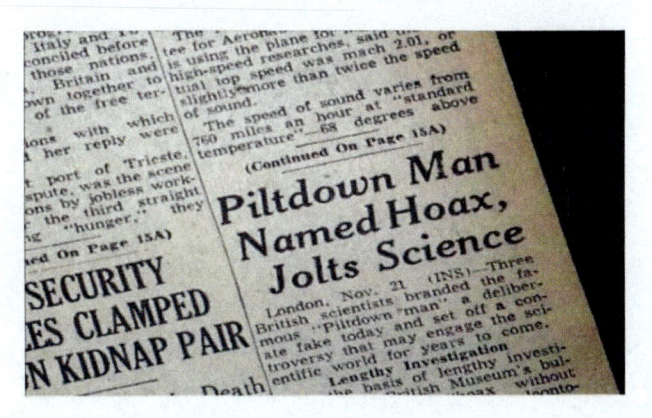

) Then there's the Nebraskan man. Another shameless attempt gone bad. Theories based on a tooth claimed to me the missing link's tooth; but once the tooth was later found out to be a pig's tooth, the tooth suddenly disappeared but the theories are still here and taught to children. Why is this ok with the public?

) And there's Lucy. When Lucy was found, she was kept from other scientists for 8 years. Later she was found to be just another ape. Overseas in France a science article comes out titled "Goodbye Lucy" saying it's been shown to be just an ape, while in America a documentary comes out stating Lucy is proof of Darwinism.

406

There's even a movie pushing this lie of Lucy being the missing link. ("missing" being the key word here. They have to entertain people with the idea of evolution, dinosaurs and a whirling ball earth because they have no physical evidence.)

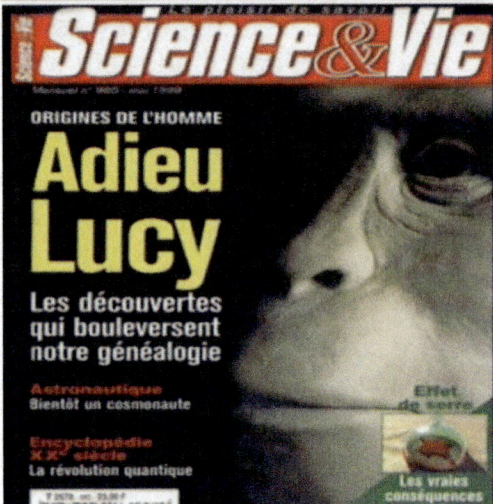

Here's pictures of the bones found and a model of the guesswork on how Lucy looked.

) Another BS evolution claim was in a Spanish town in 1882, where part of a small skull was found and said to be one of the oldest at 900,000 to 1 million years old. French scientists had a look at it and it was a baby donkey's skull.

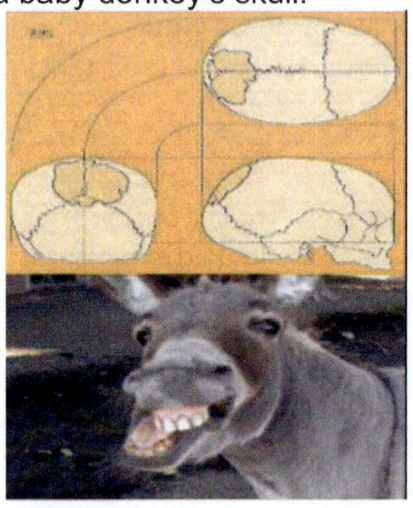

) Let's continue with Professor Ernest Haeckel who was caught faking evidence for evolution, which was called Haeckel's fraud, and his defense was "Other evolutionists have committed similar offenses." Hmmm!

) One German Professor Reimer Prashant claimed carbon dating dated fossils at 36,000 years old, but in 2005, a panel of Frankfurt University heads found out his evidence was fraudulent and fossils were around a few 1000s years old.

Dr. A.J. White Physical Chemistry "As a chemist I could see that the accuracy of any dating methods relied on a number of assumptions, some of which are unprovable and others unknowable........

The assumption of evolution is, therefore, the main evidence for evolution.

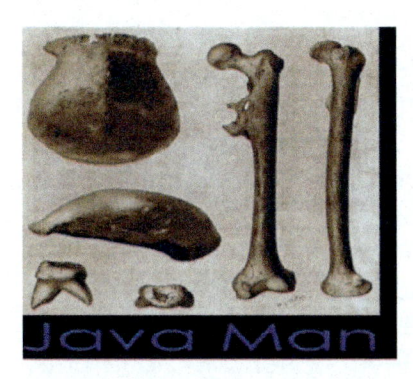

) Java Man by Eugene Dubois, a student of Ernest Haeckel, found some fossils, bones and teeth, and, within 10 years, was in scores of books, articles, etc. But come to find out the teeth were of different ages, the bones belong to different sexes of different apes. The find was kept from peer review for 30 years. But when finally looked at by other scientists it was proven yet another hoax. The thigh bone being human while the skull and teeth belong to apes. Hmm. If you have curvature, I mean fossil evidence, you don't have to fake any. And why not let other scientists peer review it? Can you guess what I'm going to say? Truth fears no investigation!!!

) One scientist claims dinosaur bones were just bones of different animals. Natural Geographic, who did a piece on it, had to later admit their article on these dinosaur fossils were man made.

) Another fossil fraud was in 1999. The Archaeoraptor, promoted by National Geographic to be the true missing link, was later found to be a bird fossil with what was claimed to be a dinosaur fossil.

Scientific American
www.scientificamerican.com

How Fake Fossils Pervert Paleontology [Excerpt]

Nov 15, 2014 — Archaeoraptor was soon dubbed the 'Piltdown bird' and the 'Piltdown chicken' by the press, in reference to the biggest fossil hoax of all time, ...

The evolution "Tree of Life" is built on assumptions and speculations. It's filled with missing links and fraudulent "evidence". There's many disagreements surrounding the evolutionary tree among evolutionists scientists. If scientists went off solid physical evidence, then there would be far less of that.

From James Perloff's book "The Case Against Darwin" he states "One comic pointed out: 'The princess kissed the frog, and he turned into a handsome prince. We call it a fairy tale. Darwin says frogs turn into princes, and we call it science."

There are others but you get my drift. That's why I ask, where and who provides the "evidence" of evolution. And, despite what people claim, 99% of scientists do not agree with evolution, but we'll get to those in a little while. Only the ones they're pushing to the cameras and some of the sheople scientists with degrees in repeating. ;)

WORLD'S LEADING BIOLOGIST, RICHARD DAWKINS, SHOWS HIS COMPELLING EVIDENCE FOR EVOLUTION... A CARTOON OF WHALES WITH FEET.

PROFESSING THEMSELVES TO BE WISE, THEY BECAME FOOLS - ROMANS 1:22

"As an undergraduate, I was taught to remember, not to think. Sure, I was given tools which I could use to think, but I wasn't actually taught to think. Then, as a Ph.D. researcher I worked in a very narrow field (as do all Ph.D. researchers), and so the breadth of a question like "What is the definition of scientific?" was absolutely irrelevant to me. Upon graduation and working as a research scientist for 17 years and as a leader of other scientists, the question has never arisen, nor apparently needed to have been asked. My point is that most scientists don't really know what is or isn't scientific, because it rarely affects what they do."   Stephen Grocott Inorganic Chemistry

So, in this chapter, we're going to have another look at a huge deception that many of us bought, me included. I was an evolution ball earth believing atheist when I awakened up to flat earth, which made me research creation science which made me question the theory of evolution a lot more deeper. That's when I discovered more lies about who we are and where we're at.

It's a matter of matter being intelligent

"Supposing there was no intelligence behind the universe, no creative mind. In that case, nobody designed my brain for the purpose of thinking. It is merely that when the atoms inside my skull happen, for physical or chemical reasons, to arrange themselves in a certain way, this gives me, as a by-product, the sensation I call thought. But, if so, how can I trust my own thinking to be true? It's like upsetting a milk jug and hoping that the way it splashes itself will give you a map of London. But if I can't trust my own thinking, of course I can't trust the arguments leading to Atheism, and therefore have no reason to be an Atheist, or anything else. Unless I believe in God, I cannot believe in thought: so I can never use thought to disbelieve in God" C.S. Lewis on Reasoning to Atheism

At what point does matter gain/create consciousness? How can matter execute anything other than stillness and decay? When we dream our imagination creates matter and characters and dialog (within our consciousness), but when we have to wake up because we're physical creatures, it all goes away. But what if God is the only consciousness that can create and doesn't have to wake up? Just a thought, but not an impossible one, because we do it every night.

Why are we the highest conscious animal on this plain and no other? Shouldn't there be others if evolution is true? Why us? We're the only creature called "beings".

Life is intelligent, dead matter is not, therefore life requires an 'intelligent' explanation not a material one. How can mindless mass develop a body, with the measurements of the legs, arms, toes and fingers so perfectly done, and not have directions? So many body parts in twos with excellent measurements. It's a legit question. It would have to think of a reason and a plan, a design.

As Dr. Ariel A. Roth said: "How could these develop without the foresight of a plan for a working system? Can order arise from the turmoil of mixed-up, undirected changes? For complicated organs that involve many necessary changes, the chances are implausibly small. Without the foresight of a plan, we would expect that the random evolutionary changes would attempt all kinds of useless combinations of parts while trying to provide for a successful evolutionary advancement. Yet as we look at living organisms over the world, we do not seem to see any of these random combinations. In nature, it appears that we are dealing largely, if not exclusively, with purposeful parts. Furthermore, if evolution is a real ongoing process, why don't we find new developing complex organs in organisms that lack them? We would expect to find developing legs, eyes, livers, and new unknown kinds of organs, providing for evolutionary advancement in organisms that lacked desirable advantages."

Machines are fussy things, always wanting all the parts to function. Cells and living organisms are bio-machines, they also require numerous parts to work otherwise it is useless.

Imagine a lizard evolving into a hummingbird. Its wings are fully evolved but the peak is not. Poor thing, hovering above a flower but can't do anything with it. Or its peak is fully functional but can't make it to the flower. OH think of the stress it would have. Luckily there's no evidence that this poor creature ever existed. No fossils of feathers with primitive scales almost gone or scales with feathers starting to protrude from them were found. Just a hummingbird and another creature, the lizard.

The bombardier beetle sprays its victims with a mixture of chemicals that creates acid. The beetle has separate compartments in its body so it won't fry itself in the process. Author and Dr. Andrew McIntosh talks about the bombardier beetle in the matter of missing parts:

"All of the above requirements would have to be in place at the same "evolutionary moment"! There is no way any "intermediate" could survive because of the risk of either (1) blowing him/herself to smithereens (because he has the combustible mixture and the catalyst, but no exhaust system), or (2) slowly eroding his/her insides by having a combustible mixture, all the necessary exhaust tubes, but no catalyst, or (3) being eaten by predators despite trying to blow them away with catalysts through a fine exhaust system, but no combustible mixture! For the creature to function, everything must all be in place together — as a good Rolls Royce engineer knows — for aircraft gas turbines to work!

Which came first, the need for food or the digestive system? At what point does matter think 'I might need food, let me build a digestive system because it takes 1000s or millions of years to make this system that I somehow already know how to make?' How did it get the kick start and know how? These are good questions. Think about them. At what point does matter suddenly or gradually have to eat, and when it does it has to build a digestive system which takes how long? Or why would it build one if it didn't need food? And if it couldn't survive without food then it wouldn't live long enough to build one over millions of years or whatever the ridiculous number the claim is now.

THE MOST ADVANCED MACHINE ON EARTH AND THEY WILL TELL YOU IT HAD NO DESIGNER

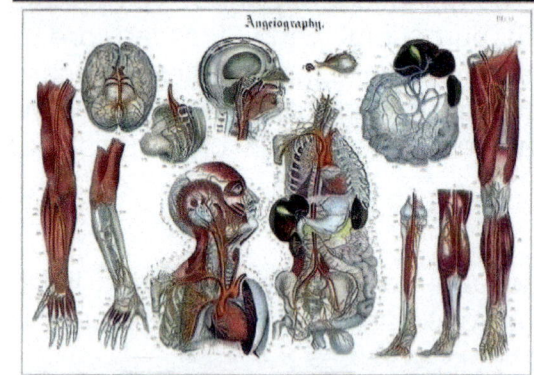

How about the digestive acid, track, etc, did this evolve at the same speed as the stomach, and how did the lifeless matter that somehow developed life, know how to do this? Where did this blueprint come from and how was the data passed on? Reproducing passes on these blueprints, but they had to come from somewhere.

How can non-conscious mindless matter produce morals, happiness, sadness, love and hate? And how is it necessary for survival? If it's to find a mate then why not become a self producing organism so you have no worries with getting laid? If it can do all these magnificent things with no consciousness or programmer, then why not that?

What I'm asking is legit questions. Where is the evidence that matter is self creating, or that it can self-organize into living organisms, or that rational consciousness can emerge from non-conscious matter, or how moral realities can emerge from mindless natural matter?

Does anyone think that a computer could create itself? We're more complex than a computer. Rocks were created naturally but the Great Wall of China was not. If life is ever created in a lab, that would also be an intelligent creator.

Physical reality shows that life has some direction or goal in mind, a great heresy to those who believe evolution.

Darwin's assumptions

Darwinism of course was never proven. The fittest survive. What exactly does that mean, the fittest? It's not the strongest; it's not the cleverest— weakness and stupidity is literally everywhere and survives. A caterpillar is weaker and not as clever as a fox, yet both remain and flourish. Each having its own role in the circle of life.

Now, don't get me wrong, I understand natural selection, I realize the slow deer gets eaten first and the low effort thinker, trusting his government, gets depopulated with the clot shot, but that doesn't change a lizard into a bird or a monkey into a human being does it? No, it does not. It doesn't turn a fish into a horse, no more than a 'shooting star' wraps a flat ocean into a ball and whirls it.

If we are nothing but stardust, a set of chemicals and matter resulting from great supernovas, what brought that dust to life? Did it come alive all by itself? How? To me, the more I ask myself these questions, the more illogical their theory becomes.

Science demonstrates that over time organisms lose genetic information, not gain it. Information can't write itself. There is no known observable process by which new genetic information can be added to the genetic code of an organism. Then how can evolution take place? How can a rock become an ape and then a human being without adding new genetic information?

How does complex DNA-coded language become in existence? How is this knowledge created? As Professor Gitt said, "No information can exist without an initial mental source. No information can exist in purely statistical processes."

In Dr. Lee Spetner good book titled "Not by Chance: Shattering the Modern Theory of Evolution" he states "In all the reading I've done in the life-sciences literature, I've never found a mutation that added information.....All point mutations that have been studied on the molecular level turn out to reduce the genetic information and not increase it."

This matches physical reality as well. You don't hear the doctor say "your child has a mutation and it's absolutely wonderful, you'll be thrilled with it." Mutations delete information from the genetic code, never create higher, more complex information.

An organism will grow thicker fur or thick soles on its feet etc., but it will not become another creature altogether. You have a polar bear in the coolest climate, then you have brown bears and grizzlies in warmer climates, then you have black bear in even warmer climates, then you have Spanish black bear in the hot climates. But you still have a bear. It doesn't turn into a desert snake or whatever. Prove me wrong.

What proof do we have that lizards turned into birds? Wouldn't it need genetics to do this? Where is the thought process coming from? There is no structure in reptile scales that support feathers and no missing link to show there ever was. Why aren't reptiles turning into birds now? Why stop? All we truly have is a full cold blooded lizard and a full warm blooded bird, no in-betweens, no connection made with either creature. What proof do they have of these extraordinary claims?

The Zetetic Method

What Is "Intelligent Design"?

Intelligent design refers to a scientific research program as well as a community of scientists, philosophers and other scholars who seek evidence of design in nature. The theory of intelligent design holds that **certain features of the universe and of living things are best explained by an intelligent cause**, not an undirected process such as natural selection.

Through the study and analysis of a system's components, a design theorist is able to determine **whether various natural structures are the product of chance, natural law, intelligent design,** or some combination thereof. Such research is conducted by observing the types of information produced when intelligent agents act. Scientists then seek to find objects which have those same types of informational properties which we commonly know come from intelligence.

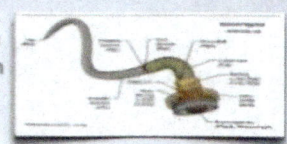

INTELLIGENT DESIGN THEORY
The study of patterns in nature that are best explained as the result of intelligence

---

Intelligent design proponents believe "there is good evidence that some features of nature--like the intricate molecular motors within cells and the finely-tuned laws of physics--are best explained as the products of an intelligent cause, not chance and necessity."

John G. West, "UPDATE: Sun Sentinel Suppresses Accurate Definition of Intelligent Design,"
http://www.evolutionnews.org/2006/02/orlando_sentinel_suppresses_ac.html

---

All the different kinds of humans fit their environment, but they're still humans, they aren't turning into something else. Monkeys fit their environment, and they're still here. No in-betweens? Hmmm! Monkeys and humans are thriving but no missing links are found. Does anyone else find that odd? It's been suggested that perhaps the next stage killed the last stage and so on but that doesn't change the missing link being missing does it? And humans have been living next to monkeys for how long now? How did monkeys last this long but no other? Why are they still here? We MUST recognize a BS story when we hear it.

Not only are there no missing links for human beings but for all animals too. There has to be missing links for everything. Think about it. Where's the missing link for the elephants, horses, ostrich, etc., etc., etc., etc...............There should be millions of missing

The Zetetic Method

links, but instead all animals are found whole and complete, no half-devolved legs, wings, etc. Oh what solid evidence do we have for such a claim that we come from a primordial soup? Where can I find it? Is it behind the missing curvature?

Why else would they fake it if it's out there? Piltdown man, Nebraska man and Lucy, etc. How can they tell you what happened millions or billions of years ago, they can't even figure out 9-11 was an [I'm whispering here] inside job? A lot of them fell for the covid scam. I hold no stock in puppet scientists or repeating sheep "scientists."

Darwin, in his book "Origin of Species," admitted that the lack of the missing link fossils were a problem and was hoping they'd find them in the future. I encourage people to read that book or any evolution book and any globe book and think about what is being said and question it deeply. Ask yourself how much of it is built on assumptions and how much is actually proven. Truth fears no investigation but others do. I'm encouraging you to investigate, but use your brain to question it WHILE you do it.

"If evolution has proceeded over the eons of time postulated, we should expect a great number of intermediates between the major types of organisms, but we can scarcely find any. Charles Darwin was fully aware of the problem and openly admitted to it in his Origin of Species, stating, "Why then is not every geological formation and every stratum full of such intermediate links? Geology assuredly does not reveal any such finely graduated organic chain; and this, perhaps, is the most obvious and gravest objection that can be urged against my theory." Dr. Ariel A. Roth Biology

People should have no fear of backlash for questioning theories or the scientists that present them. If science and scientists alike are about truth, then they shouldn't fear the investigation of it.

Author Robbie Davidson in his book "Scientism Exposed" put it nicely: "The problem remains for the Agnostic, Atheist and Anti-theist—if there never was a Creator there could not have been any creation, yet we have a verifiable creation. To put it simply, 0 x 0 can never = 1. Those who posit a Creatorless universe cannot explain how matter and energy just happened to exist [acknowledging that these are fundamentally two forms of the same phenomenon]. Matter and energy lack the ability to create themselves.

Something with a conscious will and amazing power had to precede them in reality, and create the most fundamental building blocks of existence. Those who at present do not believe must conclude that random coincidence caused random events through infinitely long periods of time to enable random mutations which caused the first cell which through statistically inconceivable amounts of time led to humankind. They assert this even though it violates the Second Law of Thermodynamics or entropy."

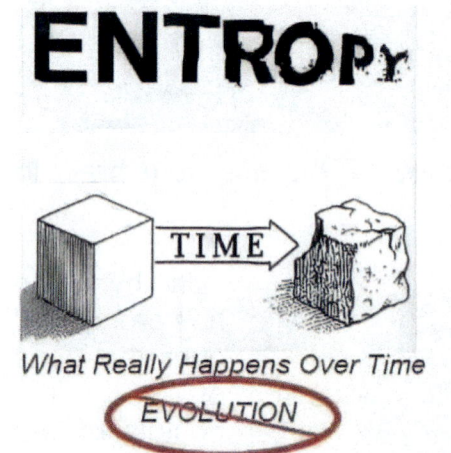

An American evolutionary biologist named Richard Lewontin claimed "Evolution is a fact. Birds arose from nonbirds and humans from nonhumans. No person who pretends to any understanding of the natural world that can deny these facts any more than she or he can deny that the earth is round, rotates on its axis, and revolves around the sun." Now that seems like one of those things you have to prove when you say it. But it never is. Perhaps some CGI images would help prove it.

Atheists, like ball earthers (I used to be both), cling ever so tightly to the impossible. A small dot that went BANG!! and expanded into chaos which, luckily for us, settled into predictable order. Then slowly and mindlessly, became what we see today. A world where everything is perfectly designed for life; everything in its correct location for the perfect temperature in this ecosystem to sustain life. Where each creature has its role and reproductive system and immune system, both seeming to do their own thing with a know how. Where consciousness, thoughts and feelings are created out of............?

If doing nothing caused the Big Bang then wouldn't it be happening now? I wonder, if I created a bang, would something come out of it as marvelous as life.

Here's a GREAT quote and point from Dr. Ker C. Thomson Geophysics on the second law of Thermodynamics:

"We simply note that one of the surest generalizations in all of physics and chemistry is the second law of thermodynamics which, as we have already shown, completely devastates any idea that matter unaided by mind or outside involvement will proceed to higher levels of organization.

Now we come to the evolutionists' quibble that the second law was different in the past from now. This is simply an adult wish fulfillment on the part of the evolutionist espousing such notions. Unless he assumes what he is trying to prove, he is left at this point with no reliable evidence to support his thesis. Science relies on measurements. Measurements we make now oppose evolution totally. To point for support to conditions in the distant past, where they can't be measured, puts the evolutionists in the same intellectual camp as those who believe in the tooth fairy.

Despite the arguments against evolution presented above and particularly in the last paragraph, the evolutionist clinging to his faith may say "Well, we are here, aren't we?" One may point out to him that he has just finished engaging in circular reasoning. That is, he has obviously attempted to support evolution by assuming that evolution is true and is what has led to his human existence and presence here.

When the circularity of his reasoning is pointed out to him, the evolutionist may then grope for evidence in the fossil record. But again he is trotting out another batch of circular reasoning. This is so because evolution is used to interpret the fossil record, so it cannot be used to justify evolution. To do so puts the proponent in the intellectual booby hatch. Whatever the explanation for the fossil record may be, it cannot be one that in effect denies the second law of thermodynamics.

In fact, the most obvious feature of the fossil record is not upward synthesis but rather death and decay. We find strong evidence for the steady loss of species within the fossil record. This is more in consonance with the second law of thermodynamics than with the upward growth posited by evolution."

You can dress up and put on cologne all you want, but
that doesn't make dating carbon a "sure thing"

"I once asked how sedimentary rocks were dated and was told by "indicator fossils." When I followed with "how were indicator fossils dated," I was told, "by the rock formations they are found in." Try as I might, the teacher could not see that this was circular reasoning!" Dr. Evan Jamieson Chemist Hydrometallurgy

Scientists have stated that the first living cells emerged between 4 and 3.8 billion years ago. But there's no proof or record of this event. How would they even come up with such a claim? Better yet, why would we even believe it? Some scientists don't even trust carbon dating. The dates can vary and are not always reliable.

Question: How do you debunk carbon dating?

Answer: Find door knobs embedded in a 300 million year old coal formation.

As one scientist said: "They use carbon dating ... to prove that something was millions of years old. Well, we have the eruption of Mt. Saint Helens and the carbon dating test that they used then would have to then prove that these were hundreds of millions of years younger, when what happened was they had the exact same results on the fossils and canyons that they did the tests on that were supposedly 100 millions of years old. And it's the kind of inconsistent tests like this that they're basing their "facts" on."

Dr. Edmond W. Holroyd Meteorology: "For now we have numerous examples in which radiometric dating gives the wrong answers, such as 13 to 3 million years for Mount St. Helens lava, historically dated at about 20 years old. Potassium-argon dating, upon which most of the geologic column and especially hominid fossils are dated, is particularly prone to "excessive argon" which gives inflated ages."

https://www.siliconrepublic.com › innovatio...

Carbon dating accuracy called into question after major flaw discovery

In a paper published to the Proceedings of the National Academy of Sciences, the team led by archaeologist Stuart Manning identified variations in the **carbon** 14 cycle at certain periods of time...

https://reasons.org › explore › publications ...

How Trustworthy is Carbon Dating? - Reasons to Believe

First developed by W. F. Libby and others in 1949, radiocarbon **dating** revolutionized archaeology-- and other scientific fields--by establishing robust dates for organic materials of a biological origin like wood, bone, or shell. **Carbon**-14 (14 C) is a naturally occurring radioisotope of **carbon** and is found in trace amounts on Earth.

https://www.smithsonianmag.com › science...

Thanks to Fossil Fuels, Carbon Dating Is in Jeopardy. One Scientist May ...

To radiocarbon date an organic material, a scientist can measure the ratio of remaining **Carbon**-14 to the unchanged **Carbon**-12 to see how long it has been since the material's source died

GUIDE TO CREATION BASICS

Did you know?

Mount St. Helens deposited over 600 feet of sedimentary layers in only a few hours, showing that it doesn't take millions of years.

CARBON -14 DATING IS NOT RELIABLE.

WE HAVE A LOWER LEG OF A MAMMOTH DATING AT 15,380 YEARS OLD, WHILE ITS SKIN DATES 21,300 YEARS OLD.

Biologist Gary Parker, who's articles and website I love to read, talks about his experience in college that turned him from evolutionist to creationist: "In one graduate class, the professor told us we didn't have to memorize the dates of the geologic system since they were far too uncertain and conflicting. Then in geophysics we went over all of the assumptions that go into radiometric dating. Afterward, the professor said, "If a fundamentalist ever got hold of this stuff, he would make havoc out of the radiometric dating system. So, keep the faith." That's what he told us. "Keep the faith.""

Starfish and jellyfish fossils are said to be 100s of millions of years old, but they're still here. Where's the evolution here? Is there solid proof?

The coelacanth fish fossils were found in "Jurassic" rock and said to be extinct for 70 million years, but as physical evidence would have it, it's still around and in fishermen's nets. And it is in complete form just like the fossil. Unreliable carbon dating and false claims go hand and hand.

It seems carbon dating is only used if the answer benefits the narrative.

prehistoricfossils.com
https://prehistoricfossils.com › starfi...

Fossil Starfish for Sale – Brittle Stars too!

The fossil record for starfish is ancient, dating back to the Ordovician around 450 million years ago. Starfish fossils are rare, as starfish tend to ...

shop.minimuseum.com
https://shop.minimuseum.com › fos...

Fossil Starfish

Starfish have existed in the fossil record for hundreds of millions of years, making them one of the oldest groups of animals on the...

I was on a cave tour in Sequoia National Park once when the guide said that it was once claimed that a certain formation took millions of years, so they put up a sign saying so. Later however, other scientists found out it took thousands of years so a new sign went up. Then later on, they found out it didn't take long at all and took down the sign and replaced it with nothing. I then researched this and found this, to my delight, from Dr. Keith H. Wanser professor of physics: "A sign above the entrance until 1988 said the caverns were at least 260 million years old. In recent years, the age on the sign was reduced to 7–10 million years, then 2 million years, and now the sign is gone — perhaps as a result of observations that stalactite growth rates of several inches a month are common.

In May 1998 I observed stalactites longer than six inches growing from the edge of the concrete boarding platform at the Arlington, Virginia, metro rail station, which was only completed in June 1991."

So why claim it in the beginning? Don't get me wrong, I understand about "new information found" and all of that, but if we went off physical facts then more claims would be based on facts and not guesswork. Here's an example:

The Big Bang, Bolton Davidheiser, Ph. D. "The Big Bang idea began with astronomer Georges Lemaitre. According to Isaac Asimov, Lemaitre conceived this mass to be "no more than a few light-years in diameter." (at least 12 trillion miles). By 1965 that figure was reduced to 275 million miles, by 1972 to 71 million miles, by 1974 to 54 thousand miles, by 1983 to "a trillionth the diameter of a proton", and now, to nothing at all! A singularity!"

Scientists seem to have a problem with saying "I don't know." It takes an intelligent person to say those words. I guess it's easier to look intelligent than to actually be intelligent. And repeating is not intelligence. Here's a prime example of what I mean. Here's a quote from a low effort thinker that believes his theories though he can't prove or observe any of them. All he can truly do is repeat, like a parrot that has been trained to do so. He is simply a clown on a pedestal for the world to clap at and follow. "Evolution as such is no longer a theory for a modern author. It is as much a fact as that the Earth revolves around the sun." Ernst Mayr

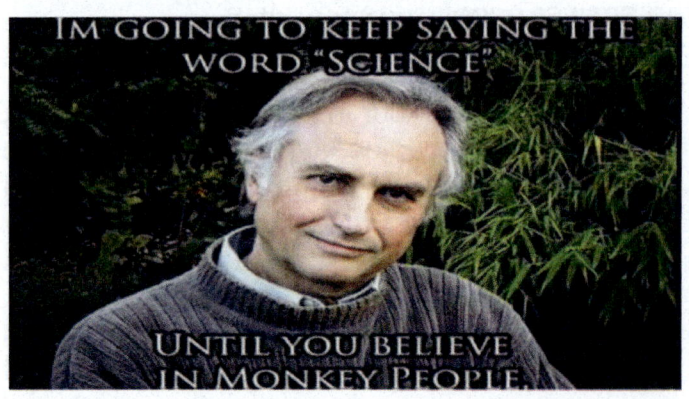

Here's someone who I used to like very much when I was sleeping while awake, Richard Dawson. I've read a few of his books, one being "The God Delusion." Now I realize who is really having a delusion.

Richard Dawkins "Put Your Money on Evolution" in New York Times says: "It is absolutely safe to say that if you meet someone who claims not to believe in evolution, that person is ignorant, stupid, or insane (or wicked, but I'd rather not consider that.)"

In his book Selfish Genes, we hear about survival of the fittest. But are we sure of this? People give to help without anything in return all the time, no selfishness there. As the point, scientist Stephen Grocott made: "If no one created me, if I am just highly evolved pond scum, then surely I am my own authority. Who or what determines right or wrong? Isn't it just relative? Isn't it different for different people and changing as society evolves? If I can get away with something for my benefit (i.e., for my evolutionary advantage), if genes are "selfish" as I have been taught, then why not push beyond the limits? Why care about the poor people, the old, the maimed, the victims in other countries? Why not abort the babies in utero, why not kill the old and useless, why not kill the dumb ones and also the unemployed if we have enough machines to do the labor? If there are no absolutes (i.e., set by something outside man and not by man) then why not agree with one Australian philosopher (working at an Australian University) who proposes infanticide for excess children? How can you logically argue against this if man really does set his own rules? I know that at the moment this is against man's rules but man's rules change. Remember, a generation ago abortion and euthanasia were both illegal and taboo subjects."

"Those details that become commonly accepted as "facts" are often changed in light of more recent discoveries. This has happened on numerous occasions, with little notice that the supposed prior facts were not facts at all. In other words, there is not one theory of evolution, but a body of opinions, speculations, and methods for interpretation of observational facts so that they fit into the philosophy of naturalism." Dr. Keith H. Wanser professor of physics

The Zetetic Method

Having almost the same DNA can have dogs and other canines breeding and different breeds of horses and donkeys can breed, and so on and so on. But can humans and monkeys breed? No, even though they share the same amount of DNA, 98%, as wolves and dogs share. Why not? Maybe because monkeys are the first link. Maybe humans can breed with the last link instead. Oh no wait, they're not here. They left and took all evidence of their existence with them. I guess we'll never know. We can have faith though in government scientists. I'm sure they wouldn't lie about it. Look at these similar percentages from two different web searches.

Dogs and wolves have many outward similarities. After all, the two species descend from a common ancestor. In fact **the two species share 98.8% of the same DNA**. They can even interbreed (although their offspring are typically not fertile).

https://schertzanimalhospital.com › ...
Dogs and Wolves: More Different Than They are Alike?

Humans and chimps share a surprising 98.8 percent of their DNA. How can we be so similar--and yet so different?

https://www.amnh.org › permanent
Comparing Chimp, Bonobo and Human DNA | AMNH

The lonely cell

Dr. John P. Marcus Biochemistry puts it nicely: "Truly, the thought of even one single functional protein arising by chance requires blind faith that will not or cannot grasp the numbers! Such thoughts are pure fantasy and have nothing to do with science.... The stories that are put forward are like fairy tales with some science thrown in to make them sound educated.

Our hypothetical nucleic acid synthesis system is therefore analogous to the scaffolding used in the construction of a building. After the building has been erected the scaffolding is removed, leaving no physical evidence that it was ever there. Most of the statements in this section must therefore be taken as educated guesses. Without having witnessed the event, it seems unlikely that we shall ever be certain of how life arose."

a·bi·o·gen·e·sis
/ˌābīōˈjenəsəs/
noun

1. the original evolution of life or living organisms from inorganic or inanimate substances.
"to construct any convincing theory of abiogenesis, we must take into account the condition of the Earth about 4 billion years ago"

2. HISTORICAL
old term for spontaneous generation.

Living organisms are only produced by other living organisms of the same kind. Abiogenesis is the theory that life can come from non-life. Evolutionists believe this happened at the 'beginning' of life. This of course can't be recreated and has no evidence. Wouldn't it be happening now?

Some scientists say that some cells being alike in all species is one proof of evolution. Is it though? Seems like a bold statement. A library is full of different books, all created, that have different subject matter, different pictures, different meanings and messages, but all are made of the same material and the same alphabet. Some are powerful classic books, others not so much, some are only mediocre yawns used for door stops or gag gifts, like this book here. But they all are created using the same material and alphabet. Paper and ink are useless without intelligence intervening. Do accidents create books of information? No! Then why pretend they do?

With all the websites in the world, most are made with the same codes yet are completely different sites. Some are similar and some are completely different. Some are the best like mind. :) But do the similar ones prove a "biological" relationship if you will? No, but they all prove a designer, and they each have their purpose.

If computers aren't built and programmed by chance then how could the more complex cells be by chance? How can they reproduce themselves without any knowledge or direction? Matter does not direct anything or create. Without consciousness, it's dead weight and nothing more. There has to be an outside force, like the created world in our dreams has us to exist.

How can a random process construct a reality with highly complex cells and systems and all of which have purpose and rely on each other? All elements, DNA, proteins, etc etc are more complex than anything produced by an intelligent man.

The first cell receiving life where none had existed before. Its amino acids formed and became proteins for life, even though salt water, sunlight and oxygen destroy amino acids, all without an intelligent agent or programmer.

And cells need protein and a genetic code. Cells need a whole team of other cells to play their role. If one of the other cells is missing then it doesn't work. They would all have to evolve at the same time without guidance.? What are the chances they all evolved not only in the same place but this would have to happen over and over all across the world.

A genetic code for a simple bacteria is more complex that the code for Windows. Nobody thinks a computer came by chance. And evolution and natural selection needs things to be alive, correct? How did dead matter or soup evolve or do anything?

"If biodiversity is as necessary for normal ecosystem operation as appears to be the case, it suggests that these services, and organisms providing them, had to have been simultaneously present right from the beginning." Henry Zuill Biology Professor of Biology

Even if all the correct cells needed for life somehow came together (and it would have to come together worldwide, because life is world wide, ocean and land based) you would still have to bring them to life and give them directions on what to do and how to do it. You can pile the materials for a building together but you're not getting a building, and letting it sit there for eons is not going to create a building. This requires skill and an intelligent designer to do this, correct? Even the simplest organisms are complex. Complexity is a problem for evolution because it requires intelligence, and all parts must be present for functioning.

(I'm trying to get better at painting and this painting is one of my stepping stones, (not that we ever stop learning) and I'm seizing the opportunity to post it, mediocre as it is.)

If you pile different color paints and brushes on a canvas, over a time period (pick any length of time you desire), would it create a painting of subject matter or just a mess? If I told you that that's all I did here, was throw it into a soup and look at what showed up on my canvas, you'd call me a liar, and you'd be right.

When you look at a painting or a statue or read a poem, you don't believe it was developed by chance do you? You recognize an intelligent designer's work. Think of the complexity that's all around you in nature and in the mirror. Is the painting not by chance but you are? What logic is this?

Like one scientist said: "If God exists, science will never find Him as long as it refuses to consider God as a part of reality. Scientists will never find the truth if they're biased."

All organisms in life have a task and a role in life. That doesn't need a designer? Even scientists can't produce life in a lab, so how can blind chance? And if scientists did, it would prove a creator. How does complexity evolve without the advantage of foresight? As one scientist said but I can't remember who: "Evolution needs increasing complexity, increasing information. We don't see it occurring today and no one was there to observe it in the past. Evolutionists counter by saying that it is too slow to observe. Even if this were true, it still means that evolution is non-scientific because it is not observable or testable."

From James Perloff's book "The Case Against Darwin" he makes a great point:
"But let's say that somehow, by chance, a cell really forms in a primeval ocean, complete with all the necessary proteins, amino acids, genetic code, translation devices, a cell

membrane, etc. Presumably his first little cell would have been rather fragile and short-lived. But it must have been quite a cell, because within the span of its lifetime, it must have evolved the complete process of cellular reproduction. Otherwise, there never would have been another cell.

And where did sexual reproduction come from? Male and female reproductive systems are different. Why would nature evolve a male reproductive system? Until it was fully functional, it would serve no purpose and would still serve no purpose unless there was, conveniently available, a female reproductive system, which must also have risen by chance."

The first cell would not have any DNA or genetic information, so the cell would have died with no information to pass on or a way of reproduction or the know-how. It would simply end with its own death. Also, there are countless other cells, amino acids, proteins, things I can't spell or pronounce, that would be involved for life to happen. Grab any biology book and read a designer's handy work. All of this requires organization and intellectual information.

We live in a world, that's like a cell, completely organized. The Big Bang Theory is questioned when the fact is shown that explosions destroy and disorganized things and causes chaos rather than organized life and an organized greenhouse for it to live in.

"And like no explosion ever, this explosion created everything and, supposedly, still is." Eric Dubay

So, 4,6 billion years ago the earth cooled down and then the rain started, and it lasted for millions of years, until the oceans of the earth formed! Where did all that water come from? I am sure it came out of nowhere, too. Clouds just formed by some miracle and that was it. If all life came from the pond scum why are they all different yet the species are the same? Eyes the same apart from each other, etc.?

entropy

The theory of evolution is questioned when we look at entropy again, the second law of Thermodynamics. This law states that systems left on their own without any intelligent interference, will decay and wither away, not get better and more organized with complex cells and membranes. Evolution states just the opposite. One is hearsay, the other is based on an observable physical fact.

How could intelligence and morality develop from matter when the proven laws of Thermodynamics stops this from happening? Evolution requires things to get better and more organized over time. But wires, plastic, metal, etc. laying around doesn't gradually build itself into a computer and program itself, which is useless without someone to use it. We see proof of entropy everywhere where intelligence is not involved.

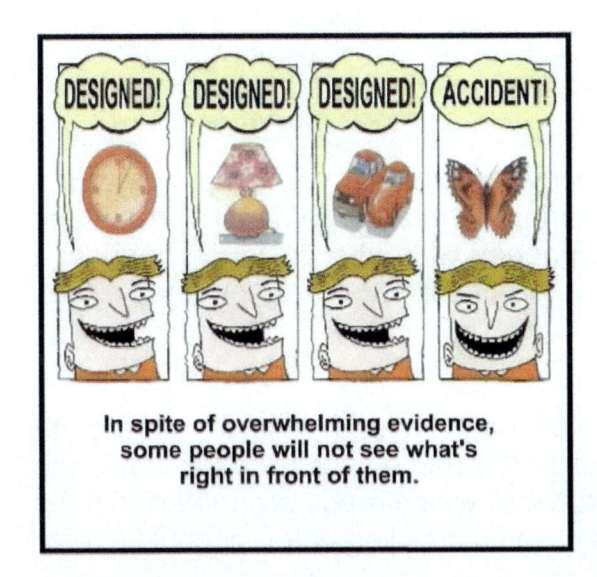

In spite of overwhelming evidence, some people will not see what's right in front of them.

Like an example Eric Dubay gave in one of his videos, can you imagine if you walked into the thick forest and stumbled into a new car among the trees. Would you imagine that various elements in the forest had come together, by chance, over millions of years to produce such a machine? No! It has intelligent design written all over it. And the car doesn't even come close to being as complex as your body or cells are. Think about it.

The eyeball is another design that is complex and requires a lot of different parts to evolve at the same time and rate. And how does it get the blueprints for this and with what know how? Like blood clotting, which has to be developed the same time as the body, or the body will bleed to death and never live long enough to reproduce.

There's so many parts of the eyeball and head and brain that would have to evolve together quickly, or the whole rigging would be useless. Why would the body grow something it can't use? Once again, how long is the quote that evolution takes?

Not even technology can produce vision like our eyes can. Even Darwin said the thought of the eye made him cold all over. Nobody's saying a camera came into being by accident are they? Darwin said of the eye: "To suppose that the eye with all its inimitable contrivances for adjusting the focus to different distances, for admitting different amounts of light, and for the correction of spherical and chromatic aberration, could have been formed by natural selection, seems, I confess, absurd in the highest degree...The difficulty of believing that a perfect and complex eye could be formed by natural selection , though insuperable by our imagination, should not be considered subversive of the theory."

Even something simple as a clay pot or an axe has an intelligent designer. Archeologists know there was a civilization when they find one of these simple tools. But then the cell, without a mind set or programmer, created a system within itself to absorb sunlight before it could destroy it and use it for food and energy? How did it obtain such skills, a thinking man wonders. Wouldn't it have to have blueprints from past species in evolution? And if so the same questions would go to that cell, correct?

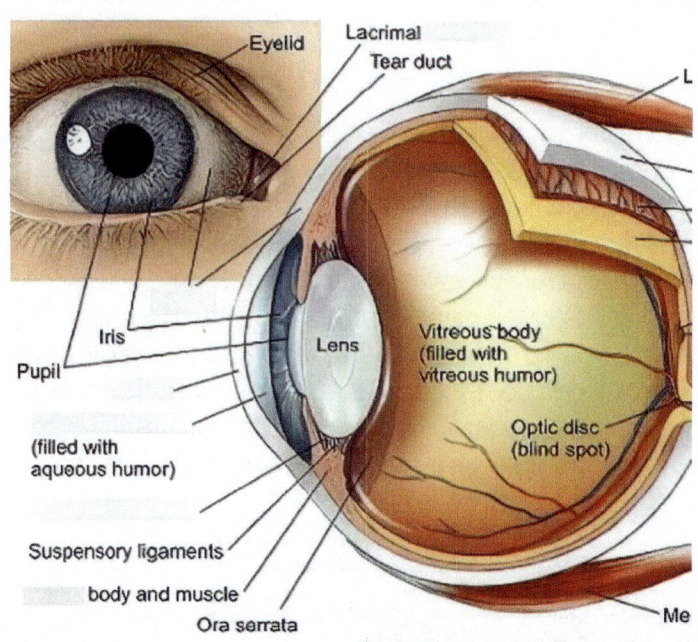

"Anyone who can contemplate the eye of a house fly, the mechanics of human finger movement, the camouflage of a moth, or the building of every kind of matter from variations in arrangement of proton and electron, and then maintain that all this design happened without a designer, happened by sheer, blind accident-such a person believes in a miracle far more astounding than any in the bible."   Author David Raphael Klein

How about the immune system? If cells fight off bad bacteria cells to protect the organism, then which came first, the protective cell or the bad guy cells? Why would the organism evolve a protective cell unless the bad guy cell was already around? And if the bad guy cell was already around then the organism would be killed before it could evolve one. How long does evolution take again?
   The mindless unguided evolution then directs the cell and diversifies all the DNA into 10 million different species on a whirling ball. So, we got our life, intelligence, consciousness and morality from nothing that was slowly guided by nothing to become what it is today? Sorry but I'll need to see the receipt on that one. If Scientism is not a religion, I'll eat my hat.
   Oxygen would oxidize a lot of these chemicals and destroy them, so scientists are claiming there was no oxygen in the environment at that time. But if that was the case then how could the ozone layer have existed? And if it did not, according to the globe theory, everything would die. And, as physical evidence would have it, all life exists and needs oxygen. Hmmm

Darwinism and the globe model are taught in schools but the obstacles and problems and the case against them, never are. As Dr. Roth once said: "And today the modern synthesis — Neo-Darwinism — is not a theory, but a range of opinions which, each in its own way, tries to overcome the difficulties presented by the world of facts."

How about when you dream at night and create that world of characters, places and what appears as matter (which, when touched, have texture), did those characters have to evolve? My point is if God is a consciousness, no Big Bang or magic is needed (If you don't think magic is needed for your Big Bang theory then try to prove it with real evidence), just like it's not needed at night when we create in our dreams, or imagine things during the day. To me, that is way more plausible then the Big Bang evolution theory, by far!!! Our dreaming at night proves it's a possibility that consciousness creates. And a proven flat earth destroys the Big Bang theory and shows a Creator.

"My brain is only a receiver, in the Universe there is a core from which we obtain knowledge, strength and inspiration. I have not penetrated into the secrets of this core, but I know that it exists." Nikola Tesla

One has to wonder how a useful protein can be formed by natural processes without an intelligent designer. If scientists do anything in the laboratory or a builder makes anything or a computer builder makes/programs a computer, all that would be an intelligent designer, or the computer's "god." But none of these things can compare to any life form, especially ours. A computer, etc., etc. never existed without us. And we would never exist without whom? That's another question for another time.

How can a protein form naturally from raw materials without DNA and the translation and forming mechanisms present too? Some cells need translators to interact with other cells they need to do their job and stay alive. So which came first the cells or the translators or the other cells if all of them need each other? What good is a book without a reader? Who created these and with what knowledge?

Longevity has shown to be in genetics. Some people's genetics have everyone in the family living til ripe old ages. Some are not so lucky. Diseases run in the family sometimes. If evolution made the organism to be all about survival, then why put a cap on it? Why not continue living, why give us a limit and why not weed out the family diseases?

Here's a great experiment from Stephen Grocott, Inorganic Chemists, that's fun for the whole family: "Sterilize a frog and put it in a sterile blender — buzz. Seal up the mixture in a sterile container and leave it as long as you want. You won't get life, despite the fact that you started with the best possible mixture of so-called precursors to life. Repeat the experiment a million times — in the sun, in the dark; with oxygen, without; with clay, without; with UV, without. It won't make any difference. Thermodynamics clearly states that the mixture will decompose to simpler, lower energy, less information-containing molecules. The complexity of the simplest imaginable living organism is mind-boggling. You need to have the cell wall, the energy system, a system of self-repair, a reproduction system, and means for taking in "food" and expelling "waste," a means for interpreting the complex genetic code and replicating it, etc., etc. The combined telecommunication systems of the world are far less complex, and yet no one believes they arose by chance."

The word evolution has many meanings, but only one which is scientific:
1) Cosmic evolution- the origin of time, space and matter. The Big Bang
2) Chemical evolution- the origin of higher elements from hydrogen.
3) Stellar and planetary evolution- origin of stars and planets.
4) Organic evolution- origin of life.
5) Macroevolution- Changing from one kind of animal into another.
6) <u>Microevolution- Variations within kinds. Only this one has been observed, which makes it physical reality and no faith needed.</u>

The rest is taken on faith. When asked for proof of the others, you get yet more unproven claims. I don't have enough faith anymore to be a whirling ball atheist. Atheists keep saying religious people go off faith, never thinking about what they actually believe in. They believe in things that have no evidence to support them. When I was a whirling ball atheist I ran off more faith than anything, yet I argued my beliefs like I had some sort of knowledge. Now I see physical evidence and don't have much need for faith. Why have faith, when you can see the evidence? I'll leave faith to the blind.

To believe we must ignore the fact that there are no obvious testable, observable phenomena on the origin of life. To say, then, that evolution explains the origin of life is circular reasoning, as the outcome is largely determined by the assumptions made.

"Whoever thinks macroevolution can be made by mutations that lose information is like the merchant who lost a little money on every sale but thought he could make it up on volume." Biophysicist Dr. Lee Spetner

The Zetetic Method

> One of my favorite shows back in the seventies was *The Rockford Files*, starring James Garner. One episode was called "The Great Blue Lake Land and Development Company." Rockford battled a crooked real estate firm that was selling parcels of desert land as prime "lakefront property"—assuring customers that, in the future, a lake would be added and the land developed. "Take a look at that!" the salesman would tell his sucker, pointing at barren, wind-swept sand. "There's the shopping center! And, oh! Look over there! There's the country club where you'll be enjoying barbecues every Saturday!"
>
> Evolution's sales pitch is a bit like that. Professor Probability takes us to a plot of empty land with a pond on it, and offers it to us for $40 million.
>
> "$40 million?!" we ask. "But there's nothing here!"
>
> "There will be," winks the professor. "Why, in time, the chemicals in that pond will turn into bacteria, the bacteria into fish, the fish into men, and the men will build a whole civilization. Why, this land will become a city, teeming with hotels and amusement parks. I tell you, my friend, at $40 million this pond is a bargain!"

I got this hilarious gem from a wonderful book called "The Case Against Darwin" by James Perloff

If evolution was for survival and organisms trying to save energy for survival, etc, then why does a cow have four stomachs? A horse and others like animals have the same diet, do just find with one. Why would a giraffe grow a long neck but not a zebra? Why not evolve to eat grass, seeing as how it's the most abundant plant on this earth plain? That would make lunch time for lions a lot safer would it not, increasing the survival rate of not getting horned to death.

People say you can't disprove evolution. LMAO! But what real physical evidence backs it up I ask? The evidence for an intelligent designer is overwhelming but none for evolution or whirling ball. If you can't disprove a magic Genie, that doesn't make it exist does it? But you can rub lamps all over the world and see nothing of the sort and if you can't prove real magic (emotional belief in it is not proof) then it doesn't exist until you do so. When evidence points against it, then there's no reason to believe it exists at all.

The claim that all scientist believe in evolution

I've heard SO MANY atheists claim that ALL scientists are atheist and evolution believers. This is far from the truth and shows their laziness when it comes to research. All those who claim this deserve the title of "dumb dumb." I guess it's easier to make false claims than to prove any. The scientists that you see on the tell-a-vision are doing just that, telling a vision. There are plenty of scientists that believe in evolution but can't prove it. Same with the flying ball theory. Any scientists that are pushed in front of the screen or given lime light, you should be aware of.

I searched for scientists that didn't believe in evolution and was quite surprised at the numbers. I wish I would have looked into this subject when I was younger, instead of going off faith based globe and evolution theories. There's even a book titled "In Six Days: Why 50 scientists Choose to Believe in Creation" by John F. Ashton. And the Creation Research Society has 600 members holding science degrees. To state that all scientists are atheist and evolution is ignorance in its full form.

And there's way more than that. I'll share a few here from that book and other places I've found. The book has 50 chapters written by 50 scientists. Then I'll share a few who believe in evolution but are doubtful of the theory.

I have put more quotes in this chapter than any other because of the amount of scientists who didn't fall for the evolution propaganda. Here are a few quotes I hope you read from some scientists who disagree with the theory of evolution:

) "In essentially all cases, their research has not been supported by government funding. This is in contrast to the many millions of dollars of government-funded research by scientists who hold evolutionary presuppositions, which has been used to support their beliefs. In spite of these handicaps, a remarkable body of evidence refuting evolutionary notions has been assembled by creationists." Dr. Keith H. Wanser professor of physics

) "A growing number of respectable scientists are defecting from the evolutionist camp ... moreover, for the most part these 'experts' have abandoned Darwinism, not on the basis of religious faith or biblical persuasions, but on scientific grounds, and in some instances, regretfully." Wolfgang Smith, Ph.D., physicist and mathematician

) "Hundreds of scientists who once taught their university students that the bottom line on origins had been figured out and settled are today confessing that they were completely wrong. They've discovered that their previous conclusions, once held so fervently, were based on very fragile evidence and suppositions which have since been refuted by new discoveries. This has necessitated a change in their basic philosophical position on origins. Others are admitting great weaknesses in evolution theory." Luther D Sutherland, Darwin's Enigma: Fossils and Other Problems, 4th edition

) "We have had enough of the Darwinian fallacy. It is time that we cry: 'The emperor has no clothes." K.Hsu, geologist at the Geological Institute at Zurich

) "Let me be blunt on this matter. Evolutionists around the world have had to learn the hard way that evolution cannot stand up against creationism in any fair and impartial debate situation where the stakes are the hearts and minds of intelligent, undecided but nevertheless objective and open-minded audiences. Experience will prove that the same is true for the age issue as well. Evolutionist's beliefs regarding the origin and development of life cannot withstand the scrutiny of an informed opposition and neither can evolutionists claim to the effect that the universe has existed for ten to twenty billion years and the earth for 4.5 billion years. To delay the collapse of widespread public acceptance of such claims, it will be necessary for evolutionist scientists to carefully avoid debate." Paul Ackerman "It's a Young World After All". From Creation Day 3, May, 1999 John MacArthur

) Dr. Lee Spetner
"The case against evolution is summed up by Berkeley University law professor Philip Johnson, who makes the following points: (1) evolution is grounded not on scientific fact, but on a philosophical belief called naturalism; (2) the belief that a large body of empirical evidence supports evolution is an illusion; (3) evolution is itself a religion; (4) if evolution were a scientific hypothesis based on a rigorous study of the evidence, it would have been abandoned long ago."

) ""Problems in Evolutionary Theory" was a class that made me realize the difficulties those who discount the possibility of a Creator have with their own theories. The problems with evolutionary theory were real, and there were no simple convincing resolutions." Dr. Timothy G. Standish professor of biology

) "In naturalistic evolution, life is believed to have originated as high fluxes of energy passed through a chemical soup of fortuitous composition. The problem here is much more difficult than that faced by the 'Maxwell demon', because life requires structures of incredible complexity, not just high energy levels.
   The presumed high-energy fluxes do not provide structure or intelligence any more than the proverbial explosion in a print shop will produce a novel." Jeremy L. Walter Mechanical Engineering

) "Once we see, however, that the probability of life originating at random is so utterly minuscule as to make it absurd, it becomes sensible to think that the favorable properties of physics on which life depends are in every respect deliberate….It is therefore almost inevitable that our own measure of intelligence must reflect …higher intelligences…even to the limit of God…such a theory is so obvious that one wonders why it is not widely accepted as being self-evident. The reasons are psychological rather than scientific." Sir Fred Hoyle, well-known British mathematician, astronomer and cosmologist

) "For the past five years I have closely followed creationist literature and have attended lectures and debates on related issues. Based solely on the scientific arguments pro and con, I have been forced to conclude that scientific creationism is not only a viable theory but that it has achieved parody, if not superiority over the normative theory of biological evolution. That this should now be the case is somewhat surprising, particularly in view of what most of us were taught in primary and secondary school." He goes on, "In practical terms, the past decade of intense activity by scientific creationists has left most evolutionist professors unwilling to debate the creationist professors. Too many of the evolutionists have been publicly humiliated in such debates by their own lack of erudition and by the weakness of their theory." Robert E. Smith, a member of the western Missouri affiliate of the American Civil Liberties Union. From Creation Day 3, May, 1999 John MacArthur

) "Darwinian theory is the creation myth of our culture. It's the officially sponsored, government financed creation myth that the public is supposed to believe in, and that creates evolutionary scientists as the priesthood... So we have the priesthood of naturalism, which has great cultural authority, and of course has to protect its mystery that gives it that authority—that's why they're so vicious towards critics." Phillip Johnson, On the PBS documentary "In the Beginning: The Creationist Controversy"

) "One of the reasons I started taking this anti-evolutionary view was ... it struck me that I had been working on this stuff for twenty years and there was not one thing I knew about it. That's quite a shock to learn that one can be so misled for so long. ...so for the last few weeks I've tried putting a simple question to various people and groups of people. Question is: Can you tell me anything you know about evolution, any one thing that is true? I tried that question on the geology staff at the Field Museum of Natural History and the only answer I got was silence. I tried it on the members of the Evolutionary Morphology Seminar in the University of Chicago, a very prestigious body of evolutionists, and all I got there was silence for a long time and eventually one person said, 'I do know one thing — it ought not to be taught in high school'." Dr. Colin Patterson, Senior Palaeontologist

) "Unfortunately many scientists and non-scientists have made Evolution into a religion, something to be defended against infidels. In my experience, many students of biology – professors and textbook writers included – have been so carried away with the arguments for Evolution that they neglect to question it. They preach it ... College students, having gone through such a closed system of education, themselves become teachers, entering high schools to continue the process, using textbooks written by former classmates or professors. High standards of scholarship and teaching break down. Propaganda and the pursuit of power replace the pursuit of knowledge. Education becomes a fraud." George Kocan, Evolution isn't Faith But Theory, Chicago Tribune 9 Monday April 21 1980

) Professor of Organic Chemistry Dwain Ford:
"Evidence for intelligent design is widespread in nature. For example:
1. The motorized rotating flagellum of some bacteria.
2. Blood clotting and its control.
3. The high degree of organization within a typical cell.
4. Cell division and its control.
5. The system for protein synthesis. 6. The human eye.
7. The respiratory chain bases in the highly organized mitochondria.
8. The biosynthetic pathway in which acetyl CoA is the key compound."

) "Darwin recognized the fact that paleontology then seemed to provide evidence against rather than for evolution in general or the gradual origin of taxonomic categories in particular." George G. Simpson American paleontologist

Now here are evolutionists who are not that assure of the theory themselves it seems:

) Sir Arthur Keith, British evolutionist Quoted in Meldan Why We Believe in Creation:

"Evolution is unproved and unprovable. We believe it only because the only alternative is special creation, which is unthinkable."

) "I suppose the reason we leaped at The Origin of Species was because the idea of God interfered with our sexual mores." Sir Julian Huxley, evolutionist Quoted in Henry M Morris "The Troubled Waters of Evolution" (San Diego: Creation-Life Publishers, 1974, 58) Why I Believe,

) "Why I Believe Evolution is a time honored scientific tenet of faith." Professor David Allbrook, professor of anatomy University of Western Australia, "Evolution, Possible or Impossible?"

) "The more one studies paleontology [the fossil record] the more certain one becomes that evolution is based on faith alone." Professor Louis T More, evolutionist The Dogma of Evolution, Princeton: University Press

) "There are only two possibilities as to how life arose. One is spontaneous generation arising to evolution; the other is a supernatural creative act of God. There is no third possibility. Spontaneous generation, that life arose from non-living matter was scientifically disproved 120 years ago by Louis Pasture and others. That leaves us with the only possible conclusion that life arose as a supernatural creative act of God. I will not accept that philosophically because I do not want to believe in God. Therefore, I choose to believe in that which I know is scientifically impossible; spontaneous generation arising from evolution." Dr. George Wald, professor emeritus of biology at Harvard University. Nobel Prize winner in biology

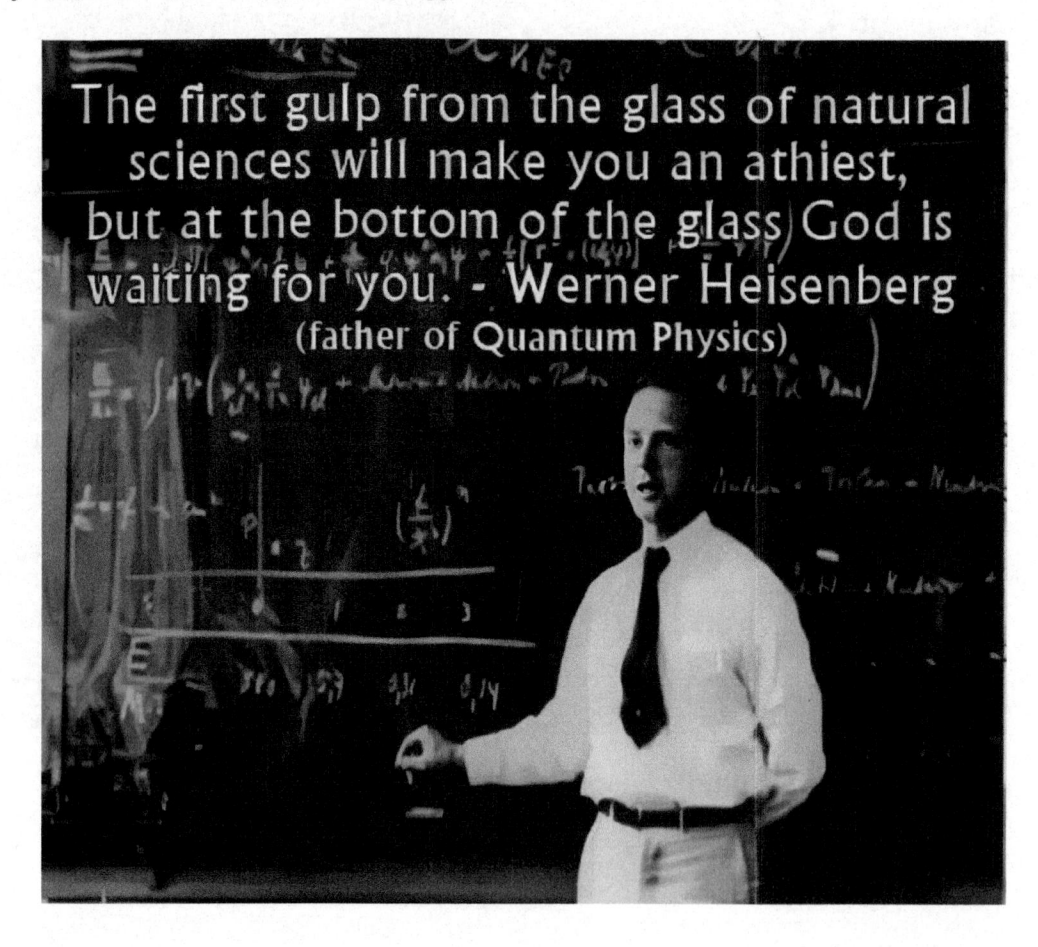

> The first gulp from the glass of natural sciences will make you an athiest, but at the bottom of the glass God is waiting for you. - Werner Heisenberg (father of Quantum Physics)

The case with fossils

There Are No Intermediate Fossils
The "intermediate life forms" in this conjectural picture never existed.

"And, let it be noted that the petrifaction of fossils is not surprising, seeing that the earth was wholly sunk under the waters for a whole year. Even geologists confess that the degree of petrifaction is no proof of the antiquity of a fossil. 'The mere amount of change, then, which the fossil has undergone, is not by any means a proof of the length of time that has elapsed since it was buried in the earth; as that amount depends so largely on the nature of the material in which it was entombed, and on the circumstances that have since surrounded it." Jukes

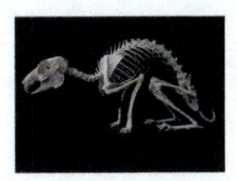

How the animal's skeleton looks like

How scientists would recreate the animal

The animal

When a volcano erupts it creates a layer of lava and ash that cools. This will bury creatures and fossilize them. A flood will also do this. We will talk about a great flood a little later but for now let's talk about the fossils found.

There are fossils of extinct animals and not so extinct found here and there, all kinds of animals. But what's never found is the missing link of any species.

Even for plants, no intermittent fossils. Professor of tropical botany at Cambridge University E. J. H. Corner, stated as regard to plant evolution: "I still think that, to the unprejudiced, the fossil record of plants is in favor of special creation. If, however, another explanation could be found for this hierarchy of classification, it would be the knell of the theory of evolution. Can you imagine how an orchid, a duckweed and a palm have come from the same ancestry, and have we any evidence for this assumption? The evolutionist must be prepared with an answer, but I think that most would break down before an inquisition. Textbooks hoodwink."

There has to be if the theory of evolution is true. How could they not? Where's the proof of the common ancestor?

A lizard is found and a fish is found but never a fish during its process of turning into a lizard. Once again, how long does evolution take? Millions of years supposedly. Think of the millions of missing links there should be. If we don't have those then why do we believe such claims? Shouldn't we demand proof?

Why would, let's stick to our lizard fish, a fish spend generations upon generations growing a pair of legs, lungs, a digestive system for land food, natural sun protection, a different set of eyes and a different immune system to handle land based bad guy cells, when it has what it needs in the ocean? When developing these things, they would be useless until all are fully developed/evolved, correct? When was the last time a body grew something useless, unless it was a deformity? Why is this still not happening?

So are we to believe that a fish slowly developed lungs while it swim around for generations, with its useless half evolved legs dangling there, all organs and limbs trying to evolve at the same rate with no guidance? OH, think of the little freak swimming around.

They make claims like "the fish walked out of water, but never go into any detail do they? Nor prove anything of the sort. Where are the intermittent fossils? Like the globe theory, when they can't prove their claims they confuse you with unproven math and dazzle you with over the top claims while showing you fake "evidence."

Fish would die quickly out of water. It would have to develop lungs and legs, which would be useless for a long time. Where's the fossil of a partly hip boned fish? There should be plenty. Eyes that can't see or legs that go through generations without walking or lungs that take generations to develop to use? Why would the body make something it couldn't use? It'd be a waste of energy and resources. Why not stay in the gigantic oceans where there's plenty?

How about the useless arms of a T-Rex? LMAO! What a clown claim that is.

What are the chances of some organisms getting the idea (how could it even get "ideas"?) to develop wings in not just one part of the world but all across this great plain? Same with scales, legs, lungs, etc., etc.

Evolution is like a bunch of letters thrown around until a Shakespeare piece develops. By way of an unconscious process known as chance.

ATHEISM

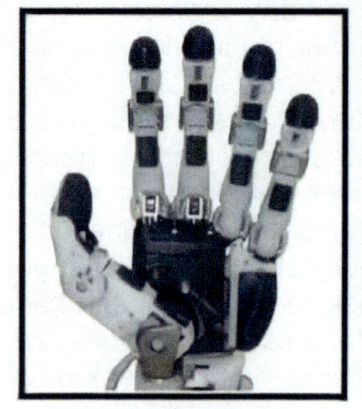

intelligent design   **coincidence**

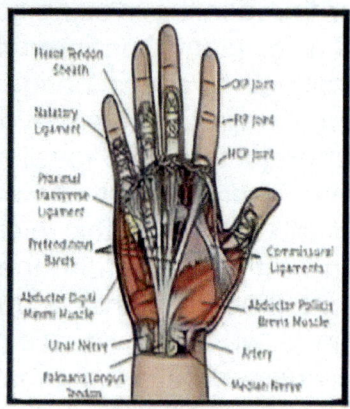

It was once claimed that the appendix was useless but later on, that was found out to be false, it's part of the immune system. It has a purpose but you can live without it still. The tail bone was once said to be left over from our monkey days and had no need but later on it was found out to be a very necessary tool. If you don't believe me, go to the doctor and tell them you want it removed because you're no longer a monkey, and see what the doctor says.

"I believe that one day the Darwinian myth will be ranked the greatest deceit in the history of science." Swedish biologist Søren Løvtrup

In order for reptiles to turn into mammals, almost the entire system of not only the body but also the behavior, has to change with it. Reptiles are cold blooded, lay eggs, and don't suckle their young and are covered in scales. Mammals are the total opposite of all that while covered in fur. Is there any proof at all of reptiles doing this 180° turn to become a cow or whatever? There's also no fossil to support any of these claims. There should be fossils from every species on earth around. But fossils that are found, are found in its full form, never an in-between fossil. Amphibian eggs have to be in water while mammals are born on land. (Other than whales, etc that is.) How would this gradually change and why is it still like that if it evolved? Again, if there's no in-betweens fossils then why are we buying monkey people? You would HAVE to believe it because you have no proof to know it.

A Dino Tale

If a meteorite wiped out life on earth, then did everything have to start over? Did evolution have a start over? Or was it just dinosaurs? If dinosaur bones are oil then how are they finding dinosaur bones? Hmm

There's a factory in China called the Ocean Art company that makes dinosaur bones and has said their main customer is the United States and European markets and museums. You don't say!

I would like independent scientists, who don't have their head stuck up the government's ass with financial tides, to peer review the ones that "are found", but instead only certain scientists are allowed to see it. Hmmm, what are they afraid of, maybe another moon rock like hoax found out by independent scientists?

There was the time they found a giant jaw bone and the Scientism priest preached that it was a dinosaur bone. Went touring, parading it around. Come to find out it was a whale's jaw bone. Awkward!

The Zetetic Method

There's one small dinosaur "museum" that has this huge metal skull and painting of the huge dinosaur, however, as you leave out the exit door, there's a very small picture of the actual skull that was found with a hammer sitting right near it. The skull is not even as long as the hammer. LMAO! The rest of the body was make believe and the skull size was a blunt lie.

They'll find a bone or two and give you an entire animal with the sound it would make and everything. Even when I was a kid I thought it was ridiculous but still it fascinated me. But I grew up.

African elephants, with it's big mouth, can take up to 80% of its day eating to sustain its bulk. How then can a brontosaurus, with its little mouth, possibly have enough time in a day to eat to sustain its enormous body, which is bigger than the African elephants? How?

Elephants eat **between 149 and 169 kg (330-375 lb.) of vegetation daily**. Sixteen to eighteen hours, or nearly 80% of an elephant's day is spent feeding. Elephants consume grasses, small plants, bushes, fruit, twigs, tree bark, and roots.

https://seaworld.org › animals › diet

All About Elephants - Diet & Eating Habits - SeaWorld.org

How did Native Americans and other world wide natives not find so many fossils while living off the land? Really? There was no discovery pier until the 19th century. According to the world book encyclopedia, before the 1800s no one "knew" that dinosaurs existed. All of a sudden they're being found right and left and kept from peer review. Why! Remember, TRUTH FEARS NO INVESTIGATION!!!

The Zetetic Method

DINOSAUR HOAX

To this day, nobody has ever excavated a complete dinosaur skeleton. Hence, the various species of dinosaurs are all artist's imaginations. Before the 1800's, nobody had ever heard of a "dinosaur," nor had anyone anywhere throughout the ages discovered a single "dinosaur fossil." This includes every single culture from around the world, from the Native Americans to the Ancient Egyptians. The prehistoric monsters seen in museum exhibits are all plaster casts; "real" dinosaur bones are only allowed to be seen by a special group of government appointed Paleontologists. The whole dinosaur industry is propaganda—created as a way to validate Darwin's false theory of evolution.

The Great Flood

If the world was flooded as ancient people claim, here's what we would find. (This list was compiled by Kent E. Hovind, an 'educated' fundamentalist Christian, and I added the rest)

1) The world would have hundreds of layers of strata. (And it does have layers, all across this great plain of ours. Like different soils in a jar of water that has been shaken up and allowed to settle. If it took millions of years. Why are the boundary lines of each later flat?)

"By contrast, the catastrophic processes observed during and following the eruption of Mount St. Helens in the Cascades of Washington state produced a scale model of the Grand Canyon in a very brief period of time. Sediments were rapidly deposited and then suddenly eroded by pyroclastic steam, water, and mud flows in the area northwest of the summit. Now the canyon walls resemble others that are assumed to be of great age, even though they are known to be less than 20 years old." Jeremy L. Walter Mechanical Engineering

2) The world should have billions of fossils including coal and oil found in those layers. (It does. And I've found seashells on top of mountains)

3) There should be huge canyons and deltas showing evidence of rapid erosion. (There is)

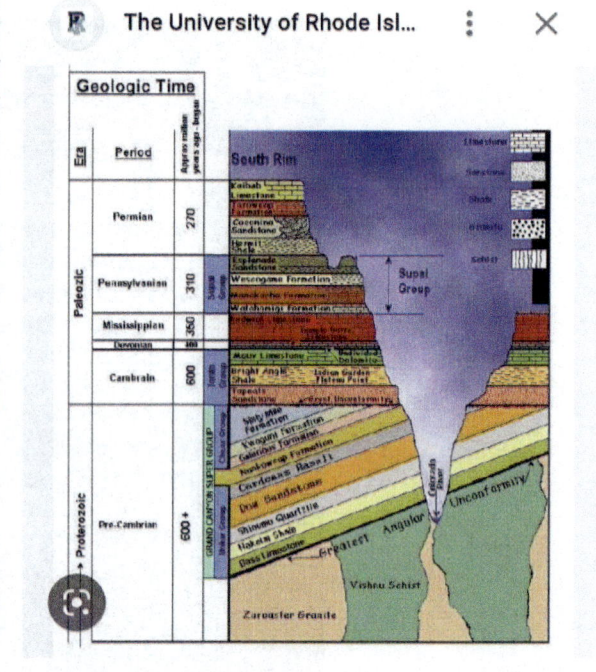

Geology of the Colorado Plateau: Grand Canyon...

4) There should be legends of this world wide flood found in cultures all across the earth. (There just so happens to be.)

5) There should be petrified trees in the vertical position extending through many layers. (There is. They say that the sediments surrounding them took up to millions of years to build up. Really! How long does a dead tree stand before it falls?)

The Zetetic Method

"Petrifaction of wood has been shown to occur rapidly in highly silicified waters, and would likely have been accelerated by the conditions of a worldwide flood. Indeed, a U.S. patent has been granted on a process to rapidly petrify wood so as to make it fire-and-wear resistant." Dr. Keith H. Wanser professor of physics

Layers of limestone in the Grand Canyon have fossils in them. The same limestone is found in Pennsylvania, England and the Himalayas in the same position. Then we have the chalk beds, like Dover, Europe, Middle East, Kazakhstan and other places that have similar fossils. All as if the world flooded and the water separated the sediments, suddenly burying living things, some with vegetation still in its mouth.

We are told that fossilization takes 10,000 or more years. This is yet another claim that can't be proven. Are we relying on carbon dating for this claim? Can't be lab experiments that went on for 10,000 years. And the dead must be rapidly buried in sediment that can harden and exclude oxygen, otherwise it would decay too quickly to become a fossil. Wouldn't that require something like a flood that buries the dead quickly otherwise it would start decaying. How long does roadkill last? How could it last until it was slowly covered up? Like cave paintings that are supposedly hundred and some thousand years old but are just now wearing out. Hmm! Are we sure about that age? I no longer trust our "established scientists" so my questions are unanswered as far as I'm concerned.

I can't prove that dinosaurs didn't exist, how could I? But the "evidence" that is brought to the table, saying that they did exist, is not enough for me to accept that claim, especially when some of it is falsified. When you have been caught lying and with fraudulent evidence in a court of law, you get in trouble, but not in science? Why not? Why haven't the scientists, who lied about the whirling ball theory, evolution, dinosaur theory and this covid/vaccine scam, been called out on their fraudulent ways?

Many evolutionists have said it's the opposable thumb that has helped us evolve into intelligent beings. But as physical evidence would have it, some other animals have it as well. Apes, monkeys and raccoons. But none of their intelligence compares to human beings. How can we be the most conscious animal on this plane and not have been here the longest? Let reality be your teacher, not claims!!!

There are these "miracles" everywhere in life and on earth showing that it's by design and not a "Big Bang" with gradual knowledge collected.

If "THEY" want me to believe anything "THEY" say, they need to provide real evidence and stop discrediting themselves with fraudulent data and falsified evidence. That might work on low effort thinkers but not someone who uses the gift the Creator has given us, a higher level of consciousness, thinking.

The BLACK SWAN

There's so much evidence in an intelligent designer that I feel embarrassed to have ever believed in evolution. I don't have enough faith to be an Atheist or believe in dinosaurs on a whirling ball anymore.

Science is supposed to be knowledge derived from observation, study and experimentation; NOT speculations, assumptions, opinions and agendas. What observations, etc. do we have then to support the theories of the whirling ball, evolution, giant lizards with illogical bodies and the Big Bang theory? How do we know that humans turn into apes or fish into land animals without any scientific evidence? Why lie and falsify evidence? WHY I ASK??? What gain is there in dumbing us down? Control maybe? One should seriously ask this and not just sweep this 'elephant' under the rug.

The Black Swan here is a few things:
1. The measurements, mathematics, patterns in nature, spirals all through nature with precise measurements, layers with precise measurements, radial symmetry and bilateral symmetry throughout nature. The measurements on a micro level and a macro level shows an intelligent design. Mankind can't design what we see, and they are intelligent beings, so how could 'nothing' do it?

If I throw a bunch of marbles on the floor I have no faith that it will create a mathematical structure with precise measurements that hold purpose. Mathematics points to logic, logic points to a mind and a mind belongs to someone.

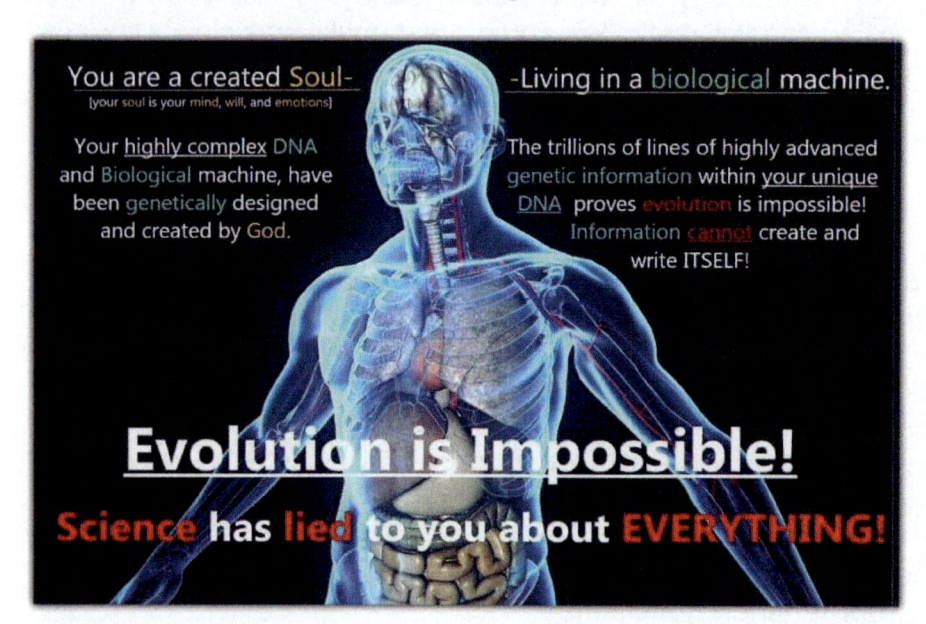

2 Death is the physical proof of an intelligent energy/designer.

When a person dies, let's say at 5:05pm, the same matter is there that was present at 5:04pm, so what changed? Where's the difference? If there's intelligent conscious energy in you, and matter doesn't think, direct and do things, which means there is, then that consciousness energy has decided that your body is no longer inhabitable and has either left your body or your body is no longer transmitting that energy from whatever source. Which makes matter a tool being used by something that's not matter. Then when the matter is left to its own device, it decays. THUS INTELLIGENCE IS ENERGY!

3. The actions all around you that you don't control. Your food doesn't rearrange itself into body parts, DNA or useful tools for the body. Nor does your food know how to fight viruses, disease, etc. The body knows how to do such things and YOU didn't teach it, did ya? Something is directing it.

4. If all signatures are missing from a computer, can you prove it was created and programmed? Would you assume it was created if we lived 200 years ago and you found it in the woods, or would you assume it was slowly formed over time? Stupid question huh? Think about that next time you look in the mirror and say 'nothing created me.'

Good poem I discovered on evolution, thought I'd share it.
EVOLUTION POEM BY J.W.H. From 'The Anti-Infidel,' March 1887

"One school in attempting to
bridge o'er the chasm,
Invented germinal cell
"Protoplasm,"
Which was first inorganic, but
afterwards seen
To grow into "Sponges" and
"Polyps" marine; From thence by "Absorption,"
"Accretion," and growth,
Giving birth to the "Bivalves" or
"Molluscs," or both.
These creatures by striving grew
fins, tails and claws,
In spite of Dame Nature's implacable laws.
They sprouted and turned into
reptiles amphibious;
Of obstacles placed in the way
quite oblivious.
Urged on by "Necessity" upwards
they grew,
Day by day giving birth to some
quadruped new,
Evolving, re-forming without
intermission
"As played upon by the surrounding condition."
Then "Like produced un like"
without hesitation,
Earthy atom transformed into
rich vegetation.
Animalcule left their aquatic
abode,
And into the Forests by thou-

sands they strode.
Frogs changed into birds at the
voice of the Sirens,
And everything living "changed
with their environs."
The Lichens from every restric-
tion then broke,
And evolved both the
Lepidodendron* and Oak.
'I was a wonderful time and a
wonderful sight
To see how each day brought new
objects to light.
The stratified rock the strange
story relates,
How the "Invertebrata"* begat
Vertebrates;
And the "Ichthyosaurus"[1] one
night in a freak,
Gave birth to the "Mastodon"[1]—
(minus the beak), While the tidy Acidian evolved
from the Oyster,
Emerging somewhat like a monk
from his cloister
The Bear from the Mole in the
past we descry,
While the Bumble Bee came "by
descent" from the Fly.
Then the Lemur begat the grim
Ape Catarrhine,
From thence came the others "in
process of time."
Their tails being "chaffed,"[1]
became shortened, 'till soon
We arrive at the hairy-faced,
tailless Baboon.
These quarreled and fought in
the Forests primeval,
Impelled by an inherent spirit of
evil.
The Pentadactilians ignoring all trammels,
Produced the most curious Ter-
restrial Mammals;
While the Porpoise and Sea-
Horse plunged into the deep,
Determined henceforward to

water to keep.
"By the use and disuse" of their
parts, as it suited,
They wandered (to no spot
particularly rooted).
One half the world took with the
other to strive, 'Till naught but the "Fittest"
were
found to "Survive."
At last Man appeared; but,
amazingly strange!
From that moment the animals
never could change.
"Like" at last "produced like," and
the laws became fixed.
Which explains why the Species
since never got mixed."

J.W.H.

CHAPTER 15
GOTTA HAVE FAITH

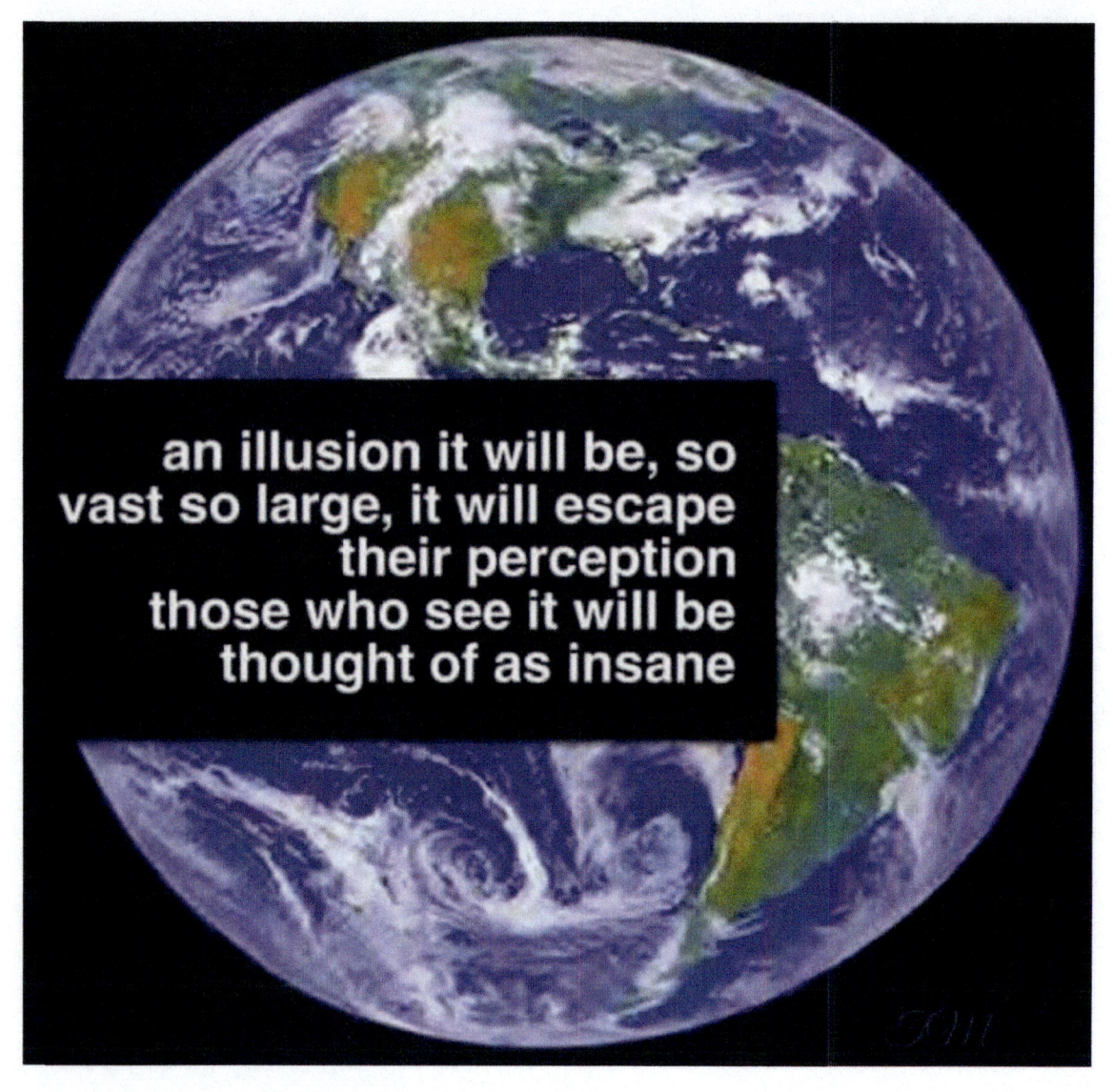

an illusion it will be, so vast so large, it will escape their perception those who see it will be thought of as insane

"The truth only hurts when you want to believe a lie." Jennifer McVey

"Globe believers think they have science on their side. They don't recognize that they have taken several great leaps of faith in their lifetime, especially the atheists.

Ultimately its worshipers are directed towards worshiping the state itself. The globe as religion was deliberately constructed so as to be the glue which binds all the people of our world under one faith and one government. And it succeeded massively." Not sure where I copied this from.

REAL SCIENCE DOESN'T CARE IN YOUR BELIEF SYSTEM, PSEUDO-SCIENCE ON THE OTHER HAND REQUIRES IT

Science is NOT on the side of the globe believers by any means. If it was so, then they could prove their stance on their arguments, but that is not the case. All they ever do is regurgitate theories in circles. A to prove B and B to prove A and A and B to prove C.

If science backed up the globe model, Neil Degrasse Tyson would debate Eric Dubay, but instead he will not. He knows his Pseudo-science is a limp noodle that cannot stand a measurement challenge.

Atheists like Christopher Hitchens, Richard Dawkins, and Sam Harris, all reject religion because it requires faith and no real proof, yet they all fall under the same exact paradigm of religion that they condemn because they do the exact same with scientism. They are exponents of one faith while downing another faith. Flat Earth is Post-Faith. All physical reality, from Earth to life, points to a Creator.

Life here requires a stationary enclosed world to live on. We experience nothing but a flat and motionless Earth. If not taught so, we would not naturally assume that we are spinning faster than the speed of sound upside down on a ball. We should not be the one proving that it is flat, but rather them proving that it is a globe.

As I've stated before, "In all observable ways there is so much truth in our favor that we do not have to believe in a flat stationary earth because we do nothing but observe it and even fly over it. However the globe is something of a different matter isn't it? You have to believe."

Can you provide logical, observable and repeatable demonstrations that prove what you believe in? Have you ever authentically questioned your own beliefs and proven them to yourself?

The government's scientism have got people so fooled with their indoctrination, that they'll make fun
of people who dare to question it. We would like to change this by snapping people out of their brain washed slumber.

For those who say they don't buy the flat earth BS, well that's fine because it's not for sale, so there's that. The lie is what's for sale, not the physical reality. The curvature is not there, your beliefs mean nothing to that physical fact. There are men these days who think they're women, but the physical facts say differently doesn't it? So what makes people think it's any different with curvature? Believe what is, not what you think. Being fooled is one thing, we are all fooled about one thing, or rather many things in life. But to stay fooled when physical observable provable facts are brought to your attention is just plain denial, and there's nothing healthy about that. To hold on to the deception because someone of authority said so, is sheep like and just plain sad. A tremendous problem arises when we are not aware of our assumptions, because then we think that we have no bias.

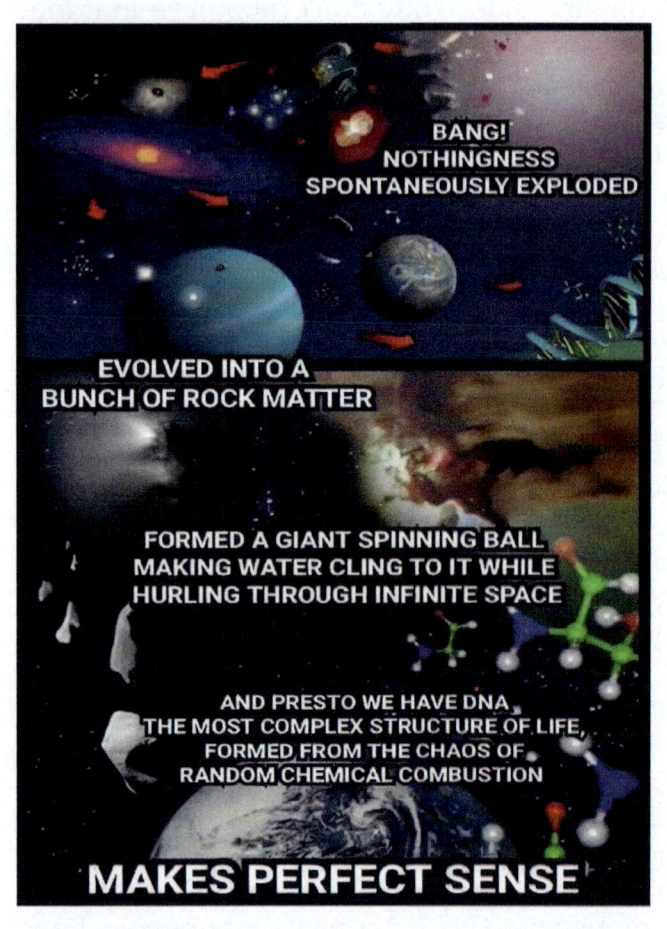

People constantly start arguing with me about flat earth yet they know nothing about the model. They will make the claims "sunsets not work on a flat earth" or "if the earth was flat, you could see the sun all the time" or "if the earth was flat the ocean would pour off." I hear ridiculous things like this all the time. Why not learn the model you're arguing against? Why not ask questions (and listen with the intent to understand) instead of arguing with claims? Many flat earthers say that they became a flat earther because they tried to prove the globe earth and couldn't. That flat earth was more observable and provable.

People have simply become intellectually lazy, letting other people think for them. Repeating instead of thinking. It's sad and pathetic. And I get tired of the conversation rather quickly because of it. I don't care what people believe or think unless it matches physical reality.

"Give me the storm and tempest of thought and action, rather than the dead calm of ignorance and faith! Banish me from Eden when you will; but first let me eat of the fruit of the tree of knowledge!" Robert Green Ingersoll

REQUIRING FAITH AND A BELIEF SYSTEM
The Globe: Gotta have faith
The Flat Earth: See that it is so

Before I close let me show a few examples of why the globe model requires faith and a belief system to exist whereas the flat earth model does not:
1) If we stepped outside and looked at the sun and said "the sun is 1.3 millions times bigger than the earth and we're revolving around it," that requires faith and belief, because observable physical reality shows it's smaller and revolving around the North Star Polaris. And hottest when directly above you shows it's not 93,000,000 miles away, but local.

2) If we fly over the ocean and say "The ocean's wrapped around a ball," that requires more faith and belief because observable physical reality shows it's flat and remains at eye level just like at the beach, which means there is no downward curvature.

3) If we say "We're spinning, wobbling and flying," that also requires a whole lot of faith and belief, because observable physical reality shows us no star parallax, North Star displacement or movement felt.

4) Faith in the nature of the planets and their distances. All we see is celestial lights, everything else is pure hearsay from people who have already lost credibility to those paying attention. If they were different distances, then you would see the difference in shifts but you do not.

5) Saying a ball is surrounded by an atmosphere while wobbling, spinning and flying without losing any pressure is a claim that should be backed up with solid evidence or should not be believed in at all, but most believe it but can't prove it therefore they're dealing in faith.

6) Not to mention the entire space program itself. After all the fake photos and videos you have to have faith in NASA'S 'evidence.' From the International Space Station to the spacewalks.
   Faith, in full bloom, is needed for all of these. We have to question what exactly we believe and what exactly we know.

The acceptance of the globe and its popularity is no argument for the accuracy of the theory. The Powers That Be can't make this world a whirling air bubbled rock shooting through space, but what they can do is convince the population that this is happening by changing your perception of the world.

"I can't believe he said the Earth was flat and motionless. Burn his book!"

The effect of melodrama, 1830, by Louis Leopold Boilly

If you believe these things, you simply cannot claim that science backs your beliefs. You can claim the narratives of Scientism and its priesthood back your claims, but science does not.

Max Plank, one of the most noted scientists of the last century said "Anyone who has been seriously engaged in scientific work of any kind realizes that over the entrance to the gates of the temple of science are written the words: 'Ye must have faith.' It is a quality which the scientist cannot dispense with."

The BLACK SWAN

If you CAN'T prove that it's the ocean that's wrapped around a ball instead of being flat as we see and photograph it, and if you CAN'T prove that this gigantic Earth is wobbling, spinning and flying instead of the sun moving, as we see it doing so, then that means you're going off FAITH and thus have proven my black swan.

CONCLUSION

"Nobody wakes up and decides to start claiming the earth is flat and endures endless ridicule for the hell of it.

It is rather an unavoidable conclusion after thoroughly examining the evidence."

Eric Dubay

"The very concept of a belief becomes antiquated and unnecessary, permanently replaced by common-sense, evidence, experience and endless exploration." Eric Dubay

"The first to awaken are often disgraced long before they are embraced. Being awakened from a slumber is not always welcome by those clinging to the final moments of sleep." Jeannine Sanderson

"Those who are able to see beyond the shadows and lies of their culture will never be understood, let alone believed, by the masses." Plato

Unthinking Respect for Authority is the Greatest Enemy of Truth

CONCLUSION

Well it seems our spinning wobbling flying ball theory didn't hold up too well with the Zetetic Method. No physical based evidence found in reality. Those who say the earth is flat are called lunatics and science deniers, but the physical evidence shows us where the lunacy really lies. Obvious to a child; obvious to any mentality not helplessly subjected to a system.

Don't let the "Powers That Be" stop you from gaining knowledge. Knowledge is what we know, not what we think. It's not what we don't know that hurts us, it's what we do know that isn't so.

I asked, at the beginning of this book, if we were all crazy or not, after reading this do you think we are?

"Being considered "crazy" by those who are still victims of cultural conditioning is a compliment." Jason Hairston

We do not believe what our eyes tell us because we have been taught a counterfeit system which demands that we believe what has never been confirmed by observation or experiment.

This is the result of a failed education system and a successful indoctrination system. The only way out is to clear your head and THINK about what you're been told and the reality of it, and see what matches.

How strong is a theory when it can be debunked with a high powered camera, or a simple plane ride? The whole whirling ball model relies on the curvature of 8 inches per square mile. But this claim of curvature has been destroyed, thus the whole theory lay in ruins.

I'll ask again, how can we take a system of assumptions and theoretical science and call it knowledge? Any person who loves truth goes off consistent evidence, reasoning and logic, can no longer maintain that the earth is a globe.

There's so much observable provable evidence of a flat motionless plane, there's no way anyone could deny solid observable proof other than through ignorance and cognitive dissonance. I'll say this again, if we're on a spinning wobbling flying ball then we WOULD NOT HAVE TO TAKE SOMEONE'S WORD FOR IT! There would be physical based evidence everywhere.

You cannot swing a dead cat without hitting some flat earth evidence. The globers say there's none all while surrounded by flat water, earthly plains that debunk curvature math, a flat airplane ride, a horizon line that remains at eye level, etc. etc. It's literally everywhere. But we see nothing for the globe model do we? We do however, see CGI, trickery videos, empty claims, assumptions, math that can't be proven for what it stands for and contradictions. Math is not physical reality, it can help prove physical reality that's already there, but it's not physical reality. It can help explain your IDEA but not manifest it.

Aristotle said "It is the mark of an educated mind to be able to entertain a thought without accepting it."

This is something a lot of people are incapable of. Instead, all they do is attack character and regurgitate indoctrination beliefs. I discuss flat earth vs globe earth with them all the time and am sick of it. Globe earthers constantly say to us "you do not have any proof of a flat earth or a working model." This is pure nonsense and obviously they don't know anything about the flat earth model that they're arguing against, which is odd because it matches observable physical really.

Before people say these things, they should take one hard look at the globe model, and then take out all the assumptions and theories posing as facts, then see what they have left; then tell me who doesn't have a working model. If anyone thinks they can prove any of this wrong, ask yourself can you prove your proof or just tell me what you believe.

"Let us not ignore this undeniable fact that conclusions which result from calculations barely upon hypotheses, are absolutely worthless, even though they come from the pen of an "F.R.A.S." or from a learned and titled "Sir." Author Karl Smith

It seems that a flat, stationary plane is currently the only Earth model with physical empirical evidence that we can all verify. Can't say the same for globe Earth, hollow Earth or the short lived theory of Concave Earth. Theories may be false, but facts we cannot refute.

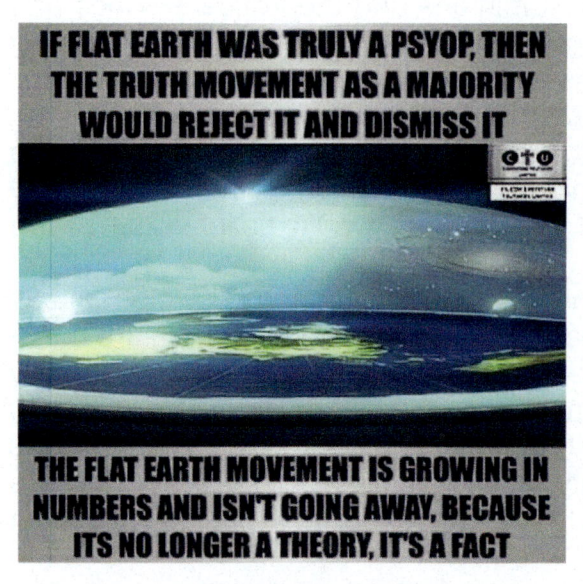

> **IF FLAT EARTH WAS TRULY A PSYOP, THEN THE TRUTH MOVEMENT AS A MAJORITY WOULD REJECT IT AND DISMISS IT**
>
> **THE FLAT EARTH MOVEMENT IS GROWING IN NUMBERS AND ISN'T GOING AWAY, BECAUSE ITS NO LONGER A THEORY, IT'S A FACT**

I hope you truly think about what I've said in this book. I'm not a good speaker and even worse writer. But what I've said is observable and provable. The heliocentric model, like evolution, is based on assumptions and speculations that what we are told is correct. But reality shows us, it is not. You have fake pictures just like you have fake fossils, like in the Peltdown Man.

No observable curvature or star parallax and a greenhouse effect all slams the ball.

Flat earth shows that we are not talking monkeys on a flying ball. We are the highest conscious being on a designed earth. But for what reason is the real question.

Email me through my website, Flatearthlogic.net, if you think you can debunk me. I will be looking for physical solid evidence, not repeated claims. NASA'S cgi and videos are not proof and should not be needed if we're indeed on a whirling ball.

If you send me an email that says "I can debunk your stupid book" but you don't even attempt to do so in the same email, then I won't reply back, because I know that you can't and that's why you didn't even try to in your useless email. Seems logical right?

I will address everything you say but if you don't return that courtesy and instead deflect what I've said, like most do, then I'll just ignore you because you will have proven that a intelligent conversation is not your goal or perhaps, you're just handicapped in that area.

I'll recommend some books and websites at the end of this book.

Is there a way out of this mess of lies and deception? Sure there is. Teach your kids to think instead of accepting claims. Tell them to demand proof! If they do, the lies would stop in a short time. A lie only has power when people believe. Use your common sense filter that consists of logic and reasoning, that way, no one can lie to you about reality.

Please take the message to heart and more importantly to thought. You have no reason to believe you are a talking monkey on a whirling ball. What I have done and recommend for you is to research the heliocentric globe model and see how much of that is observable and provable to you. Then, when you get done with that disappointment, research the geocentric flat earth model and see what you yourself can observe and can prove. Again, if you seek truth, drop your opinions. The time of awakening is here and the future is ours to write. TRUTH WANTS TO BE INVESTIGATED!!!

Thank you for your time
Lloyd Benjamin Hunt
Flatearthlogic.net

RECOMMENDATIONS

RECOMMENDED READING
"The greatest deception men suffer is from their own opinions." Leonardo Da Vinci

Flat earthers have been censored like no other. Even more so then the 9/11 truthers it seems. Not only have they taken real flat earth videos out of the search engine of YouTube, but they have gone to the trouble of replacing them with fake flat earthers who are there to discredit us and make us look like fools, and they fill the search engine up with "debunking" videos, that actually do no such thing.

> ANYWAY I JUST THINK ITS A LITTLE SUSPICIOUS THAT ITS THE ONLY EVENT IN HISTORY THAT CAN PUT YOU IN JAIL IF YOU START ASKING QUESTIONS

The only subject that I know of that is censored even more than flat earth is the Holocaust. It's even illegal to research it in 20 different countries including Germany. I've looked into it and...... I won't touch that right now.

If you type in any name of a real flat earth video, for instance, let's say "200 Proofs the Earth is not a Spinning Ball" by Eric Dubay, you will never see it, but instead you'll get disinformation videos, one behind the other. That's what this section is for.

I'm not trying to convert people to Flat Earth. I want people to think, that is all. A by-product of thinking will be your realization that the Earth is flat. If the physical evidence has been pointed out to you, then you're no longer a victim. You're being willingly fooled. And I'm ok with that. To each his own.

These days I hardly read fiction. It's mostly science books from 50 to 150 years ago, and more modern books from people who have done experiments and research and have woken up to massive lies told to us by our "Powers That Be" and are trying to wake others, such as what I'm trying to do with this book.

These books have more logical and provable arguments then these modern indoctrination books, they call science books, could ever have, with their unprovable theories. In the words of Eric Dubay "When you're creating a bullshit story you don't have physical evidence." Simple and to the point.

These older books offer experiments and ways you can prove them correct. Modern scientists tell you theories you have no way of observing or proving. They offer hypotheses and assumptions as evidence.

One of the old science books talks about the government slipping into the science departments bringing in their pseudo-scientists and ruining science. Government - word for word from ancient Greek. Govern = control, mente = mind.

And now here we are. The highest conscious being on this designed plane, thinking that we're talking monkeys on a spinning wobbling flying ball hurtling through endless space in a Goldie Locks zone. This causes us to hand over, not only our common sense with certain matters, but also our freedoms. Sad but very true.

The Zetetic Method

"One has no right to love or hate anything if one has not acquired a thorough knowledge of its nature." Leonardo Da Vinci

They are not useful tools when trying to prove the globe model. I learned this while researching flat earth and at the same time trying to prove globe earth.

David Wardlaw Scott said: "Many fiction are handbooks of useful instruction, and require to be read not only with one but with many grains of salt."

Here is a list of books that do just that. I've read around over 35 by now, here are some of them. Many of my quotes came from these books. They've made me realize things that were there all along; observable things, yet I was blind to them, because I was busy going off my belief system instead of my mind which is what the "education" system trained me to do.

Believing and not thinking clearly is the protocol that we are trained in. I hope you read these books and get something out of them. I've stolen many points from them. I'm sure the authors wouldn't mind. Like me, they were trying to wake up the masses.

Here are just a few of many books I've read on the matter of flat earth and a couple on evolution.

"Study without desire spoils the memory, and it retains nothing that it takes in." Leonardo Da Vinci

1. "The Zetetic Method: Proving the Earth Flat" by Lloyd Hunt (shameless plug, Haha)
2. "200 proofs the earth is not a spinning ball" by Eric Dubay
3. "The greatest lie on earth: proof that our world is not a moving globe" (second edition) by Edward Hendrie
4. "100 proofs the earth is not a globe" by William Carpenter (love this guy)
5. "Zetetic Astronomy" by Samuel Rowbothan
6. "Terra Firma" by David W. Scott
7. "Zetetic Cosmogony" by Thomas Winship
8. "16 Emergency Landings that Prove a Flat Earth" by Eddie Alencar
10. "The Flat Earth Conspiracy" by Eric Dubay
11. "Flat Earth Investigations into a massive 500 year Heliocentric lie" by James W. Lee
11. "Flat Earth" by Guy Stenton III
12. "The Flat Earth Conspiracy" by Eric Dubay
13. "The Firmament" by Gracie Robertson
14. "Kings Dethroned" by Gerrard Hickson
15. "Your science teacher is wrong: And how you can prove it" by John Andrew Reed
16. "Is Earth a whirling ball" by Karl A. Smith
17. "Dark moon: Apollo and the whistle blowers" by Mary Bennett and David Percy
18. "Earth not a globe" by Samuel Rowbothan
19. "Heaven and Earth" by Gabrielle Henriete

20. ""The great Earth puzzle" by TJ Hegland
21. "Is the bible from heaven? Is the Earth a globe?" by Alex Gleason (the famous map maker)
22. "Flat Earth Concordance" by Paul Raines
23. "Bible cosmology: The world according to the Bible and the ancients" by D. Haughey
24. "The terrestrial plane: The true figure of the Earth" Accurately and scientifically demonstrated by Fredk H. Cook
25. "The Earth is flat: Be afraid, be very afraid" by Casper Stith
26. "Einstein, the Earth Mover" https://www.scribd.com/document/412066837/Albert-Einstein-the-Earth-Mover
27. "Darwin's Black Box: The biochemical challenge to evolution" by Michael J. Behe
28. "Tornado through a junkyard" by James Perloff
29. "The case against Darwin: Why the evidence should be examined" by James Perloff
30. "Evolution: The greatest deception in modern history" by Roger Gallop
31. "In Six Days: Why 50 scientists Choose to Believe in Creation" by John F. Ashton
32. "The Genesis Flood" by Henry Morris and John C. Whitcomb Jr.
33. "Not By Chance: Shattering the Modern Theory of Evolution" by Dr. Lee Spetner

Websites

1. Flatearthlogic.net
2. Ericdubay.com
3. flatearth101.com
4. atlanteanconspiracy.com
5. https://ifers.forumotion.com/
6. https://youtube.com/@FlatEarthEric

Nobody does anything alone. I like to thank the people who helped me. Thanks to all the flat earthers, with their comments, videos and experiments, that help provide evidence and points to share in this book. Thanks NASA for providing clearly manipulated videos and images to help discredit you. And thanks to the many authors that put a lot of work into their books to get the message out. The awakening is here thanks to you. And to Dorothy Davis and Rocky Pinard for their editing help and encouragement. And to Frank Yazzie for listening to my endless chatter about flat earth. But most of all I'd like to thank Eric Dubay for waking this sleeping "being" up. Thanks to you I no longer walk around in an ignorant slumber.

The Zetetic Method

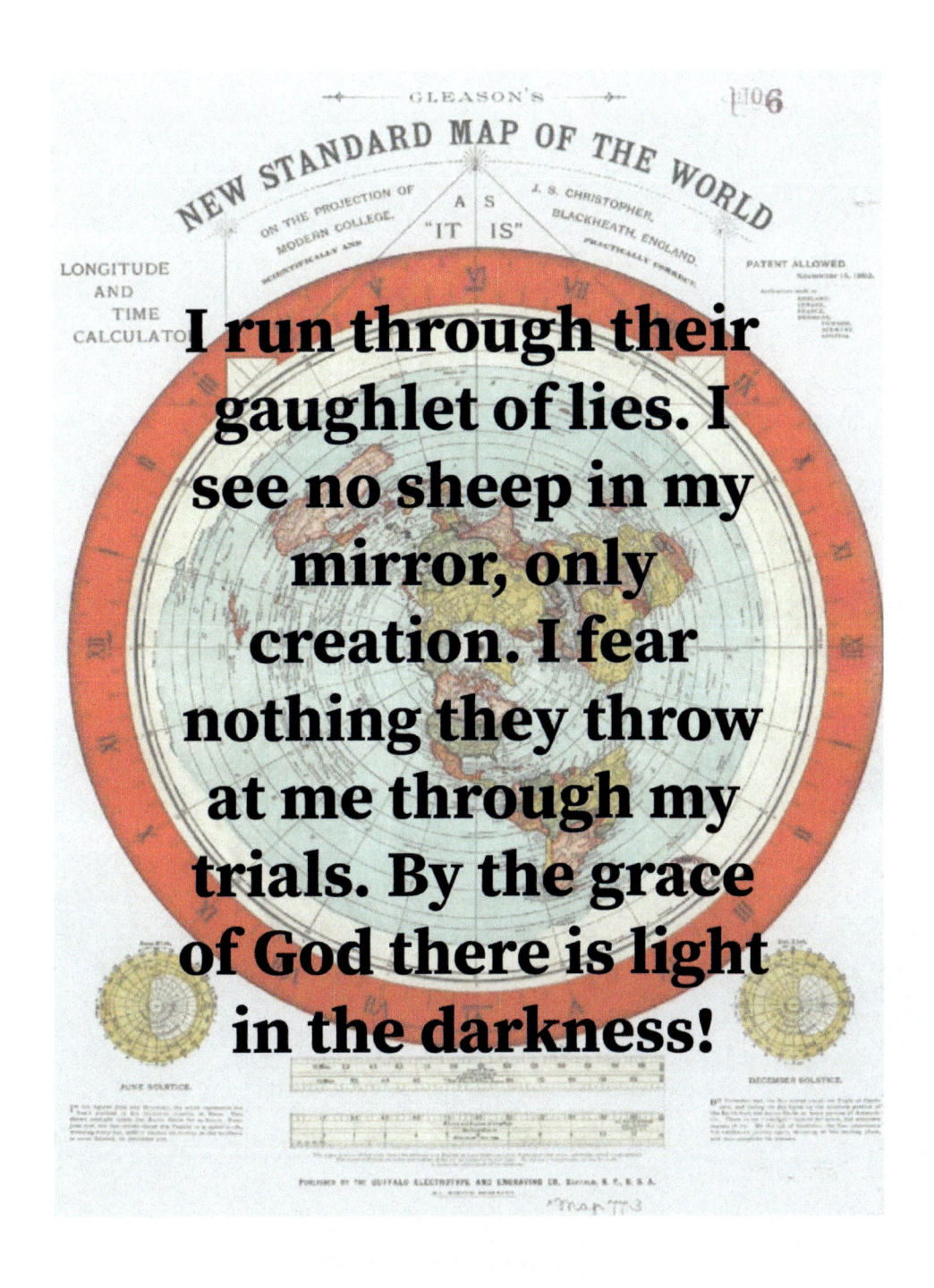

I run through their gaughlet of lies. I see no sheep in my mirror, only creation. I fear nothing they throw at me through my trials. By the grace of God there is light in the darkness!

Printed in Great Britain
by Amazon